READINGS IN CHILD DEVELOPMENT

IRVING B. WEINER
DAVID ELKIND

UNIVERSITY OF ROCHESTER

JOHN WILEY & SONS, INC. NEW YORK · LONDON · SYDNEY · TORONTO

Copyright © 1972, by John Wiley & Sons, Inc.

All rights reserved. Published simultaneously in Canada.

Library of Congress Cataloging in Publication Data

Weiner, Irving B   comp.
Readings in child development.

1. Child study — Addresses, essays, lectures.
I. Elkind, David, 1931-   joint comp.   II.   Title.

BF721.W35   155.4'08   72-1801
ISBN 0-471-92574-8
ISBN 0-471-92573-X   (pbk.)

Printed in the United States of America

10 9 8 7 6 5 4 3 2 1

READINGS IN CHILD DEVELOPMENT

Preface

This book of readings is intended to introduce students to the broad range of facts and issues in child development. To achieve this end we have devoted several chapters each to the four major stages of childhood — infancy, the preschool years, middle childhood, and adolescence; and for each stage we have included material on four core topics in developmental psychology — physical and mental growth, personality and social development, individual and group differences, and abnormal development. By arranging the chapters in this way we hope to help the reader appreciate both the overall continuity of child development and the stage-specific nature of various developmental events.

Although our focus is on particular stage-topic combinations in child development, many of the readings we have chosen overlap. Some are concerned with more than one topic during a single developmental stage, while some pursue a single topic through two or more developmental stages. Taken together, however, these selections fill in the broad picture of child development that we have tried to paint here and in our textbook, *Child Development: A Core Approach.*

In choosing articles for inclusion we have concentrated on concise reviews of the literature in various subject areas, in order to provide the reader with a survey of what is known about child development and also with a source of references to guide his further study. Some of these literature reviews are embedded in reports of research studies or clinical case observations, thereby illustrating for the reader the two major sources of data on which developmental psychologists rely. Each chapter begins with a brief introduction in which we describe the articles we have chosen and indicate their relevance to learning about child development.

We thank Carolyn Hart and Mrs. Loretta Forbes Schafer for their help in preparing the manuscript. We are also grateful to the authors and publishers who have granted us permission to reprint their copyrighted materials; each is acknowledged in the selection they have allowed us to use.

Irving B. Weiner
David Elkind

Contents

READINGS IN CHILD DEVELOPMENT

1
APPROACHES TO THE STUDY OF CHILD DEVELOPMENT

To introduce this book of readings on child development we have selected two articles that place this subject within the broader context of psychology as a social and behavioral science. In the first of these articles, Elkind describes and compares two major ways in which psychologists have approached child study: a primarily developmental approach and a primarily experimental approach. As elaborated in the article, these approaches differ in their relative emphasis on (a) molar versus molecular aspects of child behavior, (b) behaviors inititated from within the person versus behaviors controlled from without, and (c) what children are like versus how they get to be like they are.

In the second selection Martin begins by distinguishing between psychology as a study of persons and as a study of behavior. He uses the work of Skinner to illustrate psychology as the study of behavior, and his discussion of Skinner's position, although written in 1960, captures the essence of some current and very weighty philosophical issues. Martin's comments have particular implications for humanistic versus mechanistic conceptions of the nature of man, and for whether man is to be viewed as master of or mastered by his destiny. Turning to child study, Martin points out that the scientific study of man during much of the twentieth century has tended to disregard or denigrate man's mind and his capacity to think; however, he contines, there are increasing indications that this trend is being reversed, especially in the area of child study. Martin's anticipation that the mind will be rediscovered and that a cognitive theory of behavior and development will emerge is validated in many of the readings included in this book.

DAVID ELKIND

Developmental and Experimental Approaches to Child Study

Two of the many new trends that have marked the course taken by American psychology over the past decade are the rapid rise of developmental psychology as a discipline and the equally rapid growth of experimental child psychology. The reasons for these trends are multiple but most certainly include the pressures toward curricular reform which arose from the attacks upon American education in the nineteen fifties and the pressures towards social reform which arose from the civil rights movement and the "War on Poverty." Both of these pressures created demands for people trained in child development and in research with children. These demands, coupled with government support, made training in child development and research with children possible on a scale that would have seemed megalomaniacal if someone had suggested it a decade earlier.

While developmental and experimental child psychology are both concerned with young people, however, their approaches to child study stem from quite different traditions. The developmental psychologist, whose tradition is European in its nativistic, biological holism, tends to view the child as a growing organism. For the developmentalist, the child's growth is a mater of epigenesis, increasing differentia-

tion and hierarchical integration of progressively elaborated structures which makes the child a different organism in kind from the adult. The experimental child psychologist, whose tradition is English in its empiricist, physicalistic associationism, sees the child as a naive organism. For the child experimentalist, growth is a matter of gaining increasing sophistication as a consequence of accumulated experience — a circumstance which makes the child different only in degree from the adult.

The purpose of present paper is neither to attack, nor to defend either of these orientations. Rather, what I wish to do is to outline what seem to be three basic differences in their approaches to child behavior. Only when we truly appreciate the differences between these two orientations can we hope to integrate them in a meaningful and productive way. In the following pages these two orientations will be compared with regard to their conceptions of: a) the unit of psychological analysis; b) the relative activity or passivity of the subject; and c) the importance of content and process. A final section will suggest a possible underlying cause for the orientational differences in these domains.

Before proceeding however, it is perhaps well to say that I am aware of the fact that there is no single generally accepted theory of learning which unites

*From J. Hellmuth (Ed.), *Cognitive Studies*, Vol 1, 1970. Reprinted by permission of the author and Brunner/Mazel, Inc.

all child experimentalists and that the same holds true for developmental psychologists. It may well be the case that differences within learning and developmental theories can in some cases be greater than the differences between such theories. Likewise, the experimentalist may well employ age differences in his investigations just as the developmentalist often uses experimental control and manipulation of variables. There is, nonetheless, a very real difference in orientation (Kaplan, 1967; Russell, 1957) between the child experimentalist and developmentalist which justifies treating them as distinct and worthy of comparison. In short, I am using the terms child experimentalist and developmentalist in the broad sense of a set of attitudes or assumptions about the nature of child study and not in the more narrow senses either of a particular theory or research methodology.

The Unit of Analysis

Every science begins with one or more fundamental units of analysis and investigation. In physics one such element is the atom while in biology the comparable element is the cell. Progress within a particular science often comes about because new data or theoretical constructions challenge the previous interpretations of these basic concepts. The conception of the atom, for example, has undergone a series of metamorphoses and the modern view bears little resemblance to the notions of the Greek "atomists." Likewise, within biology, the concept of the cell has been radically transformed, particularly within the last few decades. Today with the "breaking" of the DNA

code and the knowledge of the relation between genes and enzymes, even the concept of "protoplasm," is regarded as quaint.

The choice of a unit of analysis within a science is, therefore, of very great significance for it is the unit which often determines the direction and hence the fruitfulness of the research enterprise. Although in most sciences the choice of the unit is relatively straightforward, it poses very real problems in the social sciences and especially in psychology, which stands somewhere between the social and biological domains. The problem is of course that at the level of the individual or of the group there are so many possible units of analysis that it is difficult to find common genotypes such as the atom which can account for the variety of phenotypic phenomena encompassed by the discipline. Within psychology, for example, we study intellectual abilities, personality traits, social attitudes, learning sets and so on without having any generally accepted unit which could be said to underly all of these elements and integrate their various manifestations. One of the major divergences between the experimental and developmental orientations rests in their choice of a unit of analysis.

Within the field of learning the basic unit is regarded as more or less complex association between behavioral and environmental events. The behavioral event can be a simple response such as lever pressing or a more complex pattern of mediating internal responses which are said to account for directed thinking (Berlyne, 1965). Likewise the environmental event can be a simple signal, a complex visual array or even a drug injection. Whether the behavioral and environmental events are conceived in a broad or narrow sense is less significant than the fact that they are said to form a unit which in principle should be able to account for a considerable variety of human behaviors. Looked at in this broad sense, that is in the sense wherein response and stimulus can be defined in simple or complex terms, it is reasonable to say that for the experimentalist, the basic unit of behavioral analysis is the S-R, or S-O-R, bond.

Within developmental psychology, however, the unit of behavioral analysis is regarded differently as becomes readily apparent when one reads developmentalists such as Freud (1953), Piaget (1950) or Werner (1957). The unit is not an S-R bond (in the broad sense described above) but rather a system or organization that possesses certain properties. Since the unit of developmental psychology is perhaps less well known or at least not as well highlighted as the unit of the learning theory orientation, it might be well to describe it with illustrative examples.

In Freud's (1938) book on the interpretation of dreams there is some admittedly associationistic psychology but there is also a good description of the "dream work," i.e., the rules and principles which govern primary process thought such as condensation and displacement. Primary process thought is described in terms of its own structures and its interrelated rules of organization. It is, then a *system* of thinking which can be used to interpret a wide variety of behaviors from dreams to slips of the tongue. In the work of Piaget (1950) the same holds true. Piaget has been progressively elaborating the *systems* of thinking

which exist at different age levels and has tried to specify these terms of their group or logical properties. The system of concrete operations, for example, which emerges at about the age of six or seven, is characterized by the following set of operations:

Associativity $\quad A + (B + C) =$
$\qquad\qquad\qquad (A + B) + C$
Combinativily $\quad A\ Y\ B = AB$
Identity $\qquad\quad A + A = 0$

As in the case of Freud, Piaget believes that these systems are the basic units of analysis and should be the starting point for interpreting many different forms of behavior at the age levels where they are present.

The foregoing difference between the experimental and developmental approaches with respect to their basic units of analysis is not absolute but relative. Within the developmental framework, it is more usual to think of systems as primary and of particular structures, such as Piaget's operations and schemas, as secondary and derivative parts of these larger organizations. Within the experimental orientation, in contrast, it is more usual to think in terms of S-R bonds as primary and their associated systems, such as habit family hierarchies, as derivative. The difference between the developmental and experimental orientations does not lie, then, in the fact that one advocates organizations and the other atomistic elements. In both the experimentalist and developmentalist orientations there are both wholes and parts and the difference lies in that the developmentalist derives the parts from the whole while the reverse holds true for the experimentalist.

It must also be said that the difference

in choice of a unit for the two orientations does not necessarily imply anything with respect to their origin in nature or nurture. While it is usual to suppose that S-R bonds are derived from nurture whereas mental systems derive from nature, such presuppositions cannot hold up under close scrutiny. If the system is held to be native or innate as, for example, some modern linguists (e.g. Chomsky, 1957) assert with respect to language structures, this innateness can only be relative. The emergence of structures common to different individuals is not independent of the environment but rather presupposes what Hartmann (1951) has called a "normal expectable environment." When the environment deviates markedly from the norm, the expected system may not appear or may appear in a distorted form. The language of the autistic child, to the extent that such autism is environmentally induced, demonstrates the relativity even of supposed innates structures to environmental influence.

The role of the environment in altering structures and systems is illustrated in some experiments reported by Waddington (1962). When the fly grub (Drosophilia) is placed on a high salt diet sufficient to kill a large number of them, those that survive become somewhat modified in their body structure. Under the high salt diet, some of these Drosophilia develop enlarged anal papillae. After twenty generations, a large proportion of the population was able to survive the high salt diet. Two results were found. The overall size of the papillae were increased and the readiness to become enlarged under high salt condition was also increased. When the new popula-

tion was put back on the old, low salt diet, the change in papillae size did not entirely reverse itself. Waddington calls this "genetic assimilation" and points out that it resembles the inheritance of acquired characteristics inasmuch as it demonstrates that a structure acquired under changed environmental conditions does not revert to its original state when the environment is restored to its previous condition. There is, of course, selection operating and that is why these findings are not evidence in support of Lamarck.

Piaget (1929) has reported similar results with molluscs moved from quiet ponds to lakeside and back again. The swirls common to the lake molluscs were gradually acquired by the pond molluscs which Piaget transported to the lake shores. When this new generation of molluscs was returned to the banks of quiet ponds, the swirls common to the lake molluscs were retained after many generations. In short these studies give evidence that the environment can force selection in certain directions and that in some cases at least the results are partially irreversible. Hence we have a kind of inheritance of acquired characteristics which is mediated by selection.

These data are of importance because they suggest that the structures that are sometimes said to be innate and independent of the environment may, at an earlier point in time, have been a product of genetic assimilation. It is because of this incessant feedback between genetically determined structures and the environment that the term "innateness" loses its fixed connotation. Every structure has a history both within the organism and within the species and may have been at one time or another determined, at least in part, by environmental Intrusions. It is for this reason that Piaget (1968) says that "every structure has a genesis and every genesis gives rise to structure."

It would be hard then, to make a case for the innateness of the structures or systems advocated by the developmentalist as the basic units of behavior. In a like manner, S-R bonds cannot be attributed solely to experience. The phenomena of generalization, for example, seems to presuppose structural systems which are themselves not learned. An animal which acquires a size discrimination will generalize this response to sets of stimuli other than those upon which it was originally practiced. Generalization is a system principle which cannot be explained entirely by reference to experience or training. In a more general way, White (1965) has recently brought together a larger group of investigations which seem to show that in many different areas of learning there are significant changes between the ages of four and six. One interpretation of these findings is that the maturation of new mental systems alters the mode of learning. In short, learning and S-R bonds cannot be acquired without the intervention of organismic systems just as organismic systems cannot appear without the nutriments and directions provided by the environment.

Accordingly, the distinction between systems on the one hand and S-R bonds on the other does not reside in their relative innateness or acquiredness since both can be shown to depend, at some point in the history either of the individual or of the species, upon genetic as well as upon environmental factors. The real difference between these two units lies in their mode of definition. The S-R bond or habit must always be defined with reference to some form of environmental input whereas a system can be defined entirely in terms of its principles of organization. The mode of definition, however, says nothing with respect to the origins of these units. The fact, say, that Piaget's concrete operations can be defined without reference to environmental input does not imply that they are innate anymore than the fact that the S-R bond can be defined without reference to organismic systems implies that it is entirely acquired.

Passivity and Activity

Another major difference between the experimental and developmental orientations lies in the dimension of activity and passivity. In the sense in which these terms are used here, activity refers to self directed and self initiated behavior whereas passivity refers to behavior which has been or can be directed and initiated from without. By and large, the experimentalist prefers to study passive behaviors whereas the developmentalist seems to prefer the study of active behaviors. This is not surprising inasmuch as the experimentalist wants to test the effects of his experimental manipulations whereas the developmentalist wants to observe the effects of endogenous growth processes.

The distinction between active and passive behaviors must not be confused, as it often is, with certain assumptions about the nature of the organism. Because the experimentalist concerns himself with those behaviors which he can control and direct, this does not mean that he attributes passivity to the organism as a whole. He has merely selected from the individual's passive behavior repertoire and does not deny that the individual also has a repertoire of self initiated and directed behaviors. In the same manner, the fact that the developmentalist studies spontaneous behavior manifestations in no way connotes that he denies the existence of a repertoire of behaviors that can be controlled by environmental manipulation. In short, it is unfair and incorrect to say of the experimentalist that he views the organism as passive and that the developmentalist views him as active. For both the experimental and developmental psychologist the organism is both active and passive and their difference lies in which of these behavior reservoirs they choose to tap and not in their vision of the organism as a whole.

This difference in selection from active or passive behavior repertoires on the part of developmentalists and experimentalists, while quite relative, has nonetheless both methodological and practical consequences. Although the experimentalist does not gainsay the endogenous factors such as maturation and exploratory and curiosity drives which can initiate and direct behavior, he is unwilling to accept any change in behavior as being due to such factors until it has been shown that comparable changes cannot be produced by environmental manipulation. Without such a demonstration, says the experimentalist, the attribution of behavior changes to intrinsic factors, smacks of mysticism rather than science. One might just as well attribute the changes to some mythical cherubs who go about their merry work of instilling behaviors in the wee hours of the morning when no one is about. So, while the experimentalist can accept active, self initiated behaviors in principle he demands proof that there are no immediate environmental determinants of such behaviors.

The developmentalist, on the contrary, is much more willing to accept changes in behavior as being due to endogenous factors without testing whether or not the changes can be brought about by environmental manipulation. What is more important, from his point of view, is to determine whether or not the changes are indeed developmental. Piaget (1951) long ago laid down the criteria for such a determination on the cognitive plane. The criteria are as follows: a) In a true developmental sequence one finds both *anticipations* (types of behavior usually observed at a later age suggested in the behavior of young children) and adherences (remnants of behaviors from an earlier age suggested in the actions of older children); b) A true developmental sequence will be evidenced by a certain uniformity of responses within age groups which is greater than any uniformities between age groups; c) Finally, the direction of change from early to late childhood should be towards the adult norm. When these criteria have been established in a given area of behavior, one can be reasonably sure that a true developmental sequence has been observed. A somewhat different criterion has been suggested by Werner (1957), who speaks of it as the orthogenetic principle which holds that behavior is developmental to the extent that it manifests progressive differentiation and hierarchial integration with increasing age.

The preference for observing passive or active behaviors on the part of experimentalist and developmental psychologists is also reflected in their respective conceptions of control. Within the experimental orientation, the concept of control is one of manipulation. Everything in the situation except the environmental change or changes under investigation are kept constant in accord with Mill's maxim that a constant cannot be a source of change. The developmentalist, in contrast, has a somewhat different conception of control. He argues that if nothing is controlled, if everything is left to vary at random, other than the task itself, and if one still finds that the behaviors manifest the criteria described by Piaget and Werner, then such regularities must be regarded as genuine characteristics of the organism. The maxim here is that uncontrolled variation cannot be regarded as a cause of observed regularities.

Finally, the preference of the experimentalist for passive behaviors and of the developmentalist for active ones is also reflected in their approach to applied problems. There is, however, a paradox here. For, while the experimentalist prefers to study the passive behaviors of his subjects, he tends to be activist in his own behavior with respect to applied problems. He wants to teach young children to read, to program learning and to modify disturbed behavior. And, it must be added, he has had some notable successes in these areas. The developmentalist, who prefers the active behaviors of his subjects, tends to be passive in his approach to applied problems. He places emphasis on enriching the environment and providing the child with the opportunity to be active and self directive (as say, in the discovery method). In a phrase, the experimentalist wants to modify behavior to make it fit the environment whereas the developmentalist wants to modify the environment to fit behavior.

Content and Process

Psychology, like every other science, has both its inductive and its deductive moments. Developmental psychology has, until fairly recently, been primarily concerned with the inductive or "what" aspect of behavior. This has sometimes been called the "developmental descriptive" approach in that it concerns itself with the nature or content of children's minds at different age levels and with describing these contents as completely as possible. Comparative analysis of contents at successive age levels often leads to inductive generalizations regarding the principles which govern the growth of mental contents. Piaget, for example, on comparing the ideas of children at different age levels about the physical world, suggested that as young people grow older their ideas become more relative, realistic and objective than they were in preceding epochs of their lives (Piaget, 1951).

The experimental orientation has, on the other hand, been primarily deductive in its approach. (Skinner is of course a quite notable exception but the premises which govern his methodology if not his conceptualizations are deductive in their orientation.) Starting from a set of principles regarding the nature of learning, consequences are deduced which are then put to test. Within this hypothetic-deductive context, the processes involved in learning, the "how" of S-R bonding is the prime focus of concern as are the variables and parameters that affect this bonding. Content is, from this point of view, a confounding factor which must be eliminated insofar as this is possible. Hence the use of nonsense syllables in memory experiments, geometric forms in concept attainment studies and so on.

This distinction, between the content orientation of the developmentalist and the process orientation of the experimentalist, is necessarily relative. The developmental psychologist is interested in processes, but of a somewhat different sort than those that concern the experimentalist. To appreciate this difference it is necessary to recall that psychology must of necessity deal with several different time scales. There is the scale of milliseconds, seconds and minutes with which neurophysiologists and psychophysicists are frequently involved when studying rate of response, thresholds and so on. Next there is the scale of hours and days which forms the background for most psychological investigations of learning, memory and problem solving. Finally, there is the scale of months and years which is the province of the developmental psychologist. I do not want to enter the continuity versus discontinuity argument here, but only to point out that there is no a priori reason why, if some processes take seconds and others hours and days, why still other processes could not take months and years.

Although it is difficult to do experimental work on these developmental processes in humans, some experimental work of this kind has been done with animals. The visual deprivation studies of Riesen (1961) demonstrate the effects of certain kinds of stimuli upon the development of sensory capacities. In a recent study by Young (1963) it was also shown that apes raised in a hemmed-in environment developed myopia as a result. But this process took months and not just hours or days and is, therefore, more difficult to manipulate and study experimentally. A good many of the studies aimed at teaching children conservation (e.g. Greco, 1959; Smedslund, 1959; Wohlwill, 1959, 1960) over a short period of time seem to have confused the products of developmental processes with those of short term learning processes. This probably explains why so many of these training studies have been failures.

While the developmentalist is concerned with both processes *and* content, the same does not seem to hold true for the experimentalist whose prime concern is with process. The experimentalist's reluctance to deal with content probably stems from the inherent difficulty in quantifying meaningful material. That this is not an insurmountable obstacle has been shown by Osgood, Suci and Tannenbaum (1957) in their work on the semantic differential — a notable step forward in the experimental study of content. The work of Attneave and Arnoult (1956) in the quantification of perceptual forms is another example of a successful attempt to measure what seems to be unmeasurable.

In closing this section on content and process, it is perhaps appropriate to point out that while the neglect of content in animal investigations can be defended, the same may not be true in studies with children. Content clearly has attentional and motivational properties that are relevant to the learning process. The banality and boredom of the "Look Spot Run" type primer in contrast with the attractiveness of comic books for young readers is but one example of the importance of content in human learning. It is to be hoped that the efforts of workers such as Osgood and Suci and Attneave and Arnoult will, in the future, encourage other experimentalists to systematically explore the role which content plays in learning.

DISCUSSION

In the foregoing pages it has been pointed out that the experimental and developmental approaches differ in their choice of psychological units and in their preferences for studying active as opposed to passive behaviors and contents as opposed to processes. While, as I have tried to indicate, these differences are only relative, they nonetheless exist and need to be accounted for. In part these differences can be explained in terms of the different traditions out of which the orientations originate. But what is the central difference between the biological, holistic and nativistic tradition on the one hand and the physicalistic, associationistic and environmental tradition, on the other hand? It is with this question that the present concluding section is concerned.

One essential difference, or so it seems to the writer, lies in the perspectives which are regarded as permissible under these two traditions. More particularly, the difference may revolve around the investigator's willingness to take his subject's point of view and to construct concepts and study relations from this perspective. By and large, the experimentalist tradition sees such an approach as inherently invalid and unscientific — more art than science. The developmentalist, in contrast, regards taking the subject's point of view as a legitimate procedure, and at least some of his concepts (such as Piaget's "conservation" concept) only make sense when the subject's point of view is taken into account. In the following paragraphs, I want to show how the willingness or unwillingness to take the subject's point of view can account for the differences in orientation that have been noted in the preceding sections. Let us take up the experimental orientation first.

The Experimental Orientation

One of the basic premises of the experimental orientation is that of an absolute separation between: (a) the stimulus and the response on the one hand and (b) the observer and what is being observed on the other. From this standpoint, the subject of investigation always appears separate from the stimuli which impinge upon him. In a Skinner box, for example, the animal is a separate entity from the lever which he presses and animal and lever must be defined independently of one another. Likewise, the investigator regards himself as entirely separate from the objects of his investigation.

This separation between subject and object and experimenter and data is an inevitable consequence of an investigator who stands outside the objects of his investigations and refuses to project himself into his subjects or to anthropomorphize. It follows, from such a position, that the major problem is to determine how the separate stimuli and behaviors get linked together in adaptive ways. The choice of an S-R bond as a basic unit of inquiry is a logical consequence of this standpoint. Likewise, the preference for observing passive behaviors can be derived from the same perspective. When subjects are looked at only from the outside, it is much easier to deal with those behaviors which can be initiated or controlled from without than to try and surmise what goes on inside the "black box" to account for spontaneous behaviors. Finally, when subjects are viewed from without, content becomes unimportant because to deal with meaning and understanding on the part of the subject presupposes that one can take the subject's point of view.

In short, the experimentalists' insistence on standing outside the subject-object, stimulus response interaction leads inevitably to the choice of an S-R bond as a unit, and to the preference for passive over active behaviors and for process over content.

The Developmental Orientation

The developmentalist, while he recognizes the value of the observer's perspective, also sees value in attempting to put himself in the subject's position and in attempting to see things from the subject's point of view. The greatest difficulty is always of objectifying this perspective and of integrating it with the perspective of the outside observer. Piaget's (1952, 1954) work on the *Origins of Intelligence in Children* and *The Construction of Reality in the Child* is a remarkable example of how such observa-

tions can be made and integrated. The *Origins* book presents an interpretation of intellectual development from without while the *Construction* book presents the same development from the standpoint of the child. Both types of interpretation are tied at every point to concrete observations.

It is the developmentalists' willingness to take the point of view of his subject which helps account for his choice of system as a unit of psychological analysis. As soon as one takes the subject's point of view, it becomes clear that many events are happening simultaneously and that they do not come in a hodge-podge but are rather patterned and organized. Consequently systems have to be postulated to account for this patterning and organization. Likewise, the preference for the study of active as opposed to passive behaviors derives, it would seem, directly from putting one's self in the subject's position and seeing things from his point of view. Once in the subject's perspective it becomes clear that stimuli are always interpreted and that there are compulsions to activity from within, such as curiosity, need for practice and exercise, needs for exploration which lead to self initiated and directed behaviors. Finally, from the standpoint of the subject, content is important because it determines his interest, motivation and comprehension.

In summary, then, it is suggested here that one of the central differences between the experimental and developmental orientations lies in their respective unwillingness or willingness to take the subject's point of view and to formulate concepts and rules of behavior from this perspective. While the problem of the experimenter's projection of himself into his subject's position Is full of dangers from a scientific standpoint, it may nonetheless be necessary for a full accounting of human behavior. The task is to make such an approach scientifically acceptable. When that is done, the major differences between the developmental and experimental orientation will, in all probability, disappear and we will have a unified discipline of child psychology that is at once experimental and developmental.

References

Attneave, F., & Arnoult, M.D. "The quantitative study of shape and pattern perception." *Psychological Bulletin*, 53: 452-471, 1956.

Chomsky, N. *Syntactic Structures.* The Hague: Mouton, 1957.

Freud, S. "The interpretation of dreams." In A. A. Brill (Ed.) *The Basic Writings of Sigmund Freud.* New York: Modern Library, 1938.

Freud, S. "Formulations regarding the two principles of mental functioning." In *Collected Papers*, Vol. IV. London: Hogarth, pp. 13-21, 1953.

Greco, P. "L'apprentissage dans une situation a structure operatoire concrete: les inversions successives de l'ordre lineaire par des rotations de 180°." In J. Piaget (Ed.) *Etudes d'Epistemologie Genetique*, Vol. 8. Paris: Universitaries de France, pp. 68-182, 1959.

Hartman, H. "Ego psychology and the problem of adaptation." In D. Rapaport (Ed.) *The Organization and Pathology of Thought.* New York: Columbia University Press, 1951.

Kaplan, B. "Meditations on genesis." *Human Development*, 10: 65-87, 1967.

Osgood C. E., Suci, G. J., and Tannenbaum, P. H. *The Measurement of Meaning.* Urbana: University of Illinois Press, 1957.

Piaget, J. "L'adaptation limnaea stagnalis au milieu lacoustres de la Suisse commande." *Revue Suisse de Zoologie*, 36: 263-531, 1929.

Piaget, J. *The Psychology of Intelligence.* London: Routledge & Kegan Paul, 1950.

Piaget, J. *The Child's Conception of the World.* London: Routledge & Kegan Paul, 1951.

Piaget, J. *The Origins of Intelligence in Children.* New York: International Universities Press, 1952.

Piaget, J. *The Construction of Reality in the Child.* New York: Basic Books, 1954.

Piaget, J. *Six Psychological Studies.* New York: Random House, 1968.

Riesen, A. H. "Stimulation as a requirement for growth and function in behavioral development." In D. W. Fiske and S. R. Maddi (Eds.) *Functions of Varied Experience.* Homewood, Ill.: Dorsey Press, 57-80, 1961.

Russell, W. A. "An experimental psychology of development: Pipe dream or possibility." In D. B. Harris (Ed.) *The Concept of Development.* Minneapolis: University of Minnesota Press, 162-174, 1957.

Smedslund, J. "Apprentissage des notions de la conservation et de la transitivité du poids." In J. Piaget (Ed.) *Etudes d' Epistemologie Genetique,* Vol. 9. Paris. Presses Universitaires de France, pp. 85-124, 1959.

Waddington, C.H. *The Nature of Life.* New York: Atheneum, 1962.

Werner, H. "The concept of development from a comparative and organismic point of view." In D.B. Harris (Ed.) *The Concept of Development.* Minneapolis: University of Minnesota Press, 125-148, 1957.

White, S.A. "Evidence for a hierarchical arrangement of learning processes." In L.P. Lipsitt and C.C. Spiker (Eds.) *Advances in Child Development and Behavior.* New York: Academic Press, 187-220, 1965.

Wohwill, J.F. "A study of the development of the number concept by scalogram analysis." *Journal of Genetic Psychology,* 97: 345-377, 1960.

Wohwill, J.F. "Un essai l'apprentissage dans le domaine de la conservation du nombre." In J. Piaget (Ed.) *Etudes d' Epistemologie Genetique,* Vol. 9. Paris: Presses Universitaires de France, pp. 125-35, 1959.

Young, F. A. "The effect of restricted visual space on the refractive error of the young monkey eye." *Investigative Ophthalmology,* 2: 571-577, 1963.

WILLIAM E. MARTIN

Rediscovering the Mind of the Child: A Significant Trend in Research in Child Development*

A spate of anniversary celebrations of university departments, institutes, organizations, and individuals that have been identified with the systematic study of the behavior and development of the child provides evidence that child development, as an area of research, has come of age. An assessment of present status leads inevitably to an examination of the past and to speculation about the future. (1) Predictions of where we are going are compounded largely of our knowledge of where we have been and where we are. Because of its multidisciplinary orientation, research in child development has been, and continues to be, responsive to the influences, both substantive and methodological, of the physical, biological, and social sciences, and of psychology. Such mixed parentage and multiple mothering render it extremely hazardous to make definitive statements of either a retrospective or prospective nature. It would therefore seem to be the better part of valor to restrict myself to a consideration of the influences of only one of the sciences, psychology, particularly as it relates to one significant trend in research in child development, namely, the rediscovery of the mind of the child. I should like first to review the factors

*From the *Merrill-Palmer Quarterly*, 1959-1960, 6, 67-76. Reprinted by permission of the author and the Merrill-Palmer Institute.

responsible for the state of mindlessness that seems to have prevailed until recent years and then turn to some indications that the concept of man as a *rational* being may be reasserting itself.

Most of us, in our training and in our experience, have been subjected to two somewhat conflicting influences: one, the scientific study of behavior, or behavioral science; two, the scientific study of personality, or, to use the words of Jacques Barzun, misbehavioral science.

As a spokesman for the science of behavior, I shall use B.F. Skinner. I am not unaware that he would be considered by some as representative of an extreme point of view. But he presents his case with such candor, simplicity, and directness, and with such lack of pretense, that he deserves our respect and our attention. Unlike some of his fellow behaviorists and unlike the emperor in the classic story, he is fully cognizant of the fact that he wears no clothes.

The essence of the Skinnerian view of a behavioral science is expressed in these words:

The external variables of which behavior is a function provide for what may be called a causal or functional analysis. We undertake to predict and control the behavior of the individual organism. This is our "dependent variable"—the effect for which we are to find the cause. Our *"independent variables"—the causes of behavior—*are the external conditions of which behavior is a function. Relations between the two—the *"cause—and—effect relationships" in behavior—*are the laws of a science. A synthesis of these laws expressed in quantitative terms yields a comprehensive picture of the organism as a behaving system.

This must be done within the bounds of a natural science . . . *(12, p. 35).*

It is clear that the subject matter of a science of behavior is behavior, not persons. The task is a purely empirical one: to determine the environmental conditions under which given behaviors can be elicited or modified. There is no theory. Contrary to the statments of some experimental psychologists, empirical laws do not constitute a theory. It is quite the other way around: A theory— or at least a "good" theory— "enables us to *derive* empirical laws" (5, p. 126) which are then subject to confirmation by experimental test.

The object of behavioral science is to predict and control. Again, to quote Skinner:

The scientific "system," like the law, is designed to enable us to handle a subject matter more efficiently. What we call the scientific conception of a thing is not passive knowledge. Science is not concerned with contemplation. When we have discovered the laws which govern a part of the world about us, and when we have organized these laws into a system, we are then ready to deal effectively with that part of the world. By predicting the occurrence of an event we are able to

prepare for it. By arranging conditions in ways specified by the laws of a system, we not only predict, we control: we "cause" an event to occur or to assume certain characteristics (12, p. 14).

Inner states of the organism, mental or physical, play no part in analysis and prediction. They exist—at least physical states do; but they are irrelevant. With characteristic frankness, Skinner says at one point: "The 'emotions' are excellent examples of the fictional causes to which we commonly attribute behavior" (12, p. 160). It follows that we cannot speak of intelligence, except possibly as what an intelligence test measures—probably not even that; perhaps we can speak only of a given behavior as being more or less adaptive with respect to some environmental variable.

Implicit in this formulation is a "nothing—but" view of the human being. Man is an empty organism. He has no nature, only a history. He is the product of that history. The outcome in terms of behavior is determined and determinable, or predictable.

It is under the influence of such a science of behavior that psychology is said to have first lost its soul, later its consciousness, and now seems in danger of losing its mind altogether. It has been a protestant reformation. It has almost succeeded in bringing into existence the Brave New World that Aldous Huxley once described with tongue in cheek. It should come as no surprise that Skinner has already contributed to our civilization a mechanical baby tender and now promises us teaching machines.

But what of a science of persons? Here concern is not so much with behavior as it is with the behaver. Behavior is only the symptom or clue to what it is the individual is striving to obtain or attain. The basic problem is one of motivation. And motivation is usually characterized by conflict—between what one wishes to do and what one feels he should do, between impulse, one's biological inheritance, and conscience, one's social inheritance. The individual is a battleground with two contending forces neither of which is realistic or rational. This conflict can never be fully resolved; it is part of the human condition. There can be, at best, a balance of power, a truce, a cold war.

The task, as in behavioral science, is to arrive at some relational statements between cause and effect. The effect is still behavior. But the cause is now within the organism, not in the environment. The environment provides only the stage on which the human comedy is played.

The purpose of a science of persons is not to predict but to explain. In a recent paper Scriven has pointed to a clear—cut distinction between prediction and explanation:

> What we are trying to provide when making a prediction is simply a claim that, at a certain time, *an event or state of affairs will occur. In explanation we are looking for a cause, an event that not only occurred earlier but stands in a special relation to the other event. Roughly speaking, the prediction requires only a correlation, the explanation more. The difference has as one consequence the possibility of making predictions from indicators other than causes—for example, predicting a storm from a sudden drop in the barometric pressure. Clearly we could not say that the drop in pressure in our house caused the storm: it merely presaged it. So we can sometimes predict what we cannot explain. But can we ever explain what we could not have predicted, even if we had had the information about the antecedent conditions? . . . This seems less likely, roughly because finding causes is harder than finding correlations. Yet it is possible, and, in some areas of knowledge, common. For sometimes the kind of correlation we need for prediction is absent, but a causal relationship can be identified (11,p. 480).*

A science of persons is forever bemused with the question, "Why did the child behave as he did?" It seldom wonders, "How will he behave in the future?" The universe of behavior is characterized by regularity; the universe of persons is characterized by irregularity. Parents, teachers, and all those who work with children soon learn not to be surprised by anything. They learn to expect the unexpected. And they are usually not disappointed.

It is interesting to note that Freud, with all of his understanding of human behavior, was reluctant to predict the future. In his later years he wrote: "If the patient who has made such a good recovery never produces any more symptoms calling for analysis, it still, of course, remains an open question how much of this immunity is due to a benevolent fate which spares him too searching a test" (6, p. 321).

The wish to predict leads to a search for empirical laws; the wish to explain leads to the formulation of theory. The empiricist observes and induces. The theoretician contemplates and deduces. The empiricist tests his prediction; the theoretician tests his explanations.

At first glance, a science of persons would seem to present a "something—more" view of the human being. He has a nature as well as a history. His nature influences his history or at least the impact of history upon himself. Two children will thus react quite differently to the same experience because they differ in their nature. The human being is not an empty organism. He is not the victim of his environment.

But, in another sense, he seems to be the victim of biological determinism. His conflicts are inherent in his biology. On the one hand, his impulses are biological: First, there are the primary drives; then, later drives evolve as he attempts to satisfy the primary drives. On the other hand, his conscience is a consequence of his biological helplessness in the early years. His dependency leads inevitably to the incorporation of some rules of conduct or values. It is the price to be paid for acceptance into the human society. Man's biological nature determines the impact of environmental events and makes certain stages in development and a given ordering of these stages. It is essentially a fatalistic view.

Confronted with strong and conflicting biological and societal demands, man is essentially a tragic figure. Being human is his problem. There is no real solution. He must admit to the necessities of the human condition. What little freedom he possesses he can maintain only to the extent that he differentiates between the necessities that actually exist and those that only seem to exist (10, p. 236).

Science, whether directed toward behavior or the behaver, reflects and is reflected in modern society. It provides either the basis or the justification for our approach to children—whether we are training or studying them. A science of behavior emphasizes the importance of environmental manipulation and scheduling and thus the mechanization and routinization of experience. Similarly, it stresses performance in the individual. Doing something, doing it efficiently, doing it automatically—these are the goals. It is the mechanization of man as well as the mechanization of the environment. The result is the triumph of technology: a pushbutton world with well—trained buttonpushers. This, for many, is the American dream come true. It is also the Russian dream. For they compete with us largely in the area of technology. American visitors to the Soviet Union see a society which in many ways aspires to be like us—and is succeeding. This identity of values and goals is no accident. For Pavlov, the father of behavioral science, is also the major, if not the only, influence on social science in modern Russia.

A person—oriented science has somewhat different goals. It attempts first to reduce environmental demands upon the individual and thus minimize tension within the individual, and second to provide as much satisfaction of basic needs as possible, by providing a maximum of material comfort and outlet for impulse expression. The emphasis is upon adjustment. The major characteristic of training and education is permissiveness. We are perhaps less concerned with what the child does than with how he feels. We want him to be happy. It might be said that the emphasis is upon the irrationality of man.

While these two approaches to the

scientific study of man differ greatly, they have one significant factor in common. They both rob the human being of the one characteristic that was once thought to be unique in man, that is, the fact that he has a mind and he has a capacity for thought. It has been and is a period of anti—intellectualism. As Howard Mumford Jones has said: ". . . the eighteenth century of Voltaire has yielded to the twentieth century of Senator McCarthy. Ours is an age which is proud of machines which think and suspicious of any man who tries to do so" (8, p. 172).

A personal experience provides an illustration of the current attitude toward intelligence and the intellectual. To a good friend of mine, a prominent businessman, I once expressed my inability to understand the tendency of the community to regard teachers, particularly university professors, as subversive, or potentially so, and to ensure their loyalty by requiring oaths of various kinds. His explanation was that teachers were more intelligent and therefore more susceptible to subversion. I had previously believed that intelligence was an asset. It now appeared that it was a liability.

Thinking, to the extent that it leads to new ideas and pressure for change is, by definition, a subversive activity. Therein lies, perhaps, the great resistance to any notion of special training for the gifted child. It is argued that such a program would lead to an intellectual elite which would be a threat to our democratic way of life. It seems to be forgotten that the founders of our way of life were intellectuals. Recall a few of them: Jefferson, Madison, Monroe, Hamilton. They were men of ideas. Although there were both liberals and conservatives among them, using present—day labels, I doubt that they would find the going easy in our modern society. A society which values mindlessness is not likely to look with favor upon men who think. Rather we seem to have turned our destiny over to a managerial elite, men of action, not men of thought. We flee the individual responsibility of being intelligent and seek the haven of the group, or the committee, or even the subcommittee, for the latter of which Dr. Belaunde, the current president of the United Nations General Assembly, has given the following definition: "a group appointed by the unwilling on behalf of the unprepared to carry out the unnecessary." Part of the discomfiture that one finds in some of the countries of western Europe, particularly in France, derives from the feeling that they are caught between two great powers both of which value machines above men, action above thought, science and technology above humanism.

We cannot conclude that science is responsible for this state of affairs. We can only say that, in its present form, whether behavior- or person-oriented, is is congruent with and supportive of our present condition. As the English novelist, C. P. Snow (13), who was trained as a scientist, has observed: "We are living in the middle of two cultures which have scarcely any contact at all — the traditional non-scientific culture and an up-and-coming scientific one. They are startlingly different, not only in their intellectual approach, but even more so in their climate of thought and their moral attitudes." Whether we continue the cold war or arrive at some form of co-existence with the Communist world, the competition in science and technology will be so great that the gap between the two cultures can only increase. We face the problem of bridging the gap between the scientist or technologist and the humanist. The best hope — perhaps the only hope — lies in the restoration of mind to the science of man. We not only need scientists who think; we need scientists who admit that man thinks.

Fortunately, there are indications that students of man are finding a model of the human being as machine or as a tragic figure helpless to cope with his fate less and less satisfactory. Let me review briefly some developments which portend the rediscovery of mind.

1. There is increasing recognition of consciousness. The child is not only subjected to experience; he experiences, and he is aware of his experiences. Subjective experience is once more being admitted as a proper variable for the student of child development. Significantly, one of our leading philosophers has now publicly called for a reinstatement of the introspective and phenomenological methods in psychology:

The phenomenal data of one's own experience are of course susceptible to direct verification, they are open to immediate inspection. And in keeping with our common-sense convictions, we have every reason to identify these directly inspected or inspectable states imputed to us by others. . . . What will not work in this connection is a purely peripheralistic behaviorism. . . . . Peripheral stimulus situations and response patterns may serve as . . . indicators of central (i.e., mental) states, but they cannot be identified with them (5, p. 124).

In a similar vein, Bridgman (3), the father of operationalism, has presented in a current book a statement of his point of view which exposes the naivete of some of his most ardent disciples. As one reviewer puts it, first quoting the author:

"Not only should we never think of the microscopic world without thinking of microscopes, but we should never think of the microscopic world without thinking of ourselves using the microscope" (p. 154). By "ourselves" he means the "nervous machinery in our heads." In the second place, to describe this physiological contribution to the knower in objective, behavioristic terms, as many psychologists do, is not adequate; introspectional language has a legitimate, though somewhat restricted, use. For example, the operation by which I determine that I have a toothache is quite different from the operation by which I determine that you have a toothache. This distinction . . . is so sharp and spectacular that it must never be forgotten. Finally, the most desirable description of any analysis is one given in the first person; for the investigator cannot get away from the fact that it is he himself who is knowing something, and what he knows is often in very significant ways determined by this fact (2, pp. 31-32).

It appears that at long last Watsonian behaviorism is dead. At least, we have a license from the most respectable of all modern philosophers, the logical positivists, to inquire into the mind of the child. We can treat him not merely as reactor but also as knower. We can assume that he has cognitions. We can inquire into those cognitions and their origins. Of course, we use his behavior to infer his mental states. The point is that we use it as a means, not the end of our investigation.

2. A second sign that we are on the way to rediscovering the mind of the child is the contemporary interest in the effects of early sensory deprivation on cognitive functioning. Earlier studies of institutionalized children by Goldfarb (*see* 9) found that they, as contrasted with rejected children, showed grave defects in their intellectual processes. They seemed to find it particularly difficult to organize their experiences in any meaningful way and to abstract relationships from them. Current interest in deprivation seems to have been triggered off by the "brain-washing" of UN military personnel in the Korean conflict by their Chinese captors. Paradoxically, it took this appalling and loathsome event to remind us that man has a brain and that without a mental image, a model of his environment, he cannot deal effectively with that environment. Without a cognitive map, he cannot develop strategies for evaluating experience, "for finding out what leads to what and with what likelihood" (4, p. 93).

Furthermore, without external stimulation, man has no way of checking, monitoring, or verifying his cognitive model of the environment. There are thus two ways in which we can reduce the human being to helplessness. We can deprive him of external stimulation, as is done in brain-washing. Or we can deprive him of those sensory experiences that are necessary for the development of cognitive maps. It is the latter problem that is, of course, of greater interest to students

of child development. Forgays, a Rutgers University psychologist, has engaged in research that shows some of the conditions under which the child develops the most useful cognitive maps. He is testing the hypothesis that a rich and constantly-changing environment is essential to the formation of models and strategies that will enable the individual to deal intelligently with the complex world in which he lives and will continue to live.

Both the behavioral and the misbehavioral sciences, the first with its concern for regularity and orderliness, the second with its emphasis upon feelings of security in children and the avoidance of stress, have led us to prescribe continuity, stability, and homogeneity as essential ingredients of the learning environment. If the world were a great deal simpler, if it smacked more of a psychological laboratory, perhaps we could agree. But the world is not a laboratory. We need to have, and to develop in our children, resources for dealing with the unexpected, the accidental, and the unusual. It may be that we can ensure a degree of security for children by minimizing the quantity and variety of stimulation and thus eliminating stress. But this ill prepares them for the complex, ever-changing world with which they must deal as adults. Confronted with that world, it should come as no surprise that they experience anxiety and react with either hostility or withdrawal. The choice is between being an angry young man or a beatnik.

Certainly, the inner resources of the brain-washed proved to be insufficient in some cases. It was not that they lacked courage; it was that they lacked mental power. The bland environmental diet on which they had been reared had given them little or no opportunity for developing that mental power. Their disintegration provides a tragic example of a science of man that refuses to recognize that he is first and above all, a creature of thought, at least potentially. If we rob him of his mind, we rob him of his humanity.

3. A third indicator that the age of mindlessness may be coming to an end is provided by the growing number of studies of children's thinking. Piaget, of course, has been engaged in research on mental development for more than thirty years. But, with his devotion to the *methode clinique*, his disdain for statistical methods and sampling, his lack of concern for environmental variables, and his habit of playing the role of logician and epistemologist, his work has been received in the United States with something less than enthusiasm. Recently, however, there appears to have been a breakthrough. Two large-scale programs of research in the Piaget tradition on cognitive processes of children are in process at Harvard University, one under the direction of Bruner in the Laboratory of Social Relations, the second in the Laboratory for Research in Instruction of the Graduate School of Education.

4. Finally, there is the growing protest against the invoking of drive reduction as the primary, if not the exclusive, dynamism of behavior. The notion that all of man's energies are devoted to the reduction of tension has become more and more distasteful and — what is more important — more and more in disagreement with our observations of children. Harlow, the eminent experimental psychologist, puts it this way:

In the course of human events many psychologists have children, and these children always behave in accord with the theoretical position of their parents. For purposes of scientific objectivity the boys are always referred to as "Johnny" and the girls as "Mary." For some eleven months I have been observing the behavior of Mary X. Perhaps the most striking characteristic of this particular primate has been the power and the presistence of her curiosity-investigatory motives. . . . *The frustrations of Mary X appeared to be in large part the results of physical inability to achieve curiosity-investigatory goals. In her second month, frustrations resulted from inability to hold up her head indefinitely while lying prone in her crib or on a mat and the consequent loss of visual curiosity goals. Each time she had to lower her head to rest, she cried lustily. At nine weeks attempts to explore (and destroy) objects anterior resulted in wriggling backward away from the lure and elicited violent negative responses. Once she negotiated forward locomotion, exploration set in, in earnest, and, much to her parents' frustration, shows no sign of diminishing.*

Can anyone seriously believe that the insatiable curiosity-investigatory motivation of the child is a second-order or derived drive conditioned upon hunger or sex or any other internal drive? The S-R theorist and the Freudian psychoanalyst imply that such behaviors are based on primary drives. An informal survey of neobehaviorists who are also fathers (or mothers) reveals that all have observed the intensity or omnipresence of the curiosity-investigatory motive in their own children. None of them seriously believes that the behavior derives from a second-order drive (7, pp. 28–29).

Thus, there is evidence from a variety of sources that there is in the making a cognitive theory of behavior and development. It will view the child not merely as a passive victim of either his environmental history or of his biological nature but as one who strives to be the master of both his nature and his history. It will thus emphasize the unique characteristic which makes that mastery a possibility, namely, intelligence. It will be a science of man that includes man. To the development of such a science, research workers in child development should have a significant contribution to make. For they are, by training and by commitment, both scientists and humanists. As such, they are in a most favorable position to humanize science and to bring an end to the mechanization of the human being. We face the question of whether man is to be the master or slave of his technology. The answer lies in the extent to which we can succeed in developing and utilizing our most important human resource, the ability to think. That we seem to be rediscovering in our research and theory the mind of the child provides hope that the answer will be in our favor.

References

1. Anderson, J.E. Child development: An historical perspective. *Child Development,* 1956, **27,** 181-196.
2. Benjamin, A.C. Review of P.W. Bridgman, *The way things are. Science,* 1959, **130,** 31-32.
3. Bridgman, P.W. *The way things are.* Cambridge, Mass.: Harvard University Press, 1959.
4. Bruner, J.S. The cognitive consequences of early sensory deprivation. *Psychosomatic Medicine,* 1959, **21** 89-95.
5. Feigl, H. Philosophical embarrassments of psychology. *American Psychologist,* 1959, **14,** 115-128.
6. Freud, S. Analysis terminable and interminable. In *Collected papers.* Vol. 5, pp. 316-357. London: Hogarth Press, 1950.
7. Harlow, H.F. Mice, monkeys, men, and motives. *Psychological Review,* 1953, **60,** 23-32.
8. Jones, H.M. Address given at the seventy-fifth anniversary of the University of Colorado, as quoted in *The Nation,* 1951, **172,** 229.
9. Martin, W.E., & Stendler, Celia B. (Eds.) *Readings in child development,* Pp. 397-403. New York: Harcourt, Brace, 1954.
10. Martin, W.E., & Stendler, Celia B. *Child behavior and development.* (Rev. ed.) New York: Harcourt, Brace, 1959.
11. Scriven, M. Explanation and prediction in evolutionary theory. *Science,* 1959, **130,** 477-482.

12. Skinner, B.F. *Science and human behavior.* New York: Macmillan, 1953.
13. Snow, C.P. *The search.* New York: Scribner's, 1958.

2
INFANCY:
PHYSICAL AND MENTAL GROWTH

The infancy period, roughly the first two years of life, is a period of very rapid physical and intellectual growth. Some aspects of this growth are better understood than others, and some, such as whether responses can be conditioned in newborn infants, are shrouded in controversy. It is not possible to provide a comprehensive selection of articles that would cover all aspects of the infancy period. Instead, we have chosen for this chapter two papers surveying some central issues in infant development and some central features of cognitive maturation in infancy.

The paper by Kessen describes several developmental issues current in the study of infant behavior, with an emphasis on evidence that infants from early in life (a) have many adaptive capacities, (b) influence their environment in addition to being influenced by it, and (c) are different from one another. Elkind summarizes useful information about the measurement of infant intelligence and about the importance of the infancy period for intellectual growth, and he describes the emergence in infants of the ability to conceptualize objects, space, time, and causality.

The issues described in these two articles continue to have an important place in developmental psychology. Kessen's concerns with individual differences, with the reciprocal nature of parent-child interaction, and with the question of early learning are reflected in many current research studies of young children. Likewise, questions about the nature of the IQ, the effects of early childhood education, and the significance of nutrition in mental growth, as dealt with by Elkind, remain unresolved and controversial. Each of these subjects is elaborated further in readings we have chosen for Chapters 3 (Rheingold, Ainsworth and Bell), 4 (Bell, Moss), and 6 (Wechsler, Elkind).

WILLIAM KESSEN

Research on the Psychological Development of Infants: An Overview*

The infant has not always been treated kindly by American psychologists. Although almost all theories — whether in the tradition of Watson, Freud, or Koffka — celebrate the importance of infant behavior, and claim that the baby is striking proof of the validity of their views, systematic empirical study of the child in his crucial first year has been an on-again, off-again affair. And for a number of reasons, not the least of which is the difficulty of seeing young children in the large numbers that we have at our command in studying the pre-school child or the adolescent. Once a child leaves the hospital after the lying-in period, he is not again easily available for research until he appears in nursery school. It may also be that the infant is so clearly one of us — in that he is human, and so clearly and incomprehensibly different, in that he is a baby — that we have, on occasion, escaped our frustration by constructing theoretical babies instead of observing real ones.

Happily, these disabilities no longer block research. There is evidence, and not only in the United States, that psychologists are studying the infant more closely than ever before. Merely to call the names of investigators and refer to some of their

findings would consume many pages. This is not to say, by the way, that the theoretical or constructed child has disappeared. Far from it! Behind each empirical investigation, there is a model, and this model colors and sometimes dominates the interpretation that is given the empirical protocols.

I would like to be able to present a neat, clear (even if artificial) dichotomy or trichotomy of theoretical positions concerning infancy — I recall with some nostalgia our antique friend "maturation *versus* learning" — but the current situation in the psychological study of infancy does not accept such simple classification. It is only a modest exaggeration to say that a recitation of theoretical subtleties would approach the complexity of a recitation of research findings. In the face of this kind of variety, I cannot hope to lay out a complete or even a fair summary of current research and thought about the behavior of the infant, Rather, I will present for your comment, review, and evaluation, a short set of propositions about babies and studies of babies; under each of these loose-jointed statements, we can examine a part of the research and speculation that has appeared over the last several years.

The first proposition or summary statement that I will propose is that *a comparative psychology of infancy can be anticipated*. Harlow's well-known

*From the *Merrill-Palmer Quarterly*, 1963, 9, 83-94. Reprinted by permission of the author and the Merrill-Palmer Institute.

work (1958) on affectional systems in the monkey, though incomplete, is as stimulating a body of research as has been done on animal development over the last decade. Less widely known, but of at least equal theoretical impact, are T. C. Schneirla's (1959) speculations about approach and avoidance and their relation to stimulus intensity. Hess (1959), among others, has presented data and commentary on the phenomena of imprinting. Seymour Levine (1957) has contributed a number of papers on the effect of infantile stress on later behavior. These names only begin a list of the researchers who are working on developmental problems with infra-human animals.

Two general comments are warranted here. The animal work which is now going on in developmental psychology is not "dry-as-dust" laboratory demonstration. Moreover, little of this work leads to procedures routinely applicable to children, in the way that some current studies of reinforcement are; nor is the current animal work aimed at elaboration of the obvious. The psychologists studying animal development are in advance of their colleagues in human developmental studies, not only in regard to novel empirical techniques, but more important, in their willingness to take an intellectual chance or risk a speculation. The second note to be appended to the work with animals is the classical one, namely, the possibility of experimental manipulation of more than a trivial sort. We have only seen the beginning of work with animals, and particularly with primates, that will permit us to examine experimentally propositions that would otherwise remain available only to limited observational examination. Studies of the relation of infant to parent, for example, can be investigated along all relevant dimensions only by the use of animals. This is not to say that once we have found the rhesus we can abandon the human being, but the thoughtfulness and energy of investigators currently working in animal research will have no small impact on current research in the psychology of development.

But let me put aside the allure of precision and control possible with animal work and confine the rest of my general propositions to those about human behavior.

The first proposition about children to be considered, and perhaps the most obvious, is that *infants are various* — young children are different from one another. I may see a straw man when I speak against the notion that human infants at birth, like well-made cigarettes, cannot be distinguished from one another; but there is still abroad in psychology — at least in the academical variety — the feeling that children at birth are, by and large, pretty much undifferentiated protoplasm or no more than merely randomly varying beings. Whatever the present state is of the pure, undifferentiated position in the sociology of knowledge, evidence is accumulating that parents and nurses were right all along — stable differences in behavior can be detected in the first days of life. Hammond (1957) has shown the stability of physical growth patterns. Richmond and his colleagues at Syracuse (1955) have reported psychophysiological stabilities in the newborn. Thomas, Chess, Birch, and Hertzig (1960), although they have published only preliminary reports, have stated that on nine variables — among them, reactivity and irritability — they have found stability in children followed longitudinally over a period of two years. There are some suggestions in Bell's work (1960), and there are some findings in our work on newborns at Yale (1961), which tend to support a strong generalization that stable individual differences in a large number of behaviors — sucking, general movement, reactivity — exist very early in life. Yet, impressive as it is, the work on the assessment of individual differences among human infants has not, like some of the animal work, been "built out" from novel observations and speculations. Rather, it has come largely from the essential and tedious work of constructing adequate response measures. These advances in technology or method are clear and welcome, but they leave open two larger questions about individual differences.

First, what is the long-range stability or relevance of these differences? It is good to know that the newborn shows stable differences in activity level from his colleague in the next crib, but the importance of this observation is markedly reduced if the difference does not show up in some form later. Among the investigators, other than the Birch group, who have done some interesting speculative work on this score, is the French psychologist Stambak (1956). She has segregated two groups of infants — hypertonic and hypotonic — and has discussed the relation of this tendency to be active or quiet to such important developmental changes as onset of walking. In addition, the Czech group (Papousek, 1961) is investigating the stability of the infant's behavior during conditioning over the first six months of life. Such studies are provocative curtain-raisers on the intricate question of behavioral stability in infancy.

There is a second question about which we have very little evidence. How are these early behavioral variations related to variations in the environment? How do different combinations of infant and caretaker mesh together? We can tag babies as active or quiet; we can make this discrimination in the first five or ten days of life. We can suspect, too, that some mothers like active babies and some mothers like quiet babies. What do you get when you combine an active baby with a mother who wanted a quiet one or a quiet baby with a mother who wanted an active one? We have very little to go on here, not only because of the obvious technical difficulties of longitudinal studies of this kind, and not only because of the fluidity of our ideas about what is important in the home, but also because, until recently, we have not had reliable ways of describing the young child's environment. The technical advance in the methods of describing newborn behavior have not been matched by methods for describing the home. But here, again, there is promise. Schaefer, Bell, and Bayley (1959) have proposed a parent attitude scale. The important interview work of Sears, et al., (1957) provides a framework for the description of parents' behavior. Rheingold (1960) has recently specified some of the dimensions of variation between home and institution. These papers point the way toward the time when a genuine analysis can be made of the interaction between mother and child. The word "genuine" reflects the hope that this analysis will not be a contaminated one; that we can make assessments of the status of the newborn, independent of observing the mother, and make assessment of the mother, independent of observing the child.

The next summary proposition that I want to suggest warrants detailed examination. I submit that *the young infant is not incompetent* or, by Andre-Thomas' (1954) catching phrase, "the neonate is not a neophyte."

We have passed the time, not so very long ago, when the newborn was considered to be sensorily bereft (e.g., Preyer's contention that children are born deaf), but the notion of newborn incompetence persists. It has perhaps its strongest statement in the work of the psychoanalysts, especially Spitz (1959), who maintains the existence of a non-differentiated phase in early life, where the newborn does not code inputs at all. In this view of the infant, by no means limited to psychoanalysts, both the baby's sensory capacities and his response capacities are held to be severely limited. The trend of recent research is clearly against this conception of the child. Research on newborn behavior over the last five years has invariably added to the newborn's list of abilities. Peiper (1956) in his encyclopedic treatment, Andre-Thomas (1954) and his colleagues in Paris, Madame Ste. Anne-Desgassies, and Prechtl (1958) are among the workers who have discussed the extended sensory and response range of the newborn in some detail. Gorman and his associates (1959) have recently found in a study of acuity that the newborn has visual resolving powers which are not markedly inferior to those of the older child. From the

research available on the competence of the newborn, let me present three studies in some detail as illustrative and somewhat representative of this newer view of the newborn.

The first study, by Blauvelt (1960), deals with the precision of at least one response the newborn makes. Following up earlier work of Prechtl on head-turning, Blauvelt has studied the baby's response to a very simple stimulation, in which the experimenter moves her finger from the tragus of the baby's ear—the baby lying on its back in the crib—toward the baby's mouth and then away again in a flat elliptical course. It turns out that the baby tracks this movement by turning his head at a speed and to a position that will reduce the distance between his mouth and the stimulating finger. He tracks this movement without special tuition; it is, if you like, built-in. The infant can pick up approaching stimulation and reduce the distance to it very quickly; he can "find" the approaching breast or bottle. What is impressive about this response is the precision of it. This is not the response of a wild newborn, flailing around uselessly and without direction; this is an organism making a precise and exact tracking response. It is a limited skill, to be sure, and certainly not widely generalizable to other activities, but it illustrates the responding precison of some newborn.

The second study illustrative of newborn competence may be one of the most important empirical research products of the last decade in infancy work. Bronshtein, Antonova, Kamenetskaya, Luppova, and Sytova (1958) have described a technique for assessing the limits of sensory differentiation in the infant that promises a precision in psychophysical description that has heretofore been possible only for the much older child. Briefly, the procedure is this. You permit or induce the child to suck and record his rhythmic response. If, during sucking, you sound a brief tone, say of 512 cycles/sec., the baby stops sucking. When the tone stops, the baby begins to suck again. To a second stimulation of the same tone, he will stop sucking. This sequence can be repeated four or five times for sounds and then when you sound your 512-cycle tone he goes on sucking without interruption. He has adapted to that sound. If, however, you now present a different tone, say one of 1,024 cycles, he will stop sucking. If he continues to suck on the application of the second stimulus, this is presumptive evidence that he cannot discriminate the two stimuli. If he does stop sucking on the second stimulus, if it "undoes the adaptation," then there is evidence that he can discriminate these two stimuli. If this technique is as sensitive as the Russians suggest, we will be able to find out more about the sensory capacities of the young infant than we can find out about the sensory capacities of young five- or six-year-olds. Bronshtein presents data to indicate that the infant makes clearly differential responses to variations in pitch, light intensity, and other stimulus changes. Lipsitt, at Brown, has adapted this technique to a study of olfactory stimulation and has found that not only is sucking inhibited and adapted in this fashion but so also is movement. Just as the Blauvelt study illustrates the possible response flexibility of the newborn, so the Bronshtein and Lipsitt studies indicate the remarkable amount of stimulus

coding the newborn is capable of. The world of the infant is not a vast confusing "blob."

Consider yet a third study. In our work at Yale (1963), we have found that if you put a nipple in a baby's mouth, he will stop general movement at once, and when you take it out he will start moving again. This effect appears in the absence of nutrient; the nipple does not supply food—it only provides an opportunity to suck. And, this inhibition of movement takes place in the fourth or third or second, or even first day of life. The child is able to deal with a complex and vitally important input—namely, nipple or sucking—by a very regular response. Nor, apparently, does he have to learn either how to suck or how to quiet. There is of course the argument that he learned the responses *in utero*, but we have hardly advanced beyond Hippocrates' statement of that argument 2,500 years ago.

These studies suggest that the newborn has far greater capacities for sensory discrimination than could have been guessed a decade ago, and though less impressive, the evidence is beginning to indicate that he has surprising response competencies as well. But the evidence for newborn resourcefulness poses a peculiar paradox. To put the question very bluntly, if the human newborn is so capable, why does he not learn more? If he is so capable, why is he so stupid? These questions form the bridge to my next general proposition, one which seems so insecure that I have phrased it in the form of yet another question.

There is early adaptation, but is there early learning? The conflict represented in this question can be expressed simply enough. On the one hand the behavior of baby seems to change over the first few days of life. There are many examples; let me cite just one.

Peiper maintains that there are three techniques of infantile sucking. One of them is the response that most mammals use to get milk out of a breast; it is a lapping response that involves pressing the nipple against the roof of the mouth with the tongue and squeezing milk out of it. Another one is to reduce pressure inside the mouth so as to pull the milk in by a discrepancy in pressure. This is the way most babies suck from bottles. And the third, fairly infrequent technique—confined to bottlefed babies for obvious reasons—is to bite hard at the back of the nipple and squirt milk into the mouth. This variation is interesting because babies apparently come to use one of these different patterns very quickly. They learn, if "learn" is appropriate, the kind of sucking to use.

The difficulty with calling this kind of change "learning" arises from our failure to demonstrate early learning in a controlled setting. If the newborn is capable of this natural learning it should be possible for a psychologist to teach him something in a systematic learning study. And yet the evidence, controlled evidence for newborn learning, hardly exists. There is research by Marquis (1931), recently replicated in the USSR, showing that the baby adapts to a feeding rhythm, but the evidence does not support the conclusion that learning according to the usual theoretical models takes place in the period of early infancy. The Russians, with their strong demand for environmental control of behavior, have tried a large number of times to condition young infants. Sometimes they are successful; oftentimes they

are not. Russian studies do not report conditioning in children under eight or nine days of age, and most conditioning studies indicate that it may take weeks or even months to condition an infant child in the Pavlovian mode (Dashkovskaya, 1953). How do we interpret this curious discrepancy between the fact that the human baby seems to adapt his sucking style and to his feeding routines on the one hand, and the difficulty that all investigators have had in demonstrating newborn learning on the other?[1]

The following three options seem available to us: First, in spite of my statements about newborn competence, there may be genuine neurological incapacity in the newborn. There is no such thing as early learning, in the usual sense, because the child is not complete. A case for this position can be made. There are data on myelinization, on changes in pattern of EEG, on developments of vision and prehension, on the appearance of smiling—to take the most obvious case—all of which can be used to bolster the view that the young infant is a neurologically deficient organism. Under this reading, how do we account for the changes in behavior that do take place? Perhaps by maintaining that the caretaker becomes more competent. This would be a case of training the parent to adapt more effectively to the child rather than teaching the child to adapt to his environment. And to the data from Bronshtein and Lipsitt on the ability of the young infant to make sensory discriminations,

[1] The argument for early adaptation by the infant can probably be made much more forcefully, but a natural history of the first months of life remains to be written.

we would have to say, "True, infants can make sensory discriminations, but there is no associative coding; there is a deficiency in the hooking of links together."

The second answer, and the one I think that would be given by the learning analysts (Gewirtz, 1961), is that nobody has tackled the problem of early learning. In particular, holders of this position would maintain that the procedures of classical conditioning as used by the Russians are the wrong tactics. What we should do if we want to demonstrate early learning is to use instrumental techniques; that is, to make some effective reinforcement contingent on the occurrence of some response of the infant. For example, let the baby turn his head and then give him something to suck on. This is a testable propostion and it is being tested.

I would like to suggest a third possibility—an unpopular one. In brief, there may be experiential effects that are not learning. To put it another way, not all adaptation of the infant represents either classical conditioning or instrumental learning. I think it is inappropriate to maintain that all changes in behavior that can be related to the child's contact with the environment are the result of reinforcement contingencies. Of course, the instrumental learning position can be made to fit them, but it seems to me that such a forced fit results in theoretical vagueness and a weakening of the instrumental position.

Perhaps in pulling apart the problem of behavioral change in early infancy to exaggerate the variation among options, I have only shown that the resolution of the problem will require revisions in method, new knowledge of infantile neurophysiology, and a reworking of contemporary learning theory.

But consider now another interesting problem which illuminates some theoretical disagreements among students of infancy. Two theoretical positions have occupied this field—the psychoanalytic and the learning-theoretical. Justice can be done to neither in a summary presentation; Rapaport (1959) and Wolff (1960) present the psychoanalytic presuppositions in detail and with force; Gewirtz (1961) has prepared a closely reasoned argument for a learning analysis.[2] Now, there is a new entrant into the field of theories of mother attachment. John Bowlby in a series of recent papers (1958) has borrowed from the investigators of instinct in animals, a notion that sounds very much like imprinting and has suggested that the child's responses of sucking, clinging, and following lead to mother-attachment. Just sucking, and just clinging, and just following on the part of the child, without obvious reinforcement or redistribution of cathexis, will result in a union between child and mother; much as the chick will imprint on a blinking light. Not only does Bowlby discuss what ties the child to his mother—namely, these three responses—but be also discusses what links the mother to the child. Not only does the child become attached to the mother because of sucking, clinging, and following, but the mother is drawn or

---

[2] It should be noted in passing that a learning analysis is both stronger and in a better position for compromise with other views by virtue of a retreat from the drive-reduction interpretation of reinforcement and by recent animal studies which show stable secondary reinforcement effects.

attached—Bowlby does not use the word "imprinting"—to the child by the child's smiling and crying. Smiling and crying are held to be congenital or innate releasers of maternal behavior.

It is difficult to evaluate this position and I am hard pressed to invent a satisfactory test for it. Perhaps we must call on animal research to work out the implications of Bowlby's assertions. But the main value of this new view will probably be the value of all theories of development—that they jog thinking, they make people run a study just to see what happens. Certainly Bowlby's ideas have had that effect. His own research with Robertson on separation (1952), the work done by Schaffer (1959) on hospitalization of young children, and an unpublished study by Ainsworth (1961) have demonstrated the provocative effect of these speculations. One of the achievements of the work done by Ainsworth, in Uganda, is that, instead of discussing mother attachment as a unitary notion, she has, in these longitudinal field observations of the child between four weeks of age and fourteen months, described some ten or twelve indexes of the child's attachment to the mother, and in this way has made possible a more subtle analysis of the relation than we have had heretofore.

It is interesting to note, as an adjunct to the problem of mother-attachment, that something very curious indeed seems to happen to children near the middle of the first year. Ambrose's (1961) results on smiling indicate that at 17—25 weeks, general social smiling begins to decay and the child begins to smile only at its caretakers. Schaffer's work indicates that children who are hospitalized before they are 28 weeks old, accept hospital routines and separation easily; children hospitalized after 28-weeks-of-age show striking symptom patterns of distress and refusal to accept normal hospital care. Ainsworth finds that almost all of her criteria of mother attachment begin to show transition in the period from 17 to 30 weeks, with much of the change occurring in the narrow band between 25 and 28 weeks. Somewhere in the middle of the first year, the child appears to shift from being attached to human beings at large to being attached to one, or two, or three human beings.

The Ainsworth study is comparable in its impact to Rheingold's (1956) study of caretaking in institutionalized infants— both of these studies represent the payoff for the theoretical positions underlying them. The psychology of infancy undoubtedly profits from being in a state of theoretical dis-equilibrium, and the diversity of ideas about the nature of the child's attachment to his mother will almost certainly be productive of important empirical advances.

Consider one last generalization about infancy. It is one where contention, compromise, and reciprocation among theoretical positions has already resulted in general agreement. *The infant is active, and the relation of infant and caretaker is reciprocal.*

It is on this issue that the psychologist's view of the child has changed most dramatically in recent years. The model of the child which was drawn form Pavlov through Watson, and supported by the development of learning psychology in the United States, was of a recipient organism—a reactive one. Behavior at any particular time is the function of the current stimulating environment. This remains technically a sound view, but the effect of it on the psychology of the infant was to diminish our appreciation of how complicated and subtle is the child.

Not only can the child be usefully seen as active, rather than merely as reactive, but is may also be useful to think of even the infant as a problem-solver. Certainly the child, like the adult, can be seen as encountering problems in his environment. At least from the age of six months, the child's behavior can be discussed in terms of discrepancy, goal-seeking, means to an end, and so on. One student of children has not deviated from this view of the active searching child. Piaget and his students have seen the child, especially the infant, as being in a constant exchange with the environment, meeting its demands, and what American investigators somehow forgot, making its own demands on that environmemt.

The shift in point-of-view—to set the antithesis sharply—has been from the child who is a passive receptacle, into which learning and maturation pour knowledge and skills and affects until he is full, to the child as a complex, competent organism who, by acting on the environment and being acted on in turn, develops more elaborated and balanced ways of dealing with discrepancy, conflict, and dis-equilibrium. This shift, I believe, is of incalculable implication and seems to have been accepted to some degree by almost all students of children. Bowlby emphasizes the control by the child in crying and smiling; psychoanalytic theory makes more space for autonomous ego functions; child psychologists dedicated to a learning analysis speak of the child as active; and I suspect Piaget thinks of how he knew it all the time. But this shift only sets the problem for the psychology of the infant; questions abound. What is a "problem" for the infant? What is an environmental discrepancy for the newborn, for the six-month old, for a walker? Do Piaget's speculations about assimilation, accommodation, and equilibration have more than a metaphorical value? Can child psychologists follow the lead of psychologists of cognition in adults, who use computer analogies? Can we build a theory of cognitive development without the use of terms like reinforcement, drive, or dissonance resolution?

Only one thing seems certain. We are better equipped, with attitude and technique, to make a systematic and meaningful analysis of infant behavior than ever before. The current psychology of infant behavior, by and large, is managing to steer skillfully between the Scylla of "Oh, Oh, look what the baby did!" and the Charybdis of "But the theory says thus and so." We are engaging in hot, theoretical debate, but more and more the debate refers back to the child—back to the theory-illuminated facts.

References

Ainsworth, M.D. The development of infant child interaction among the Ganda. Paper read at Tavistock Study Group of Mother-Infant

Interaction, London, 1961.

Ambrose, J.A. The development of smiling response in early infancy. In Foss, B. M. (Ed.), *Determinants of infant behavior*. New York: Wiley, 1961.

Andre-Thomas. Ontogenese de la vie psycho-affective et de la douleur. *Encephale*, 1954, 43 289-311.

Bell, R. Q. Relations between behavior manifestations in the human neonate. *Child Develpm.*, 1960, 31 463-477.

Blauvelt, H. and J. McKenna. Capacity of the human newborn for mother-infant interaction. II. The temporal dimensions of a neonate, response. *Psychiat. Res. Rep.*, 1960, 13 128-147.

Bowlby, J. The nature of the child's tie to his mother. *Int. J. Psychoanal.*, 1958, **39**, 1-24.

Bronshtein, A. I., T.G. Antonova. A. G. Kamenetskaya, N. N. Luppova, and V. A. Sytova. On the development of the functions of analyzers in infants and some animals at the early stage of ontogenesis. In *Problems of evolution of physiological functions*. OTS Report No. 50-61066. Translation obtainable from U.S. Dept. of Commerce, Moscow: Acad. Sci., 1958.

Dashkovskaya, V.S. First conditioned reactions in newly born children in normal state and in certain pathological states. *Zh. vyssh. nervn. Deiatel.*, 1953, 3(2), 247-259.

Gewirtz, J. L. A learning analysis of the effects of normal stimulation, privation, and deprivation on the acquisition of social motivation and attachment. In Foss, B. M. (Ed.)., *Determinants of infant behavior*. New York: Wiley, 1961.

Gorman, J. J., D. G. Cogan, and S. S. Gellis. A device for testing visual acuity in infants. *Sight-Saving Rev.*, 1959, **29**, 80-84.

Hammond, W. H. The constancy of physical types as determined by factorial analysis. *Hum. Biol.*, 1957, **29**, 40-61.

Harlow, H. F. The nature of love. *Amer. Psychologist*, 1958, 13 673-685

Hess, E.H. Imprinting. *Science*. 1959, **130** 133-141.

Kessen, W. and A. M. Leutzendorff. The effect of non-nutritive sucking on movement in the human newborn. *J. comp. Physiol. Psychol.*, 1963.

Kessen, W., E. J. Williams, and J. P. Williams. Selection and test of response measures in the study of the human newborn. *Child Develpm.*, 1961, 32 7-24.

Levine. S. Infantile experience and resistance to psychological stress. *Science*, 1957, **126**, 405.

Marquis, D. P. Can conditioned responses be established in the newborn infant? *J. genet. Psychol.*, 1931, 39 479-492.

Papousek, H. A physiological view of early ontogenesis of so-called voluntary movements. In P. Sobotka (Ed.), *Functional and meta-*

bolic development of the central nervous system. Prague: State Pedagogic Publ., 1961.

Peiper, A. *Die Eigenart der Kindlichen Hirntatigkeit* (2nd Ed.). Leipzig: Thieme, 1956.

Prechtl, H. F. R. The directed head turning response and allied movements of the human baby. *Behaviour*, 1958, **13**, 212-242.

Rapaport, D. The structure of psychoanalytic theory: A systematizing attempt. In Koch, S. (Ed.), *Pyschology: a study of a science. vol. 3.* New York: McGraw-Hill, 1959.

Rheingold, H.L. The modification of social responsiveness in institutional babies. *Monogr. Soc. Res. Child Develpm.*, 1956, **21** (2)

Rheingold, H. L. The measurement of maternal care. *Child Develpm.*, 1960, **31**, 565-575.

Richmond, J. B. and S. L. Lustman. Autonomic function in the neonate: I. Implications for psychosomatic theory. *Psychosom. Med.*, 1955. **17**, 269-275.

Robertson, J. and J. Bowlby. Responses of young children to separation from their mothers. *Courrier de la Centre Internationale de L'Enfance*, 1952, **2**, 131-142.

Schaefer, E. S., R. Q. Bell, and N. Bayley. Development of a maternal behavior research instrument. *J. genet. Psychol.*, 1959, **95**, 83-104.

Schaffer, H. R. and W. M. Callender. Psychologic efforts of hospitalization in infancy. *Pediatrics*, 1959, **24** 528-539.

Schneirla, T. R. An evolutionary and developmental theory of biphasic process underlying approach and withdrawal. In M. R. Jones (Ed.), *Nebraska symposium on motivation:* 1959 Lincoln: Univer. of Nebraska Press, 1959.

Sears, R. R., E. E. Maccoby, and H. Levin. *Patterns of child rearing.* New York: Harper & Row, 1957.

Spitz, R. A. *A genetic field theory of ego formation; its implications for pathology.* New York: Internat. Univer. Press, 1959.

Stambak, M. Contribution a l'etude du developpement moteur chez le nourrisson. *Enfance*, 1956, **9**(4), 49-59.

Thomas, A., S. Chess, H. Birch, and M. E. Hertzig. A longitudinal study of primary reactive patterns in children. *Comprehensive Psychiat.*, 1960, **1**, 103-112.

Wolff, P. H. *The developmental psychologies of Jean Piaget and psychoanalysis.* New York: International Universities, 1960.

DAVID ELKIND

Cognition in Infancy and Early Childhood*

Cognition has to do with knowledge and with the processes by which it is acquired and utilized. Research on the development of cognition has gone in several different directions depending upon the theoretical orientation of the investigator in question. These orientations can be loosely grouped within two broad categories. On the one hand there is the orientation which starts from the assumption that knowledge and the capacity to acquire it exists in some amount and can be measured. This is the *mental test* approach. A second orientation starts from the premise that knowledge and the processes of acquisition change or develop with age and the task of psychology is to describe and explain this development. This second orientation might be called *developmental*. It should be said that these two approaches do not necessarily contradict one another. The mental test approach is concerned with assessing individual differences whereas the developmental approach concerns itself with normative trends. Yet individual differences can only be assessed with reference to norms while norms are always abstractions from individual variations. In fact, many of the tasks which

appear on intelligence tests are also used in the study of the nature and content of cognitive processes. In short, the difference between the orientations is relative rather than absolute and is more a matter of differing emphasis rather than differences in kind.

Defined in this broad fashion, these two orientations with respect to cognition in infancy and early childhood encompass a tremendous amount of research. Selection is obviously necessary not only because of the sheer amount of material but also because few investigators abide by the age limits of our present concern, so that many studies deal with age groups which overlap the infancy and early childhood periods. In the present chapter no attempt has, therefore, been made to be encyclopedic. On the contrary, the aim has been to select issues and areas of research that seem important and whose examination might lead to reevaluation and/or new insights into problems of theory or fact. Such an approach will, of necessity, involve some new categorizations and terminology as well as a moderate amount of speculation. Hopefully it will be of more use and interest than a simple compilation of the available literature.

The first section of the chapter will deal with the mental test approach to cognition in infancy and early childhood. Three issues will be taken up: the prediction of later mental ability on the basis of

*From Chapter 6 of Y. Brackbill (Ed.), *Infancy and Early Childhood*, 1967. Reprinted by permission of the author and The Free Press, a Division of the Macmillan Company.

infant tests of intelligence, infancy as a critical period in intellectual development, and, finally, the many faces of causality with respect to intelligence in young children. The second section of the chapter will deal with the developmental approach and will take up problem solving, memory, and conceptualization during the early years of life.

THE PROBLEM OF INFANT INTELLIGENCE

If any psychological finding has a claim to being axiomatic it is the observation that so called infant tests of intelligence are poor predictors of later intellectual level. Virtually everyone who has reviewed the research in this area (e.g., Goodenough, 1949; Jones, 1954; Bayley, 1955; Cronbach, 1962; Landreth, 1962) agrees that the usefulness of infant tests as predictors of later intelligence varies as a joint function of (a) age of initial testing; (b) the time interval between initial examination and retest (including the events which occur within that interval). By and large the earlier the test is given, the lower the correlation with later tests of mental ability, and the shorter the interval between test and retest, the larger the correlation. Tests, for example, given prior to the third year are of little predictive value with respect to intelligence scores attained in middle childhood (Bayley, 1940). On the other hand tests given during the third year correlate significantly with IQs attained at age six (Ebert & Simons, 1943; Honzik, et al., 1948).

Reactions to this state of affairs have been of two sorts. On the one hand there are those who accept these findings as inevitable because of the different capacities assessed by infant as opposed to noninfant tests of intelligence. These writers reject the notion of intelligence as a fixed capacity or quantum of mental energy that remains relatively constant throughout life. As Bayley (1955) writes, "I see no reason to think of intelligence as an integrated entity or capacity which grows throughout childhood by steady accretions" (Bayley, 1955, p. 807). In a similar vein Goodenough suggests that it may not even be justified to speak of intelligence in infancy and speaks of "The unsettled question as to whether or not true intelligence may be said to have emerged before symbolic processes exemplified in speech have become established. Attempting to measure infantile intelligence may be like trying to measure a boy's beard at the age of three" (1949, p. 310).

Other writers, however, have reacted differently to this anomalous situation. While granting the validity of the findings regarding quantitative prediction of intellectual standing from infant tests, they claim that qualitative estimates of intelligence made in infancy may still be of value. That is to say, although one may not be able to predict the later quantitative scores on the bases of scores attained in infancy, one can make successful predictions from the infants' general level of functioning. Thus if infants were categorized in gross terms as mentally retarded, below average, average, above average, and superior with respect to intellectual ability and on the basis of infant tests, the predictive power of these tests for later intellectual standing would be considerably improved. From a practical standpoint, such predictions would be of value to institutions, as adoption agencies, which are in great need of infant predictive indices.

The evidence for the predictive validity of such qualitative evaluations, although not overwhelming, is sufficiently impressive to warrant further exploration. Since these studies are less well known than those which demonstrate the lack of quantitative relationship between infant and later intelligence, a few of them will be reviewed here. In one study, Illingworth (1961) sought to demonstrate that at the low end of the intelligence continuum a diagnosis of mental level in infancy will have considerable predictive value with respect to later ability. Illingworth found that in a sample of 122 infants given a diagnosis of mental inferiority in infancy, 30 died and 65 out of the 87 survivors had an IQ score of less than 70 when tested several years later. Despite these findings, however, Illingworth does not believe that, with the exception of mental subnormality, there will ever be a high correlation between infant tests of intelligence and IQ scores attained at later age levels.

This pessimism is not entirely shared by Simon and Bass (1956) who studied 56 infants tested before the age of one year and again prior to school age. When the infant test scores and the scores attained at the preschool level were grouped according to three categories— dull normal and defective; average; above average and superior—a significant relationship between the two sets of categorizations was obtained. These writers found, however, that this relationship was largely a function of having included children at the two extremes of retarda-

tion and superiority in the sample. Macrae (1955) using more subjects (102) and more categories (superior, above average, average, below average, and mentally defective) obtained similar results. The children were initially tested before the age of three with the Gesell Schedule and were retested after the age of five with the WISC. Of the 102 cases examined, only five cases deviated more than one category, and there was not a single instance of a deviation of more than one category. Furthermore, in striking contrast to all of the findings using quantitative scores, the predictive value of the infant tests was affected neither by the age at which the infant test was given nor by the interval between test and retest.

Escalona and Moriarity (1961) introduced clinical appraisal of total test performance into their calculations of the predictive value of infant intelligence tests. The subjects were 58 infants selected for "normalcy" on the bases of medical, social, and developmental criteria. Infant measures were (a) Gesell Schedule scores, (b) Cattell IQ scores, and (c) clinical appraisal based on total test performance. The subjects were again tested between the age of six and nine years with the WISC. The results indicated that for this sample, no method of appraisal predicted later intelligence range when utilized prior to the age of twenty weeks. For tests administered between twenty and thirty-two weeks of age there was a positive but not significant relationship with later measures of IQ. When clinical appraisal of test scores made during this same age period (twenty to thirty-two weeks) were related to later intellectual standing, significant correlations were obtained. The authors conclude, "When infant assessments were examined for their ability to distinguish between subjects who would later be of average or above intelligence, clinical appraisal (but neither of the test scores) achieved these discriminations at a highly significant level" (1961, p. 604).

Knobloch *et al.* (1963) also found that clinical assessment was a successful way of predicting later intellectual level and argued for giving up the test-score method of infant evaluation.

Although these studies are not free from methodological defects—a statement which also holds true for the studies dealing with quantitative scores—the results do suggest that if the full range of intellectual variation is taken into account and this variation is dealt with categorically rather than numerically, then the assessment of infant intelligence can predict intellectual level at later ages. Put differently, one might say that infant examinations may be useful in predicting gross differences in later intellectual level and particularly at the extremes (superior and mentally retarded range). For practical purposes, such as advising adoptive parents, such gross discriminations are much better than nothing and seem to justify the continued use of infant assessment methods for predicting later intelligence.

Do these findings refute the axiom that infant tests are poor predictors of later ability? Not necessarily. If intelligence is conceived in strictly quantitative terms as a score on a particular test, then the axiom still holds true. Infant tests cannot apparently predict later intelligence test *scores*. If, on the other hand, intelligence is conceived as a *ranking*

relative to other children of the same age, then infant tests do seem to be able to predict the child's later standing with respect to his peers. Considering the fact that all intelligence scores are in reality ranks since they do not represent units-recalling six digits does not mean that one has two units more of memory than the person who recalls only four—the question boils down to just how much precision one is willing to settle for. If one is adopting a child even some precision is better than none.

INFANCY AND EARLY CHILDHOOD AS A CRITICAL PERIOD IN INTELLECTUAL GROWTH

The concept of the "critical period" seems to derive mainly from the work of ethologists such as Konrad Lorenz (1957) who used the term to describe some extraordinary circumstances of animal behavior. What Lorenz and others have observed is that there is a period during infancy when social attachments need to be made if they are to be lasting. Apparently these attachments are made regardless of species and Lorenz and other ethologists tell of chicks who follow them around as if they were the mother hen. Extensive work on this phenomenon has been done by Scott (1963) with dogs. Scott has shown that for dogs the period of socialization begins at approximately twenty days of age and continues for a few weeks thereafter. If social relationships are not established during this period it becomes increasingly difficult to do so later. Dogs with no experience of humans during this period are "wild" whereas those handled by humans during the same period are "tame."

It seems likely that something similar is apt to hold for the human infant. Schaffer and Emerson (1964) have, for example, shown that evidences of social attachments among infants begin to appear during the third quarter of the first year. The signs of such attachment are evidences of distress when a familiar person leaves the room, or when a stranger enters it. Infancy is not only a period when the child establishes social attachments, it is also a period in which it establishes a fundamental feeling tone about the social world. Erikson (1963) describes this attitude as one of *basic trust,* the feeling that the social world is reliable and that one's needs will be met. This attitude derives from the normal experiences of infancy in which the baby is cared for on an unconditional acceptance basis. In the absence of this unconditional acceptance and care, the child develops a sense of mistrust, the feeling that the world is a dangerous, fearful, and unreliable place, which then undermines all his later attempts to establish healthy interpersonal relationships.

These conditions, the establishment of emotional attachment and basic trust, thus seem to have their critical periods during the first year of life. If this is true then cognitive development must also have a critical period in infancy. This follows because for the infant, much more than for the older child and adult, intellectual and affective functions are undifferentiated. That is to say, anything which affects the child's affective equilibrium also affects his cognitive functioning. For the adult, whose intellectual abilities are fully developed, even severe neuroses may only dampen intellectual

functioning. But for the growing organism whose intellectual capacities are in the process of development, emotional disturbance can be catastrophic. As the work of Ribble (1943), Goldfarb (1945), and Spitz (1945) suggests, lack of appropriate social and affective stimulation in infancy leads to devastating consequences in both the personality and intellectual spheres. It is for this reason that infancy can be regarded as a critical period in intellectual development. At this age social and emotional deprivation are equally intellectual deprivation.

It is not, however, simply deprivation which affects later personality and intellectual development. On the contrary, research is beginning to show that the nature and quality of the stimulation provided infants may have enduring effects. Although such research is only now gaining momentum, it promises to reveal much about the early influences on intellectual growth. To illustrate this line of research and some of the most interesting conclusions several representative studies will be reviewed in detail.

In one of the continuing reports from the Berkeley growth study Bayley and Schaefer report on the intercorrelations between maternal and child behaviors and intelligence over an age span of eighteen years. The patterns of correlations for the 61 subjects tested repeatedly during the first eighteen years of their lives were complex and varied with the age and the sex of the individuals involved. What emerged from the study was the importance of what might be called "parental emotional temperature"—from extreme warmth to extreme coldness—shown during the early years of the child's life for later intellectual development:

Hostile mothers have sons who score high in intelligence in the first year or so, but have low IQs from age 4 through 18 years. The highly intelligent boys, in addition to having loving mothers, were characteristically happy, inactive and slow babies who grew into friendly, intellectually alert boys and well adjusted, extraverted adolescents. The girls who had loving, controlling mothers were happy, responsive babies who earned high mental scores. However, after three years, the girls' intelligence scores show little relation to either maternal or child behavior variables, with the exception of negative correlations with maternal intrusiveness. The girls' childhood IQs are correlated primarily with education of the parents and with estimates of the mother's IQ (1964, p. 71).

Bayley and Schaefer conclude that these results support the hypothesis of genetically determined sex differences. Their results suggest that the effect of the environment, particularly maternal behaviors, exerts a constant influence on the developing mental capacities of boys but not of girls. Apparently this study presents some empirical evidence for the proverbial hardiness of the female sex in comparison to males. If these results are accepted, the boy would seem to be much more susceptible to environmental influence than are girls. From a clinical point of view, this might explain why many boys than girls have learning problems and get into trouble with the law.

Another study concerned with parent-child relationships has been reported by Kagan and Freeman (1963) on the basis of data from the Fels longitudinal research investigation. As in the Bayley and Schaefer report, the obtained relationships were complex and varied with age and sex. Kagan and Freeman, however, were concerned with a different parameter of parental behavior. This parameter, which might loosely be called *parental control*, involved such activities as restriction, coercion, protectiveness, criticism, acceptance, and affection. On the basis of their findings, Kagan and Freeman concluded that "Maternal justification of discipline during the ages 4 through 7 continued to be associated with higher IQ scores for both boys and girls even when mother's education was controlled. Moreover, for girls, early criticism was positively associated with IQ at ages 3½ ($r = .52$), 5½ ($r = .51$), and 9 ($r = .46$) with maternal education held constant" (1963, pp. 905–906).

Both Bayley and Schaefer and Kagan and Freeman are careful to point out the dangers of interpreting correlation as causation. It may be the case, for example, that the obtained correlations are mediated by other variables not directly studied. What does seem clear is that there is a host of parental behavior dimensions such as emotional temperature and control which may influence intellectual growth. When these dimensions begin to be combined in the same investigation we can expect the results to be even more involved and complex. And that, after all, is as it should be since human behavior is no simple matter.

In some cases, the parental parameters are bound to overlap. It is hard to imagine a warm mother who is also critical. But such conflicting, or apparently conflicting, patterns do seem to occur as in the cold, hostile mothers who breast feed their babies out of a sense of duty rather than affection (Henstein, 1963). Children who receive this kind of double communication often develop serious emotional difficulties in later life. We are thus now only beginning to appreciate the variety of parental behavior dimensions which may influence intellectual growth. It is still too early to say with assurance that warmth or coldness, coercion or affection will have this or that effect upon the child until we can measure the whole spectrum of parental behaviors in combination. Although the two studies reported here are only a start in that direction, they do underscore the intricate chain of causation that underlies what were once thought to be simple and straightforward relationships between the intelligence of parents and their children.

Before closing this section on infancy as a critical period in the development of intelligence, it might be well to point out that some writers, namely Fowler (1962), have stressed the positive aspects of this hypothesis. Fowler's point is that infancy and early childhood have been neglected by educators and parents out of, to Fowler's view, a mistaken belief that education was not appropriate during the early years and that it might even interfere with the child's personality development. Quite the contrary, claims Fowler. He argues that gifted persons have routinely shown early cognitive skills such as reading or playing instruments prior to the age of three. Fowler claims that this is due to earlier intellectual stimulation and training experienced by such persons. To substantiate his claim, Fowler reports work with his daughter whom he taught to read at an early age and who at the age of eight had an IQ of 150 to 170. Fowler admits that

the girl does manifest mild emotional problems although in general she gets along quite well. Fowler, like Watson (1928) and, apparently, Bruner (1960) seems to take an extreme environmentalist position which asserts that one can after all make a silk purse out of a sow's ear. The current revival of interest in the Montessori methods (1964) suggests that Fowler is not alone in his belief in the importance of early education.

The issues raised by Fowler are of extreme importance. Assuming that one can train children earlier than we have been accustomed to doing, what would be the purpose of such training? Is intellectual development purchased at the expense of something more valuable? And if it is not, is the educational system prepared to handle children who read and do mathematics when they enter kindergarten? In short the matter is not just a philosophical or scientific one, but an eminently practical issue. For the early education of children presupposes a fundamental change in the hierarchy of the educational system. What sense does it make to provide early education for children if they will then only be bored when they go to school. Those who wish to educate at an early age must face the fundamental fact of educational existence, to wit, that the wheels of change regarding educational practice grind exceedingly slowly.

We began this section with the statement that infancy and early childhood are a "critical period" in the development of intellectual functioning. Research dealing with emotional deprivation and with maternal interaction patterns does seem to indicate that intelligence is vulnerable in the early years just because it is not yet differentiated from affective components of personality. This is not to say that infants are mere passive lumps to be molded by experience and parental behaviors—far from it. Considering the variety of parental behaviors one has to assume that infants are surprisingly hardy critters who will develop relatively well under an amazingly wide variety of conditions. What we need to know are the lethal parental behavior combinations and dosages as well as the optimal ones. Research such as that of Bayley and Schaefer and of Kagan and Freeman is a start in the direction of attaining that knowledge. . . .

CATEGORICAL CONCEPTS DURING THE FIRST TWO YEARS OF LIFE

Kant wrote that although one could not deny the reality of the external world, one could not at the same time deny that everything regarded as external was at least in part dependent upon the thinking and perceiving subject. That is to say, the world we know is always limited by our organs of knowing. There are, for example, many forms of stimulation, such as high-frequency sounds, that are not within the sphere of our experience but are very much within the sphere of certain animal species such as dogs. Many other such examples could be cited, and von Uexkull (1957) has given vivid illustrations of perceptual worlds other than our own. Our knowledge of the world is, according to Kant, not simply limited by the sense organs but also by the innate organizing tendencies of the mind. Just as we cannot escape being sensitive to some stimuli and not to others, so can we not escape organizing our world within a spatial, temporal, and causal framework. We have, in Kant's view, really no choice in the matter, and all our experience is organized within such a framework. Kant, however, wrote as if these categories were the same in children as in adults, i.e., *a priori*. What Jean Piaget (1954) has shown is that although the child does seem to organize his experience within the categories described by Kant, the categories themselves go through a gradual process of construction.

This is not to say that the infant is aware of space, time, and causality as we know them. Far from it! On the other hand, it is possible for an observer to see in the infant's actions a causal, temporal, or spatial framework of which the infant is probably not aware. The situation is a little analogous to certain computers that can be programmed to play chess or write novels. To say that the computer operates in an intelligent way is not the same thing as saying that it is conscious of its intelligence, but only that it behaves *as if* it were. The same is true for infants in whom we can observe intelligent behavior without, at the same time, having to assert that the infant is aware of its intelligence. With these cautionary remarks in mind we can proceed to the development of the categorical concepts in infancy.

The Concept of the Object

Although not a categorical concept in the Kantian sense, the concept of the object is one of the fundaments of all categorical thinking and of all later conceptual developments and so must be dealt with. Although to the adult objects such as a chair or a table seem to be "out there" and to be separate from their physical properties (hardness, texture, color) and action properties (to be sat upon, leaned against, stood on), this is not the case for the very young infant.

In his brilliant studies of his own three infants during their first years of life, Piaget (1954) has provided evidence of the enormous labors involved in constructing the concept of an object. For Piaget the infant does not have a true object concept until he can represent it as evidenced by his pursuit of that object in its absence. This point is not reached, however, until the middle of the second year of life and is prefaced by a series of behaviors that gradually lead up to this representation. During the first few months after birth objects are really not distinguished from the actions associated with them. An object is simply something to suck, to grasp, to push, or merely to look at. When the object disappears, say the bottle removed before the infant has satisfied his hunger, he may continue to suck as if the sucking would reconstitute the object. Likewise, when the mother leaves the room, the infant continues to look at the point where the mother disappeared as if watching would bring the image back.

Between the third and seventh and eighth months after birth the child comes increasingly to differentiate the object from his own actions and to recognize that it has movements or trajectories of its own. One evidence of this differentiation is that the older infant now looks at the place where an object will land, after it has been dropped, rather than its position before it has dropped. Still another evidence of this differentiation is

the recognition at this age level of an object from seeing only a part of it. This does not mean, according to Piaget, that the child conceives of a whole object, part of which is hidden. On the contrary, Piaget believes that the infant regards an object emerging from behind a screen to be in the *process of formation*. Still another interesting behavior at this age level is the child's ability to neglect an object and then return to it after an interval of time. All of these observations suggest that the object is coming to be regarded as something which exists independently of the infant's perceptual and motor activity. This point is not fully reached, however, until several additional skills are mastered.

One of the next advances in attainment of the object concept, which Piaget says occurs between the age of eight and ten months, occurs when the infant begins to search for objects that have been hidden behind a screen. What marks this stage distinctively is that the child actually removes the screen himself. Piaget, for example, describes hiding a cigar case under a cushion after which his son Laurent (age nine months, seventeen days) immediately raised the cushion in order to find the object. (Prior to this age the child ceased to pursue an object hidden before his eyes.) The behavior of this stage was, however, governed by a very important restriction which Piaget describes as follows: "The child looks for and conceives of the object only in a special position, the first place in which it was hidden and found" (1954, p. 50). That is to say, if the object is first hidden under one screen and then under another, both displacements visible to the child, the child nonetheless looks under the first and not the second screen.

During the second year of life the child gradually advances to the stage where he can recognize the position of an object even after it has been hidden in three successive positions. This ability, to take account mentally of the successive displacements of a hidden object, is for Piaget the mark of a true object concept. Such behavior suggests that the child can deal with objects as independent of his own perception and as having independent positions and trajectories in space.

Space Concepts

Many of the observations that Piaget used to describe the development of the object concept can equally well be employed to illustrate the attainment of space concepts. In the development of space, however, Piaget makes it clear just how complex and intricate are the unconscious coordinations by which the infant gradually orients himself and things within a spatial framework. One can get a rough idea of some of the difficulties involved by imagining oneself in a strange city whose narrow, winding streets are unmarked and for which there is no map or guide available. To learn the plan of the city one would have to make one's own map in a sort of trial-and-error fashion. Constructing a kind of map space is only one of the many problems of space conceptualization faced by the infant.

According to Piaget (1954) the infant progresses during the first two years of life from an initial sense of *practical space* to a *subjective space* and eventually to an *objective space*. To understand the differences between these three forms of

spatial concept, we must begin by noting that any spatial concept involves the coordination of positions in a systematic way. These positions may either be of things or of the child in relation to things. Practical, subjective, and objective space correspond to different levels of differentiation and integration of these two kinds of positions.

Up to about the age of three months the infant can be observed to move his glance from one to another of a series of objects. From the point of view of the observer this type of visual behavior already implies a notion of space. It is still a practical notion because the child deals with positions in terms of his activity, looking, and the positions of objects are still not separated from the movement needed to perceive those positions. There are thus as many practical spaces or positions as different activities. The child might thus be said to have a buccal (mouth) space, a tactile space, a visual space, kinesthetic space, and so on. Practical space is revealed whenever the child shows an awareness of the position or displacement of things with respect to a particular activity as in the following example:

From 0;2 Laurent knows how to carry to his mouth an object grasped independently of sight and how to adjust it empirically. . . . At 0;3 he puts a clothespin in his mouth, adjusting its position so that he may suck it (Piaget, 1954, p. 107).

Beginning about the fourth month of life and extending until about the tenth, the child evolves what Piaget calls a *subjective* space. What seems to occur is that the various practical spaces begin to be coordinated one with the other. In Piaget's view the central condition for the establishment of these coordinations is the development of prehension, the ability to deal with things manually. Once prehension emerges, the child begins to grasp for what he sees, tastes, or feels and in this way gradually begins to bring together the spatial information obtained from each of the different sensory avenues. As a result he is able "to relate certain of his own movements to those of the environment" (Piaget, 1954, p. 11). Here is an example of this type of coordination:

At 0;6 he (Laurent) directs his eyes towards an object after having touched it. But he cannot see it because of various screens (Piaget, 1954, p. 115).

From the age of about nine or ten months and extending into the second year the young child gradually elaborates what Piaget calls an *objective* space. At this age the coordination of positions and displacements of subjective space come gradually to be divorced from the child's activity as a whole and to be regarded as independent of his own influence. At the same time the child also begins to see himself and his positions as but one object among many objects in the spatial field. The crucial evidence for the attainment of objective space is that the child's recognition of the movements and displacements of things in the environment is reversible. This means simply that the child recognizes that an object moved from one position to another can be moved back again. Although this would

seem to be the simplest of ideas, it is in fact extraordinarily complex. When the child does demonstrate the recognition of this, it indicates a fundamental change in spatial organization. Instead of regarding objects as having fixed positions, he suddenly comes to see positions as more or less temporary *states* of objects. This transition from a static to a dynamic way of viewing reality also occurs in the verbal and logical plane, as we will see later.

Although Piaget derived his notions of practical, subjective, and objective space from his observations on his three infants, older children seem to manifest similar stages in the mastery of more complex spatial problems. In a study by Meyer (1940) preschool-age children's spatial concepts were tested by having them fit wooden forms together and by determining their understanding of the rotations of a pivoted bar. With these tasks Meyer claims to have found Piaget's stages repeated between the ages two and five. In brief, Meyer found that up to the age of two or two and a half, children showed only a *practical* space in the sense that they regarded objects only as something to satisfy their needs. Between the ages of three and four Meyer found what resembled Piaget's *subjective* space in the sense that although the children were still centered on their own activities, they also manifested some interest in the objects themselves, independent of their own immediate needs. After the age of four Meyer reported that the children manifested *objective* space in the sense that they considered themselves as but one object among many and that they attempted to adjust their own behavior to the position of objects.

Time Concepts

As in the case of the object and space, Piaget finds a gradual development in infancy from a practical time to a subjective and finally to an objective time by the end of the second year of life. During the first few months of life the infant shows a practical grasp of time in the sense that it knows how to coordinate its movements in time and how to perform certain actions before others in a regular order. Piaget notes, for example, that even at two months the infant turns its head when it hears a sound and tries to perceive what it has heard. These sequences, although suggesting some temporal ordering, do not imply that the child has any awareness of time. This is to say, the actions could occur in a reflex fashion without any sense of causal connection between the two.

Beginning about the age of three months the infant begins to construct what Piaget calls a *practical* time series. By this he means that the child begins to perform a series of actions that are not determined entirely by the external stimulations acting upon him. At this stage the infant adds to the simple reflex series of the previous stage the results of his past experience so that his action no longer appears reflexive but rather purposive. Consider the following illustration:

abs 169 At 0;3 (13) Laurent, already accustomed for several hours to shake a hanging rattle by pulling the chain attached to it . . . is attracted by the sound of the rattle (which I have just shaken) and looks simultaneously at the rattle and at the hanging chain. Then while staring at the rattle, (R), he drops from his right hand a sheet he was sucking, in order to reach with the same hand for the lower end of the hanging chain (C). As soon as he touches the chain, he grasps and pulls it, thus reconstructing the series C-R (Piaget, 1954, p. 330).

What this illustration shows is that the child knew he had to drop one thing in order to attain another just as he knew he had to pull the chain in order to shake the rattle. It is the use of intermediary means to a goal that differentiates the purposive from the pure reflexive act and that suggests a temporal as well as a causal series. Piaget also argues that it is at this stage that one sees the beginning of memory formations. The child now not only recognizes the mother but also localizes her in the recent past. If she comes into the room and sits down while the infant is playing, the infant may note this and return to its play. Moments later it may again look toward where the mother is seated giving evidence of a recent memory.

From about the eighth or ninth month and extending through the second year, the child gradually constructs what Piaget calls an *objective* time. Some of the observations relevant to the attainment of the object-time notion are significant here. First of all, the child begins to search for hidden objects, which means he has ordered a series of perceptions of memories within a temporal sequence. As he grows older the child begins to be able to take account of successive displacements of the hidden object which implies a still more elaborate temporal organization of perceptual memories. Finally, toward the middle of the second year a "true" objective sense of time appears to the extent that the child begins to symbolize or represent temporal sequences and durations by means of words.

Causality

The development of elementary causal conceptions in the infant follows the pattern we have become familiar with in discussing the other categories. Beginning as practical causality in which psychological efficacy and physical force are undifferentiated, the infant progresses to the more or less complete practical separation of physical and psychic causality by the end of the second year. During the first few months of life the child's reflex behaviors are the only indices of causal connections. As Piaget puts it:

Whether the nursling at the age of one or two months succeeds in sucking his thumb after having attempted to put it into his mouth or whether his eyes follow a moving object, he must experience, though in different degrees, the same impression: namely, that without his knowing how a certain action leads to a certain result, in other words that a certain complex of efforts, tension, expectation, desire, etc., is charged with efficacy (1954, p. 229).

For Piaget then causality during the early months of life consists in little more than the feeling of effort experienced in connection with the resistance of things.

From about the third to the seventh or eighth month a new level of causal behavior emerges which Piaget calls *magico-phenomenalistic causality.* This it will be recalled is the period in which active prehension emerges and, hence, the co-

ordination of vision and other sense modalities with movement. At this stage the infant becomes witness to, and takes interest in, three types of action: movements of the body, movements which depend upon body movements, and movements that are independent of the child's actions. In Piaget's view, the infant begins to discover causal relations in the process of observing the three types of movement. Children at this level of development "find their hands" and begin to associate the feeling of efficacy with the visual perception of hand movements. Likewise, the feeling of effort when pushing or shaking a rattle comes to be associated with the sight of the movement of the rattle and with its sound. Piaget calls this stage "magico-phenomenalistic" because the child fails to distinguish the sphere of its efficacy from the sphere of movements wherein it lacks efficacy. The infant, for example, may shake its leg on seeing a doll at a distance as if this act would move the doll. Piaget also argues that even when the child of this stage pulls a string to make a toy rattle, he does not realize that there is an intermediary between his action and the effect. It is the fact that the infant behaves as if his gestures alone could produce physical results that accounts for Piaget's attaching the magico-phenomenalistic label to this period. (Traces of this kind of casuality can still be seen in adults who try to influence the course of a bowling or billiard ball with "body English.")

Beginning at about the seventh or eighth months of life and extending to the latter half of the second year Piaget found what he regarded as the gradual attainment of an objective sense of causality. By objective with respect to causality Piaget means that the child comes to distinguish between physical and psychological causes. At the outset of this period the child only dissociates causality from his own actions without at the same time attributing causality to objects. Then, at about one year of age, "the child recognizes causes that are entirely external to his activity and for the first time he establishes among events perceived links of causality independent of the action itself" (Piaget, 1954, p. 279). Here is an example:

At 1; (28) Jacqueline touches with her stick a push cat placed on the floor, but does not know how to pull it to her. The spatial contact between the stick and the cat seem to her sufficient to displace the object. . . . Finally at 1;3 (12) Jacqueline utilizes the stick correctly; objective and spatialized causality are therefore applied to the physical conditions of the problem (Piaget, 1954, p. 284).

Finally, toward the middle of the second year of life the objectification of causality is completed with the beginnings of representation. What this means is that at this point the child begins to take account of causes that are outside his immediate sphere of perception, something he did not do heretofore. He comes at this final point in the development of practical causality to be, in Piaget's words, "capable of reconstructing causes in the presence of their effects alone." Here is one example of representative causal behavior:

At 1;4 (4) Laurent tries to open a garden gate but cannot push it forward because it is held back by a piece of furniture. He cannot account either visually or by any sound for the cause that prevents the gate from opening, but after having tried to force it he suddenly seems to understand, he goes around the wall, arrives at the other side of the gate, moves the armchair which holds it firm and opens it with a triumphant expression (Piaget, 1954, p. 296).

At this final point the child shows clearly that causality is no longer merely perceptual and that by means representation he can reconstruct causes and anticipate consequences not immediately present.

It might be well, at this point, to summarize in a general way the process of conceptualization that occurs during the first two years of life as disclosed by the work of Piaget. What Piaget argues is that the infant begins in an egocentric universe in which there is nothing other than that which directly concerns his own activities and needs. It is thus a world that, in terms of the object and space, does not transcend the images and spatial relations that are immediately given in perception. It is a world, moreover, in terms of time and causality, that does not go beyond the immediate present. With increasing age the child gradually becomes aware of a world that is independent of his perception and action and that manifests laws and sequences that are independent of his will. By the end of the period, with the aid of representation, he recognizes the existence of objects not present to perception and the relativity of spatial position while his notions of time and causality expand backward to the past and press forward to the future. The egocentric universe has thus been transformed into an objective world.

At the same time, however, it must be recognized that this achievement holds only on the plane of perception and action. For, at the age of about two, the child begins to construct a new universe on the level of verbalization and representation. And, in the process of constructing this verbal, representational universe he again begins egocentrically and only gradually extricates himself to discover the objective verbal and representational world. For Piaget, each new, higher level of conceptual functioning demands a new structuring of experience. This is as arduous as that undertaken at the previous level of mental functioning. . .

References

Bayley, N. Mental growth in young children. *Yearb. nat. Soc. Stud. Educ.*, 1940, 39, Part II.

Bayley, N. On the growth of intelligence. *Amer. Psychol.*, 1955, 10, 805-818. Reprinted in Y. Brackbill & G. G. Thompson (Eds.), *Behavior in infancy and early childhood: A book of readings.* New York: Free Press, 1967.

Bayley, N., & Schaefer, E. Correlations of maternal and child behaviors with the development of mental abilities: Data from the Berkeley growth study. *Monogr. Soc. Res. Child Develpm.*, 1964, 29, No. 97.

Bruner, J. S. *The process of education.* Cambridge: Harvard Univer. Press, 1960.

Cronbach, L. J. *Educational psychology.* (2nd ed.) New York: Harcourt, Brace & World 1962.

Ebert, E., & Simons, K. The Brush Foundation study of child growth and development. I. Psychometric tests. *Soc. Res. Child. Develpm. Monogr.*, 1943, 8, No. 2.

Erikson, E. H. *Childhood and society.* (2nd ed.) New York: Norton, 1963.

Escalona, S. K., & Moriarity. A. Prediction of school age intelligence from infant tests. *Child Develpm.*, 1961, 32, 597-605.

Fowler, W. Cognitive learning in infancy and early childhood. *Psychol. Bull.*, 1962, 59, No. 2, 116-152.

Goldfarb, W. Psychological privation in infancy and subsequent adjustment. *Amer. J. Orthopsychiat.*, 1945, 15, 247-255.

Goodenough, F. L. New evidence of environmental influence on intelligence. *Yearb. nat. Soc. Stud. Educ.*, 1940, 39, No. 1, 307-365.

Goodenough, F. L. *Mental testing.* New York: Rinehart, 1949.

Heinstein. M. I. Behavorial correlates of breast-bottle regimes under varying parent-infant relationships. *Soc. Res. Child Develpm. Monogr.*, 1963, 28, No. 4.

Honzik. M.P., MacFarlane, J. W., & Allen, L. The stability of mental test performance between two and eighteen years. *J. exp. Educ.*, 1948, **17**, 309-324.

Illingworth. R. S. The predictive value of developmental tests in the first year, with special reference to the diagnosis of mental subnormality. *J. child Psychol. Psychiat.*, 1961, **2**, 210-215.

Jones, H. The environment and mental development. In L. Carmichael (Ed.), *Manual of child psychology*, New York: Wiley, 1954.

Kagan, J., & Freeman, M. Relation of childhood intelligence, maternal behaviors and social class to behavior during adolescence. *Child Develpm.*, 1963, **34**, 899-911.

Knobloch, H., & Pasamanick, B. Further observations on the development of Negro children. *J. genet. Psychol.*, 1953, **83**, 137-157.

Knobloch, H., & Pasamanick, B. Predicting intellectual potential in infancy. *Amer. J. Dis. Childh.*, 1963, 107, No. 1, 43-51.

Landreth, C. *The psychology of early childhood.* New York: Knopf. 1962.

Lorenz, K. Comparative study of behavior. In C. H. Schiller (Ed.), *Instinctive behavior,* New York: Inter. Univer. Press, 1957.

MacRae, J. M. Retests of children given mental tests as infants. *J. genet. Psychol.*, 1955, **87**, 111-119.

Meyer, L. E. Comprehension of spatial relations in preschool children. *J. genet. Psychol.*, 1940, **57**, 119-151.

Montessori, M. *The Montessori method.* New York: Schocken, 1964.

Piaget, J. Judgement and reasoning in the child. *London: Routledge, & Kegan Paul, Ltd., 1951. (a)*

Piaget, J. *Play, dreams and imitation in childhood.* New York: Norton, 1951. (b)

Piaget, J. *The construction of reality in the child.* New York: Basic Books, 1954.

Piaget, J., & Inhelder, B. *The child's conception of space.* New York: Humanities Press, 1956.

Ribble, M. A. *The rights of infants,* New York: Columbia, 1943.

Schaffer, H.R., & Emerson, P. E. The development of social attachments in infancy. *Soc. Res. Child Develpm. Monogr.*, 1964, **29**, No. 3.

Scott, J. P. The process of primary socialization in canine and human infants. *Soc. Res. Child Develpm. Monogr.*, 1963, **28**, No. 1.

Simon, A. J., & Bass, L. G. Toward a validation of infant testing. *Amer. J. Orthopsychiat.*, 1956, **26**, 340-350.

Spitz, R. A. Hospitalism: An inquiry into the genesis of psychiatric conditions in early childhood. *Psychoanalytic Study of the Child.* New York: Inter. Univer. Press, 1945.

von Uexkull, J. A. stroll through the world of animals and men. In C. H. Schiller (Ed.), *Instinctive behavior,* New York: Inter. Univer. Press, 1957.

Watson, J. B. *Psychological care of infant and child.* New York: Norton, 1928. Reprinted in part in Y. Brackbill & G. G. Thompson (Eds.), *Behavior in infancy and early childhood:* A book of readings. New York: Free Press, 1967.

3
INFANCY:
PERSONALITY AND SOCIAL DEVELOPMENT

Personality can be regarded as the sum of an individual's socially relevant behavior and thought. Personality and social development accordingly begin in infancy with the onset of a child's habitual ways of relating to people and his characteristic patterns of thinking and feeling about people. These aspects of personality are manifest primarily through what is called expressive behavior, and the evolution of *expressive* behavior in many ways chronicles the evolution of personality.

The following two articles are concerned with the emergence of expressive behavior during infancy. In the first of these articles Rheingold describes how and when such expressive behaviors as smiling begin to appear and how these behaviors contribute to an infant's becoming a social being. She elaborates four important principles governing social behavior in human infants, and she also includes some interesting cross-species comparisons in the development of social awareness and social interaction.

In the second article Ainsworth and Bell discuss the manner in which expressive behaviors become selectively directed to form *attachments* between an infant and important people in his life, especially his mother. Once an infant becomes attached to his mother, his sense of well-being and his security in exploring his environment are strongly affected by whether she is present.

HARRIET L. RHEINGOLD

The Development of Social Behavior in the Human Infant*

The assignment to write a paper often forces one to search for some system by which to organize what one thinks important on the given topic. Thus, in a recent paper (Rheingold, in press) I proposed four general principles of behavior under which the facts and current theories about human infancy could be organized. The principles were (1) that the infant is responsive to stimulation; (2) that the infant is an active organism; (3) that the infant's behavior is modifiable; and (4) that the infant in turn modifies the environment, particularly the social environment. The principles, it is obvious, apply to the behavior of older as well as younger organisms and to the behavior of one species as well as another. That they also apply to the behavior of the infant testifies to their generality. As a consequence, developmental psychology may be integrated with a more comprehensive science of behavior.

In the present paper, the same four principles will be used but now applied to the development of *social* behavior in the infant. Although the development of social behavior in the human infant will be the primary focus of attention, some data on the development of social behav-

ior in a few other mammalian species will be included. A complete comparative psychology of the development of social behavior will not result, but the form it could take will be suggested.

The advantages of a comparative approach are several: It provides a wider and more objective theater for viewing the behavior of the human infant. It supplies a corrective for inexact generalizations from animal to man. It serves, also, to bring knowledge about man's behavior into closer association with knowledge about the behavior of his mammalian relatives. . . . .

The four principles stated earlier, revised for the present purpose, may now be presented as follows:

1. The infant is responsive to stimuli arising from social objects.
2. The infant is active in initiating social contacts.
3. The infant's social behavior is modified by the responses of others (social objects) to him.
4. The infant's social responses modify the behavior of others in his group.

THE INFANT IS RESPONSIVE TO SOCIAL STIMULI

The infant's sensitivities determine the stimuli arising from social objects to

*From *Monographs of the Society for Research in Child Development*, 1966, 31 (No. 5), 1-17. Reprinted by the permission of the author and the Society for Research in Child Development.

whlch he can respond; his capabilities determine the responses he can make to these stimuli. The task here is to enumerate both the sensory systems of the infant that are stimulated by the presence and behavior of other members of his group, and the responses he gives to the stimulation.

The human infant, from birth, is responsive to a wide range of external stimulation. He possesses almost all the sensory systems he will have as an adult, and every sense he does possess functions, at least to some extent. In this respect he differs from the young of other mammals, such as the rodents and carnivores, which with few exceptions are functionally blind and deaf at birth. As a consequence, the human infant, from the beginning, lives in a broader environment.

We now ask, to what stimuli arising from social objects is the human infant responsive? Certainly the visual stimuli presented by people, that is, the sight of social objects, evoke responses in him almost from the day of birth. He not only sees them, but, as he grows older, he actively looks at them and subjects them to considerable visual exploration (Wolff, 1963). He smiles and vocalizes and, on occasion, also cries at their appearance. As his motor skills mature, he first reaches out, then grasps, and finally holds on to people. Somewhat later, he crawls and creeps to them on visual cues (e.g., Bayley, 1933; Cattell, 1940; Griffiths, 1954). During the first month, he also attends to the voices of social objects (Bayley, 1933), quiets at the sound, and then may smile and vocalize (Griffiths, 1954; Wolff, 1963). But he is 4 months of age before he can turn his head in the direction of a voice (Cattell, 1940). Furthermore, he appears sensitive to the tone of the voice and, by 8 months of age, to what the voice says.

The human infant is also responsive to the tactile and kinesthetic stimulation provided by social objects. During the first month of life, he quiets when picked up (e.g., Bayley, 1933) and smiles if his hands are rhythmically moved (Wolff, 1963). Much more of a definitive nature cannot be said; his responses to tactile and kinesthetic stimulation from the social object, in the absence of accompanying visual and auditory stimulation, have not yet been systematically studied.

Attractive as the possibility may be to some, there is at present no evidence that the infant responds to olfactory stimuli presented by social objects.

Quite different from the human infant's are the sensitivities and responses of other mammalian infants to stimuli arising from members of their own species. (For a review of the sensory and motor development of many young mammals, see Cruikshank, 1954.) For example, 8 minutes after birth, the newborn kitten, on its own, makes contact with its mother's body. It cannot be sensitive to the visual stimuli presented by the mother because its eyes do not open until the seventh day. No, it is sensitive to the thermal and auditory stimuli she presents (Tilney & Casamajor, 1924); it is these stimuli that give direction to its head movements. Prominent, too, in the newborn kitten's environment, are its littermates. They also offer thermal and tactile stimuli to which the kitten responds, for kittens, like rodent and dog pups, pile up on each other in the mother's absence, become quiet, and sleep (Bolles & Woods, 1964; Rheingold, 1963; Scott & Marston,

1950). During the first 2 weeks of life, the rodent and carnivore infants' chief social responses are effecting and maintaining contact with mother and littermates. In the third week, tactile and thermal stimuli are no longer dominant; now the kitten and the pup respond to visual, auditory, and olfactory stimuli emanating from social objects. Especially the sight of others stimulates approach and play behavior.

The rhesus infant, however, contrasts with the human, on the one hand, and with the rodent and carnivore infants, on the other. He sees and hears,[1] but his primary responses to social stimuli—aside from nursing, which characterizes all mammalian infants and is not separately discussed—are grasping and clinging (Harlow, 1960), responses that secure thermal, tactile, and kinesthetic stimulation.

In contrast to the human infant, the early responsiveness of other mammals, for example, the rodent, carnivore, and subhuman primate families, appears to depend on different sensitivities—thermal, tactile, and kinesthetic. Associated with these sensitivities are capabilities for locomotion and grasping, which bridge the distance between these infants and others, and effect, instead of visual ties, ties of contact.

The most physically helpless infant, the human, who can neither cling nor locomote, seems, nevertheless, effective in bridging the distance—the distance he cannot travel—between himself and members of his group primarily by the use of vision and hearing and by responses such as looking, smiling, and vocalizing, which hold them at his side. Thus, Ainsworth (1964), Rheingold (1961), and Walters and Parke (1965) have pointed to the role of distance receptors in the genesis and maintenance of social responsiveness in the human infant.

The sensitivities and capabilites of still other mammalian infants should at some time be considered. What can we make of the ungulate infant that not only sees *and* locomotes almost from birth, but also uses visual cues to guide his locomotion?

In focusing our attention on the immature mammal's social behavior, we are likely to ignore that very early in life he tends to give the same responses to nonsocial as to social objects. Thus, the human infant looks at a variety of visual arrays and often smiles and vocalizes to them as well (Piaget, 1952; Preyer, 1893; Rheingold, 1961; Salzen, 1963). When a few months older, he reaches out to them, and in another few months crawls to them. Other young mammals, once they have left their mothers, also approach, manipulate, and play with both inanimate and animate objects (Bolles & Woods, 1964; Harlow, 1962). This observation will be discussed later.

The analysis of the infant's sensitivity to social stimuli has glossed over too lightly the complexity of the social object. Social objects are indeed complex stimulus objects, and often stimulate more than one sense. Their dimensions, nevertheless, are assumed to be specifiable. To discover the effective dimensions, the investigator reduces the complexity

---

[1] Animals may possess good sensory perception in several modalities but, nevertheless, predominantly use only a few. To possess a sense does not mean that it is characteristically utilized Thus, the rhesus infant sees but responds to social objects primarily by grasping.

of the social object by the experimental manipulation of its structure and behavior. Thus, Rosenblatt and Lehrman (1963), in measuring maternal behavior, used as a standard stimulus for rat mothers any living infant rat 5 to 10 days of age. Replicas and models have also been used; well known are Schneirla and Rosenblatt's (1961) brooder for kittens, Harlow's (1958) terry-cloth cylinder for rhesus infants, and Igel and Calvin's (1960) surrogate mother for dogs. Still farther removed from the real-life social object are the replicas of human faces and parts of faces used to study smiling in human infants (e.g., Ahrens, 1954; Spitz & Wolf, 1946). At an even more abstract level of analysis, Welker (1959), in an attempt to identify the stimuli that facilitate huddling in a litter of pups, measured the effect of contact upon the pup's locomotion under varying room temperatures.

This partial account suggests the diversity of avenues through which the social stimuli of one's own species come to the infant, and the diversity of responses he gives them. It goes without saying that infants of different species differ in their sensory apparatuses, in the state of maturity of each appartus at birth, and in the rate of development of each subsequent to birth. They differ as well in their capabilities, that is, in the response classes activated by stimulation from social objects. Diverse though their sensory apparatuses and capabilities may be, however, infants of every mammalian species do sense members of their own group—most often, of course, the mother—and do respond to them.

THE INFANT INITIATES SOCIAL BEHAVIOR

The infant not only responds to social stimuli, he also initiates social contacts. No one will dispute the statement. Yet here, in the absence of evidence from controlled studies, we will often have to rely on everyday and naturalistic observation. Still, observation is clear on this point: The infant is no more passive in his social behavior than he is in other kinds of behavior.

Human infants frequently look at people before they are looked at, smile before they are smiled to, vocalize before they are spoken to, and cry. As a consequence, they attract the attention of individuals and draw them closer. They expose themselves, thus, to social stimulation and, by their own efforts, increase the amount of stimulation in their environments.

What of other mammalian infants? Infant rats on the thirteenth day of life begin to groom each other. A day later, when their eyes start to open, they "play" with each other, "running into one another, jumping, climbing, burrowing, chasing, wrestling" (Bolles & Woods, 1964, p. 433).

Puppy dogs, too, make physical contacts with their mothers and littermates, not waiting to be contacted. In the third week of life, as vision guides their responses, they mouth and bite, first the mouths of littermates, then other parts of their littermates' and the mothers' bodies. In the fourth week, they paw, box, tumble, tussle, and chase each other; in brief, they play. At this age, too, pups go to the mother's head, instead of her belly, whine and cry, raise a paw to her, and lick her face (Rheingold, 1963; Scott & Marston, 1950).

Kittens, too, when 3 weeks of age, leave the home site and approach the female to nurse. They also romp around her, pounce on her, paw her, and toy with her tail. They respond the same way to their littermates. When 4 weeks of age they initiate almost all the contacts they have with the mother, while she now tries to avoid them (Schneirla, Rosenblatt, & Tobach, 1963).

Rhesus infants, while still very young, approach other infants (Rowell, Hinde, & Spencer-Booth, 1964). Harlow (1962), in reporting his playroom and playpen studies of the infant rhesus, gave details of the infant's initiation of social contacts with other infants. He identified three compnents, "One of these is a visual-exploration component, in which the animal orients closely to, and peers intently at . . . the other animal. A second is oral exploration, a gentle mouthing response, and the third pattern is that of tactual exploration" (p. 216). These behaviors were characteristic of surrogate-raised infants and were labeled "presocial." Rough-and-tumble play followed, in which both partners participated in pushing, pulling, mauling, and biting each other. The persistent initiation of contact by rhesus infants—with mothers who reject them—is by now well known (Harlow, Harlow, & Hansen, 1963).

Similarly, infant langur monkeys, observed in the wild, climb on adult females during the first 3 months of life. At 5 months of age, they chase and wrestle with other young. They initiate play with adult females by jumping on them, racing around them, pulling their fur, and pushing up against them; later they initiate playful contact even with adult males (Jay, 1963).

In general, the principle of infant initiation of social behavior is important because it assigns a measure, a rather large measure of responsibility to the infant for the genesis of his own social behavior. The brevity of treatment accorded this principle here should not be taken as a measure of its importance.

THE INFANT'S SOCIAL BEHAVIOR IS MODIFIABLE

The third principle states that the infant's social behavior is modifiable, that it is maintained and altered by the responses of social objects to his behavior. The position taken here is that behavior in the immature organism is not fixed but flexible. Nevertheless, I do not wish to set in opposition the processes of maturation and learning; rather, I take the now accepted position that any behavior, no matter how simple or how early its appearance, is already the result of an interaction of genetic material and environmental condition. To claim that the infant's behavior is modifiable, claims nothing about the origin of the behavior, whether innate or learned, for it is always possible to begin the study of learning with any behavior or response the organism already possesses. The purpose here is to examine some social responses of the immature organism that appear to be modifiable by the behavior of social objects in his environment.

The composition of the social group into which the infant is born determines the potential evoking and reinforcing agents of his social behavior and the agents who will provide discriminative stimuli for subsequent social responses. Every member of the group, and seldom is the mother the only member, is potentially a caretaker, if we do not limit the term "caretaker" too narrowly. They are the organisms toward whom he will display social behavior and who will display social behavior toward him; they are the organisms to whose behavior he will respond and the organisms who will respond to his behavior. It is clear then, that an account of the nature of the infant's social group would have been as appropriate to the discussion of the first two principles as to this principle.

What of the social group into which the human infant most commonly is born in our culture? His is usually a single birth. In this respect, he is different from the rodent and carnivore infant, which is one of many and will have almost constant contact with many littermates. He is also different from the ungulate and primate infants, which early associate with other infants born about the same time. The human infant usually joins a small group composed of mother, father, and perhaps a few older siblings. These few members contrast with the packs and troops that some other mammals form. The primate group, for example, is often composed of several males of varying orders of dominance, several females with young, and many juveniles of all ages. The human infant's, therefore, is a smaller world as far as day-by-day experience go. Yet, on occasion, his social environment becomes more varied and more extensive; he has relatives of all ages, and babysitters, and sometimes he is trans-

ported to environments rich in both physical and social stimulation.

No recital of how the infant's social behavior is modified can be complete without taking into account the sensitivities and capabilities of the social objects in the infant's environment, factors raised here for the first time, but important for the whole discussion. Social objects do not respond to all the infant's behavior; presumably some of these lacks can be traced to varying degrees of sensitivity to the infant's behavior. The nature of the response, it is evident, depends upon what the social objects can do, that is, their capabilities. Needless to say, adequacy of care for any specific species is not here at issue; by hypothesis, all the behavior of present species must be equally adaptive. But one may still ask, what is the nature of the response the members of the group give the infant? In passing, I cannot refrain from calling attention to the numerous and ingenious tools and artifacts man has devised to supplement and sometimes supplant the responses he can make to the infant.

We turn now to the major topics of this section: (1) the infant's social behavior is modified by the responses of social objects to his social behavior, and (2) the processes by which modification is effected. It has previously been stated that the infant past the neonatal stage often gives similar responses to both the animate and inanimate objects in his envrionment. It is now proposed that he learns to discriminate between social object—that is, members of his own group— and nonsocial objects by the different nature of the responses he receives from both classes.

Let us consider the case for the human

infant and use his smiling as an example of responsiveness to social objects. The choice is dictated by the early appearance of smiling and by the attention it has received from developmental psychologists. During the first few weeks of life, the literature reports smiles that are evoked only by stimuli arising from social objects, their voices and their appearances (see Ambrose, 1960; and Gewirtz, 1965, for reviews), and by rhythmic movements of the infant's arms, when these are initiated by a person (Wolff, 1963). There is one exception: Ahrens's (1954) report of an infant smiling at patterns of dots during the second month of life.

I pass over without comment the next few weeks, during which the smile appears more quickly and more frequently, to make a few observations that seem not to have received the attention they deserve. The first is that sometime during the third month, and still more apparent during the fourth month, the smile becomes one component in a chain of responses evoked primarily by visual stimuli. In this chain, the first response is intent regard accompanied by a reduction or even a cessation of physical activity. The next response is facial brightening, and then smiling. The smile is followed by an increase in physical activity. Then, as the infant kicks, waves his arms, or arches his back, he vocalizes (Gesell & Thompson, 1934, p. 261; Washburn, 1929).

This sequence of response I have labeled "the smiling respones." It seems important to make the point, first, because it relates intent visual regard and vocalizing with the smile and, second, because at this period of time the response is given not only to social objects

but also to such disparate objects as toys (Piaget, 1952; Rheingold, 1961), the infant's own hand (Piaget, 1952), and a swinging lamp (Preyer, 1893). In *The Origins of Intelligence in Children*, Piaget (1952) reported a number of observations on the development of vision in his son, Laurent. From these observation—and you must remember that smiling was not their focus — I tallied every instance in which Piaget reported a smile *and* the object that evoked it. In eight reports, from 1 month 15 days to 2 months 4 days, the stimulus object was a person. At 2 months 11 days, we find the first reports of smiling to nonsocial objects. On the day, the infant smiled to a handkerchief, a rattle, and other toys, both in motion and motionless. In the next 23 reports of smiles, at ages up to 4 months when the section on vision ended, in only six was the stimulus a social object. In 17 of the 23 smiling espisodes in the third and fourth months, the stimulus was a nonsocial object. The smiling response, therefore, cannot be equated with the social response; the nature of the stimulating object must define whether the response is social or nonsocial.

The evidence suggests that, during a stage in the development of the *seeing* human infant, smiles are primarily evoked by visual arrays possessing certain, as yet unspecified, stimulus properties, whether presented by social or nonsocial objects. Schneirla (1959) pointed to low intensity as the effective stimulus property (p. 33), Bowlby (1958), to "certain inherently interesting stimulus patterns" (p. 361), and Salzen (1963), to any contrast or change in brightness. The role of learning in the development of the smiling response at this stage is not yet clear (Gewirtz, 1965). Some of the reinforcing effects of sensory feedback may be unconditioned (Skinner, 1953), although they soon do become conditioned. At any rate, I am less concerned with the origin of the smiling response than with an analysis of the stimulus properties that evoke it.

In the next stage of development, beginning sometime after 4 months of age, the smiling response is evoked more and more often by animate objects, less and less often by inanimate objects; it is evoked by people, seldom by things, These stages, of course, are not precisely fixed in time or mutually exclusive. It must be admitted, further, that in delineating this stage I am predicting what seems reasonable; the studies have not yet been performed.

Two processes can account for the developing discrimination. First, the social object, being animate, possesses, and therefore more regularly presents, the set of effective stimuli. Second, the social object, being animate *and* human, that is a member of one's own species, is *responsive* to the infant's smiling. The infant's smiling evokes responses from persons much of the time, from things not at all. A smile is often met with a smile, and sometimes also with words and touches. At the least, the human observer will move closer, stay longer, and pay attention. It is upon this characteristic of human interchange that Bowlby (1958) based his statement on the adaptive value of the infant's smile for his own survival.

Controlled studies have shown that, when these naturally occurring interactions between infant and adult are experimentally programmed, the social response of infants can in fact be modified by responses from social objects. For example, the number of vocalizations 3-month-old infants give to the sight of a person has been systematically increased (Rheingold, Gewirtz, & Ross, 1959; Weisberg, 1963), as well as the number of smiles in 4-month-old infants (Brackbill, 1958).

These studies suggest that instrumental conditioning may be the process by which the discrimination between people and things is learned, that is, the events contingent upon the infant's response increased the subsequent occurrence of the response. While in general I believe the evidence supports this conclusion, other mechanisms may also be operating. As long as infants are fed and made warm and dry by human hands, we cannot rule out the possibility that social objects are discriminated on the basis of secondary reward value (Keller & Schoenfeld, 1950). Recently, Sears (1963) wrote, "One apparent result of this mutually satisfying relationship is the creation of secondary rewards or reinforcers for both members of the pair. That is, the mother's talking, patting, smiling, her gestures of affection or concern, are constantly being presented to the baby in context with primary reinforcing stimulations such as those involved in eating, fondling, and caressing" (p. 30). Multicausality is not rare in behavior theory, and important responses may well be overdetermined.

One final word on the discrimination between people and things: Exploratory behavior has been defined (Berlyne, 1960, p. 78) as a response that increases the organism's exposure to his environment. Social behavior, specifically the smiling response, increases the infant's exposure to the sight and sound of persons because of their response to it. The smiling response, like exploratory behavior, maximizes the inflow of stimulation and, thus, of information from the object in question. Although it is possible to simplify too much, still, some more powerful and general principles of behavior may result from categorizing at least some classes of social behavior as exploratory. Exploratory behavior could describe the larger class; social behavior, the class in which the object is not a thing but another living organism.

In the next stage of the smiling response—and here, as elsewhere, the stages are characterized by extensive temporal overlapping—the infant discriminates between familiar and strange social objects. As early as the third month, an infant may sober upon the appearance of a strange person (Gesell & Thompson, 1934). In speaking of this discrimination, I do not refer solely to distress responses. Observation and experimental evidence do not consistently support the conclusion that infants at a certain age are afraid of strangers. First, in my experience, distress responses are not typical of the majority of infants; they occur in some infants for short periods of time, and in only a few infants for longer periods of time. In our laboratory, 9-month-old infants smile easily to the entire staff. In spite of the amount of attention paid the phenomenon, we still do not have, even at this late date, normative data on a representative sample of infants. Second, as for evidence: Morgan (1965) found that when the stranger did not touch the infant but smiled, talked, and moved his head as if playing peekaboo, infants 4 to

12 months of age tended to react positively. Gewirtz (1965), measuring the occurrence and frequency of smiles to a relatively strange person presenting an expressionless face, found no abrupt decline in a large sample of children from 1 to 18 months of age; those living in environments in which they had considerable contact with a smaller number of adults, a condition often thought to be correlated with fear of strangers, declined the least.

The distress response aside, it seems likely that most infants give the smiling response to strange persons more slowly and less fully than to familiar ones. We expect the response to be sensitive to such variables as the familiarity of the surrounding environment, the distance from the mother, the brusqueness of the stranger's approach, and the intrusiveness of his behavior. In most instances, whatever the complex set of stimuli that constitutes strangeness may be, its effect wears off fairly quickly. It is interesting to note, in passing, that we tend to call the stimulus "novel" when it evokes approach behavior and "strange" when it evokes withdrawal and distress behavior.

A preference for the familiar—often overlooked these days in our concern with the control exerted over behavior by the novel—is under certain, as yet unknown, conditions characteristic of all animals of all ages; it is a component of the pattern of behavior known as "wildness." In part, the preference for the familiar can be labeled "perceptual learning," previous exposure being required for the discrimination (Kimble, 1961); in part, it would appear to be a matter of the known reinforcers being more reinforcing.

In the next developmental stage, the infant discriminates between one familiar person and another. His social responses—here, specifically, the smiling response—may occur more quickly and more frequently and in greater intensity to persons other than the mother, to perhaps the father or a sibling, as Ainsworth (1964) noted. The same observation was made by Schaffer and Emerson (1964) in recording the infant's response to the departure of known persons. The very constancy of the mother's presence, the fact that her flow of stimuli are often not contingent upon acts of the infant, as well as the aversive nature of some of the necessary caretaking activities, may operate against maximum social interchange. In contrast, the responses of fathers and siblings are intermittent, are more often—we can surmise—contingent on the infant's behavior, and are more often playful, that is offering stimulation for its own sake, characteristics that should make for more powerful reinforcement. The appearance of these other persons, then, would possess discriminative stimuli for future reinforcement; they provide cues for the occurrence of interesting stimulation.

The development of the smiling response has been presented in detail as an example of the principle that the infant's social behavior is modified by the responses of people to *his* social behavior. What of the modification of other classes of social behavior in other mammals?

For the infant mammal, too, it is obvious that its behavior toward members of its group must be modified by the responses the social objects give in turn. After the period of close physical attachment to the mother in the rodent, carnivore, and primate young, the infant approaches and contacts both animate and inanimate objects in its environment (Bolles & Woods, 1964; Harlow, 1962; Rheingold, 1963). In time, his responses to them become differentiated, as do his responses to littermates, juveniles, and adults. The infant mammal, too, like the human infant, discriminates early between strange and familiar organisms, and then between different familiar organisms.

The social behavior of animal infants has also been modified in laboratory studies. Rhesus infants raised on surrogate mothers do not develop normal social behavior (Harlow, 1963); rhesus infants raised in bare cages cling to each other (Harlow, 1963); kittens raised on brooder mothers are inept in making contact with their own mothers (Schneirla et al., 1963). Deprivation of normal experiences appears then to markedly affect the development of social behavior in infants.

Suggestive also are the results of some studies of the social responsiveness of dog to man. Puppies ran more often and faster to a passive human being than to one who patted and made a fuss over them. This behavior was modified by deprivation of social contact and, further, occurred in animals reared in isolation which therefore had no history of receiving food at the hands of people. A passive person thus appears to be a primary reinforcer of social approach behavior in the puppy (Bacon & Stanley, 1963; Stanley, 1965; Stanley & Elliot, 1962; Stanley, Morris & Trattner, 1965).

THE INFANT MODIFIES THE BE-HAVIOR OF OTHERS

The fourth principle states that the infant, by his appearance and behavior, modifies the behavior of other social objects. He not only evokes responses from them but maintains and shapes their responses by reinforcing some and not others. From our individual experiences, we know how effective he can be! He is so effective because he is relatively helpless yet active and because he is so attractive to his beholders. The amount of attention and the number of responses directed to the infant are enormous—out of all proportion to his age, size, and accomplishments. Under ordinary circumstances, in any human group containing an infant, the attention directed toward him is usually considerable. Although I have no data to cite for the human group, the facts in primate groups have been well documented (e.g., DeVore, 1963; Jay, 1963; Rowell et al., 1964). For the langur monkey, Jay (1963) has reported, "From birth the newborn is a focal point of interest for all adult and subadult females in the troop. Females gather around the mother as soon as they notice the newborn. . . .A group of from four to ten females quickly surrounds and grooms the mother. . . .Each time she sits, three or four females crowd in front of her to touch, smell, and lick the newborn. . . .An infant may be held by as many as eight or ten females and carried as far as 75 feet from its mother in the first two days of life" (pp. 288-289). Similarly, for the baboon, DeVore (1963) wrote,

The birth of a new infant absorbs the attention of the entire troop. From the moment the birth is discovered, the mother is continuously surrounded by the other baboons, who walk beside her and sit as close as possible when she rests. . . .After a week or 10 days, older juveniles and females who sit beside the mother and groom her quietly for several minutes may be allowed to reach over and touch the infant lightly. Young juveniles and older infants sit near the mother and watch her newborn intently, but are seldom able to approach the mother because of the older troop members around her. . . . Older juvenile or subadult females appear to be most highly motivated toward the newborn infant, and the moment a mother sits one or more of these females is likely to stop whatever she is doing and join the mother. . . . Juvenile and young adult males express only perfunctory interest in the infant, but older males in the central hierarchy frequently come and touch the infant (pp. 313-314).

Appearance aside, the helplessness of most mammalian infants, of course, demands caretaking responses. The nature and frequency of caretaking have been documented for many mammals (e.g., Rheingold, 1963), including the human infant (e.g., Rheingold, 1960). Rosenblatt and Lehrman (1963) have shown that the maintenance of maternal responses, although partly dependent on the mothers's physiological condition, is also partly dependent on stimulation by the young. And Harlow et al. (1963) have shown how some rhesus infants, by their repeated efforts to attach themselves to rejecting rhesus mothers, eventually made the mothers passably accepting of them. The infant also evokes nurturant behavior in others than the mother. Noirot (1964) has shown how maternal or caretaking behavior was increased in both male and female mice by brief contact with an infant mouse. The above passages from Jay and DeVore make the same points.

Further, the infant's positive social responses evoke responsiveness in kind from others in his environment. The human infant's smiles, for example, are met by smiles; his vocalizations, by vocalizations; his playful overtures, by play. Here, too, may be mentioned the distress cries of the infants; surely they modify the behavior of others. Generally, they exert a powerful effect upon the members of almost all mammalian groups. So aversive, especially to humans, is the crying of the infant that there is almost no effort we will not expend, no device we will not employ, to change a crying baby into a smiling one—or just a quiet one.

Although the mechanisms have not yet been specified, there seem to be strong reinforcing effects in caring for the needs of the helpless and dependent. Caretakers appear to find satisfying the operations of feeding, bathing, and putting the infant to sleep. We have long paid attention to how the infant's behavior is modified by the behavior of his caretakers; only now are we beginning to ponder on how the infant's behavior may modify the behavior of his caretakers.

CONCLUSION

The four principles, in summary, provide a framework for classifying and organizing knowledge of the development of social behavior in the human and other mammalian infants. They may also provide the distance required to gain a fresh perspective on the development of social behavior. They bypass controversies, especially the troublesome one of innate versus learned behavior. They are not, of course, explanatory principles, but they do leave the door open for an analysis of the processes by which behavior is modified. The four principles, furthermore, do not represent four stages in development; rather, they exist together and are intimately related. Within each principle, however, there are stages of development, here only hinted at. Finally, they take cognizance of species-characteristic behavior in their dependence upon the sensitivities, capabilities, and social organization of each animal.

The principles, in addition, may serve to correct for premature and incautious generalizations from one species to another. More and more rarely now do we make the error of construing the behavior of animals in human terms; we must guard as carefully, in the absence of supporting evidence, against the error of construing the behavior of humans in animal terms.

In this presentation, it has been assumed that no extra theories, laws, or constructs are necessary to account for the behavior of the infant as distinct from the behavior of older organisms, to account for social behavior as distinct from other classes of behavior, or to account for the behavior of one species as distinct from the behavior of other species. Much can be gained, I believe, by an integration of all mammalian behavior into a science of behavior . . . .

References

Ahrens, R. Beitrag zur Entwicklung des Physiognomie und Mimikerkennens. *Zeitschrift fur experimentalle und angewändte Psychologie,* 1954, **2,** 412-454.

Ainsworth, Mary D. Patterns of attachment behavior shown by the infant in interaction with his mother. *Merrill-Palmer Quarterly,* 1964, **10,** 51-58.

Ambrose, J. A. The smiling and related responses in early human infancy: an experimental and theoretical study of their course and significance. Unpublished doctoral dissertation, Univer. of London, 1960.

Bacon, W. E., & Stanley, W. C. Effect of deprivation level in puppies on performance maintained by a passive person reinforcer. *Journal of comparative and physiological Psychology,* 1963, **56,** 783-785.

Bayley, Nancy. *The California first-year mental scale.* (Univer. of Calif. Syllabus Series, No. 243.) Berkeley: Univer. of Calif. Press, 1933.

Berlyne, D. E. *Conflict, arousal, and curiosity.* New York: McGraw-Hill, 1960.

Bolles, R. C., & Woods, P. J. The ontogeny of behaviour in the albino rat. *Animal Behaviour,* 1964, **12,** 427-441.

Bowlby, J. The nature of the child's tie to his mother. *International Journal of Psycho-analysis,* 1958, **39,** 350-373.

Brackbill, Yvonne. Extinction of the smiling response in infants as a function of reinforcement schedule. *Child Development,* 1958, **29,** 115-124.

Cattell, Psyche. *The measurement of intelligence of infants and young children.* New York: Psychol. Corp., 1940.

Cruikshank, Ruth M. Animal infancy. In L. Carmichael (Ed.), *Manual of child psychology.* (2d ed.) New York: Wiley, 1954, pp. 186-214.

DeVore, I. Mother-infant relations in free-ranging baboons. In Harriet L. Rheingold (Ed.), *Maternal behavior in mammals.* New York: Wiley, 1963, pp. 305-335.

Gesell, A., & Thompson, Helen. *Infant behavior: its genesis and growth.* New York: McGraw-Hill, 1934.

Gewirtz, J. L. The course of smiling by groups of Israeli infants in the first 18 months of life. In *Studies in psychology: Scripta Hierosolymitana,* **14,** Jerusalem: Hebrew Univer. Press, in press.

Griffiths, Ruth. *The abilities of babies.* New York: McGraw-Hill, 1954.

Harlow, H. F. The nature of love. *American Psychologist,* 1958, **13,** 673-685.

Harlow, H. F. Primary affectional patterns in primates. *American Journal of Orthopsychiatry,* 1960, **30,** 676-684.

Harlow, H. F. Development of the second and third affectional systems in macaque monkeys. In T. T. Tourlentes, S. L. Pollack, & H. E. Himwich (Eds.), *Research approaches to psychiatric problems: a symposium.* New York: Grune & Stratton, 1962, pp. 209-238.

Harlow, H. F. The maternal affectional systems. In B. M. Foss (Ed.), *Determinants of infant behavior II.* London: Methuen, 1963, pp. 3-29.

Harlow, H. F., Harlow, Margaret K., & Hansen, E. W. The maternal affectional system of rhesus monkeys. In Harriet L. Rheingold (Ed.), *Maternal behavior in mammals.* New York: Wiley, 1963, pp. 254-281.

Igel, C. J., & Calvin, A. D. The development of affectional responses in infant dogs. *Journal of comparative and physiological Psychology,* 1960, **53,** 302-305.

Jay, Phyllis. Mother-infant relations in langurs. In Harriet L. Rheingold (Ed.), *Maternal behavior in mammals.* New York: Wiley, 1963, pp. 282-304.

Keller, F. S., & Schoenfeld, W. N. *Principles of psychology.* New York: Appleton-Century-Crofts, 1950.

Kimble, G. A. *Hilgard and Marquis' conditioning and learning.* New York: Appleton-Century-Crofts, 1961.

Morgan, G. A. Some determinants of infants' responses to strangers during the first year of life. Unpublished doctoral dissertation, Cornell Univer., 1965.

Noirot, Eliane. Changes in responsiveness to young in the adult mouse. IV. The effect of an initial contact with a strong stimulus. *Animal Behavior,* 1964, **12,** 44-445.

Piaget, J. *The origins of intelligence in children.* Trans. by Margaret Cook. New York: Int. Univer. Press, 1952.

Preyer, W. *The senses and the will.* Trans. by H. W. Brown. New York: Appleton, 1893.

Rheingold, Harriet L. The measurement of maternal care. *Child Development,* 1960, **31,** 565-575.

Rheingold, Harriet L. The effect of environmental stimulation upon social and exploratory behaviour in the human infant. In B. M. Foss (Ed.), *Determinants of infant behaviour.* London: Methuen, 1961, pp. 143-177.

Rheingold, Harriet L. Maternal behavior in the dog. In Harriet L. Rheingold (Ed.), *Maternal behavior in mammals.* New York: Wiley, 1963, pp. 169-202.

Rheingold, Harriet L., Gewirtz, J. L., & Ross, Helen W. Social conditioning of vocalizations in the infant. *Journal of comparative and physiological Psychology,* 1959, **52,** 68-73.

Rosenblatt, J. S., & Lehrman, D. S. Maternal behavior in the laboratory rat. In Harriet L. Rheingold (Ed.), *Maternal behavior in mammals.* New York: Wiley, 1963, pp. 8-57.

Rowell, T. E., Hinde, R. A., & Spencer-Booth, Y. "Aunt"-infant interactions in captive rhesus monkeys. *Animal Behaviour,* 1964, **12,** 219-226.

Salzen, E.A. Visual stimuli elicting the smiling response in the human infant. *Journal of genetic Psychology,* 1963, **102,** 51-54.

Schaffer, H. R., & Emerson, Peggy E. The development of social attachments in infancy. *Monographs of the Society for Research in Child Development,* 1964, **29,** No. 3 (Serial No. 94).

Schneirla, T. C. An evolutionary and developmental theory of biphasic processes underlying approach and withdrawal. In *Nebraska symposium on motivation.* Lincoln: Univer. of Nebraska Press, 1959, pp. 1-42.

Schneirla, T. C., & Rosenblatt, J. S. Behavioral organization and genesis of the social bond in insects and mammals. *American Journal of Orthopsychiatry,* 1961, **31,** 223-253.

Schneirla, T. C., Rosenblatt, J. S., & Tobach, Ethel. Maternal behavior in the cat. In Harriet L. Rheingold (Ed.), *Maternal behavior in mammals.* New York: Wiley, 1963, pp. 122-168.

Scott, J.P., & Marston, Mary-'Vesta. Critical periods affecting the development of normal and mal-adjustive social behavior of puppies. *Journal of genetic Psychology,* 1950, **77,** 25-60.

Sears, R. R. Dependency motivation. In M. R. Jones (Ed.), *Nebraska symposium on motivation.* Lincoln: Univer. of Nebraska Press, 1963, pp. 25-64.

Skinner, B. F. *Science and human behavior.* New York: Macmillan, 1953.

Spitz, R. A., & Wolf, Katherine M. The smiling response: a contribution to the ontogenesis of social relations. *Genetic Psychology Monographs,* 1946, **34,** 57-125.

Stanley, W. C. The passive person as a reinforcer in isolated beagle puppies. *Psychonomic Science,* 1965, **2,** 21-22.

Stanley, W. C., & Elliot, O. Differential human handling as reinforcing events and as treatments influencing later social behavior in Basenji puppies. *Psychological Reports,* 1962, **10,** 775-788.

Stanley, W. C., Morris, D. D., & Trattner, Alice. Conditioning with a passive person reinforcer and extinction in Shetland sheep dog puppies. *Psychonomic Science,* 1965, **2,** 19-20.

Tilney, F., & Casamajor, L. Myelinogeny as applied to the study of behavior. *Archives of Neurology and Psychiatry,* 1924, **12,** 1-66.

Walters, R. H., & Parke, R. D. The role of the distance receptors in the development of social responsivenes. In L. P. Lipsitt & C. C. Spiker

(Eds.), *Advances in child development and behavior.* Vol. 2. New York: Academic Press, 1965, pp. 59-96.

Washburn, R. W. A study of the smiling and laughing of infants in the first year of life. *Genetic Psychology Monographs,* 1929, **6,** 396-537.

Weisberg, P. Social and nonsocial conditioning of infant vocalizations. *Child Development,* 1963, **34,** 377-388.

Welker, W. I. Factors influencing aggregation of neonatal puppies. *Journal of comparative and psysiological Psychology,* 1959, **52,** 376-380.

Wolff, P. H. Observations on the early development of smiling. In B. M. Foss (Ed.), *Determinants of infant behaviour II,* London: Methuen, 1963, pp. 113-134.

MARY D. SALTER AINSWORTH AND SILVIA M. BELL

Attachment, Exploration, and Separation: Illustrated by the Behavior of One-Year-Olds in a Strange Situation*

Within the last decade the term "attachment" has appeared with increasing frequency in both empirical and theoretical segments of the developmental psychology literature (see Cairns 1966; Gewirtz 1961, 1969; Maccoby & Masters, in press; Robson 1967; Schaffer & Emerson 1964; Schwarz 1968). The term, as originally introduced by Bowlby (1958, 1969) and as used by Ainsworth (1963, 1964, 1967), implies an ethological and evolutionary viewpoint, and hence has conno-

*From *Child Development,* 1970, 41, 49-68. Reprinted by permission of the author and the Society for Research in Child Development.

tations not necessarily shared by those with other theoretical orientations. Infant-mother attachment has been conceived as related to separation anxiety (see Bowlby 1960), fear of the strange and strangers (see Morgan & Ricciuti 1969; Schaffer 1966), and exploration (see Ainsworth 1967; Ainsworth & Wittig 1969). It is believed that the interrelationships between these behaviors throw light upon the biological function of infant-mother attachment; that they do is strongly suggested by field studies of ground-living nonhuman primates. Although comparable reports of human infants in their natural home environment are not yet forthcoming, interaction between attachment behavior, exploration, separation anxiety, and fear of the strange may be observed in a controlled laboratory environment — the strange or unfamiliar situation.

It is the purpose of this paper to highlight some distinctive features of the ethological-evolutionary concept of attachment, by citing reports of the interactions between the infant's attachment behavior and other behaviors mentioned above; to illustrate these interactions by a report of the behavior of 1 year olds in a strange situation; and to note parallels between strange-situation behavior and behavior reported in other relevant observational, clinical, and experimental contexts.

Let us begin with some definitions and key concepts distinctive of the ethological-evolutionary viewpoint, as proposed by Bowlby (1958, 1969) and Ainsworth (1964, 1967, 1969). *An attachment* may be defined as an affectional tie that one person or animal forms between himself and another specific one—a tie that binds them together in space and endures over time. The behavioral hallmark of attachment is seeking to gain and to maintain a certain degree of proximity to the object of attachment, which ranges from close physical contact under some circumstances to interaction or communication across some distance under other circumstances. *Attachment behaviors* are behaviors which promote proximity or contact. In the human infant these include active proximity- and contact-seeking behaviors such as approaching, following, and clinging, and signaling behaviors such as smiling, crying, and calling.

The very young infant displays attachment (proximity-promoting) behaviors such as crying, sucking, rooting, and smiling, despite the fact that he is insufficiently discriminating to direct them differentially to a specific person. These initial behaviors indicate a genetic bias toward becoming attached, since they can be demonstrated to be either activated or terminated most effectively by stimuli which, in the environment of evolutionary adaptedness, are most likely to stem from human sources. When these behaviors, supplemented by other active proximity-seeking behaviors which emerge later — presumably through a process of learning in the course of mother-infant interaction — become organized hierarchically and directed actively and specifically toward the mother, the infant may be described as having become attached to her.

The intensity of attachment behavior may be heightened or diminished by situational conditions, but, once an attachment has been formed, it cannot be viewed as vanishing during periods when attachment behavior is not evident. Therefore, it seems necessary to view attachment as an organization of behavioral systems which has an internal, structural portion that endures throughout periods when none of the component attachment behaviors have been activated.

Viewed in the context of evolutionary theory, infant-mother attachment may be seen to fulfill significant biological functions, that is, functions that promote species survival. The long, helpless infancy of the human species occasions grave risks. For the species to have survived, the infant has required protection during this period of defenselessness.

It is inferred, therefore, that the genetic code makes provision for infant behaviors which have the usual (although not necessarily invariable) outcome of bringing infant and mother together.

Exploratory behavior is equally significant from an evolutionary point of view. As Hamburg (1968) has pointed out, a prolonged infancy would miss its adaptive mark if there were not also provisions in the genetic code which lead the infant to be interested in the novel features of his environment — to venture forth, to explore, and to learn. The implication is that the genetic biases in a species which can adapt to a wide range of environmental variations provide for a balance in infant behaviors (and in reciprocal maternal behaviors) between those which lead the infant away from the mother and promote exploration and acquisition of knowledge of the properties of the physical and social environment, and those which draw mother and infant together and promote the protection and nurturance that the mother can provide.

The interaction between exploratory and attachment behaviors has been highlighted in field studies of ground-living nonhuman primates (e.g., Southwick, Beg, & Siddiqi 1965; DeVore 1963; Goodall 1965; Schaller 1965) as well as studies of such species in captive colonies (see Hinde, Rowell, & Spencer-Booth 1964, 1967) and in laboratories (e.g., Harlow 1961; Harlow & Harlow 1965; Mason 1965.) Although at first infant and mother are in almost continuous close contact, soon they are in collusion to make more elastic the bonds that unite them. The infant ventures forth to investigate his environment and to play with other infants, and gradually spends more

and more time "off" his mother. His expeditions take him further and further away from her, and she becomes increasingly permissive and retrieves him less promptly and less frequently. Alarm or threat of separation, however, quickly bring mother and infant together again.

Naturalistic studies of the attachment-exploration balance are very time consuming; the interaction between the two sets of behaviors must be observed over a wide range of situations. A short-cut alternative is to utilize a controlled strange or unfamiliar situation in which the child, with and without his mother, is exposed to stressful episodes of different kinds. So powerful is this technique in evoking behavioral changes that it is likely to be used with increasing frequency in studies of mother-infant interaction. The ethological-evolutionary view of the attachment-exploration balance is a useful model to use when planning and when interpreting the findings of strange-situation studies.

Of strange-situation studies already reported in the literature, only two have been guided by an ethological-evolutionary point of view. Harlow (1961) used a strange situation to demonstrate the security function of surrogate cloth mothers for infant rhesus macaques. Ainsworth and Wittig (1969) made a preliminary report of the attachment-exploration balance in human 1 year olds. Other studies — Arsenian (1943), Cox and Campbell (1968), Rheingold (1969) — focused on exploratory behavior and reported that the presence of the mother supports it, but paid scant attention to attachment behavior and its hierarchical manifestations in reunion episodes as well as during separation.

The strange-situation procedure provides more than an opportunity to observe how exploratory behavior is affected by mother-present, mother-absent, or other conditions. It is a laboratory microcosm in which a wide range of behaviors pertinent to attachment and to its balance with exploratory behavior may be elicited. Attachment behaviors may be seen as complicated by "negative" behaviors, such as avoidance and aggression. And yet, since the laboratory situation provides but a very small sample of mother-infant interaction, strange-situation findings are not self-interpreting. Perception of the implications of the behaviors that occur in it is facilitated by reference to the findings of other studies — naturalistic, clinical, and experimental. For this reason the ensuing report of a strange-situation study is presented as a useful *illustration* of the shifting balance between exploratory and attachment behavior implicit in the ethological-evolutionary view of attachment. The discussion which follows the presentation refers to relevant findings of other studies. The propositions offered in conclusion comprehend these other relevant considerations as well as the findings of the illustrative strange-situation study.

THE STRANGE SITUATION

In the course of a longitudinal, naturalistic investigation of infant-mother attachment during the first year of life, there was little opportunity in the home environment to observe the balance of attachment and exploratory behaviors under conditions of novelty and alarm. Therefore, a laboratory situation was devised as a test situation to which the Ss were introduced when nearly 1 year old. It was desired to observe the extent to which the infant could use his mother as a secure base from which he could explore a strange environment, with fear of the strange kept in abeyance by her presence. It was also intended to observe the extent to which attachment behavior might gain ascendancy over exploratory behavior under conditions of alarm introduced by the entrance of a stranger and under conditions of separation from the reunion with the mother.

Method

Subjects. The 56 Ss were family-reared infants of white, middle-class parents, who were originally contacted through pediatricians in private practice. One subsample of 23 Ss, who had been observed longitudinally from birth onward, were observed in the strange situation when 51 weeks old. The second subsample of 33 Ss, studied in the context of an independent project (Bell in press), were observed when 49 weeks old.

Procedure. The strange situation was comprised of eight episodes which followed in a standard order for all subjects. The situation was designed to be novel enough to elicit exploratory behavior, and yet not so strange that it would evoke fear and heighten attachment behavior at the outset. The approach of the stranger was gradual, so that any fear of her could be attributed to unfamiliarity rather than to abrupt, alarming behavior. The episodes were arranged so that the less disturbing ones came first. Finally, the situation as a whole was intended to be no more disturbing than those an infant was likely to encounter in his ordinary life experience. A summarized account of the procedure has been given elsewhere (Ainsworth & Wittig 1969) but will be reviewed here.

The experimental room was furnished — not bare — but so arranged that there was a 9 x 9-foot square of clear floor space; marked off into 16 squares to facilitate recording of location and locomotion. At one end of the room was a child's chair heaped with and surrounded by toys. Near the other end of the room on one side was a chair for the mother, and on the opposite side, near the door, a chair for the stranger. The baby was put down in the middle of the base of the triangle formed by the three chairs and left free to move where he wished. Both the mother and the female stranger were instructed in advance as to the roles they were to play.

In summary, the eight episodes of the situation are as follows:

Episode 1 (M, B, O). Mother (M), accompanied by an observer (O), carried the baby (B) into the room, and then O left.

Episode 2 (M, B). M put B down in the specified place, then sat quietly in her chair, participating only if B sought her attention. Duration 3 minutes.

Episode 3 (S, M, B). A stranger (S) entered, sat quietly for 1 minute, conversed with M for 1 minute, and then gradually approached B, showing him a toy. At the end of the third minute M left the room unobtrusively.

Episode 4 (S, B). If B was happily engaged in play, S was nonparticipant. If he was inactive, she tried to interest him in the toys. If he was distressed, she tried to distract him or to comfort him. If he

could not be comforted, the episode was curtailed — otherwise it lasted 3 minutes.

Episode 5 (M, B). M entered, paused in the doorway to give B an opportunity to mobilize a spontaneous response to her. S then left unobtrusively. What M did next was not specified — except that she was told that after B was again settled in play with the toys she was to leave again, after pausing to say "bye-bye." (Duration of episode undetermined.)

Episode 6 (B alone). The baby was left alone for 3 minutes, unless he was so distressed that the episode had to be curtailed.

Episode 7 (S, B). S entered and behaved as in episode 4 for 3 minutes, unless distress prompted curtailment. (Ainsworth & Wittig 1969, planned a somewhat different procedure for episode 7, which was attempted for the first 14 Ss but, as it turned out, approximated the simpler procedure reported here, which was used for the remaining Ss.)

Episode 8 (M, B). M returned, S left, and after the reunion had been observed, the situation was terminated.

The behavior of the Ss was observed from an adjoining room through a one-way vision window. Two observers dictated continuous narrative accounts into a dual channel tape recorder which also picked up the click of a timer every 15 seconds. (This represents the procedure we now consider standard. For the first 14 Ss, however, the dual channel recorder was not available, so one observer dictated, while the other made written notes. For the second subsample of 33 Ss, author Bell was the sole observer.) The protocols were subsequently transcribed and consolidated, then coded. Reliability of observation was checked by separate codings of the dictated reports made by the two authors in four cases observed by both. Product-moment coefficients of 0.99 were found for each of locomotor, manipulatory and visual exploration, and one of 0.98 for crying.

The narrative record yielded two types of measure. A frequency measure was used for three forms of exploratory behavior — locomotor, manipulatory, and visual — and for crying. A score of 1 was given for each 15-second time interval in which the behavior occurred. The maximum was 12 for an episode, since the standard length of an episode was 3 minutes, and longer or shorter episodes were prorated. Frequency measures were obtained for episodes 2 through 7. Product-moment reliability coefficients for two independent coders for eight randomly selected cases were as follows: exploratory locomotion, 0.99; exploratory manipulation, 0.93; visual exploration, 0.98; crying, 0.99.

The second measure was based upon detailed coding of behaviors in which the contingencies of the mother's or stranger's behavior had to be taken into consideration. The codings were then ordered into 7-point scales on the assumption that not only could the same behavior be manifested in different degrees of intensity, but that different behaviors could serve the same end under different intensities of activation. There were five classes of behavior thus scored.

Proximity- and contact-seeking behaviors include active, effective behaviors such as approaching and clambering up, active gestures such as reaching or leaning, intention movements such as partial approaches, and vocal signals including

"directed" cries.

Contact-maintaining behaviors pertain to the situation after the baby has gained contact, either through his own initiative or otherwise. They include: clinging, embracing, clutching, and holding on; resisting release by intensified clinging or, if contact is lost, by turning back and reaching, or clambering back up; and protesting release vocally.

Proximity- and interaction-avoiding behaviors pertain to a situation which ordinarily elicits approach, greeting, or at least watching or interaction across a distance, as when an adult entered, or tried to engage the baby's attention. Such behaviors include ignoring the adult, pointedly avoiding looking at her, looking away, turning away, or moving away.

Contact- and interaction-resisting behaviors included angry, ambivalent attempts to push away, hit, or kick the adult who seeks to make contact, squirming to get down having been picked up, or throwing away or pushing away the toys through which the adult attempts to mediate her interventions. More diffuse manifestations are angry screaming, throwing self about, throwing self down, kicking the floor, pouting, cranky fussing, or petulance.

These four classes of behavior were scored for interaction with the mother in episodes 2, 3, 5, and 8, and for interaction with the stranger in episodes 3, 4, and 7.

Search behavior was scored for the separation episodes 4, 6, and 7. These behaviors include: following the mother to the door, trying to open the door, banging on the door, remaining oriented to the door or glancing at it, going to the mother's empty chair or simply looking at it. Such behaviors imply that the infant is searching for the absent mother either actively or by orienting to the last place in which she was seen (the door in most cases) or to the place associated with her in the strange situation (her chair.)

In scoring these five classes of behavior, the score was influenced by the following features: the strength of the behavior, its frequency, duration, and latency, and by the type of behavior itself — with active behavior being considered stronger than signaling. Detailed instructions for scoring these behaviors as well as for coding the frequency measures are provided elsewhere.[1]

Reliability coefficients (rho) for two independent scorers for 14 randomly selected cases were, for behaviors directed to the mother, as follows: proximity- and contact-seeking, 0.93; contact-maintaining, 0.97; proximity- and interaction-avoiding, 0.93; contact-resisting, 0.96; search, 0.94.

Findings

The findings to be reported here are of behaviors characteristic of the sample as a whole. Individual differences were conspicuous, instructive, and significantly

correlated with other variables. Some of these have been reported elsewhere (Ainsworth & Wittig 1969; Ainsworth & Bell in press; Bell in press) but they cannot be considered here.

Exploratory Behavior. Figure 1 shows how three forms of exploratory behavior vary in successive episodes from 2 through 7. There is a sharp decline in all forms of exploratory behavior from episode 2 when the baby was alone with his mother to episode 3 when the stranger was present also. (This and all other interepisode differences reported here are significant at the .01 level or better, as tested by the binomial test, unless noted otherwise.) Exploration remains depressed through episode 4 when the baby was left with the stranger. Visual and manipulatory exploration (visual at the .02 level) recover significantly in episode 5, aided by the mother's attempts to interest the baby again in play, although similar efforts by the stranger in episodes 4 and 7 were ineffective. Visual and manipulatory exploration decline again in episode 6 after the mother departs for a second time, leaving the baby alone. All forms of exploratory behavior decline to their lowest point in episode 7 after the stranger had returned but while the mother was still absent.

To supplement the visual exploration score, which measured visual orientation to the physical environment, visual orientation to the mother and to the stranger were also coded. The only noteworthy findings may be summarized as follows: In episode 2, the baby looked at the toys and other aspects of the physical environment much more frequently than at the mother, at whom he glanced only now and then, keeping visual tabs on her;

[1] The following materials have been deposited with the National Auxiliary Publications Service: instructions for conducting the strange situation procedure, instructions to the mother, instructions for coding behaviors for frequency measures, and instructions for coding socially interactive behaviors. Orders NAPS Document 00762 from ASIS National Auxiliary Publications Service, c/o CMM Information Sciences, Inc., 22 West 34th Street, New York, New York 10001; remitting $3.00 for microfiche or $1.00 for photocopies.

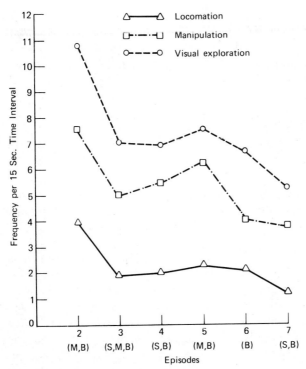

Figure 1. *Incidence of exploratory behavior.*

in episode 3, the stranger, the most novel feature of the environment, was looked at more than the toys, and the mother was looked at no more frequently than before.

Crying. Figure 2 suggests that the strange situation does not in itself cause alarm or distress, for crying is minimal in eposode 2. Crying does not increase significantly in episode 3 (p = .068), which suggests that the stranger was not in herself alarming for most Ss, at least not when the mother was also present. The incidence of crying rises in episode 4 with the mother's first departure; it de-

clines upon her return in episode 5, only to increase sharply in episode 6 when she departs a second time, leaving the baby alone. It does not decrease significantly when the stranger returns in episode 7, which suggests that it is the mother's absence rather than mere aloneness that was distressing to most of the babies, and that the greater incidence of crying in episode 6 than in episode 4 is largely due to a cumulative effect.

Search Behavior During Separation. The mean strength of search behavior was moderate in episode 4 (3.0), significantly stronger in episode 6 (4.6),

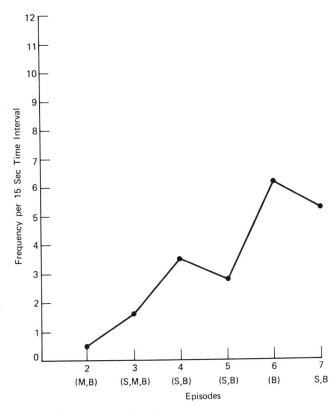

Figure 2. *Incidence of crying.*

and moderate again in episode 7 (2.5). Although this might suggest that search behavior is especially activated by being left alone and reduced in the presence of the stranger, this interpretation is not advanced because of the contingencies of the stranger's behavior and her location near the door. Some infants (37 percent) cried minimally if at all in episode 6, and yet searched strongly. Some (20 percent) cried desperately, but searched weakly or not at all. Some (32 percent) both cried and searched. All but four Ss reacted to being left alone with either one or other of these attachment behaviors.

Proximity-Seeking and Contact-Maintaining Behaviors. Figure 3 shows that efforts to regain contact, proxmity or interaction with the mother occur only weakly in episodes 2 and 3 but are greatly intensified by brief separation experiences. Contact-maintaining behavior is negligible in episodes 2 and 3, rises in the first reunion episode (5), and rises even more sharply in the second reunion episode (8). In the case of both classes of behavior the increase from episodes 2 through 5 to 8 is highly significant ($p <$ .001). Some Ss showed these behaviors in relation to the stranger also. Thus, for example, a few infants approached the stranger in each of the episodes in which the stranger was present, but substantially fewer than those who approached the

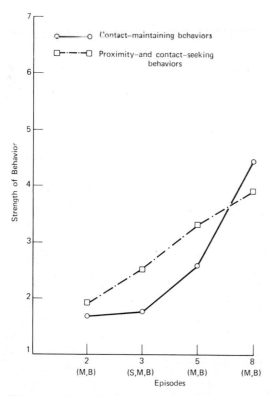

Figure 3. *Strength of proximity-seeking and contact-maintaining behaviors directed toward the mother.*

mother. Some infants were picked up by the stranger in episodes 4 and 7—in an attempt to comfort them—and some of these did cling to her and/or resist being put down again. Nevertheless proximity-seeking and contact-maintaining behaviors were displayed much less frequently and less strongly to the stranger than to the mother.

Contact-Resisting and Proximity-Avoiding Behaviors. Table 1 shows the incidence of contact-resisting and proximity-avoiding behaviors directed to both mother and stranger. Contact-resisting behavior directed toward the mother oc-

curred very rarely in the preseparation episodes because the mother had been instructed not to intervene except in response to the baby's demands, and therefore episodes 2 and 3 are omitted from the table. In the reunion episodes, some Ss resisted contact with the mother, but many did not. Therefore Table 1 shows the incidence of this behavior rather than its mean strength.

About one third of the sample showed contact-resisting behavior to the mother in episode 5, at least to some degree, and about one half showed it in episode 8. All but one infant who scored relatively high

Table 1 Incidence of Contact-Resisting and Proximity-Avoiding Behavior to Mother and Stranger

Strength of Behavior	Behavior to Mother		Behavior to Stranger		
	Episode 5	Episode 8	Episode 3	Episode 4	Episode 7
Resist Contact					
6−7	4	6	0	6	7
4−5	5	8	5	3	12
2−3	9	13	2	3	3
1	38	29	49	44	34
Avoid Proximity					
6−7	7	5	4	1	1
4−5	17	13	7	3	6
2−3	3	7	7	1	2
1	29	31	38	51	45

(4 or higher) in contact-resisting behavior received a comparably high score on contact-maintaining behavior. Thus, at least when directed to the mother, contact-resisting behavior seems to represent classic ambivalence—wanting to be held, wanting to be close, and at the same time angrily resisting contact.

Contact and interaction with the stranger were also resisted but somewhat less frequently than with the mother. Six Ss showed fairly strong contact- or interaction-resisting behavior (scores of 4 or higher) with both stranger in episode 7 and with mother in episode 8, but, for the most part, babies who tended to resist the mother did not resist the stranger and vice versa.

Proximity- and interaction-avoiding behavior did not occur in relation to the mother in the preseparation episodes, for the mother's nonparticipant role made no claim on the baby's attention. But, as shown in Table 1, it occurred to some degree in about half the sample in each of the reunion episodes, 5 and 8. About one third of the sample avoided the stranger at some time in episode 3—ignoring her, avoiding meeting her eyes, or moving further away from her. The incidence of these behaviors declined in episode 4, and even in episode 7 remained less than in episode 3. About half the sample avoided neither mother nor stranger, but those who showed this behavior in any strength (score of 4 or over) to one did not show it to the other.

DISCUSSION

These findings illustrate the complex interaction between attachment behavior, response to novel or unfamiliar stimulus objects and situations, and responses to separation from the attachment object and to subsequent reunion. First, let us consider response to novelty. It is now commonly accepted that novelty may elicit either fear and avoidance or approach and exploration, depending both on the degree of novelty and upon circumstances. One of the conditions which facilitates approach and exploration of the novel is the presence, in reasonable but not necessarily close proximity, of the mother—the object of attachment. The infants of the present sample showed little alarm in the pre-separation episodes of the strange situation. Their attachment behavior was not activated; they tended not to cling to the mother or even to approach her. They used her as a secure base from which to explore the strange situation. This finding is not new. Similar observations have been reported by Arsenian (1943), Cox and Campbell (1968), Ainsworth and Wittig (1969), and Rheingold (1969) for human subjects, and by Harlow (1961) for rhesus macaque infants. The presence of the mother can tip the balance in favor of exploring the novel rather than avoiding it or withdrawing from it.

Absence of the mother tends to tip the balance in the opposite direction with a substantial heightening of attachment behavior and concomitant lessening of exploration. During the mother's absence, proximity-promoting behaviors (crying and search) are evident. The mother's return in the reunion episodes did not serve to redress the balance to its previous level. Attachment behaviors—proximity- and contact-seeking and contact-maintaining behaviors—remained heightened. Crying did not immediately subside in many cases and, despite the mother's attempts to evoke a renewed interest in exploring the properties of the toys, exploration remained depressed below its initial level.

It was assumed that separation episodes totaling 9 minutes at most would not have any lasting effect on the balance between attachment and exploratory behavior, and indeed the posttest behavior of the infants tended to confirm this assumption. Nevertheless these minuscule separations evoke behaviors which are similar in kind to those provoked by longer separations, although differing in duration and intensity. The behavior of these 1-year-old humans in response to separations lasting only a few minutes bears remarkable resemblance to the behavior of infant monkeys in response to separation for longer periods—a week (Spencer-Booth & Hinde 1966) or a month (Kaufman & Rosenblum 1967). In these experiments the mother was removed, and the infant left in his familiar social group. Attachment behavior, including distress calling and search for the mother, was heightened, and exploratory and play behavior was depressed during the separation. The infants responded more intensely to frightening stimuli during separation than when the mother was present. As separation continued there was some lessening of the intensity of distress and search, and some recovery of exploration and play—a recovery not manifest by the human infants in this sample in their very brief separation. When the mother was restored, however, the infant monkeys clung to her more and explored less than they had before separation—differing in this from non-separated controls—and these effects lasted for three months or more.

The response of infant monkeys to experimental separations strongly resembles the behavior of young children, aged from 8 months to 3 years, when they undergo separations of several days, weeks, or even months away from home in hospitals or residential nurseries. Robertson and Bowlby (1952), Bowlby (1953), Schaffer (1958), and Heinicke and Westheimer (1965) have shown that the child is at first acutely distressed, protests the separation, and attempts to regain the mother by all means at his disposal. This initial phase of response tends to give way to despair, which in turn may give way—if the separation endures long enough—to a brightening of affect and renewed responsiveness to companions and to things in the environment. Attachment behavior directed toward the mother may have disappeared, but reunion with the mother tends to reactivate it and indeed to intensify it beyond its preseparation level. This heightened level tends to persist for a more of less prolonged period, usually much longer than the separation itself. During the period after reunion when the child's attachment behavior is heightened, he is focused on his mother, attends less to other people and to things in his environment, explores less, and presumably learns less. An unduly prolonged heightening of attachment behavior may be viewed as a distortion of the attach-

ment-exploration balance. Some long-term follow-up studies (e.g., Bowlby, Ainsworth, Boston, & Rosenbluth, 1956) suggest that this kind of behavior, often described as overdependent, may in some instances be a lasting effect of long, depriving separations.

Let us turn from attachment behavior to consider those behaviors that work against contact- and proximity-seeking, namely, contact-resisting and proximity- and interaction-avoiding behaviors. Contact-resisting behavior, as directed toward the mother, usually occurred in conjunction with contact-seeking behavior, and hence, as suggested earlier, implies an ambivalent response. Ambivalent or rejecting and angry responses are reported as common in young children returning home after brief separations (e.g. Heinicke & Westheimer 1965). Separation heightens aggressive behavior of this kind as well as attachment behavior, and predisposes the child toward angry outbursts upon minimal provocation. Spencer-Booth and Hinde (1966) report similar increase of aggression in monkeys: Unusually intense tantrums occur in response to any discouragement of contact-seeking behavior during the period of reunion after separation. Some of our strange-situation Ss showed contact-resisting behavior toward the stranger. Although in some cases this may indicate fear of the strange person, it seems likely that in some, perhaps most, it is a manifestation of aggression evoked by the mother's departure.

Proximity-avoiding behavior, on the other hand, seems likely to stem from different sources in the case of the stranger than in the case of the mother, even though the overt behavior seems the same in both cases. Ignoring the stranger, and looking, turning, or moving away from her probably imply an avoidance of the unfamiliar and fear-evoking person. This is suggested by the fact that these responses are more frequent (as directed toward the stranger) in episode 3, when the stranger has first appeared, than in later episodes. Similar avoidance of the mother cannot be due to unfamiliarity, and seems unlikely to be caused by fear. Such behavior occurs in the reunion episodes, and is more frequent than avoidance of the stranger.

Proximity- and interaction-avoiding behavior in relation to the mother is shown in striking form by some young children upon reunion after separations lasting for weeks or months. Robertson and Bowlby (1952) and Heinicke and Westheimer (1965) report that some children do not seem to recognize their mothers upon reunion, and that for a longer or shorter time they remain distant from her and treat her like a stranger. Bowlby (1960) has termed this kind of distanciation "detachment." During a prolonged separation, detachment tends to succeed protest and despair reactions, and after reunion it may persist for a long time—even indefinitely in cases in which separations have been very long and depriving. Such behavior has not yet been reported in nonhuman primates—perhaps because their experimental separations have been brief, perhaps because of species differences.

Avoidance responses of the kind observed in the strange situation in relation to the mother—looking away, turning away—may be detachment in the making and so constitute a primitive kind of defense. The constellation of individual differences in the strange-situation sample supports this hypothesis, although it is impossible here to present detailed evidence.

It may be pertinent, however, to refer to a similar looking-away response found in two experiments on the conditioning and extinction of attachment behaviors. Brackbill (1958) worked with the smiling response. During the conditioning period she provided contingent reinforcement for smiling by responding socially to the baby each time he smiled—and smiling increased in frequency. During the extinction period she met the baby's smile with an impassive face. Not only did the frequency of smiling decrease, but when the experimenter failed to respond to a smile, the baby fussed and looked away. It became increasingly difficult to catch the baby's eye. He looked away from the person who had previously reinforced his attachment behavior but who no longer did so. Similar results are reported for an experiment on babbling by Rheingold, Gewirtz, and Ross (1959).

These findings highlight the fact that in extinction—as indeed learning theorists have often themselves emphasized—there is an active process of blocking the response by another, antithetical behavior, rather than or in addition to the weakening of the strength of smiling (or babbling) behavior itself. This suggests that detached behavior may consist of responses, incompatible with attachment behavior, which have, often temporarily, gained the greater strength. That attachment can endure despite a period of detachment is shown by the strength with which attachment behavior can break through into overt expression in the case of young children who do not at reunion seem to recognize their mothers, but who subsequently manifest much heightened proximity-seeking and contact-maintaining behavior.

In summary, continuities have been noted between attachment and exploratory behavior and their activating and terminating conditions, observed in the microcosm of the laboratory strange-situation, and similar behaviors and conditions as reported by field studies, clinical studies, and experimental studies for both humans and nonhuman primate subjects. It is urged that the concept of attachment and attachment behavior employed as a guide in future studies be given a broad enough perspective to comprehend the spectrum of findings relevant to attachment which have been sampled in this discussion.

References

Ainsworth, M. D. The development of infant-mother interaction among the Ganda. In B. M. Foss (Ed.), *Determinants of infant behavior II.* London: Methuen, 1963. Pp. 67-112.

Ainsworth, M. D. Patterns of attachment behavior shown by the infant in interaction with his mother. *Merrill-Palmer Quarterly*, 1964, **10**, 51-58.

Ainsworth, M. D. S. *Infancy in Uganda: infant care and the growth of love.* Baltimore: Johns Hopkins University Press, 1967.

Ainsworth, M. D. S. Object relations, dependency and attachment: a theoretical review of the infant-mother relationship. *Child Development*, 1969, **40**, 969-1025.

Ainsworth, M. D. S., & Bell, S. M. Some contemporary patterns of mother-infant interaction in the feeding situation. In J. A. Ambrose (Ed.), *The functions of stimulation in early post-natal development.* London: Academic, in press.

Ainsworth, M. D. S., & Whittig, B. A. Attachment and exploratory behavior of one-year-olds in a strange situation. In B. M. Foss (Ed.), *Determinants of infant behaviour IV.* London: Methuen, 1969. Pp. 111-136.

Arsenian, J. M. Young children in an insecure situation. *Journal of Abnormal and Social Psychology*, 1943, **38**, 225-249.

Bell, S. M. The development of the concept of the object as related to infant-mother attachment. *Child Development*, in press.

Bowlby, J. Psychopathological processes set in train by early mother-child separation. *Journal of Mental Science, 1953*, **99**, 265-272.

Bowlby, J. The nature of the child's tie to his mother. *International Journal of Psychoanalysis*, 1958, **39**, 350-373.

Bowlby, J. Separation anxiety. *International Journal of Psychoanalysis,* 1960, **41**, 69-113.

Bowlby, J. *Attachment and loss.* Vol. 1. *Attachment.* London: Hogarth, 1969; New York: Basic Books, 1969.

Bowlby, J., Ainsworth, M. D., Boston, M., & Rosenbluth, D. The effects of mother-child separation: a follow-up study. *British Journal of Medical Psychology,* 1956, **29**, 211-247.

Brackbill, Y. Extinction of the smiling response in infants as a function of reinforcement schedule. *Child Development,* 1958, **29**, 115-124.

Cairns, R. B. Attachment behavior of mammals. *Psychological Review,* 1966, **73**, 409-426.

Cox, F. N., & Campbell, D. Young children in a new situation with and without their mothers. *Child Development,* 1968, **39**, 123-131.

DeVore, I. Mother-infant relations in free-ranging baboons. In H. L. Rheingold (Ed.), *Maternal behavior in mammals* New York: Wiley, 1963. Pp. 305-335.

Gerwirtz, J. L. Mechanisms of social learning: some roles of stimulation and behavior in early human development. In D. A. Goslin (Ed.), *Handbook of socialization theory and research.* Chicago: Rand McNally, 1969. Pp. 57-212.

Goodall, J. Chimpanzees of the Gombe Stream Reserve. In I. DeVore (Ed.), *Primate behavior: field studies of monkeys and apes.* New York: Holt, Rinehart & Winston, 1965. Pp. 425-473.

Hamburg, D. A. Evolution of emotional responses: evidence from recent research on non-human primates. In J. Masserman (Ed.), *Science and psychoanalysis.* Vol. 12. New York: Grune & Stratton, 1968. Pp. 39-52.

Harlow, H. F. The development of affectional patterns in infant monkeys. In B. M. Foss (Ed.), *Determinants of infant behavior.* London: Methuen, 1961. Pp. 75-97.

Harlow, H. F., & Harlow, M. K. The affectional systems. In A. M. Schrier, H. F. Harlow, & F. Stollnitz (Eds.), *Behavior of nonhuman primates.* Vol. 2. New York: Academic, 1965. Pp. 287-334.

Heinicke, C. M., & Westheimer, I. *Brief separations.* New York: International Universities Press, 1965.

Hinde, R. A., Rowell, T. E., & Spencer-Booth, Y. Behavior of socially living rhesus monkeys in their first six months. *Proceedings of the Zoological Society of London,* 1964, **143**, 609-649.

Hinde, R. A., Rowell, T. E., & Spencer-Booth, Y. The behaviour of socially living rhesus monkeys in their first two and a half years. *Animal Behaviour,* 1967, **15**, 169-196.

Kaufman, I. C., & Rosenblum, L. A. Depression in infant monkeys separated from their mothers. *Science,* 1967, **155**, 1030-1031.

Maccoby, E. E., & Masters, J. C. Attachment and dependency. In P. Mussen (Ed.), *Carmichael's manual of child psychology*, in press.

Mason, W. A. Determinants of social behavior in young chimpanzees. In A. M. Schrier, H. F. Harlow, & F. Stollnitz (Eds.), *Behavior of nonhuman primates.* Vol. 2. New York: Academic, 1965. Pp. 287-334.

Morgan, G. A., & Ricciuti, N. N. Infants' responses to strangers during the first year. In B. M. Foss (Ed.), *Determinants of infant behavior IV.* London: Methuen, 1969. Pp. 253-272.

Rheingold, H. L. The effect of a strange environment on the behavior of infants. In B. M. Foss (Ed.), *Determinants of infant behavior IV.* London: Methuen, 1969. Pp. 137-166.

Rheingold, H. L., Gewirtz, J. L., & Ross, H. W. Social conditioning of vocalizations in the infant. *Journal of Comparative and Physiological Psychology*, 1959, **52**, 68-73.

Robertson, J., & Bowlby, J. Responses of young children to separation from their mothers. II. Observations of the sequences of response of children aged 16 to 24 months during the course of separation. *Courrier Centre International de l'Enfance*, 1952 2, 131-142.

Robson, K. S. The role of eye-to-eye contact in maternal-infant attachment. *Journal of Child Psychology and Psychiatry*, 1967, **8**, 13-25.

Schaffer, H. R. Objective observations of personality development in early infancy. *British Journal of Medical Psychology*, 1958, **31**, 174-183.

Schaffer, H. R. The onset of fear of strangers and the incongruity hypothesis. *Journal of Child Psychology and Psychiatry*, 1966, **7**, 95-106.

Schaffer, H. R., & Emerson, P. E. The development of social attachments in infancy. *Monographs of the Society for Research in Child Development*, 1964, **29**, (3, Serial No. 94).

Schaller, G. B. The behavior of the mountain gorilla. In I. DeVore (Ed.), *Primate behavior: field studies of monkeys and apes.* New York: Holt, Rinehart & Winston, 1965. Pp. 324-367.

Schwarz, J. C. Fear and attachment in young children. *Merrill-Palmer Quarterly*, 1968, **14**, 313-322.

Southwick, C. H., Beg, M. A., & Siddiqi, M. R. Rhesus monkeys in North India. In I. DeVore (Ed.), *Primate behavior field studies of monkeys and apes.* New York: Holt, Rinehart & Winston, 1965. Pp. 111-159.

Spencer-Booth, Y., & Hinde, R. A. The effects of separating rhesus monkey infants from their mothers for six days. *Journal of Child Psychology and Psychiatry, 1966*, **7**, 179-198.

Walters, R. H., & Parke, R. D. The role of the distance receptors in the development of social responsiveness. In L. P. Lipsitt & C. C. Spiker (Eds.), *Advances in child development and behavior.* Vol. 2. New York: Academic, 1965. Pp. 59-96.

4
INFANCY:
INDIVIDUAL AND GROUP DIFFERENCES

One characteristic of scientific progress is the gradual recognition of the complexity of the subject under study. This is certainly true in the case of the study of human infants, who were once considered to be as alike as peas in a pod but are no longer so considered. Today differences among individual infants and among babies who differ in sex, ethnic origin, and sociocultural background are an ever-increasing focus of investigation. The complex nature of infant behavior is shown in another way as well. As suggested in the Kessen paper in Chapter 2, it is recognized today that the effect of an infant's behavior on his parents can be every bit as potent as the effect of their behavior on him.

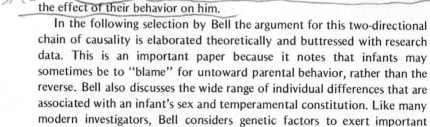

In the following selection by Bell the argument for this two-directional chain of causality is elaborated theoretically and buttressed with research data. This is an important paper because it notes that infants may sometimes be to "blame" for untoward parental behavior, rather than the reverse. Bell also discusses the wide range of individual differences that are associated with an infant's sex and temperamental constitution. Like many modern investigators, Bell considers genetic factors to exert important influences on individual differences in behavior.

The second paper by Moss is a report of a research investigation and a summary of other studies concerned with the relationship between an infant's state — including his age, sex, and activity level — and the quantity and quality of the mothering he receives. The Bell and Moss papers taken together exemplify contemporary awareness of the complexity of individual differences in infants and of the role of parental and genetic influences in these differences.

RICHARD Q. BELL

A Reinterpretation of the Direction of Effects in Studies of Socialization*

It is not too surprising to find that most research on parent-child interaction has been directed to the question of effects of parents on children. The historian Palmer (1964) maintains that our political and social philosophy emerged in a period when there were many revolutionary or protorevolutionary movements ranging from the Carolinas to Sweden, movements directed not just against monarchical absolutism but against all constituted bodies such as parliaments, councils, assemblies, and magistracies. These institutions tended to be hereditary, either in theory or through firmly established practice. In taking a strong stand against hereditary determination of position in our society we have also stressed the malleability and susceptibility to improvement of the child. Although scientific research on parents and children is a fairly recent phenomenon, it still shows the primary influence of this broad social philosophy by emphasizing parents and educational institutions as determinants of human development.

Until recent years there have been very few findings which would indicate that this is not a fruitful approach. The prolonged helplessness of the human infant, in comparison to the early competence of some other animal infants, fits in

with the picture of an organism designed to be taught and modified by the parent in the early years. It seems eminently plausible to visualize the human parent as the vehicle for the transmission of culture and the infant as simply the object of an acculturation process. The parent is the initial agent of culture, the child the object.

Because of this general view, it is often overlooked that even John Locke, to whom we are indebted for the concept of the infant as a tabula rasa, placed great emphasis in his advice to parents on early observation of congenital characteristics (Kessen, 1965, p. 67). Locke questioned the existence of innate ideas, not all innate characteristics. Currently, at least one major work on the socialization of the child has acknowledged that there are probably constitutional differences between children which affect behavior (Sears, Maccoby, & Levin, 1957, 454-455), and that the model of a unidirectional effect from parent to child is overdrawn, a fiction of convenience rather than belief (Sears et al., 1957, p. 141). The model was adopted in order to proceed with research, leaving the validity of the approach to be judged by the results.

This paper summarizes data indicating that a unidirectional approach is too imprecise and that another formulation is possible which would accommodate our social philosophy as well as new data

*From the *Psychological Review*, 1968, 75, 81-95. Reprinted by permission of the author and the American Psychological Association.

from studies of man and other animals. Before proceeding, usage of two terms must be explained. Individual behavior sequences cannot be referred to as exclusively genetically or experientially determined. It is possible, however, to employ experimental operations in such a way that a *difference* between two groups or between two conditions applied to the same subjects can be attributed to genetic or experiential differences. Thus the terms *genetically, congenitally,* or *experientially determined* are abstractions derived from experimental operations. For brevity, a *congenital effect* will refer to both genetic and congenital determination.

The same consideration applies to the question of whether parent and child effects can be separated. In the ordinary interaction of any parent and child we can speak only of an event sequence. However, by experimental operations we can isolate parent effects and child effects. In the remainder of this paper a child or parent effect will refer to such a derivative of an experimental operation. No implication about origin of the behavior need be drawn in this case since such studies can take as their starting point any behavior which is available at the time in the repertoire of parent or child.

We must also keep in mind that demonstration of a child effect indicates only that it plays *some* role in parent behavior. The development of the parent behavior is not explained by such a demonstration. In the same vein, Epstein (1964) has pointed out relative to studies of learning that evidence of the modifiability of a response provides no explanation of its origin.

RECENT DATA DISCORDANT WITH PARENT-EFFECT MODEL

Discordant data at the human level are still meager. This is because most research efforts have been directed to the task of testing parent effects and have not always been designed so as to permit clear interpretation of "negative" results. It will be necessary to rely upon informal observations and data generated unintentionally.

Rheingold (1966, pp. 12-13) has pointed to a compelling fact observable under ordinary circumstances in any human group containing an infant. "The amount of attention and the number of responses directed to the infant are enormous—out of all proportion to his age, size, and accomplishments." The effect of the appearance of helplessness and the powerful stimulus of distress cries were also noted. "So aversive, especially to humans, is the crying of the infant that there is almost no effort we will not expend, no device we will not employ, to change a crying baby into a smiling one—or just a quiet one."

Studies of variations in parental behavior with different children provide one other kind of data discordant with a parent-effect model. A mother of identical schizophrenic quadruplets was found to be uniformly extreme in restrictiveness with her daughters but not uniform in affection when rated against a theoretical normal group (Schaefer, 1963). Yarrow (1963, pp. 109-110) has reported that the same foster mother showed differences in behavior with infants assigned to her at different times. In one particularly dramatic case extreme differences in maternal care existed for two infants of the same sex and age assigned to a foster mother at the same time. Characteristics of the infants appeared to have evoked very different behavior in this foster mother and in other members of her family.

Reports of lack of uniformity of behavior of parents towards their children are not confined to intensive case studies. Stott (1941) reported a correlation of only .22 between sibling reports of a positive or negative home environment. Lasko (1954, p. 111) correlated maternal characteristics across 44 sibling pairs and found that mothers were not consistent in affection but were in restrictiveness, a finding which is in agreement with the report on the quadruplets. In a parent-effect model, it is easy to explain differences between the behavior of two parents with the same child, but awkward to accommodate a difference in the behavior of one parent toward two children. The latter difficulty is due to the fact that the parent-effect model assumes a fixed and invariantly applied repertoire. The usual method of explaining differences in behavior of a parent with different children is to postulate effects associated with ordinal position or sex of siblings. The reports on infants in foster homes could not be explained this way.

Levy (1958, p. 8) was unable to find consistency in maternal greeting behavior when the infant was brought from the nursery for a feeding, until it was noted that this behavior was a function of the state of the infant. The present author carried out separate chi-square analyses of Levy's data for each of three successive observations. There were no differences on the initial observation, but for the second and third observations it was found that infants awake or awakening were greeted, whereas those asleep were not ($p < .01$; $p < .05$, respectively). Other data in the same volume support Levy's contention that specific maternal behavior could be accounted for more by the infant's behavior than by the mother's general "maternal attitude," whether the latter was estimated from interview material or from actual observation of her behavior. Another finding with a similar implication was reported by Hillenbrand (1965). The amount the infant consumed in breast-feeding during the newborn period was highly correlated with the number of weeks the mother continued feeding at the breast, whereas the latter measure showed no correlation with personality characteristics of the mother.

One other study at the human level is best accommodated by a bidirectional model (Bell, 1964). Scores on one parent-attitude scale have been found consistently higher in mothers of children with congenital defects than in mothers of normals. Differences between groups of parents were ascribed to the effects on parents of a limitation in coping ability associated with the congenital disorder in affected children.

Research on lower animals provides stronger evidence of the stimulating and selective effect of the young. A volume edited by Rheingold (1963) covers maternal behavior from the deer mouse to the baboon and provides a number of observations on the importance of the young in shaping interactions. An example is the report of two instances in which the clinging of rhesus infants fostered with nonlactating females induced maternal responsiveness and biochemically normal lactation (pp. 268-269). In other studies offspring effects have been manipulated experimentally. Lactation in the rat has been maintained for long periods by supplying new litters of pups; number and age of pups were effective parameters (Bruce, 1961). Licking and nest-building occurred when 1-day-old pups were presented to female mice without previous experience; short-term stimulus-specific decrements in the maternal response followed repeated presentation of 1-day-old pups, but recovery of response was shown to an older pup (Noirot, 1965). This study is the most recent in a series supporting the hypothesis that changes in the interest of the female mouse in the litter from birth to weaning depend mainly upon changes in stimuli coming from the young.

It has been shown by cross-fostering that pups from one strain of mice induced more retrieving and licking behavior than pups from another strain (Ressler, 1962). The open-field behavior of rat foster mothers has shown effects of the experience of rearing pups subjected to direct treatments such as shock (Dennenberg, 1963), or indirect treatments such as subjecting their true mothers to premating and gestational stress (Joffe, 1965).

In a classic study, Beach and Jaynes (1956) manipulated appearance and behavior of offspring so as to identify specific classes of stimuli controlling parent behavior. Visual, olfactory, tactile, thermal, and movement cues from rat pups were shown to be capable of inducing maternal retrieving, being effective individually and in combination.

It is evident from the foregoing brief review that students of animal behavior have been much more aware of offspring effects on parents than investigators of human parent-child interaction; this more comprehensive view of parent-offspring interaction may be a simple consequence of availability; all phases of development are accessible to direct observation and manipulation. It is also possible that our political and social philosophy has limited scientific outlook at the human more than the animal level. The animal mother is not seen as an agent of socialization, nor her offspring as a tabula rasa.

There are many implications of this research on animal behavior. For the present purpose two are most salient. If variations in offspring behavior affect animal parents from which we expect fairly rigid patterns, even greater effects would be expected on human parental behavior, which is presumably more plastic and susceptible to all classes of influence. The other point is brought out by the variety of offspring stimulus parameters being opened up by animal studies; it should not be difficult to accept the notion of offspring effects if we consider the fact that offspring are at least sources of stimuli. Some stimulus control of human parental behavior should be expected since we take for granted the general likelihood of finding stimulus control over behavior in general.[1]

[1] The author is indebted to Leon J. Yarrow for suggesting this point.

MODIFIERS OF PARENT RESPONSE

Congenital Determinants

Three propositions concerning congenital determinants of later behavior will be advanced in this section. Some studies of human subjects will be cited which provide relatively clear evidence. Only reasonable inferences can be made from others. All in all, these studies suggest but by no means document the propositions which are advanced concerning child effects. The present objective is to take the first steps toward developing an alternative to existing socialization theory. A limited scheme which is merely plausible and parsimonious will serve the purpose. Provisional acceptance of this scheme will make it possible to provide concrete illustrations of how some recent findings in the research literature may be reinterpreted.

It will first be assumed that there are congenital contributors to human assertiveness, which will be taken to mean maintenance of goal-directed behavior of high magnitude in the face of barriers. Reasoning, threat of withdrawal of love, and appeals to personal and social motives can all be used to arrest ongoing child behavior in excess of parental standards, providing the child is not extreme in assertiveness. With a child who is strongly assertive a parent may more often fall back on quick tangible reinforcement or nonreinforcement. At times when the child, the parent, or both are stressed, the parent falls back further to distraction, holding, frightening verbalization, and physical punishment. The foregoing effects on parent behavior also are considered likely to issue from the behavior

of hyperactive, erratic, and unpredictable children, and it is assumed that there are congenital determinants of this kind of behavior as well.

It is further assumed that a different kind of behavior is shown by parents of children congenitally low in assertiveness, activity, or sensory-motor capability. Drawing attention to stimuli, rewarding an increase in behavior, urging, prompting, and demanding are examples of parent response to these child characteristics.

It is also assumed that there are congenital contributors to differences in person orientation. Children high in person orientation attend to the behavior of their parents and reinforce social responses, emanating from them. Children low in person orientation induce less nurturance from parents, and their behavior is controlled less by variations in social response of parents. They are interested in physical activity and inanimate objects. Their stimulus characteristics primarily mobilize those elements in the parent nurturance repertoires pertaining to providing and withholding physical objects and activities. Since love-oriented control techniques are less useful with these children and material reinforcers cannot always be flexibly applied, their parents more frequently show further recourse to physical punishment.

Support for a congenital contribution to assertive behavior is seen in the finding that sex differences in socialization training are pronounced in primitive cultures in which large animals are hunted (Barry, Bacon, & Child, 1957). Furthermore, in all of the 224 primitive cultures surveyed by Murdock (1937), males were accorded roles involving fighting. Greater skeletal muscle development in males is probably an important factor, since even newborn males possess more muscle tissue, females more fat, relative to total body weight (Garn, 1958). It appears reasonable that some potential for use of muscles in physically assertive behavior can also be assumed. We would not expect the exclusive allocation of the fighting role to males if they possessed only greater skeletal muscle mass with no accompanying potential for use, or if there were equal distribution of this potential between the sexes. Males in our advanced societies do not carry spears, but it is improbable that our congenital dispositions have changed as rapidly as our cultural evolution. Even theoretical systems committed to the study of parent effects have acknowledged the probable existence of constitutional bases for sex differences in overt aggressiveness (Sears et al., 1957, p. 484).

One other line of evidence is from twin studies. Direct observation of monozygotic and dizygotic twins each month during the first year of life has shown significant heritability for an item from the Bayley Infant Behavior Profile labeled "goal directedness," which denotes absorption with a task until it is complete (Freedman, 1965). Vandenberg (1962) has pointed out that such twin contrasts in early infancy are more likely to detect genetic contributions than studies of children and adults because later social functioning shapes behavior in ways remote from the circumstances under which genetic selection took place. However, even in studies of school-age children which use the admittedly insensitive self-report questionnaires, significant heritability has been shown for groups of

items interpreted as reflecting vigor (Vandenberg, 1962) and dominance (Gottesman, 1965).

Stronger evidence exists for a congenital contribution to person orientation; not only in the twin studies just cited but in several others summarized by Scarr (1965), heritability has been shown for social responsiveness or sociability, the findings cutting across age, sex, social class, and even cultural differences.

Some specific ways in which congenital factors may affect person orientation can be suggested on the basis of data from other studies. Schaffer and Emerson (1964) concluded that avoidance by some infants of being held, carried on the lap, stroked, or kissed was not accounted for by propensities of the mothers, but was due to the infant's restlessness and negative response to the restraint involved in these contacts. Infants who avoided contact showed lower intensity in later social contacts, though neither timing nor breadth of contacts was affected. There was a nonsignificant tendency for those who avoided early contacts to be males. The study is suggestive rather than conclusive because the sample of infants who avoided contacts was small.

Moss (1967) reports from day-long naturalistic observations in the home at 3 and 12 weeks that male infants were more irritable (crying, fussing), and slept less than females. This would mean that, on the average, the mother-son interaction was more one of physical caretaking, the mother being engaged in a variety of efforts to soothe males. Walters and Parke (1965) summarize evidence that the development of social response is relatively independent of the primary-drive reduction which might be expected to follow from such physical acts of care-taking. In fact, there are many reasons for expecting that greater irritability in the males would not favor development of social responses positively valued by parents (i.e., smiling, visual regard, noncrying vocalizations): (a) appearance of the mother at the time of crying could lead to an increase in the rate of crying, as reported for institutional infants by Etzel and Gewirtz (1967); (b) ministrations which follow the mother's appearance would necessarily contain some stimulation of an aversive nature, as in diaper changing or efforts to release ingested air, a point made by Rheingold (1966, p. 11); (c) nonaversive reinforcing elements in caretaking would be less likely to reinforce the infant's positively valued social responses since an irritable infant probably emits less of this behavior; (d) the mother would have less time available for purely social stimulation, and might simply wish to avoid the infant when he is quiet.

These possibilities are all consistent with Moss' (1967) finding that by the 12th week, mothers provided less stimulation of an interactional-social nature (imitation) for male than for female infants. It might also be argued that mothers imitated female infants more because of the earlier maturation of social responsiveness in females, an alternative explanation in congenital terms. Mothers could have begun differential sex-role training in social responsiveness sometime in the intervening period, but a ready explanation for initiating such training in just this period is not available. The data do not permit decisions on these different explanations, but the one selected for the present thesis seems at least as defensible

as the others: Greater irritability in males led to less stimulation from mothers of the kind which should produce positively valued social responsiveness. This, in turn, may be extended developmentally using data from Bayley and Schaefer (1964, p. 44): Males were rated as less responsive to persons during 11 out of 12 developmental examinations between 10 and 36 months. Goodenough's (1957) report of sex differences in object and person orientation is typical of many other reports in the literature which indicate that males show less social orientation by the preschool period.

The research of Pasamanick, Robers, and Lilienfeld (1956) provides evidence that complications of pregnancy and delivery are associated with later behavior disorders of children, including hyperactive behavior, and that males are more frequently affected. The foregoing studies permit an inference that there is a congenital contributor to early response to social reinforcement. If hyperactive or restless infants do not respond as well as other infants to some of the early social reinforcers, it would be reasonable to expect that their later behavior would be controlled less adequately by use of love-oriented techniques which depend for their efficacy on the strength of the social bond. It could also be inferred that they would be less person-oriented, as a consequence of the less intense primary social bond.

Stechler (1964) lists a number of recent prospective studies which confirm the general validity of Pasamanick's approach, and reports his own finding that neonatal apnea was associated with low developmental quotients in the first 2 years of life. Higher irritability or crying during the newborn period and lower developmental quotients later in infancy have been reported for infants whose mothers reported fears or anxiety during pregnancy (Davis, Holden, & Gray, 1963; Ferreira, 1960; Ottinger & Simmons, 1964). We have already mentioned a study of congenital handicaps which limit sensory-motor development (Bell, 1964). Reports of congenital contributors to sensory-motor development are not limited to populations showing pathology. Kagan and Garn (1963) have reported that chest width measured from roentgenographic films of parents or their children is positively correlated with the children's perceptual-motor and language development in the preschool years.

To summarize, there is direct evidence of congenital factors contributing to two classes of child behavior which are likely to have very different effects on parents: impaired sensory-motor development, and behavior disorders involving hyperactivity. From twin studies there is evidence of a congenital contributor to person orientation and to facets of behavior which appear related to assertiveness. On the other hand, the evidence for congenital contributors to sex differences in person orientation and assertive behavior is mostly inferential. This is particularly true for assertive behavior: No relevant data on early development of sex differences could be located in the literature. In view of this, the arguments relative to assertiveness are merely advanced to indicate that congenital determination is at least reasonable. If we accept this, albeit provisionally, we can further assume that variation within the sexes on congenital grounds could also occur. Polygenetic rather than simple

all-or-none determination would be favored by modern genetic theory.

Differentiation of Parent Responses

Parents do not have fixed techniques for socializing children. They have a repertoire of actions to accomplish each objective. Furthermore, activation of elements in the repertoire requires both cultural pressures and stimulation from the object of acculturation. Characteristics that most infants and children share, such as helplessness, evoke responses.

Another major effect of the child is shown in the parent's selective performance of elements from the caretaking repertoire. It is assumed that there are hierarchies of actions, that different children induce responses from different parts of these hierarchies. Others escalate the actions of their parents so that at one time or another, or in sequence, the entire hierarchy relevant to a certain class of child behavior may be elicited. The child in turn reinforces or fails to reinforce the parent behavior which is evoked. The repertoire changes as a function of cultural demands and also as a result of stimulation and reinforcement received from the child.

Two types of parent control repertoires must be differentiated. *Upper-limit control behavior* reduces and redirects behavior of the child which exceeds parental standards of intensity, frequency, and competence for the child's age. *Lower-limit control behavior* stimulates child behavior which is below parental standards. In other words, parent control behavior, in a sense, is homeostatic relative to child behavior. To predict interaction in particular parent-child pairs it is necessary to know the behavior characteristics of the child, the cultural demands on the parent, and the parents' own individual assimilation of these demands into a set of expectations for the child. Nonetheless, for purposes of illustration we might say that the average parent would show an increase in upper-limit control behavior in response to excessive crying in the infant, or in response to impulsive, hyperactive, or overly competent or assertive behavior in the young child. These widely different behaviors are only considered similar with respect to their effect on upper-limit control. Parental lower-limit control behavior would be stimulated by lethargy in the infant, by low activity, overly inhibited behavior, and lack of competence in the young child. Again, these are different behaviors but are assumed to be similar in effect.

It is customary to observe or rate parental behavior without reference to stimulation provided by the young. When this is done, a parent showing extreme upper-limit behavior in several areas is likely to be described as "punitive," or "restrictive," one showing extreme lower-limit behavior as "intrusive," or "demanding." Both could be considered "controlling," but according to the present conceptual scheme designed to accommodate child effects, the history of preceding interaction sequences could be quite different. The need for differentiating these two types of control is indicated not only by the present theoretical considerations but also by the empirical finds that punitive and strict behavior is not correlated with intrusive and demanding behavior in parents of young children (Schaefer, 1959, p. 228).

REINTERPRETATION OF RECENT LITERATURE

The child-effect system of explanation which has just been developed states that parent behavior is organized hierarchically within repertoires in the areas of social response and control. Reasonable bases exist for assuming that there are congenital contributors to child behaviors which (a) activate these repertoires, (b) affect the level of response within hierarchies, and (c) differentially reinforce parent behavior which has been evoked.

This system will be applied next to current findings in several major areas in which parent and experiential family effects on children have been given almost exclusive consideration. The findings in most cases are from recent studies which replicate or are consistent with previous studies, or in which results are more defensible than usual because of careful attention to sampling, procedural controls, and measurement. In most cases the authors of these papers were careful not to claim that causes and effects could be clearly differentiated. The question of direction of effects may be raised nonetheless, to ascertain whether the findings are relevant to the theory which motivated the research.

Though in the discussion which follows, the evidence is organized to support the validity of a child-to-parent effect, this should not be taken to mean that an "either—or" approach to the study of parent and child effects is preferred to an interactional view. This reinterpretation is only an expedient considered necessary to direct attention to the possibility of child effects. If this possibility is admitted we can then begin the task of thinking of parent *and* child effects. The primary goal of an expanded model of the socialization process is to uncover interactions of child and parent effects as well as main effects attributable to either source.

Lefkowitz, Walder, and Eron (1963) found in 8-year-olds that peer ratings of aggression were highest and parent reports of the child's use of confession lowest where use of physical punishment was reported by the parents. Bandura and Walters (1959) reported more physical punishment used in a group of male 15- to 16-year-old repeated offenders than in nondelinquents. One theory being tested in each case was that use of punishment in the home produces frustration and conflict or affords a model of aggression which in turn produces aggressive behavior in the child. An alternative explanation is that these children were congenitally assertive. Congenital assertiveness activated upper-limit control repertoires in parents and techniques within the repertoire were escalated toward physical punishment. Congenital hyperactivity could produce similar results.

Reviewing the area of moral development, Hoffman (1963) found consistent results in studies dealing with reaction to transgression. His interpretation was that an internalized moral orientation, indicated by confession, guilt, or reparation efforts, was fostered by an affectionate relation between the parent and child, in combination with disciplinary techniques which utilized this relation by appealing to the child's personal and social motives. One alternative explanation is that the children showing little internalization of a

moral orientation were congenitally low in person orientation. Because of this their mothers were less affectionate and did not appeal to the child's personal or social values.

A study of sex-role development by Mussen and Rutherford (1963) reports findings which replicated those in a previous study. Boys 5-6 years old scoring high in masculinity on the IT test, in comparison with lows, revealed high father nurturance, punishment, and power in doll play. A high power score indicated that father figures were both highly rewarding and punishing. These findings generously supported all major contending theories: developmental identification, defensive identification, and role-theory. A congenital explanation would be that the highs were more masculine in the sense that they showed lower person orientation and higher assertiveness. The father responded with affection because the son's assertiveness and interests in physical activity and toys were sex appropriate, reinforcing his own identification vicariously through his boy. Much as he felt affectionate toward his masculine boy he found he retreated to punishment frequently because the child, being assertive and less responsive to social stimuli, could not be controlled readily by love-oriented techniques.

In the area of intelligence, Bing (1963) found that mothers of children who showed higher verbal than spatial or numerical ability had a more close and demanding relation with their children both in interviews and observation situations than did mothers of children who showed discrepant nonverbal abilities. These findings confirmed the hypothesis that discrepant verbal ability is fostered by a close relation with a demanding and somewhat intrusive mother, discrepant nonverbal abilities being enhanced by allowing the child a considerable degree of freedom. An alternative explanation would be that the high-verbal children were high in person orientation and low in assertiveness. This is a reasonable combination of characteristics if one assumes that congenital determinants of assertiveness and person orientation are independent or at least not highly positively correlated. These children reinforced their mothers' social responses and elicited nurturant behavior. The resultant interaction intensified verbal expression because this is the primary channel of communication. The fact that these children were low in assertiveness led to lower-limit control behavior reflected in the mother's demanding and intrusive behavior.

Schaefer's (1959) summary of his own work and that of others indicates that a major portion of the variance in parent behavior can be accounted for under two dimensions described as love-hostility and autonomy-control. This is a useful finding, offering the possibility of descriptive parsimony, regardless of the question of direction of effects. However, the two-dimensional model might represent a system of effects of children on parents. The hostility extreme of the love-hostility dimension (strictness, punishment, perceiving the child as a burden) could be characterized as a parent upper-limit control pattern in response to overly assertive, unpredictable, or hyperactive behavior. The love extreme could reflect positive evaluation of children showing more modal behavior but not behavior

extreme in the opposite direction.

In support of this we find in longitudinal data from the Berkeley Growth Study (Schaefer & Bayley, 1963) that calm children were evaluated positively by their mothers during the first 3 years. Children who were rapid and active were perceived as a burden during the first 15 months. The next set of measurements available for both mothers and children covered the period when the child was between 9 and 12 years. Mothers of children rated as rapid at this time were themselves rated as irritable and perceiving the child as a burden. No rating of calmness was available. A rating of the child's inactivity in this same period could not be considered a simple inverse of the activity rating made in the first 3 years, either from the standpoint of wording or correlation pattern across the sexes. If we assume that it primarily differentiated degree of inactivity running from the highly inactive to modal levels of activity, this rating becomes relevant to the autonomy versus control dimension.

The autonomy extreme of the autonomy-control dimension might reflect parents' granting autonomy to children who conform to parental expectations of capability and assertiveness. The control extreme (intrusiveness, anxiety, achievement demand, anxiety relative to the child's behavior and health) would be considered parental lower-limit control behavior in response to children low in assertiveness or sensory-motor capability. In support of this we find that mothers of male and female inactive children during the period 9-14 years were rated as intrusive and as high in achievement demand, but low in granting autonomy to the child. All relations cited from this study (Schaefer & Bayley, 1963) were consistent for both sexes and significant beyond the .05 level for combined male and female samples according to the present author's analysis of tabular material on pages 109-110 and 121-122. Data from earlier age periods could not be brought to bear on a child-effect interpretation of the autonomy-control dimension because of very differing relations between maternal and child behavior in mother-son versus mother-daughter pairs.

Social class differences in parent behavior may also be interpreted as influenced by child effects. According to Bronfenbrenner's (1958) analysis, middle-class parents show less use of physical punishment and more use of love-oriented techniques than lower-class parents. There was no clear evidence of a change in this finding in the period from 1932 to 1952, as there was for other child-rearing techniques. Complications of pregnancy and delivery are more frequent in the lower classes (Pasamanick & Knobloch, 1960), and on this basis we could expect more hyperactivity in children from lower-class samples. From the earlier discussions relative to hyperactivity we would expect to find in lower-class parents more upper-limit control behavior, of which physical punishment is a salient example, and less use of love-oriented techniques. It is clear that studies of social-class differences in the future should control for complications of pregnancy and delivery. Some class differences may be reduced in magnitude or altered qualitatively when the samples are made comparable with respect to complications of pregnancy and delivery.

Another area receiving considerable attention in the research literature is that of family structure effects such as birth order, sex of siblings, and family size and density. Data from several studies would support the assumption that differences in parent behavior with different children in the family may be primarily due to increased experience and change in availability to children as the family grows (Conners, 1963; Lasko, 1954; Waldrop & Bell, 1964). However, this does not make it possible to dismiss the possibility of child effects. Second- or later-born neonates show higher skin conductance than firstborn (Weller & Bell, 1965). There is collateral evidence that this indicates heightened arousal and greater maturity in this early period, though there is no information available on later development. Another paper summarizes data indicating that the physiology of pregnancy and delivery is quite different for the mother with her first versus later births (Bell, 1963), raising the possibility that some differences in parent behavior with first- versus later-born children may be a response to congenital differences in the child.

A similar child effect could be operative with increases in family size and density. Since greater dependency was found in preschool children coming from large families with short intervals between siblings it was assumed that these children were simply more deprived of maternal attention (Waldrop & Bell, 1964). While this may have been true in part, further study revealed that newborns from large dense families were more lethargic (Waldrop & Bell, 1966). In this case information on later development was available and the finding was that measures of lethargy in the newborn period were correlated with later dependency. In short, there may be congenital factors operating in determining family structure effects, and credence cannot be given to an interpretation solely in terms of experiental factors until influences identifiable in pregnancy, delivery, and the newborn period are isolated.

EXAMPLES OF STUDIES DIFFICULT TO REINTERPRET

In contrast to these studies, there are others yielding data which could not be reinterpreted as a function of congenital effects contributed by the child. For example, there are studies which substitute experimenters for parents and assign children at random to experimental groups in which different "parental" treatment is administered. In one study, experimenters played the role of parents who did or did not control access to food and toy resources in familylike interactions with pre-school children (Bandura, Ross, & Ross, 1963): Children imitated parents who controlled resources. In a study of moral development, experimenters behaved with different groups of children in such a way as to create differences in the child's control over punishment and in the cognitive clarity of a task which preceded a contrived transgression (Aronfreed, 1963). Self-critical and reparative responses following transgression were maximized by prior cognitive clarity and child control. These studies used a flexible approach which can be applied to a wide variety of parent-effect parameters very rapidly. One limitation is that we do not obtain data on the cumulative effects of parents on children. The other problem is that of ownness. It is encouraging in this respect that Stevenson, Keen and Knights (1963) in studies of social reinforcement with 4- and 5-year-olds, found effects common to fathers and male experimenters, and effects common to mothers and female experimenters. This reassures us that at least with young children it may be possible to produce results with experimenters similar to effects parents have on their own children.

One other approach involves experimental manipulation of the behavior of parents and measurement of the effects on children. This is an approach that is only slightly less flexible than the foregoing and can be carried out very rapidly. Merrill (1946) manipulated parent behavior by providing mothers in two matched groups with different feedback relative to the behavior of their children. As in the previous approach which substituted experimenters for parents, the possibility of pseudo-parent effects being produced by latent child effects is minimal where the children are assigned to experimental groups at random, or on the basis of some relevant matching variable. On the other hand, since the parent is present in the interaction, the child may respond in term of past expectancies rather than to the manipulated behavior of the parent as such. This operates against obtaining differences in child behavior in different treatments, but where differences are obtained they can be interpreted as free of child effects.

Offspring effects can also be isolated. An example is provided in a summary of a series of studies carried out by Siegel (1963). Retardates aged 10 and 15 were classified into high- and low-verbal ability groups. Children in each group were then placed in brief interaction situations with adults who had no previous contact with them. The adults were to assist children in learning how to assemble a puzzle. Generally, adult responses and questions with low-verbal children were more frequent but shorter and more redundant. Labeling children of similar verbal ability as high or low had no effect on the adult behavior. Support was provided for the hypothesis that linguistic level of children exerts a control over adult verbal behavior.

A second variant of the first design is suggested by the research of Yarrow (1963), already discussed, which took advantage of the assignment of young infants to foster mothers for temporary care while adoption procedures were pending. It is necessary only to measure infant characteristics prior to assignment to foster mothers and then make the assignment systematically so that each foster mother's behavior with at least two different kinds of infants could be measured.

One other approach would make it possible to obtain effects with natural parents. Clinicians frequently report that successful medication of children who are hyperactive and impulsive produces pronounced reactive changes in parent and even total family behavior. Addition of pre- and postmedication measures of parent-child and family interaction to a well controlled study of drug effects should make it possible to evaluate this and other possible child effects.[2]

Other approaches have been mentioned in the introductory section of this paper (Bell, 1964; Levy, 1958). A detailed discussion of all possible research designs is beyond the scope of this paper, which is primarily concerned with a substantive question of how studies of socialization may be interpreted. This brief recapitulation of designs is to serve the purpose of emphasizing the fact that offspring and parent effects can be separately identified and experimentally manipulated. This will require less reliance on correlation studies of parent and child behavior upon which theories of socialization have been largely based up to the present. Even correlations obtained between parent and child behaviors from longitudinal studies offer no means of ascertaining the direction of effects, unless specially designed for the purpose. Kagan and Moss (1962) have pointed out that the problem of whether maternal hostility is a reaction to child aggression or vice versa is not solved by the demonstration of long-term relations between these maternal and child behaviors in follow-up studies.

[2] This adaptation of drug studies was suggested by Paul H. Wender.

References

Aronfreed, J. M. The effects of experimental socialization paradigms upon two moral responses to transgression. *Journal of Abnormal and Social Psychology*, 1963, **66**, 437-448.

Bandura, A., Ross, D., & Ross, S. A. A comparative test of the status envy, social power, and secondary reinforcement theories of identificatory learning. *Journal of Abnormal and Social Psychology,* 1963, **67,** 527-534.

Bandura, A. & Walters, R. H. *Adolescent aggression.* New York: Ronald Press, 1959.

Barry, H. III, Bacon, M. K., & Child, I. L. A cross-cultural survey of some sex differences in socialization. *Journal of Abnormal and Social Psychology,* 1957, **55** 327-332.

Bayley, N., & Schaefer, E. S. Correlations of maternal and child behaviors with the development of mental abilities: Data from the Berkeley Growth Study. *Monographs of the Society for Research in Child Development,* 1964, **29,** (6, Whole No. 97).

Beach, F. A., & Jaynes, J. Studies of maternal retrieving in rats. III. Sensory cues involved in the lactating females' response to her young. *Behaviour,* 1956,**10,** 104-125.

Bell, R. Q. Some factors to be controlled in studies of behavior of newborns. *Biologia Neonatorum,* 1963, **5,** 200-214.

Bell, R. Q. The effect on the family of a limitation in coping ability in a child: A research approach and a finding. *Merrill-Palmer Quarterly,* 1964, **10,** 129-142.

Bing, E. Effect of childrearing practices on development of differential cognitive abilities. *Child Development,* 1963, **34,** 631-648.

Bronfenbrenner, U. Socialization and social class through time and space. In E. E. Maccoby, T. M. Newcomb, E. L. Hartley (Eds.), *Readings in social psychology.* New York: Holt, Rinehart & Winston, 1958. Pp. 400-425.

Bruce, H. M. Observations on the suckling stimulus and lactation in the rat. *Journal of Reproduction and Fertility,* 1961, **2,** 17-34.

Conners, C. K. Birth order and needs for affiliation. *Journal of Personality,* 1963, **31.** 408-416.

Davids, A., Holden, R. H., & Gray, G. B. Maternal anxiety during pregnancy and adequacy of mother and child adjustment eight months following childbirth. *Child Development,* 1963, **34,** 993-1002.

Denenberg, V. H. Early experience and emotional development. *Scientific American,* 1963, **208,** 138-146.

Epstein, W. Experimental investigations of the genesis of visual space perception. *Psychological Bulletin,* 1964, **61,** 115-128.

Etzel, B., & Gewirtz, J. Experimental modification of caretaker-maintained high rate operant crying in a 6- and a 20-week-old infant *(Infans Tyrannotearus). Journal of Experimental Child Psychology,* 1967, **5,** 303-317.

Ferreira, A. J. The pregnant woman's emotional attitude and its reflection on the newborn. *American Journal of Orthopsychiatry,* 1960, **30,** 553-561

Freedman, D. C. Hereditary control of early social behavior. In B. M. Foss (Ed.) *Determinants of infant behaviour III.* New York: Wiley, 1965. Pp. 149-159.

Garn, S. M. Fat, body size, and growth in the newborn. *Human Biology,* 1958, **30,** 265-280.

Goodenough, F. W. Interest in persons as an aspect of sex difference in early years. *Genetic Psychology Monographs,* 1957, **55,** 287-323.

Gottesman, I. I. Genetic variance in adaptive personality traits. Paper presented at the 73rd annual convention of the American Psychological Association, September 1965, Chicago, Illinois.

Hillenbrand, E. D. The relationship of psychological, medical, and feeding variables to breast feeding. Unpublished master's thesis, George Washington University, 1965.

Hoffman, M. L. Childrearing practices and moral development: Generalizations from empirical research. *Child Development,* 1963, **34,** 295-318.

Joffe, J. M. Genotype and prenatal and premating stress interact to affect adult behavior in rats. *Science,* 1965, **150,** 1844-1845.

Kagan, J., & Garn, S. M. A constitutional correlate of early intellectual functioning. *Journal of Genetic Psychology,* 1963, **102,** 83-89.

Kagan, J., & Moss, H. A. *Birth to maturity.* New York: Wiley 1962.

Kessen, W. (Ed.) *The child.* New York: Wiley, 1965.

Lasko, J. K. Parent behavior toward first and second children. *Genetic Psychology Monographs,* 1954, **49,** 97-137.

Lefkowitz, M. M., Walder, L. O., & Eron, L. D. Punishment, identification and aggression. *Merrill-Palmer Quarterly,* 1963, **9,** 159-174.

Levy D. M. *Behavioral analysis: Analysis of clinical observations of behavior as applied to mother-newborn relationships.* New York: Thomas. 1958.

Merrill, B. A measurement of mother-child interaction. *Journal of Abnormal and Social Psychology,* 1946, **41,** 37-49.

Moss, H. A. Sex, age, and state as determinants of mother-infant interaction. *Merrill-Palmer Quarterly,* 1967, **13,** 19—36.

Murdock, G. P. Comparative data on the division of labor by sex. *Social Forces,* 1937, **15,** 551—553.

Mussen, P., & Rutherford, E. Parent-child relations and parental personality in relation to young children's sex-role preferences. *Child Development,* 1963, **34,** 589—607.

Noirot, E. Changes in responsiveness to young in the adult mouse. III. The effect of immediately preceding performances. *Behavior,* 1965, **24,** 318—325.

Ottinger, D. R., & Simmons, J. E. Behavior of human neonates and prenatal maternal anxiety. *Psychological Reports,* 1964, **14,** 391–394.

Palmer, R. R. *The age of the democratic revolution:* Vol. II. *The struggle.* Princeton: Princeton University Press, 1964.

Pasamanick, B., & Knobloch, H. Brain damage and reproductive casualty. *American Journal of Orthopsychiatry,* 1960, **30,** 298–305.

Pasamanick, B., Robers, M.E., & Lilienfeld, A. M. Pregnancy experience and the development of behavior disorders in children. *American Journal of Psychiatry,* 1956, **112,** 613–618.

Ressler, R. H. Parental handling in two strains of mice reared by foster parents. *Science,* 1962, **137,** 129–130.

Rheingold, H. L., (Ed.) *Maternal behavior in mammals.* New York: Wiley, 1963.

Rheingold, H. L. The development of social behavior in the human infant. In H. W. Stevenson (Ed.), Concept of development: A report of a conference commemorating the fortieth anniversary of the Institute of Child Development, University of Minnesota. *Monographs of the Society for Research in Child Development,* 1966, **31,** (5, Whole No. 107).

Scarr, S. The inheritance of sociability. *American Psychologist,* 1965, **20,** 524. (Abstract)

Schaefer, E. A circumplex model for maternal behavior. *Journal of Abnormal and Social Psychology,* 1959, **59,** 226–235.

Schaefer, E. Parent-child interactional patterns and parental attitudes. In D. Rosenthal (Ed.), *The Genain quadruplets.* New York: Basic Books, 1963. Pp. 389–430.

Schaefer, E., & Bayley, N. Maternal behavior, child behavior, and their intercorrelations from infancy through adolescence. *Monographs of the Society for Research in Child Development,* 1963, **28** (3, Whole No. 87).

Schaffer, H. R., & Emerson, P. E. Patterns of response to physical contact in early human development. *Journal of Child Psychology and Psychiatry,* 1964, **5,** 1–13.

Sears, R. R., Maccoby, E. E., & Levin, H. *Patterns of child rearing.* Evanston, Ill.: Row, Peterson, 1957.

Siegel, G. M. Adult verbal behavior with retarded children labeled as "high" or "low" in verbal ability. *American Journal of Mental Deficiency,* 1963, **68,** 417–424.

Stechler, G. A longitudinal follow-up of neonatal apnea. *Child Development,* 1964, **35,** 333–348.

Stevenson, H. W., Keen, R., & Knights, R. M. Parents and strangers as reinforcing agents for children's performance. *Journal of Abnormal* and Social Psychology, 1963, **67**, 183—186.

Stott, L. H. Parent-adolescent adjustment: Its measurement and significance. *Character and Personality*, 1941, **10**, 140—150.

Vandenberg, S. G. The hereditary abilities study: Hereditary components in a psychological test battery. *American Journal of Human Genetics*, 1962, **14**, 220—237.

Waldrop, M., & Bell, R. Q. Relation of preschool dependency behavior to family size and density. *Child Development*, 1964, **35**, 1187—1195.

Waldrop, M., & Bell, R. Q. Effects of family size and density on newborn characteristics. *American Journal of Orthopsychiatry*, 1966, **36**, 544—550.

Walters, R. H., & Parke, R. D. The role of the distance receptors in the development of social responsiveness. In L. P. Lipsitt & C. C. Spiker (Eds.), *Advances in child development and behavior.* Vol. 2. New York: Academic Press, 1965. Pp. 59—96.

Weller, G. M., & Bell, R. Q. Basal skin conductance and neonatal state. *Child Development*, 1965, **36**, 647—657.

Yarrow, L. J. Research in dimensions of early maternal care. *Merrill-Palmer Quarterly*, 1963, **9**, 101-114.

HOWARD A. MOSS

Sex, Age, and State as Determinants of Mother-Infant Interaction*

A major reason for conducting research on human infants is derived from the popular assumption that adult behavior, to a considerable degree, is influenced by early experience. A corollary of this assumption is that if we can precisely conceptualize and measure significant aspects of infant experience and behavior we will be able to predict more sensitively and better understand adult functioning. The basis for this conviction concerning the enduring effects of early experience varies considerably according to the developmental model that is employed. Yet there remains considerable consensus as to the long term and pervasive influence

*From the *Merrill-Palmer Quarterly*, 1967, **13**, 19-36. Reprinted by permission of the author and the Merrill-Palmer Institute.

of the infant's experience.

Bloom (1964) contends that characteristics become increasingly resistant to change as the mature status of the characteristic is achieved and that environmental effects are most influential during periods of most rapid growth. This is essentially a refinement of the critical period hypothesis which argues in favor of the enduring and irreversible effects of many infant experiences. Certainly the studies on imprinting and the effects of controlled sensory input are impressive in this respect (Hess, 1959; White and Held, 1963). Learning theory also lends itself to support the potency of early experience. Since the occurrence of variable interval and variable ratio reinforcement schedules are highly probable in infancy (as they are in many other situations), the learnings associated with these schedules will be highly resistant to extinction. Also, the pre-verbal learning that characterizes infancy should be more difficult to extinguish since these responses are less available to linguistic control which later serves to mediate and regulate many important stimulus-response and reinforcement relationships. Psychoanalytic theory and behavioristic psychology probably have been the most influential forces in emphasizing the long-range consequences of infant experience. These theories, as well as others, stress the importance of the mother-infant relationship. In light of the widespread acceptance of the importance of early development, it is paradoxical that there is such a dearth of direct observational data concerning the functioning of infants, in their natural environment, and in relation to their primary caretakers.

Observational studies of the infant are necessary in order to test existing theoretical propositions and to generate new propositions based on empirical evidence. In addition, the infant is an ideally suitable subject for investigating many aspects of behavior because of the relatively simple and inchoate status of the human organism at this early stage in life. Such phenomena as temperament, reactions to stimulation, efficacy of different learning contingencies, perceptual functioning, and social attachment can be investigated while they are still in rudimentary form and not yet entwined in the immensely complex behavioral configurations that progressively emerge.

The research to be reported in this paper involves descriptive-normative data of maternal and infant behaviors in the naturalistic setting of the home. These data are viewed in terms of how the infant's experience structures potential learning patterns. Although the learning process itself is of primary eventual importance, it is necessary initially to identify the organizational factors, in situ, that structure learning opportunities and shape response systems.

A sample of 30 first-born children and their mothers were studied by means of direct observations over the first 3 months of life. Two periods were studied during this 3-month interval. Period one included a cluster of three observations made at weekly intervals during the first month of life in order to evaluate the initial adaptation of mother and infant to one another. Period two consisted of another cluster of three observations, made around 3 months of age when relatively stable patterns of behavior were likely to have been established. Each cluster included two 3-hour observations and one 8-hour observation. The 3-hour observations were made with the use of a keyboard that operates in conjunction with a 20-channel Esterline-Angus Event Recorder. Each of 30 keys represents a maternal or infant behavior, and when a key is depressed it activates one or a combination of pens on the recorder, leaving a trace that shows the total duration of the observed behavior. This technique allows for a continuous record showing the total time and the sequence of behavior. For the 8-hour observation the same behaviors were studied but with the use of a modified time-sampling technique. The time-sampled units were one minute in length and the observer, using a stenciled form, placed a number opposite the appropriate behaviors to indicate their respective order of occurrence. Since each variable can be coded only once for each observational unit, a score of 480 is the maximum that can be received. The data to be presented in this paper are limited to the two 8-hour observations. The data obtained with the use of the keyboard will be dealt with elsewhere in terms of the sequencing of events.

The mothers who participated in these observations were told that this was a normative study of infant functioning under natural living conditions. It was stressed that they proceed with their normal routines and care of the infant as they would if the observer were not present. This structure was presented to the mothers during a brief introductory visit prior to the first observation. In addition, in order to reduce the mother's self-consciousness and facilitate her behaving in relatively typical fashion, the observer emphasized that it was the infant who was being studied and that her actions would be noted only in relation to what was happening to the infant. This approach seemed to be effective, since a number of mothers commented after the observations were completed that they were relieved that they were not the ones being studied. The extensiveness of the observations and the frequent use of informal conversation between the observer and mother seemed to contribute further to the naturalness of her behavior.

The observational variables, mean scores and sample sizes are presented in Table 1. These data are presented separately for the 3-week and the 3-month observations. The inter-rater reliabilities for these variables range from .74 to 1.00 with a median reliability of .97. Much of the data in this paper are presented for males and females separately, since by describing and comparing these two groups we are able to work from an established context that helps to clarify the theoretical meaning of the results. Also, the importance of sex differences is heavily emphasized in contemporary developmental theory and it is felt that infant data concerning these differences would provide a worthwhile addition to the literature that already exists on this matter for older subjects.

The variables selected for study are those which would seem to influence or reflect aspects of maternal contact. An additional, but related consideration in the selection of variables was that they have an apparent bearing on the organization of the infant's experience. Peter Wolff (1959), Janet Brown (1964), and Sibylle Escalona (1962) have described qualitative variations in infant state or activity level and others have shown that the response patterns of the infant are highly influenced by the state he is in (Bridger, 1965). Moreover, Levy (1958) has demonstrated that maternal behavior varies as a function of the state or activity level of the infant. Consequently, we have given particular attention to the variables concerning state (cry, fuss, awake active, awake passive, and sleep) because of the extent to which these behaviors seem to shape the infant's experience. Most of the variables listed in Table 1 are quite descriptive of what was observed. Those which might not be as clear are as follows: *attends infant*—denotes standing close or leaning over infant, usually while in the process of caretaking activities; *stimulates feeding*—stroking the infant's cheek and manipulating the nipple so as to induce sucking responses; *affectionate contact*—kissing and caressing infant; *stresses musculature*—holding the infant in either a sitting or standing position so that he is required to support his own weight; *stimulates/arouses infant*—mother provides tactile and visual stimulation for the infant or attempts to arouse him to a higher activity level; and *imitates infant*— mother repeats a behavior, usually a vocalization, immediately after it is observed in the infant.

The sex differences and shifts in behavior from 3 weeks to 3 months are in many instances pronounced. For example, at 3 weeks of age mothers held male infants about 27 minutes more per 8 hours than they held females, and at 3 months males were held 14 minutes longer. By the time they were 3 months of age there was a decrease of over 30% for both sexes in the total time they were held by their mothers. Sleep time also showed marked sex differences and changes over time. For the earlier observations females slept about an hour longer than males, and this difference tended to be maintained by 3 months with the female infants sleeping about 41 minutes longer. Again, there was a substantial reduction with age in this behavior for both sexes; a decrease of 67 and 86 minutes in sleep time for males and females, respectively. What is particularly striking is the variability for these infant and maternal variables. The range for sleep time is 137-391 minutes at 3 weeks and 120-344 minutes at 3 months, and the range for mother holding is 38-218 minutes at 3 weeks and 26-168 minutes for the 3-month observation. The extent of the individual differences reflected by these ranges seem to have important implications. For instance, if an infant spends more time at a higher level of consciousness this should increase his experience and contact with the mother, and through greater learning opportunities, facilitate the perceptual discriminations he makes, and affect the quality of his cognitive organization. The finding that some of the infants in our sample slept a little over 2 hours, or about 25% of the observation time and others around 6 hours or 75% of the time, is a fact that has implications for important developmental processes. The sum crying and fussing, what we term irritability level of the infant, is another potentially important variable. The range of scores for this behavior was from 5-136 minutes at 3 weeks and 7-98 at 3 months. The fact that infants are capable through their behavior of shaping maternal treatment is a point that has gained increasing recognition. The cry is a signal for the mother to

Table 1 Mean Frequency of Maternal and Infant Behavior at 3 Weeks and 3 Months

Behavior	3-week observation		3-month observation[a]	
	Males[b] (N = 14)	Females (N = 15)	Males[b] (N = 13)	Females (N = 12)
Maternal variables				
Holds infant close	121.4	99.2	77.4	58.6
Holds infant distant	32.3	18.3	26.7	27.2
Total holds	131.3	105.5	86.9	73.4
Attends infant	61.7	44.2	93.0	81.8
Maternal contact				
(holds and attends)	171.1	134.5	158.8	133.8
Feeds infant	60.8	60.7	46.6	41.4
Stimulates feeding	10.1	14.0	1.6	3.6
Burps infant	39.0	25.9	20.9	15.3
Affectionate contact	19.9	15.9	32.8	22.7
Rocks infant	35.1	20.7	20.0	23.9
Stresses musculature	11.7	3.3	25.8	16.6
Stimulates/arouses infant	23.1	10.6	38.9	26.1
Imitates infant	1.9	2.9	5.3	7.6
Looks at infant	182.8	148.1	179.5	161.9
Talks to infant	104.1	82.2	117.5	116.1
Smiles at infant	23.2	18.6	45.9	46.4
Infant vaiables				
Cry	43.6	30.2	28.5	16.9
Fuss	65.7	44.0	59.0	36.0
Irritable (cry and fuss)	78.7	56.8	67.3	42.9
Awake active	79.6	55.1	115.8	85.6
Awake passive	190.0	138.6	257.8	241.1
Drowsy	74.3	74.7	27.8	11.1
Sleep	261.7	322.1	194.3	235.6
Supine	133.7	59.3	152.7	134.8
Eyes on mother	72.3	49.0	91.0	90.6
Vocalizes	152.3	179.3	207.2	207.4
Infant smiles	11.1	11.7	32.1	35.3
Mouths	36.8	30.6	61.2	116.2

[a]Four of the subjects were unable to participate in the 3-month observation. Two moved out of the area, one mother became seriously ill, and another mother chose not to participate in all the observations.

[b]One subject who had had an extremely difficult delivery was omitted from the descriptive data but is included in the findings concerning mother-infant interaction.

Table 2 Changes in Behavior Between 3 Weeks and 3 Months ($N = 26$)

Maternal variables	t-values	Infant variables	t-values
Higher at 3 weeks		*Higher at 3 weeks*	
Holds infant close	4.43****	Cry	2.84***
Holds infant distant	.56	Fuss	1.33
Total holds	4.00****	Irritable (cry and fuss)	1.73*
Maternal contact		Drowsy	9.02****
(holds and attends)	.74	Sleep	4.51****
Feeds infant	3.49***		
Stimulates feeding	3.42***		
Burps infant	3.28***		
Rocks infant	1.08		
Higher at 3 months		*Higher at 3 months*	
Attends infant	5.15****	Awake active	2.47**
Affectionate contact	2.50**	Awake passive	5.22****
Stresses musculature	3.42***	Supine	1.75*
Stimulates/arouses infant	2.63**	Eyes on mother	3.21***
Imitates infant	4.26****	Vocalizes	3.56***
Looks at infant	.38	Infant smiles	6.84****
Talks to infant	2.67**	Mouths	3.69***
Smiles at infant	4.79****		

$*p < .10$ $**p < .05$ $***p < .01$ $****p < .001$

respond and variation among infants in this behavior could lead to differential experiences with the mother.

Table 2 presents t values showing changes in the maternal and infant behaviors from the 3-week to the 3-month observation. In this case, the data for the males and females are combined since the trends, in most instances, are the same for both sexes. It is not surprising that there are a number of marked shifts in behavior from 3 weeks to 3 months, since the early months of life are characterized by enormous growth and change. The maternal variables that show the greatest decrement are those involving feeding behaviors and close physical contact. It is of interest that the decrease in close contact is paralleled by an equally pronounced increase in attending behavior, so that the net amount of maternal contact remains similar for the 3-week and 3-month observations. The main difference was that the mothers, for the later observation, tended to hold their infants less but spent considerably more time near them, in what usually was a vis-a-vis posture, while interacting and ministering to their needs. Along with this shift, the mothers showed a marked increase in affectionate behavior toward the older infant, positioned him more so that he was required to make active use of his muscles, presented him with a greater amount of stimulation and finally, she exhibited more social behavior (imitated, smiled, and talked) toward the older child.

The changes in maternal behavior from 3 weeks to 3 months probably are largely a function of the maturation of various characteristics of the infant. However, the increased confidence of the mother, her greater familiarity with her infant, and her developing attachment toward him will also account for some of the changes that occurred over this period of time.

By 3 months of age the infant is crying less and awake more. Moreover, he is becoming an interesting and responsive person. There are substantial increases in the total time spent by him in smiling, vocalizing, and looking at the mother's face, so that the greater amount of social-type behavior he manifested at three months parallels the increments shown in the mothers' social responsiveness toward him over this same period. The increase with age in the time the infant is kept in a supine position also should facilitate his participation in vis-a-vis interactions with the mother as well as provide him with greater opportunity for varied visual experiences.

Table 3 presents the correlations between the 3-week and the 3-month observations for the maternal and infant behaviors we studied. These findings further reflect the relative instability of the mother-infant system over the first few months of life. Moderate correlation coefficients were obtained only for the

Table 3 Correlations Between Observations at 3 Weeks and at 3 Months ($N = 26$)

Maternal variables	$r =$	Infant variables	$r =$
Holds infant close	.23	Cry	.28
Holds infant distant	.04	Fuss	.42**
Total holds	.18	Irritable (cry and fuss)	.37*
Attends infant	.36*	Awake active	.25
Maternal contact		Awake passive	.26
(holds and attends)	.25	Drowsy	.44**
Feeds infant	.21	Sleep	.24
Stimulates feeding	.37*	Supine	.29
Burps infant	.20	Eyes on mother	−.12
Affectionate contact	.64****	Vocalizes	.41**
Rocks infant	.29	Infant smiles	.32
Stresses musculature	.06	Mouths	−.17
Stimulates/arouses infant	.23		
Imitates infant	.45**		
Looks at infant	.37*		
Talks to infant	.58***		
Smiles at infant	.66****		

$*p < .10$ $**p < .05$ $***p < .01$ $****p < .001$

class of maternal variables concerning affectionate-social responses. It thus may be that these behaviors are more sensitive indicators of enduring maternal attitudes than the absolute amount of time the mother devoted to such activities as feeding and physical contact. The few infant variables that show some stability are, with the exception of vocalizing, those concerning the state of the organ-ism. Even though some of the behaviors are moderately stable from three weeks to three months, the overall magnitude of the correlations reported in Table 3 seem quite low considering that they represent repeated measures of the same individual over a relatively short period.

Table 4 presents t-values based on comparisons between the sexes for the 3-week and 3-month observations. A

Table 4 Sex Differences in Frequency of Maternal and Infant Behaviors at 3 Weeks and 3 Months

Maternal variables	t-values		Infant variables	t-values	
	3 weeks	3 months		3 weeks	3 months
Male higher			*Male higher*		
Holds infant close	1.42	1.52	Cry	1.68	1.11
Holds infant distant	2.64**		Fuss	2.48**	3.47***
Total holds	1.65	1.12	Irritable (cry		
Attends infant	2.66**	1.10	and fuss)	2.23**	2.68**
Maternal contact			Awake active	1.66	.57
(holds and attends)	2.09**	1.57	Awake passive	2.94***	1.77*
Feeds infant	.06	.27	Drowsy		.41
Burps infant	1.67	.69	Supine	2.30**	1.07
Affectionate contact	.90	1.00	Eyes on mother	1.99*	.75
Rocks infant	1.21		Mouths		.64
Stresses musculature	2.48**	1.67			
Stimulates/arouses					
infant	2.20**	1.53			
Looks at infant	1.97*	1.36			
Talks to infant	1.02	.79			
Smiles at infant	.57				
Female higher			*Female higher*		
Holds infant distant		.05	Drowsy		.03
Stimulates feeding	.62	1.47	Sleep	3.15***	2.87***
Rocks infant		.82	Vocalizes	1.34	.23
Imitates infant	.80	1.76*	Infant smiles	.02	.08
Smiles at infant		.44	Mouths		2.57**

$* p < .10$ $** p < .05$ $*** p < .01$

number of statistically significant differences were obtained with, in most instances, the boys having higher mean scores than the girls. The sex differences are most pronounced at 3 weeks for both maternal and infant variables. By 3 months the boys and girls are no longer as clearly differentiated on the maternal variables although the trend persists for the males to tend to have higher mean scores. On the other hand, the findings for the infant variables concerning state remain relatively similar at 3 weeks and 3 months. Thus, the sex differences are relatively stable for the two observations even though the stability coefficients for the total sample are low (in terms of our variables).

In general, these results indicate that much more was happening with the male infants than with the female infants. Males slept less and cried more during both observations and these behaviors probably contributed to the more extensive and stimulating interaction the boys experienced with the mother, particularly for the 3-week observation. In order to determine the effect of state we selected the 15 variables, excluding those dealing with state, where the sex differences were most marked and did an analysis of covariance with these variables, controlling for irritability and another analysis of covariance controlling for sleep. These results are presented in Table 5. When the state of the infant was controlled for, most of the sex differences were no longer statistically significant. The exceptions were that the t-values were greater, after controlling for state, for the variables "mother stimulates/arouses infant" and "mother imitates infant." The higher score for "stimu-

lates/arouse" was obtained for the males and the higher score for "imitates" by the females. The variable "imitates" involves repeating vocalizations made by the child, and it is interesting that mothers exhibited more of this behavior with the girls. This response could be viewed as the reinforcement of verbal behavior, and the evidence presented here suggests that the mothers differentially reinforce this behavior on the basis of the sex of the child.

In order to further clarify the relation between infant state and maternal treatment, product-moment correlations were computed relating the infant irritability score with the degree of maternal contact. The maternal contact variable is based on the sum of the holding and attending scores with the time devoted to feeding behaviors subtracted out. These correlations were computed for the 3-week and 3-month observations for the male and female samples combined and separate. At 3 weeks a correlation of .52 ($p < .01$) was obtained between irritability and maternal contact for the total sample. However, for the female subsample this correlation was .68 ($p < .02$) and for males only .20 (non. sig.). Furthermore, a somewhat similar pattern occurred for the correlations between maternal contact and infant irritability for the 3-month observation. At this age the correlation is .37 ($p < .10$ level) for the combined sample and .54 ($p < .05$ level) for females and $-.47$ ($p < .10$ level) for males. A statistically significant difference was obtained ($t = 2.40, p < .05$ level) in a test comparing the difference between the female and male correlations for the 3-month observation. In other words maternal contact and irritability positively covaried for females at both

Table 5 Sex Differences after Controlling for Irritability and Sleep Time Through Analysis of Covariance[a]

Maternal or Infant Behaviors	Sleep time controlled for		Sex with higher mean score	Irritability controlled for		Sex with higher mean score
	3 weeks	3 months		3 weeks	3 months	
Variables	t	t		t	t	
Holds infant close	.30	1.22		.64	1.70	
Holds infant distant	.59	−.20		.92	−.20	
Total holds	.43	.88		.86	1.08	
Attends infant	1.12	1.36		1.91*	.94	Males
Maternal contact (holds and attends)	.62	1.04		1.20	1.12	
Stimulates feeding	.55	−1.12		−.09	−1.06	
Affectionate contact	−.46	.91		.56	1.27	
Rocks	.35	−.70		.44	−1.44	
Stresses musculature	1.84*	.71	Males	1.97*	1.40	
Stimulates/arouses infant	2.09**	1.82*	Males	2.43**	2.31**	Males
Imitates infant	−.91	−2.73**	Females	−.63	−2.14**	Females
Looks at infant	.58	1.35		1.17	1.02	
Talks to infant	−.48	.24		.70	.89	
Infant supine	.82	−.03		1.36	.69	
Eyes on mother	.87	.58		1.76*	−.37	Males

*p < .10   **p < .05

[a]A positive t-value indicates that males had the higher mean score, and a negative t-value indicates a higher mean score for females.

ages; whereas for males, there was no relationship at 3 weeks, and by 3 months the mothers tended to spend less time with the more irritable male babies. It should be emphasized that these correlations reflect within group patterns, and that when we combine the female and male samples positive correlations still emerge for both ages. Since the males had substantially higher scores for irritability and maternal contact than the females, the correlation for the male subjects does not strongly attenuate the correlations derived for the total sample, even when

the males within group covariation seems random or negative. That is, in terms of the total sample, the patterning of the males scores is still consistent with a positive relationship between irritability and maternal contact.

From these findings it is difficult to posit a causal relationship. However, it seems most plausible that it is the infant's cry that is determining the maternal behavior. Mothers describe the cry as a signal that the infant needs attention and they often report their nurturant actions in response to the cry. Furthermore, the cry is a noxious and often painful stimulus that probably has biological utility for the infant, propelling the mother into action for her own comfort as well as out of concern for the infant. Ethological reports confirm the proposition that the cry functions as a "releaser" of maternal behavior (Bowlby, 1958; Hinde, et al., 1964; Hoffman, et al., 1966). Bowlby (1958) states:

It is my belief that both of them (crying and smiling), act as social releasers of instinctual responses in mothers. As regards crying, there is plentiful evidence from the animal world that this is so: probably in all cases the mother responds promptly and unfailingly to her infant's bleat, call or cry. It seems to me clear that similar impulses are also evoked in the human mother. . . . .

Thus, we are adopting the hypothesis that the correlations we have obtained reflect a causal sequence whereby the cry acts to instigate maternal intervention. Certainly there are other important determinants of maternal contact, and it is evident that mothers exhibit considerable variability concerning how responsive they are to the stimulus signal of the cry. Yet it seems that the effect of the cry is sufficient to account at least partially for the structure of the mother-infant relationship. We further maintain the thesis that the infant's cry shapes maternal behavior even for the instance where the negative correlation was noted at 3 months for the males. The effect is still present, but in this case the more irritable infants were responded to *less* by the mothers. Our speculation for explaining this relationship and the fact that, con-

versely, a positive correlation was obtained for the female infants is that the mothers probably were negatively reinforced for responding to a number of the boys but tended to be positively reinforced for their responses toward the girls. That is, mothers of the more irritable boys may have learned that they could not be successful in quieting boys whereas the girls were more uniformly responsive (quieted by) to maternal handling. There is not much present in our data to bear out this contention, with the exception that the males were significantly more irritable than the girls for both observations. However, evidence that suggests males are more subject to inconsolable states comes from studies (Serr and Ismajovich, 1963; McDonald, Gynther, and Christakos, 1963; Stechler, 1964) which indicate that males have less well organized physiological reactions and are more vulnerable to adverse conditions than females. The relatively more efficient functioning of the female organism should thus contribute to their responding more favorably to maternal intervention.

In summary, we propose that maternal behavior initially tends to be under the control of the stimulus and reinforcing conditions provided by the young infant. As the infant gets older, the mother, if she behaved contingently toward his signals, gradually acquires reinforcement value which in turn increases her efficacy in regulating infant behaviors. Concurrently, the earlier control asserted by the infant becomes less functional and diminishes. In a sense, the point where the infant's control over the mother declines and the mother's reinforcement value emerges could be regarded as the first manifestation of socialization, or at least represents the initial conditions favoring social learning, Thus, at first the mother is shaped by the infant and this later facilitates her shaping her behavior of the infant. We would therefore say, that the infant, through his own temperament or signal system contributes to establishing the stimulus and reinforcement value eventually associated with the mother. According to this reasoning, the more irritable infants (who can be soothed) whose mothers respond in a contingent manner to their signals should become most amenable to the effects of social reinforcement and manifest a higher degree of attachment behavior. The fact that the mothers responded more contingently toward the female infants should maximize the ease with which females learn social responses.

This statement is consistent with data on older children which indicate that girls learn social responses earlier and with greater facility than boys. (Becker, 1964). Previously we argued that the mothers learned to be more contingent toward the girls because they probably were more responsive to maternal intervention. An alternative explanation is that mothers respond contingently to the girls and not to the boys as a form of differential reinforcement, whereby, in keeping with cultural expectations, the mother is initiating a pattern that contributes to males being more aggressive or assertive, and less responsive to socialization. Indeed, these two explanations are not inconsistent with one another since the mother who is unable to soothe an upset male infant may eventually come to classify this intractable irritability as an expression of "maleness."

There are certain environmental settings where noncontingent caretaking is more likely and these situations should impede social learning and result in weaker attachment responses. Lennenberg (1965) found that deaf parents tended not to respond to the infant's cry. One would have to assume that it was more than the inability to hear the infant that influenced their behavior, since even when they observed their crying infants these parents tended not to make any effort to quiet them. The function of the cry as a noxious stimulus or "releaser" of maternal behavior did not pertain under these unusual circumstances. Infants in institutions also are more likely to be cared for in terms of some arbitary schedule with little opportunity for them to shape caretakers in accordance with their own behavioral vicissitudes.

Although we have shown that there is a covariation between maternal contact and infant irritability and have attempted to develop some theoretical implications concerning this relationship, considerable variability remains as to how responsive different mothers are to their infants' crying behavior. This variability probably reflects differences in maternal attitudes. Women who express positive feelings about babies and who consider the well-being of the infant to be of essential importance should tend to be more responsive to signals of distress from the infant than women who exhibit negative maternal attitudes. In order to test this assumption, we first derived a score for measuring maternal responsiveness. This score was obtained through a regression analysis where we determined the amount of maternal contact that would be expected for each mother by controlling for her infant's irritability score. The expected maternal contact score was then subtracted from the mother's actual contact score and this difference was used as the measure of maternal responsivity. The maternal responsivity scores were obtained separately for the 3-week and the 3-month observations. The parents of 23 of the infants in our sample were interviewed for a project investigating marital careers, approximately 2 years prior to the birth of their child, and these interviews provided us with the unusual opportunity of having antecedent data relevant to prospective parental functioning. A number of variables from this material were rated and two of them, "acceptance of nurturant role," and the degree that the baby is seen in a positive sense" were correlated with the scores on the maternal responsivity measure.[2] Annotated definitions of these interview variables are as follows:

"Acceptance of nurturant role" concerns the degree to which the subject is invested in caring for others and in acquiring domestic and homemaking skills such as cooking, sewing, and cleaning house. Evidence for a high rating would be describing the care of infants and children with much pleasure and satisfaction even when this involves subordinating her own needs.

The interview variable concerning the "degree that the baby is seen in a positive sense" assesses the extent to which the subject views a baby as gratifying, pleasant and non-burdensome. In discussing what she imagines infants to be like she

[2] Dr. Kenneth Robson collaborated in developing these variables, and made the ratings.

stresses the warmer, more personal, and rewarding aspects of the baby and anticipates these qualities as primary.

Correlations of .40 ($p < .10$ level) and .48 ($p < .05$ level) were obtained between the ratings on "acceptance of nurturant role" and the maternal responsivity scores for the 3-week and 3-month observations, respectively. The "degree that the baby is seen in a positive sense" correlated .38 ($p < .10$ level) and .44 ($p < .05$ level) with maternal responsivity for the two ages. However, the two interview variables were so highly intercorrelated ($r = .93$) that they clearly involve the same dimension. Thus, the psychological status of the mother, assessed substantially before the birth of her infant, as well as the infant's state are predictive of her maternal behavior. Schaffer and Emerson (1964) found that maternal responsiveness to the cry was associated with the attachment behavior of infants. Extrapolating from our findings, we now have some basis for assuming that the early attitudes of the mother represent antecedent conditions for facilitating the attachment behavior observed by Schaffer and Emerson.

The discussion to this point has focused on some of the conditions that seemingly affect the structure of the mother-infant relationship and influence the reinforcement and stimulus values associated with the mother. Next we would like to consider, in a more speculative vein, one particular class of maternal behaviors that has important reinforcing properties for the infant. This discussion will be more general and depart from a direct consideration of the data. There has been mounting evidence in the psychological literature that the organism has a "need for stimulation" and that variations in the quantity and quality of stimulation received can have a significant effect on many aspects of development (Moss, 1965; Murphy, et al., 1962; White and Held, 1963). Additional reports indicate that, not only does the infant require stimulation, but that excessive or chaotic dosages of stimulation can be highly disruptive of normal functioning (Murphy, et al., 1962). Furthermore, there appear to be substantial individual differences in the stimulation that is needed or in the extremes that can be tolerated. As the infant gets older he becomes somewhat capable of regulating the stimulation that is assimilated. However, the very young infant is completely dependent on the caretaking environment to provide and modulate the stimulation he experiences. It is in this regard that the mother has a vital role.

The main points emphasized in the literature are that stimulation serves to modulate the state or arousal level of the infant, organize and direct attentional processes, and facilitate normal growth and development. Bridger (1965) has shown that stimulation tends to have either an arousing or quieting effect, depending on the existing state of the infant. Infants who are quiet tend to be aroused, whereas aroused infants tend to be quieted by moderate stimulation. Moreover, according to data collected by Birns (1965), these effects occur for several stimulus modalities and with stable individual differences in responsivity. (We found that mothers made greater use of techniques involving stimulation—"stresses musculature" and "Stimulates/arouses"—with the males who as a group were more irritable than

the females.)

The capacity for stimulus configurations to direct attention, once the infants is in an optimally receptive state also has been demonstrated by a number of studies. Young infants have been observed to orient toward many stimuli (Razran, 1961; Fantz, 1963), and certain stimuli are so compelling that they tend to "capture" the infant in a fixed orientation (Stechler, 1965). Other studies have demonstrated that infants show clear preferences for gazing at more complex visual patterns (Fantz, 1963). Thus, stimulation can influence the set of the infant to respond by modifying the state of the organism as well as structure learning possibilities through directing the infant's attention. White (1959) has systematically described how stimulation contributes to the learning process in infants. He points out that the infant is provided with the opportunity to activate behavioral potentials in attempting to cope with control stimulation. Motor and perceptual skills eventually become refined and sharpened in the process of responding to stimulus configurations and it is this pattern of learning which White calls "effectance behavior."

Not all levels of stimulation are equally effective in producing a condition whereby the infant is optimally alert and attentive. Excessive stimulation has a disruptive effect and according to drive reduction theorists the organism behaves in ways aimed at reducing stimulation that exceeds certain limits. Leuba (1955), in an attempt to establish *rapprochement* between the drive reduction view and the research evidence that shows that there is a need for stimulation, states that there is an optimal level of stimulation that is required, and that the organism acts either to reduce or to increase stimulation so as to stay within this optimal range.

The mother is necessarily highly instrumental in mediating much of the stimulation that is experienced by the infant. Her very presence in moving about and caring for the infant provides a constant source of visual, auditory, tactile, kinesthetic and proprioceptive stimulation. In addition to the incidental stimulation she provides, the mother deliberately uses stimulation to regulate the arousal level or state of the infant and to evoke specific responses from him. However, once the infant learns, through conditioning, that the mother is a source of stimulation he can in turn employ existing responses that are instrumental in eliciting stimulation from her. Certain infant behaviors, such as the cry, are so compelling that they readily evoke many forms of stimulation from the mother. It is common knowledge that mothers in attempting to quiet upset infants, often resort to such tactics as using rocking motion, waving bright objects or rattles, or holding the infant close and thus provide warmth and physical contact. The specific function of stimulation in placating the crying infant can be somewhat obscured because of the possibility of confounding conditions. In our discussion so far we have indicated that stimulation inherently has a quieting effect irrespective of learning but that crying also can become a learned instrumental behavior which terminates once the reinforcement of stimulation is presented. However, it is often difficult to distinguish the unlearned from the learned patterns of functioning, since the infant behavior (crying) and the outcome

(quieting) are highly similar in both instances. Perhaps the best means for determining whether learning has occurred would be if we could demonstrate that the infant makes anticipatory responses, such as the reduction in crying behavior to cues, prior to the actual occurrence of stimulation. In addition to the cry, the smile and the vocalization of the infant can become highly effective, and consequently well-learned conditioned responses for evoking stimulation from adult caretakers. Rheingold (1956) has shown that when institutional children are given more caretaking by an adult they show an increase in their smiling rate to that caretaker as well as to other adults. Moreover, for a few weeks after the intensive caretaking stopped there were further substantial increments in the smiling rate, which suggests that the infant after experiencing relative deprivation worked harder in attempting to restitute the stimulation level experienced earlier.

It seems plausible that much of the early social behavior seen in infants and children consists of attempts to elicit responses from others. We mentioned earlier that it has been stressed in recent psychological literature that individuals have a basic need for stimulation. Since the mother, and eventually others, are highly instrumental in providing and monitoring the stimulation that is experienced by the infant, it seems likely that the child acquires expectancies for having this need satisfied through social interactions and that stimulation comes to serve as a basis for relating to other. Indeed, Schaffer and Emerson (1964) have shown that the amount of stimulation provided by adults is one of the major determinants of infants' attachment behavior. Strange as well as familiar adults who have been temporarily separated from an infant often attempt to gain rapport with the infant through acts of stimulation. It is quite common for the father, upon returning home from work, to initiate actions aimed at stimulating the child, and these actions are usually responded to with clear pleasure. Because of the expectancies that are built up some of the provocative behaviors seen in children, particularly when confronted with a non-responsive adult, could be interpreted as attempts to elicit socially mediated stimulation.

The learning we have discussed is largely social since the infant is dependent on others, particularly the mother, for reinforcements. This dependency on others is what constitutes attachment behavior, and the specific makeup of the attachment is determined by the class of reinforcements that are involved. The strength of these learned attachment behaviors is maximized through stimulation, since the mother is often the embodiment of this reinforcement as well as the agent for delivering it. The social aspect of this learning is further enhanced because of the reciprocal dependence of the mother on the infant for reinforcement. That is, the mother learns certain conditioned responses, often involving acts of stimulation, that are aimed at evoking desired states or responses from the infant.

In conclusion, what we did was study and analyze some of the factors which structure the mother-infant relationship. A central point is that the state of the infant affects the quantity and quality of maternal behavior, and this in turn would seem to influence the course of future social learning. Furthermore, through controlling for the state of the infant, we were able to demonstrate the effects of pre-parental attitudes on one aspect of maternal behavior, namely, the mother's responsiveness toward her infant. Many investigators, in conducting controlled laboratory studies, have stressed that the state of the infant is crucial in determining the nature of his responses to different stimuli. This concern is certainly highly relevant to our data, collected under naturalistic conditions.

References

Becker, W. C. Consequences of different kinds of parental discipline. In M. L. Hoffman & Lois W. Hoffman (Eds.). *Review of child development research: I.* New York: Russell Sage Found., 1964. Pp. 169-208.

Birns, B. Individual differences in human neonates' responses to stimulation. *Child Develpm.*, 1965, **36**, 249-256.

Bloom, B. S. *Stability and change in human characteristics.* New York: Wiley, 1964.

Bowlby, J. The nature of a child's tie to his mother. *Internat. J. Psychoanal.*, 1958, **39**, 350-373.

Bridger, W. H. Psychophysiological measurement of the roles of state in the human neonate. Paper presented at Soc. Res. Child Develpm., Minneapolis, April, 1965.

Brown, Janet L. States in newborn infants. *Merrill-Palmer Quart.*, 1964, **10**, 313-327.

Escalona, Sibylle K. The study of individual differences and the problem of state. *J. Child Psychiat.*, 1962, **1**, 11-37.

Fantz, R. Pattern vision in newborn infants. *Science*, 1963, **140**, 296-297.

Hess, E. H. Imprinting. *Science*, 1959, **130**, 133-141.

Hinde, R. A., Rowell, T.E., Spencer-Booth, Y. Behavior of living rhesus monkeys in their first six months. *Proc. Zool. Soc., London*, 1964, **143**, 609-649.

Hoffman, H., et al. Enhanced distress vocalization through selective reinforcement. *Science*, 1966, **151**, 354-356.

Lenneberg, E. H., Rebelsky, Freda G., & Nichols, I. A. The vocalizations of infants born to deaf and to hearing parents. *Vita Humana*, 1965, **8**, 23-37.

Leuba, C. Toward some integration of learning theories: The concept of optimal stimulation. *Psychol. Rep.*, 1955, **1**, 27-33.

Levy, D. M. *Behavioral analysis.* Springfield, Ill.: Charles C Thomas, 1958.

McDonald, R.L., Gynther, M. D., & Christakos, A. C. Relations between maternal anxiety and obstetric complications. *Psychosom. Med.*, 1963, **25**, 357-362.

Moss, H. A. Coping behavior, the need for stimulation, and normal development. *Merrill-Palmer Quart.*, 1965, **11**, 171-179.

Murphy, Lois B., et al. *The widening world of childhood.* New York: Basic Books, 1962.

Noirot, Eliane. Changes in responsiveness to young in the adult mouse: the effect of external stimuli. *J. comp. physiol. Psychol.*, 1964, **57**, 97-99.

Razran, G. The observable unconscious and the inferable conscious in current Soviet psychophysiology: Interoceptive conditioning, semantic conditioning, and the orienting relex. *Psychol. Rev.*, 1961, **68**, 81-146.

Rheingold, Harriet L. The modification of social responsiveness in institutional babies. *Monogr. Soc. Res. Child Develpm.*, 1956, **21**, No. 2 (Serial No. 23).

Schaffer, H. R. & Emerson, Peggy E. The development of social attachments in infancy. *Monogr. Soc. Res. Child Develpm.*, 1964, **29**, No. 3 (Serial No. 94).

Serr, D. M. & Ismajovich, B. Determination of the primary sex ratio from human abortions. *Amer. J. Obstet. Gyncol.*, 1963, **87**, 63-65.

Stechler, G. A longitudinal follow-up of neonatal apnea. *Child Develpm.*, 1964, **35**, 333-348.

Stechler, G. Paper presented at Soc. Res. Child Develpm., Minneaplis, April, 1965.

White, B. L. & Held, R. Plasticity in preceptual development during the first six months of life. Paper presented at Amer. Ass. Advncmnt. Sci., Cleveland, Ohio, December, 1963.

White, R. W. Motivation reconsidered: the concept of competence. *Psychol. Rev.*, 1959, **66**, 297-323.

Wolff, P. H. Observations on newborn infants. *Psychosom. Med.*, 1959, **21**, 110-118.

5
INFANCY:
ABNORMAL DEVELOPMENT

The articles selected for this chapter are concerned with three types of abnormal psychological development associated primarily with the infancy period: mental retardation, psychosocial deprivation, and infantile autism. Mental retardation, although it may not be identified until the preschool years or even later, is most frequently an inborn condition. In the Zigler article the author first reviews two lines of theory and research in mental retardation: one a defect orientation suggesting that retarded youngsters are *qualitatively* different from other children, and the other a developmental orientation suggesting that they are only *quantitatively* different. Zigler then describes the important ways in which motivational and emotional factors, in addition to intellective factors, color the life of the retarded child.

Psychosocial deprivation refers to a wide variety of developmental arrests—physical, intellectual, emotional, and interpersonal—that infants may suffer when they do not receive adequate stimulation from their environment. Caldwell discusses the concept of deprivation and traces the evolution of our present knowledge about its effects on young children.

Infantile autism is an extremely serious and fortunately rare developmental disorder beginning at or soon after birth. Because it interferes with a broad range of basic perceptual, language, and interpersonal skills, and because its origin has remained a challenging mystery, infantile autism has commanded considerable attention. The paper by Rimland, abstracted from his excellent book on this subject, describes the typical behavior patterns of autistic children, with particular attention to how they differ from retarded children.

EDWARD ZIGLER

Familial Mental Retardation: A Continuing Dilemma*

The past decade has witnessed renewed interest in the problem of mental retardation. The interest has resulted in vigorous research activity and the construction of a number of theories which attempt an explanation of attenuated intellectual functioning. However, much of the research and many of the theoretical efforts in the area appear to be hampered by a variety of conceptual ambiguities. Much of this ambiguity is due to the very heterogeneity of phenomena included within the rubric of intellectual retardation. A portion of this ambiguity also appears to be the product of many workers' general conceptual orientation to the area of mental retardation.

The typical textbook pictures the distribution of intelligence as normal or Gussian in nature, with approximately the lowest 3 percent of the distribution encompassing the mentally retarded (see Fig. 1a). A homogeneous class of persons is thus constructed, a class defined by intelligence-test performance which results in a score between 0 and 70. This schema has misled many laymen and students, and has subtly influenced the approach of experienced workers in the area. For if one fails to appreciate the arbitrary nature of the 70-I.Q. cutoff

point, it is but a short step to the formulation that all persons falling below this point compose a homogeneous class of "subnormals," qualitatively different from persons having a higher I.Q. The view that mental retardates comprise a homogeneous group is seen in numerous research studies in which comparisons are made between retardates and normal individuals with groups defined solely on the basis of an I.Q. classification.

This practice gives rise to a "difference," or "defect," orientation to mental retardation. Such an approach historically included the notion of moral defect and had many origins, ranging from the belief that retardates were possessed by a variety of devils to the empirical evidence of the higher incidence among them of socially unacceptable behaviors, such as crime and illegitimacy. More recently, the notion of defect has referred to defects in either physical or cognitive structures. This defect approach has one unquestionably valid component. There is a sizable group of retardates who suffer from any of a variety of known physical defects. For example, mental retardation may be due to a dominant gene, as in epiloia; to a single recessive gene, as in gargoylism, phenylketonuria, and amaurotic idiocy; to infections, such as congenital syphilis, encephalitis, or rubella in the mother; to chromosomal defects, as in mongolism: to toxic agents, as in retardation caused by radiation in utero, lead

*From Science, 1967, 155, 292-298. Reprinted by permission of the author and the American Association for the Advancement of Science.

poisoning, or Rh incompatibility; and to cerebral trauma.

The diverse etiologies noted above have one factor in common; in every instance, examination reveals an abnormal physiological process. Persons who are retarded as a result of an abnormal physiological process *are* abnormal in the orthodox sense, since they suffer from a known physiological defect. However, in addition to this group, which forms a minority of all retardates, there is the group labeled "familial"—or, more recently, "cultural-familial"—which comprises approximately 75 percent of all retardates. This group presents the greatest mystery and has been the object of the most heated disputes in the area of mental retardation. The diagnosis of familial retardation is made when an examination reveals none of the physiological manifestations noted above, and when retardation of this same type exists among parents, siblings, or other relatives. Several writers have extended the defect notion to this type of retardate as well, although they differ as to what they propose as the specific nature of the defect. On the basis of differences in performance between retardates and normals on some experimental tasks, rather than on the basis of physiological evidence, they have advanced the view that all retardates suffer from some specifiable defect over and above their general intellectual retardation.

Some order can be brought to the area of mental retardation if a distinction is maintained between physiologically defective retardates, with retardation of known etiology, and familial retardates, with retardation of unknown etiology. For the most part, work with physiologic-ally defective retardates involves investigation into the exact nature of the underlying physiological processes, with prevention or amelioration of the physical and intellectual symptoms as the goal. Jervis[1] has suggested that such "pathological" mental deficiency is primarily in the domain of the medical sciences, whereas familial retardation represents a problem to be solved by behavioral scientists, including educators and behavioral geneticists. Diagnostic and incidence studies of these two types of retardates have disclosed certain striking differences. The retardate having an extremely low I.Q. (below 40) is almost invariably of the physiologically defective type. Familial retardates, on the other hand, are almost invariably mildly retarded, usually with I.Q.'s above 50. This difference in the general intellectual level of the two groups of retardates is an important empirical phenomenon that supports the two-group approach to mental retardation, the approach supported in this article.

A TWO-GROUP APPROACH

Hirsch[2] has asserted that we will not make much headway in understanding individual differences in intelligence, and in many other traits, unless we recognize that, to a large degree, such differences reflect the inherent biological properties of man. We can all agree that no genotype spells itself out in a vacuum, and that the phenotypic expression is finally the result of environment interacting with the genotype. However, an appreciation of the importance of genetic differences allows us to bring considerable order to the area of mental retardation.

We need simply to accept the generally recognized fact that the gene pool of any population is such that there will always be variations in the behavioral or phenotypic expression of virtually every measurable trait or characteristic of man. From the polygenic model advanced by geneticists, we deduce that the distribution of intelligence is characterized by a bisymmetrical bell-shaped curve, which is characteristic of such a large number of distributions that we have come to refer to it as the normal curve. With the qualification noted below, this theoretical distribution is a fairly good approximation of the observed distribution of intelligence. In the polygenic model of intelligence,[2-4] the genetic foundation of intelligence is not viewed as dependent upon a single gene. Rather, intelligence is viewed as the result of a number of discrete genetic units. (This is not to assert, however, that single gene effects are never encountered in mental retardation. As noted above, certain relatively rare types of mental retardation are the product of such simple genetic effects.)

Various specific polygenic models have been advanced which generate theoretical distributions of intelligence that are in keeping with observed distributions.[3,5,6] An aspect of polygenic models of special importance for the two-group approach is the fact that they generate I.Q. distributions of approximately 50 to 150. Since an I.Q. of approximately 50 appears to be the lower limit for familial retardates, it has been concluded[4,5,7] that the etiology of this form of retardation reflects the same factors that determine "normal" intelligence. With this approach, the familial retardate may be viewed as normal, where "normal" is defined as meaning an integral part of the distribution of intelligence that we would expect from the normal manifestations of the genetic pool in our population. Within such a framework it is possible to refer to the familial retardate as less intelligent than other normal manifestations of the genetic pool, but he is just as integral a part of the normal distribution as are the 3 percent of the population whom we view as superior, or the more numerous group of individuals whom we consider to be average.[8]

The two-group approach to mental retardation calls attention to the fact that the second group of retardates, those who have known physiological defects, represents a distribution of intelligence with a mean which is considerably lower than that of the familial retardates. Such children, for the most part, fall outside the range of normal intelligence—that is, below I.Q. of 50—although there are certain exceptions. Considerable clarity could be brought to the area of mental retardation through doing away with the practice of conceptualizing the intelligence distribution as a single, continuous, normal curve. Perhaps a more appropriate representation of the empirical distribution of intelligence would involve two curves, as Fig. 1b illustrates. The intelligence of the bulk of the population, including the familial retardate, would be depicted as a normal distribution having a mean of 100, with lower and upper limits of approximately 50 and 150, respectively. Superimposed on this curve would be a second, somewhat normal distribution having a mean of approximately 35 and a range from 0 to 70. (That the population encompassed by the second curve in Fig. 1b extends beyond the 70-I.Q. cutoff point is due to the fact that a very small number of individuals with known defects—for example, brain damage—may be found throughout the I.Q. continuum.) The first curve would represent the polygenic distribution of intelligence; the second would represent all those individuals whose intellectual functioning reflects factors other than the normal polygenic expression—that is, those retardates having an identifiable physiological defect. This two-group approach to the problem of mental retardation has been supported by Penrose,[4] Roberts,[9] and Lewis.[10] The very nature of the observed distribution of I.Q.'s below the mean, especially in the range of 0 to 50 (see Fig. 1c), seems to demand such an approach. This distribution, in which we find an overabundance of individuals at the very low I.Q. levels, is exactly what we would expect if we combined the two distributions discussed above, as is the general practice. . . .

DEVELOPMENTAL VERSUS DEFECT ORIENTATION

Once one adopts the position that the familial mental retardate is not defective or pathological but is essentially a normal

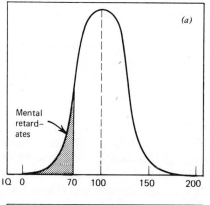

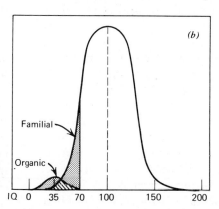

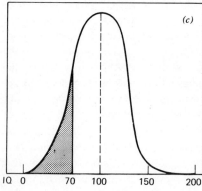

Figure 1. (a) Conventional representation of the distribution of intelligence. (b) Distribution of intelligence as represented in the two-group approach. (c) Actual distribution of intelligence. [After Penrose (4)].

individual of low intelligence, then the familial retardate no longer represents a mystery but, rather, is viewed as a particular manifestation of the general developmental process. According to this approach, the familial retardate's cognitive development differs from that of the normal individual only in respect to its rate and the upper limit achieved. Such a view generates the expectation that, when rate of development is controlled, as is grossly the case when groups of retardates and normals are matched with respect to mental age, there should be no difference in formal cognitive processes related to I.Q. Stated somewhat differently, this means that the familial retardate with a chronological age of 10, an I.Q. of 70, and thus a mental age of 7, would be viewed as being at the same developmental level intellectually as a child with a chronological age of 7 and an I.Q. of 100.

In contrast, according to the defect orientation, all retardates suffer from a specific physiological or cognitive defect over and above their slower general rate of cognitive development. This view generates the expectation that, even when the rate of cognitive development is controlled, as in the situation where mental ages are matched, differences in intellectual functioning which are related to I.Q. will be found. On their face, the repeated findings of differences in performance between groups of normals and retardates matched as to mental age have lent credence to the defect theory and have cast doubt on the validity of the developmental theory.

The developmental theorist's response to these frequently reported differences has been to point out that performance on any experimental task is not inexorably the product of the subject's cognitive structure alone but reflects a variety of emotional and motivational factors as well. To the developmentalist, then, it seems more reasonable to attribute differences in performance between normals and retardates of the same mental age to motivational differences which do not inhere in mental retardation but are, rather, the result of the particular histories of the retarded subjects.

It should be noted that most theories in the area of mental retardation are basically defect theories. These differ among themselves, however. A major difference involves the theoretician's effort to relate the postulated defect to some specific physiological structure. The theoretical language of some theoreticians is explicitly physiological, that of others is non-physiological, while that of others remains vague. Particular defects that have been attributed to the retarded include the following: relative impermeability of the boundaries between regions in the cognitive structure[11, 12]; primary and secondary rigidity caused by subcortical malformations, respectively[13]; inadequate neural satiation related to brain modifiability or cortical conductivity[14]; malfunctioning disinhibitory mechanisms[15]; improper development of the verbal system, resulting in a dissociation between verbal and motor systems[16, 17]; relative brevity in the persistence of the stimulus trace[18]; and impaired attention-directing mechanisms.[19]

Where the hypothesized defect is an explicit physiological one, it would appear to be a simple matter to obtain direct evidence that the defect does or does not exist. Such evidence would come from biochemical and physiological analyses as well as from pathological studies of familial retardates. A number of such studies have, of course, been carried out. Although there is an occasional report of some physical anomaly, the bulk of the evidence has indicated that the familial retardate does not suffer from any gross physiological defects. Indeed, if such evidence were readily available the defect theorist would cease relying on the more ambiguous data provided by studies of molar behavior. Failure to find direct evidence of a defect in familial retardates has not deterred and should not deter theorists from postulating such defects.

In spite of the negative physiological evidence, workers such as Spitz[14] maintain that all retardates, including familial retardates, are physically defective, and that our failure to discover defects in familial retardates is due to the relatively primitive nature of our diagnostic techniques. This view is bolstered by Masland,[20] who has also noted the inadequacies of such techniques. It is perfectly legitimate for the defect theorist to assert that, although not at present observable, the physical defect that causes familial retardates to behave differently from normals of the same mental age will someday be seen. These theorists operate very much as the physicists of a not-too-distant era did when they asserted that the electron existed even though it was not directly observable. Analogously, defect theorists in the area of mental retardation undertake to validate the existence of a defect by first asserting that it should manifest itself in particular phenomena—that is, in particular behaviors of the retarded—and then devising experiments in which, if the predicted behavior is observed, the existence of the hypothesized defect is confirmed. Not only is this approach legitimate but, as noted above, it has become increasingly popular as well. A relatively comprehensive review of the literature emanating from the general defect position is now available.[21] In the following paragraphs I briefly summarize the major defect positions.

An influential defect position is that of the Russian investigator A. R. Luria,[16] whose work has now also influenced investigators in England and the United States. In the Soviet Union no distinction is made between retardates having known organic impairment and that larger group whose retardation is of unknown etiology, nor are genetic or cultural factors considered to be determinants of mental retardation. All grades of mental retardation are attributed to central-nervous-system damage believed to have occurred initially during the intrauterine period or during early childhood. Thus the diagnosis of mental retardation necessarily involves specification of a defect in some neurophysiological system; in fact, in the Soviet Union, professionals who work with the mentally retarded are called "defectologists."

Luria's interest in defective functioning appears to be an outgrowth of his more basic concern with the development of the higher cognitive processes in man. The influence of both Vygotsky and Pavlov may be seen in his work, which has been primarily concerned with the highly intricate development of the role of speech and language in regulating the child's behavior. In his comparisons between normal and retarded children, Luria has demonstrated that the behavior of retardates resembles that of chronologically younger normal children in that verbal instructions do not result in smooth regulation of motor behavior. Luria has found that retarded subjects have considerable difficulty with tasks requiring verbal mediation. Thus, Luria has inferred that the major defect in the retarded child involves an underdevelopment or a general "inertness" of the verbal system, and a dissociation of this system from the motor or action system. This dissociation is vaguely conceptualized as resulting from a disturbance in normal cortical activity.

The view that the behavior of a retardate resembles that of a chronologically younger child is, of course, consistent with the general developmental position. However, several English and American investigators[17, 22] have demonstrated that, even with mental age level controlled, retardates have more difficulty on tasks requiring verbal mediation than normal subjects have. On the other hand, other such investigations have failed to provide support for Luria's position.[23] To date, findings related to this position can best be described as equivocal.

Another major defect position is that of Herman Spitz,[14] who has extended the Kohler-Wallach[24] cortical satiation theory to the area of mental retardation. According to Spitz, all retardates suffer from inadequate neural or cortical functioning; the inadequacy is best characterized by a certain sluggishness, or less-than-normal modifiability, in the functioning of cortical cells. Thus, Spitz believes that in retardates it takes longer to induce temporary, as well as permanent, electrical, chemical, and physical changes in stimulated cortical cells, and furthermore, that once such a change is produced, it is less readily modified than in the case of normal persons.

Spitz's evidence in support of his theory has come primarily from comparisons of the performance of retardates and normals of the same chronological age on a variety of perceptual tasks—for example, figural after-effects and Necker-cube reversals. The heuristic value of Spitz's position may be seen in his recent efforts to extend his postulates beyond the visual perception area and employ them to generate specific predictions concerning the phenomena of learning transposition, generalization, and problem solving. The evidence in favor of Spitz's position is far from clear-cut, however. Spivack[25] has pointed out that Spitz's findings are in marked contrast to those of other investigators. The very nature of many of Spitz's measures—for example, a verbal report—raises the troublesome issue of how well they reflect the perceptual responses being investigated. It should be noted that, in respect to this point as well as to other criticisms, Spitz himself has become one of the most cogent critics of his own efforts.

Many of Spitz's findings could be encompassed by the general developmental postion. The developmental theorist would argue that it is not surprising that one gets different results for normals and for retardates matched with respect to chronological age, since such groups are at different developmental levels (as defined by mental age). One would be tempted to say that Spitz's work has little relevance to the issue of whether familial retardates suffer from a defect over and above their slower and more limited rate of cognitive development. However, Spitz has been quite explicit in his views that the differences he obtains are not developmental phenomena but reflect a physical deficit that should manifest itself even in comparisons with normal subjects matched in mental age to the retardates.

Ellis[18] has also advanced the view that the retardate is basically different from the normal individual and that this difference is a result of central-nervous-system pathology from which all retardates suffer. Ellis views this central-nervous-system pathology as producing a short-term memory deficit which, in turn, underlines the inadequacy of much of the retardate's behavior. The theoretical model presented by Ellis includes two major constructs, stimulus trace and neural integrity.

The stimulus trace, the mechanism underlying short-term memory functions, is conceptualized as a neural event or response which varies with the intensity, duration, and meaning of the stimulus situation confronting the subject. The stimulus-trace construct is thus anchored to stimulus characteristics on the one hand and to the subject's responses to these characteristics on the other. The neural-integrity construct is conceptualized as the determinant of the nature of stimulus-trace activity, and is defined by "measures of behavioral adequacy." The typical measure of neural integrity employed by Ellis is the I.Q. Thus, a person of low I.Q. is said to suffer from a lack of neural integrity. This lack, in turn, delimits or restricts stimulus-trace activity, and such restriction results in a variety of inadequate behaviors.

In support of this theory, Ellis has noted findings from numerous experiments involving short-term retention phenomena. These include studies on serial learning, delayed-reaction tasks, fixed-interval operant behavior, electroencephalographic investigations, reaction time, and factor analyses of the WISC test (the Wechsler Intelligence Scale for Children), as well as several studies of discrimination learning in brain-damaged animals.[18] In respect to his own experimental tests, Ellis's reliance on the I.Q. as the measure of neural integrity has produced two types of comparisons: comparison of retardates and normals of the same chronological age and comparison of retardates and normals of the same mental age. In either comparison Ellis's model would predict that the retardates would be inferior on tasks involving short-term retention, due to their lower I.Q. In general, the findings obtained with groups matched as to chronological age have supported Ellis's position, while those obtained with groups matched as to mental age have not.

It should be noted that the demonstration that retardates do less well than normals of the same chronological age on tasks requiring short-term memory is a somewhat circular undertaking. It is circular to the extent that a deficit in short-term memory would influence the I.Q. score itself through its effect on certain of the intelligence subtests—for example, the digit-span test. Again, it should be emphasized that the discovery of a difference between normals and retardates of the same chronological age is just as amenable to a general developmental interpretation as to the view that all retardates suffer from central-nervous-system pathology, since the mental age of such retardates is necessarily lower than that of normal subjects in the control group.

Perhaps the oldest of the more influential defect positions is the Lewin-Kounin[11], [12] formulation that familial retardates are inherently more "rigid" than normal individuals of the same mental age. This position differs from the others discussed above in that the defect is conceptualized as inhering in a hypothesized cognitive structure without reference or reduction to any specific physiological entities. By the term *rigidity*, Lewin and Kounin were referring not to behaviors, as such, but rather to characteristics of the cognitive structure. These theorists felt that the essential defect, in retardation, was the lowered capacity for dynamic rearrangement in the "psychical system." This "stiffness" in cognitive functioning was conceptualized as being due to the relative impermeability of the boundaries between cells or regions of the cognitive structure. *Rigidity*, then, referred primarily to the nature of these boundaries, and to the resulting degree of communication or fluidity between regions.

Principal support for this position was contained in a series of experiments conducted by Kounin,[11] in which he found differences between familial retardates and normals of the same mental age on a variety of tasks involving transfer phenomena, sorting, and concept-switching. Although the Lewin-Kounin position continues to receive some support,[26] a fairly sizable amount of work[27], [28] now indicates that the differences discovered by Kounin between retardates and normals of the same mental age were due to differences in motivational variables rather than to an inherent cognitive rigidity of the retardate.

Lewin and Kounin appear to be the only defect theorists who have dealt adequately with the problem of etiology, which becomes a crucial issue in the controversy over the two theories. Their formulation was limited to familial retardates, and only such retardates were employed in Kounin's experiments. The other defect theorists have tended to argue that the distinction between familial and organic retardates is misleading, and, as a result, they have used groups of retardates of both types in their experiments. This presents an almost insurmountable problem when one attempts to evaluate the degree to which any uncovered differences in behavior support the major theoretical premise which underlies most defect approaches. This premise, clearly seen in the work of Luria, Spitz, and Ellis, is that all retardates, familials and organics alike, suffer from some specifiable defect. However, until the etiological issue is attended to in the research design, there is no way of assessing how much of the revealed difference between normals and retardates of the same mental age is a product of the gross organic pathology known to exist in the organic retardates included in the retarded group and how much is a product of the defect thought by the defect theorists to exist in all retardates.

The general developmental approach is applicable only to the familial retardate, and this approach does not speak to the issue of differences discovered between normal children and organic retardates. The developmental theorist also believes that, even when a difference in behavior is found between normals and familial retardates of the same mental age, it need not be attributed to any defect which inheres in familial mental retardation. Such differences are viewed as the possible outcome of differences in a variety of motivational factors which exist between the two groups. A sampling of the literature which lends credence to this view follows.

MOTIVATIONAL AND EMOTIONAL FACTORS

The view of those of us who believe that many of the reported differences between retardates and normals of the same mental age are a result of motivational and emotional differences which reflects differences in environmental histories does not imply that we ignore the importance of the lower intelligence per se. In some instances the personality characteristics of the retarded individual will reflect environmental factors that have little or nothing to do with intellectual endowment. For example, many of the effects of institutionalization may be constant, regardless of the person's intelligence level. In other instances we must think in terms of an interaction; that is, a person with low intellectual ability will have certain experiences and develop certain behavior patterns differing from those of a person with greater intellectual endowment. An obvious example of this is the greater amount of failure which the retardate typically experiences. What must be emphasized is the fact that the behavior pattern developed by the retardate as a result of such a history of failure may not differ in kind or ontogenesis from patterns developed by an individual of normal intellect who, because of some environmental circumstance, also experiences an inordinate amount of failure. By the same token, if the retardate can somehow be guaranteed a history of greater success, we would expect his behavior to be more normal, regardless of his intellectual level. Within this framework, I now discuss several of the personality factors which have been known to influence the performance of the retarded.

It has become increasingly clear that our understanding of the performance of the institutionalized familial retardate will be enhanced if we consider the inordinate amount of social deprivation these individuals have experienced before being placed in institutions. [20,30] A series of recent studies[30-34] has indicated that one result of such early deprivation is a heightened motivation to interact with a supportive adult. These studies suggest that, given this heightened motivation, retardates exhibit considerable compliance with instructions when the effect of such compliance is to increase or maintain the social interaction with the adult. These findings would appear to be consistent with the often-made observation that the retarded seek attention and desire affection.[35,36]

Recent findings suggest that the perseveration so frequently noted in the behavior of the retarded is primarily a function of these motivational factors rather than a result of inherent cognitive rigidity, as suggested by Lewin[12] and Kounin.[11] Evidence is now available indicating (i) that the degree of perseveration is directly related to the degree of deprivation the individual experienced before being institutionalized,[30] and (ii) that institutionalized children of normal intellect are just as perseverative as institutionalized retardates, while noninstitutionalized retardates are no more perseverative than noninstitutionalized children of normal intellect.[31,32]

Although there is considerable evidence that social deprivation results in a heightened motivation to interact with a supportive adult, it appears to have other effects as well. The nature of these effects is suggested in observations of fearfulness, wariness, or avoidance of strangers on the part of retardates, or of suspicion and mistrust.[36,37] The experimental work done by Zigler and his associates on the behavior of institutionalized retarded individuals has indicated that social deprivation results in both a heightened motivation to interact with supportive adults (a positive-reaction tendency) and a wariness of doing so (a negative-reaction tendency). The construct of a negative-reaction tendency has been employed to explain certain differences between retardates and normals reported by Kounin, differences that have heretofore been attributed to the greater cognitive rigidity of retarded individuals. For instance, it has been demonstrated[38] that, once the institutionalized familial retardate's wariness has been allayed, he becomes much more responsive than the normal individual to social reinforcement. Thus, a motivational rather than a cognitive factor would seem to underlie certain rather mysterious behavioral phenomena frequently observed in familial retardates—for example, a tendency to persist longer on the second of two highly similar tasks than on the first.

Both positive- and negative-reaction tendencies have been recently investigated in a series of studies, with children of normal intellect,[39] directed at further validation of the "valence position." Stated most simply, this position asserts that the effectiveness of an adult as a reinforcing agent depends upon the valence he has for the particular child whose behavior is being reinforced. (An adult's valence for a child refers to the degree to which that adult is sought or avoided by the child.) This valence is determined by the child's history of positive and negative experiences with adults. The studies noted above have produced considerable evidence that prior positive contacts between the child and the adult increase the adult's effectiveness as a reinforcer, while negative contacts decrease it. If the experimentally manipulated negative encounters in these experiments are viewed as experimental analogs of encounters institutionalized retardates actually have experienced, then the often-reported reluctance of such children to interact with adults and their wariness of such encounters become understandable. Thus it would appear that their relatively high negative-reactive tendency motivates them toward behaviors, such as withdrawal, that reduce the quality of their performance to a level lower than that which one would expect on the basis of their intellectual capacity alone.

Another factor frequently mentioned as a determinant in the performance of the retarded is their high expectancy of failure. This failure expectancy has been viewed as an outgrowth of a lifetime characterized by confrontations with tasks with which they are intellectually ill-equipped to deal. The work of Cromwell and his colleagues[40] has lent support to the general proposition that retardates have a higher expectancy of failure than normals have, and that this results in a style of problem-solving in which the retardate is much more highly motivated to avoid failure than to achieve success. However, the results of experimental work with retardates to investigate the success-failure dimension are still somewhat inconsistent, suggesting that even such a relatively simple proposition as this one is in need of further refinement.

Recent studies[31, 33, 41] have indicated that the many failures experienced by retardates generate a cognitive style of problem-solving characterized by outer-directedness. That is, the retarded child comes to distrust his own solutions to problems and therefore seeks guides to action in the immediate environment. This outer-directedness may explain the great suggestibility so frequently observed in the retarded child. Evidence has now been presented indicating that, relative to normals of the same mental age, the retarded child is more sensitive to verbal cues from an adult, is more imitative of the behavior of adults and of his peers, and does more visual scanning. Furthermore, certain findings[31] suggest that the noninstitutionalized retardate is more outer-directed in his problem solving than the institutionalized retardate is. This makes considerable sense if one remembers that the noninstitutionalized retardate lives in an environment that is not adjusted to his intellectual shortcomings and, therefore, probably experiences more failure than the institutionalized retardate.

Another nonintellective factor important in understanding the behavior of the retarded is the retardate's motivation to obtain various types of reinforcement. The social-deprivation work discussed indicates that retardates have an extremely strong desire for attention, praise, and encouragement. Several investigators[40, 42] have suggested that, in normal development, the effectiveness of attention and praise as reinforcers diminishes with maturity and is replaced by the reinforcement inherent in the awareness that one is correct. This latter type of reinforcer appears to serve primarily as a cue for self-reinforcement.

Zigler and his associates[27,43,44] have argued that various experiences in the lives of the retarded cause them to care less about being correct simply for the sake of creectness than normals of the same mental age. In other words, these investigators have argued that the position of various reinforcers in the reinforcer hierarchies of normal and retarded children of the same mental age differ.

Clearest support for the view that the retardate cares much less about being correct than the middle-class child of normal intellect does is contained in a study by Zigler and deLabry.[43] These investigators found, as Kounin[11] did, that when the only reinforcement was the information that the child was correct, retardates were poorer on a concept-switching task than middle-class normal children of the same mental age. However, when Zigler and deLabry added another condition, reward with a toy of the child's choice for concept-switching, they found that the retardates performed as well as the middle-class normal children. Since the satisfaction of giving the correct response is the incentive typically used in experimental studies, one wonders how many of the differences in performance found between retardates and normals are actually attributable to differences in capacity rather than to differences in the values such incentives may have for the two types of subjects.

Much of this work on motivational and emotional factors in the performance of the retarded is very recent. The research on several of the factors discussed is more suggestive than definitive. It is clear, however, that these factors are extremely important in determining the retardate's level of functioning. This is not to assert that these motivational factors cause familial mental retardation but to say, rather, that they lead to the retardate's behaving in a manner less effective than that dictated by his intellectual capacity. An increase in knowledge concerning motivational and emotional factors and their ontogenesis and manipulation would hold considerable promise for alleviating much of the social ineffectiveness displayed by that rather sizable group of persons who must function at a relatively low intellectual level.

SUMMARY

The heterogeneous nature of mental retardation, as well as certain common practices of workers in the area, has resulted in a variety of conceptual ambiguities. Considerable order could be brought to the area if, instead of viewing all retardates as a homogeneous group arbitrarily defined by some I.Q. score, workers would clearly distinguish between the group of retardates known to suffer from some organic defect and the larger group of retardates referred to as familial retardates. It is the etiology of familial retardation that currently constitutes the greatest mystery.

A number of authorities have emphasized the need for employing recent polygenic models of inheritance in an effort to understand the familial retardate. While appreciating the importance of environment in affecting the distribution determined by genetic inheritance, these workers have argued that familial retardates are not essentially different from individuals of greater intellect, but represent, rather, the lower portion of the intellectual curve which reflects normal intellectual variability. As emphasized by the two-group approach, retardates with known physiological or organic defect are viewed as presenting a quite different etiological problem. The familial retardate, on the other hand, is seen as a perfectly normal expression of the population gene pool, of slower and more limited intellectual development than the individual of average intellect.

This view generates the proposition that retardates and normals at the same general cognitive level—that is, of the same mental age—are similar in respect to their cognitive functioning. However, such a proposition runs headlong into findings that retardates and normals of the same mental age often differ in performance. Such findings have bolstered what is currently the most popular theoretical approach to retarded functioning—namely, the view that all retardates suffer from some specific defect which inheres in mental retardation and thus makes the retardate immutably "different" from normals, even when the general level of intellectual development is controlled. While these defect or difference approaches, as exemplified in the work of Luria, Spitz, Ellis, and Lewin and Kounin, dominate the area of mental retardation, the indirect, and therefore equivocal, nature of the evidence of these workers has generated considerable controversy.

In contrast to this approach, the general developmental position has emphasized systematic evaluation of the role of experiential, motivational, and personality factors. As a central thesis, this position asserts that performance on experimental and real-life tasks is never the single inexorable product of the retardate's cognitive structure but, rather, reflects a wide variety of relatively nonintellective factors which greatly influence the general adequacy of performance. Thus, many of the reported behavioral differences between normals and retardates of the same mental age are seen as products of motivational and experiential differences between these groups, rather than as the result of any inherent cognitive deficiency in the retardates. Factors thought to be of particular importance in the behavior of the retardate are social deprivation and the positive- and negative-reaction tendencies to which such deprivation gives rise; the high number of failure experiences and the particular approach to problem-solving which they generate; and atypical reinforcer hierarchies.

There is little question that we are witnessing a productive, exciting, and perhaps inevitably chaotic period in the history of man's concern with the problem of mental retardation. Even the disagreements that presently exist must be considered rather healthy phenomena. These disagreements will unquestionably generate new knowledge which, in the hands of practitioners, may become the vehicle through which the performance of children, regardless of intellectual level, may be improved.

References and Notes

1. G. A. Jervis, in *American Handbook of Psychiatry*, S. Arieti, Ed. (Basic Books, New York, 1959), vol. 2, pp. 1289-1313.
2. J. Hirsch, *Science* 142, 1436 (1963).
3. I. L. Gottesman, in *Handbook of Mental Deficiency*, N. R. Ellis, Ed. (McGraw-Hill, New York, 1963), pp. 253-296.
4. L. S. Penrose, *The Biology of Mental Defect* (Sidgwick and Jackson, London, 1963).
5. C. Burt and M. Howard, *Brit. J. Statist. Psychol.* 9, 95 (1956).
6. C. Burt and M. Howard, *ibid.* 10, 33 (1957); C. C. Hurst, in *Proc. Roy, Soc. London Ser. B* 112, 80 (1932); R. W. Pickford, *J. Psychol.* 28, 129 (1949).
7. G. Allen, *Amer. J. Mental Deficiency* 62, 840 (1958); C. Burt, *Amer. Psychologist* 13, 1 (1958).
8. G. E. McClearn, in *Psychology in the Making*, L. Postman, Ed.

(Knopf, New York, 1962), pp. 144-252.

9. J. A. F. Roberts, *Eugenics Rev.* **44**, 71 (1952).
10. E. O. Lewis, *J. Mental Sci.* **79**, 298 (1933).
11. J. Kounin, *Character and Personality* **9**, 251 (1941); *ibid.*, p. 273.
12. K. Lewin, *A Dynamic Theory of Personality* (McGraw-Hill, New York, 1936).
13. K. Goldstein, *Character and Personality* **11**, 209 (1942-43).
14. H. H. Spitz, in *Handbook of Mental Deficiency*, N. R. Ellis, Ed. (McGraw-Hill, New York, 1963), pp. 11-40.
15. P. S. Siegel and J. G. Foshee, *J. Abnormal Soc. Psychol.* **61**, 141 (1960).
16. A. R. Luria, in *Handbook of Mental Deficiency*, N. R. Ellis, Ed. (McGraw-Hill, New York, 1963), pp. 353-387.
17. N. O'Connor and B. Hermelin, *J. Abnormal Soc. Psychol.* **59**, 409 (1959).
18. N. R. Ellis, in *Handbook of Mental Deficiency*, N. R. Ellis, Ed. (McGraw-Hill, New York, 1963), pp. 134-158.
19. D. Zeaman and B. J. House, *ibid.*, p. 159.
20. R. L. Masland, *Amer. J. Mental Deficiency* **64**, 305 (1959).
21. E. Zigler, in *Review of Child Development Research*, M. L. Hoffman and L. W. Hoffman, Eds. (Russell Sage Foundation, New York, in press), vol. 2.
22. N. A. Milgram and H. G. Furth, *Amer. J. Mental Deficiency* **67**, 733 (1963); *ibid.* **70**, 849 (1966).
23. D. Balla and E. Zigler, *J. Abnormal Soc. Psychol.* **69**, 664 (1964); M. Rieber, *Amer. J. Mental Deficiency* **68**, 634 (1964).
24. W. Kohler and H. Wallach, *Proc. Amer. Phil. Soc.* **88**, 269 (1964).
25. G. Spivack, in *Handbook of Mental Deficiency*, N. R. Ellis, Ed. (McGraw-Hill, New York, 1963), pp. 480-511.
26. M. Budoff and W. Pagel, "Learning potential and rigidity in the adolescent mentally retarded," paper presented before the Society for Research in Child Development, Minneapolis, Minn., March 1965.
27. E. Zigler, in *Readings on the Exceptional Child*, E. P. Trapp and P. Himelstein, Eds. (Appleton-Century-Crofts, New York, 1962), pp. 141-162.
28. E. Zigler, in *International Review of Research in Mental Retardation*, N. R. Ellis, Ed. (Academic Press, New York, 1966), vol. 1, pp. 77-105.
29. A. D. B. Clarke and A. M. Clarke, *Brit. J. Psychol.* **45**, 197 (1954); D. Kaplun, *Proc. Amer. Ass. Mental Deficiency* **40**, 68 (1935).
30. E. Zigler *J. Abnormal Soc. Psychol.* **62**, 413 (1961).
31. C. Green and E. Zigler, *Child Develop.* **33**, 499 (1962).

32. E. Zigler, *J. Personality* **31**, 258 (1963).
33. E. Zigler, L. Hodgden, H. Stevenson, *ibid.* **26**, 106 (1958).
34. R. Shepps and E. Zigler, *Amer. J. Mental Deficiency* **67**, 262 (1962); H. Stevenson and L. Fahel, *J. Personality* **29**, 136 (1961); E. Zigler and J. Williams, *J. Abnormal Soc. Psychol.* **66**, 197 (1963).
35. W. M. Cruickshank, *J. Clin. Psychol.* **3**, 381 (1947); E. E. Doll, *Readings on the Exceptional Child*, E. P. Trapp and P. Himelstein, Eds. (Appleton-Century-Crofts, New York, 1962), pp. 21-68.
36. E. A. Hirsh, *Amer. J. Mental Deficiency* **63**, 639 (1959); B. L. Wellman, *Childhood Educ.* **15**, 108 (1938).
37. M. Woodward, *Brit. J. Med. Psychol.* **33**, 123 (1960).
38. P. Shallenberger and E. Zigler, *J. Abnormal Soc. Psychol.* **63**, 20 (1961); E. Zigler, thesis, Univ. of Texas, Austin, 1958.
39. H. Berkowitz, E. C. Butterfield, E. Zigler, *J. Personality Soc. Psychol.* **2**, 706 (1965); H. Berkowitz and E. Zigler, *ibid.,* p. 500; N. McCoy and E. Zigler, *ibid.* **1**, 604 (1965).
40. R. L. Cromwell, in *Handbook of Mental Deficiency*, N. R. Ellis, Ed. (McGraw-Hill, New York, 1963), pp. 41-91.
41. J. Turnure and E. Zigler, *J. Abnormal Soc. Psychol.* **69**, 427 (1964).
42. E. Beller, *J. Genet. Psychol.* **87**, 25 (1955); J. Gewirtz, *Monographs Soc. Res. Child Develop. No. 59* (1954), p. 19; G. Heathers, *J. Genet. Psychol.* **87**, 37, (1955); E. Zigler, *Amer. J. Orthopsychiat.* **33**, 614 (1963).
43. E. Zigler and J. deLabry, *J. Abnormal Soc. Psychol.* **65**, 267 (1962).
44. E. Zigler and E. Unell, *Amer. J. Mental Deficiency* **66**, 651 (1962).

BETTYE M. CALDWELL

The Effects of Psychosocial Deprivation on Human Development in Infancy*

As an explanation for certain distortions in human development, the concept of deprivation has been very appealing to scientists from diverse backgrounds and with varied areas of application. Whenever any approximation of a minimal level of necessary input can be established, the deprivation model appears to be appropriate as a frame of reference; furthermore, it appears to be relevant for all living organisms and to the entire gamut of developmental influences from biochemical to psychosocial. Also it seems to carry within it the promise of remediation, for if one can specify the substance of which the organism has been deprived, then one should hopefully be able to supply the missing ingredients in the proper quantities at the correct time.

The natural logic inherent in the concept of deprivation—i.e., that an insufficiency of a particular substance or experience would lead to untoward developmental consequences—has stimulated a vast amount of fruitful research. It is probably accurate to say that, in general, the sequential investigations have followed something of an evolutionary pattern in terms of choice of the de-

pendent variable. The first of these is usually life itself, with sublethal effects gradually added to the list of possible consequences in an order that progresses from somatic toward psychosocial. Thus, historically, in terms of the consequences of nutritional deprivation, early studies tended to stress the effects of malnutrition on stature or brain weight—with research into its effects on mental development very current and that concerned with socio-emotional development more contemplated than consummated. Something of a similar evolution has occurred on the side of the independent variable. That is, early efforts were devoted primarily to demonstrations of the consequences of deprivation of some biochemical substance (e.g., oxygen) with research attention to psychosocial deprivation on a large scale being of fairly recent origin.

Within this broad domain of scientific concern with the consequences of deprivation, it is possible to offer some generalizations about findings that have emerged. When the investigations have utilized an *experimental* model, as is the case in animal studies where the independent variable can be precisely quantified and manipulated, findings have tended to be fairly consistent across a broad range of developmental influences. However, when hypotheses are tested in

*From the *Merrill-Palmer Quarterly*, 1970, 16, 260-277. Reprinted by permission of the author and the Merrill-Palmer Institute.

humans, forcing reliance upon a *field study* model with the hope of finding different levels of the independent variable in nature, consistency disappears and polemics materialize. In field studies the complexity of the concept of deprivation immediately becomes apparent. Not only is it difficult to disentangle one type of deprivation from another (e.g., nutritional and psychosocial), but to be precise about the time of maximum exertion of effect of one or another component is almost impossible. That is, prenatal malnutrition tends to be correlated with postnatal malnutrition and also with prenatal and postnatal psychosocial deprivation; in field studies it is virtually impossible to determine which is associated with any observed primary effect.

When one uses psychosocial factors as both independent and dependent variables in a deprivation model design, it becomes increasingly difficult to arrive at any firm generalizations. Animal studies have not yielded completely consistent data either within or across species, as discussed by Griffin and Harlow (1966). And at the human level, with the inevitable forfeiture of the experimental method, data have been both scanty and conflicting.

Some of the variance may relate to the difficulty involved in precisely defining what it is we are talking about when we speak of "psychosocial deprivation." Although an overly pedantic attempt at definition would be both unnecessary and tedious, it would perhaps help the following discussion if some attention were given to current thinking about the concept of psychosocial deprivation. Undoubtedly the most serious attempt at definition has been made by Richardson

(1966, pp. 55-56), who discussed the slipperiness of the concept as follows:

Two kinds of evidence can lead us to suspect deprivation. The first is whether the child is able to perform at a given age within the level of expectations and demands that are common to his tribe, society, or national group.

The second kind of evidence needed to judge a case of deprivation involves the child's upbringing and experiences. . . . If a child does not receive the elements of upbringing or experience essential for development, this is evidence of deprivation.

These two kinds of evidence—of whether a child fails to live up to expectations and of whether he has not had the experiences necessary to prepare him to meet these expectations—are both needed to make a judgement.

Richardson is describing the kind of inference that is always required whenever information about a particular variable is sought after the fact—in this case, after the deprivation has presumably occurred. However, such a definition would not be necessary for a contemporary assessment of deprivation with follow-up sustained long enough to permit the effects of the independently defined deprivation to appear. Unfortunately, investigations of the consequences of psychosocial deprivation are often begun retrospectively. And yet contemporaneous assessments of children in potentially depriving environments should be a major research strategy. If one adhered rigidly to the Richardson concept of deprivation, such investigations would be precluded.

In addition to the tendency to become

alert to deprivation only after its presumed consequences have begun to appear, there is undoubtedly another reason for the tendency to want to support the presumed presence of deprivation with proof of effect. Conceptually we are always troubled by false negatives—in this case by the appearance of some children who appear to develop reasonably well in an environment judged to be depriving in terms of a crucial component—children who grow big and strong on an inadequate diet, who grow up bright and alert after a history of having been blue and almost lifeless for five minutes following birth, who develop high achievement motivation in a sociocultural context characterized by apathy and defeat. An immediate and possibly valid explanation likely to be offered is that the crucial variable may not hit all children with the same impact; i.e., some children in a family get more food than others, or perhaps the anoxic baby had oxygen reserves that could not be measured, or perhaps the last child had a special relationship with a powerful nonfamily member. Thus it could be asserted that it is safer to infer deprivation only when one sees evidence that it has hit its target. This author regards such concern for cushioning the concept as unnecessary. During the middle ages it is doubtful that the occurrence of a plague was questioned just because half the population managed to live. The fact that deprivation defined in terms of a complex set of elements of experience needed for development exists but occasionally misses its target does not require proof of effect for presence of influence to be inferred. Such a requirement runs the risk of purporting to study the effects of an independent variable (deprivation) on a dependent variable (development) by getting information about the magnitude of the independent variable from the measure of the dependent variable. Developmental misses are informative about the range of human adaptability; they do not require any more conceptual elasticizing for psychosocial factors than for any other type of presumed developmental influence. As we learn to identify more of "the elements of . . . experience essential for development," to determine whether they are critical only in the presence or absence of other variables or only if the phenomenological field and the objective field are isomorphic, it will become easier to refine the definition of deprivation and thus engage in anterospective studies of development in which psychosocial deprivation might occur.

EVOLUTION OF PRESENT KNOWLEDGE IN THE FIELD

With respect to the effects of psychosocial deprivation on the human infant, there has unfortunately been more speculation than investigation, or perhaps less speculation than unwarranted inference. Research with this age group is extremely difficult to conduct, not only because of the above described tangles inherent in the deprivation concept but also because of a shortage of assessment techniques suited to the young child and of qualified persons to apply them. Nor has there ever been a readily available series of large numbers of potential research subjects—at least not readily available to persons interested in this area. The well-child clinic has been the only major resource, and by and large it has not been utilized for such studies. And, as now constituted in most communities, it would produce a biased sample.

Much of the early work done in the area owes its impetus to the reports of Spitz (1945, 1946), who launched what might be called the "maternal deprivation" decade. His report that infants who were abruptly separated from their mothers often went into a state of depression and showed a sharp decline in cognitive functioning seemed to catalyze worldwide interest in the subject. Implicit in this work was the importance of the emotional relationship existing between mother and infant. The publication of Bowlby's monograph (1952), summarizing the existing world literature on the subject while still concentrating on the *maternal* component of the deprivation, made concern with the psychosocial environment during infancy official and instigated very salutary international changes in institutional practices. Historians can always recognize precursors to an idea whose time has come, and Stone (1954) pointed out that curiosity about the consequences of what is here being called psychosocial deprivation is very old indeed. In fact, just prior to the time Spitz published his first report, Ribble (1943) had been stressing the importance of the mother for the healthy development of the infant. However, she appeared to be placing greater emphasis on the physical stimulation provided by the mother and thereby missed her chance to parent a trend.

It did not take long until disclaimers appeared, occasionally caustic and polemic (e.g., Pinneau, 1951, 1955), but more often simply suggesting that proponents of the maternal deprivation concept might be overstating things in their insinuation that negative consequences were inevitable and irreversible. As the exciting animal work of the mid-fifties and early sixties came to be known, perhaps especially the work of Harlow and his associates (1958, 1961), the adjective in "maternal deprivation" began to be downgraded and more attention paid to the noun. Casler, for example, published a monograph (1961) in which he almost superciliously ridiculed the notion that the "maternal" part of the concept was important for anything other than the sensory stimulation supplied thereby.

The coup de grace to the indiscriminate espousal of the concept of maternal deprivation was supplied not by polemics but by careful analyses of empirical studies (see especially Yarrow, 1961, 1964; and Ainsworth, 1962) which challenged the notions of inevitability and irreversibility of effect and which pointed out some of the common design flaws inherent in most of the available studies. From these analyses, from other empirical work appearing at the time, and from new social concerns which suddenly galvanized in the early sixties, the concept of maternal deprivation as an independent variable was broadened to take in the entire psycho-social-cultural domain. Again, as is customarily the pattern in the early stages of evolution of an idea, there was a tendency to indict an entire package rather than look immediately for those aspects which were most crucial. Thus Riessman's book (1962) launched a new term—cultural deprivation—and the types of studies which followed seemed almost unconcerned with anything as specific and personal as a young child's relationship with his mother. The suspected irritants were much more social and cosmic! At the same time, developmental concerns (the dependent variable side of the paradigm) seemed to shift from socioemotional to cognitive. The publication of *Intelligence and Experience* by Hunt (1961), organizing a wealth of evidence relating to the effects of experience on intelligence, and by implication, of deprivation of crucial components of experience, seemed to help shift interest from any narrow selection of influences to an examination of a full array of experiential parameters.

In the brief history here traced, it was interesting to note how quickly the infant got lost. Not the importance of infancy, by any means, just the infant. In fact, he seemed to disappear between Spitz and Bowlby! For while Spitz's work had dealt with infants whom he had observed both prior to and after separation from the mother, most of the studies found by Bowlby and referred to in his volume were retrospective and involved later reports of persons who had been separated from their mothers during infancy. Bowlby, Ainsworth, and Rosenbluth (1956) later carried out a follow-up study using children who had been separated from their mothers during infancy, but the assessments were carried out during the middle-childhood period. And yet most of the available literature on maternal deprivation seemed to suggest that the critical period for producing maximum separation effects was during infancy.

In another vein, studies which began to appear in the early sixties contrasting the developmental picture of children who were culturally deprived (to use the term then fashionable) and non-deprived groups tended to show that by the time the children reached public school age they already functioned at a lower level than their non-deprived peers. This could only be interpreted as indicating that the depressing effect of the environment had already been at work during the early years of life, even though the research groups had not studied their subjects during that period.

Field Studies of Early Deprivation

Some of the early leads regarding psychosocial deprivation during infancy came from studies concerned with effects of different child-rearing practices, with information occasionally offering misleads rather than heuristic clues. In an early study of child-rearing practices in different ethnic and social class groups, Davis and Havighurst (1946) suggested that the early family environment of the lower-class child was perhaps more comfortable, in terms of parental practices, than that of the middle-class child. Lower-class parents reported themselves, in interviews, to be more indulgent in terms of early feeding practices and to be less concerned with early toilet training than did middle-class parents. Also they were interpreted as being more willing to grant independence as their children grew older. Class differences were more striking than race differences. Williams and Scott (1953), using only Negro families, found essentially the same pattern of class differences.

Less than a decade later, however, data from the study of Maccoby and Gibbs (1954) suggested just the reverse pattern. That is, maternal interviews with parents of five-year-olds brought forth the information that, during infancy as well as at the time of the interviews, the middle-class parents were more lenient and permissive than the lower-class parents. A number of independent researches subsequently carried out tended, in general, to support the findings of the Maccoby and Gibbs study or else to find no appreciable differences between social class groups (see Caldwell, 1964). Bronfenbrenner (1958) suggested that the tenor of the postwar period was in favor of permissiveness and that middle-class parents, with their greater susceptibility to opinions of the "experts," had probably assimilated the recommendations more rapidly than lower-class parents. At any rate, certainly no data have emerged since the early fifties to suggest that in any significant way the child from what might be considered deprived social circumstances has any particular psychological advantage in his early family environment.

Most of these studies used as contrast groups samples that perhaps did not differ very drastically along a hypothetical continuum from deprived to non-deprived. For example, in the Maccoby and Gibbs (1954) study, the groups might be described as upper-lower versus lower-middle. In more recent years, however, careful studies of groups that could be characterized as truly deprived have been carried out, most notable of which are perhaps Wortis et al. (1963), Pavenstedt (1965), and Malone (1966). In the Wortis et al. study, observations were carried out during infancy making this perhaps the most relevant study for the present discussion. They found that what might have been called permissiveness in another decade appeared to be more a lack

of concern. Weaning and toilet training, rather than being carried out slowly and in line with the child's indications of maturity, were handled inconsistently and in the manner that caused the least trouble for the mother. These mothers were extremely intolerant of any expressions of aggression from the children but were relatively unconcerned about manners, noise, and cleanliness in general. Also the mothers themselves were depressed and withdrawn and in general pessimistic about life. Independently assayed, i.e., not judged on the basis of development of the children, psychosocial deprivation was a demonstrable reality. Here it should be mentioned parenthetically that all the children in this study had been born prematurely, thus compounding biological insult with psychosocial deprivation. The children involved in this study, now in the middle childhood years, are currently being followed to learn about their school achievement and general social and emotional adjustment (Wortis, personal communication).

Caldwell and Richmond (1967) have reported on a small sample of low-income mothers whose maternal behavior was observed and rated sequentially and whose children were examined at the same points in time. These data offer leads regarding the relation between certain discrete maternal behaviors that would be considered depriving and the development of the children during the infancy period. The results showed that, on a number of scales purporting to measure some aspect of affiliative (emotionally supportive) maternal behavior, mothers who were rated lowest on these scales had children with lower IQ's at 12,

18, and 24 months of age. Similar associations were found for a series of scales measuring different facets of achievement motivation in the mothers. In general, at 12 months of age, the correlations between affiliative and achievement-oriented maternal behavior and development tended to be low and positive, with both the number of coefficients attaining statistical significance and their magnitude increasing as the children approached two years of age.

With the intensified interest in cognitive development in the sixties has come a renewed interest in instrument development for the early infancy period. This interest, coupled with concern for psychosocially deprived children, has led to a number of new studies examining early differences between infants being reared in suspect environments and those being reared in environments labeled by fiat as adequate (i.e., middle-class homes). Two recent studies have produced somewhat contradictory results. Wachs (1967) found social class differences as early as 12 months on an ordinal scale developed by Uzgiris and Hunt (1964) which measures attainment of the concept of object permanence. On the other hand, Golden and Birns (1968) were unable to demonstrate social-class differences in test scores of Negro infants during the first two years of life on either a standard test of infant development (the Cattell) or an experimental procedure developed to measure more subtle aspects of cognitive functioning. They did, however, report that the children from lower social class groups were more difficult to test, with one-fourth of the children from welfare families requiring more than one session to complete the testing. This finding

whether due to motivational factors or to difficulty in adjusting to the interpersonal components of the test, somewhat weakened the authors' conclusions of no social-class differences in performance.

A most interesting and important study by Decarie (1965), although carried out in quite a different context, has yielded important data relating to the effects of psychosocial deprivation during infancy. She was concerned with determining whether Piaget's concept of "object permanence" bore a relation to the psychoanalytic concept of "object relations", developing an experimental procedure to measure the former and adapting certain items from the Griffiths Scale of Mental Development (1953) to measure the latter. For her population she used 30 home-reared infants, 30 in adoptive homes, and 30 residing in an institution. Her results showed clearly the damaging effects of the psychosocial deprivation inherent in the institutional atmosphere, as on both the measures of object permanence and object relations the institutional infants (examined repeatedly up to 22 months of age) lagged behind the other two groups, showed deviant as well as delayed developmental profiles, and were far more variable than the other two groups. Significantly, the children in adoptive homes, all of whom had undergone at least one separation and relocation, generally occupied an intermediate position between the institution and home-reared infant.

The important question of what happens developmentally during the period between roughly the end of the first year and age three, at which time at least a few children come under research scrutiny, remains a research problem of top priority. Early studies (again often done outside the deprivation model but offering data relevant to inferences in this area) tended to show no *major* differences between infants presumed to be non-deprived and a group that might be considered deprived of one or more developmental supports. For example, Knobloch and Pasamanick (1953) showed that Negro infants were slightly accelerated in motor development during the first year of life and certainly showed no major deficit in functioning during this period. Yet data coming from various compensatory education programs (see Hodges & Spicker, 1967) dealing with deprived and non-deprived preschool children, have *consistently* shown a deficit in functioning levels in the deprived groups during the preschool or kindergarten period. Deutsch has suggested (1965) that, rather than diminishing when the children reach the age of formal public education, the discrepancy increases with age.

All the available studies are consistent in their implications. During the first year of life infants from deprived and non-deprived homes appear to develop at about the same rate; we tend to lose track of them from roughly one to three years of age; when found again at age three the deficit is striking (and depressingly resistant to sustained change). Such findings suggest that the optimal time for trying to reverse the deprivation is during the two year hiatus when subjects are seldom visible to research scrutiny. The programs described by Caldwell and Richmond (1968), Robinson (1968), and Gordon (1967) have been designed to try to develop intervention strategies appropriate for this crucial period.

Undoubtedly the most significant re-cent addition to information in this area is that provided by Bayley (1965). With carefully trained examiners giving the revised Bayley Scales of Mental and Motor Development to 1,409 infants from a representative sample of the total American population, she has established performance curves for relevant subgroups of infants between one and fifteen months of age. There were *no* significant differences on the mental scales as a function of social class, sex, race, or parental education up to 15 months of age. However, on the motor scales Negro infants tended to score higher than whites, with the differences significant at most evaluation points up to 12 months of age but not thereafter. The drop that occurs for the children from lower social class backgrounds thus can be pinpointed as occurring somewhere between 15 months and three years of age. Similar data had been reported earlier by Hindley (1960) for a small group of British children within the age range of six to eighteen months.

Experimental Studies Relevant to the Deprivation Model

With human subjects, one cannot point to a truly experimental study that involves deprivation. The only pattern ethically open to the investigator is to try to reverse deprivation—i.e., to enrich—and examine the effects. The earliest important study of this nature was that of Skeels and Dye (1939), the project that became the "sleeper" of its time. Briefly, these authors transferred 13 young children who were showing retarded development in an orphanage to an institution for the mentally retarded. In this new environment, hardly one likely to be thought of as enriching, the infants were cared for by adolescent and young adult mentally retarded girls. Instead of being part of the crowd of infants having to share the scanty amount of adult attention available in the orphanage, the children were suddenly cynosures in a population probably starved for small, dependent creatures in need of love and attention. The story has the happiest of endings. Most of the children, after receiving even this distorted brand of enrichment, soon became adoptable and, when found and studied some 30 years later (Skeels, 1966), were found to have been able to maintain themselves in the community and to have produced offspring that functioned within the normal range. At the time of this writing, this is the *only* enrichment study known to this author which has had such an extended follow-up.

Early on the heels of the first speculations about maternal deprivation (at a time when no one would have said anything good about the Skeels and Dye work), Rheingold (1956) carried out an important study aimed at determining whether the amelioration, if not the removal, of psychosocial deprivation would produce favorable developmental consequences. She served as a sort of congregate mother for two sequential groups of four infants residing in an institution and selected eight matched subjects as controls. After two months of her special mothering of them, the infants were examined on certain eye-hand tests selected from the Cattell Infant Test and on certain aspects of social development. The experimentally mothered infants were found on retest to be more socially responsive, not only to their special caretaker but to other people on the ward as well, and to be slightly though nonsignificantly advanced in postural and motor behavior.

Rheingold and Bayley (1959) re-examined these infants when they were approximately two years old. At this time they could detect no differences between the two groups of babies, either in terms of social behavior or performance on a developmental examination. The authors concluded that, while the early enrichment was enough to produce concurrent changes, it could not sustain them for a prolonged period. To this author, however, the investigators seemed too conservative in their conclusion, as the enriched babies were found on the follow-up to vocalize more than the control babies. The relationship between early vocalizations and later language is far from understood, but in view of the unyielding consistency with which deprived children are shown to function less adequately in the language area, any type of social experience which is associated with an increase in vocalization is worthy of further study.

There are a few additional experimental studies which might be cited as relevant, but most of them have involved what this author would consider "artificial" enrichment or else have involved such brief follow-up as to make inferences based on them much too hazardous. For example, Casler (1965) has investigated the effects of kinesthetic stimulation on institutional infants prior to adoption; Dennis and Sayegh (1965) tried accelerating fine motor performance in only a two-week experimental period; Ourth and Brown (1961) had mothers provide extra stimulation for their infants during the neonatal period and compared frequency of crying in this group and a routine ward control group; White and Held (1966) reported the consequences for institutional infants of extra handling, motility, and enriched visual surroundings. While all such studies are important, they do not give us the kind of hard data needed to understand the effects of "real life" deprivation, or the removal of it, on sustained development. The current enrichment projects involving infant subjects (Gordon, 1967; Caldwell & Richmond, 1968; Painter, 1968; Schaefer, 1968) will in time provide some much needed information about the long-term effects of enrichment upon the cognitive and socio-emotional development of infants. . . .

References

Ainsworth, M. *Reversible and irreversible effects of maternal deprivation on intellectual development.* Child Welfare League of America, 1962, pp. 42-62.

Bayley,N. Comparisons of mental and motor test scores for age 1-15 months by sex, birth order, race, geographical location, and education of parents. *Child Develpm.*, 1965, **36**, 379-411.

Bowlby, J. *Maternal care and mental health.* Geneva, Switzerland: World Health Organization, 1952.

Bowlby, J., Ainsworth, M., Boston, M., & Rosenbluth, D. The effects of mother-child separation: a follow-up study. *Brit. J. med. Psychol.*, 1956, **29**, 211-247.

Bronfenbrenner, U. Socialization and social class through time and space. In E. E. Maccoby, T. M. Newcomb, & E. Hartley (Eds.), *Readings in social psychology*. New York: Holt, Rinehart & Winston, 1958, pp. 400-425.

Caldwell, B. M. The effects of infant care. In M. L. Hoffman & L. W. Hoffman (Eds.), *Review of child development research*, Vol. I. New York: Russell Sage, 1964, pp. 4-87.

Caldwell, B. M. & Richmond, J. B. Social class level and stimulation potential of the home. In J. Hellmuth (Ed.), *Exceptional infant*, Vol. I, 1967, pp. 455-466.

Caldwell B. M. & Richmond, J. B. The Children's Center in Syracuse, New York. In L. L. Dittman (Ed.), *Early child care: the new perspectives*. New York: Atherton Press, 1968, pp. 326-358.

Casler, L. Maternal deprivation: a critical review of the literature. *Soc. Res. Child Develpm. Monogr.*, 1965, **71** (Whole No. 2), 64 pp.

Casler, L. The effects of extra tactile stimulation on a group of institutionalized infants. *Genet. Psychol. Monogr.*, 1965, **71** (Whole

No. 1), 137-175.

Davis A. & Havighurst, R. J. Social class and color differences in child-rearing. *Amer. Sociol. Rev.*, 1946, **11**, 698-710.

Decarie, T. G. *Intelligence and effectivity in early childhood*. New York: International Univer. Press, 1965.

Dennis, W. & Sayegh, Y. The effect of supplementary experiences upon the behavioral development of infants in institutions. *Child Develpm.*, 1965, **36**, 81-90.

Deutsch, M. The role of social class in language development and cognition. *Amer. J. Orthopsychiat.*, 1965, **35**, 78-88.

Golden, M. & Birns, B. Social class and cognitive development in infancy. *Merrill-Palmer Quart.*, 1968, **14**, 139-149.

Gordon, I. J. Home stimulation for disadvantaged infants. Unpublished manuscript, 1967.

Griffin, G. A. & Harlow, H. F. Effects of three months of total social deprivation on social adjustment and learning in the Rhesus monkey. *Child Develpm.*, 1966, **37**, 533-547.

Griffiths, R. *The abilities of babies*. New York: McGraw-Hill, 1954

Harlow, H. F. The nature of love. *Amer. Psychologist*, 1958, **13**, 673-685.

Harlow, H. F. & Harlow, M.K. A study of animal affection. *Natural History*, Dec., 1961, 48-55.

Hodges, W. L. & Spicker, H. H. The effects of preschool experiences on culturally deprived children. In W. W. Hartup & Nancy L. Smothergill, *op. cit.*, pp. 262-289.

Hunt, J. McV. *Intelligence and experience*. New York: Ronald Press, 1961.

Knobloch, E. & Pasamanick, B. Further observations on the behavior development of Negro children. *J. genet. Psychol.*, 1953, **83**, 137-157.

Maccoby, E. & Gibbs, P. K. Methods of child-rearing in two social classes. In W. E. Martin & Celia B. Tendler (Eds.), *Readings in child development*, New York: Harcourt, Brace, 1954, pp.380-396.

Malone, C. A. Safety first: comments on the influence of external danger in the lives of children of disorganized families. *Amer. J. Orthopsychiat.*, 1966, **36**, 3-12.

Painter, G. *Infant education*. San Rafael, Cal.: Dimensions Publishing Co., 1968.

Pavenstedt, E. A comparison of the child-rearing environment of upper-lower and very low-lower class families. *Amer. J. Orthopsychiat.*, 1965, **35**, 89-98.

Pinneau, S. R. A critique on the articles by Margaret Ribble, *Child Develpm.*, 1951, **21**, 203-228.

Pinneau, S. R. The infantile disorders of hospitalism and anaclitic depression. *Psychol. Bull.*, 1955, **52**, 429-452.

Rheingold, H. L. The modification of social responsiveness in institutional babies. *Soc. Res. Child Develpm. Monogr.*, 1956, **21** (Whole No. 63, No. 2).

Rheingold, H. & Bayley, N. The later effects of an experimental modification of mothering. *Child Develpm.*, 1959, **30**, 363-372.

Ribble, M. A. *The rights of infants.* New York: Columbia Univer. Press, 1943.

Richarson, S. A. Psychosocial and cultural deprivation in psychobiological development: psychosocial aspects. In *Deprivation in psychobiological development.* Pan American Health Organization, Scientific Publication No. 134, 1966.

Riessman, F. *The culturally deprived child.* New York: Harper & Row, 1962.

Robinson, H. B. The Frank Porter Graham Child Development Center. In L. L. Dittman (Ed.), *Early child care: the new perspectives.* New York: Atherton Press, 1968, pp. 302-312.

Schaefer, E. S. & Furfey P. Intellectual stimulation of culturally deprived infants. Unpublished Progress Report, 1968.

Skeels, H. M. Adult status of children with contrasting early life experiences. *Soc. Res. Child Develpm. Monogr.*, *1966*, **31**, (Whole No. 3), pp. 1-65.

Skeels, H. M. & Dye, H. B. A study of the effects of differential stimulation on mentally retarded children. *Pro. Amer. Ass. ment. Defic.*, *1939*, **44**, 114-136.

Spitz, R. A. Hospitalism: an inquiry into the genesis of psychiatric conditions in early childhood. In O. Fenichel, et al. (Eds.), *Psychoanalytic studies of the child*, Vol. 1. New York: International Univer. Press, 1945, 53-74.

Spitz, R. A. Hospitalism: a follow-up report. In O. Fenichel, et al., *op. cit.*, Vol. 2, 1946, pp. 113-117.

Stone, L. J. A critique of studies of infant isolation. *Child Develpm.*, 1954, **25**, 9-20.

Uzgiris, I. C. & Hunt, J. McV. A scale of infant psychological development. Unpublished manuscript 1964.

Wachs, T. D. Cognitive development in infants of different age levels and from different environmental backgrounds. Unpublished manuscript, 1967.

Weisberg, P. Social and nonsocial conditioning of infant vocalizations. *Child Develpm.*, 1963, **34**, 377-388.

White, B. L. & Held, R. Plasticity of sensorimotor development in the human infant. In I. F. Rosenblith & W. Allinsmith (Eds.), *The causes of behavior*, Vol. 2. Boston: Allyn and Bacon, 1966, pp. 60-70.

Williams, J. R. & Scott, R. B. Growth of Negro Infants: IV. Motor development and its relationship to child-rearing practices in two groups of Negro infants. *Child Develpm.*, 1953, **24**, 103-121.

Wortis, H., et al. Child-reading practices in a low socioeconomic group. *Pediatrics*, 1963, **32**, 298-307.

Yarrow, L. J. Maternal deprivation: toward an empirical and conceptual reevaluation. *Psychol. Bull.*, 1961, **58**, 459-490.

Yarrow, L. J. Separation from parents during early childhood. In M. L. Hoffman & L. W. Hoffman (Eds.), *Review of child development research*, Vol. 1. New York: Russell Sage, 1964. pp. 89-130.

BERNARD RIMLAND

The Syndrome of Early Infantile Autism*

In 1943 Leo Kanner, then director of the Child Psychiatry Clinic at Johns Hopkins Hospital and author of the definitive textbook in child psychiatry, published his first description of a rare and remarkable behavior disorder in children. His paper, titled *Autistic Disturbances of Affective Contact*, was based on the striking similarities he had perceived in the case histories and behavior of eleven children brought to the clinic over a period of years. A year later he followed his initial detailed report with a brief paper in which he named the new syndrome "early infantile autism." Kanner

applied this title because the children had been unusual "from the beginning of life," and because their aloof, withdrawn, "autistic" personalities caused them always to appear to be living in a private, inaccessible dream-world; isolated, seemingly by choice, from contact with others. (See Bruch [1959] for an interesting glimpse into Kanner's clinic at the time the diagnosis was formulated.) . . .

COURSE AND SYMPTOMS OF THE DISEASE

Because of its rarity, little is known about the conditions under which infantile autism occurs. By far the largest group of cases has been that reported by Kanner

*From Chapter 1 of B. Rimland, *Infantile Autism*, 1964. Reprinted by permission of the author and Appleton-Century-Crofts.

and his colleagues at the Johns Hopkins Hospital clinic. Much of the available information comes from the reports of Kanner's first 100 cases (Kanner, 1954a; Kanner and Lesser, 1958). The present writer's survey of the available literature supports the data provided on the first 100 cases.

Infantile autism occurs primarily in first-born males. The sex ratio is about three or four boys to one girl (Kanner, 1954a; Keeler, 1957; Anthony 1958). Eighty of the first 100 cases were boys, twenty were girls. Fifteen of the 100 had no siblings, forty-three were first-born, twenty-three second-, thirteen third-, and six were fourth- or fifth-born.

Pregnancy and Birth. Complications of pregnancy are reported to be no more common than usual in births producing autistic children (Kanner, 1954a; Kanner & Lesser, 1958). Keeler (1957), however, reports that many of the mothers of his cases (number not specified) had experienced bleeding in the first trimester of pregnancy; and that others had a history of miscarriage and stillbirths. One of the ten cases seen by van Krevelen (1963) had a history of maternal bleeding in the first trimester, and another was afflicted with rubella in the fifth month.

Twelve of Kanner's first 100 cases had been born prematurely. (The base rate for prematurity among whites in the United States is about seven per cent.) Keeler also notes an elevated incidence of prematurity in autistic children, and observes that for most a lack of movement was reported before birth.

The First Two Years. The child is usually exceptionally healthy and attractive, quite often precocious and alert in appearance. Very little that is unusual is noticed in the first months, except perhaps that feeding may be a problem. Some autistic infants are reported to have been apathetic and unresponsive in the first few months, while others have been given to implacable crying. Typically, it is not until about the fourth month that even a person experienced with babies may first notice anything unusual. The first awareness of any problem is often the observation that the child fails to make the usual anticipatory movements prior to being picked up. He also fails to make the usual adjustments of his body to adapt to the person carrying or holding him. Head-banging is common, both in the crib and while being held; the latter behavior causing considerable discomfort and chargrin to the adult holding him. Case histories of very young autistic infants have been supplied by Plenter (1955), Lazure (1959), Eveloff (1960) and Lewis and Van Ferney (1960).

Between the fourth and eighteenth months several disturbing symptoms will have begun to appear. These include prolonged rocking and head-banging in the crib, apathy and disinterest in the surroundings, unusual fear of strangers, obsessive interest in certain toys or mechanical appliances, highly repetitive and ritualistic play, insistence on being left alone and that the physical environment remain unchanged, and very unusual language behavior. Speech, of a very unusual sort, may have started early. Because speech is of special importance in early infantile autism, it will be discussed separately below, in conjunction with separate discussions of other behaviors of special interest.

By the time the child is eighteen months to two years old the parents will have become quite concerned, especially if another child has been born which acquaints them with the much different normal pattern of development. One of the most disturbing of the symptoms is what has been called "autistic aloneness." The child may sit for hours staring into space, motionless, as if deep in thought. The autistic child looks highly intelligent and always appears to be mentally occupied during these periods of self-imposed isolation. Sometimes a fleeting, pensive smile will cross his face. The child's attention cannot be attracted by calling his name or speaking. No sign of attention is given.

Even more disturbing is the child's utter lack of interest in people. Most autistic children act is if other people did not exist (e.g., Chapman, 1957; G. Arnold, 1960; Loomis, 1960), but a few appear to have an active aversion to others (e.g., Plenter, 1955). Coupled with the disinterest in persons is frequently an active interest in inanimate objects.

Specific Problems and Behaviors. Professional help is often sought after the child has reached the second birthday. Not only has the child's development become of concern, he has become exceedingly difficult to live with.

Toilet training is ordinarily difficult to establish, though sometimes it can take place early. It is not uncommon for toilet training to start early, then be completely absent for several more years.

Feeding problems are almost the rule. Some children have ravenous appetites; others eat very little. Almost all have odd eating habits and preferences, however. Some children will take only milk. An autistic girl reported by Rattner and Chapman (1959) subsisted entirely on milk for her first six years. Others will never touch milk. One child went for several days without taking liquid until it was discovered he would drink only from a transparent container. Witmer's case would *not* drink from a transparent container, nor would he drink water. Other children have been reported utterly to refuse to drink liquids which were not a certain precise temperature. Absolute refusal to use the hands is also sometimes reported, which means spoon feeding. Creak (1952) reports an autistic child who loved chocolate, but would eat it only if cut into squares; round chocolate was not acceptable. Certain autistic children are exceedingly neat and clean in their habits, becoming upset at untidiness. One such child began eating with a spoon with perfect precision at nine months. One girl would eat only sandwiches she made herself, starting at three years of age.

Repetitive behavior and fetishlike preoccupation with mechanical objects such as vacuum cleaners, stoves, light switches, and faucets is a common symptom. Any attempt to divert the child from this type of pursuit is met by an intense and violent temper tantrum: "... when he was lifted from the couch, put upon his feet and made to walk, he burst into a paroxysm of rage. His eyes became bloodshot; even his gums bled" (Witmer, 1920, p. 100). One child who loved to bounce in a "jump chair" wore out three reinforced canvas chair covers and broke the chair's steel frame before he became too large for it at age three. At age four this child became obsessed with water heaters and would look at one for hours, find pictures of water heaters in magazines, and carried one (actually a defunct flashlight cell) with him at all imes, for several months.

Insistence on the preservation of sameness in the environment is one of the two most widely accepted diagnostic signs, the self-imposed isolatiom—"autistic aloneness"—being the other. Cases of extreme emotional reactions—violent tantrums or disconsolate weeping—are also commonly reported where no semblance of an external cause can be identified. In other cases a cause, often merely an accidental displacement of a piece of furniture, can be found (Kanner, 1951). A refusal to change clothes, especially pajamas, is often reported. Bedtime rituals are often long and elaborate.

Suspected Deafness. Once the parents have begun to realize that their child's behavior is not normal, they almost without exception consider the possiblity of a hearing defect. The parents have often been unable to attract the child's attention by speaking to him or calling his name. The child is often described as being "in a shell," or as "so completely wrapped up in his thoughts you can't talk to him." An unusual noise will sometimes evoke a reaction, while at other times even loud and unexpected noises will have little or no effect (e.g., Goldfarb, 1956; Anthony, 1958).

The child's ability to repeat tunes and to say some of the things he has heard belie the possibility of a hearing defect.

Differentiation from Mental Deficiency

Mental retardation is the next suspicion, but again certain contradictory observations are regarded as not supporting this classification.

Appearance. Kanner emphasizes that the children simply do not look retarded. He has frequently commented on the "strikingly intelligent physiognomies" of autistic children. Others have also noted that the dull, vacuous expression of the feeble-minded is not found in autistic children. Instead they appear always to be concentrating on something else. (Pictures of autistic children appear in the papers by van Krevelen [1952], Bakwin [1954], and Plenter [1955]. Oppenheim's case [1961], probably autistic; and the twins described by Kallman et al., [1940], possibly autistic, are also pictured.).

Early Skilled Performance. Another reason for not considering the children feeble-minded is the outstanding performance they display in many areas ordinarily considered closed to the mentally deficient. Early use of language, and early, or at least undelayed, motor ability is common. Some cases have been reported of delayed walking with sudden onset of good performance, as though the child could have walked earlier but did not. Other signs which help differentiate the autistic child from most of the mentally deficient are their excellent memories and musical abilities. The spatial abilities of autistic children are also frequently reported as being unusually good.

Memory. Coupled with the elaborate insistence that no change take place in the environment is, in many autistic children, a truly phenomenal ability to recall the exact state of the environment. Kanner describes autistic children who screamed in implacable fury when one block was experimentally turned in a jumble of blocks and toys left on the floor during the child's absence. Each block had to be returned to its exact place before the child was satisfied.

Once blocks, beads or sticks have been put together by the child in a certain way, they are often regrouped later in exactly the same way, even though there was no definite design. The child's memory is phenomenal in this respect. After the lapse of several days, a multitude of blocks could be rearranged, most astonishingly ... in precisely the same unorganized pattern, with the same color of each block turned up, with each picture or letter on the upper surface of each block facing the same direction as before. The absence of a block, or the presence of a supernumerary block was noticed immediately ... (1951, p.24).

Extraordinary memory seems almost the rule with these children. One child was able to reproduce an aria in a foreign language after hearing it only once. Another child was able to repeat the questions and answers of a Protestant catechism and name the Presidents at the age of two. According to Kanner and Lesser:

The astounding vocabularies of the speaking children, the unusual memory for events, the excellent rote memory for poems and names, and the precise recollection of complex patterns and sequences, be-speak good intelligence in the sense in which this word is commonly used. Binet or similar testing can rarely be carried out because of limited accessbility, but the children perform surprisingly well on the Seguin Formboard (1958, p. 720).

Spatial Ability. The high level of spa-
tial ability of the child with infantile autism is reflected in his good performance on the Seguin Formboard, and on jig-saw puzzle tasks. It has been noted by a number of writers that autistic children can sometimes assemble jig-saw puzzles as readily when the picture is facing down as when it is visible. May (1958) reported his young twin autistic sons to have engineered a ladder by pulling bureau drawers part way out to use as steps. The child's previously mentioned insistence upon sameness in the physical environment, including the arrangement of randomly scattered blocks and toys, indicates an unusual degree of spatial memory.

Motor and Manual Ability. Most writers regard the children as quite agile and graceful. Benda (1952, p. 501) states, "The autistic child is, surprisingly often, a beautiful child who impresses by his fast and graceful movements...." Waal's case (1955) at 2½ was as agile and dexterous as a four-year-old. The boy described by Loomis (1960) walked at eight months and was "really a high trapeze artist" at two. Rank and MacNaughton's case (1950) was "quick and Light" with excellent motor coordination.

While refusal to use the hands is a fairly common symptom, the children who do use their hands are remarkably dexterous. Creak (1952) and Rothenberg (1960) have each reported cases of three-year-old autistic boys who could balance a dime on edge. Other children have been very skilled at spinning and twirling jar lids and other round objects from an early age. One boy who was obsessed with balls was able, at fourteen months, to catch a ball with either one or both hands. He could throw a ball across a room to within an inch or two of the hand of the adult playing catch with him. A twelve-year-old boy, taught the numbers on a typewriter, could type the series to 1000 without error at an estimated 60 word-per-minute rate.

The child will sometimes induce an adult to act as his "hands" by leading the adult to the object desired or task to be performed and somehow communicating his wants (Rank and MacNaughton, 1950; Sherwin, 1953).

Musical Ability. Astonishing musical ability is found in these children quite frequently, in some cases accompanied by perfect pitch (Kanner, 1943; etc.; Scheerer, Rothmann & Goldstein, 1945; van Krevelen, 1952a; Sherwin, 1953; Keeler, 1958; May, 1958; see also Michaux et al., 1957). One of Kanner's earliest autistic cases, a member of the small minority who may be considered recovered, has become a composer in adulthood. A case reported recently by Anatasi and Levee (1960) as an adult *idiot savant* musician of great skill, gives every indication of having been an autistic child.

One of the three musically talented children reported by Sherwin (1953) was able to reproduce the notes of the scale "with extraordinary accuracy" at 14 months. At 17 months he spontaneously repeated in full an aria from Don Giovanni. Between his 18th and 36th months this child sang "a remarkable repertoire of music, consisting of symphonies by Mozart and Haydn, songs by Schubert and Brahms, selections from Carmen, a Tschiakowsky Piano Concerto and diversified well-known songs" (p. 825).

Special Abilities in Autism and Idiot Savant Performance

Despite these signs of what Kanner calls "good cognitive potential," many autistic children do eventually become institutionalized as mentally deficient. It may be these children who figure in the stories which are heard now and then of psychologists being startled to find above-average test performance on certain tasks by mute and uncomprehending individuals who have shown no other sign of intelligence (Eisenberg, 1956; Kanner, 1949).

The possibility that some *idiot savants* may actually be cases of early infantile autism has been discussed by several writers, e.g., Scheerer, Rothmann & Goldstein (1954), Rosen (1953), Sarason and Gladwin (1958), van Krevelen (1958), Goldstein (1959), and Anastasi and Levee (1960). The occurrence of isolated areas of extraordinary mental ability in individuals showing a low order of ability in all other areas does fit the picture of autism very well. *Idiot savants* have been noted with special abilities in calculation, music, art, mechanics, mental calendar manipulation, and memory. This list applies very well to the autistic child's often-reported special interests and abilities. It is interesting to conjecture that the silent, unreachable autistic child may indeed be "lost in thought"—reliving an experience in minute detail, hearing music long since forgotten or perhaps never heard by others, or playing games with numbers or objects manipulatable only in the recesses of his brain.

Of exceptional interest are the not uncommon reports of autistic children who become quite adept at reading aloud, but who have no apparent comprehension of what the words mean (Kanner, 1952; Benda, 1960). Other autistic children write but do not speak (G. Arnold, 1960; Oppenheim, 1961). The Oppenheim case, unlike that of Arnold, appeared to be able to communicate through writing. It is possible that Oppenheim's is not a true case of infantile autism.

The Speech of Autistic Children. One of the most striking characteristics of early infantile autism is the baffling use of language by those autistic children who use speech. Because of his early speech, the child is frequently regarded as being highly precocious or "a budding genius." Words are learned with great rapidity in these cases, and sometimes the child is suddenly found to be using complete sentences at one year of age, even before the component words have been used singly. The language acquisition of one autistic child between his seventh and twelfth month was reported as follows: "mamma," "dada," "bear," "spoon," "hungry," "done," "ball," and "C'mon, let's play ball."

The speech is generally of a peculiar noncommunicative kind, however, and is ordinarily produced in an empty high-pitched, parrotlike monotone. Whispering is very common, little or no expression is used, and, as it generally turns out, the speech is elicited only as specific responses to certain stimuli, and not as a means of communication. Naming of objects, for example, is common, but asking or answering questions is rare or absent. Desires are communicated by leading an adult by the hand to what is wanted. "No!" is often indicated by emphatically grunting and waving the arms.

Kanner has written extensively on the speech of autistic children (1946 and 1951, especially). He describes their speech in terms of "affirmation by repetition," "pronominal reversal," "extreme literalness," "metaphorical usage," "part-whole confusion," and "delayed echolalia."

The words *I* and *yes* are strikingly and consistently absent, often until the sixth or seventh year in the speaking autistic children. The boy discussed by Nesnidalova and Fiala (1961) did not use *I* until his tenth year. *You* is used for *I* (*pronominal reversal*), and *Yes* is indicated by repeating the question (*affirmation by repetition*). "Do you want some milk?" thus means, "I want some milk," or, "Yes, I want some milk."

An example of *literalness* is found in the boy whose father tried to encourage the use of the word *Yes* by carrying the child on his shoulders as a reward for saying it. The boy learned to say *Yes*, but only as an indication that he wanted his father to carry him, the original literal meaning to the child. To another boy *down* meant *the floor*. One boy was upset because his father spoke of hanging a picture *on* the wall, rather than *near* the wall.

Metaphorical use of language is illustrated by the boy who used the sentence, "Don't throw the dog off the balcony" to indicate "No." His mother had long before used this sentence to dissuade him from dropping a toy dog from a railroad station balcony. Another boy, at seven, used "He knocked me down" to indicate a blow, pat, spank, or bump, deliberate or accidental, caused by an adult or child of either sex.

Part-whole confusion is seen in the expression, "Do you want some catsup, Honey?" as used by one three-year-old autistic boy to ask for dinner, his favorite food being meat seasoned with catsup. The expression "bumped-the-head" was used by this child as a request for comforting, even though it was a hand or knee he offered for therapy.

Delayed echolalia is another common speech symptom. The child will simply repeat a phrase or sentence, often out of context and with no apparent purpose. "It's all dark outside," was reiterated constantly by an autistic child, day and might. Many autistic children repeat radio and television commercials endlessly (G. Arnold, 1960; van Krevelen, 1960). Arnold's case also reproduced video commercials in writing, with perfect spelling, at four.

Only about half of all autistic children are able to use speech. The others are either completely mute or may speak only once or twice in a lifetime. Kanner describes two cases in which a sentence has been used at ages four or five, in situations perceived by the children as emergencies. but never before or after (1949). One "emergency" was a prune skin stuck in the child's mouth, which elicited a panicky "Take it out!" Rothenberg's laconic case "Jonny" had said only "I can't" and "Go to hell" by age ten. The case reported by Anastasi and Levee did not learn to speak until age five. . . .

References

Anastasi, Anne, & Levee, R. F. Intellectual defect and musical talent: A case report. *Amer. J. ment. Defic.*, 1960, **64**, 695-703.

Anthony, J. An experimental approach to the psychopathology of childhood: Autism. *Brit. J. med. Psychol.*, 1958, **31** 211-225.

Arnold, G. E. Writing instead of speaking. *Curr. Probl. phoniat. Logoped.*, 1960, **1**, 155-162. of the word Yes

Bakwin, H. Early infantile autism. *J. Pediat.*, 1954, **45** 492-497.

Benda, C. E. *Developmental disorders of mentation and cerebral palsies*. New York: Grune & Stratton, Inc., 1952.

Benda, C. E. Childhood schizophrenia, autism and Heller's disease. In P. W. Bowman & H. V. Mautner (Eds.), *Mental retardation: Proceedings of the first international conference on mental retardation*. New York: Grune & Stratton, Inc., 1960. Pp. 469-492.

Bruch, Hilde. Studies in schizophrenia: The various developments in the approach to childhood schizophrenia. Psychotherapy with schizophrenics. *Acta psychiat. neurol. Scand., Kbh.*, 1959, **34** (Suppl. 130)

Chapman, A. H. Early infantile autism in identical twins: Report of a case. *AMA, Arch. Neurol. Psychiat.*, 1957, **78**, 621-623.

Creak, Mildred, & Ini, Sylvia. Families of psychotic children. *J. child Psychol. Psychiat.*, 1960, **1**, 156-175.

Eveloff, H. H. The autistic child. *AMA Arch. gen. Psychiat.,* 1960, **3**, 66-81.

Goldfarb, W. Receptor preferences in schizophrenic children. *AMA arch.. Neurol. Psychiat.,* 1956, **76,** 643-652.

Goldstein, K. Abnormal mental conditions in infancy. *J. nerv. ment. Dis.,* 1959, **128,** 538-557.

Kallman, F. J., Barrera, S. E., & Metzger, H. Association of hereditary microphthalmia with mental deficiency. *Amer. J. ment. Defic.,* 1940, **45,** 25-36.

Kanner, L. Autistic disturbances of affective contact. *Nerv. Child,* 1943, **2,** 217-250.

Kanner, L. Early infantile antism. *J. Pediat.,* 1944, **25,** 211-217.

Kanner, L. Irrelevant and metaphorical language in early infantile autism. *Amer. J. Psychiat.,* 1946, **103,** 242-246.

Kanner, L. Problems of nosology and psychodynamics of early infantile autism. *Amer. J. Orthopsychiat.,* 1949, **19,** 416-426.

Kanner, L. The conception of wholes and parts in early infantile autism. *Amer. J. Psychiat.,* 1951, **108,** 23-26.

Kanner, L. Emotional interference with intellectual functioning. *Amer. J. ment. Defic.,* 1952, **56,** 701-707.

Kanner, L. To what extent is early infantile autism determined by constitutional inadequacies? *Proc. Ass. Res. Nerv. & Ment. Dis.,* 1954, **33,** 378-385.

Kanner, L., & Lesser, L. I. Early infantile autism. *Pediat. Clinics N. Amer.,* 1958, **5,** 711-730.

Keeler, W. R. In discussion. In *Psychiat. Reports of Amer. Psychiat. Ass.,* 1957, No. 7, 66-88.

Lazure, D. Un cas de reaction psychotique chez un enfant d'age prescholaire. (A case of psychotic reaction in a child of pre-school age.) *Canad. Psychiat. Ass. J.,* 1959, **4,** 19-22.

Lewis, S. R., & Van Ferney, S. Early recognition of infantile autism. *J. Pediat.,* 1960, **56,** 510-512.

Loomis, E. A., Jr. Autistic and symbiotic syndromes in children. *Monogr. Soc. Res. Child Developm.,* 1960, **25,** 39-48.

May, J. M. *A physician looks at psychiatry.* New York: John Day, 1958.

Michaux, L., Duche, D., Stein, C., & Mlle Lepage. Dispositions musicales precoces chez une fille de cing ans grande arrieree de l'intelligence et de la parole. (Avec presentation de malade.) *Rev. Neuropsychiat. Infant,* 1957, **5**:5-6, 284-291.

Oppenheim, Rosalind C. They said our child was hopeless. *Sat. Eve. Post,* June 17, 1961, **23,** 56-58.

Plentner, A. M. De ziekte van Kanner. *Ned. Tijdschr. Geneesk,* 1955, **99,** 428-434.

Rank, Beata, & MacNaughton, Dorothy. A clinical contribution to early ego development. *Psychoanal. Stud. Child.* New York: Internat. Univ. Press, 1950, 5, 53-65.

Rattner, L. J., & Chapman, A. H. Dangers of indiscriminate hospitalization of the preschool child. *J. Dentistry Child,* 1959, **26,** 55-62.

Rosen, V. H. On mathematical "Illumination" and the mathematical thought process. *Psychoanal. Stud. Child.* New York: Internat. Univ. Press, 1953, **8,** 127-154.

Rothenberg, Mira. The rebirth of Jonny. *Harper's Magazine,* 1960, **220** (Feb.) 57-66.

Sarason, S. B., & Gladwin, T. Psychological and cultural problems in mental subnormality: A review of research. *Genet. Psychol. Monogr.,* 1958, **57,** 3-289.

Scheerer, M., Rothmann, Eva, & Goldstein, K. A. A case of "Idiot Savant": An experimental study of personality organization. *Psychol. Monogr.,* 1945, **58** (Whole No. 269).

Sherwin, A. C. Reactions to music of autistic (schizophrenic) children. *Amer. J. Psychiat.,* 1953, **109,** 823-831.

van Krevelen, D. A. Early infantile autism. Z. f. Kinderpsychiat., 1952, **19,** 91-97.

van Krevelen, D. A. Personal Communication Jan. 7, 1963.

Waal, N. A special technique of psychotherapy with an autistic child. In G. Caplan (Ed.), *Emotional problems of early childhood.* New York: Basic Books, 1955. Pp. 431-449.

Witmer, L. Orthogenic cases, XIV-Don: A curable case of arrested development due to a fear psychosis the result of shock in a three year old infant. *Psychol. Clinic,* 1919-22, **13,** 97-111.

6
THE PRESCHOOL YEARS:
PHYSICAL AND MENTAL GROWTH

During the preschool years (roughly ages two to five) children are still small enough to be cute and lovable as they were as infants but are also mature enough to begin demonstrating significant capacities for independence and originality. Hence early childhood is an attractive age, and the way in which many preschoolers combine cherubic innocence with a devilish propensity for trouble has a very special appeal to adults. In recent years, however, attention to the charm and innocence of the preschool child has been replaced with an emphasis on his intellectual potential. Prominent examples of this trend include television's Sesame Street, government programs like Head Start that are aimed at helping culturally disadvantaged children prepare for school, and the interest of many well-to-do parents in sending their children to Montessori schools in the hopes that they too will get a head start.

In the first of the following two articles, David Wechsler, author of the widely used Wechsler Scales for assessing intelligence, explains what IQ means and how it is measured. He covers in his discussion such important considerations as the constancy of IQ scores and the extent to which they are affected by cultural and socioeconomic factors. Although Wechler's article was written in response to criticisms of IQ testing in the schools, and hence focuses on school-age children, the current emphasis on the intellectual potential of preschool children makes it highly relevant to this chapter. The second article, by Elkind, goes on to describe more broadly the cognitive abilities of young children and the implications of these emerging abilities for preschool educational programs.

DAVID WECHSLER

The I. Q. Is an Intelligent Test*

It is now two years since the New York City school system eliminated the I.Q. from pupil's records. Banned under the pressure of groups that claimed the I.Q. was unfair to the culturally deprived, it has been replaced by achievement tests. Meanwhile a great deal of effort is being put into developing new, nonverbal scales to measure schoolchildren's abilities while eliminating the troublesome factor of language.

Neither of these substitutes is an adequate replacement for the I.Q. In my opinion, the ban was misdirected in the first place and we should restore the I.Q. to its former position as a diagnostic tool as soon as possible. The substitutes simply do not test enough of the abilities that go to make up individual intelligence.

To understand what I.Q. tests do, and why they are valuable, we must first be clear about what intelligence is. This is a surprisingly thorny issue. Too much depends upon how one defines intelligence. In this respect psychologists are in no better agreement than the lay public. Divergency of view stems largely from differences in emphasis on the particular abilities thought to be central to the definition one envisages. Thus, an educator may define intelligence primarily as

the ability to learn, a biologist in terms of ability to adapt, a psychologist as the ability to reason abstractly and the practical layman as just common sense.

One difficulty is similar to what a physicist encounters when asked to state what he means by energy, or a biologist what he means by life. The fact is that energy and life are not tangible entities; you cannot touch them or see them under a microscope even though you are able to describe them. We known them by their effects or properties.

The same is true of general intelligence. For example, we must assume that there is something common to learning to count, avoiding danger and playing chess which makes it possible for us to say that they are evidence of intelligent behavior, as against learning to walk, being accident prone and playing bingo, which seemingly have little if anything to do with it.

Intelligence, operationally defined, is the aggregate capacity of the individual to act purposefully, to think rationally and to deal effectively with his environment. Although it is not a mere sum of intellectual abilities, the only way we can evaluate it quantitatively is by the measurement of various aspects of these abilities.

Any test is primarily a device for eliciting and evaluating a fragment of behavior. An intelligence test is one by which an examiner seeks to appraise this bit of behavior insofar as it may be called

*From the *New York Times Magazine*, June 26, 1966. Reprinted by permission of the author and the New York Times Company.

intelligent. Various abilities can be used for this purpose because manifestations of ability are the means by which a subject can communicate and demonstrate his competences. To this end it is not so much the particular ability that is tested which is important, as the degree to which it correlates with posited criteria. A test is considered a good measure of intelligence if it correlates, for example, with learning ability, ability to comprehend, evidence of capacity to adjust and so on. If it does so to a satisfactory degree it is said to be valid. But, even when a test has been established as valid, there still remains a question: For what class of subjects is it valid? The answer will depend in a large measure upon the population on which the test was standardized—for example, middle-class white children, Southern Negro children or recently arrived Puerto Ricans.

Thus I.Q. tests are attacked on the ground that they are over weighted with items depending on verbal ability and academic information. Individuals with limited educational backgrounds are obviously penalized, and non-English-speaking subjects are admittedly incapable of taking the tests at all. This is an important stricture and test makers, contrary to some opinion, are fully aware of it. One way of "solving" the problem would be to provide separate normal or average scores for different populations, but apart from the practical difficulty of obtaining such norms, there is always the stricture that they bypass rather than meet the central issue. A compromise approach is practiced in some school systems, where intelligence tests continue to be used—under the more acceptable name of "aptitude tests."

Almost from the start, psychologists have sought to cope with the problem of literacy and language disability by devising nonverbal tests of intelligence. Thus, soon after the Binet tests were introduced more than a half-century ago, two American psychologists, Pintner and Paterson, developed the Non-Language Individual Performance Scale for non-English-speaking subjects. Similarly, when the Army ALPHA (the main verbal test of World War I) was devised for the military services, a companion nonverbal test (the Army Beta) was prepared along with it.

The Pintner-Paterson scale required the subject to give evidence of his capacities by filling in appropriate missing parts on familiar pictures, putting together form boards, learning to associate signs with symbols, etc. The Army Beta consisted of such tasks as following mazes, reproducing picture designs, counting cubes, etc.—with directions presented to the subject by gesture or mime.

Many similar tests—the so-called "culture-free' or "culture-fair" tests—have followed. The most recent one reported is the Johns Hopkins Perceptual Test devised by Dr. Leon Rosenberg and associates at the Johns Hopkins School of Medicine. This test was initially developed for children who did not speak or who were handicapped by certain functional or organic disorders; it has also been recommended as a more effective intelligence test for the very young and for culturally deprived children.

The Johns Hopkins Perceptual Test consists of a series of designs from which a child is asked to choose appropriate patterns to match others shown to him.

Its primary merit is that it eliminates the factor of language. It is also claimed to be less dependent than verbal tests upon acquired skill, which, of course, depend to some extent upon a child's environmental experience. But this test, like other performance tests, does not measure a sufficient number of the abilities that go to make up the total picture of intelligent behavior.

Contrary to claims, the results of performance tests have been generally disappointing. The findings indicate that while they may be useful in certain situations, and for certain diagnostic groups, they prove quite unsatisfactory as alternates for verbal scales. They correlate poorly with verbal aptitudes and are poor prognosticators of over-all learning ability as well as school achievement. Above all, they have turned out to be neither culture-free nor culture-fair.

Culture-free tests fail to attain their end because, in the first place, the items usually employed are themselves subject to particular environmental experiences. A circle in one place may be associated with the sun, in another with a copper coin, in still another with a wheel. In some places a dog is a pet, in others a detested animal. Pictures, in the long run, are just symbols and these may be as difficult to understand and recognize as words; they have to be interpreted, as anyone who has attempted to learn sign language knows. Putting together blocks may be a challenge or a threat, working fast a sign of carelessness or an incentive to competition. Nonverbal, even more than verbal tests, need to be related to particular environments and, from a practical point of view, are both limited in range and difficult to contrive.

Finally, many performance items when increased in difficulty tend to become measures of special abilities rather than having any significant correlation with over-all measures of intelligence. Thus, while tests of visual motor coordination may be useful items on intelligence tests for young children they are no longer effective at later ages. Copying a diamond is a good test at the 7-year level, but whether a child of 12 can produce a complicated design has little to do with his general intelligence and represents at most a special ability.

The effect of culture on test performance is a subject that demands serious concern, but here one deals with the problem of what one understands by the word "culture." In the United States there is a strong trend among contemporary writers to identify the term with socio-economic levels. This is in contrast to the historic and broader meaning of the term, which covers all human as well as environmental influences that serve to characterize the intellectual and moral status of a civilization.

Not all the poor are culturally deprived. Although standards may differ widely, "culturally different" does not mean "culturally deprived." The Jews and Italians who lived on the Lower East Side had their culture, and so have the Negroes in the slums of Harlem. They differ widely in respect to almost any variable one might employ, and culture is no exception. What this implies is that "culture" no more than color of skin should be a basis for assessing individuals.

The comments relating to the question of cultural impact apply with equal force to the problem of racial and national differences. One may start with the hypothesis that such differences exist and not necessarily be overwhelmed by their importance. This, in the writer's opinion, is a reasonable position.

The opinion is based on studies done in the field and, in particular, on data from World War I and World War II United States Armed Forces testing programs. The data from World War I included not only tables for the over-all draft population but for a great many subgroupings. Among these were separate test-score summaries according to national origin of the draftees, and a particularly detailed one comparing Negroes and whites. As might have been expected, differences between groups compared were found, and as might also have been expected invidious comparisons were immediately made and exploited. Particularly emphasized were the lower scores made by Negroes as compared with those made by white soldiers. Neglected, on the other hand, were the differences found between occupational levels and the more general ones between urban and rural populations.

It was not too difficult to correct the erroneous inferences made by the racists. But, in disposing of the racial claims, some authors went much beyond what the data warranted. Eventually, statements were made that other test findings revealed no significant differences between any national or racial groups — a fact which is equally questionable, and in any event still needs to be demonstrated. In the author's opinion, national and racial differences do exist — probably of both genetic and environmental orgins, in varying degree. But the fact is that these differences are not large or relevant in the individual case.

We now come to the biggest bugaboo of intelligence testing — the I.Q. itself. The scientific literature on it is as large as its assailants are numerous. It has been attacked by educators, parents, writers of popular articles and politicians. During the Korean War it was investigated by Congress. Now that we are once more having trouble with draft quotas, the I.Q. will most likely be investigated again. It is doubtful whether the I.Q. can be brought into good grace at this time, but perhaps much of the fire sparked by the I.Q. can be quenched by an objective explanation of what it really is.

An I.Q. is just a measure of relative brightness. It merely asserts that, compared with persons of his own age group, an individual has attained a certain rank on a particular intelligence test. For example, a 10-year-old takes the Stanford-Binet test and attains a certain score, which happens to be that for the statistically average 8-year-old. We then divide the child's mental age (8) by his chronological age (10) and obtain a quotient, which we multiply by 100 simply to remove the inconvenience of decimal points. The result is called the Intelligence Quotient (or I.Q.) — in this case, 80. This particular figure tells us that, as compared with others in his age group, the child has performed below normal (which would be 100).

When this procedure of comparative grading is applied to a geography or bookkeeping test — when a teacher apportions class grades on a bell curve or sliding scale — nobody gets excited. But when it is used with a mental test the reaction is quite different.

Opposition is generally focused not on the way that I.Q.'s are computed, but, more pointedly, on the way they are interpreted and utilized. One interpretation that has caused understandable concern is the notion that a person is "born with" an I.Q. which remains immutable. This is an allegation proclaimed by those who are opposed to the I.Q. rather than a view maintained by psychologists. What is asserted by psychologists, and supported by test-retest findings, is that I.Q.'s once accurately established are not likely to vary to any considerable degree. This does not mean that an I.Q. never changes, or that the conditions under which it was obtained may not have affected its validity.

The so-called constancy of the I.Q. is relative, but compared with other commonly used indexes, it is surprisingly stable. It is much more stable, for instance, than an individual's electrocardiogram or his basal metabolism level, which are accepted without question.

There are always exceptional cases which cannot be overlooked or by passed. But one does not throw out the baby with the bath water. When for any reason a subject's I.Q. is suspect, the sensible thing to do is to have him retested. I.Q.'s, unlike the laws of the Medes and the Persians, are not irrevocable, but they should be respected.

While retest studies show that I.Q.'s are relatively stable, they also reveal that in individual cases large changes may occur — as much as 20 points or more. Thus, conceivably, an individual could move from the "dull normal" group to "average," or vice versa.

Much depends upon the age at which the original test was administered and the interval between testings. In general, I.Q.'s obtained before the age of 4 or 5

are more likely to show discrepancies between test and retest; those in the middle years least. Discrepancies are also likely to be larger as the intervals between retests increase. All this evidence points to reasons for not making a definite intelligence classification on the basis of a single test, and more especially on one administered at an early age. This precaution is necessary not because the tests are unreliable but because rates of mental maturity are often factors that have to be taken into account. Such variations tend not only to penalize slow developers but also to overrate early bloomers.

Various skills are required for effective test performance at different age levels. The fact that they are not present at a particular age level does not indicate that a child who lacks them is necessarily stunted. It may only be that these skills have not as yet emerged. Early training has a bearing on test readiness, but it is not true that if a child has not had this training at one age, he will not develop the skills required at a later age. On the other hand, deliberately teaching a child skills in order to have him "pass" an intelligence test, as now seems to be the vogue, is not the answer to acquiring a high I.Q.

An important conclusion to be drawn from the above is that more, rather than less, testing is needed. Unfortunately, when this is suggested, one encounters the objection that extended testing programs in public schools would be too costly. The expensiveness of school testing has been greatly exaggerated, especially when considered in relation to the over-all cost of keeping a child in school (an average of $600 to $700 per child per year in most parts of the country).

Particularly neglected is the individual intelligence examination, which at present is administered in most public schools only to "problem cases." In the author's opinion, an individual intelligence examination ought to be given to all children as they enter school. Most private schools require such an examination, and there is good reason why the public schools should also provide it.

Allowing $50 per examination administered once over a four-year period, the cost would be a minuscule addition to the school's budget. In return, a systematic individual examination could serve as a means of evaluating a child's assets and liabilities before he was subjected to the hazards of arbitrary placement. Finally, it must be borne in mind that intelligence tests are intended as a means not merely for detecting the intellectually retarded, but also for discovering the intellectually gifted.

In discussions of the merits and limitations of intelligence tests, one important aspect, frequently overlooked, is their basic aim. This objective is most effectively summed up in the late Professor Irving Lorge's definition of what intelligence tests aim to measure — namely, "the ability to learn and to solve the tasks required by a particular environment."

This definition implies a multiple approach to the concept of intelligence and intelligence testing. In the latter process, one is of necessity engaged in evaluating an individual's particular abilities. Of course, in doing so, one obtains information regarding a subject's liabilities and handicaps. This information is both useful and important, but is really only an incidental aspect of what one wishes to discover from an intelligence test.

When it is asserted that intelligence tests are unfair to the disadvantaged and minorities, one must be mindful of the fact that they are simply recording the unfairness of life. They show also, for example, that our mental abilities, whoever we may be, decline with advancing age — (of course, this decline is in many cases counterbalanced by increased experience.)

Intelligence tests were not devised for the handicapped alone but for everybody. What then can be the reason for believing they may not be suitable for the major segments of our population — or for prohibiting their administration to the majority of children in a school system? The current New York City I.Q. ban is a case in point, and especially discouraging when one sees what is being used instead.

The tests that have been substituted are a series of achievement tests — in particular, reading tests. Of all the possible choices, one can hardly imagine a worse alternative. For of all areas in which the disadvantaged child is handicapped, reading heads the list. The main difference between an intelligence (or aptitude) test and an achievement test is that the former is less tied to curriculum content. If it is true that a low score on an intelligence test presents a misleading picture of a pupil's learning capacity, how much more unfair would be an even lower score on an achievement test. It is possible that the I.Q. was banned in New York because those who supported the ban wished primarily to combat what they believed to be a widespread view that the I.Q. is "somehow a fixed, static and genetic measure of learning ability." One may wonder, however, whether political pressures may not have played some role in the decision - and one may hope that the ban will soon be retracted.

The I.Q. has had a long life and will probably withstand the latest assaults on it. The most discouraging thing about them is not that they are without merit, but that they are directed against the wrong target. It is true that the results of intelligence tests, and of others, too, are unfair to the disadvantaged, deprived and various minority groups but it is not the I.Q. that has made them so. The culprits are poor housing, broken homes, a lack of basic opportunities, etc., etc. If the various pressure groups succeed in eliminating these problems, the I.Q.'s of the disadvantaged will take care of themselves.

DAVID ELKIND

Early Childhood Education: A Piagetian Perspective*

The current national interest in early childhood education coincides with an equally strong national interest in the work of the Swiss psychologist, Jean Piaget. The simultaneous rise of interest in early childhood and in Piaget is, of course, not accidental. Piaget's research and theories regarding the development of intelligence in children have revolutionized our conception of how the mind grows and functions. It is not surprising, therefore, that those concerned with improving the quality of early childhood education should look to the work of Piaget for direction and guidance.

What, then, does the research and theory of Jean Piaget suggest with regard to the education of young children? Unfortunately, there is more than one answer to that question, and Piaget has been quoted as being in support of both the academic (structured learning) approach to childhood education as well as the traditional, informal, or what I call "growth," preschool programs. The situation is not helped by the fact that Piaget speaks to educational issues in a general and broad sense and has not given "nuts and bolts" descriptions as to how the practice of education is to be carried out.

Accordingly, the implications for preschool education outlined here are of

*From *The Principal*, 1971, 51, 48-55. Reprinted by permission of the author and the National Association of Elementary School Principals.

necessity my responsibility, and reflect my understanding of what Piaget's work suggests as to the education of young children. As a starting point for introducing those implications, I want to briefly summarize those aspects of Piaget's work that deal with: (a) the thinking; (b) the language; and (c) the egocentrism of the young child. I am emphasizing the psychological characteristics of the child as a basis for drawing educational implications for preschool programs because Piaget, like Rosseau, believes that sound pedagogy at any age level must begin with a thorough understanding of the child. A consideration of the thought and language of young children is, from this point of view, prerequisite to any informed program of early childhood education.

THINKING IN YOUNG CHILDREN

In the broadest sense, thinking is a kind of miniaturized and internalized action system that allows us to do in our heads what before we had to do with our hands. Thinking allows us to anticipate the consequences of our actions and to exert a higher order regulation over them. It doesn't always work, of course, and many of us have had the experience of reaching for and taking that extra piece of cake or cigarette even while we were thinking of the consequences of our actions. In general, however, thinking is a higher order system which can, but may not always, regulate our real actions.

In young children this internalization process has not gone too far and they must experiment in fact with problems that older children and adults can deal

with in their heads. On a simple pencil maze, for example, a young child will put his pencil to the paper as soon as the task is described to him and will proceed along whichever path he happens to see first. Older children, however, spend a few moments looking at the maze as a whole and do not put pencil to paper until they have found the correct path by mental experimentation. The young child acts where the older child thinks (but again, not always, as teachers and parents know full well. Unfortunately the capacity to think does not insure the tendency to use the capacity.)

Perhaps the most significant educational fact about the young child's relatively undeveloped thinking is that he cannot abide by *rules*. What are rules if they are not internalized guides and regulations of action? When older children play a game with rules, such as checkers, each child must wait his turn, must move only one of his set of checkers, and must move it one space at a time and in a particular direction. In such a game there are no external cues as to how the child is to behave, for all that exists is a board with squares and some checkers. Guidance and direction for playing checkers has to come not from without, but from within the child's head. Young children (unless they are exceptionally bright) do not play games with rules such as checkers, because they have not yet fully internalized the action system which is thought.

The young child's difficulty with rules can be illustrated both with research and anecdotal data. In one series of studies, Piaget and his colleagues studied the classificatory behavior of young children. When young children are presented with a series of figures that are alike or the same in certain ways (squares, circles, rectangles, colored red, green and blue), and they are asked to put them together in certain ways, they do characteristic things. Many children just put the objects together in "heaps" because they happen to see them together. Other children build "shapes" of a house or boat and group the pieces that way. Other children create "chains" and arrange a series such as the following: blue square, red square, red circle, green circle, green rectangle, and so on. What is missing in all of these solutions is clearly some overriding and guiding rule which would allow the child to group the materials in a systematic way.

Anecdotal evidence points in the same direction. When young children play "games" with adults, they have one overriding concern, which is to win. They pay little or no attention to rules and make up their own to suit their ends. But they pay no more attention to the rules which they have fabricated than they do to the rules that have been imposed by adults. We see the same phenomena in the social domain, where young children have to be reminded constantly to say "please" and "thank you." The use of such expressions again presupposes the awareness of general rules such as "when you ask for something say please." Young children routinely fail to say "please" or "thank you" because they have never internalized the rules for using these expressions and not because of stupidity or stubbornness.

The fact of the young child's inability to operate according to internalized rules has considerable educational significance. All formal education involves the inculca-

tion of rules. Writing, spelling, reading, arithmetic and art all involve basic rules which are the foundation of the subject. From this point of view, therefore, it makes very little sense to begin formal instruction in tool subjects until one has some assurance that the children can internalize and operate according to rules. Prior to that stage, education has of necessity to be *preparatory* in the sense of familiarizing the child with the contents of the rules he will be learning later. Learning numbers and letters, drawing, practice in classifying and ordering materials, all acquaint the child with the materials and contents that he will order according to rules at some later time. In short, one clear implication of Piaget's research regarding young children's thinking is that formal instruction be delayed until about the age of six or seven, when most children can learn rules.

LANGUAGE IN YOUNG CHILDREN

The most generally accepted view of the relation between thought and language is that they constitute separate but related systems. One evidence for this separateness is the fact that the basic language system, including rules of syntax and grammar, is acquired by the age of four or five, long before the child can master rules within the plane of thought or action. Moreover, the language system seems to be more or less completely formed by the age of eight or nine, whereas the growth of mental processes does not cease until adolescence. Likewise, the fact that someone can speak gibberish or think in images shows that there can be language without thought and thought without language.

The separateness of the thought and language systems and the fact that they mature at different rates have special consequences for young children. At the preschool level, the discrepancy between the relative immaturity of the thought and of the language systems is most pronounced. For, whereas the child of four or five has a fairly large vocabulary (5000 words or so), and has the basis of grammar and syntax, he has not as yet internalized his thinking, and his concepts of basic relations such as "left" and "right" are quite immature. Because of this discrepancy in level of maturity, there is little coordination between thought and language in young children.

This lack of coordination is easy to observe. Piaget noted, for example, that young children frequently engage in parallel play. Such play occurs when two children talk _at_ rather than _to_ one another. One child might describe his trip to the lake while the other will talk about his uncle George. Neither child is really talking to the other, and their language is more a kind of accompaniment to their activities that it is a true effort of communication. That is why young children frequently talk or sing to themselves (as Pooh bear does) when they are playing alone. In such situations, the young child's language does not guide his activities or vice versa; they merely keep one another company, so to speak.

The educational implications of this lack of fit between the thought and language in the young child were recognized intuitively by gifted educators, such as Maria Montessori, long before the factual evidence regarding the lack of coordination was available. Montessori argued persuasively that the child ought to learn motor and perceptual discriminations _before_ he was given words with which to label the discriminations. Implicit in this de-emphasis on giving language to preschool children was the recognition that young children know many more words than they can understand, and that the education of young children should emphasize coordinating thought and language and should not take this coordination for granted.

Piaget's research, and Montessori's educational experiences, were of course directed towards children who had been exposed, from birth, to the language of the dominant culture in which they were reared. In America today, however, we have many young children who come to school or preschool from a different language environment. Many Mexican-American youngsters in the Southwest come to school having heard only Spanish in their lives, and many Indian children know only their native language. Many black youngsters come to school speaking a different English dialect, no less diverse or complex but different, than that spoken by their teachers in school.

The educational problems of such children are doubly complex because one has not only to help the child coordinate language with experience, but also, in effect, to teach him a second language. Several alternative strategies are available in this situation. One of these is to ignore the second language and to teach children in their native language. This is being done in many preschool programs in the Southwest for Mexican-American and for Indian youth. A similar program might be instituted for black children. In many cases, however, attempts have been made to solve both problems at the same time by teaching black children to coordinate their experience with words from the dominant dialect. The success of these programs on a long-range basis has yet to be determined.

EGOCENTRISM IN THE YOUNG CHILD

One of the most significant of Piaget's discoveries is that the young child is unable in many situations to distinguish his own from other peoples' point of view. It is this inability of the young child to put himself in another person's position and to see things from that perspective which Piaget calls *egocentrism*. The phenomenon of egocentrism is easy to demonstrate. If you ask a preschool child to show his right and his left hands, he may be able to do this. But, if you stand opposite him, and ask him to show you your right hand and left hand, he will say that your right is on the same side as his.

A young child's egocentrism can be demonstrated in other ways as well. In one study, pairs of children were seated on opposite sides of a table which was divided by a screen. One of the children (the speaker) had to describe a design to the child sitting opposite him (the listener) so that the listener could select the correct design from a pile in his possession. The results showed that while four-year-old subjects were able to understand the problem, they were unable to really help the listener find the correct design. They gave personal clues (such as "Mommy's hat"), which were totally useless to the listener in finding the correct design. When the speaker became the listener,

however, he could effectively use the clues he himself had devised. In general then, the egocentrism of the young child, his inability to put himself in another person's position, is a well-established phenomenon.

From an educational perspective, there is one aspect of the young child's egocentrism that is of particular significance. Basically, the young child is unable to take another child's point of view because he doesn't clearly distinguish between his feelings and thoughts and those of others. Put differently, the child believes that everybody sees the world as he does, and he therefore is not aware of the need to see it in any other way. When young children make up words, as they often do, this aspect of egocentrism is very clear. One preschooler created the word "stocks" to represent both socks and stockings, and used it without explanation as if everyone knew what he was talking about. This assumption, that there is a kind of universal awareness to which everyone is tuned in, is illustrated by the child who said, when asked whether a bad tooth hurt, "Yes, can't you feel it?" In short, the child fails to take anyone else's point of view because, in part at least, he believes that everyone sees and experiences the world as he does.

With respect to education, egocentrism means that the young child believes that he knows everything just as he thinks adults do. To be sure, children ask a great many questions. But the questions are often rhetorical and the child is ready to answer it himself if you give him the chance. Indeed perhaps the majority of children's questions are of the kind with which we are all familiar. A friend asks us where *we* are going on our vacation in hopes that we will ask the same question in return so that he can describe *his* vacation plans. Where young children ask questions they often hope we will ask them the question in return. Of course sometimes children admit that they do not know something but feel that they "forgot." Sometimes children ask questions in order to be "reminded" of information which they possess but could not retrieve.

Young children then, believe that they know everything even if they admit they have forgotten some things. Teaching children with this kind of an orientation is quite different from teaching older children who, by virtue of being able to see things from the perspective of others, can recognize how much they do not know and need to learn. But the young child does not see any necessity for acquiring new information since he believes it is already stored in his head. Formal, or direct education, involving the inculcation of facts and rules, is inappropriate for such a child because he does not accept the underlying contract in such an arrangement, namely, that he has something to learn from the teacher.

The picture of the child presented by Piagetian research, and complemented by the contribution of many other workers suggests, therefore, that any program for preschool education must start from these fundamental facts about young children: (a) they do not think or act according to rules; (b) their language is not coordinated with their thinking; (c) they believe they know or can eventually recall everything. Before we proceed to the educational implications of these facts about the psychology of young children, we need to look at some

widespread myths about the psychology of young children which have, in my opinion, led to some rather misguided preschool programs. These myths include: (a) the myth of the facile learner, (b) the myth of intellectual precocity, (c) the myth of early "stimulation," and (d) the myth of revolutionary new insights regarding young children.

(a) The Myth of the Facile Learner. One of the arguments one hears for introducing formal teaching into preschool education comes from those who say the young child is an eager learner. What they leave unsaid is the kind of learning most characteristic of young children, namely, rote learning. Young children learn stories, TV commercials, knock-knock jokes and what-have-you with the alacrity of a magpie. Such learning is, however, largely unconscious and is acquired without conscious intent. In contrast, any effort to teach preschool children content, such as people's names, which does not interest or amuse them, fails miserably. The preschool child is a facile learner, but what he learns he learns by rote and what he learns is dictated pretty much by himself. From an educational standpoint, it is facility in rule, rather than rote, learning that is crucial to successful formal instruction.

(b) The Myth of Intellectual Precocity. One of the arguments made for formal instruction in the preschool years is that intellectual growth is most rapid during these years and that the child has attained half of his intellectual powers by the age of four. The only basis for this statement is the fact that one can, from a knowledge of a child's IQ at age four, predict with 50% accuracy what his IQ will be at age 17. But the ability to predict a test score does not really tell you how much or what kind of ability a child has at a young age. Certainly intellectual growth is rapid in the early years, but can one really say that he knows half of all that he will ever know and possesses half of his total mental powers at age four? Not only does such a statement defy common sense, but is indefensible on scientific grounds because our measurement of mental abilities is far too crude for any such statement to be substantiated.

(c) **The Myth of Early Stimulation.** Because the early years of life have come to be regarded as crucial for later intellectual development, many workers have argued for the importance of stimulating young children as much as possible in order to maximize their intellectual growth. The situation here, I am afraid, is not unlike a comparable situation which occurred when psychoanalytic theory was in vogue. In the name of psychoanalysis, some parents refused to scold, correct or punish their offspring for fear it would injure their delicate psyches. Today we are in danger of the opposite extreme, wherein parents are encouraged to intellectually over-stimulate their children in hopes that this will make them intellectual giants.

The fact is, of course, that most young children, regardless of background, are probably *over-* rather than under-stimulated. Young children do not process information as readily as adults and cannot take in information in the same size "chunks" as adults do. A trip to the grocery store, the purchase of a new shirt or sweater are experiences which it takes a young child considerable time to assimilate. Moreover, at this age, when the whole world is new to the child, he often knows best what kind of stimuli and how much he needs for his mental growth. Young children many times have more fun with simple toys of their own devising (pots and pans, boxes that "store-bought" toys came in), than they do with the complicated gadgets fabricated by adults. In the educational domain, the same holds true, and if, as Montessori made clear, we properly "prepare" the environment for young children — i.e., provide them with the stimulus nutriment they need — then that is the major part of the teaching task for this age group. On the other hand, overstimulating young children because of adherence to some currently fashionable myths about how young children think and learn could be harmful.

(d) **The Myth of Revolutionary New Insights Regarding Young Children.** Perhaps the most pernicious myth of all regarding early childhood is that there have been revolutionary new breakthroughs in our knowledge about young children. In fact, however, this is just not true. All the data about the child being a facile learner, about his having "half" his intelligence by age four, about the significance of early stimulation have, for the most part been known for decades. Montessori wrote detailed accounts of the kinds of learning engaged in by young children. Thorndike, more than a half a century ago, pointed out that the three-year-old had half his adult intellectual potential. Likewise the McGraws carried out elaborate research on the effects of early training and stimulation on the growth of motor skills. What is new is not the facts, but their *interpretation*.

To claim, as some early educational

workers do, that significant "new" information about preschool children is available which supports giving them formal instruction in tool subjects, is simply not true. The facts about how children think and grow have been accumulating for centuries. Gifted and sensitive workers like Froebel, Pestalozzi, Montessori and Piaget have all interpreted this information as indicative of informal education for young children. What is new is that these facts are now interpreted as favoring formal training for young children. To call these new *interpretations* of old data new *facts* is deceptive and misleading.

EDUCATIONAL IMPLICATIONS

Implicit or explicit in the writings of Piaget are the considerations that young children cannot operate according to rules, that their language is not well coordinated with their thought and that they are egocentric. Any program of preschool education must, of necessity, start from a thorough understanding and consideration of these facts. They suggest that formal instruction, in the sense of the inculcation of rules, is inappropriate for young children. This is true both because children cannot fully appreciate rules and because, thanks to their egocentrism, they do not see the need for them. On the other hand, the relative lack of coordination between the young child's language and thinking make this a natural starting point for educational intervention. Much of traditional or *growth* preschool education, including the informal programs recently imported from England, as well as Montessori and Piaget based programs, emphasize this

language-thought coordination approach.

In the growth preschool, teachers recognize the special qualities of young children and treat them accordingly. Educational materials are concrete and action-oriented. Show-and-tell helps children coordinate their experiences with language, as well as teaching children, by listening quietly to others, to overcome their egocentrism. Projects like "making peanut butter" give children practical information in a direct way and demonstrate the fundamental rule of preschool teaching, namely, that children need to be *shown*, not told, information. Preparation for formal education is given by providing children with materials they can classify, quantify, discriminate and which help them learn the alphabet and letters. In this way the growth school responds to the child's needs to internalize rules through action, to coordinate language and experience, and to overcome his egocentrism.

Before closing this paper, I want to say something about some of the pressures which have made professionals as well as parents responsive to providing formal educational programs for young children. In the case of the professionals, I believe that we have another instance of what we have seen in so many other domains, namely, a tendency to do what we *can* do without sufficient regard for what we *should* do. Government-sponsored preschool programs made it possible for professionals to try out formal educational programs with young children. At least some of these programs, or so it seems to me, were undertaken without sufficient consideration for the human rights of the children involved.

As for parents, the pressures are complex and multiple. There are the *status* pressures to have children who read early and do well in school. Then there are the *personal* pressures which make parents want to give their children the educational advantages they never had. Finally, and most importantly, there are the *guilt* pressures suffered by mothers who feel that they should be taking care of their preschoolers instead of putting them in a preschool or day-care center. If the mother can reassure herself that her child is reaping educational benefit from the preschool, then she need not feel so guilty about wanting to go to work or to get out of the house. As women come to appreciate that the "maternal instinct" is a fable and that young children suffer no emotional trauma by spending their days in a nursery or care center, the need to rationalize sending their children to preschool for rather narrow educational purposes will diminish.

The problem with all of these pressures for academic preschool programs is that they arise out of parental rather than child needs. As the current educational system is set up, there is no reason, from the child's point of view, for him to read, write or do mathematics until first grade. It is parental need that demands that children acquire these tool skills earlier. In all probability, and there is evidence to support this probability, early training in tool skills is pretty much like early training in motor skills. Some children

can be taught to read and write earlier than six or seven years of age, but the effort involved will be considerably greater than that required if he were taught at a later age. Moreover, the results are not long-lived, and children who are taught to read early, as opposed to those who read early on their own, are no different than their peers in reading ability at the age of nine or ten.

CONCLUSION

In this paper I have tried to point out three aspects of the thinking and language of young children that have been described by Jean Piaget and the implications of these facts for the education of young children. I have also tried to describe some of the myths which are currently widespread about young children. These myths suggest a rather different kind of preschool education than that suggested by the work of Piaget and other workers familiar with young children. America is currently moving toward making preschool education available for all those parents who want it for their children. It would be a tragic mistake if the development of such programs was guided by faddish concerns and parental anxieties rather than by what we know about the emotional and intellectual needs of young children.

7
THE PRESCHOOL YEARS:
PERSONALITY AND SOCIAL DEVELOPMENT

The expressive behaviors acquired in infancy begin during the preschool years to reflect individual personalities with specific attitudes, preferences, and coping styles that will characterize a child throughout his life. There is a tremendous expansion in the numbers and types of people with whom a child comes in contact and in the nature of the interactions he has with them, and there is an equally rapid expansion in the cognitive and motor skills that he is capable of mastering. Personality development in the preschool years accordingly revolves around the formation of a child's basic capacities to deal effectively with interpersonal and achievement-related situations.

In the first of the two selections that follow, Baumrind refers to these basic capacities as *instrumental competence*, by which she means behavior that is socially responsible and independent. Baumrind elaborates the nature of instrumental competence, discusses sex differences in how competence develops, and specifies child-rearing practices that appear to facilitate the emergence of socially responsible and independent behavior in young children.

Whereas Baumrind's concept of instrumental competence touches on achievement behavior, Crandall in her review article focuses specifically on the beginnings of achievement-oriented behavior in the preschool years. She summarizes what is known about the personality characteristics, test performance, and achievement motivation of boys and girls who achieve more than their peers, and she describes the effects of early environmental stimulation and various parental actions on the achievement behavior of children both during and after the preschool years.

DIANA BAUMRIND

Socialization and Instrumental Competence in Young Children*

For the past 10 years I have been studying parent-child relations, focusing upon the effects of parental authority on the behavior of preschool children. In three separate but related studies, data on children were obtained from three months of observation in the nursery school and in a special testing situation; data on parents were obtained during two home observations, followed by an interview with each parent.

In the first study, three groups of nursery shcool children were identified in order that the childrearing practices of their parents could be contrasted. The findings of that study (Baumrind, 1967) can be summarized as follows:

1. Parents of the children who were the most self-reliant, self-controlled, explorative and content were themselves controlling and demanding; but they were also warm, rational and receptive to the child's communication. This unique combination of high control and positive encouragement of the child's autonomous and independent strivings can be called *authoritative* parental behavior.

2. Parents of children who, relative to the others, were discontent, withdrawn and distrustful, were themselves detached and controlling, and somewhat less warm than other parents. These may be called *authoritarian* parents.

3. Parents of the least self-reliant, explorative and self-controlled children were themselves noncontrolling, nondemanding, and relatively warm. These can be called *permissive* parents.

A second study, of an additional 95 nursery school children and their parents also supported the position that "authoritative control can achieve responsible conformity with group standards without loss of individual autonomy or self-assertiveness (Baumrind, 1966, p. 905)." In a third investigation (Baumrind, 1971, in press) patterns of parental authority were defined so that they would differ from each other as did the authoritarian, authoritative, and permissive combinations which emerged from the first study.

PATTERNS OF PARENTAL AUTHORITY

Each of these three authority patterns is described in detail below, followed by the subpatterns that have emerged empirically from my most recent study. The capitalized items refer to specific clusters obtained in the analysis of the parent behavior ratings.

*From *Young Children*, 1970, 26, 104-119. Reprinted by permission of the author and the Association for the Education of Young Children.

The *authoritarian* parent[1] attempts:

to shape, control and evaluate the behavior and attitudes of the child in accordance with a set standard of conduct, usually an absolute standard, theologically motivated and formulated by a higher authority. She values obedience as a virtue and favors punitive, forceful measures to curb self-will at points where the child's actions or beliefs confict with what she thinks is right conduct. She believes in inculcating such instrumental values as respect for authority, respect for work, and respect for the preservation of order and traditional structure. She does not encourage verbal give and take, believing that the child should accept her word for what is right (Baumrind, 1968, p. 261).

Two subpatterns in our newest study correspond to this description; they differ only in the degree of acceptance shown the child. One subpattern identifies families who were Authoritarian but Not Rejecting. They were high in Firm Enforcement, low in Encourages Independence and Individuality, low in Passive-Acceptance, and low in Promotes Nonconformity. The second subpattern contained familes who met all the criteria for the first subpattern except that they scored high on the cluster called Rejecting.

The *authoritative* parent, by contrast with the above, attempts:

to direct the child's activities but in a rational, issue-oriented manner. She encourages verbal give and take, and shares with the child the reasoning behind her policy. She values both expressive and instrumental attributes, both autonomous self-will and disciplined conformity. Therefore, she exerts firm control at points of parent-child divergence, but does not hem the child in with restrictions. She recognizes her own special rights as an adult, but also the child's individual interests and special ways. The authoritative parent affirms the child's present qualities, but also sets standards for future conduct. She uses reason as well as power to achieve her objectives. She does not base her decisions on group consensus or the individual child's desires; but also, does not regard herself as infallible or divinely inspired (Baumrind, 1968, p. 261).

Two subpatterns corresponded to this description, differing only in the parents' attitudes towards normative values. One subpattern contained families who were Authoritative and Conforming. Like the Aurthoritarian parents described above, these parents had high scores in Firm Enforcement and low scores in Passive-Acceptance. However, they also had high scores in Encourages Independence and Individuality. The second subpattern contained parents who met the criteria for the first subpattern, but who also scored high in Promotes Nonconformity.

The *permissive* parent attempts:

to behave in a nonpunitive, acceptant and affirmative manner towards the child's impulses, desires, and actions. She consults with him about policy decisions and gives explanations for family rules.

[1] In order to avoid confusion, when I speak of the parent I will use the pronoun "she," and when I speak of the child, I will use the pronoun "he," although, unless otherwise specified, the statement applies to both sexes equally.

She makes few demands for household responsibility and orderly behavior. She presents herself to the child as a resource for him to use as he wishes, not as an active agent responsible for shaping or altering his ongoing or future behavior. She allows the child to regulate his own activities as much as possible, avoids the exercise of control, and does not encourage him to obey externally-defined standards. She attempts to use reason but not overt power to accomplish her ends (Baumrind, 1968, p. 256).

We were able to locate three subpatterns reflecting different facets of this prototypic permissiveness. One subpattern, called Nonconforming, typified families who were nonconforming but who were not extremely lax in discipline and who did demand high performance in some areas. The second subpattern, called Permissive, contained families who were characterized by lax discipline and few demands, but who did not stress nonconformity. The third subpattern contained families who were both non-conforming and lax in their discipline and demands; hence, they are referred to as Permissive-Nonconforming.

INSTRUMENTAL COMPETENCE

Instrumental Competence refers to behavior which is socially responsible and independent. Behavior which is friendly rather than hostile to peers, cooperative rather than resistive with adults, achievement- rather than nonachievement-oriented, dominant rather than submissive, and purposive rather than aimless, is here defined as instrumentally compe-

tent. Middle-class parents clearly value instrumentally competent behavior. When such parents were asked to rank those attributes that they valued and devalued in children, the most valued ones were assertiveness, friendliness, independence and obedience, and those least valued were aggression, avoidance and dependency (Emmerich & Smoller, 1964). Note that the positively valued attributes promote successful achievement in United States society and, in fact, probably have survival value for the individual in any subculture or society.

There are people who feel that, even in the United States, those qualities which define instrumental competence are losing their survival value in favor of qualities which may be called *Expressive Competence.* The author does not agree. Proponents of competence defined in terms of expressive, rather than instrumental, attributes value feelings more than reason, good thoughts more than effective actions, "being" more than "doing" or "becoming," spontaneity more than planfulness, and relating intimately to others more than working effectively with others. At present, however, there is no evidence that emphasis on expressive competence, at the expense of instrumental competence, fits people to function effectively over the long run as members of any community. This is not to say that expressive competence is not essential for effective functioning in work as well as in love, and for both men and women. Man, like other animals, experiences and gains valid information about reality by means of both noncognitive and cognitive processes. Affectivity deepens man's knowledge of his environment; tenderness and receptivity enhance the character and effectiveness of any human being. But instrumental competence is and will continue to be an essential component of self-esteem and self-fulfillment.

One subdimension of instrumental competence, here designated *Responsible vs. Irresponsible,* pertains to the following three facets of behavior, each of which is related to the others:

(a) **Achievement-Oriented vs. Not Achievement-Oriented.** This attribute refers to the willingness to persevere when frustration is encountered, to set one's own goals high, and to meet the demands of others in a cognitive situation versus withdrawal when faced with frustration and unwillingness to comply with the teaching or testing instructions of an examiner or teacher. Among older children, achievement-orientation becomes subject to autogenic motivation and is more closely related to measures of independence than to measures of social responsibility. But in the young child, measures of cognitive motivation are highly correlated with willingness to cooperate with adults, especially for boys. Thus, in my study, resistiveness towards adults was highly negatively correlated with achievement-oriented behavior for boys, but not for girls. Other investigators (Crandall, Orleans, Preston & Rabson, 1958; Haggard, 1969) have also found that compliance with adult values and demands characterize young children who display high achievement efforts.

(b) **Friendly vs. Hostile Behavior Towards Peers.** This refers to nurturant, kind, altruistic behavior displayed toward agemates as opposed to bullying, insulting, selfish behavior.

(c) **Cooperative vs. Resistive Behavior**

Towards Adults. This refers to trustworthy, responsible, facilitative behavior as opposed to devious, impetuous obstructive actions.

A second dimension of child social behavior can be designated *Independent vs. Suggestible.* It pertains to the following three related facets of behavior:

(a) **Domineering vs. Tractable Behavior.** This attribute consists of bold, aggressive, demanding behavior as opposed to timid, nonintrusive, undemanding behavior.

(b) **Dominant vs. Submissive Behavior.** This category refers to individual initiative and leadership in contrast to suggestible, following behavior.

(c) **Purposive vs. Aimless Behavior.** This refers to confident, charismatic, self-propelled activity versus disoriented, normative, goalless behavior.

The present review is limited to a discussion of instrumental competence and associated antecedent parental practices and is most applicable to the behavior of young children rather than adolescents. Several ancillary topics will be mentioned, but not discussed in depth, including:

The relation of IQ to instrumental competence. My own work and that of others indicate that, in our present society, children with high IQs are most likely to be achievement-oriented and self-motivated. The correlations between IQ and measures of purposiveness, dominance, achievement-orientation and independence are very high even by ages three and four.

The relation of moral development and conscience to instrumental competence. This area of research, exemplified by some of the work of Aronfreed,

Kohlberg, Mussen, and Piaget, is of special importance with older age groups and will be covered tangentially when the antecedents of social responsibility are explored.

The relation of will to instrumental competence. This topic, which overlaps with the previous one, has received very little direct attention during the past 30 years. In the present review, this area is discussed to some extent along with antecedents of independence.

The antecedents of creative or scientific genius. Socialization practices which lead to competence are not the same as those associated with the development of high creativity or scientific genius. Most studies, such as those by Roe (1952) and Eiduson (1962), suggest that men of genius are frequently reared differently from other superior individuals. It has been found, for example, that as children men of genius often had little contact with their fathers, or their fathers died when they were young; they often led lonely, although cognitively enriched, existences. Such rearing cannot be recommended, however, since it is unlikely that the effects on most children, even those with superior ability, will be to produce genius or highly effective functioning.

The development of instrumental competence in disadvantaged families. The assumption cannot be made that the same factors relate to competence in disadvantaged families as in advantaged families. The effect of a single parental characteristic is altered substantially by the pattern of variables of which it is a part. Similarly, the effect of a given pattern of parental variables may be altered by the larger social context in which the family operates. The relations discussed here are most relevant for white middle-class families and may not always hold for disadvantaged families.

DEVELOPMENT OF INSTRUMENTAL INCOMPETENCE IN GIRLS

Rapid social changes are taking place in the United States which are providing equal opportunity for socially disadvantaged groups. If a socially disadvantaged group is one whose members are discouraged from fully developing their potentialities for achieving status and leadership in economic, academic and political affairs, women qualify as such a group.

There is little evidence that women are biologically inferior to men in intellectual endowment, academic potential, social responsibility or capacity for independence. Constitutional differences in certain areas may exist, but they do not directly generate sex differences in areas such as those mentioned. The only cognitive functions in which females have been shown consistently to perform less well than males are spatial relations and visualization. We really do not know to what extent the clearly inferior position women occupy in United States society today should be attributed to constitutional factors. The evidence, however, is overwhelming that socialization experiences contribute greatly to a condition of instrumental *incompetence* among women. It follows that if these conditions were altered, women could more nearly fulfill their occupational and intellectual potential. The interested reader should refer to Maccoby's excellent "Classified Summary of Research in Sex Differences" (1966, pp. 323-351).

Few women enter scientific fields and very few of these achieve eminence. According to the President's Commission on the Status of Women in 1963, the proportion of women to men obtaining advanced degrees is actually dropping. Yet there is little convincing evidence that females are constitutionally incapable of contributing significantly to science. Girls obtain better grades in elementary school than boys, and perform equally to boys on standard achievement tests, including tests of mathematical reasoning. By the high school years, however, boys score considerably higher than girls on the mathematical portion of the Scholastic Aptitude Test (Rossi, 1969). It is interesting to note that a high positive relation between IQ and later occupational levels holds for males, but does not hold for females (Terman & Oden, 1947). According to one study of physics students, girls have more scholastic aptitude and understanding of science and scientific processes than boys (Walberg, 1969). As Rossi has argued:

If we want more women to enter science, not only as teachers of science but as scientists, some quite basic changes must take place in the way girls are reared. If girls are to develop the analytic and mathematical abilities science requires, parents and teachers must encourage them in independence and self-reliance instead of pleasing feminine submission; stimulate and reward girls's efforts to satisfy their curiosity about the world as they do those of boys; encourage in girls not unthinking conformity but alert intelligence that asks why and rejects the easy answers (Rossi, 1969, p. 483).

Femininity and being female is socially devalued. Both sexes rate men as more worthwhile than women (e.g., McKee & Sherriffs, 1957). While boys of all ages show a strong preference for masculine roles, girls do not show a similar preference for feminine roles, and indeed, at certain ages, many girls as well as boys show a strong preference for masculine roles (Brown, 1958). In general, both men and women express a preference for having male children (Dinitz, Dynes, & Clarke, 1954). Masculine status is so to be preferred to feminine status that girls may adopt tomboy attributes and be admired for doing so, but boys who adopt feminine attributes are despised as sissies. Feminine identification in males (excluding feminine qualities such as tenderness, expressiveness and playfulness) is clearly related to maladjustment. But even in females, intense feminine identification may more strongly characterize maladjusted than adjusted women (Heilbrun, 1965). Concern about population control will only further accelerate the devaluation of household activities performed by women, and decrease the self-esteem of women solely engaged in such activities.

Intellectual achievement and self-assertive independent strivings in women are equated with loss of femininity by men and women alike. Women, as well as men, oppose the idea of placing women in high-status jobs (Keniston & Keniston, 1964). One researcher (Horner, 1969) thinks that women's higher test anxiety reflects the conflict between women's motivation to achieve and their motivation to fail. She feels that women and girls who are motivated to fail feel ambivalent about success because intellectual achievement is equated with loss of femininity by socializing agents and eventually by the female herself.

Generally, parents have higher achievement expectations for boys than they do for girls. Boys are more frequently expected to go to college and to have careers (Aberle & Naegele, 1952). The pressure towards responsibility, obedience and nurturance for girls, and towards achievement and independence for boys which characterizes United States society also characterizes other societies, thus further reinforcing the effect of differential expectations for boys and girls (Barry, Bacon, & Child, 1957). In the United States, girls of nursery school age are not less achievement-oriented or independent than boys. By adolescence, however, most girls are highly aware of, and concerned about, social disapproval for so-called masculine pursuits. They move toward conformity with societal expectations that, relative to males, they should be nonachievement-oriented and dependent.

Girls and women consistently show a greater need for affiliation than do boys and men. The greater nurturance toward peers and cooperation with adults shown by girls is demonstrable as early as the preschool years. In general, females are more suggestible, conforming and likely to rely on others for guidance and support. Thus, females are particularly susceptible to social influences, and these influences generally define femininity to include such attributes as social responsibility, supportiveness, submissiveness and low achievement striving.

There are complex and subtle differences in the behavior of boys and girls from birth onward, and in the treatment of boys and girls by their caretaking adults. These differential treatments are sometimes difficult to identify because, when the observer knows the sex of the parent or child, an automatic adjustment is made which tends to standardize judgments about the two sexes. By the time boys enter nursery school, they are more resistant to adult authority and aggressive with peers. Thus, a major socialization task for preschool boys consists of developing social responsibility. While preschool girls (in my investigations) are neither lacking in achievement-orientation nor in independence, the focal socialization task for them seems to consist of maintaining purposive, dominant and independent behavior. Without active intervention by socializing agents, the cultural stereotype is likely to augment girls' already well-developed sense of cooperation with authority and eventually discourage their independent strivings towards achievement and eminence. As will be noted later, there is reason to believe that the socialization practices which facilitate the development of instrumental competence in both girls and boys have the following attributes: a) they place a premium on self-assertiveness but not on anticonformity, b) they emphasize high achievement and self-control but not social conformity, c) they occur within a context of firm discipline and rationality with neither excessive restrictiveness nor overacceptance.

SOCIALIZATION PRACTICES RELATED TO RESPONSIBLE VS. IRRESPONSIBLE BEHAVIOR

The reader will recall that I have defined

Responsible vs. Irresponsible Behavior in terms of: a) Friendliness vs. Hostility Towards Peers, b) Cooperation vs. Resistance Towards Adults, and c) High vs. Low Achievement Orientation. Socialization seems to have a clearer impact upon the development of social responsibility in boys than in girls, probably because girls vary less in this particular attribute. In my own work, parents who were authoritative and relatively conforming, as compared with parents who were permissive or authoritarian, tended to have children who were more friendly, cooperative and achievement-oriented. This was especially true for boys. Nonconformity in parents was not necessarily associated with resistant and hostile behavior in children. Neither did firm control and high maturity-demands produce rebelliousness. In fact, it has generally been found that close supervision, high demands for obedience and personal neatness, and pressure upon the child to share in household responsibilities are associated with responsible behavior rather than with chronic rebelliousness. The condition most conducive to antisocial aggression, because it most effectively rewards such behavior, is probably one in which the parent is punitive and arbitrary in his demands, but inconsistent in responding to the child's disobedience.

Findings from several studies suggest that parental demands provoke rebelliousness only when the parent both restricts autonomy of action and does not use rational methods of control. For example, Pikas (1961), in a survey of 656 Swedish adolescents, showed that differences in the child's acceptance of parental authority depended upon the reason for the parental directive. Author-

ity based on rational concern for the child's welfare was accepted well by the child, but arbitrary, dominering or exploitative authority was rejected. Pikas' results are supported by Middleton and Snell (1963) who found that discipline regarded by the child as either very strict or very permissive was associated with rebellion against the parent's political views. Finally, Elder (1963), working with adolescents' reports concerning their parents, found that conformity to parental rules typified subjects who saw their parents as having ultimate control (but who gave the child leeway in making decisions) and who also provided explanations for rules.

Several generalizations and hypotheses can be drawn from this literature and from the results of my own work concerning the relations of specific parental practices to the development of social responsibility in young children. The following list is based on the assumption that it is more meaningful to talk about the effects of *patterns* of parental authority than to talk about the effects of single parental variables.

1. *The modelling of socially responsible behavior facilitates the development of social responsibility in young children, and more so if the model is seen by the child as having control over desired resources and as being concerned with the child's welfare.*

The adult who subordinates his impulses enough to conform with social regulations and is himself charitable and generous will have his example followed by the child. The adult who is self-indulgent and lacking in charity will have his example followed even if he should preach generous, cooperative behavior.

Studies by Mischel and Liebert (1966) and by Rosenhan, Frederick, and Burrowes (1968) suggest that models who behave self-indulgently produce similar behavior in children and these effects are even more extensive than direct reward for self-indulgent behavior. Further, when the adult preaches what he does not practice, the child is more likely to do what the adult practices. This is true even when the model preaches unfriendly or uncooperative behavior but behaves towards the child in an opposite manner. To the extent that the model for socially responsible behavior is perceived as having high social status (Bandura, Ross & Ross, 1963), the model will be most effective in inducing responsible behavior.

In our studies, both authoritative and authoritarian parents demanded socially responsible behavior and also differentially rewarded it. As compared to authoritative parents, however, authoritarian parents permitted their own needs to take precedence over those of the child, became inaccessible when displeased, assumed a stance of personal infallibility, and in other ways showed themselves often to be more concerned with their own ideas than with the child's welfare. Thus, they did not exemplify prosocial behavior, although they did preach it. Authoritative parents, on the other hand, both preached and practiced prosocial behavior and their children were significantly more responsible than the children of authoritarian parents. In this regard, it is interesting that nonconforming parents who were highly individualistic and professed anticonforming ideas had children who were more socially responsible than otherwise. The boys were achievement-oriented and the girls

were notably cooperative. These parents were themselves rather pacific, gentle, people who were highly responsive to the child's needs even at the cost of their own; thus, they modelled but did not preach prosocial behavior.

2. *Firm enforcement policies, in which desired behavior is positively reinforced and deviant behavior is negatively reinforced, facilitate the development of socially responsible behavior, provided that the parent desires that the child behave in a responsible manner.*

The use of reinforcement techniques serves to establish the potency of the reinforcing agent and, in the mind of the young child, to legitimate his authority. The use of negative sanctions can be a clear statement to the child that rules are there to be followed and that to disobey is to break a known rule. Among other things, punishment provides the child with information. As Spence (1966) found, nonreaction by adults is sometimes interpreted by children as signifying a correct response. Siegel and Kohn (1959) found that nonreaction by an adult when the child was behaving aggressively resulted in an increased incidence of such acts. By virtue of his or her role as an authority, the sheer presence of parents when the child misbehaves cannot help but affect the future occurrence of such behavior. Disapproval should reduce such actions, while approval or nonreaction to such behavior should increase them.

In our studies, permissive parents avoided the use of negative sanctions, did not demand mannerly behavior or reward self-help, did not enforce their directives by exerting force or influence, avoided confrontation when the child disobeyed, and did not choose to or did not know how to use reinforcement techniques. Their sons, by comparison with the sons of authoritative parents, were clearly lacking in prosocial and achievement-oriented behavior.

3. *Nonrejecting parents are more potent models and reinforcing agents than rejecting parents; thus, nonrejection should be associated with socially responsible behavior in children, provided that the parents value and reinforce such behavior.*

It should be noted that this hypothesis refers to nonrejecting parents and is not stated in terms of passive-acceptance. Thus, it is expected that nonrejecting parental behavior, but not unconditionally acceptant behavior, is associated with socially responsible behavior in children. As Bronfenbrenner pointed out about adolescents, "It is the presence of rejection rather than the lack of a high degree of warmth which is inimical to the development of responsibility in both sexes (1961, p. 254)." As already indicated, in our study authoritarian parents were more rejecting and punitive, and less devoted to the child's welfare than were authoritative parents; their sons were also less socially responsible.

4. *Parents who are fair, and who use reason to legitimate their directives are more potent models and reinforcing agents than parents who do not encourage independence or verbal exchange.*

Let us consider the interacting effects of punishment and the use of reasoning on the behavior of children. From research it appears than an accompanying verbal rationale nullifies the special effectiveness of immediate punishment, and also of relatively intense punishment

(Parke, 1969). Thus, by symbolically reinstating the deviant act, explaining the reason for punishment, and telling the child exactly what he should do, the parent obviates the need for intense or instantaneous punishment. Immediate, intense punishment may have undesirable side effects, in that the child is conditioned through fear to avoid deviant behavior, and is not helped to control himself consciously and willfully. Also, instantaneous, intense punishment produces high anxiety which may interfere with performance, and in addition may increase the likelihood that the child will avoid the noxious agent. This reduces that agent's future effectiveness as a model or reinforcing agent. Finally, achieving behavioral conformity by conditioning fails to provide the child with information about cause and effect relations which he can then transfer to similar situations. This is not to say that use of reasoning alone, without negative sanctions, is as effective as the use of both. Negative sanctions give operational meaning to the consequences signified by reasons, and to rules themselves.

Authoritarian parents, as compared to authoritative parents, are relatively unsuccessful in producing socially responsible behavior. According to this hypothesis, the reason is that authoritarian parents fail to encourage verbal exchange and infrequently accompany punishment with reasons rather than that they use negative sanctions and are firm disciplinarians.

SOCIALIZATION PRACTICES RELATED TO INDEPENDENT VS. SUGGESTIBLE BEHAVIOR

The reader will recall that Independent

vs. Suggestible Behavior was defined with reference to: a) Domineering vs. Tractable Behavior, b) Dominance vs. Submission, c) Purposive vs. Aimless Activity, and d) Independence vs. Suggestibility. Parent behavior seems to have a clearer effect upon the development of independence in girls than in boys, probably because preschool boys vary less in independence.

In my own work independence in girls was clearly associated with authoritative upbringing (whether conforming or nonconforming). For boys, nonconforming parent behavior and, to a lesser extent, authoritative upbringing were associated with independence. By independence we do not mean anticonformity. "Pure anticonformity, like pure conformity, is pure dependence behavior (Willis, 1968, p. 263)." Anticonforming behavior, like negativistic behavior, consists of doing anything but what is prescribed by social norms. Independence is the ability to disregard known standards of conduct or normative expectations in making decisions. Nonconformity in parents may not be associated in my study with independence in girls (although it was in boys) because females are especially susceptible to normative expectations. One can hypothesize that girls must be trained to act independently of these expectations, rather than to conform or to anticonform to them.

It was once assumed that firm control and high maturity demands lead to passivity and dependence in young children. The preponderance of evidence contradicts this. Rather, it would appear that many children react to parental power by resisting, rather than by being cowed. The same parent variables which increase the probability that the child will use the parent as a model should increase the likelihood that firm control will result in assertive behavior. For example, the controlling parent who is warm, understanding and supportive of autonomy should generate less passivity (as well as less rebelliousness) than the controlling parent who is cold and restrictive. This should be the case because of the kinds of behavior reinforced, the traits modelled and the relative effectiveness of the parent as a model.

Several generalizations and hypotheses can be offered concerning the relations between parental practices and the development of independence in young children:

1. *Early environmental stimulation facilitates the development of independence in young children.*

It took the knowledge gained from compensatory programs for culturally disadvantaged children to counteract the erroneous counsel from some experts to avoid too much stimulation of the young child. Those Head Start programs which succeed best (Hunt, 1968) are those characterized by stress on the development of cognitive skills, linguistic ability, motivational concern for achievement, and rudimentary numerical skills. There is reason to believe that middle-class children also profit from such early stimulation and enrichment of the environment. Fowler (1962) pointed out, even prior to the development of compensatory programs, that concern about the dangers of premature cognitive training and an overemphasis on personality development had delayed inordinately the recognition that the ability to talk, read and compute increases the child's self-respect and independent functioning.

Avoidance of anxiety and self-assertion are reciprocally inhibiting responses to threat or frustration. Girls, in particular, are shielded from stress and overstimulation, which probably serves to increase preferences for avoidant rather than offensive responses to aggression or threat. By exposing a child to stress or to physical, social and intellectual demands, he or she becomes more resistant to stress and learns that offensive reactions to aggression and frustration are frequently rewarding. In our studies, as the hypothesis would predict, parents who provided the most enriched environment, namely the nonconforming and the authoritative parents, had the most dominant and purposive children. These parents, by comparison with the others studied, set high standards of excellence, invoked cognitive insight, provided an intellectually stimulating atmosphere, were themselves rated as being differentiated and individualistic, and made high educational demands upon the child.

2. *Parental passive-acceptance and overprotection inhibits the development of independence.*

Passive-acceptant and overprotective parents shield children from stress and, for the reasons discussed above, inhibit the development of assertiveness and frustration tolerance. Also, parental anxiety about stress to which the child is exposed may serve to increase the child's anxiety. Further, willingness to rescue the child offers him an easy alternative to self-mastery. Demanding and nonprotective parents, by contrast, permit the child to extricate himself from stressful situations and place a high value on tolerance of frustration and courage.

According to many investigators (e.g., McClelland, Atkinson, Clark, & Lowell, 1953), healthy infants are by inclination explorative, curious and stress-seeking. Infantile feelings of pleasure, originally experienced after mild changes in sensory stimulation, become associated with these early efforts at independent mastery. The child anticipates pleasure upon achieving a higher level of skill, and the pleasure derived from successfully performing a somewhat risky task encourages him to seek out such tasks.

Rosen and D'Andrade (1959) found that high achievement motivation, a motivation akin to stress-seeking, was facilitated both by high maternal warmth when the child pleased the parent and high maternal hostility and rejection when the child was displeasing. Hoffman, et al., (1960), found that mothers of achieving boys were more coercive than those who performed poorly, and it has also been found (Crandall, Dewey, Katkovsky, & Preston, 1964) that mothers of achieving girls were relatively nonnurturant. Kagan and Moss (1962) reported that achieving adult women had mothers who in early childhood were unaffectionate, "pushy" and not protective. Also, Baumrind and Black (1967) found paternal punitiveness to be associated positively with independence in girls. Finally, in my recent study, there were indications for girls that parental nonacceptance was positively related to independence. That is, the most independent girls had parents who were either not passive-acceptant or who were rejecting.

Authoritarian control and permissive noncontrol both may shield the child from the opportunity to engage in vigorous interaction with people. Demands which cannot be met, refusals to help, and unrealistically high standards may curb commerce with the environment. Placing few demands on the child, suppression of conflict, and low standards may understimulate him. In either case, he fails to achieve the knowledge and experience required to desensitize him to the anxiety associated with nonconformity.

3. *Self-assertiveness and self-confidence in the parent, expressed by an individual style and by the moderate use of power-oriented techniques of discipline, will be associated with independence in the young child.*

The self-assertive, self-confident parent provides a model of similar behavior for the child. Also, the parent who uses power-oriented rather than love-oriented techniques of discipline achieves compliance through means other than guilt. Power-oriented techniques can achieve behavioral conformity without premature internalization by the child of parental standards. It may be that the child is, in fact, more free to formulate his own standards of conduct if techniques of discipline are used which stimulate resistiveness or anger rather than fear or guilt. The use of techniques which do not stimulate conformity through guilt may be especially important for girls. The belief in one's own power and the assumption of responsibility for one's own intellectual successes and failures are important predictors of independent effort and intellectual achievement (Crandall, Katkovsky, & Crandall, 1965). This sense of self-responsibility in children seems to be associated with power-oriented techniques of discpline and with critical attitudes on the part of the adult towards the

child, provided that the parent is also concerned with developing the child's autonomy and encourages independent and individual behavior.

In my study, both the authoritative and the nonconforming parents were self-confident, clear as well as flexible in their childrearing attitudes, and willing to express angry feelings openly. Together with relatively firm enforcement and non-rejection, these indices signified patterns of parental authority in which guilt-producing techniques of discipline were avoided. The sons of nonconforming parents and the daughters of authoritative parents were both extremely independent.

4. *Firm control can be associated with independence in the child, provided that the control is not restrictive of the child's opportunities to experiment and to make decisions within the limits defined.*

There is no logical reason why parents' enforcing directives and making demands cannot be accompanied by regard for the child's opinions, willingness to gratify his wishes, and instruction in the effective use of power. A policy of firm enforcement may be used as a means by which the child can achieve a high level of instrumental competence and eventual independence. The controlling, demanding parent can train the child to tolerate increasingly intense and prolonged frustration; to broaden his base of adult support to include neighbors, teachers and others; to assess critically his own successes and failures and to take responsibility for both; to develop standards of moral conduct; and to relinquish the special privileges of childhood in return for the rights of adolescence.

It is important to distinguish between

the effects on the child of restrictive control and of firm control. *Restrictive control* refers to the use of extensive proscriptions and prescriptions, covering many areas of the child's life; they limit his autonomy to try out his skills in these areas. By *firm control* is meant firm enforcement of rules, effective resistance against the child's demands, and guidance of the child by regime and intervention. Firm control does not imply large numbers of rules or intrusive direction of the child's activities.

Becker (1964) has summarized the effects on child behavior of restrictiveness vs. permissiveness and warmth vs. hostility. He reported that warm-*restrictive* parents tended to have passive, well-socialized children. This author (Baumrind, 1967) found, however, that warm-*controlling* (by contrast with warm-*restrictive*) parents were not paired with passive children, but rather with responsible, assertive, self-reliant children. Parents of these children enforced directives and resisted the child's demands, but were not restrictive. Early control, unlike restrictiveness, apparently does not lead to "fearful, dependent and submissive behaviors, a dulling of intellectual striving, and inhibited hostility," as Becker indicated was true of restrictive parents (1964, p. 197).

5. *Substantial reliance upon reinforcement techniques to obtain behavioral conformity, unaccompanied by use of reason, should lead to dependent behavior.*

To the extent that the parent uses verbal cues judiciously, she increases the child's ability to discriminate, differentiate, and generalize. According to Luria (1960) and Vygotsky (1962), the child's ability to "order" his own behavior is based upon verbal instruction from the adult which, when heeded and obeyed, permits eventual *cognitive* control by the child of his own behavior. Thus, when the adult legitimizes power, labels actions clearly as praiseworthy or changeworthy, explains her rules and encourages vigorous verbal give and take, obedience is not likely to be achieved at the cost of passive dependence. Otherwise, it may well be.

It is self-defeating to attempt to shape, by extrinsic reinforement, behavior which by its natue is autogenic. As already mentioned, the healthy infant is explorative and curious, and seems to enjoy mild stress. Although independent mastery can be accelerated if the parent broadens the child's experiences and makes certain reasonable demands upon him, the parent must take care not to substitute extrinsic reward and social approval for the intrinsic pleasure associated with mastery of the environment. Perhaps the unwillingness of the authoritative parents in my study to rely solely upon reinforcement techniques contributed substantially to the relatively purposive, dominant behavior shown by their children, especially by their daughters.

6. *Parental values which stress individuality, self-expression, initiative, divergent thinking and aggressiveness will facilitate the development of independence in the child, provided that these qualities in the parent are not accompanied by lax and inconsistent discipline and unwillingness to make demands upon the child.*

It is important that adults use their power in a functional rather than an interpersonal context. The emphasis should be on the task to be done and the rule to be followed rather than upon the special status of the powerful adult. By focusing upon the task to be accomplished, the adult's actions can serve as an example for the child rather than as a suppressor of his independence. Firm discipline for both boys and girls must be in the service of training for achievement and independence, if such discipline is not to facilitate the development of an overconforming, passive life style.

In our study, independence was clearly a function of nonconforming but nonindulgent parental attitudes and behaviors, for boys. For girls, however, nonconforming parental patterns were associated with independence only when the parents were also authoritative. The parents in these groups tended to encourage their children to ask for, even to demand, what they desired. They themselves acquiesced in the face of such demands provided that the demands were not at variance with parental policy. Thus, the children of these parents were positively reinforced for autonomous self-expression. In contrast to these results, the authoritarian parents did not value willfulness in the child, and the permissive parents were clearly ambivalent about rewarding such behavior. Further, the permissive parents did not differentiate between mature or praiseworthy demands by the child and regressive or deviant demands. These permissive parents instead would accede to the child's demands until patience was exhausted; punishment, sometimes very harsh, would then ensue.

SUMMARY

Girls in western society are in many ways systematically socialized for instrumental incompetence. The affiliative and cooperative orientation of girls increases their receptivity to the influence of socializing agents. This influence, in turn, is often used by socializing agents to inculcate passivity, dependence, conformity and sociability in the young females at the expense of independent pursuit of success and scholarship. In my studies, parents designated as authoritative had the most achievement-oriented and independent daughters. However, permissive parents whose control was lax, who did not inhibit tomboy behavior, and who did not seek to produce sex-role conformity in girls had daughters who were nearly as achievement-oriented and independent.

The following adult practices and attitudes seem to facilitate the development of socially responsible and independent behavior in both boys and girls.

1. Modelling by the adult of behavior which is both socially responsible and self-assertive, especially if the adult is seen as powerful by the child and as eager to use the material and interpersonal resources over which he has control on the child's behalf.

2. Firm enforcement policies in which the adult makes effective use of reinforcement principles in order to reward socially responsible behavior and to punish deviant behavior, but in which demands are accompanied by explanations, and sanctions are accompanied by reasons consistent with a set of principles followed in practice as well as preached by the parent.

3. Nonrejecting but not overprotective or passive-acceptant parental attitudes in which the parent's interest in the child is abiding, and, in the preschool

years, intense; but where approval is conditional upon the child's behavior.

4. High demands for achievement, and for conformity with parental policy, accompanied by receptivity to the child's rational demands and willingness to offer the child wide latitude for independent judgment.

5. Providing the child with a complex and stimulating environment offering challenge and excitement as well as security and rest, where divergent as well as convergent thinking is encouraged.

These practices and attitudes do not reflect a happy compromise between authoritarian and permissive practices. Rather, they reflect a synthesis and balancing of strongly opposing forces of tradition and innovation, divergence and convergence, accommodation and assimilation, cooperation and autonomous expression, tolerance and principled intractability.

References

Aberle, D. F. & Naegele, K. D. Middle-class fathers' occupational role and attitudes toward children. *American J. Orthopsychiatry*, 1952, **22**, 366-378.

Bandura, A., Ross, D. & Ross, S. A. A comparative test of the status envy, social power, and the secondary-reinforcement theories of identificatory learning. *J. abnorm. soc. psychol.,* 1963, **67**, 527-534.

Barry, H., Bacon, M. K. & Child, I. L. A crosscultural survey of some sex differences in socialization. *J. abnorm. soc. psychol.*, 1957, **55**, 327-332.

Baumrind, D. Effects of authoritative parental control on child behavior. *Child Develpm.*, 1966, **37**, 887-907.

Baumrind, D. Child care practices anteceding three patterns of preschool behavior. *Genetic psychol. Monogr.*, 1967, **75**, 43-88.

Baumrind, D. Authoritarian vs. authoritative parental control. *Adolescence*, 1968, **3**, 255-272.

Baumrind, D. Current patterns of parental authority. *Developmental psychol. Monogr.*, 1971, **4**(1), in press.

Baumrind, D., & Black, A. E. Socialization practices associated with dimensions of competence in preschool boys and girls. *Child Develpm.* 1967, **38**, 291-327.

Becker, W. C. Consequences of different kinds of parental discipline. In M. L. Hoffman & L. W. Hoffman (eds.), *Review of Child Development Research*. Vol. 1. New York: Russell Sage Foundation, 1964, 169-208.

Bronfenbrenner, U. Some familiar antecedents of responsibility and leadership in adolescents. In L. Petrullo & B. M. Bass (eds.),

Leadership and interpersonal behavior. New York: Holt, Rinehart & Winston, 1961, 239-271.

Brown, D. Sex role development in a changing culture. *Psychol. Bull.,* 1958, **55** 232-242.

Crandall, V., Dewey, R., Katkovsky, W. & Preston, A. Parents' attitudes and behaviors and grade school children's academic achievements. *J. genet. psychol.,* 1964, **104,** 53-66.

Crandall, V., Katkovsky, W. & Crandall, V. J. Children's beliefs in their own control of reinforcements in intellectual-academic achievement situations. *Child Develpm.,* 1965, **36,** 91-109.

Crandall, V., Orleans, S., Preston, A. & Rabson, A. The development of social compliance in young children. *Child Develpm.,* 1958, **29,** 429-443.

Dinitz, S., Dynes, R. R. & Clarke, A. C. Preference for male or female children: Traditional or affectional. *Marriage and Family Living,* 1954, **16,** 128-130.

Eiduson, B. T. *Scientists, their psychological world.* New York: Basic Books, 1962.

Elder, G. H. Parental power legitimation and its effect on the adolescent. *Sociometry,* 1963, **26,** 50-65.

Emmerich, W. & Smoller, F. The role patterning of parental norms. *Sociometry,* 1964, **27,** 382-390.

Fowler, W. Cognitive learning in infancy and early childhood. *Psychol. Bull.,* 1962, **59,** 116-152.

Haggard, E. A. Socialization, personality, and academic achievement in gifted children. In B. C. Rosen, H. J. Crockett & C. Z. Nunn (eds.), *Achievement in American Society.* Cambridge, Mass.: Schenkman Publishing, 1969, 85-94.

Heilbrun, A. B. Sex differences in identification learning. *J. genet. psychol.,* 1965, **106,** 185-193.

Hoffman, L., Rosen, S. & Lippit, R. Parental coerciveness, child autonomy, and child's role at school. *Sociometry,* 1960, **23,** 15-22.

Horner, M. Fail: Bright women. *Psychology Today,* 1969, **3**(6).

Hunt, J. McV. Toward the prevention of incompetence. In J. W. Carter, Jr. (ed.), *Research Contributions from Psychology to Community Mental Health.* New York: Behavioral Publications, 1968.

Kagan, J. & Moss, H. A. *Birth to Maturity: A Study in Psychological Development.* New York: John Wiley, 1962.

Keniston, E. & Keniston, K. An American anachronism: the image of women and work. *Am. Scholar,* 1964, **33,** 355-375.

Luria, A. R. Experimental analysis of the development of voluntary action in children. In *The Central Nervous System and Behavior.* Bethesda, Md.: U.S. Department of Health, Education, & Welfare, National

Institutes of Health, 1960, 529-535.

Maccoby, E. E. (ed.). *The Development of Sex Differences.* Stanford, Calif.: Stanford University Press, 1966.

McClelland, D., Atkinson, J., Clark, R. & Lowell, E. *The Achievement Motive.* New York: Appleton-Century-Crofts, 1953.

McKee, J. P. & Sherriffs, A. C. The differential evaluation of males and females. *J. Pers.,* 1957, **25,**356-371.

Middleton, R. & Snell, P. Political expression of adolescent rebellion. *Am. J. Sociol.,* 1963, **68,** 527-535.

Mischel, W. & Liebert, R. M. Effects of discrepancies between observed and imposed reward criteria on their acquisition and transmission. *J. Pers. & soc. Psychol.,* 1966, **3,** 45-53.

Parke, R. D. Some effects of punishment on children's behavior. *Young Children,* 1969, **24,** 225-240.

Pikas, A. Children's attitudes toward rational versus inhibiting parental authority. *J. abnorm. soc. Psychol.,* 1961, **62,** 315-321.

Roe, A. *The Making of a Scientist.* New York: Dodd, Mead, 1952.

Rosen, B. C. & D'Andrade, R. The psychological origins of achievement motivation. *Sociometry,* 1959, **22,** 185-218.

Rosenhan, D. L., Frederick, F. & Burrowes, A. Preaching and Practicing: effects of channel discrepancy on norm internalization. *Child Develpm.,* 1968, **39,** 291-302.

Rossi, A. Women in science: why so few? In B. C. Rosen, H. J. Crockett, & C. Z. Nunn (eds.), *Achievement in American Society.* Cambridge, Mass.: Schenkman Publishing, 1969, 470-486.

Siegel, A. E. & Kohn, L. G. Permissiveness, permission, and aggression: the effects of adult presence or absence on aggression in children's play. *Child Develpm.,* 1959, **36,** 131-141.

Spence, J. T. Verbal-discrimination performance as a function of instruction and verbal reinforcement combination in normal and retarded children. *Child Develpm.,* 1966, **37,** 269-281.

Terman, L. M. & Oden, H. H. *The Gifted Child Grows Up.* Stanford, Calif.: Stanford University Press, 1947.

Vygotsky, L. S. *Thought and Language.* Cambridge, Mass.: M.I.T. Press, 1962.

Walberg, H. J. Physics, femininity, and creativity. *Develpml. Psychol.,* 1969, **1,** 47-54.

Willis, R. H. Conformity, independence, and anti-conformity. In L. S. Wrightsman, Jr. (ed.), *Contemporary Issues in Social Psychology.* Belmont, Calif.: Brooks/Cole Publishing, 1968, 258-272.

VIRGINIA CRANDALL

Achievement Behavior in Young Children*

No one knows exactly why or when children begin to want to do something *well*. Although observers often note that the infant of a year or less struggles to turn himself over, to pull himself up, to walk, to grasp an object, and to acquire speech, most investigators concerned with "achievement motivation" or "achievement behavior" would not classify these early efforts as motivated by a desire to "achieve." What criteria, then, distinguish certain purposeful behaviors as achievement behaviors? Crandall, Katkovsky and Preston (1960a) suggest that "achievement behavior is behavior directed toward the attainment of approval or the avoidance of disapproval [from oneself or from others] for competence of performance in situations where standards of excellence are applicable." Somewhat similarly, in describing achievement *motivation*, McClelland and his colleagues (1953) state: "The child must begin to perceive performance in terms of standards of excellence" and to experience pleasant or unpleasant feelings about meeting or failing to meet these standards. Early efforts at locomotion, prehension and speech are not usually cate-

gorized as achievement behavior because children of such very young ages do not yet have the cognitive ability to apply "standards of excellence" to their own behavior. Psychologists would generally agree that the child must be able to note a discrepancy between his present level of competence and a higher level of skill and to predict that more proficiency will produce greater pleasure, pride or approval from others than his present skill will now permit. Thus, it is at the point when the child attempts to *perfect* a skill, to accomplish something *more efficiently* or *quickly*, to produce a *better* product, to do something *well*, that his efforts are defined as achievement behavior.

Achievement motivation would seem to have its origin in learning experiences during early childhood. McClelland, et al. (1963) maintain that feelings of pleasure originally attendant upon mild changes in sensory stimulation become associated with early efforts at independent mastery. That is, the child learns to anticipate that certain levels of skill will produce feelings of pleasure if they are perceived as moderately above his present performance level just as he tends to enjoy moderate increments in kind, quality, intensity, and patterning of other forms of stimulation. But these authors state further that "stronger achievement motives probably required for most (though not necessarily all) children some

*From *Young Children*, 1964, 20 77-99. Reprinted by permission of the author and the Association for the Education of Young Children.

structuring of performance standards, some *demands* by the parents and the surrounding culture" (1953, p. 78; see also 1958 pp. 437-452). Crandall, Preston and Rabson (1960) place primary, rather than secondary, emphasis on such demands, rewards and punishments when considering the genesis of the achievement need. They argue that direct social reinforcement of the child's accomplishment is necessary if the child is to learn to value achievement activities as potential sources of satisfaction and security. Only later, and for some children, do approval from others for good performance become unnecessary and feelings of pride or self-approval constitute sufficient reinforcement to maintain or increase their achievement behaviors.

Individual differences have been found (Crandall, Preston & Rabson 1960) among three-, four- and five-year olds in the frequency and persistence with which tasks requiring skill and effort are attempted. Sears and Levin (1957) also report that four- and five-year-old children varied in their aspirations to tackle succeeded or failed tasks and Tyler, Rafferty and Tyler (1962) found individual differences among nursery school children in their attempts to get recognition for achievement behavior. Finally, McClelland (1958) reports that individual differences in achievement motivation (measured with a test involving the drawing of "doodles") had appeared by the age of five. These studies suggest that the desire to achieve must have been established to some degree by the time these children were tested or observed, but that it is more fully developed in some preschool children than in others. No research, however, has attempted to investigate the approximate age or conditions under which achievement behavior begins to emerge.

First-, second-, and third-grade children spend more time and strive more intensely in some kinds of achievement activities than in others (Crandall, 1961). Thus, achievement efforts of young grade school children not only vary from child to child, but also vary for any one child from one achievement area to another (i.e., intellectual, physical skills, mechanical and artistic activities). It is possible that similar differentiation occurs even earlier, but no research of this nature has been reported.

EARLY ENVIRONMENTAL STIMULATION

Recent investigations have focused on stimulation in the preschool child's physical and social environment as a possible determinant of intellectual achievement (Bruner, 1961; Deutsch, 1964; Hunt, 1961; Hunt, 1963).

A group of researchers under the direction of Martin Deutsch (e.g., Deutsch, 1962; Deutsch, 1964; Deutsch & Brown, 1964; John, 1963; John, 1964) have studied Negro and white children on the edge of a large slum area in New York. These investigators found concept formation, auditory and visual discrimination, language acquisition and IQ scores related to such factors as race, social class, nursery school or kindergarten attendance, and father's presence or absence from the home. One of the elements common to all these factors, they reason, is the social and physical stimulus deprivation or enrichment concomitant to the child's status on each of these dimensions.

Forgays (1963) presented four-year-old children with discrimination problems in which their only incentive was the opportunity to obtain tactual, visual or auditory stimulation. Middle class children learned these problems more rapidly than lower class subjects, presumably because of their early exposure to more stimulating surroundings.

Most of the researchers associated with these studies have recommended that environmental intervention might increase the achievement of children from deprived backgrounds. The idea is not new. As early as 1907, Montessori (1912; 1959), in her work with three-to-six-year-old children from the slums of Rome, provided her pupils with a wide variety of materials to play with and tasks of graded difficulty to choose from at will. By the time these children were five years of age, many of them were reading and writing. Fowler (1962; 1963) demonstrated that two-, three- and four-year-old children can be taught to read by providing a very shallow gradient of stimuli consisting primarily of printed verbal and pictorial material. In his excellent review (1962) of earlier attempts to teach children of preschool ages to read, Fowler states ". . . of 25 children who learned to read before the age of 3-0 . . ., 72 per cent had definitely enjoyed a great deal of unusually early intellectual stimulation. . . . There was no evidence of a child reading early where stimulation was absent."

Nursery school attendance is an obvious source of enrichment of the child's environment and, thus, of his intellectual achievement. Results from studies of pre-school attendance are too complex, however, to be reviewed here. In general, they seem to indicate that substantial increases in IQ cannot be expected from nursery school attendance unless the child has come from an environment which is unusually static and unstimulating (e.g., an orphanage). Even then, results attributed to the environmental stimulation of nursery school may have been artifacts of test unreliability, practice effects of repeated testing, and/or the greater rapport of nursery school children with adult examiners who tested them. Wellman's summary (1943) of studies conducted at the Iowa Child Welfare Research Station and the reviews of Hunt (1961), Jones (1954), and Swift (1964) are recommended to the interested reader. Now let us focus directly on the achieving child himself.

ACHIEVING CHILDREN

Personality Characteristics

What are the personality attributes of children who display more achievement behavior than their peers? A longitudinal study (Sontag, Baker & Nelson, 1958) based on ratings of children's behavior in nursery and elementary school, as well as in the home, showed that both boys and girls whose IQs increased during the preschool years were independent of adults and competitive with peers. In addition, the girls were less "feminine" in their behavior than girls with decreasing IQs and did not need immediate rewards for good behavior, but could delay gratification until some more distant time. Later, during the elementary school

years, both male and female IQ "ascenders" were again found to be competitive
in the scholastic situation and independent, initiating more activities on their
own and more frequently attempting to
overcome obstacles by themselves. Boys
with increasing IQs were also more aggressive and more anxious than boys whose
IQs declined. "Ascending" girls displayed
more sibling rivalry, had parents who
emphasized the importance of school
achievement and, at the preschool ages,
these girls were able to delay gratification. This ability to delay rewards for
more long-term goals has also been shown
to be associated with higher achievement
motivation scores (Mischel, 1961).

Independence, then, was a consistent
characteristic of children who showed
increases in IQ scores. Such independence
was also present in the three-to-five-year-
old achieving children of another study
(Crandall, Preston & Rabson, 1960). That
is, the more time these children chose to
spend in achievement activities during
nursery school, the less they sought emotional support and instrumental help
from the staff or from their mothers in
the home.

In spite of the fact that independence
is related to achievement, a similar sample
of children who displayed more achievement efforts in nursery school were
found to be compliant to the requests
and demands of the adult staff (Crandall,
Orleans, Preston & Rabson, 1958). Haggard (1957) also reports that compliance
to adult pressures and values was found
among children at the elementary age
level who were high academic achievers.
In this longitudinal study of gifted children, Haggard investigated a variety of
personality characteristics associated with
academic achievement and reports that to
some degree these factors change with
age. In the third grade,

*High achievers were sensitive and re-
sponsive to socialization pressures . . . and
were striving to live up to adult expectations . . . Their conformity in this respect
seems to have given them a high degree of
security and confidence in their relations
with adults, even though they expressed
some underlying resentment toward
authority figures. In general, however,
they showed a high degree of inner
harmony, being rather adept at emotional
control. . . . In their behavior with others,
they were somewhat more tense, competitive, and aggressive; had developed
good work habits and were persistent in
them; got along better with their parents,
teachers, and peers; and showed a higher
level of over-all adjustment than did the
low academic achievers. . . .*

*By Grade VII, various changes had
taken place in the children who remained
high academic achievers. Although they
continued to respond to the socialization
pressures of adults and to strive toward
adult standards of behavior, they had
developed strong antagonistic attitudes
toward adults. . . . They increasingly rejected adults as persons. At the same
time, they showed a marked increase in
the level of their anxiety and a corresponding decrease in their intellectual
originality and creativity. Although there
was no such difference in anxiety and
creativity between high and low achievers
in Grade III, a marked difference existed
between these groups by Grade VII. . . .
They also became more aggressive, persistent, hard driving, and competitive, and
they showed signs of willingness to be*

aggressive and destructive in order to defeat and win over other persons. . . .

It would appear, then, that achieving children, in contrast to peers who perform less well, do not need to depend upon adults but are somewhat compliant and conforming to their demands and accept and incorporate adults' high evaluations of the importance of achievement. They are also able to work without being immediately rewarded for their efforts, show initiative, self-reliance, and emotional control. While achieving children of preschool and early elementary age are somewhat aggressive and competitive, their social relationships are generally good. Achievement, however, seems to be exacting its toll. By later elementary school or junior high age, aggression and competition have become accentuated, relationships with siblings, peers and adults show some disruption, and the children are less creative and more anxious. Research on high school students, beyond the scope of this paper, indicates that these attributes become increasingly pronounced at later ages. Does this mean that the effort to achieve "produces" the less desirable personality attributes? Or does it mean that only if children have acquired such a personality constellation will they then be able to achieve in our highly competitive, post-Sputnik educational system? Cause and effect relationships cannot be determined from these data, but it is obvious that our "education for excellence" is accompanied by certain psychological costs.

Anxiety and Test Performance

Much research has been directed toward determining the effects of anxiety on achievement performance. High levels of anxiety seem to impede optimum performance on the complex problem solving tasks presented in intelligence tests and scholastic-achievement tests. The process is assumed to be one in which the anxious child is overly concerned with the tester's or teacher's evaluation of his performance and is thus less free to attend to the material presented to him in a learning situation and less able to report it in a testing session. It may also be that the less intelligent or less academically proficient child has had more difficulty, fewer rewards, and more failure experiences and, as a result, has *become* more anxious.

Several studies of elementary school children have investigated the relationship between anxiety and test performance (Crandall, Katkovsky & Preston, 1962; Feldhusen & Klausmeier, 1962; Hafner & Kaplan, 1959; Keller & Rowley, 1962; 1964; McCandless & Castaneda, 1956; Reese, 1961; Sarason, Davidson, Lighthall, Waite & Ruebush, 1960; Stanford, Dember & Stanford, 1962). Among *early* elementary school children the findings generally show that more anxious children tend to perform more poorly on achievement and intelligence tests, although the relationships are weak and vary greatly from one investigation to the next. Among fifth- and sixth-grade students, greater anxiety has been found to relate somewhat more frequently to poor test performance, and the relationships are usually stronger for girls than for boys. Where differences in anxiety scores are reported for the two sexes, girls are consistently more anxious, or at least admit to more anxiety, than boys. The lack of strong and consistent inverse relationships between anxiety test scores and achievement test scores except in sixth-grade girls, led Keller and Rowley (1962) to maintain that anxiety may only affect academic achievement in relatively high-anxious groups. Since the two longitudinal studies cited previously found that achieving children were more anxious than their nonachieving peers, it may be that moderate amounts of anxiety do not interfere with intellectual performance. There may be, however, some critical level of anxiety (such as that attained by sixth-grade girls) beyond which intellectual efforts are adversely affected.

The characteristics of the learning or testing situation and of the task must also be taken into account. Grimes and Allinsmith (1961) found that anxious or compulsive children in highly structured classrooms performed as well on standardized reading and intelligence tests as their less anxious peers but were not as productive in classrooms where less structure was imposed on the learning situation. Sarason et al. (1960) report that high-anxious children performed better on a "gamelike" intelligence test than on a more typical "test-like" instrument. Thus, it might be concluded that when the task or the situation is so structured that it does not engage the anxiety of the usually anxious child, he will be freed to perform more optimally.

Achievement Motivation and Attitudes Directly Related to Achievement Activities

In addition to general personality attributes which have been found to distinguish achieving from nonachieving children, some studies have also shown that achieving children score higher on measures of achievement motivation. Usually an index of achievement motivation is obtained by asking the child to tell stories about pictures or about dolls or to complete a story after a situation has been described to him. Winterbottom (1958) found that eight-to-ten-year-old boys who obtained the highest achievement motivation scores on a story-telling measure were rated by their teachers as showing more motivation to achieve in general, and in sports and schoolwork in particular. Achievement motivation scores, however, did not differentiate the boys who were rated as actually performing more successfully in those activities from the boys who were rated as less successful in their attempts. In a longitudinal study of six-to-ten-year-old children, higher achievement motivation scores were obtained by children whose IQ scores had increased over that age period, while those children with decreasing IQ scores had lower scores on the motivational measure (Kagan, Sontag, Baker & Nelson, 1958). High achievement motivation also characterized nine-to-eleven-year-old boys (Rosen & D'Andrade, 1959) who displayed greater proficiency on achievement tasks consisting of block stacking, anagrams and constructing patterns. Finally, Cox (1962) reports that fourth- and fifth-grade Australian children with higher achievement motivation scores were superior on school examination performance and were more often in the "superior stream" than in the "inferior stream" (comparable to ability groups in this country).

On the other hand, Crandall, Katkovsky and Preston (1962) did not find achievement motivation scores to be any higher among early elementary children who performed more adequately on reading and arithmetic achievement tests and IQ tests. Nor did children with high achievement motivation scores choose to spend more time or strive harder in intellectual achievement activities than did children with lower scores. Murstein and Collier (1962) also report that seventh-grade children with higher motivation scores did not perform better on arithmetic problems or a canceling task than did children with lower motivation scores.

These disparities may arise in part from difficulty in the method by which achievement motivation has been assessed. That is, among very young children the stories told to pictures or doll play situations are often so meager as to allow for only the crudest scoring. Or it may be that findings vary by such situational factors as whether or not motivation has been "aroused," and the probability of reward which the situation offers. Little work of this nature has been done, however, with subjects under college age.

It may be that more specific attitudes, beliefs and expectations concerning achievement activities of different kinds would also contribute to the understanding of achievement behavior. For example, the degree to which children expect that they will be successful in intellectual achievement attempts has generally been found to influence their actual intellectual achievement performance. In studies conducted at the Fels Institute, junior high students who expected to obtain good grades in mathematics and English were, in fact, those

students who did perform better in these courses, particularly where high success-expectancy was combined with high IQ. But when IQ and expectancy were in conflict, the children's expectations of success were even more highly related to their grades than were their intelligence test scores! Children who were confident about being successful also actually performed more competently on standardized achievement tests, and Battle (in press) found that if a child expected to do well in mathematics he persisted longer on a difficult mathematics problem.

It should be pointed out, however, that among the junior high students studied by the Fels group and the first- and second-grade pupils studied by Sears (1964), the positive relationship of expectancy to performance was somewhat weaker for the poor students than for those who were doing well in school, thus leading to the conclusion that some of the poorer students were giving unrealistically high estimates of their own ability.

Sex Differences

Girls seem to have more difficulty than boys in evaluating their ability accurately. Additional findings from the Sears study (1964) indicate that fifth- and sixth-grade girls' concepts of their own mental ability are rather inconsistently related to their performance on intelligence and achievement tests, and the author also states that "girls generally show *less good* self-concepts than boys." Brandt (1958) also finds that girls are less accurate or realistic than boys in their self-concepts. Crandall, Katkovsky and Preston (1962) even report that among first-, second- and third-grade girls, the brighter the girl, the less successful she expected to be on intellectual tasks, and the lower her IQ score, the more successful she expected she would perform in intellectual activities!

In the same study, the authors also observed the children in free play. They report that the girls who spent most time and were striving hardest in intellectual activities had received higher scores on a measure of their desire to be good at intellectual activities. Thus, the extent of their effort semed to be determined by their *wish* to do well. Among the boys, however, expectancy of intellectual success was closely and realistically related to IQ scores, and boys who thought they could do well were those who were observed to strive hardest in intellectual activities in free play. In addition, these boys held higher standards for their own performance and thought that they, rather than fate, luck or other people, caused their own intellectual successes and failures. This belief in self-responsibility for, or control over, intellectual successes and failures was also found in elementary children who had higher report card grades and achievement test scores (Crandall, Katkovsky & Crandall, in press).

An investigation (Crandall & Rabson, 1960) of both nursery school and early elementary school children revealed that there were no differences between boys and girls in the *amount* of achievement efforts they displayed at either age level, but among the elementary children boys chose more often than girls to return to a previously failed task in an attempt to master it. The girls, however, avoided returning to the previously failed task and were more dependent on both peers and adults for help and approval and more often withdrew from threatening situations in free play.

There is some possibility that girls achieve for different reasons than boys. A number of studies suggest that girls' achievement efforts may more often be directed at obtaining affection or approval from others than from the self-approval attendant upon successful task accomplishment. For example, Sears (1962) found that among elementary school boys there were consistent, moderate relationships between achievement motivation and the boys' scholastic achievement test scores. Among the girls of that study, however, *affiliative* motives, rather than their achievement motivation, related most directly to their academic achievement test scores.

Tyler, Rafferty and Tyler (1962) demonstrated that girls who made more attempts in nursery school to obtain recognition for achievement also made more attempts to obtain love and affection. Boys' behavior, however, showed no such relationships. Similarly (Crandall, Dewey, Katkovsky & Preston, 1964), elementary-school girls who displayed more achievement efforts were those who sought the most approval from the staff of the Day Camp where they were being observed, while achievement efforts and approval-seeking showed no such relationship among the boys.

Thus, young girls may be using achievement striving to obtain love and approval from others. If this is the case, it is not surprising that in our culture which values achievement so highly, girls have become anxious regarding achievement, attempt to obtain approval for their achievement efforts, are prone to avoid the risk of failing, are dependent on adult help, and cannot rate their own competence accurately, often "underselling" it. For girls, the effort to achieve seems to exact fairly strong psychological penalties as the necessary price of affection and approval.

PARENTAL INFLUENCES ON CHILDREN'S ACHIEVEMENT BEHAVIOR

While there are many aspects of the social environment which contribute to children's achievement behavior, perhaps the most crucial of these for the very young child is found in interaction with his parents. Since it has already been noted that achieving children are also independent, it might be assumed that parents of these children make early and strong demands for independent behavior. Studies on this point, however, show inconsistent results. On the one hand, high achievement motivation was found in eight-to-ten-year-old boys whose mothers reported on a questionnaire that they had expected early independent behavior (Winterbottom, 1958), and high intelligence and achievement test scores were obtained by third-grade boys whose mothers had expected early or moderately early independence (Siss & Wittenborn, 1962). Yet Chance (1961) reports that first-grade children performed more proficiently on academic achievement tests if their mothers expected independent behaviors to occur relatively *late* in childhood. When Rosen and D'Andrade (1959) observed parents as their boys (nine-to-eleven) worked on achievement tasks, they discovered that fathers of boys with high achievement motivation allowed their sons more independence, but mothers allowed them less. Still another study (Crandall, Preston & Rabson, 1960) did not find independence training, as observed in the home, to be related in either direction to the children's achievement efforts in nursery school.

Part of the disparity in these findings may lie in the differences between mothers' retrospective reports on written questionnaires (Chance, 1961; Siss & Wittenborn, 1962; Winterbottom, 1958) and the direct observation of mothers' current independence training techniques used in the latter two studies. Part of the difference may be due to the ages of the children studied. In addition, a recent investigation (Rosen, 1964) has found that boys who received early independence training evidence greater incorporation of their mothers' achievement values — whether these values are strong or weak, positive or negative. Thus, if, by chance, the groups of mothers tested in the foregoing investigations happened to vary from study to study in the achievement orientations they held, the relationships found between independence training and the achievement motivation or behavior of their sons might well be affected. It is interesting to note, however, that mothers' direct reinforcement of achievement attempts (i.e., training specifically aimed at encouraging achievement behavior), was effective in producing higher achievement motivation (Rosen & D'Andrade, 1959) and more achievement efforts (Crandall et al., 1960).

Mothers' attempts to accelerate their children's cognitive and motor development have also been investigated. Moss and Kagan (1958) found that mothers who "pushed" their children's development had sons whose intelligence test scores at three years of age were higher than those of less acceleratory mothers, and IQ ascenders in the elementary years also had more acceleratory mothers (Sontag, Baker & Nelson, 1958).

Investigations by Crandall, Katkovsky and Preston (1960b) indicate that parental influences differ greatly depending on the sex of parent and child and the area of achievement behavior under consideration. For example, children's efforts to achieve in the mechanical area were most often associated with attitudes the parents held toward their children of the same sex, while parental influences in the physical skills area seemed to come from both the same-sex and the opposite-sex parent. That is, both boys and girls spent more time and worked harder at sports and gross motor activities if their parents of the same sex had participated frequently with them and instigated them toward these pursuits. The physical skills efforts, however, of both boys and girls were also associated with the importance fathers placed on their children's competence in this area, and high achieving boys had mothers who were rejecting and non-nurturant while girls had fathers who were low in affection.

In the intellectual area the children's efforts were most often associated with attitudes held by parents of the opposite sex and with the context of the child's relationship to that parent. The intellectually striving boys had *mothers* who considered intellectual competence highly important for their sons and whose relationships with them were ones of active involvement. That is, these mothers not only praised their sons' intellectual achievement efforts and were especially nurturant and affectionate, but they were also overtly rejecting and punitive. Conversely, girls who displayed such intellectual efforts in the free-play situation had *fathers* who were generally affectionate and nurturant but criticized, as well as praised, their daughters' achievement efforts. The girls' fathers were also more satisfied than dissatisfied with their daughters' efforts and they, as well as the mothers, evaluated the girls' intellectual competence as high. However, like the boys' mothers, these girls' mothers were also overtly rejecting.

The Rosen and D'Andrade (1959) study found that both parents of those boys with high achievement motivation scores held high standards for their sons and were more competitive, more interested, and demonstrated more involvement during the sons' performance. The mothers (but not the fathers) were likely to reward their sons with warmth and approval and showed some tendency, also, to punish with hostility and rejection. The authors conclude, "In a way, it is this factor of involvement that most clearly sets the mothers of high *n* Achievement boys apart from the mothers of low *n* Achievement boys."

In sum, the foregoing studies suggest that high levels of active parental involvement, particularly along cross-sex, parent-child lines provide the basis for achievement motivation, performance on intelligence tests, and intellectual achievement behaviors evidenced in free play. It should be noted that in each case, part of that involvement was reflected in negatively-valued parental behaviors or attitudes such as rejection, criticality, hostility, or "pushing" the child beyond his ability, and that this was particularly true of *mothers* of achieving children of either sex.

Other investigations of the parental behaviors associated with high academic achievement in children have also found proficiency in the classroom associated with parent-child relationships usually characterized as undesirable. For example, mothers of achieving girls were less affectionate and less nurturant (Crandall, Dewey, Katkovsky & Preston, 1964) and mothers of achieving boys were less accepting (Barwick & Arbuckle, 1962) and more coercive (Hoffman, Rosen & Lippitt, 1958) than were those of other children who performed more poorly. Haggard (1957), too, reports that high achieving children in the early elementary years "saw their parents as being somewhat overprotective, pressuring for achievement, and lacking in emotional warmth (frequently they were correct)."

The attitudes which parents hold about their own personal achievements have been found to affect their attitudes toward their children's achievements and to influence their own behavior with their children in achievement activities. Since neither of these analyses is directly concerned with the *children's* achievement behavior, they will not be discussed here. The interested reader is referred to Katkovsky, Preston & Crandall, 1964a; 1964b.

The salience of early maternal behaviors to achievement development was demonstrated in a longitudinal study by Kagan and Moss (1962). Intellectual achievement in adult males was strongly related to high maternal protection and low maternal hostility during the first three years of the boy's life, followed by acceleration of the child's achievement efforts during ages three to ten. The achieving adult women, however, had had mothers who were hostile toward them and lacking in protectiveness during the first three years of life while they simultaneously accelerated their daughters' achievement development during that period and again during the ages six to ten. Thus, variations in maternal behavior in the very early years have effects so far-reaching as to produce differences in achievement behavior many years later in adulthood.

CONCLUSION

This discussion has not attempted to present a comprehensive picture of all the social and cultural, peer, sibling and school factors which have been found to relate to children's achievement behavior. This summary has focused principally on the achieving child himself since it is ultimately the orientations he has developed which determine whether he will attempt to achieve when he is faced with a potential achievement situation. External forces can have impact only indirectly as they influence his motivations and attitudes.

Similarly, in studying the determinants of children's achievement behavior, it seems imperative that we must eventually establish the specific orientations the young child holds which promote, guide or limit his achievement efforts. Then the link can be established between social and environmental factors and these orientations and we will better understand how and why such external forces are influencing his behavior. While research of this kind has been done with older subjects, almost none has been attempted with preschool children. The difficulty here is primarily one of measurement, and does not reflect indifference to the developmental aspects of achievement attitudes. Attitudes and motivations have previously been assessed almost exclusively through verbal measures, and very young children lack the necessary verbal skills. In addition, our real attack on the origins of achievement orientations, facilitating or impeding effects on their emergence, and their specificity or generality across kinds of activity as they make their initial appearance cannot really be investigated until nonverbal measures are developed.

This report has reflected the almost-exclusive emphasis on behaviors of an intellectual nature which characterizes research in achievement. Some few research attempts reveal that many children seek approval for, or feel proud of, their competence in sports, crafts, leadership ability, art and many other fields of endeavor. We know very little about the determinants of these kinds of achievement efforts. The paucity of research in these domains of behavior is probably a reflection of the overweaning emphasis on intellectual achievement which has grown out of present international rivalries; it is indeed unfortunate that such exigencies have turned our attention away from such important aspects of achievement development.

References

Barwick, Janice, & Arbuckle, D. The study of the relationship between parental acceptance and the academic achievement of adolescents. *J. educ. Res.,* 1962, **56,** 148-151.

Battle, Esther. Motivational determinants of academic task persistence. *J. abnorm. soc. Psychol.,* in press.

Brandt, R. M. The accuracy of self-estimate: a measure of self-concept. *Genet. psychol. Monogr.,*1958, **58,** 55-99.

Bruner, J. S. The cognitive consequences of early sensory deprivation. In P. Solomon (Ed.), *Sensory Deprivation.* Cambridge: Harvard Univ. Press, 1961.

Chance, June E. Independence training and first graders' achievement. *J. consult. Psychol.,* XXV, 1961, 149-154.

Cox, F. N. An assessment of the achievement behavior system in children. *Child Develpm.,* 1962, **33,** 907-916.

Crandall, V. Parents as identification models and reinforcers of children's achievement behavior. Progress report, NIMH Grant M-2238, January, 1961 (mimeographed).

Crandall, V., Dewey, Rachel, Katkovsky, W., & Preston, Anne. Parents' attitudes and behaviors and grade school children's academic achievements. *J. genet. Psychol.,* 1964, **104,** 53-66.

Crandall, V., Katkovsky, W., & Preston, Anne. A conceptual formulation of some research on children's achievement development. *Child Develpm.*, 1960, **31**, 787-797. (a)

Crandall, V., Katkovsky, W., & Preston, Anne. Parent behavior and children's achievement development. Paper read at American Psychol. Assn., Chicago, 1960. (b)

Crandall, V., Katkovsky, W., & Preston, Anne. Motivational and ability determinants of young children's intellectual achievement behaviors. *Child Develpm.*, 1962, **33**, 643-661.

Crandall, V., Orleans, Sonya, Preston, Anne, & Rabson, Alice. The development of social compliance in young children. *Child Develpm.*, 1958, **29**, 429-443.

Crandall, V., Preston, Anne, & Rabson, Alice. Maternal reactions and the development of independence and achievement behavior in young children, *Child Develpm.*, 1960, **31**, 243-251.

Crandall, V., & Rabson, Alice. Children's repetition choices in an intellectual achievement situation following success and failure. *J. genet. Psychol.*, 1960, **97**, 161-168.

Crandall, Virginia, Katkovsky, W., and Crandall, V. J. Children's beliefs in their own control of reinforcements in intellectual-academic situations. *Child Develpm.*, in press.

Deutsch, Cynthia. Auditory discrimination and learning: social factors. Paper presented at Arden House Conference on Preschool Enrichment of Socially Disadvantaged Children, December, 1962.

Deutsch, M. Facilitating development in the pre-school child: social and psychological perspectives. *Merrill-Palmer Quarterly*, in press.

Deutsch, M., & Brown, B. Social influences in Negro-white intelligence differences. *J. soc. Issues*, in press.

Feldhusen, J.F., & Klausmeier, H.J. Anxiety, intelligence and achievement in children of low, average, and high intelligence. *Child Develpm.*, 1962, **33**, 403-409.

Forgays, D.G. Subject characteristics and the selective influence of enriched experience in early life. Symposium paper presented at American Psychol. Assn., Philadelphia, August, 1963.

Fowler, W. Cognitive stimulation, IQ changes and cognitive learning in three-year-old identical twins and triplets. *Amer. Psychologist*, 1961, **16**, 373. (Abstract)

Fowler, W. Teaching a two-year-old to read: An experiment in early childhood learning. *Genet. Psychol. Monogr.*, 1962, **66**, 181-283.

Fowler, W. Structural dimensions of the learning process in early reading. Symposium paper presented at American Psychol. Assn., Philadelphia, August, 1963.

Grimes, J., & Allinsmith, W. Compulsivity, anxiety and school achievement. *Merrill-Palmer Quarterly,* **VII,** 1961, 247-271.

Haggard, E.A. Socialization, personality, and achievement in gifted children. *Sch. Rev.,* Winter Issue, 1957, 318-414.

Hoffman, Lois, Rosen, S., & Lippett, R. Parental coerciveness, child autonomy, and child's role at school. Paper read at American Psychol. Assn., Washington, August, 1958.

Hunt, J. McV. *Intelligence and Experience.* New York: Ronald Press, 1961.

Hunt, J. McV. The epigenesis of intrinsic motivation and the stimulation of early cognitive learning. Paper read at American Psychol. Assn., Philadelphia, August, 1963.

John, Vera P. The intellectual development of slum children: some preliminary findings. *Amer. J. Orthopsychiat.,* 1963, **33,** 813-822.

John, Vera. The social context of language acquisition. *Merrill-Palmer Quarterly,* in press.

Jones, H.E. The environment and mental development. In L. Carmichael (Ed.), *Manual of Child Psychology.* New York: Wiley, 1954. Pp. 631-696.

Kagan, J., & Moss, H.A. *Birth to Maturity: A Study in Psychological Development.* New York: John Wiley, 1962.

Kagan, J., Sontag, L.W., Baker, C.T., & Nelson, Virginia L. Personality and IQ change. *J. abnorm. soc. Psychol.,* 1958, **56,** 261-266.

Katkovsky, W., Preston, Anne, & Crandall, V.J. Parents' attitudes toward their personal achievements and toward the achievement behaviors of their children. *J. genet. Psychol.,* 1964, **104,** 67-82. (a)

Katkovsky, W., Preston, Anne, & Crandall, V.J. Parents' achievement attitudes and their behavior with their children in achievement situations. *J. genet. Psychol.,* 1964, **104,** 105-121. (b)

Keller, E.D., & Rowley, V.N. Anxiety, intelligence and scholastic achievement in elementary school children. *Psychol. Rep.,* 1962, **11,** 19-22.

Lunneborg, P.W. Relations among social desirability, achievement, and anxiety measures in children. *Child Develpm.,* 1964, **35,** 169-182.

McCandless, B., & Castaneda, A. Anxiety in children, school achievement, and intelligence. *Child Develpm.,* 1956, **27,** 379-382.

McClelland, D.C. The importance of early learning in the formation of motives. In J. Atkinson (Ed.), *Motives in Fantasy, Action and Society.* Princeton: D. Van Nostrand Co., Inc., 1958. Pp. 437-452.

McClelland, D.C. Risk taking in children with high and low need for achievement. In J. Atkinson (Ed.), *Motives in Fantasy, Action and Society.* Princeton: D. Van Nostrand Co., Int., 1958. Pp. 306-321.

McClelland, D., Atkinson, J., Clark, R., & Lowell, E. *The Achievement Motive.* New York: Appleton-Century-Crofts, Inc., 1953.

Mischel, W. Delay of gratification, need for achievement, and acquiescence in another culture. *J. abnorm. soc. Psychol.*, 1961, **62**, 543-552.

Montessori, Maria. *The Montessori Method.* New York: Frederick A. Stokes, 1912.

Montessori, Maria, *Education for a New World.* Wheaton, Ill.: Theosophical Press, 1959.

Moss, H.A., & Kagan, J. Maternal influences on early IQ scores. *Psychol. Rep.*, 1958, **4**, 665-661.

Murstein, B.I., & Collier, H. The role of the TAT in the measurement of achievement as a function of expectancy. *J. proj. Tech.*, 1962, **26**, 96-101.

Reese, H.W. Manifest anxiety and achievement test performance. *J. educ. Psychol.*, 1961, **52**, 132-135.

Rosen, B.C. Family structure and value transmission. *Merrill-Palmer Quarterly*, Jan. 1964, 59-76.

Rosen, B., & D'Andrade, R. The psychosocial origins of achievement motivations. *Sociometry*, 1959, **22**, 185-218.

Ruebush, B.K. Interfering and facilitating effects of test anxiety. *J. abnorm. soc. Psychol.*, 1960, **60**, 205-212.

Sarason, S., Davidson, K., Lighthall, F., Waite, R. & Ruebush, B. *Test Anxiety in Elementary School Children: A Report of Research.* New York: Wiley, 1960.

Sears, Pauline S., & Levin, H. Level of aspiration in preschool children. *Child Developm.*, 1957, **28**, 317-326.

Sears, Pauline S. Correlates of need achievement and need affiliation and classroom management, self-concept and creativity. Unpublished manuscript, Laboratory of Human Development, Stanford University, 1962.

Sears, Pauline S. Self-concept in the service of educational goals. *Calif. J. Instructional Improvement*, Spring, 1964.

Siss, R., & Wittenborn, J. R. Motivational attitudes of mothers and teachers and their influence upon the educational achievement of third grade boys. Paper read at American Psychol. Assn., St. Louis, August, 1962.

Sontag, L.W., Baker, C.T., & Nelson, Virginia. Mental growth and personality development: a longitudinal study. *Child Develpm. Monogr.*, 1938, No. 2 (Whole No. 68).

Stanford, D., Dember W., & Stanford, L. A children's form of the Alpert-Haber Achievement Anxiety Scale. *Child Develpm.*, 1963, **34**, 1027-1032.

Swift, Joan W. Effects of early group experiment: the nursery school and day nursery. In M.L. Hoffman & L.W. Hoffman (Eds.), *Review of Child Development Research.* New York: Russell Sage, 1964.

Tyler, F.B., Rafferty, Janet, & Tyler, Bonnie. Relationships among motivations of parents and their children. *J. genet. Psychol.*, 1962, **101**, 69-81.

Wellman, Beth L. The effects of preschool attendance upon intellectual development. In R. G. Barker, J. Kounin & H.F. Wright (Eds.), *Child Behavior and Development.* New York: McGraw-Hill, 1943. Pp. 229-243.

Winterbottom, Marian. The relation of need for achievement to learning experiences in independence and mastery. In J. Atkinson (Ed.), *Motives in Fantasy, Action and Society.* Princeton: Van Nostrand, 1958.

8
THE PRESCHOOL YEARS:
INDIVIDUAL AND GROUP DIFFERENCES

Preschool children are particularly vulnerable to orientations, attitudes, and values of parents and others in their immediate family. This is true not only because preschool children are young and impressionable, but also because their attachment to parents or caretakers is extremely intense and has not yet been diluted by attachments to peers, teachers, or other adults. The impact of parents on young children is formidable and cannot easily be outweighed by relatively brief excursions to nursery school or day care centers.

The two articles reprinted here deal with some of the research and issues in the socialization of young children. Variations in socialization are one of the most important factors determining individual differences among young children, and the two articles reprinted here deal with some of the research and issues in this area. In the first paper Clausen describes some of the kinds of socialization practices, attitudes, and orientations that make for individual differences among children. He also points out some of the developmental tasks of this age period, and he identifies areas where more research and information are badly needed.

The second paper, by Herzog and Sudia, concerns a more limited but very important issue, namely, the effects of father absence on child growth and development. In many ways this paper is a model of objective, thoughtful reporting. The authors refuse to be influenced by the "common sense" view of the effects of father absence and make clear how difficult it is to assess the effects of this variable in a meaningful and objective way. In doing so they also demonstrate in general the complexities of assessing the effects of even a relatively simple family variable and the danger of accepting, without examination, some "common sense" assumptions about the effects on children of such variables as father absence.

JOHN A. CLAUSEN

Perspectives in Childhood Socialization*

Our primary concern in this presentation is not with methodology or research strategy but with the cumulative nature of childhood socialization. The child undergoing socialization may not be aware of the significance of influences that impinge on him or even of the beginnings of shifts in his interests and identifications, yet he has an unmatched view of his own life history. He knows how tired he gets of hearing the same old admonitions from parents or teachers; he can recall how breathtakingly fresh a particular discovery was for him years ago. He has a sense of who he is and what he wants, and both come into play over the course of socialization. Parents, too, can view their children's development over the long run. They live with hopes and fears for each child. At times they see their relationships with a child grow suddenly tense and anger-laden; they know the bewilderment of having their own values and goals challenged and occasionally discarded. As a prelude to more detailed consideration of the perspectives of the child and his socialization agents, we shall begin with a brief overview of the problems posed when one considers socialization as a cumulative

*From Chapter 4 of J. A. Clausen (Ed.), *Socialization and Society*, 1968. Reprinted by permission of the author and Little, Brown & Company.

process, beginning at birth and taking place in a variety of settings.

From the beginning, each child presents a more or less unique constellation of constitutional attributes. His size, physical attractiveness, intellectual capacity, and temperament are to a considerable degree influenced by the genes he inherits. Any of these attributes can, however, be modified by intrauterine developments or birth injury as well as by diet, disease, and the nature of the psycho-social environment in which he grows.

His original social matrix—family, social class, ethnic background—not only provides him with initial orientations and trained abilities but carries also an implicit social stereotype of attributed characteristics. Within this matrix, the child develops characteristic ways of interpreting and responding to others. He becomes more or less dependent on others; that is, he may tend to act in his own behalf in many situations or he may look to others to meet his needs. Tendencies to assertiveness, openness to new experience, acceptance of authority—or to opposite responses—gradually become established.

Thus the child brings to each new situation or social role certain behavioral tendencies that are typical for him, some of which were built up in previous social roles, while others are manifestations of his original dispositions. Socialization agents will respond both to the social stereotype derived from appearance and background and to the child's characteristic patterns of behavior.

Within the various milieus and settings in which his socialization takes place, the child is exposed to very different "assumptive worlds." From the time he begins to master language, he is presented with interpretations of himself and of the people around him: his own attractiveness, worthiness, and what he should believe about the nature of his world and the sources of power in it; their motives, their trustworthiness, and their expectations. An adult who comprehends the nature of cultural diversity may be able to operate comfortably in several assumptive worlds; a child whose ability to symbolize is only rudimentary can hardly be expected to do so. Words themselves have different connotations in different social milieus, whether they be the more abstract references to thoughts and feelings used in one group or, in another, the simple direct references to action spiced with words forbidden in conventional middle-class speech. One's language, like his body build and facial features, serves to identify and categorize him. It will inevitably reflect, during the early years, the usage prevalent in one's original social matrix. Only very recently has it been recognized that the Negro child who speaks the dialect derived from the subculture of field slaves must, in effect, master two languages in order to learn to read. For example, linguists working in the Center of Applied Linguistics note that in learning to read the sentence, "John will be there," the southern Negro child living on a farm or in an urban slum must not only make the translation from

print to sound but must learn to equate this sentence with the comparable one in his native tongue, "John go be dere."

Quite apart from the specific aims of socialization agents, the child confronts different constellations of values, beliefs, people, and opportunities depending on where his family is located socially, geographically, and temporally. Some of the most salient features of these constellations are beginning to become clear, though the problems of conceptualization are far from solved.[1] Style of life, including patterns of eating, sleeping, living together, dealing with life problems; preferred modes of association and activities; evaluations made and those received from others; long-range goals; degree of identification with one's neighbors and associates; values for one's children; personality attributes making for success in one's occupation; perception of potential opportunities for the attainment of prized adult statuses—these are but a few of the aspects of life experience that differ sharply according to position in the social structure. They affect the child's perception of school and peer-group socialization settings as well as the nature of family life and parental socialization efforts, and they influence the probability of achieving an integrated identity and an effective role repertoire.

The child must manage to incorporate

[1] An exploration of the features and consequences of social-class differences was undertaken in the report "Linking Social Class and Socialization: Toward a Framework for Analysis and Research" prepared by Harold Proshansky (Ed.), on the basis of a literature review and work-group discussions at the University of Michigan (see Appendix B, Multilithed or Mimeographed Reports).

and to some extent integrate experience from situation to situation and from setting to setting. He must become skilled at discerning not only what is wanted of him by any given socialization agent but the degree of leeway that is available to him, the congruity of any given demand with others made upon him, and the costs of noncompliance with any particular influence attempt. He must learn to restrain or give play to his dispositions differentially; that is, to learn when to act aggressively and when to act submissively, when he can effectively challenge authority and when to accede to it. He must manage his relationships across settings in such a way as to meet quite different sets of expectations.

It is obvious that there are limits to the degree to which the child can bridge conflicting demands or incompatible expectations. Within these limitations he can compartmentalize his roles and the performances they demand. He can be carefree, daring, and somewhat aggressive in the peer group and yet serious, compliant, and reserved in his role as student. He cannot, however, avoid situations where the two sets of demands conflict. At times he must choose where his primary commitment or involvement lies, declaring greater allegiance to the aims of, and his personal ties with, one group as against another. Here we encounter a very difficult problem of conceptualization. To be fully incorporated into a group, an individual must know and understand the role of group member, must be capable of performing that role, and must be motivated to do so.[2] Adequate socialization experience is a necessary, but not a

sufficient, prelude to full membership status; the individual must elect to maintain a degree of commitment to the group and its purposes, but such commitment is not an automatic resultant of socialization.

With this general overview, let us turn to a more detailed examination of the aims and tasks of childhood socialization as viewed by various agents and by the child and as influenced by characteristics of the settings within which socialization takes place. We shall draw largely upon research findings that relate to a single setting at a single point in time. To round out the examination we shall rely heavily upon common experiences and problems in socialization. The problems that confront parents, teachers, and children appear in a different guise than do those posed by the social scientist who wishes his research to bear on theoretical issues. If our task is to extend theory so that it can cope with the phenomena that make the socialization process problematic for participants, we shall have to try to take the perspectives of those participants into account. Some of what we have to say will inevitably seem obvious. Moreover, it is difficult to combine the perspective of researcher with that of a participant in socialization; primary attention will go to the latter. Along the way, we shall try to point out issues and questions begging for research and at the end will offer more general observations about needed research.

THE TASKS OF CHILDHOOD SOCIALIZATION

[2] For a fuller discussion, see Brim (1960).

Most parents are certainly not aware,

when their first infant arrives, of the socialization tasks they must carry out or even of the nature of the expectations they will develop for the child within a matter of weeks. Rather surprisingly, there has been little research on the general orientations that adults who are not yet parents have toward children and how these orientations influence their parental behaviors on the one hand and are modified by the parental experience on the other. Most married couples desire children and, indeed, a good many say they would like at least three or four children (Westoff, Potter, and Sagi, 1963). Moreover, the expressed desire for several children is not, in general, markedly diminished by having experience with one, despite the protests of many new parents concerning the stress and turmoil of caring for an infant. We know from Sears, Maccoby, and Levin (1957) that pregnancies subsequent to the first are somewhat less likely to bring "delight" to the prospective mother, yet in the entire child-rearing literature there is but one study (Lasko, 1954) that examines the affectional relationship between mother and child and patterns of child care during the first few years for *two children from the same family.* There are, of course, many retrospective reports by mothers of the ways in which they improved their maternal performance with experience; to report otherwise might seem an admission of limited capacity to learn.

Few parents appear to be casual about their offspring, but some seem quite preoccupied with envisioning the future and bending their energies to control it, while others seem to live much more in the immediate present. All parents are to

a degree future oriented until their children are well along toward adulthood, but in the first two years many of the tasks that face them and the child have an immediacy that makes long-term future orientations less directly significant than are current task definitions.

There are certain generic tasks to be accomplished in childhood socialization, whatever the culture. Most of these are carried out through the interaction of parents and child, each having his part to play and each only partly aware of what is taking place. The notion of developmental tasks is not new, and the present formulation overlaps considerably with that propounded nearly twenty years ago by Robert J. Havighurst (1948) and further developed in a subsequent work (1953). For Havighurst a developmental task is one typically arising at a certain period of life and requiring mastery by the individual if he is to be a successful and happy human being (Havighurst, 1953, pp. 2–4). Such tasks may be posed by physical maturation, by cultural pressures, or by the individual's own striving. Whereas Havighurst delineated a series of specific tasks, such as learning to walk and learning to take solid food, we have tried in the following pages to indicate the generic tasks to be accomplished, especially as these engage the energies of both parent and child. Whether or not they are accomplished in the family, however, we would state categorically that these tasks must be achieved if the individual is to be successfully socialized *in any society.* Obviously one could elaborate a much finer set of task categories or conceivably could reduce the number here presented. Each type or group of tasks might indeed be regarded as a set of age-graded expectations of increasing complexity, appropriate to the child's abilities and to the requirements of his particular milieu, to be worked on by the child and his socialization agents over the long course of childhood.

The tasks of childhood socialization within the family constitute the first steps toward achieving the performance requirements that are posed for the participant in a given society. But from the perspectives of parent and child they will be seen somewhat differently than from the perspective of societal functioning. Many of the activities or tasks are more properly to be regarded as a series of stages or sequences beginning with initial parental demands and the child's first partial responses and building up to the demand for and achievement of fully acceptable performances at later ages.

Parental Aims and Activities

We may note the following major responsibilities which parents must to some degree fulfill if the child is to survive and to achieve sufficient competence to be acceptable to his parents and to others:

1. Provision of sustenance and nurturance for the infant.

2. Training and channeling of physiological needs — for food, elimination, sleep, etc. — to suit the convenience of parents and (ultimately) to meet cultural standards.

3. Teaching, skill training, and providing opportunities for practice of motor skills, language, cognitive skills, social skills, and technical skills in order to facilitate care, insure safety, and develop potentials for autonomous behavior.

4. Orienting the child to his immedi-

ate world of kin, community, and society in a variety of social situations and settings.

5. Transmitting cultural goals and values; motivating the child toward parental and societal goals.

6. Promoting interpersonal skills, concern for and responsiveness to the feelings of others.

7. Controlling the scope of the child's behaviors, limiting "transgressions," correcting errors, providing guidance and interpretations (and here we crosscut several of the above tasks).

Most of these responsibilities or tasks are further defined in any society by norms that specify how and when parents are to carry them out; that is, a mother is expected to be nurturant in a particular way, "good parents" invest time and effort and follow accepted techniques to make sure that their children learn particular skills, avoid particular kinds of transgressions by certain ages. In all societies there appear to exist ideals of "good child" and "good parent," even though there may be a great deal of latitude in many realms of parent-child interaction.[3]

For each of these statements of parental aims and activities, we can offer a corollary task or achievement for the

---

[3] We take these norms and ideals largely for granted; they seem a part of human nature, and to a degree they probably are. But there are cultural variations both in the ideals themselves and in the ways in which they are exemplified and transmitted. The study of such "collective representations" as they appear in literature, mythology, and other symbolic forms has been of recent origin in the United States but has been a major emphasis in France. See, for example, Chombart de Lauwe (1962).

child. These are summarized in Table 1. The parents' provision of nurturance, affection, and warmth should permit the child to develop a sense of trust and at very least to adapt his bodily movements to those of his caretaker. Failure to adapt, either because of biological deficits in the child or anxiety and tension in the caretaker, will cause a great deal of frustration for both infant and caretaker. Descriptions by psychiatric clinicians suggest that failure to achieve mutual gratification in the nurturing relationship is likely to be associated with a long train of emotional difficulties for the child (see, for example, Sullivan, 1953).

Parental training aimed at the channeling of the child's physiological needs has as its counterpart the demand that the child control his biological impulses, expressing them only in acceptable modes and giving up unacceptable ones. As every parent knows, there can be a great deal of give-and-take and effort on the part of both parent and child before the child willingly accepts the solid foods offered him, gives up the breast or the bottle, and consistently uses the approved toilet arrangements. There *may* be much effort expended, but then again, there may not. Much depends on the vigor and skill with which parents pursue their aims and on

Table 1 **Types of Tasks of Early Childhood Socialization in the Family**

Parental Aim or Activity	Child's Task or Achievement
1. Provision of nurturance and physical care.	Acceptance of nurturance (development of trust).
2. Training and channeling of physiological needs in toilet training, weaning, provision of solid foods, etc.	Control of the expression of biological impulses; learning acceptable channels and times of gratification.
3. Teaching and skill-training in language, perceptual skills, physical skills, self-care skills in order to facilitate care, insure safety, etc.	Learning to recognize objects and cues; language learning; learning to walk, negotiate obstacles, dress, feed self, etc.
4. Orienting the child to his immediate world of kin, neighborhood, community, and society, and to his own feelings.	Developing a cognitive map of one's social world; learning to fit behavior to situational demands.
5. Transmitting cultural and subcultural goals and values and motivating the child to accept them for his own.	Developing a sense of right and wrong; developing goals and criteria for choices, investment of effort for the common good.
6. Promoting interpersonal skills, motives, and modes of feeling and behaving in relation to others.	Learning to take the perspective of another person; responding selectively to the expectations of others.
7. Guiding, correcting, helping the child to formulate his own goals, plan his own activities.	Achieving a measure of self-regulation and criteria for evaluating own performance.

the child's readiness. In many societies it appears that such matters do not tend to become important issues (Hart, 1955); yet in all societies children do learn the necessary measures of control and channels of gratification.

The child's learning to walk and talk are such natural phenomena that it may seem strange to view them as tasks. They are achievements, but how much difference does parental teaching and skill training really make? Maturational readiness is certainly a requisite to effective training; no amount of parental pushing can overcome this stubborn fact.[4] Given such readiness, the child will learn a language that he hears every day whether or not a special effort is made to teach him. On the other hand, such effort (or simply exposure to the rich use of language) is likely to mean increased stimulus and increased opportunity to practice rudimentary skills once they are learned. Only children and firstborn children, for example, tend to acquire the use of language somewhat earlier and somewhat more precisely than do their later-born peers (McCarthy, 1954; Koch, 1956), and one surmises that this is largely due to the greater amount of verbal stimulation from parents at the time when language acquisition is possible. Social-class differences in language learning (McCarthy,

1954) would seem to come about, in part at least, for the same reason.

Stimulation and the provision of models for the child is important, but so is opportunity to perform. The mother who always dresses and feeds her child does not maximize the child's ability to dress and feed himself. A good many tasks can probably be learned by children much earlier than we permit them to learn, partly because their early efforts are so ineffective that it seems simpler to give assistance or do the whole job oneself. For some tasks this may make little difference in the child's development; the time will come when he will insist on dressing himself, for example. But for other tasks, continued parental intervention may prevent both skill learning and development of a sense of competence and autonomy. More important than task performance per se will be the ability to exercise judgement in his own behalf, to make decisions and experience their consequences. What we call "dependency" is not a simple trait but a generalization from a variety of manifestations of the child's inability to act for himself and therefore to rely habitually upon others. Unfortunately, little of the research conducted on dependency examines developmental sequences of skill learning and task performance in the child.

One of the parent's most frequently recurrent tasks is to explain the dangers and behavioral requirements of places, activities, and social situations to the child. In part this is a matter of answering questions — who, when, why? In part it is a matter of explaining how one behaves in a wide variety of situations. From such interchanges and from direct exploration

[4] The early research of McGraw (1935) using twins indicated the ineffectiveness of instituting motor-skill training before maturational readiness. More recent studies of the effects of early stimulation and environmental enrichment suggest that perceptual skills may be enhanced by such stimulation at much younger ages than previously believed. Maturation still sets limits, but they are not so sharply defined.

of his environment, the child builds up a picture of the nature of his world, both physical and social. Here again a question (confronted regularly by parents but largely ignored by research) arises as to optimum autonomy at any given age or skill level. Small children must be protected from environmental dangers, but in an environment where dangers will be encountered they must learn to exercise judgement and handle themselves skillfully. Margaret Mead's observations on the skills of Manus children, who live over water and must early learn to balance themselves in canoes, is a case in point (Mead, 1930). The over-protective mother in such a situation may prevent early accidents but produce a child who is less well equipped to avoid later ones. Or her child may develop such timidity as to limit his performance in a variety of situations. The temperament and energy level of the child will themselves tend to modify the caretaker's role.

In general, the responses that others make to the child in any situation teach him to fit his behavior to situational demands. This is not of course, a single task or even sequence of tasks. It is a matter of lifelong learning. And as Gregory Bateson (1947) and others have so clearly pointed out, success in this process depends on the child's learning to learn — on his becoming aware of cues and applying himself to the task of making sense of them.[5]

What parents want for their child will frequently become apparent in the con-

cerns they express about the child's behavior at a given age. Current problems with the child may be exasperating largely because they constitute difficulties with which the parent must cope, such as the two- to three-year-old who is a dynamo of uncontrollable energy, who is into everything and seemingly quite unresponsive to parental admonition. But far more often, current problems are exasperating (and anxiety provoking) because they suggest future difficulties of inadequacies in meeting expectations. As Aberle and Naegele (1952) noted, many of the matters of concern to middle-class fathers are, from the father's point of view, "prognosticators of adult traits which will interfere with success in middle-class occupational life." One might add, success in the kind of middle-class occupational life that the father himself is most familiar with, for there are considerable differences in the kinds of traits most conducive to success in medicine, law, architecture, and business.

Coordinate with the parent's transmission of cultural goals or moral values and the parent's efforts to motivate the child in the pursuit of such goals and values is the child's development of a sense of right and wrong and standards for guiding his behavior. Again, this is hardly a task in the usual sense but rather a matter of cognitive achievements and of personal identifications. Here we shall simply note that far less attention has been given to the content of what is transmitted and to opportunities for incidental learning of just what is acceptable behavior than to modes of parental sanctioning.

Finally, the parent's efforts to control the scope of the child's behaviors, to provide a measure of autonomy while

---

[5]Highly relevant evidence is provided by Harlow's research on learning sets in monkeys (Harlow, 1949).

offering guidance and commentary, will be related directly to the child's achieving a measure of self-control and some criteria for the evaluation of his own performances. Parent and child must be guided by feedback in many different situations.

There are many aspects of infant care and childhood socialization that cannot, of course, be encapsulated in equivalent pairs of parental activities and child achievements. Moreover, the child's development of social skills cannot in general be directly linked to any particular parental activity, though language, social orientation, and parental guidance will all help him to learn to interpret the actions of others and to modify his own actions appropriately in different social situations. Again, the achievement of selfhood is closely linked to language learning but also to the development of moral values and to a variety of parental demands.

The Child's Perspective

Most parents probably do not explicitly formulate the various aims and activities entailed in early child rearing. Some of these are so completely taken for granted that they need not be formulated. Others become formulated in very specific terms when that which was taken for granted proves to be problematic — most often, when the child has clearly different aims from those of his parents. For the child early manifests his preferences and his will. There are many things the child wants to do, and often he is eager to learn what his parents want him to learn. On the other hand, there are skills his parents want him to learn but about which he cares little and other parental demands that are unpleasant impositions. Even a quite small child may develop strategies for avoiding certain of the learning experiences his parents attempt to arrange for him. As Jane Loevinger has succinctly pointed out: "A parent can decide to beat his child, but he cannot decide how the child will construe the beating" (Loevinger, 1959).

Parental efforts to teach cultural values and to motivate the child are likely to be seen by the child as demands to learn the things grownups regard as important. At times they also involve the child in awe-inspiring rituals that make him feel he is part of something powerful and wonderful. Parental control and limit-setting, on the other hand, may make him feel coerced and frustrated; when he is older he may feel that he is treated unfairly, particularly if the limits set for him are different from those imposed upon his friends. At times the child will not understand what his parents are driving at, expecially if behaviors that elicit amused acceptance at one time bring forth angry castigation at another.

The small child has been characterized by Kubie as "one helpless Lilliputian among hordes of brutal rival Lilliputians in a Brobdingnagian world of giants who are always giving too much protection or too little" (Kubie, 1957, p. 90). These Brobdingnagian giants can pick him up and cuddle him or shake him angrily, can coo at him or shout or scream at him. At times even loving parents may become furiously angry with him and may easily engender feelings of real terror in the child. But mostly, parents and other caretakers are sources of pleasure and security. The child wants their attention, wants to please them, wants to hold on to them. If family life is stable and nurturant, the child is not likely to prefer the company of others to the company of his parents until the approach of adolescence. As late as the initial year of junior high school, for example, our own unpublished data reveal that 74 per cent of the subjects of the Oakland Growth Study would choose both of their parents to be with on a desert island if they could have only three people with them.

In many ways, socialization can be seen as the imposition of restraints and frustrations on the child, especially if one concentrates attention on the demands of weaning, toilet training, and restraining aggression. For most children, however, frustration is probably less acute and less pervasively characteristic of childhood than is the zest for learning to control their bodies and to explore their world. If such exploration brings approval and if accomplishments are praised, the child gains both confidence and competence. If parental response is negative, the child may be dissuaded from certain of his explorations or he may come to treasure the times when he is not under the surveillance of his parents and hence is free to pursue forbidden sources of satisfaction.

In any event, as he is being cared for, guided, and given opportunity to learn, the child is coming to know not only his world but himself. The self is undoubtedly more than reflected appraisals, but a major contribution to self-feeling comes from the child's learning to "take the role of the other." He is able to imagine himself in the place of his parents, his siblings, or someone else who observes and comments on his behavior. In so doing, he begins to bring into his own awareness the social process and the norms that govern others. He also takes over or reflects the dominant tone of those whose commentaries and behaviors he models. We have only the most meager systematic data, largely from students of language learning, on this tremendously important state of development. The young child frequently comments aloud on his current actions, thus providing a monologue which is directed as much to himself as to an outside audience. In time his commentaries become subvocal, but he continues to respond to his own behavior as to the behavior of others, evaluating it in much the same terms that are used by those most significant to him.

Siblings are most often part of the early socialization setting, and their role can be an important one.[6] An older sibling can provide a role model, a companion, a competitor, and an ally. A younger sibling gives his older brother or sister a new perspective, if not a role model, and an opportunity to feel protective, grown-up. The child without siblings is likely to be more adult oriented, less skilled in his later relations with peers unless he has had substantial early opportunity for play with other children.

The social interaction of the young child with his parents, siblings, playmates, and others who enter his immediate environment in the early years has been little studied. We know something of the

[6] Reviews of research evidence leave no doubt that the position of the child among his brothers and sisters significantly influences his personality development (Clausen, 1966), but we have relatively much less information about the ways in which the child's experiences are altered by his position in the family.

process of successive approximations and differentiations by which the meanings of words are learned[7] but little of the ways in which the child learns to interpret the facial expressions, tones of voice, and actions of those with whom he interacts. We have little descriptive data and no evidence regarding long-term consequences of such early learning for the human, but recent research with primates suggests that interaction with adults and with peers in early childhood is crucially important to social and sexual competence in adulthood (Harlow and Harlow, 1965).

Sequence and Scheduling — Preliminary Considerations

So long as the child's activities are confined to the family, the imposition of socialization demands will be largely dependent on the convenience and convictions of his parents. Whether the child is fed on schedule or on demand, whether it has regular hours for sleeping, for being bathed, and for other routines of care, whether it is expected to be toilet trained at one year or two, and whether it is stimulated and primed for little performances as soon as it can lisp are to a considerable degree matters of parental option in a society such as our own. It is true that parents may not recognize these as matters of decision. From their own childhood experiences, from the com-

[7] For a description of the process, see Brown (1958). The beginnings of research on more general aspects of speech socialization and on the acquisition of linguistic competence represent a promising recent development. Sée, for example, Bernstein (1964) and Hymes (1962).

ments of their parents or other persons experienced in the care of children, from pediatricians and family doctors, and from the mass media they may have derived convictions as to the right time for particular demands as well as the right way of imposing them.

Parents are also faced with problems in the scheduling of their own lives and with the fact that a child who has mastered locomotion without having mastered certain other skills and controls can be a nuisance. The mother who wishes to hold a full-time job outside the home can hardly continue to nurse her child unless she can take the child to her place of work. Societies differ greatly in the extent to which they afford alternative institutional arrangements for infant care.

The mother of three or four young children will have reason to expect a measure of self-care and self-control from the older children while she is involved in the care of the newest infant. The available research evidence (reviewed in Clausen, 1966) suggests both that more demands for self-care are made in larger families and that firstborn children tend to have greater responsibilities.

Demands for scheduling increase very markedly when the child moves outside of the family circle. Expectations of what is appropriate for a child of a given age are, of course, not purely matters of social definition. As already noted, the child's performances depend on biological maturation. None but legendary children walk or talk at six months. There is a sufficiently broad span of maturational readiness for particular childhood performances so that expectations of the larger community are not heavily imposed on the small child but normative expectations nevertheless exist. As he moves outside the home, the walking, talking child must rather quickly come to recognize that there are limits to the liberties he can take with others and their property if he is to avoid their displeasure. In small communities at least, parents whose children are lacking in control will be the subject of comment; and, if the children present a serious annoyance, they may be excluded from some circles. Parents who are unduly restrictive will also be the subject of comment, being seen as rigid, or old-fashioned, or perhaps as not understanding children. In contemporary urban society, however, most parental behaviors will be unknown, and social pressures to influence parents whose products are not wholly acceptable will be minimal. Insofar as pressures do exist, they will come from agents and agencies asked to share in the care of the child, such as nursery schools and "babysitters," or from other parents or persons whose children or sensibilities have been outraged. Research on feedback to parents and its effects is almost non-existent.

RELATIONSHIPS BETWEEN SOCIALIZATION AGENTS AND THE CHILD

As the child moves outside the family there are a number of other agents and agencies of socialization to which he will be exposed. In unsupervised play with his peers he comes to participate in autonomous groupings which have their own shared activities, codes of behavior, and controls. Through family, school, or neighborhood he may be involved in church activities, in clubs, and supervised youth groups. Some of these are selected by the child or his parents as congenial or helpful. In other instances, agents or agencies may select the child for attention because of problematic behaviors. In each instance, there are particular agents pursuing particular socialization or control goals.

Any member of society may serve as a socialization agent when he influences the behavior of another, even though he may not intend such influence or may intend it merely as leading to immediate situational change. The present analysis examines the child's interactions with a limited number of the major agents of socialization. In the course of this analysis we shall examine the nature of relationships between agent and inductee as well as the aims, techniques, and timing of socialization efforts. In general, it appears that the more intimate and enduring a relationship, the less sharply are socialization aims formulated and the less directly linked to particular techniques. This is only a hypothesis, but it appears to be supported by informal observation if not by systematic data.

Socialization techniques have been studied largely as they relate to the imposition of disciplines of early childhood training, the uses of rewards and punishments, and the expressed concerns of parents of older children. To a considerable degree, the techniques of socialization in later childhood are enmeshed in the dialectic of social interaction, in personal interactive strategies, and modes of role relationship and role induction. Timing or scheduling has likewise been considered largely for the infant and toddler except in studies of age-grading in other societies. We shall not, then, be in a position to draw on systematic research but rather to ask questions about issues that seem worthy of more adequate consideration.

Let us now examine in more detail the relational patterns and loyalties involved in the major socialization settings of childhood and, subsequently, some of the implications each set of influences has for the others. These implications or consequences will depend to a very large degree on the placement of the child's family within the social structure. Social class, size of community, religion, and race or ethnic membership markedly affect what is transmitted, techniques of transmission, and the interrelationships of socialization influences. In order to be better able to examine these effects, some further conceptualization of socialization relationships may be useful.

Role Relationships in Socialization

Relationships between socialization agents and individuals being socialized tend to be subject to normative expectations for the role performance of each participant as well as value orientations adhering to the relationship itself (for example, the moral injunctions relating to family ties). The normative expectations are often flexible, however, depending on the characteristics of the individuals involved, the demands of other roles, the nature of the social setting in which socialization takes place, and the nature of the goals being sought at any given time. It is therefore difficult to separate the purely normative definition of a role relationship from those aspects that are somewhat dependent on personal characteristics or situational considerations. The

following appear to be the most important properties or modifiers of role relationships involving socialization agents and those being socialized.[9]

(1) Affectivity, nature of the emotional tie:

   (a) Loving-hostile (accepting-rejecting)
   (b) Emotionally involved—affectively neutral

(2) Relative power of agent and inductee, including resource control (equivalent to dependence of the inductee).

(3) Relative degree of initiative (responsibility) allocated to agent and inductee.

(4) Specificity or diffuseness of the claims of each individual upon the other.

(5) Explicitness and primacy of socialization aims (or social-influence aims) of agent as against other objectives (that is, commitment of the agent to bringing about changes in the orientations, skills, feelings, etc., of the inductee).

(6) Consonance, congruence, or resonance of the goals of agent and inductee in the relationship generally and in regard to specific socialization aims.

(7) Interpersonal skills of both parties and the clarity of communication between them.

(8) Group and contextual supports for or in opposition to agent's aims and methods (normative solidarity versus alienation, subterranean values, conflict orientation).

[9] This formulation draws upon several classifications of social relationships in use within general behavioral science theory as well as upon evidence from socialization research theory.

Each of these variables is in part specified by social-structural arrangements or by the cultural expectations and value orientations that apply to a given relationship; each is also to some degree dependent on personal characteristics or orientations of the participants, some of which may be specific to a given situation or context. In the family, where the most crucial part of primary socialization takes place, parents and children are bound to each other by the strongest moral imperatives. There is usually a strong affectional bond; relationships are diffuse (primary, pervasive); parental power is high (complete in infancy, very high in childhood); the socialization role tends to have primacy, especially for the mother, though not in all situations; parental goals tend to be largely accepted during the early years; and parents and children speak the same language, even though they may not always communicate.

Psychological research on socialization has concerned itself most closely with affectivity and power or control in the parent-child relationship. Thus Schaefer (1959) has suggested that maternal behavior toward the child can be summarized as a function of the dimensions "love-hostility" and "control-autonomy." Becker (1964) has proposed a three-dimensional model for the classification of parental orientations toward the child and has examined the consequences of various disciplinary techniques when used by parents holding such orientations. He has labeled the dimensions "warmth-hostility," "restrictiveness-permissiveness," and "detachment-anxious emotional involvement." Becker summarizes research indicating that power-assertive techniques of discipline tend to be used

by hostile parents and tend to promote aggression and resistance to authority in young children. Although it seems reasonable to assume that hostility and warmth are attributes of the parent when we are considering parental behaviors with small children, there is a point at which they are likely to become attributes of the relationship. Moreover, some parental hostility even to small infants seems to reflect the parent's feeling that the child is not as loving as the parent has expected. Such feelings have been reported, for example, in instances of severe child beating (Morris and Gould, 1963). In any case it does appear that affection, emotional involvement, and the uses of power by the parent are probably the most crucial dimensions of parent-child relationships *for the small child*. Once the child has begun to learn about the world outside the family circle, however, and especially if there are siblings who can reinforce each other's invoking of points of view that differ from the parents, other aspects of the parent-child relationship must be considered.

Unfortunately, there is not a simple relationship between these aspects of socialization roles and the effectiveness of socialization efforts. Indeed, in the case of much learning by imitation, it appears that no relationship at all is required with the model; the child merely needs to see him. Situational circumstances can be extremely important as in cases of behavioral contagion. On the other hand, copying is more frequent when a positive relationship exists (Bandura and Walters, 1963) or when the model has high prestige (Lippitt *et al.*, 1952). In instances when an adult is trying to teach a child something important to that child's orientation or future functioning, existing research and theory support the generalization that, other things being equal, a positive, warm relationship will be more effective for almost any kind of learning except avoidance responses. Power not harshly used will be most effective when linked with positive affect but may be effective to a degree even when there is no emotional tie between the agent and the child, since power implies that the agent controls resources. On the other hand, power coupled with hostility may lead to coercion but seldom to consensus. Indeed, the use of power is likely to generate hostility; authoritarian parents generate more resentment than democratic ones, in our own society at least (Elder and Bowerman, 1963). The ends of social control may be served by such use of power, but the agents' socialization aims are less likely to be achieved. Don, a Hopi chief studied by Simmons (1942) was frightened by the powerful, masked Katchina gods who beat him, without intercession from his parents, at his initiation. Subsequently, he bitterly resented this collusive use of force and was alienated rather than emotionally incorporated into the social network by the act.

One may examine the scope of the activities of child and agent in a number of other respects. To what extent does the agent use his power and resources to screen out influences impinging upon the child and to limit opportunities available to it as against opening up the child to diverse experiences and opportunities? There are also matters of style or emphasis. Does the agent stress the motivations underlying the child's behaviors, or the behavioral outcomes themselves? Kohn (1963) has suggested, for example, a

marked difference between the styles manifest by middle-class and working-class parents in precisely this respect, with the middle-class parent being far more concerned about underlying motivations. One may ask, also, is the emphasis on encouraging the child to try new tasks or on evaluating his skill in performing tasks especially important to his parents?

The timing of socialization efforts must also be considered. To date, timing has been examined primarily in connection with the enhancement of achievement motivation through early demands for self-reliance (McClelland, 1961) and the effects of training relative to maturational readiness (McGraw, 1935). But it is obvious that some parents anticipate certain kinds of performance requirements to a substantial degree while others do not make specific efforts to train their children for such tasks until the children appear to be late or deficient in performance by almost any standards. Some parents, for example, provide the child with instruction and opportunities to learn to swim while of preschool age, while others become aware of the fact that their children have not learned to swim only when they encounter a situation in which it is assumed that all adolescents are swimmers. Very often, of course, differences in the timing of socialization efforts reflect differences in the priorities assigned to various activities, skills, or knowledge. Should an "immature" child start the first grade at the usual age, or will he benefit from an additional year of kindergarten in which his physical, social, and intellectual skills may blossom sufficiently to permit him to experience greater competence in the classroom? Timing also rests on assumptions about appropriateness and may involve anxieties about the child getting into trouble or getting wrong ideas if a given facet of socialization experience comes too soon — or too late.

It appears that parents can have close, warm relationships with their children and yet manifest quite different styles — quite different emphases — in their socialization efforts. It is not at all evident that any given style or approach is necessarily superior to any other. Much will depend upon the nature of the environment in which socialization takes place, the attributes of the participants, and the nature of the role performance to be desired. It is equally difficult to establish, except on the basis of personal preferences, the pros and cons of conformity or good "adjustment to one's environment." There is little question but that induction of a considerable degree of conformity can have a high payoff value for the child, so far as interpersonal relationships and social mobility in contemporary American society are concerned. On the other hand, beyond a certain minimum, such conformity may not go hand in hand with either intellectual or artistic creativity. Quite possibly, also, a person may be highly conforming in certain respects yet highly innovative in others. For example, MacKinnon (1965) has noted that highly creative architects score lower on ratings of affiliation and deference and higher on aggression and autonomy than their less creative peers. Creative architects also score lower on scales of responsibility and self control, among others. In their socialization they appear to have had unusual freedom to explore their world, clear standards of conduct but at the same time "the absence of pressures to establish prematurely one's professional identity." . . .

References

Aberle, D. F., and Naegele, K. D. Middle-class fathers' occupational role and attitudes toward children. *American Journal of Orthopsychiatry*, 1952, **22**, 366-78.

Bandura, A., and Walters, R. A. *Social Learning and Personality Development*. New York: Holt, Rinehart & Winston, 1963.

Bateson, G. Social planning and the concept of "deuterolearning." In T. M. Newcomb and E. L. Hartley, *Readings in Social Psychology*. New York: Henry Holt & Co., 1947. Pp. 121-28.

Becker, W. C. Consequences of different kinds of parental discipline. In M. L. Hoffman and Lois W. Hoffman (Eds.), *Review of Child Development Research*. Vol. 1. New York: Russell Sage Foundation, 1964. Pp. 169-208.

Bernstein, B. Elaborated and restricted codes: their social origins and some consequences. In J. J. Gumperz and D. Hymes (Eds.), *The Ethnography of Communication*. Special publication of the *Ameri-*

can *Anthropologist*, 1964, 66, No. 6, Part 2, 55-69.

Brim, O. G., Jr. Personality development at role learning. In I. Iscoe and H. Stevenson (Eds.), *Personality Development in Children*. Austin: University of Texas Press, 1960. Pp. 127-59.

Brown, C. *Manchild in the Promised Land*. New York: The Macmillan Co., 1965.

Chombart de Lauwe, Marie-José. La représentation de l'enfant dans la société urbain contemporaine. *Enfance*, 1962, No. 1, 53-67.

Clausen, J. A. Family structure, socialization, and personality. In M. L. Hoffman and Lois W. Hoffman (Eds.), *Review of Child Development Research*. Vol. 2. New York: Russell Sage Foundation, 1966. Pp. 1-53.

Elder, G. H., Jr., and Bowerman, C. E. Family structure and child-rearing patterns: the effect of family size and sex composition. *American Sociological Review*, 1963, **28**, 891-905.

Harlow, H. F. The formation of learning sets. *Psychological Review*, 1949, **56**, 51-65.

Harlow, H. F., and Harlow, Margaret. The affectational systems. In A. M. Schrier, H. F. Harlow, and F. Stollnitz (Eds.), *Behavior of Nonhuman Primates*. Vol. 2. New York: Academic Press, 1965.

Hart, C. W. M. Contrasts between prepubertal and postpubertal education. In G. D. Spindler (Ed.), *Education and Anthropology*. Stanford: Stanford University Press, 1955. Pp. 127-62.

Havighurst, R. J. *Developmental Tasks and Education*. Chicago: University of Chicago Press, 1948.

Havighurst, R. J. *Human Development and Education*. New York: Longmans, Green, 1953.

Hymes, D. H. The ethnography of speaking. In T. Gladwin and W. C. Sturtevant (Eds.), *Anthropology and Human Behavior*. Washington, D.C.: Anthropological Society of Washington, 1962. Pp. 13-53.

Koch, H. L. Sibling influence on children's speech. *Journal of Speech Disorder*, 1956, **21**, 322-28.

Kohn, M. L. Social class and parent-child relationships: an interpretation. *American Journal of Sociology*, 1963, **68**, 471-80.

Kubie, L. S. Social forces and the neurotic process. In A. H. Leighton, J. A. Clausen, and R. N. Wilson (Eds.), *Explorations in Social Psychiatry*. New York: Basic Books, 1957. Pp. 77-104.

Lasko, Joan K. Parent behavior toward first and second children. *Genetic Psychology Monographs*, 1954, **49**, 96-137.

Lippitt, R., Polansky, N., Redl, F., and Rosen, S. The dynamics of power. *Human Relations*, 1952, **5**, 37-64.

Loevinger, Jane. Patterns of parenthood as theories of learning. *Journal of Abnormal and Social Psychology*, 1959, **59**, 148-50.

McCarthy, Dorothea. Language development in children. In L. Carmichael (Ed.), *Manual of Child Psychology*. New York: John Wiley & Sons, 1954. Pp. 492-630.

McClelland, D. C. *The Achieving Society*. Princeton, N.J.: D. Van Nostrand Co., 1961.

McGraw, Myrtle B. *Growth: A Study of Johnny and Jimmy*. New York: Appleton, 1935.

MacKinnon, D. W. Personality and the realization of creative potential. *American Psychologist*, 1965, **20**, 273-281.

Mead, Margaret. *Growing Up in New Guinea: A Comparative Study of Primitive Education*. New York: William Morrow & Co., 1930.

Morris, M.G., and Gould, R. W. Role reversal: A concept in dealing with the neglected battered-child syndrome. In *The neglected battered child syndrome: Role reversal in parents.* New York: Child Welfare League of America, 1963.

Schaefer, E. S. A circumplex model for maternal behavior. *Journal of Abnormal and Social Psychology*, 1959, **59**, 226-35.

Sears, R. R., Maccoby, E. E., and Levin, H. *Patterns of child rearing*. Evanston, Ill.: Row, Peterson & Co., 1957.

Simmons, L. W. (Ed.) *Sun chief: The Autobiography of a Hopi Indian*. New Haven, Conn.: Yale University Press, 1942.

Sullivan, H. S. *The interpersonal theory of psychiatry*. New York: W. W. Norton & Co., 1953.

Westoff, C., Potter, R. G., and Sagi, P. *The third child*. Princeton, N. J.: Princeton University Press, 1963.

ELIZABETH HERZOG AND CECELIA E. SUDIA

Fatherless Homes: A Review of Research*

Over six million children in the United States today are growing up in fatherless

*From *Children*, Sept.-Oct., 1968, 177-182. Reprinted by permission of the authors and the Office of Child Development, U. S. Department of Health, Education and Welfare.

homes. People are making many adverse generalizations about these children — generalizations concerning problem behavior, intellectual ability and achievement, and emotional adjustment. To find out whether these generalizations are supported by evidence, we have reviewed research on children growing up in homes from which the father is absent.

Let it be clear at the outset that, other things being equal, we believe a two-parent home is more likely to be better for a child than a one-parent home. However, our review is not concerned with such a comparison, but merely with the effects on children of growing up in fatherless homes.

The report is not yet complete, but it is far enough along to provide some tentative findings and some firm impressions, based on review of almost 400 studies. Our primary list is limited to studies that are focused directly on the effects on children of growing up in fatherless homes, plus a few that include such a focus as part of a broader inquiry. This primary list, which we call our "core group," includes 59 studies. We tried especially to cover studies that were conducted during the last two decades, in addition to a few outstanding studies from earlier years. We did not try to cover the countless studies that include the category "broken home" as a trait used in describing a sample. Our effort, rather, was to achieve a representative sample of such studies for comparisons. Further, we limited our inquiry to homes in which the absent parent was the father, since such homes make up by far the majority of broken homes and since fatherless homes cannot be equated with motherless homes.

A systematic review of research in a given subject area means that the findings of other investigators become the raw data of the review. Although our analysis has not been primarily quantitative, we did undertake to make a rough and superficial count of the conclusions offered by the studies in our core group:

how many reported adverse effects associated with fatherless homes, how many reported no adverse effects; and in each group, how many studies appeared reasonably sound in method, how many exhibited research defects too gross to permit serious consideration, and how many lay in the dubious territory between these extremes. Obviously, our classifications regarding soundness were subjective. However, each represented a conference judgment, and we accepted the author's word in classifying conclusions. We think that most serious researchers would probably agree to our extreme groups. There would probably be disagreement about studies in the dubious group, which we coded, quite literally, with a question mark.

For convenience, we refer to the studies that report adverse traits or behavior associated with absence of a father as upholding the "classic" view, and to the others as challenging the classic view.

Our rough overall count, in effect, allowed each study to cast one vote "for" or "against" indicting the fatherless home as inflicting on its children adverse effects of some specified kind. The purpose was merely to document direction and degree of consensus without necessarily assuming that the results would prove one view right and another wrong.

Among the core group investigating the effects of continuing absence of the father, 29 studies support the classic view that fatherless homes are associated with adverse characteristics or behavior in the child; 17 challenge this position; and 13 report mixed conclusions.

Of the 29 reporting adverse effects, seven were rated as reasonably sound in method. Of the 17 challenging the classic view, seven were rated as reasonably sound.

The count cannot be taken too seriously because aspects investigated and conclusions reached were so varied and so fragmentary. Most studies of fatherless homes look at only one area, or, typically, only a few slivers of information within one area. It is interesting, however, that in the overall count the "classic" view wins handily, but among the studies rated acceptable in method, the rough score is a tie: seven for and seven against the classic view. The acceptable group comprises a larger proportion of those challenging than of those supporting the classic view.

Since juvenile delinquency is one of the adverse effects most often ascribed to broken homes, we made a separate count of those core studies that mention juvenile delinquency plus some other studies of delinquency not included in the core group. We found that seven studies upheld the classic view with regard to juvenile delinquency, although five of these did so with strong qualifications or reservations; of these, four were rated reasonably sound in method. Six studies opposed the classic view; of these, only one was rated reasonably sound.

The qualifications and reservations associated with the classic view had to do largely with confounding factors. Some investigators who found deliquent behavior significantly correlated with fatherless homes distrusted their own findings because of accumulated evidence that apprehension and treatment of juveniles are influenced by the fact of a broken home; or that the proportion of broken homes is high among low-income Negroes, who are more likely than others

to be apprehended and, once apprehended, are more likely to be institutionalized — an experience tending to promote recidivism.

All in all, the consensus concerning delinquency leans toward the classic view if one takes no account of adequacy of method, and also if one does; but the classic view in this consensus is strongly qualified by suspicions of confounding factors.

TEMPORARY FATHER ABSENCE

Some of the studies cited as evidence of the adverse effects of fatherless homes are studies of *temporary* father absence. One of those most often cited is a Norwegian study[1] of father absence that was not only temporary, but also socially approved. The fathers were naval officers who were often away for 2 years at a time. The families were rural, white, upper-middle class, strait-laced Protestant. This Norwegian study is a careful study, with carefully qualified conclusions. But, as often happens, the investigators' qualifications evaporate when it is cited by others. Eloquent pleas have been made for rescuing the boys of Harlem from the adverse efforts of fatherless homes "proved" by the Norwegian study. But there is a question about applying findings of this study to Negro boys in our urban ghettos. The question is underscored by the findings of other studies of the effects of a father's planned, temporary, socially approved absence (especially absence for military duty). Some of these studies, also carefully planned and executed, conclude that the chief problems were precipitated by the father's return rather than by his absence.[2]

The children in the Norwegian study were about 9 years old. Some studies of college men whose fathers had been away temporarily when they were growing up show systematic differences between these men and the controls, college men whose fathers were present throughout their childhood. On the other hand, at least one study shows differences in early childhood that seem to disappear later.[3] In another study, the investigator concluded that children in fatherless homes may merely take longer than children in two-parent homes to develop some characteristics, and suggested that they are more dependent than other children on peers for learning certain kinds of behavior.[4] Obviously, the age at which separation from the father occurs is important, and so is the age at which the child is studied.

Study findings are hardly needed to demonstrate that temporary father absence cannot be equated with continuing father absence; or that planned and socially approved absence cannot be equated with socially disapproved absence. Studies that control for type of father absence — and many do — consistently report differences between children whose fathers are dead and those whose parents are divorced or separated. The differences are not always in the same direction. On the whole, however, ascribed effects of the father's absence are more marked in children whose parents are divorced or separated than in children whose fathers are dead. That is, adverse effects are reported to be stronger when the cause of fatherlessness is viewed with social disfavor. In line with this generalization, some studies of families broken by divorce report more adverse effects on children in Catholic and Jewish than in Protestant families[5] and in middle-income white families than in low-income Negro families.[6]

The picture does not become more clearcut when studies of temporary father absence are separated from studies of continuing father absence. The general pattern of findings remains the same though the numbers in each group are smaller. More studies do than do not report adverse effects associated with temporary father absence; but when the count is limited to studies rated free of gross defect in method, the number in each group is the same.

We are deliberately bypassing a number of highly relevant research points, such as sample selection, presence or absence of controls, effectiveness of controls, especially for socioeconomic status, and, above all, type of father absence. We have counted at least seven types of father absence, variously defined and varyingly compared, in the studies reviewed, and these do not exhaust the variations found in real life. The different types of father absence cannot be equated, nor do they form an orderly continuum.

In many instances, it is difficult to compare the studies because they do not use the same definition of "broken home," the term most commonly used. For example, some investigators include any "ever-broken" home in the broken home group, while others exclude reconstituted homes. Thus, children with a stepparent are sometimes in the "broken" and sometimes in the "intact" group.

A further point, also obvious, must be recognized in passing: although the differences reported are statistically significant, they are not necessarily practically significant. For example, with regard to juvenile delinquency, one statewide study reports that about 2 percent of the boys in two-parent homes and about 3.5 percent of the boys in one-parent homes were classified as delinquents.[7] Another way of saying the same thing is that 98 percent of the boys in two-parent homes and 96.5 percent of the boys in fatherless homes were classified as nondelinquent. Even without the appropriate qualifications, these figures do not suggest that most boys in fatherless homes are likely to be delinquent.

FAMILY PATTERNS

One missing element in these studies is a sense of individuals in the context of families and of families in the context of a broader community. Another is the recognition of different kinds of one-parent and two-parent families. When studies are focused on two-parent families, differences in harmony and functional two-parentness are often recognized. We hear a great deal about the communications gap between generations and about the impact on the child of the parents' marital relationship and of the parents' individual emotional or behavior problems.

On the other hand, in discussions of the adverse effects of broken homes on the development of children, there often seems to be a tacit assumption that all two-parent homes are "good" homes, in which fathers are strong and zealous, all parental functions are shared, and close-knit harmony prevails. Very few studies

compare the effects on children of tense and conflict-ridden two-parent homes with the effects of harmonious, well-organized one parent homes. Even fewer studies inquire about how the image of an absent father is presented to his children. We found almost no studies that explicitly related the effect of father absence to availability and functioning of other relatives or to the economic consequences of his absence.

SEX ROLES

In studies of fatherless children, much emphasis is placed on the lack of sex role models, especially on the problem the fatherless boy has in developing adequate masculine identification. In studies of Negro boys in low-income homes, sex role problems are ascribed to the matriarchal family. Studies of middle-class children also highlight sex role problems, but without reference to matriarchy. The most frequent conclusion is that, lacking a resident male model, the boy is more likely to become feminized. He may show this by dependency and passivity, or he may show it by compensatory masculinity. If he scores too low on a test of masculinity-femininity, he is classified as feminized; if he scores high, he may be classified as showing overcompensation.

Studies concerned with masculinity and femininity pose problems both of substance and of method. The concepts used include "masculine and feminine roles," "role models," "identity," and "identification." These terms are neither strictly synonymous nor mutually exclusive, but present purposes do not require an attempt to define their areas of overlap and margins of difference. The measures most often used are scales of masculinity and femininity (referred to as M-F scales), questionnaires about family roles and relationships, and projective tests.

Many different M-F scales have been used, most of which were constructed through trial-and-error selection of the items that discriminated most effectively between males and females. These items usually include the subject's activity preference, occupational preference, avowed anxieties, and emotional reactions.

Among the projective tests used in these studies, structured doll play is conspicuous. Other projective tests employed were the IT Scale for Children and the Blacky test.

The studies reviewed were focused chiefly on boys who were growing up in fatherless homes. Differences in various directions have been reported for girls in fatherless homes compared with those in two-parent homes, but more attention has been paid to boys and their sex role identification. Only two studies focused exclusively on girls.

A preponderance of relevant studies in our core group show some M-F differences in the direction of lower masculinity scores on the part of fatherless boys. On a referendum basis, this tendency would be clear. But if only the studies rated reasonably sound in method are taken into account, the verdict is somewhat less decisive. In any case, the verdict is based only on a moderate difference between the mean scores of the groups compared. There are many individual exceptions — that is, a considerable overlap exists in the scores of children in one-parent and two-parent homes. Still a question remains about the assumptions

underlying the use of these tests in studies of fatherless families.

Many of the measures employed have been sharply challenged on points of contents and interpretation.[8, 9] However, quite aside from questions about the validity of the tests (and there are serious questions), there is a question whether one should use as a criterion of basic well-being the degree to which a fatherless boy can be classified as adequately masculine according to one of the familiar measures. If it is assumed that "real" masculinity or femininity *should* be a criterion in judging well-being, then it must be recognized that there are several aspects the familiar tests do not claim to measure — for example, the child's conception of the way a man feels and behaves and the way a woman feels and behaves, or his picture of the interrelations between men and women. A more important consideration may be the child's conception of what it means to be a human being and what to expect from and offer to other human beings.

Most tests of sex role development do not claim to assess a child's basic well-being or potential for future well-being. They are geared, rather, to testing discrete variables which, according to the theory accepted by the investigator, provide clues to future well-being. Doubts about their usefulness as a basis for generalizations concerning fatherless children are supported by the fact that typically the M-F scores of more highly educated male and female subjects are closer together than those with less education.[10]

People who are concerned primarily with broad generalizations and broad programs cannot afford to base such generalizations on fragmentary studies undertaken to test fragments of theories which are themselves under challenge. Much of the research reviewed dealing with adequate sex-role development is of this nature.

Practitioners and program planners are not obliged to wait for resolutions of theoretical controversies before seeking answers relevant to programs and services. But they *are* obliged to make sure that any conclusions accepted are based on the soundest available evidence, which has been subjected to thorough analysis and has been viewed in the context of other available evidence.

Long before theoretical controversies have been resolved and experimental testing of theories has been completed, a great deal can be learned by careful analysis of detailed descriptive studies. For that matter, theory itself might profit by a great deal more preliminary observation and description. After all, this was the basis of Piaget's theories, which have contributed substantially both to theoretical psychology and its practical application.[11]

The information about very low-income families, fatherless or fathered, that is most useful to practitioners and programs has not come from neat precise experimental testing of discrete, theory-based variables. It has come rather from less structured descriptive reports of anthropologists and anthropologically attuned sociologists such as Hylan Lewis, S. M. Miller, Lee Rainwater, and Frank Riessman, to name a few.

THREE CONCLUSIONS

This review has been a chastening experience. We have analyzed a wide range of studies, from large to small and from solid to inconsequential, using diverse and sometimes dubious instruments. There has been an almost startling lack of replication. Results do not fit together or complement each other to a substantial degree. Nevertheless, the review does provide a basis for conclusions:

1. Existing data do not permit a decisive answer to questions about the effects on children of fatherlessness. As Maccoby remarked about one small group of father absence studies, "the issue must remain open for further evidence."[10] We can add that, on the basis of what we have found so far, we would not expect adequate evidence to indicate dramatic differences stemming from fatherlessness per se. If all the confounding factors (such as socioeconomic status, race, age of child, type of father absence) could be controlled, children in fatherless homes might be classified as somewhat worse off than children in two-parent homes with regard to some (though by no means all) of the variables investigated; but the statistical differences would probably be far less dramatic than is generally assumed, and might be negligible. Even if some differences were statistically significant, we would expect their practical importance to be dwarfed by other variables.

2. To increase knowledge about the effects on children of growing up in fatherless homes and about ways of helping them to achieve their full potential, we need to look with new eyes at the family—a prescription more easily given than filled. We need to broaden the context of our investigations and to deepen our knowledge about individual roles and interactions and about family

processes. In this connection, several interrelated areas would merit more attention than they have had.

The fatherless home in the United States, for example, deserves study as a family form in itself, rather than as a mutilated version of some other form. It would be useful to give clearer recognition to the one-parent family as a family form in its own right—not a preferred form, but nevertheless one that exists and functions and represents something other than mere absence of true familiness. We need to take account of its strengths as well as its weaknesses; of the characteristics it shares with two-parent families as well as its differences; of ways in which it copes with its undeniable difficulties; and of ways in which the community supports or undermines its coping capacity.

Role models that actually influence children in both one-parent and two-parent homes also deserve more study. On the one hand, there are suggestions that many fatherless boys are not so lacking in male models as is often assumed—especially boys in very low-income families.[1][2]

On the other hand, there are questions about whether an effective male model necessarily has to be one living in the home. It is often pointed out that children learn about maleness and femaleness from many sources, including the adults in their homes, their peer groups, TV, movies, and other mass media, and especially the persons—children or adults—who influence them particularly. Less is said about the influence of siblings as such, who are conspicuous by their absence from most of the studies reviewed. Yet in theories of child development and in the life history of most people who have had brothers or sisters, siblings are important.

Granting that an adequate, affectionate, resident father is desirable for and desired by most boys and girls, a great deal more needs to be learned about the extent to which male models who are not the children's fathers, including those who do and those who do not live in the home, help or could help fill the model gap. This means that more must also be learned about male models other than the father in the lives of children who grow up in two-parent homes—homes with fathers adequate and inadequate, ever-present or intermittently present. But we need to learn on a base broader than a few discrete theory-determined variables.

The mother in the fatherless home also needs to be studied. How does she cope with her dual role as mother and father-substitute? How does she cope with her children? What picture of the absent father does she project to them? What kind of supervision and discipline is she able to exercise? What expectations does she impart to them about life and about people? What support does she have from family, friends, or community? We assume that the effect on children of the mother's behavior and attitudes is profound in any family. Unquestionably, in the absence of a father, the mother's role is especially difficult and demanding.

It is usually impossible and often would be undesirable to restore the absent father to a fatherless home. But it *is* possible to ease at least some of the mother's burdens—economic and social, if not psychological. And this may be the most direct and effective means of opening a pathway to fuller development and more life satisfaction for her children.

3. We are giving the question a wrong slant when we ask: how, and how much, are childred harmed by growing up in fatherless homes? The history of research about working mothers provides a useful example with regard to question formulation. Not so many years ago, conferences were discussing the effects on children of having a mother work outside the home. Distressed mothers, alarmed at the wide publicity given to an inadequately controlled research stody, were writing to the Children's Bureau to ask, "Am I making my child into a juvenile delinquent because I have to work?"

Today there is remarkable consensus among research investigators concerned with the subject, that whether the mother works is not in itself the crucial variable. On the contrary, analysis of available evidence indicates that the effect on her child of a mother's employment depends on a number of other factors, such as her attitudes toward working or not working; the attitudes of other family members; her relationship to her husband; her temperament; her arrangements for child care; and the age, sex, and special needs of the child.

The relevance of this example lies in the shift of focus from a single variable, assumed to be "the" determining factor of whatever results are found, to a cluster of interacting factors that, on the one hand, mediate the effect of that variable and, on the other hand, provide clues to methods of diminishing some adverse elements in its effects. We expect an analogous development with regard to children in fatherless homes.

References

1. Lynn, D. B., Sawrey, W.L.: The effects of father absence on Norwegian boys and girls. *Journal of Abnormal and Social Psychology*, September 1959.
2. Stolz, Lois Meek, et al.: Father relations of war-born children. Stanford University Press, Stanford, Calif. 1954.
3. Mischel, Walter: Father-absence and delay of gratification: cross-cultural comparisons. *Journal of Abnormal and Social Psychology*, July 1961.
4. Sears, Pauline S.: Doll play aggression in normal young children: influence of sex, age, sibling status, father's absence. *Psychological Monographs*, vol. 65, no. 6, 1951.
5. Rosenberg, Morris: *Society and the adolescent self-image*. Princeton University Press, Princeton, N.J. 1965.
6. Gurin, Gerald, Veroff, Joseph, Feld, Sheila: *Americans view their mental health*. Basic Books, New York. 1960.
7. Gregory, Ian: Anterospective data following childhood loss of a parent: I. Delinquency and high school dropout. *Archives of*

General Psychiatry, August 1965.

8. Pollack, Otto: The outlook for the American family. *Journal of Marriage and the Family,* February 1967.

9. Vincent, Clark: Implications of changes in male-female role expectations for interpreting M-F scores. *Journal of Marriage and the Family,* May 1966.

10. Maccoby, Eleanor E.: Sex differences in intellectual functioning. In *The development of sex differences* (Maccoby, Eleanor E., ed.), Stanford University Press, Stanford, Calif. 1966.

11. Hunt, J. McVicker: *Intelligence and experience.* The Ronald Press Co., New York. 1961.

12. DuBois, Hazel: Working mothers and absent fathers—family organization in the Caribbean. Unpublished paper given at the annual meeting of the American Anthropological Association, Detroit, Mich., November 1964.

9
THE PRESCHOOL YEARS:
ABNORMAL DEVELOPMENT

Two disorders, minimal brain dysfunction and childhood schizophrenia, account for most of the major psychopathology that emerges during the preschool years. Minimal brain dysfunction, like mental retardation, is usually an inborn condition present from birth; however, it has a number of particular implications for the cognitive and motor developments that take place during the preschool years, two to five, and it is by far the most frequent behavior disorder for which children of this age are brought for professional help. The Wender article that follows describes in vivid detail the characteristic behaviors of the minimally brain damaged child, including the changing manifestations of this disorder in middle childhood and adolescence. Especially important in this respect are learning disabilities attributable to brain dysfunction, which constitute a prominent disorder among school-age children.

Childhood schizophrenia is a form of schizophrenic disturbance beginning between age two and adolescence. Goldfarb summarizes a study of adaptive functions and contributing factors in early childhood schizophrenia conducted at the Henry Ittelson Center for Child Research. He elaborates in particular the behavioral impairments exhibited by schizophrenic children and the possible origins of childhood schizophrenia in neurological abnormalities and disturbed family relationships.

PAUL H. WENDER

Characteristics of the Minimal Brain Dysfunction Syndrome*

What are MBD children like? With what problems do they appear? How are they recognized?

Oscar's eight. As we look back, we've been having problems all along but we'd gotten used to them. I'm not sure that we would have come if the school hadn't complained about the same sorts of things we've been used to for a long time. He's always been a strong-willed, negative child who wanted to do things his own way. He was impossible to toilet train or even keep around the house. When he was 2 he wandered away and we had the whole neighborhood and the police looking for him . . . . We didn't find him for five or six hours and when we did he didn't seem to be the least bit upset by his little adventure. He's always been a bundle of nervous energy. He's always fidgety—he can't even watch TV for long. When he was younger you could never afford to take your eyes off him . . . the second you did he would be into things and you'd find they were broken. He wore everything out . . . toys, clothes, everything . . . . He wasn't malicious. He just has two left hands and two left feet. He tripped all over himself and when he

*From Chapter 1 of P. H. Wender, *Minimal Brain Dysfunction in Children*, 1971. Reprinted by permission of the author and John Wiley and Sons.

was growing up he was constantly bumped or scraped. Fortunately he was a pretty thick-skinned little boy, pretty tough, and never cried very much. As I said, it's always been hard to discipline him. It started with toilet training. That was a nightmare—he still wets the bed occasionally. Sometimes he's purely negative and other times he just appears to be forgetful. It's hard to tell if it's really forgetfulness. He changes so much from one day to the next—he's consistently variable. He doesn't seem to be a daydreamer but sometimes it looks like he just forgets what you told him. That shows up in the way he plays. He's never had much stick-to-itiveness and always runs from one thing to another. He never had trouble at school getting along with the other kids. He's always been really outgoing—if anything, inclined to be a bit bossy, but very friendly. He likes his teacher, too. All the teachers have thought Oscar was a nice boy but he just wouldn't listen. This year his teacher says he's always in and out of his seat, humming in class, fiddling around, bothering the other children, and just seems uninterested in learning. She feels—the way we do—that he could really learn if he tried. When he is interested in something he can really get quite good at it. The trouble with school just seems to be that he doesn't care.

The school suggested that we bring

Gary for a psychiatric examination. They thought that maybe his learning problems might have an emotional basis. The accompanying letter from the school psychologist regarding this child with a "special learning disorder" indicated that Gary had normal intelligence with "no indication of brain damage" (because "there was inappreciable scatter" on testing) The problem "seemed to be primarily motivational .... A difficulty in complying with authority figures, particularly females, seems to be the major dynamic factor. Psychotherapy for the child and his parents is recommended." The child's school history revealed few details that differentiated him from most children with "special learning disorders" who are not referred to child guidance clinics. Inquiry concerning the referring psychologist revealed that he was a proponent of the psychogenic theory of learning disability; he was apt to refer for psychiatric evaluation all children with learning problems who were not grossly retarded.

Johnny's probation officer told us to come here. He's been a bad kid for years and managed not to get booked for a long time. In the first grade he took stuff from my purse and sold stuff from around the house. The past couple years he's fallen in with a bad bunch of kids who've been leading him—other kids have always been able to boss him around. First it was a bit of stealing from the drugstores, then hubcaps, and finally this business with the car. He's always done badly in school. He was left back twice and been suspended a few times. He couldn't do anything very good in sports either. He's always been trying to get other kids to like him any way he could. He never did what we told him at home. Everything

you did would roll off his back. My husband says I spare the rod and that I don't follow through. He ought to live with Johnny. I tell him something 10 times, 20 times, 100 times and he just ignores me. It isn't like he's being ornery. It just never reaches him. I just can't get through. The father added: "He's not really a bad kid .... I wasn't good in school and I had some trouble with the cops when I was a boy .... I drank a bit too much but I've finally settled down."

Our doctor thought that Mark ought to get a neurological evaluation. He said that he might have minimal cerebral palsy and recommended us to you for a neurological evaluation and EEG. Mark was a premature baby, had jaundice after he was born, was a bit slow developing, a bit clumsy and awkward, and our doctor always felt that he might have a little bit of cerebral palsy. He's been a very nice boy. He's very affectionate—if anything, he hangs on you too much for attention and love. He's very immature and it's hard for him to do his chores. He's eight now and he really can't tie his shoelaces. He doesn't take care of his room, he just forgets to do what you tell him to. He had to repeat first grade and is having trouble now in the second. They said his I.Q. was low-normal and that he should be able to learn but he still seems to be having a great deal of difficulty. He has a lot of trouble writing and has very messy handwriting. I've tried to help him with that and with reading. He reverses a lot of letters and words and just can't stick with it. You try to get him to sit down and five minutes after you start he's up again. He's a good boy, he just has some problems. Our doctor thought that by finding out exactly what the difficulty *was we might be able to get him into some kind of treatment program.*

These vignettes are condensations of several cases and portray common variants or subtypes of the MBD syndrome. What do these children have in common? One is "all boy," one has a "special learning disorder," one appears to be a budding delinquent, and the last seems to have organic brain damage. Despite these seemingly disparate clinical pictures, it is very probable that all four of these boys have "minimal brain dysfunction."

If these children may be meaningfully grouped together, the examples illustrate that the MBD syndrome is indeed a syndrome: the behavioral and psychological abnormalities portrayed above occur in a number of areas which are not necessarily affected in any individual child. These areas will be described in more detail later. A further complication, not demonstrated in these histories, is that the affected areas often change over time, with certain abnormalities disappearing and others becoming more salient at different ages. This, too, will be elaborated. I shall also include descriptions of various clinical signs of MBD, of MBD subtypes, of social context, and of a diagrammatic means of representing the overlap of MBD with other diagnostic states in children.

CHARACTERISTIC DYSFUNCTIONS

MBD children manifest dysfunction in the following areas: motor activity and coordination; attention and cognitive function; impulse control; interpersonal relations, particularly dependence-independence and responsiveness to social influence; and emotionality. The characteristic dysfunctions in these areas are detailed below.

Motor Behavior

The principal abnormalities of motor function are a high activity level and impaired coordination (dyspraxia). As "hyperactivity" (the term often applied to the syndrome) implies, many of these children are described as motorically overactive. A history frequently reported by parents involves a child who was active and restless in infancy, stood and walked at an early age, and then, like an infant King Kong, burst the bars of his crib asunder and sallied forth to destroy his parents' house. The description of the child as a toddler is likely to mention that he "was into everything," was constantly touching—and hence, inadvertently breaking—toys and objects, and had to be watched at all times for his own protection as well as the preservation of the household. As an older child, he may be described as being incessantly in motion, driven like a motor, constantly fidgeting, unable to sit still at the dinner table or even in front of the television set. At school his teacher is apt to report that the child fidgets, is unable to sit still in his seat, gets up and walks around the classroom, talks, jostles, and annoys his fellows. Older children and adolescents will usually be aware of their excessive activity level, which they often characterize as "nervousness" or "restlessness." When successfully treated with medication, they will report a decline in these symptoms which parallels others' report of a decline in activity.

Parents sometimes report two additional early manifestations of excessive activity: "colic" during infancy and sleep problems. Stewart et al. (1966) report an increased prevalence of infant feeding problems and colic among the hyperactive children in their series.[1] The sleeping difficulties are variable: Some children go to bed late, fall asleep with difficulty, awaken frequently, and arise early. Others may have difficulty falling asleep, but sleep profoundly and are difficult to arouse.

The motoric hyperactivity is often accompanied by a verbal hyperactivity. Some children manifest a press of speech analogous to that seen in manic adults. Unless prompted by the interviewer (or parent or teacher) they are unable to maintain a cognitive focus; and if left to themselves they demonstrate a more or less typical flight of ideas. Occasionally an older child will complain of a press of thoughts: "I can't stop thinking even when I go to sleep."

Attempts to document a gross increase in motor activity with objective measuring devices have been variably successful. Bell et al. (1969), employing pedometers, were not able to demonstrate increased activity in a subsample of nursery school children rated as hyperactive by observers. Other studies do provide objective documentation for an increase in motor activity in some "hyperactive" children. Hutt et al (1963) employed a room with a grid-marked floor which permitted the

assessment of changes of location over time and the amount of time spent engaged in one activity; they were able to show that the time spent in any one activity was shorter for epileptic hyperactive children and that the mobility of such children was decreased by amphetamine. Sprague et al. (1969) measured movement by means of a stabilimetric cushion (which measured wiggling) and a telemetric device to measure head movement. Using these measures the authors were able to reliably classify retarded children into either high or low activity groups.

The reason that objective measures sometimes fail to document increased activity is probably twofold. First, the techniques employed vary. Gross motor activity (measured by the pedometer) may not be excessive, while fidgeting (measured by Sprague's technique) may indeed be increased. Second, some MBD children are in fact not hyperactive but only appear so. Some give the impression of hyperactivity because of their constant shifting of activities and lack of goal direction. In other children the striking feature is not the total amount of activity but the children's inability to inhibit activity when inhibition is appropriate; these children are no more active than other children on the playground but cannot curtail their activity in the classroom.

Lastly, there are a very few children with other features of the syndrome who are motorically hypoactive and listless. These children should be included in the MBD group not only because they possess many other characteristics of the syndrome, but also because they respond

---

[1] Although they report these figures as non-significant, a recalculation of their data using a one-tailed exact probability test reveals them to be statistically significant.

similarly to drugs.[2]

The excessive motor activity of children with the MBD syndrome decreases with age, as does the motor activity of children in general. The subjective concomitants of the syndrome may not disappear so rapidly. In a follow-up study of hyperactive children, Menkes et al. (1966) found that some patients reported persistent feelings of restlessness which lasted up to the age of 30.

Another major motor deviation seen in many, but not all, of these children is incoordination. Some MBD children have histories of advanced motor development, of having attained developmental landmarks at an early age, and of always having been good at athletics. More common is the history which describes a clumsy, inept child. He may have walked at an early age but he always had "two left feet" and constantly tripped over himself. He may have had difficulty with balance and may not have been able to ride a two-wheel bicycle until he was 9 or 10. He may have poor fine motor coordination: his handwriting is described as unusually poor, and he has had difficulty in learning to button buttons, tie shoelaces, and cut with scissors. (An example in point is that of a boy with a

WISC I.Q. of 140 who could not learn to tie shoelaces until he was 10 years old.) Many of the children have poor visual-motor coordination and have great difficulty in learning to throw and catch a ball. This area of disability in particular is psychologically painful to boys, who may report that they are picked eighteenth when baseball teams are "choosing up" sides. As will be discussed later, the characteristic psychological defense of boys takes the form of: "I don't care, I don't like baseball, basketball, ..." This may sometimes lead to feminine identification and/or rejection by the peer group.

Attentional and Perceptual-Cognitive Function

The most striking and constant perceptual-cognitive abnormality of the MBD child is shortness of attention span and poor concentration ability. Parents report that the child never plays at one game for a long period of time and rushes from one activity to another. As a toddler or a nursery school student the child pulls every toy from the shelf, plays with each desultorily, and them seems at a loss for further things to do. When he reaches school age, his teacher is likely to report: "You can't get him to pay attention for long . . . he won't finish his work . . . he doesn't do well on his own— even though he functions well on a one-to-one basis." Both parent and teacher report: "He doesn't listen [for long], doesn't mind . . . doesn't remember."

In describing the perceptual-cognitive problems of the MBD child, Strauss and Kephart (1955) observe that distracti-

---

[2] Anderson (1956) and Bender (1949) note that some children have most of the characteristics of the "hyperactive" (MBD) behavioral syndrome but lack one defining attribute: they are hypoactive. This observation jibes with my experience. Recognition of the subgroup is of practical importance, because by virtue of not being designated as hyperactive, such children do not receive appropriate therapy. This is unfortunate, since drug therapy often seems to be effective for the hypoactive subgroup as well as the hyperactive subgroup.

bility is "often the most obvious of [the MBD child's] difficulties. He finds it impossible to engage in any activity In a concentrated fashion but is always being led aside from any task at hand by stimuli which should remain extraneous but do not. In extreme cases his activity may appear to be an aimless pursuit of stimulus after stimulus as one after another of the elements in his perceptual environment attracts his attention. If we make the structuring problem easier for him . . . [by reducing extraneous stimuli and/or simplifying the task] his distractibility decreases" (p. 135). The last observation is reflected in the frequently heard assertion that the child functions quite normally "on a one-to-one basis."

Objective documentation of the attentional deficit is sparse. Hutt et al. (1963) were able to show not only that brain-damaged children had a shorter attention span for playing with one object at a time but that they were less able to experience distractions without disruption of their task. Non-brain-damaged children were more readily able to visually fixate on activities other than their main activity, that is, they were better able to direct their attention elsewhere without disrupting their ongoing task.

The quality of "forced responsiveness" to environmental stimuli is often present and reflected in an interest in and attraction to minute details. This concern with the irrelevant seems to reflect an inability to organize hierarchically, so that all aspects—of a percept or an idea—are of equal importance; as much attention is directed to the peripheral as to the essential. This approach may sometimes lend an obsessive quality to the child's actions. The obsessive quality may be strengthened by perseveration, which is another behavior manifestation seen among some MBD children. When both occur together (the repetitive performance of the trivial) the behavior is apt to be labeled "compulsive." The repetitive, stereotyped nature of the behavior is sometimes overlooked because observers focus on its interpersonal consequences and ignore its style. Much of the attention-seeking and demanding behavior of these children has a stereotyped, compulsive flavor.

It is worth mentioning that the classroom inattentiveness of these children is sometimes labeled "daydreaming." Since the rich inner life seems to be more the privilege of the schizoid than the MBD child, the report of such "daydreaming" may erroneously militate against a diagnosis of MBD. Asking a few questions of the child will usually resolve the differential diagnostic problem: whereas the schizoid child is likely to have involved and fantastical reveries, the MBD child who is "daydreaming" is apt to report that he is anticipating his afternoon postliberation pleasures.

Cognitively, these children manifest varied patterns of defects. Many children show both noncognitive difficulties (which have already been and will be further discussed) and cognitive problems; many children have hyperactivity and other aspects of the MBD syndrome without having any specific perceptual-cognitive problems; finally, many children identified on the basis of "special learning difficulties" that are the major causes of concern manifest other MBD characteristics (including "hyperactivity") only minimally or not at all.

Whether problems of attention or

"special learning problems" contribute more to the MBD child's academic troubles is hard to say, since either would be sufficient to cause difficulties. In any event, school underachievement (which is discussed below) is almost a hallmark of this syndrome. The etiological problem is compounded by the psychological consequences of early underachievement; a vicious circle is produced in which poor performance generates criticism and a poor self-image, both of which tend to decrease motivation.[3]

As with hyperactivity, the outward signs of distractibility and inattentiveness tend to disappear with age, but the problems may tend to remain in more muted form. Older MBD subjects tend to report continued difficulty in concentration. It is my impression that such individuals also manifest an absence of sustained interest in nonacademic areas: recreational activities, hobbies, jobs, initially attract the attention of these persons but (like the toys of childhood) fail to keep it.

Learning Difficulties. One complex form of psychological performance in the MBD child that should be commented on especially is school learning performance. The determinants of academic performance are numerous and complex. Capacity, motivation, and adequacy of teaching all contribute to how well a child will learn, and consequently poor school performance is not a specific diagnostic sign. Bearing this in mind, it is of considerable practical consequence to be aware that a substantial fraction of MBD children (of

the order of magnitude of one-half to two-thirds) manifest learning difficulties in school, and that *among children with normal intelligence and with good school experience MBD is a very frequent source of academic difficulty.* The most serious manifestation is difficulty in learning to read (although problems in writing—generally sloppiness—and problems in comprehension and arithmetic may be present as well). The terms "reading disability," "learning disability," and "dyslexia" designate the difficulties of an heterogeneous group of children. Included are neurotics, dysphasics, and retarded children. Probably the single most common subgroup, however, consists of children with the MBD syndrome. MBD has been implicated by several studies of adolescents with academic problems. Reviewing a successive sample of 20 MBD children over the age of 12, Laufer (1962) found the only characteristic common to all was "poor school performance despite adequate intellect" (p. 505). Working with Swedish teen-age dyslexics of normal intelligence, Frisk et al. (1967) found that approximately one-third to one-half showed current distractibility and restlessness, sleep disturbance, or impaired motor abilities, and that as children they had had an increased prevalence of speech dificulties, clumsiness, and enuresis (an aspect of poor impulse control that will be discussed below). Studying a nonselected group of "adolescent underachievers," Hammar (1967) found that approximately one-half consisted of MBD children "grown up"; when children with undiscovered retardation were eliminated, 67% of the underachievers were MBD.

From a practical standpoint it is im-

[3] For an elaboration of the mechanism of such cycles, "deviation amplifying feedbacks," see Wender (1968).

portant to be aware that not only do many MBD children present as "under-achievers" or "dyslexics," but that many children referred for nonspecified "emotional problems" have reading problems together with other MBD problems. The description of Frisk et al. of such a group is consonant with my own clinical experience: approximately one-third of their series of dyslexic children were referred for "physical or neurotic symptons, although poor adjustment and vaguely described school problems also were indicated" (p. 338). These "neurotic" symptoms were found—and this again is in keeping with my experience—to be appreciably aggravated by the unmet pressures of school and home and the child's sense of guilt and inadequacy regarding his own substandard academic performance.

From the vantage point of the clinician, considerable care must be exerted in sorting out causes and effects: he is apt to be presented with a confusing array of personal and academic problems which overlie and many even conceal the MBD difficulties which are their nidus.

Impulse Control

A very frequently described characteristic of MBD children is poor "impulse control," a decreased ability to inhibit. The principal dysfunctions included under this rather general term include: low frustration tolerance, antisocial behavior (destructiveness, stealing, lying, firesetting, sexual "acting out"), and impaired sphincter control (enuresis, encopresis). Hyperreactivity could also be included but will be discussed under emotional dysfunctions.

Low frustration tolerance, the inability to delay gratification and "impulsivity" have similar behavioral referents. The child in question is described as having little stick-to-itiveness or perseverance; he gives up readily. He rapidly becomes upset when things or people fail to behave as he would have them. He is the opposite of the child who will sit quietly in the corner attempting to solve a puzzle and brooking no interruption. The MBD child may function better when given constant adult attention, praise, and reinforcement—hence the frequent (and already cited) comment of teachers that such a child seems to function well with "one-to-one attention."

Defective impulse control is also manifested in poor planning and judgment. Foresight and organizational ability are qualities which develop, if at all, with age. MBD children manifest less of these attributes than would be age appropriate. They are more likely than most children to run off in several directions at once and to fail to see the future consequences of their action. An attribute which might be placed either under impulsivity or inattentiveness is these children's marked lack of attention to detail. This is manifested at home as disorderliness and a general lack of organization. Parents complain of untidy rooms and failure to dress neatly: unbuttoned buttons, unzipped zippers, untied shoelaces. At school it is seen in their sloppy work, their failure to finish tasks, and their approximations in reading and writing.

MBD children are often reckless and manifest no concern for bodily safety—they act without thinking, are frequently injured, and often seem to be accident prone. The reports of injuries, including head injuries, so often elicited in the histories of these children are often a manifestation of the child's illness and not a primary cause of it.[4]

Social impulsivity—antisocial behavior—is often prominent and tends to dominate the clinical picture: many of these children are wanton destroyers, compulsive stealers, and firesetters. Destructiveness is usually the sign manifested earliest in their development: the children are not malicious but are surprised breakers of toys and wearers-out of clothing—no item seems to remain intact in their possession. Stealing, a ubiquitous and multidetermined behavior of young children, tends to persist in a few MBD children for years. It may have a constant and compulsive quality (continually taking money from the household), or it may appear reactively and in a seemingly understandable way (e.g., as retaliation or in order to win the affection of other children). What is striking is the low threshold for the appearance of such behavior and its failure to respond to social controls. Similar comments apply to lying, firesetting, and sexual "acting out." Very young children are honest and the appearance of lying may be considered a developmental milestone. In the normal course of events, indiscriminate lying is followed by modulated honesty. Not so with some MBD children, in whom compulsive lying persists through adolescence. Fire fascinates primitive man and children alike, but both are generally able to curtail their attraction to it. For a few MBD children this is not the case and in them compulsive firesetting may dominate the clinical picture. "Sexual acting out," sexual promiscuity, is seen in some adolescent girls. Again, obviously, sexual drives are ubiquitous and it is only the failure of inhibition that is pathological. [This last sympton (sign, to be exact) is particularly dependent on cultural definition and may currently be in the process of being legislated out of existence.]

In MBD children in whom "antisocial" behavior is prominent, this behavior usually begins to attract increasing social and professional attention so that the other MBD abnormalities are ignored; in such instances the children are often diagnosed as "psychopathic." Although an appreciable fraction of antisocial and delinquent children may have MBD characteristics, only a small fraction of the children seen with other manifestations of the MBD syndrome conspicuously display "antisocial" characteristics as well. Even so, it may be that the association between the MBD syndrome and antisocial behavior is less than it appears to be; it is likely that hyperactive and distractible children who are otherwise agreeable are not referred to child guidance clinics and that their more distressing fellows are overrepresented.

Another common characteristic of MBD children is defective sphincter control: many of these children are enuretic or encopretic. Whether these problems should be catalogued as problems of negativism, inattentiveness, or impulse

[4] Bond and Appel (1931) reported that many of the postencephalitic children they studied had suffered head injuries, usually from being struck by automobiles as they impulsively rushed into the street. In several instances the children had incurred these injuries following their recovery from encephalitis and their development of MBD symptoms.

control is problematic. Some children are reported as having been unusually obstinate about learning these skills; supposedly they fully understood the demands, but refused to comply with them.[5] Other children apparently have failed to heed internal cues and have wet themselves while playing—they forgot. Nocturnal enuresis is common and might have been listed under motoric hyperactivity since there is some evidence that it is a direct manifestation of problems in the regulation of arousal (Broughton, 1968). True encopresis—a much less common problem—may have similar causes.

Generally, however, the encopresis is of the "false" variety; some of the children (generally the more severely disturbed ones) do have full bowel movements in their pants but usually the complaint refers to another manifestation of the MBD child's neglect of detail—in this instace a nonfastidious inattention to wiping which produces slight staining.

Interpersonal Relations

The most prominent types of MBD alterations in interpersonal relations are a considerable resistance to social demands, increased independence, and extroversion. The MBD child tends to show these patterns in his relations to his parents, parent surrogates, and peers. Probably the single most disturbing feature of these children's behavior, and the one most responsible for their referral for treatment, is their unresponsiveness to social demands. They may appear almost impossible to acculturate. In the area of response to external controls most MBD children are similarly described. They are perennial 2-year-olds. They are obstinate, stubborn, negativistic, bossy, disobedient, sassy, and impervious. All disciplinary measures seem unsuccessful: rewards, deprivation of privileges, physical punishment. "He wants his own way . . . he never learns by his own mistakes. . . . You can't reach him . . . he's almost immune to punishment." The manifestations of noncompliance change as the child grows older. During adolescence his noncompliance is apt to take the form of "passive-aggressiveness" or disengagement and ignoring of his parents. He does not oppose so much as he does not listen.

The child's peer relations are also predictable. With adults he resists controls—with peers he attempts to be controlling. He may be described as having no friends, but closer inspection reveals a pattern much different from that of the schizoid or withdrawn child. The MBD child is usually quite aggressive socially and initiates friendships successfully, but his "bossiness" and insistence that all games be played according to his own rules drive other children away.[6] He is apt to report that he is talked about, rejected, and, perhaps, bullied; these reports are not paranoid but are accurate reflections of what his own behavior

[5] Such children document the psychoanalytic proposition linking obstinacy and toilet-training problems but suggest an alternative explanation: difficult toilet training is the first sign — not the cause — of the later stubbornness.

[6] Excessive timidity is occasionally seen. This is more characteristic of the most immature, most physically inept children, who are rejected by their peers and unable to defend themselves.

compels others to do. He "makes friends easily but can't keep them." As a result he is often found to be playing with younger children, and, if a boy, with girls. A superficial report of the child's peer relations may convey the impression that he is introverted and fearful but closer inspection will usually reveal him to be an unsuccessful extrovert.

The least constant—and most perplexing—aspect of the MBD child's behavior is in the area of affection and dependence. MBD children tend to polarize along this dimension, and I suspect that their numerical distribution would be bimodal. Many are described as having been infant "touch-me-nots," who did not enjoy being cuddled, who avoided physical contact, and who wiggled off their mother's lap. As toddlers these children wandered away from home and at school age showed no separation anxiety. In another MBD subgroup, the children appear to be excessively dependent or to be vacillating between excessive dependency and independence. They may be insatiably demanding of affection, or they may alternate between such a position and one of complete indifference (in a manner similar to that seen in many institutionalized children). These children are (Bond and Appel, 1931) "mawkishly affectionate, eager to paw strangers, anxious for notice" (P. 15). Whether the polarities of dependence and independence represent "intrinsic" variance or varying psychological responses to the same underlying tendencies is uncertain. In some children the independence seems to be "pure," having been present from an early age and having been unsullied by much affectionateness (the lack of affectionateness may, in fact, be a parental complaint). Even

these children are often excessively dependent instrumentally, since poor motor skills combined with poor frustration tolerance favor parental intercession. In other children the independence seems to be reaction formation or a form of bravado. These children are reminiscent of the monkeys studied by Harlow (1958) who would venture into the more open and frightening room only after having "charged themselves" with bravery by first cuddling cloth mothers made available to them.

Emotion

The emotionality of MBD children shows four major types of dysfunction: increased lability, altered reactivity, increased aggressiveness, and dysphoria.

These children's behavior tends to be predictably unpredictable. Their spontaneous lability is reflected in statements such as: He's happy one minute, impossible to get along with the next . . . . He's got his good days and bad days and it's hard to understand why."

Reactivity to both internal and external stimuli is often altered and may take the form of either hyporeactivity or hyperreactivity: responses are normal in kind but abnormal in degree. Pain responses are often diminished. The children seem unusually undaunted and stoical regarding the frequent bumps, falls, and scrapes to which young flesh is heir. (This may be obscured by the increased attention-seeking some of them manifest—when observed they tend to squeeze every last drop of secondary gain from minor traumata.) As already mentioned with regard to social demands, parents report that physical punishment goes unnoticed. Similarly, psychological punishment—deprivation of privileges, criticism, disapprobation—is also unheeded. "You can't get through to him at all . . . punishment just rolls off his back." It may be noted that in both of the above respects, MBD children are at an opposite pole from many borderline schizophrenic children, who may have catastrophic reactions in response to mild physical injury and who are excessively sensitive to any form of punishment.

The "hyperreactivity" might have been just as logically discussed under the heading of impulse control because it is not clear if the MBD child's abnormal behavior is a manifestation of abnormal emotional reactivity or the inability to modulate normal reactivity. In any event, situations that most children would regard as pleasurable result in excessive excitement, while unpleasurable ones produce excessive anger or temper outbursts. Most young children will become excited at the supermarket or the circus; MBD children tend to become very overexcited and to lose what few controls they do have with brief and/or less intense exposure to such situations. Similarly, most children do not tolerate frustration or disappointment well; such stoical equanimity as they may acquire comes with age. But the MBD child not only has a much lower threshold for such frustration, he also has a more violent reaction to it. When things do not go his way, an MBD child is subject to temper tantrums, angry outbursts, or sullen displeasure—the type of reaction varying, among other things, with the child's age. Such loss of control can also occur in reaction to inner stimuli. Most young children become irritable and regress when fatigued or

hungry—MBD children, again, appear to have a lower tolerance for such stresses and a lower threshold for such regression. Under the influence of excitement, MBD children manifest still further disorganization and decreased responsiveness to external controls. This lack of responsiveness to others is similar in many respects to that seen in the abrupt "catastrophic" reactions of some schizophrenic children.

Although many parents characterize their MBD children as "angry," they usually describe irritability rather than hostility. Unmodulated reactivity is the referent: "He's got a low boiling point . . . when he gets angry he can't control himself. . . ." Many children are described as being "good-natured" except for infrequent angry outbursts. In others, anger or sadism seems to have been present from an early age, and does not seem entirely reactive to the unusually severe punishment which such behavior generally engenders from parents. Among those MBD children preoccupied with injury, violence and death, one is apt to find a larger fraction of children in whom the MBD syndrome exists concurrently with a borderline schizophrenic process. Sadism, too, directed toward either other children or animals, is not characteristic and its presence suggests more serious—schizophrenic—pathology. Again, the bias produced by clinic selection tends to increase the apparent prevalence of children with difficulties in control of anger, which is a socially disturbing symptom. It is less likely that unaggressive children with MBD characteristics will be referred to the child guidance clinic or the psychiatrist.

The major dysphoric characteristics are anhedonia, depression, low self-esteem, and anxiety.

Anhedonia—the inability (or reduced ability) to experience pleasure—is not always conspicuous but it is usually present: "He never gets a kick out of anything . . . he can't be bothered to do much, nothing really seems to give him pleasure . . . you can never satisfy him." The insatiability implied by the foregoing phrases is often considered to be a product of "spoiling" or excessive gratification. Many MBD children do not have a history of being excessively indulged: their insatiability seems more a sign of their lifelong nongratifiability than an effect of cultivated excessive demands. This diminished pleasure sensitivity has not been commented on in previous description of the syndrome. I would like to call the reader's attention to the anhedonia since I believe—rightly or wrongly—that it is a characteristic critically related to the etiology of the syndrome.

Many of the children are said to have "masked depression" or to have "depressive equivalents."[7] The behavioral referents of these statements include: expressions of concern about possible injury and death for their parents and themselves, expressed low self-esteem, feelings of guilt or unworthiness, and lack of zest and initiative.

A characteristic that is far from unique to MBD children but is seen in virtually all such children is low self-esteem. In older children and adolescents the self-evaluations may be concealed by bravado, but parents or teachers will report that the children often describe themselves as defective, bad, inadequate, or different. This low opinion of themselves generally occurs in the absence of any other signs or sadness or depression.

Lastly, excess anxiety is seen in a few children. The children in question usually appear to be "neurotic," that is, overconstricted or compulsive. In some, the compulsiveness appears "defensive" in function—the children's anxiety may increase considerably when their compulsive habits are interfered with. (An alternative explanation is simply that anxiety is generated by attempts to alter any fixed habit patterns.) In other instances, the compulsiveness appears to be a familial pattern and seems to have been fostered by the child's parents (who are often over-organized and rigid people themselves.) When nonfamilial, the compulsiveness may have been "hit upon" spontaneously, becoming ingrained in those children who have markedly rigid needs and demands for constancy and sameness. These latter children seem to have difficulties similar to those Goldstein (1942) has described in brain-damaged adults: in both children and adults the compulsiveness appears to prevent the anxiety that some people experience in new or different or unexpected situations. However, although the children may react quite violently to alteration of such prescribed patterns, they do not react in the "catastrophic" fashion Goldstein described in his patients.

Pervasive and prolonged anxiety is not common among MBD children. As a

---

[7] These phrases sometimes contain an implicit assertion about the etiology of the MBD syndrome. In view of the considerable controversy concerning the etiology of depression itself, the explanation by implicit identity is not as clarifying as it first seems.

chronic symptom it is more common in the seriously disturbed, borderline schizophrenic children. As an acute sympton it is seen in those children whose impulsivity has momentarily gotten them into difficulty; it is frequently and appropriately seen in children who have recently been suspended from school or called before the juvenile court.

CHANGING MANIFESTATIONS OF THE SYNDROME WITH AGE

A characteristic feature of the MBD syndrome, and one that tends to conceal its diagnosis, is the change in its manifestations as the child grows. The behavior that is salient in a toddler is different from that which is salient in an adolescent.

The reasons for these changes are several. First, there seem to be genuine physiological alterations with maturation—for example, motoric hyperactivity and enuresis apparently decrease with age. Second, there are learned psychological alterations—a child is more hostile after his tenth year of peer rejection than he is after one or 2 years of such treatment. Third, "problems" are socially defined and depend on social expectations: a fidgety nursery school child is expected (and tolerable), while a restless second grader is not; reading difficulty (learning with effort) is expected of first graders, but it may be called "dyslexia" in the third grade.

The most typical patterns during the various stages of maturation would be approximately as follows.

As an infant, the MBD child's most conspicuous problem would be physiological functioning: he is apt to be hyperalert and irritable; he is apt to have "colic," crying frequently and being difficult to soothe; he is apt to have sleep disturbances (which may be his most prominent abnormality)—he may have difficulty in falling or staying asleep, or he may awaken frequently and early.

At the toddler stage (2–4 years), the child's behavioral repertoire mushrooms, and in the case of the MBD child, the capacities for wrongdoing expand similarly. The most disturbing—and hence most frequently reported characteristics—are destructiveness (usually inadvertent) and an inability to "listen," that is, to respond to parental discipline. If unattended, the MBD child is "into everything," pulling pots and pans from cupboards, ashtrays from tables. Unless he is firmly supervised he will wander away from home, into the street, into a cleverly varied group of dangerous situations. Parental prohibitions are useless. The instant his mother's back is turned the child repeats the prohibited activity. Consistency and firmness are relatively ineffectual. The child's "affectionate" behavior is characteristic: he is a noncuddler, but at the same time that he is wiggling off laps, he is simultaneously demanding attention. He stands, so to speak, at arm's length, prodding his parent with a pole. Motoric abnormalities may or may not be present: he is likely to have some speech difficulties (immature, "babyish" speech) and is likely to trip over himself in his destructive sorties. In summary, the MBD toddler is an exaggerated 2-year-old: undisciplinable, strong-willed, demanding, and—most important from the parents' standpoint—singularly ungratifying.

As the MBD child reaches preschool age, most of the above characteristics persist, but at this age the attentional and social problems become more conspicuous. The short attention span, low frustration tolerance, and temper tantrums make sustained play and nursery school participation difficult. Indicative peer relations soon appear: the MBD child teases, dominates, annoys; in more extreme instances his aggressiveness is more direct. These attributes endear him neither to his teacher nor to his fellows, and in some instances result in his beginning his academic career as a kindergarten dropout.

When the MBD child begins the first grade, the motoric restlessness becomes salient: his teacher complains that he cannot sit still, gets up and walks around, whistles, and shuffles. Academic problems—though often present—tend to be ignored. First-graders are not expected to learn to read. Enuresis may "now" appear. Although it may have been continually present it is defined as a problem only when the child reaches an age when it is expected to disappear (usually about 6), or when he stays overnight at camp or with friends. His other nonendearing traits at home (noncompliance, tantrums, etc.) are likely to persist but to be overshadowed by his school difficulties.

At about the third grade, when the child is 9 or 10, academic and antisocial problems assume the limelight. Until that time slowness in reading could be attributed to "immaturity" or academic unreadiness. By the third grade the diagnosis is changed to that of a learning problem, or learning disorder. Reading difficulty causes the greatest concern but the child may also display problems with writing (messiness) and arithmetic. Outside of school, antisocial behavior is likely to command attention. Stealing, lying, and firesetting were tolerable in the 6-year-old but are not tolerable in the 10-year-old. When these behaviors persist—and particularly if they are severe—they make the loudest claim for intervention. In many of these young social transgressors, concurrent academic problems may be overlooked at first. When they are discovered later, after a full evaluation, the child's behavior, his "acting out," is sometimes explained as a reaction to his learning problems.

During preadolescence and early adolescence, social (antisocial) problems become the most common causes for referral. While the academic ones remain, they may now be taken for granted. This is *not* to say that the *same* child who has a reading problem predictably develops social problems. Rather, antisocial problems are among the most common problems for this age group, and MBD children constitute an appreciable fraction of these "antisocial" children. By about age 10 the child is likely to have fallen several grade levels behind in reading. Since adequate performance on most other subjects demands competent reading, the child's academic level tends to be generally retarded. Rejected by the adult establishment and the "proper" boys and girls, the MBD child may take up with other outcasts. Depending on his social class and the era, his group of delinquents will fight, steal cars, or take drugs. Even if the serious antisocial problems are not present, the persistence of the other problems constructs a common and distressing personality structure: an academically underachieving, self-centered negativistic adolescent.

The *postadolescent* fate of the MBD child is uncertain and his clinical picture cannot be drawn. Some of the possible outcomes are discussed in the chapter on prognosis. It should be emphasized that not every MBD child progresses through each of the presented patterns. Some children manifest difficulties in all developmental stages, some in only a few. As mentioned, not all MBD children have difficulties in all areas at any one stage: some will have academic problems, some will have social problems, and some will have neither. Lastly, MBD children tend to "outgrow" not only their motoric problems but their other difficulties as well. Any given MBD child may follow the developmental sequence listed and "drop out" at one particular stage. In fact it is usual for the problems to abate at or around the time of puberty. Certainly the developmental stages do not constitute a fatalistic timetable of childhood behavior disorder. . . .

References

Anderson, C. Early brain injury and behavior. *J. Amer. Med. Wom. Ass.*, 1956, **11**, 113-119.

Bell, R.Q., Waldrop, M.F., and Beller, G.M.A. A rating system for the assessment of hyperactive and withdrawn children in preschool samples. Unpublished manuscript, 1969.

Bender, L. Psychological problems of children with organic brain disease. *Amer. J. Orthopsychiat.*, 1949, **19**, 404-415.

Bond, E. D., and Appel, K. E. *The Treatment of Behavior Disorders Following Encephalitis.* New York: Commonwealth Fund, Division of Publications, 1931.

Broughton R. J. Sleep disorders: disorders of arousal? *Science,* 1969, **159**, 1070-1077.

Frisk, M., Wegelius, B., Tenhunen, T., Widholdm, O., and Hortling, H. The problem of dyslexia in teenage. *Acta Peadiat. Scand.,* 1967, **56**, 333-343.

Goldstein, K. *Aftereffects of Brain Injuries in War.* New York: Grune & Stratton, 1942.

Hammar, S. L. School underachievement in the adolescent: a review of 73 cases. *Pediatrics,* 1967, **40**, 373-381.

Harlow, H. F. The nature of love. *Amer. Psychol.,*1958, **13**, 673-685.

Hutt, C., Hutt, S. J., and Ounsted, C. A method for the study of children's behavior. *Develop. Med. Child Neurol.,* 1963, **5**, 233-245.

Laufer, M. W. Cerebral dysfunction and behavior disorders in adolescents. *Amer. J. Orthopsychiat.,* 1962, **32**, No. 3, 501-505.

Menkes, M., Rowe, J. S., and Menkes, J. H. A twenty-five-year follow-up study on the hyperkinetic child with minimal brain dysfunction. *Pediatrics,* 1967, **39**, 393-399.

Sprague, R. L., Werry, J. S., and Davis, K. V. Psychotropic drug effects on learning and activity level of children. Paper presented at Gatlinburg Conference on Research and Theory in Mental Retardation, March 13, 1969 (unpublished).

Stewart, M., Ferris, A., Pitts, N., Jr., and Craig, A. G. The hyperactive child syndrome. *Amer. J. Orthopsychiat.,* 1966, **36**, 861-967.

Strauss, A.A., and Kephart, N.C. *Psychopathology and Education of the Brain-Injured Child, Vol. II. Progress in Theory and Clinic.* New York: Grune & Stratton, 1955.

Wender, P. H. Vicious and virtuous circles: the role of deviation amplifying feedback in the origin and perpetuation of behavior. *Psychiatry,* 1968, **31**, 309-324.

WILLIAM GOLDFARB

Childhood Schizophrenia*

The classification of childhood schizophrenia refers to a group of children with a plethora of behavioral impairments whose consequences are catastrophically burdensome to the children themselves, their parents and families, and the community at large. In every case, the disabilities of the schizophrenic child are awesome in their impact on the observer. Such children are isolated from other children and cannot be managed in the usual school and community setting. The families find themselves scouring the community for suitable resources for treatment and management — most often without success. Though the incidence of schizophrenic children is not known, state and community agencies find themselves under increasing pressure to offer therapeutic assistance. . . .

The present period is one of therapeutic optimism in which a number of workers are attempting to extend the limits of therapeutic potential in the children considered untreatable in the recent past. Since it has not been demonstrated that a single cause or historical development accounts for childhood schizophrenia, it is necessary to outline a treatment regimen for each child tailored to his own needs. This individual case

*From International Psychiatric Clinics, 1964, 4, 821-845. Reprinted by permission of the author and Little, Brown.

approach — utilizing the milieu, direct individual psychotherapy and, where indicated, biologic and pharmacologic techniques — has seemed to be responsible for significant improvement in relationships and overall adjustment, though follow-up studies are still essential to determine the final effects of such treatment.[1]

In recent years, the criteria for the diagnosis of childhood schizophrenia have been delineated with increasing precision and agreement by child psychiatrists. Distinguishing diagnostic features include: major impairments in human relationship and affectional response, deficient awareness of personal identity, impaired perceptual and conceptual response, marked opposition to environmental shift, failure in communication, motility disturbance, and pronounced anxiety.

In spite of this series of criteria, and the feasibility of their employment for the diagnosis and classification of childhood schizophrenia, it is important to

[1] Of the first 25 schizophrenic children admitted to the residential service of the Ittleson Center for Child Research at about six years of age, 20 children (80 percent) were returned to the community approximately two years later. Careful follow-up data on all children discharged from the Center throughout their childhood are being obtained to determine the adaptive vicissitudes of these treated schizophrenic children as they grow into maturity.

understand that the children filtered out by this diagnostic screen are by no means a homogeneous group. These children are highly diversified among themselves in their relationships, adaptive capacities, neuropsychological competence, family backgrounds, and response to treatment efforts. The need remains for investigating the qualitative and quantitative variations in ego among schizophrenic children. Similarly, the etiology for the extensive disturbances in orientative and adaptive functions is not established, although hereditary factors (2, 9), psychogenic factors (3, 5, 12), and the factor of reproductive trauma (5, 10, 14-16) have been imputed. Etiologic investigation also is essential.

The discussion that follows describes clinical findings in childhood schizophrenia that have seemed to be particularly salient. Then, some experimental comparisons of schizophrenic and healthy children of a control group are summarized. Finally, an approach to the causal subdivision of schizophrenic children is presented. No effort will be made to review the entire subject of childhood schizophrenia; an excellent review is given by Eckstein et al. (4). Rather, the direction and outcome of a number of studies of childhood schizophrenia in a variety of behavioral functions at the Ittleson Center over the past 10 years are stressed. Reference is made to the clinical pertinence of these findings.

BEHAVIORAL VARIATIONS IN SCHIZOPHRENIC CHILDREN

In our therapeutic and field studies of schizophrenic children, we have asked what is unusual in the behavior of schizophrenic children relative to the presumptively normal child and, at the same time, is common to most of the schizophrenic children. From the beginning, we have been most impressed by the variations among a group of diagnosed schizophrenic children. They differ widely among themselves in symptoms, capacities, psychological defenses, family patterns, and potentialities for treatment. . . .

If children labeled as schizophrenic vary among themselves, if each child is himself sensitively changing and responsive to altered influence, and if, as implied, the diagnosis does not designate a specific etiology, what findings do determine the diagnosis? It can be said very simply that the diagnosis is made when the observer notes profound disturbances in essential adaptive functions. To spell out in a series of investigations the kind and range of disorder in childhood schizophrenia, a group of diagnosed schizophrenic children have been compared with a group of normal children, matched in age, sex, and adaptive equipment (5). The choice of areas for study was influenced by the therapeutic objective and experience of the Ittleson Center, a concept of personality derived from a psychoanalytic point of view, an alertness to biologic factors in the evolution of child behavior, and an interest in the psychosocial climate within which the child grows. Out of all these influences, a working research model emerged.

EGO AND THE SCHIZOPHRENIC CHILD

Central to this model was the concept

and definition of ego — a concept borrowed very largely from psychoanalysis. The word ego has been employed with many variations in emphasis and meaning. In every case, however, it refers to the human being's functions in contacting reality, testing it, and manipulating it for purposes of survival, self-realization, and need gratification. Among these functions are psychological processes such as perception, memory, conceptualization, and motor response. It may be assumed that the child inherits his potentialities for perceiving and ordering the data of perception into internal schemata and developing strategies for executing appropriate adaptive maneuvers. However, it may also be assumed that the child's potentialities for action are modified both by his biologic needs and by early and primary interpersonal experiences, as with his mother.

In the clinical and experimental investigations to be summarized, ego has been further defined as the self-directing, self-regulating part of the organism. Thus conceived, the ego is the internal organizer that makes it possible to face an inner and outer environment that is constantly changing and to cope with ever-shifting environmental demands with appropriate and efficient strategies. The ego's organizing function implies a capacity for conceptualizing on the basis of a multiplicity of experiences and a continuous process of perceptual intake for guiding the child in his coping maneuvers. On the basis of these monitoring (perceptual) and schematizing experiences, the child is enabled to generalize what is predictable and universal in his inner and outer experiences. It is noteworthy, therefore, that a sense of personal iden-

tity — that is, of the self differentiated from the non-self and continuous in time and space — is not a static unchanging entity. Rather it is the dynamic consequence of a continuous operation of vigilant receptor behavior and effective inner processes for coordinating and categorizing informational intake, and for observing uniformities and common essences in diverse experiences.

For purposes of experimental investigation, it has been assumed that in every case the diagnosis of childhood schizophrenia refers to observations of gaps in the child's ego at all levels — that is, receptive, integrative, and executive. In other words, it was postulated that the schizophrenic child is impaired in the effectiveness with which he receives information, structures the information into patterned forms, conceptualizes and categorizes the information into working schemata, and, finally, strategically executes the appropriate adjustive acts on the basis of these schemata. These gaps in ego are associated with a deep impairment in personal identity or in the clear-cut consciousness of the self differentiated from the non-self. It was hypothesized additionally that the primary defects in ego and in awareness of self lead to an elemental sense of anxiety, which we have termed primordial panic. The anxiety, in turn, was held to lead to a sequence of protective maneuvers, including withdrawal and a seeking for sameness. Based on this hypothesis, the following questions were asked: What is the schizophrenic child's overall level of ego organization? How intact is his sensory equipment? How well does he organize and give form to his sensory intake? How capably does he conceptualize and coordinate the flood of inner and outer information in order to achieve a state of orientation and complacent smooth action in the face of changing environmental circumstances? How effective and smoothly modulated is the motor executive side of his behavior? What is his status in regard to speech and communication?

Sensory Tests

Not infrequently in the histories of schizophrenic children, reference is made to suspicion of sensory loss. The possibility of deafness is a particularly common diagnostic consideration. On the other hand, some observers have raised the possibility of hypoacusis — that is, a manifestation of reduced sensory threshold.[2] Obviously, it is essential to appraise the adequacy of the child's sensory equipment before exploring his internal integration of elementary sensory experiences. Thresholds have been measured by us for vision, for hearing, and for touch. These tests demonstrate definitely that normal children and schizophrenics do not differ in elementary sensory acuity. A gross clinical test (pinprick) of painful sensation in the schizophrenic children also confirms the presence of normal pain sensation in the schizophrenic children.

Perceptual Tests

The peripheral sensory structures are thus intact in the schizophrenic children. How well, however, do they perceive relation-

[2] The implication of such a contingency in an explanation of the hypersensitive responses of schizophrenic children will be referred to in the discussion of receptor behavior.

ships in sensory experiences? Do they organize these sensory stimuli into meaningful perceptual patterns as well as do healthy children? The answer to these questions is of importance if one assumes that the smooth, graceful execution of an act and the clear consciousness of self are dependent on a constant and active organization of internal and external signals. To examine these questions, a variety of perceptual tests have been employed. Some of them assay the child's ability to differentiate body cues. Thus the esthesiometer measures threshold for discriminating two tactile stimuli presented simultaneously. The finger location test appraises a child's ability to localize the fingers of his hand. These abilities contribute to the internal integration of a clear body image. Other tests measure the ability to discriminate figure from ground and the ability to perceive wholes when fragmented stimuli are presented. In all these tests, the schizophrenic children are inferior to normals.

Conceptual Tests

If, as demonstrated, the schizophrenic child has serious deficits in ability to structure stimuli into patterns of meaningful relationships, one might anticipate impairments in the higher cognitive processes of conceptualization. Here, again, many tests have been used to assay different facets of abstraction and categorization. Typical of such conceptual tests is right-left discrimination, the ability to categorize by form and color, orientation to time, place, and person, or the representation of the human body. These tests show that the schizophrenic child finds it difficult to differentiate right and left; he is poorly oriented for time, place, and person and is deficient in grouping objects by form and shape; and, finally, he represents the human body far more primitively than normal children.

Our best measure of integrative functioning is the intelligence test. The test that has been employed is the Wechsler Intelligence Scale for Children. The intelligence quotient (IQ) in the test denotes intellectual functioning relative to a normal standardization group. It does not necessarily reveal inherent potentiality for intelligent response. It is an excellent measure of such potentiality when the child is free of affective inhibition and has had normal environmental stimulation. In the schizophrenic child, who is deviant in emotional organization and experience and impaired in overall qualities such as attention, persistence of effort, and the pleasure of fulfillment and self-actualization, the intelligence quotient is an excellent representation of current ego competence. The Wechsler scale offers one IQ to represent verbal competence (verbal IQ), another to represent competence with nonverbal materials (performance IQ) and a score combining both verbal and performance IQ's (full IQ). The schizophrenic children are inferior to the normal in each of these measures. More specifically, while our control group is in the range of normal, the schizophrenic children in our studies generally function at retarded levels. Most of the schizophrenic children function below the least able of the children in the control group.

Motor Tests

Motor coordination and locomotor balance have been measured by a variety of tests. Among these, the most extensive series of psychomotor observations are in the Lincoln-Oseretsky test, which sums many observations of fine and gross motor response. Here again the schizophrenic child is inferior to the normal child.

Speech Deviations

For a number of years at the Ittleson Center, observations have been made of the schizophrenic child's mode of communication, particularly of his voice and speech. Special techniques for the appraisal of speech have been developed (7). In these, children are rated relative to the presumptive normal in a number of aspects of voice and speech such as phonation, rhythm, articulation, gestural communication, and communication of mood and symbolic meaning. The schizophrenic children deviate from the normal in all these qualities. We have been particularly interested in their deviancies in the elements of phonation (volume, pitch, and voice quality) and rhythm (note phrasing, fluency, stress, intonation, and inflection), inasmuch as these aspects of voice and speech are the essential constituents of emotional and connotative communication. They determine the individual's capacity to signal multiple meanings beyond the mere denotative significance of word combinations. The attainment of the very large array of phonative and rhythmic variations essential for subtle emotional and connotative expression is learned in early childhood. These subtle signals are standard and represent cultural expectancies, essential to assure social cohesion. The speech of schizophrenic children always deviates from normal expectancy, but the speech deficiencies are not consistent from one schizophrenic child to another. One is thus not justified in referring to "schizophrenese" — that is, a specific and positive schizophrenic speech pattern. What is uniform is merely an absence of normal expectancy. It is also noteworthy that in the absence of such culturally standard cues for metacommunicative expression, the listener feels disengaged and the schizophrenic child is further isolated from human rapport.

These experimental studies of ego equipment demonstrate unequivocally that schizophrenic children suffer from deficiencies in orientative and manipulative functions underlying self-direction and self-regulation. The deficits in organizing and regulating self processes in turn are associated with a complex of clinical phenomena found rather universally in seriously impaired schizophrenic children; namely, seriously impaired self-awareness, aberrant perceptual behavior, and marked anxiety states. These three behavioral aberrations are dynamically linked. In brief, the deviant perceptual behavior seems to deprive the schizophrenic child of essential referential and ego-anchoring mechanisms, and the anxiety is a result of the absence of a stable self-awareness.

Awareness of Self

Self-awareness in the normal child starts with a consciousness of his body in intended action. Gradually an internalized image of the body structure and functions (body identity) is conceptualized and sustained even when the sensorimotor experiences which originally determined the body identity are absent or altered. To illustrate, a child stands and, as a result of vision and perception of muscle action and balance, communicates to himself "I am a child who can stand when I want to." Social approval, of course, enhances his natural feelings of pride in mastery and skill. In the young child, therefore, his consciousness of self can be appraised by a study of his internalized body image.

As already stated, experimental tests demonstrate that schizophrenic children are incapacitated, relative to normal, in discrimination of body perception, in the localization of these perceptions, and in their ability to give pattern and meaning to body perceptions. Therapeutic findings with schizophrenic children give many dramatic and uncontrived examples of impaired body identity.

Thus, they lack body images that are integrated, stable in time, and clear in form. One child walked about all day feeling her body. Another observed the motions of her hand in fascination and addressed it as a baby. A third child talked to her hands as friends, apparently separable from herself.

There are many examples of fragmented body concepts which contrast strikingly with the normal child's feeling of body wholeness. In addition, the normal child's complacency about his body identity is quite different from the extreme distress of the schizophrenic child who is frustrated by the feeling of non-intactness of his body and preoccupied with restitutive strivings. One little schizophrenic girl repeatedly referred to her feeling that her body was disintegrating. On one occasion she became anxious to the point of agitation and asked if her hand would fall off.

Related to this impairment in body integrity is a lack of awareness of body boundaries. In this event the child is uncertain that the body sheath will contain the inner parts of the body and fearful that the world will either invade the body or that the inner organs and tissues will escape outward. Such fantasies are often associated with extreme fear of body penetration. Or, on the other hand, the skin may be gashed deeply with no apparent awareness. Several children cutting paper with scissors have had to be watched lest they cut into their skin without the usual consciousness of body penetration. . . .

Receptor Responses

It is apparent that effective self-differentiation assumes receptor proficiency. It is therefore of interest that schizophrenic children evidence abnormal patterns of receptor behavior. Unusual hypersensitivity to sensory stimulation was first described by Bergmann and Escalona (1). In a later series of investigations at the Ittleson Center, a variety of receptor deviancies were noted. Thus the forementioned aberrations in pain behavior were studied and attention was called to the trend to diminished reaction or, even, total absence of pain reaction to physical traumas which normally elicit distress, crying, and some kind of adaptive response, e.g., defensive withdrawal or counteraggression (6). A later study (7) described a widespread deviation in receptor behavior, characterized by a tendency to avoid receptor intake through the eyes and ears and to rely to an

unusual degree on touch, taste, and smell. Stated otherwise, the child avoids contacting the world through his distance receptors and prefers the use of his proximal receptors. The schizophrenic child's pattern of receptor preferences is very different from that of the normal child, who typically hungers for visual and auditory experience from early infancy. . . .

ETIOLOGY OF SCHIZOPHRENIA

In the discussion to this point, the schizophrenic child has been shown to deviate from normal in ego functioning. In particular, the lack of normal guides for self-regulation and for the attainment of clearly delineated self-awareness, as well as the consequences of such deficits, have been stressed. What causes such deficits? Is there a single cause, such as heredity or trauma, or environment? Certainly, the kinds of ego deficit described may be produced by a variety of causes or combinations of such causes. The hypothesis we have preferred is one which postulates multiple causes or, more preferably, varying combinations of multiple contributing factors. These combinations may be considered along a mixture continuum. At one end of this continuum, somatic inadequacies within the child are the primary reason for his ego deficiencies. At the other end of the continuum, the primary factor is a deleterious psychosocial atmosphere within the family. To demonstrate such an etiologic model, one might hypothetically rank a group of schizophrenic children in order of ratio of contribution of somatic and familial factors leading to abnormality. Though only a schematic model for heuristic purposes, it agrees with clinical experience. Thus, at one pole, would be found the brain-damaged child from a normal, well-functioning family. At the other pole, would be the child who is entirely free of somatic defects but who has been reared in an extremely disturbed family unit.

Neurologic Status

To test this theory of the etiology of childhood schizophrenia, techniques have been developed to appraise the neurologic status of the children on the one hand and the psychosocial adequacy of the family on the other hand. In accord with our etiologic model, the argument is as follows:

1. Neurologic study of schizophrenic children reveals a group of children with neurologic impairment.
2. Study of the families of schizophrenic children reveals a group of families with conspicuously disordered patterns of psychosocial interaction.
3. The theory of multiple causation is supported by the pattern of interrelationships of neurologic findings in the children and the findings derived from study of the psychosocial conduct of the family.

As a first approach to an estimate of the relative incidence of neurologic impairment in schizophrenic and normal children, a series of classic neurologic tests were standardized and suitable ratings of adequacy were developed. In each test, the schizophrenic children are far inferior to normal. They demonstrate aberrations in coordination, perceptual discrimination, body imagery, muscle tone, balance, and postural and righting behavior. It is recognized that similar disorders may be produced by emotional factors. Thus, either emotional impulsivity or inhibition of assertiveness and aggression may produce physical awkwardness; or diminished body tone might conceivably be linked to exaggerated psychic passivity. Certainly, disturbances in body imagery may result from external interference with the development of self-awareness and personal identity. Nevertheless, the responses to the neurologic tests in many of the schizophrenic children are qualitatively of a kind found more typically among children with known brain damage.

The most significant assay of the neurologic status of the schizophrenic children has been made by a child neurologist with extensive experience in the evaluation and observation of neurologic ailments. . . .

Using the neurologist's diagnosis, schizophrenic children may thus be subdivided into those with neurologic impairment termed *organic* and those with no evidence of neurologic impairment termed *nonorganic*. Comparison of the behavior data of the normal, organic schizophrenic and nonorganic schizophrenic children shows a consistent gradient of capacity in most perceptual, conceptual, and psychomotor functions; namely, normals are superior to nonorganic schizophrenics, who are in turn superior to organic children. To illustrate this gradient, the mean full intelligence quotients on the Wechsler Intelligence Scale for Children in the group studied are normals 109, nonorganic schizophrenic 92, and organic schizophrenic 62.

It is noteworthy, too, that the overwhelming majority of organic schizophrenic children function at defective intellectual levels.

Notwithstanding the capacity gradient, children in both organic and nonorganic schizophrenic groups are similar in a number of attributes which differentiate them from normal and which are the basis for their inclusion in a single category of psychosis. Thus, children in both groups are profoundly confused in personal identity; and children in both groups are deviant in the way they integrate receptor experience in that they tend both to be sensitive to and to exclude visual and auditory stimuli, although the most extreme forms of auditory distress or avoidance are to be found in the organic group. Finally, although a global appraisal of speech which gives weight to symbolic features in speech shows the nonorganic schizophrenic children to be superior to the organic, the two groups are not different in some important, specific aspects of speech. Both groups are equally impaired and differ from normal in the rhythmic aspects of speech, i.e., rate, phrasing, fluency, stress, intonation, and inflection, and in the phonation aspects (volume, pitch, quality). Defects in both groups of schizophrenic children in these characteristics of speech, which are normally utilized in the communication of feelings and multilevel meanings, cause both groups to be equally deficient in clear, comprehensible communication of emotions and connotative meaning.

Influence of the Family

These findings differentiating normal from schizophrenic children and delineating roughly two clusters of children within the schizophrenic group provide a framework for the meaningful study of families. Professional opinion has been divided regarding the significance of family influence in the etiology of childhood schizophrenia. If one views childhood schizophrenia as a single disorder, one is likely to overlook the possibility that the deleterious family experience is of significance in the case of some schizophrenic children and of less significance in the case of other children. To test this possibility, studies of patterns of family interaction have been made in families of schizophrenic and of normal children. One series of investigations has used a technique for the participant observation of the psychosocial environment of the family. This technique focuses on the interactions among the family members in their various roles (e.g., husband and wife as marital partners and as parents) and on the family as a total functional unit. Ratings describing various relational responses are summed to obtain a score which represents the general adequacy of the family to meet its child-rearing function. Using this measure of the family adequacy, a gradient of family adequacy may be noted, as follows: families of normal children are superior to families of the schizophrenic group as a whole. The more interesting gradient, however, is the fact that families of normal children were highest in family adequacy, families of organic schizophrenic children were slightly but not significantly inferior to those of the normal children in adequacy, and families of nonorganic schizophrenic children were most inferior in adequacy. In the case of organic schizophrenic children from families that are normal in their patterns of psychosocial interaction, it is reasonable to assume that the intrinsic ego deficits of the children as a result of cerebral dysfunction are primary determinants in the ultimate picture of psychopathy. In the case of the nonorganic children, typically from low-adequacy families, one may assume that the disordered rearing atmosphere is the primary factor in their impaired egos. In the case of organic schizophrenic children from low-adequacy homes, both the intrinsic incompetence of the child and the deleterious effects of the family seem to contribute to the gaps in adaptive functions in the child.

Finally, as a result of comprehensive longitudinal investigation of the children and their parents in both organic and nonorganic subclusters of schizophrenic children, it has become apparent that in every case, regardless of subdiagnosis of organicity or nonorganicity, comprehensive psychodynamic understanding of the child requires a biologic and psychological appraisal of the schizophrenic child with an eye on intrinsic needs and ego potentials, and an appraisal of his family as a unit and the family individual members in terms of their own intrapsychic needs and expectations. Most important, the mutual, reciprocating impact of the schizophrenic child and his parents and siblings needs to be understood. Even the symptoms of a child with clear-cut brain damage are best explained in psychodynamic and interpersonal terms inasmuch as they are not merely direct expressions of gaps in anatomic structure. Rather, they are manifestations of what the child does in a compensatory sense as a total organism in the face of his structural limitations.

In the most recent phase of family investigation, interest has centered on those specific aspects of family conduct that contribute to the ego aberrations of the children. The study of patterns of relational behavior in the family is as pertinent in the case of the schizophrenic children with cerebral dysfunction as it is in the case of those schizophrenic children presumably free of evidences of cerebral dysfunction. Indeed, the analysis of psychosocial influences in the family is essential even if the children with brain damage are reared in normally functioning family units. Thus, in every instance of marked receptor distress or receptor avoidance associated with brain damage, the aberrant receptor responses of the child have been influenced by the family response to his structurally determined incompetence. In fact, one is not merely observing a child with a trend, for example, to hypersensitivity, but rather a complex episode that one may term a "hypersensitive child-hyperstimulating parent" transaction. In residential treatment, such children typically move toward a more normal response to receptor intake; that is, they begin to look and listen and as a result become considerably less anxious. Not infrequently, these children who have relinquished their psychotic symptoms then present more clearly a picture of simple mental retardation.

Where the Ittleson children are physiologically intact and presumably normal in potentiality for assimilating and manipulating reality, we have found that their families are consistently abnormal in the psychosocial influence on the child. It may be assumed that, although the normal child has an inherent capacity to perceive his environment clearly as a basis for organizing strategies for its manipulation, he requires a psychosocial environment that, in itself, is clear and distinct. Among the families of schizophrenic children a clearly patterned psychosocial environment is often lacking. Our clinical observations, recently confirmed by controlled study, have called attention to a type of paralysis in parental function, which has been termed parental perplexity. This parental atmosphere is characterized by extreme parental indecisiveness, a lack of parental sponta-neity and empathy with the child, the parents' inability to sense what the child's needs are and thus an inability to satisfy them at the proper moment, and an unusual absence of control and authority. In this type of unpatterned climate, positive reinforcement of desirable traits and negative reinforcement of undesirable traits are not administered. Instead, the child is left with feelings of confusion and an inclination to respond in a randomized, impoverished, and unpredictable fashion, when more focused, directed behaviors are lacking. . . .

References

1. Bergmann, P., and Escalona, S. Unusual sensitivities in young children. *Psychoanalyt. Stud. Child* 3-4: 333-352, 1949.
2. Bender, L. Childhood schizophrenia; clinical study of 200 schizophrenic children. *Amer. J. Orthopsychiat.* 17:40-56, 1947.
3. Boatman, J. J., Szurek, S. A. A clinical study of childhood schizophrenia. In Jackson, D. (Ed.), *Etiology of Schizophrenia*. New York: Basic Books, 1960.
4. Eckstein, R., Bryant, K., and Friedman, S. Childhood conditions in schizophrenia. In Bellak, L. (Ed.), *Schizophrenia*. New York: Logos Press, 1958.
5. Goldfarb, W. *Childhood Schizophrenia*. Cambridge: Harvard University Press, for the Commonwealth Fund, 1961.
6. Goldfarb, W. Pain reaction in a group of institutionalized schizophrenic children. *Amer. J. Orthopsychiat.* 28:777-785, 1958.
7. Goldfarb, W. Receptor preferences in schizophrenic children. *Arch. Neurol. Psychiat.* 76:643-652, 1956.
8. Goldfarb, W., Braunstein, P., and Lorge, I. A study of speech patterns in a group of schizophrenic children. *Amer. J. Orthopsychiat.* 26:544-555, 1956.
9. Kallmann, F. J., and Roth, B. Genetic aspects of preadolescent schizophrenia. *Amer. J. Psychiat.* 112:599-606, 1956.
10. Knobloch, H., and Pasamanick, B. Etiologic Factors in "Early Infantile Autism" and "Childhood Schizophrenia." Address, International Congress of Pediatrics in Lisbon, Portugal, Sept. 9-25, 1962.

11. Levy, D. M. The act as unit of behavior. *Fifth Annual Sandor Rado Lectures.* Columbia University, Psychoanalytic Clinic, 1961.
12. Mahler, M. On child psychosis and schizophrenia. Autistic and symbiotic infantile psychoses. In *Psychoanal. Stud. Child,* Vol. 7. New York: International Universities Press, 1952.
13. Rado, S. Hedonic control, action self and the depressive spell. In *Depression: Proceedings of the American Psychopathol. Assoc.* New York: Grune & Stratton, 1954.
14. Taft, L., and Goldfarb, W. Prenatal and perinatal factors in childhood schizophrenia. *Develop. Med. Child Neurol.* 6:32-43, 1964.
15. Vorster, G. An investigation into the part played by organic factors in childhood schizophrenia. *J. Ment. Sci.* 106:494, 1960.
16. Zitrin, A. Address to American Psychiatric Association. May 1962, Toronto, Canada.

10
MIDDLE CHILDHOOD:
PHYSICAL AND MENTAL GROWTH

Middle childhood, roughly the age period from 6-7 to 11-12, is marked by some extraordinary accomplishments in mental growth. Probably the foremost expositor of these accomplishments has been the Swiss psychologist, Jean Piaget, whose seminal studies of children's thinking have revealed many hitherto unknown and unsuspected facets of the child's mind. Piaget has also identified a number of mechanisms by which school-age children become progressively able to replace their earlier egocentric views of the world with more mature, less self-centered conceptions.

In the first of the following two selections, Piaget describes some of the major intellectual accomplishments of school-age children. As this article illustrates, Piaget and his colleagues have never based their investigations on traditional experimental procedures. Instead they have employed a flexible, nonstandardized interview technique aimed at getting at a child's genuine convictions about things. Because the results of Piaget's studies have now been replicated all over the world, we can be fairly confident that they do indeed hold true for most children.

Yet some investigators have questioned Piaget's interpretations of his findings. Elkind in the second selection summarizes Piaget's theory of mental development from infancy through adolescence and reviews some of the challenges it has evoked. Whereas Piaget interprets his findings in terms of the growth of logic, for example, others have interpreted them as attributable to developments in language or perceptual ability. The results are not all in with respect to this issue, but Piaget's contention that it is the growth of logic that underlies maturation in concept formation still appears to constitute a valid interpretation.

JEAN PIAGET

The Mental Development of the Child*

THE PROGRESS OF THOUGHT

When the egocentric forms of causality and representations of the world — i.e., those based on the child's own activity — start to decline under the influence of the factors just cited, new kinds of explication arise which derive from the preceding explications but also correct them. It is striking to note that among the first to appear are those which resemble certain theories advanced by the Greeks at the time of the decline of the mythological explications.

One of the simplest forms of rational relation between cause and effect is explication by means of identification. During the preceding age period thought was characterized by a mixture of animism and artificialism. With respect to the origin of the stars (a bizarre question to pose to children, but one which they frequently raise spontaneously) primitive types of causality are evident: for example, "The sun is born because we are born," and "It has grown because we have grown." When this gross egocentricity is on the decline, the child, while

maintaining the idea of the growth of the stars, does not consider that they are derived by human or anthropomorphic means but through other natural bodies whose formation appears, at first glance, to be more readily understandable. Thus the sun and moon have come out from the clouds; little pieces of clouds have grown and "little moons" frequently grow in front of our eyes! But clouds themselves have come out of smoke or air. Stones are formed from the earth, the earth from water, etc. When things are no longer seen as growing like living beings, their derivation is no longer traced by the child to biological processes but to trans-mutations. It is easy to see the connection between these explications and the reduction of matter theories which were in vogue in the school of Miletus (the "nature" or "physis" of things was a kind of growth for these philosophers and their "hylozoism" was closely related to the animism of the child).

Now what do these early types of explication consist of? Does childhood animism give way directly to a kind of causality based on the principle of identity? Does this well-known logical principle govern reason right away in the manner that certain philosophers[20] would have us believe? Certainly there is proof in these developments that egocentric assimilation and the principles of animism, finalism, and artificialism are in the process of becoming transformed into

*From Chapter 1 of D. Elkind (Ed.), *Six psychological studies of Jean Piaget*, 1967. Reprinted by permission of the author and Random House, Inc.

rational assimilation, i.e., into a structuring of reality by reason itself, but this rational assimilation is much more complex than pure and simple identification.

If, instead of attempting to follow children in their questions about distant realities such as the stars, the mountains, and the ocean, which can be dealt with only on the verbal plane, one questions them about tangible and plausible things, one is in for a great surpise. By the age of seven years, the child is capable of building explanations which are properly atomistic; this occurs at the period when he starts to count. To continue with our comparison, recall that the Greeks invented atomism soon after having speculated on the transmutation of substances, and note in particular that the first of the atomists was probably Pythagoras, who believed that the composition of bodies was based on material numbers or discontinuous points of substance. Of course, with rare exceptions (and there are some), the child does not generalize and differs from the Greek philosophers in that he does not construct a system. But when experience permits, he does have recourse to an explicit and quite rational atomism.

The simplest experiment in this regard consists of presenting the child with two glasses of water of the same shape and size, filled three-quarters full. Two lumps of sugar are immersed in one glass, and the child is asked in advance if the water will rise. Once the sugar is immersed, the new water level is measured and the glass is weighed, so as to show that the glass containing the sugar weighs more than the other glass. While the sugar is dissolving, the following questions are asked:

1. Once the sugar is dissolved, will anything remain in the water?

2. Will the weight remain greater or become the same as the glass containing the clear water?

3. Will the level of the sugar water descend so as to become equal to the water level in the other glass or will it remain the way it is?

The child is asked to give reasons for all his replies. After the sugar has completely dissolved, the fact that the weight and volume (level) of the sugar water remain unchanged is pointed out and the discussion continues. The reactions observed at successive ages are so clear and regular that they can be used as a diagnostic procedure in the study of mental retardation (Inhelder, 1963). To begin with, the child of less than seven years generally denies the conservation of any of the dissolved sugar and *a fortiori* that of the weight and volume associated with it. For him the fact that the sugar dissolves implies that it is entirely annihilated and no longer has any reality. It is true that the taste of the sugar water remains, but according to the very young child the taste, too, is destined for annihilation in a few hours or days in the same way that smell or a shadow disappears. At about the age of seven, by contrast, the child understands that the dissolved sugar remains in the water, i.e., there is conservation of the substance. But in what form? For some subjects, it becomes transformed into water or liquefied into a syrup which mixes with the water; an explanation by transmutation. In the case of the more advanced child, something else is proposed. The child states that he can see the piece of sugar frittering into "little crumbs" in the course of dissolving. Once it is realized that these "little bits" become constantly smaller, it is easy to understand that the water still contains invisible "little balls." And, these subjects add: "That is what makes the sweet taste." Thus atomism is born in the guise of a "metaphysics of dust" or powder, as a French philosopher has so wittily said. But it is still a qualitative atomism, since these "little balls" have neither weight nor volume and the child expects the weight to disappear and the level of the water to descend after the sugar has dissolved. At a later stage, which occurs at about nine years, the child reasons in the same way with respect to the substance but adds an essential element. Each small ball has its own weight, and if all the partial weights are added one will arrive at the weight of all the immersed sugar. By contrast, while he is capable of such a subtle *a priori* explanation for the conservation of weight, he is unable to do the same for volume and expects the level of the water to go down after the sugar has dissolved. Finally, at eleven to twelve years, the child generalizes his explanatory schema to the volume itself and declares that, since each little ball occupies its own place, the sum of these spaces will equal the space taken up by the immersed sugar so that the level of the water will not go down.

Such is childhood atomism. This example is not unique. One obtains the same explanation in reverse when a grain of popcorn is heated. For the young child the substance increases; at seven the substance is conserved without increasing — it merely swells and the weight changes; at nine to ten years the weight remains the same but not the volume; and toward twelve years, since flour is composed of invisible grains with a constant volume, these grains of powder simply move away from each other, separated by the hot air.

This atomism is remarkable not so much because of the representation of the granules, suggested by experience with powder or flour, but because of the deductive process it reveals. The whole is explained by the composition of its parts. This presupposes real operations of segmentation or partition and, inversely, of reunion or addition, as well as displacement by concentration or spreading out (like the pre-Socratics). Above all, it presupposes real principles of conservation, indicating that the operations at work are grouped into closed and coherent systems, in which the conservations represent "invariants."

We have just seen an early manifestation of the concept of permanence. It becomes associated successively with substance, weight, and volume. This is easy to demonstrate in other experiments. For example, the child is given two small balls of modeling clay of the same size and weight. One of the balls is then shaped into a flat cake, a sausage, or cut into pieces. Before the age of seven, the child believes that the quantity of matter, the weight, and the volume have changed. At seven to eight years, he sees the constancy of matter but still believes in the variability of the other qualities. Toward nine years, he recognizes the conservation of weight but not of volume, and at eleven to twelve years he recognizes the constancy of the volume. It is easy to demonstrate that, as of seven years, many other principles of conservation are also acquired. These conservations reflect the development of thinking and are completely absent in the younger child. It is only after the age of seven that one finds the conservation of lengths, surfaces, discontinuous wholes, etc. These ideas of invariance are equivalent, on the conceptual level, to what we have already seen in the sensorimotor schema of the "object," the practical invariant of action.

How are these concepts of conservation, which so profoundly differentiate the thought of the second period of childhood from the early years, elaborated? Exactly like atomism itself or, to speak more generally, like the causal explication based on partitive composition. These conservation concepts result from the interplay of operations coordinated among themselves into integrated systems whose most remarkable property, as compared with the intuitive thinking of the young child, is that of being reversible. The real reason children of this age recognize the conservation of substance or weight is not identity (the small child is just as capable of seeing that "nothing has been added or taken away" as is the older child), but the possibility of a rigorous return to the point of departure. The flat cake weighs as much as the ball, says the older child, because you can remake a ball from the cake. Later on we shall see the real significance of these operations. It is operations that result in a correction of perceptual intuition—which is always a victim of illusions of the moment—and which "decenter" egocentricity so as to transform transitory relationships into a coherent system of objective, permanent relations.

Before we continue, let us point out again the great advances achieved at this level of thinking. In addition to causality and concepts of conservation there is the mastery of time, rate, and space, concepts which are now general schemata of thought, rather than schemata of action or intuition.

The development of time concepts in children raises curious problems in connection with questions posed by contemporary science. At every age, of course, the child will be able to say of a moving object that goes from A to B to C that it was at A "before" being at B or at C and that it takes "more time" to go from A to C than from A to B. This is more or less the extent of the young child's temporal intuitions. If he is asked to compare two moving objects following parallel courses at different rates, it is apparent that: (1) the young child does not have the intuition of the simultaneity of terminal points, because he does not understand the existence of a time *common* to the two movements; (2) he does not have the intuition of the equality of two synchronous durations; (3) he does not understand the connection between duration and succession. For example, if boy X is younger than boy Y, the young child does not conclude that the second boy must necessarily have been born "after" the other. How, then, does he construct time? By the coordination of operations analogous to those which have already been discussed: placing events in successive order on the one hand and nesting the durations conceived as intervals between these events. The two systems are coherent because they fit together.

As for speed, young children of all ages correctly intuit that a moving object that passes another object is going faster than the second object. But if this passing is made invisible (by hiding the moving objects in tunnels of unequal length or by making the routes unequal but concentric circles) the intuition of speed fails. The rational concept of speed, on the other hand, conceived as a relationship between time and distance traveled evolves together with the time concept at around eight years of age.

There remains the construction of the space concept, which has immense importance both for the comprehension of the laws of development and for its pedagogical implications. Unfortunately, while we more or less understand the development of this concept in the form of a practical schema during the first two years, research with respect to the spontaneous geometry of the older child is far from being as advanced as the preceding concepts. All that we can say is that the fundamental ideas of order, continuity, distance, length, measurement, etc., only give rise in early childhood to extremely limited and distorted intuitions. Primitive space is neither homogeneous nor isotropic, nor continuous, etc.; above all, it is centered on the subject's standpoint rather than representing various points of view. It is again at approximately seven years of age that rational space is constructed by means of the same general operations whose formation we shall now discuss.

THE RATIONAL OPERATIONS

Intuition is the highest form of equilibrium attained by the thinking of young children and, in this sense, corresponds to the concrete operational thinking of middle childhood. The concrete operational kernel of intelligence merits detailed examination since it furnishes the key to an essential part of mental development.

It should be noted first that, while the concept of operation is well defined, it applies to many diverse realities. There are logical operations which underlie a system of class concepts and relations; arithmetic operations (addition, multiplication, etc., and their inverses); geometric operations (sections, displacements, etc.); temporal operations (seriation of events, i.e., the successive ordering of events and the nesting of intervals between them); mechanical operations; physical operations; etc. Psychologically, an operation is, above all, some kind of action (the act of combining individuals or numeric units, displacing them, etc.), whose origin is always perceptual, intuitive (representational), or motoric. The actions which are the starting point for operations are thus rooted in the sensorimotor schemata, i.e., in actual or mental (intuitive) experience. Before becoming operational, they constitute the substance of sensorimotor intelligence, then of intuition.

How can we explain the transition from intuitions to operations? Intuitions become transformed into operations as soon as they constitute groupings which are both composable and reversible. In other words, actions become operational when two actions of the same kind can be composed into a third action of the same kind and when these various actions can be compensated or annulled. Thus the action of combining (logical or arithmetic addition) is an operation, because several successive combinations are equivalent to a single combination (composition of additions) and because the combinations can be annulled by dissociations (subtractions).

It is remarkable to see the formation

of a whole series of these groupings by children at about age seven. They transform the intuitions into operations of all kinds and explain the transformation of thinking described earlier. Above all, it is striking to see how these groupings are formed, often very rapidly, through a sort of total reorganization. No operation exists in an isolated state; it is always formed as a function of the totality of operations of the same kind. For example, a logical concept of class (combination of individuals) is not constructed in an isolated state but necessarily within a classification of the grouping of which it forms a part. A logical family relation (brother, uncle, etc.) is constituted only as a function of a set of analogous relations whose totality constitutes a system of relationships. Numbers do not appear independently of each other (3, 10, 2, 5, etc.); they are grasped only as elements within an ordered series: l, 2, 3 . . . etc. Likewise, values exist only as a function of a total system or "scale of values." An asymmetric relationship such as $B < C$ is intelligible only in relation to the possible seriation of the set: $O < A < B < C < D$ . . . etc. What is even more remarkable is that these systems of sets are formed only in the child's thinking in connection with the precise reversibility of the operations, so that they acquire a definite and complete structure right away.

A particularly clear example of this is that of the qualitative seriation: $A < B < C$ . . . etc. During early childhood, a youngster can distinguish two sticks by their length and can judge that B is larger than A, but at this age level it is merely a conceptual or intuitive relationship and not a logical operation. If the young child

is first shown sticks $A < B$, and then sticks $B < C$ while A is hidden under the table, and he is asked if A (which has just been compared with B) is larger or smaller than C (which is on the table with B), the child refuses to make a decision and asks to see the two together because he cannot deduce $A < C$ from $A < B$ and $B < C$. This occurs, naturally, only when the differences are not so great as to remain in the memory as picture images. When will the child be able to make this deduction? Not until he can construct a series or scale of sticks on the table, and, curiously enough, he will not be able to do so before six or seven years of age. To be sure, even a young child can order sticks of very different lengths, but this is simply a matter of constructing a staircase, i.e., a perceptual figure. By contrast, if the differences are small and he has to compare the elements of each pair of sticks in order to organize them, he will start by simply arranging them in pairs: CE; AC; BD; etc., without coordinating the pairs one with the other. Later he will make little series of three or four elements but still without coordinating the several part series. Subsequently, he will succeed with the whole series but only by trial and error and without knowing how to intersperse distinct new elements once the initial series has been completely arranged. Finally, at around the age of six and a half or seven, he discovers an operational method which consists of looking first for the smallest element, then for the smallest of those that remain, etc. He thus succeeds in constructing the whole series without trial and error and is also able to intersperse new elements. He then becomes capable of reasoning: $A < B$ and $B < C$, therefore A < C. It is also immediately apparent that this construction presupposes the inverse operation (operational reversibility). Each element is conceived both as smaller than all the following elements (relation <) and as larger than all the preceding elements (relation >). This allows the subject to discover a method of construction as well as to intersperse new elements after the total initial series has been constructed.

It is very interesting to note that, while the operations of seriation (coordination of asymmetric relation) are discovered at about the age of seven with respect to length or size, it is not until about the age of nine that the child can serially order weights in an analogous fashion (for example, the seriation of balls of the same size but different weight). It is not until eleven or twelve years that he acquires the same capacity with respect to volume (tested by means of immersing objects in water). By the same token, not until he is nine does the child conclude that A < C, if A < B and B < C with regard to weight, and not until he is eleven or twelve does he draw the same conclusions with respect to volume. It is evident that these operations are closely connected with the actual construction of the concepts of weight and volume and notably with the elaboration of the principles of conservation related to them (see above).

A second example of a total system of operations is the coordination of symmetrical relations, in particular the relation among equalities: A = B; B = C; therefore A = C. Once again these groupings are linked to the construction of concepts themselves. These equality groupings appear as of the age of seven with respect

to simple lengths and quantities, but not until the age of nine with respect to equalities of weight, while equalities with respect to volume do not appear until age twelve. Here is an example illustrating the equality of weights. The child is given some bars A = B = C . . . of the same shape, size, and weight; then he is given pieces of lead, stone, etc., of different shapes but with the same weight as the bars. The child compares the lead with bar A and, to his astonishment, notes that the two weights are equal on the scale. He also sees that bar A's weight is equal to that of bar B. He is then asked whether bar B will weigh as much as the piece of lead. Up until the age of eight and a half or nine years, he refuses to concede the equality. Not until the age at which all weight relations are coordinated will he be capable of this reversible composition.

A particularly apt example of the composition of symmetrical relations is that of "brother." A small child of four or five years (let us call him Paul) has a brother, Etienne. When Paul is asked if his brother Etienne has a brother, he will frequently reply in the negative. The reason given is usually the following: "There are only two of us in the family and Etienne does not have a brother." Here we see clearly the intellectual egocentricity that characterizes intuitive thought. Not knowing how to get away from his own point of view so as to see himself from another person's point of view, the child begins by denying the symmetry of the relationship of brother to brother because of a lack of reciprocity (i.e., symmetrical reversibility). By the same token, one can see how the logical or operational coordination of this kind of relationship is connected with an individual's social coordination and with the coordination of the intuitive points of view he has experienced.

We come now to the system of logical operations essential to the genesis of general concepts or "classes," hence of all classification. The principle is simply the nesting of the parts in the whole, or, conversely, the separation of the parts with respect to the whole. Here again, one must not confuse the intuitive totalities or simple collections of objects with the operational totalities or classes which are truly logical.

An easily reproducible experiment demonstrates that operational classes are constructed much later than one might think and shows how they are linked to reversible thinking. An open box containing about twenty brown wooden beads and two to three white wooden beads is presented to the subject. After he has manipulated the beads he is asked whether there are more wooden beads or more brown beads in the box. The great majority of children below seven years can only say, "There are more brown ones." This is so because, to the extent that they dissociate the whole ("all of wood") into two parts ("white" and "brown"), they are unable to compare one of these parts with the whole, which they have mentally destroyed; they can compare only the two parts. By contrast, at about seven years this difficulty attenuates and the whole can be compared to one of its parts, each part from then on being conceived as a true part of the whole (a part equals the whole minus the other parts, by virtue of the inverse operation).

Finally we come to the question of how numbers and arithmetic operations are constructed. We know that only the first numbers are accessible to the young child because these are intuitive numbers which correspond to perceptible figures. The indefinite series of numbers and, above all, the operations of addition (plus its inverse, subtraction) and multiplication (plus its inverse, division) are, on the average, accessible only after the age of seven. The reason for this is simple enough. Number is in reality a composite of some of the preceding operations and consequently presupposes their prior construction. A whole number is in effect a collection of equal units, a class whose subclasses are rendered equivalent by the suppression of their qualities. At the same time, it is an ordered series, a seriation of the relations of order. Its dual cardinal and ordinal nature thus results from a fusion of the logical systems of nesting and seriation, which explains why true number concepts appear at the same time as the qualitative operations. It is readily understandable, therefore, that the term-by-term correspondences which we have analyzed above (II C) remain intuitive during early childhood. They do not become operational and do not constitute numerical operations until the child reaches the point where he is able to coordinate the operations of seriation and nesting of parts in wholes (classes). It is only at this point that term-by-term correspondence brings with it the enduring equivalence of corresponding collections and thus engenders true number.

We may draw a general conclusion: a child's thinking becomes logical only through the organization of systems of operations which obey the laws common to all groupings: (1) Composition: two operations may combine to give another operation of the grouping (e.g., +1 +1 = 2). (2) Reverslbility: every operation can be inverted (e.g., +1 becomes inverted to −1). (3) The direct operation and its inverse gives rise to an identical or null operation (e.g., +1 − 1 = 0). (4) Operations can combine with one another in all kinds of ways. This general structure, which mathematicians call "groups," characterizes all the systems of operations already described except that in the logical or qualitative domains (seriation of relations, nesting of classes, etc.), conditions (3) and (4) present certain peculiarities as a result of the fact that a class or relation added to itself does not change. In this case, we speak of a "grouping," which is an even more elementary and general concept than group.

The passage from intuition to logic or to mathematical operations is effectuated during the course of middle childhood by the construction of groupings and groups. Concepts and relations cannot be constructed in isolation but from the outset constitute organized sets in which all the elements are interdependent and in equilibrium. This structure, proper to mental assimilation of an operational order, assures the mind of an equilibrium considerably superior to that of intuitive or egocentric assimilation. The attained reversibility is a manifestation of a permanent equilibrium between the assimilation of things to the mind and the accommodation of the mind to things. Thus, when the mind goes beyond its immediate point of view in order to "group" relations, it attains a state of coherence and noncontradiction paralleled by cooperation on the social plane (see A). In both cases the self is subordinated to the laws of reciprocity. . . .

References

Inhelder, B. *Le diagnostic du raisonnement chez les débiles mentaux.* (2nd ed.) Neuchâtel: Delachaux and Niestlé, 1963.

DAVID ELKIND

Cognitive Development*

PIAGET'S DEVELOPMENTAL THEORY OF INTELLIGENCE

In the course of almost half a century of continuous research on children's thinking Piaget has evolved a general theory of mental growth. According to the theory, adult intelligence (adaptive thinking and action) is derived from the earliest sensorimotor coordination of infants, in a series of stages that are related to age. Piaget recognizes that there are wide individual differences in the age at which any particular stage emerges, but he believes that the sequence in which the stages appear is necessary and invariant for all children. Piaget's theory is thus a "nature" theory in the sense that the sequence of stages is determined by maturational factors, but it is also a

Table 1 *Stages of Cognitive Growth in Piaget's Theory*

Stage	Approximate Age Range (years)	Major Characteristic
Sensorimotor period	0 to 2	Object permanence, elementary causality
Pre-operational period	2 to 6	Symbolic function
Period of concrete operations	6 or 7 to 11 or 12	Concrete operations (see Table 2), "age of reason"
Period of formal operations	11 or 12 on	Formal operations (see text), complex reasoning, metaphor

"nurture theory" in the sense that the age at which any particular stage is achieved depends upon individual differences in ability, background, and experience. The developmental stages are listed in Table 1, and are briefly described below.

*From Chapter 14 of H. W. Reese and L. P. Lipsitt, *Experimental child psychology*, 1970. Reprinted by permission of the author and Academic Press.

Sensorimotor Period

During the first two years of life the infant is transformed from a relatively helpless organism with limited motility, powers of expression, and social awareness to a highly mobile, verbal, relatively socially adept child. Corresponding to these remarkable changes in motility, expression, and socialization are equally significant changes in cognitive awareness and capacity.

During the early months of life, to illustrate, the young Infant behaves as if the world about him were a kind of motion picture, a continuously changing panorama of events no one of which has any permanence. If an adult is playing with a three month old and suddenly ducks out of sight, the infant may not look after him and may attend to something else. Despite the fact that the infant appeared totally engrossed in the adult a moment before, after the adult disappears the infant behaves as if he never existed. For the infant, it is literally true that "out of sight is out of mind."

Toward the end of the first year, however, the infant begins to seek after objects that have disappeared and thus gives evidence that he now attaches permanence to objects that are no longer present to his senses. It is only toward the end of the first year, for example, that infants begin to cry at the disappearance of the mother and sometimes to display a fear of strangers. Likewise, if an infant less than six months old is removed from the home (say for a minor operation) he shows no vexatious signs after his return. If, however, the infant is eight to nine months old, his return home is marked by crying, tantrums, and clinging to mother (Schaffer, 1958). Other evidence (Charlesworth, 1966; White, 1969) also attests to the validity of Piaget's (1964) observation that a major achievement of the sensorimotor period is the construction of the concept of a permanent object, one that is believed to exist even when it is outside the child's immediate psychological world.

Other cognitive accomplishments during the sensorimotor period are equally striking and significant. During this period the infant acquires an elementary notion of causality and begins to anticipate the results of his actions. He will, for example, push his cereal off the tray of the high chair and then look at the floor where it has fallen. Toward the end of the second year his spatial concepts are also well elaborated and he usually knows the floor plan of his home quite well and can get where he wants to go (and sometimes where he is not supposed to go) with ease. All in all, then, the remarkable achievements made by the infant in the realms of motility, expression, and socialization are coupled with equally remarkable achievements with respect to his conception of objects, space, and causality.

The Pre-Operational Period

In Piaget's view, the pre-operational period (usually two to six years of age) is marked by the emergence of what he calls the *symbolic function*, or true systems of representation such as language. The symbols of the pre-operational period must not be confused with the more primitive representations of the sensorimotor stage. The infant can use both *signals*—stimuli which through conditioning come to elicit particular behaviors, like the sight of the bottle which *signals* sucking—and *signs* which are part of the object represented (e.g., the tail of the dog is a *sign* of the dog; mother's voice is a *sign* of mother). Neither signs nor signals are true symbols because they cannot be produced by the subject.

Evidence for the presence of the symbolic function during the preschool period comes from a variety of sources. First, the acquisition of language increases rapidly during the third year. Further, symbolic play appears. A child engages in symbolic play when, for example, he puts two sticks together and calls them an airplane or he calls a stone a turtle. Such designations are true symbols because they are produced by the subject and are not simply imposed upon him. In addition, the first evidence of dreams and night terrors, which suggest active symbolic activity, is obtained. Finally, "deferred imitation" begins; the child becomes able to see an action and to repeat or mimic it hours later. Here again the suggestion is that the delay is bridged by some form of internalized representation. The attainment and development of the symbolic function is thus one of the central accomplishments of the pre-operational period of cognitive development.

Period of Concrete Operations

Although children in the pre-operational stage make remarkable progress in symbolic activities, particularly language expression, their ability to deal with classes, relations, and numbers is quite limited. For example, pre-operational children have difficulty in distinguishing between "some" and "all" (Sinclair-DeZwart, 1967) and between use of a class term to represent a single member of the class and use of it to represent the class as a whole. When a pre-operational child calls his pet "doggie," he uses the term both as a proper name (e.g., as a substitute for "Spot") and as a class name ("dog") without clearly differentiating between the two uses. In the realm of number, the pre-operational child can usually discriminate up to three or four objects and may be able to count to twenty, but he cannot

coordinate his verbal counting with the enumeration of elements.

Toward the age of six or seven years, however, the child gradually attains what Piaget (1950) called *concrete operations*, internalized actions that operate in a manner analogous to elementary arithmetic operations. These operations fall into groupings such that if one operation in a grouping is present, all are present. One of the groupings that appear in this period is described in Table 2.

The emergence of these concrete operations permits achievements not possible in the pre-operational period. With respect to classes, for example, the child can now deal with their combinations. He can now say that boys and girls are children and that children minus boys is equal to girls (Elkind, 1961a; Wohlwill, 1968). He is thus, in Piagetian terms, able to *nest* classes. In a like manner, concrete operations enable children to arrive at a true concept of number and to perform the elementary operations of arithmetic. The acquisition of the number concept will be discussed in more detail later.

In short, the emergence of concrete operations, usually during the period from 6 or 7 to 11 or 12 years of age, enables the child to engage in elementary reasoning of the syllogistic variety. That is why the age of 6 to 7 has traditionally been called the "age of reason." During the elementary school period, concrete operations enable the child to elaborate his conceptions of time to include clock and historical time and to elaborate his conceptions of space to include geographical and geometrical space. Likewise, his conception of causality is expanded to include complex cause and effect sequences such as those found in mystery stories, which begin to be appreciated toward the end of childhood. Moreover, since concrete operations are internalized, the child can now solve in his head problems which as a pre-operational child he had to solve by means of trial and error actions.

Table 2 *One of the Groupings of Concrete Operations*

Operation	Description
Composition	A class (A) combined with its complement (A') gives rise to the total class (B): $A + A' = B$. E.g., boys (A) and $(+)$ girls (A') are $(=)$ children (B).
Inversion	A class (A) subtracted from the total class (B) gives rise to its complement (A'): $B - A = A'$. E.g., children (B) who are not $(-)$ boys (A) are girls (A').
Identity	For every class there is another that when combined with it gives rise to the identity element, 0: $A - A = 0$. E.g., the class of boys minus the class of boys equals the null or identity class.
Tautology	For every class there is another that when combined with it gives rise to the class itself: $A + A = A$. E.g., the class of boys plus the class of boys equals the class of boys.
Partial associativity	In some cases the order in which a set of classes is combined has no effect upon the result: $A + A' + B' = A + (A' + B')$; but $(A + A) - A \neq A + (A - A)$, since $(A + A) - A = 0$ and $A + (A - A) = A$.

Period of Formal Operations

The concrete operations of childhood enable the child to deal with the concrete reality about him in a logical way, but they have certain limitations. For one thing, even though the child can reason about concrete objects, he has difficulty in reasoning about verbal propositions. For example, if a child is first shown two different-sized dolls, A and B (where $A > B$) and then another two, B and C (where $B > C$), he can deduce that A is bigger than C without having compared the two directly. He has much more difficulty, however, if the problem is posed verbally, for example, "Helen is taller than Jane and Jane is taller than Mary. Who is the tallest of the three?" (Glick and Wapner, 1968; Piaget, 1950).

The child with concrete operations is limited in still another respect. He is limited, for the most part, to dealing with at most two classes or relations at a time. A child with *formal operations*, however, can deal with many variables simultaneously. Inhelder and Piaget (1958), for example, showed children and adolescents a variety of experimental setups, such as the experimental determination of what combination of four colorless liquids (diluted sulfuric acid, water, oxygenated water, and thiosulfate) and a reagent (potassium chloride) would turn the liquid in one container yellow. Adolescents were able to solve the problem (which required the combination of three liquids) in a systematic manner, but children combined two of the liquids at a time, often without arriving at a solution. Formal operations thus permit the adolescent to engage in the kind of thinking that is characteristic of scientific experimentation. The period of formal operations usually begins at 11 or 12 to 15 years of age.

Formal operations also make possible other achievements. For example, adolescents can conceptualize their own thoughts and think about thinking. To illustrate, if a child is asked, "Can a dog or cat be a Protestant?", he is likely to say, "No, because they won't let him into church"; but the adolescent is likely to say, "No, because dogs wouldn't understand things like that." In addition, formal operations enable adolescents to think about ideal or counterfactual situations and to understand metaphorical expressions. If a child is asked to suppose that coal is white, he is likely to reply that "coal is black," but the adolescent can accept the counterfactual premise and reason from it.

The attainment of formal operations, in contrast with the attainment of concrete operations, does not appear to be universal, and may therefore be much more dependent upon culture (Goodnow and Bethon, 1966) and perhaps competence in symbolic skills such as reading (Elkind, Barocas, and Rosenthal, 1968)....

EVALUATION OF PIAGET'S WORK

Investigators other than Piaget and his colleagues have dealt with four main issues about Piaget's research and theory. (a) *Reliability:* Several investigators have explored the reliability or reproducibility of Piaget's findings. Studies of this kind have already been cited in the discussions of Piaget's specific investigations, and since the general consensus is that the findings are reliable, the research on this issue need not be further considered here. (b) *Generalizability:* There have been studies of the generalizability of Piaget's findings to children from different social classes and cultures, and to children with sensory deficits and limited intelligence. (c) *Interpretation:* Some investigators have questioned Piaget's interpretations of the findings and have tested alternative hypotheses. This has led, in some cases, to concern with the modifiability of the child's performance in the kinds of tasks used by Piaget. (d) *Relation to Other Variables:* One group of researchers has studied the relation of performance on these kinds of tasks to other aspects of the child's behavior and thought, such as intelligence test performance and personality.

In the rest of the present section a summary of selected research on each of the last three issues will be presented, together with conclusions as to what the results seem to suggest so far.

Generalization of the Findings

Researchers have asked to what extent the results obtained by Piaget with white middle class Western European children are generalizable to children of other races and cultures. Perhaps in no other area of psychology is there so much cross-cultural and cross-social-class information available as on the Piagetian tasks. For example, conservation problems have been given to children in Canada (Dodwell, 1960, 1961; Laurendeau and Pinard, 1962), England (Lovell, 1961), Hong Kong (Goodnow and Bethon, 1966), Italy (Peluffo, 1962), Jamaica (Vernon, 1965), Prince Edward County, Virginia (Mermelstein and Shulman, 1967), and Senegal (Greenfield, 1966).

There are problems in interpreting results from cross-cultural studies, however, because of the differences in language, experience, and cultural values. If similar results are obtained cross-culturally, there is no problem; but if differences are observed, it is not easy to interpret or account for the cause of the differences.

To illustrate the kinds of issues that come up in cross-cultural research, a study by Greenfield (1966) is instructive. Greenfield worked in Senegal, French Africa, with Wolof children, who are Moslem and represent the dominant population. The subjects were from three age levels and were grouped according to residence and school—urban-school, bush-school, and bush-unschooled. They were tested on the liquid conservation task, in their native language. The results showed that no more than 50 percent of the unschooled bush children attained conservation by the age of 11 to 13 years. Both urban (Dakar) and bush school children, however, showed 100 percent conservation by the same age level. A secondary finding of this study was that when bush children rather than the experimenter poured the liquid, many more children showed conservation both immediately and on a delayed posttest. Greenfield

interpreted this result as due to the child's attributing less magic to himself than to the adult.

In a comprehensive summary of the findings of the cross-cultural studies, Goodnow (1969) arrived at the following conclusions: (a) Some tasks are more vulnerable than others to departures from urban Western schooling. The most hardy of the tasks appears to be the conservation of number, and the most vulnerable tasks appear to be those requiring "words, drawings, visual imagery" (Goodnow, 1969, p. 453). (b) The tasks that are less vulnerable to cultural differences may be those for which the child has action models. In societies where children have many measurement and measuring experiences, concepts of length and time may be more fully developed than in cultures where such experiences are less frequent. (c) "The critical skill may be versatility in the use of different sources of information and different models" (Goodnow, 1969, p. 454).

In summary, then, it is not possible to make any sweeping statements about the cross-cultural replication of Piaget's findings. Some tasks appear to be more hardy than others, and the differences that do appear seem to revolve around the ages at which the tasks are passed rather than the sequence of their acquisition. It is not known, however, whether the *processes* by which children of other cultural groups attain conservation are the same as for urban Western children. What cross-cultural studies do unequivocally show is that the "naturalness" of conservation as known in Western culture is probably a product, in part at least, of direct or indirect physical and social experience.

Tests of Piagetian Interpretations

One of the most active areas of research now current has to do with testing Piaget's interpretations of his findings, namely, that the age differences in performance are attributable to age differences in cognitive structures or mental operations. Some investigators have attempted to show that the child's performance on the conservation task is a result of misleading perceptual cues rather than a result of a cognitive deficit; others have argued that the failure to conserve has to do with language misunderstandings; and still others have attempted to show that non-conservation is due to a lack of instruction or learning.

Perceptual Interpretations. Several investigators (e.g., Bruner, 1966; Gelman, 1969; Mehler and Bever, 1967) have argued that the conservation problem presents children with misleading perceptual cues, and that conservation

involves learning to ignore such misleading perceptual information. Such a position is not really contrary to Piaget's views, since he too believes that the child must overcome misleading perceptual cues if he is to attain conservation. A conflict in interpretation arises over *how* the misleading perceptual cues are to be overcome. For Bruner (1966), it appears that a verbal formula shields the child from the illusion of non-conservation; for others, such as Mehler and Bever (1967) and Gelman (1969), what is required is a more sophisticated perceptual discrimination.

To illustrate the research on which these alternative interpretations are based, consider a study by Frank (reported by Bruner, 1966, pp. 193-202). In this investigation four to seven year old children were exposed to three tasks (see Figure 1). In the first, they observed two beakers that were either the same or different in width, height, or both width

Present	Screen	Pour	Same to drink?	If I pour into empty glass, where will water come? Point to level

Original display	Mark level of water	Pour into empty glass	Mark level of other glass	Unscreen and and explanation

Figure 1. *The three tasks used by Frank: Task 1 is at the upper left, Task 2 at the upper right, and Task 3 across the bottom of the figure. (From Bruner, 1966, Figure 3, p. 195. Reprinted by permission of the author and John Wiley & Sons, Inc.)*

and height. One was half filled with colored water. After the child had observed the two beakers, they were placed behind a screen so that only their tops were visible; the liquid was then poured from one beaker into the other, and the child was asked whether there was still the same amount of water as before. In the second task, the same beakers were used, and the child had to predict the outcome of the pouring by pointing to the level the water would reach if it were poured into the second beaker. The third task was a combination of the first and second in that the pouring was actually carried out behind the screen but the child had to predict, by marking upon the screen, the level to which he expected the water to come in the second container. Pre- and posttests of conservation of liquid quantities were also employed.

The results showed that young children, who did not exhibit conservation on the standard test, nonetheless said that the amount of liquid was unchanged when it was poured into a wider container, but only when they could not actually see the level reached (first-task condition). They also predicted that the height reached by liquid poured from a narrow container into a wide one would be the same in the wide one as it had been in the narrow one (second-task condition). Thus, their judgment that the amount of liquid would be the same when poured into a wide container was based on the false premise that the level would not change with the width of the container. This interpretation of the apparent "conservation" was corroborated when, in the third task, the screen was removed and virtually all of the four year old children changed their judgment and said that the amount of water was not the same because the level was different.

Another finding, which according to Bruner demonstrates the role of misleading cues, was that after experiencing the three screening procedures, many children who were non-conservers in the pretest became conservers in the posttest. Apparently, the screening procedures had the effect of inducing conservation, at least in some children. This result supports a perceptual interpretation of conservation, but the support might be more convincing if the children who attained conservation in this way were shown *not* to be about to attain conservation spontaneously, through the utilization of operational thought. Other studies (e.g., Wallach, Wall, and Anderson, 1967) have shown the importance of determining the child's precise level of conservation before assessing the effectiveness of a particular training procedure.

The level of development of conservation can be assessed by determining if there are any circumstances under which a child will say that a quantity is conserved across a transformation of its appearance. For example, if the child says that the ball and the sausage of clay (in the test of conservation of mass) contain different amounts of clay but that they will both contain the same amount of clay if one is rolled back into a ball, he is more advanced than a child who says that the transformation is completely irreversible. Likewise, the child who judges a quantity as conserved across a relatively small alteration in its appearance but not across a relatively large one is more advanced than a child who will not acknowledge conservation under any circumstances.

Another study of the same type was reported by Mehler and Bever (1967). These investigators gave conservation problems to children as young as two years of age. The children were shown unequal numbers of elements in different arrays. In one array the more numerous elements were close together, and the less numerous were further apart. The two and three year olds correctly judged the more numerous but shorter row to have more elements, but somewhat older children made the opposite judgment. Mehler and Bever argued that the child originally has conservation but later gets misled as he becomes more attentive to perceptual cues. Alternative interpretations can be made, however, particularly because the actual inequality of the two sets provided immediate perceptual cues to the solution. It is possible, for example, that the young children were responding on an undifferentiated basis of sheer numerosity and the older children were responding to a more differentiated perceptual impression of length. If so, the response of the two year olds would be analogous to the pseudo-conservation responses in Frank's investigation in the sense that they would be correct judgments made for reasons that, in the adult view, are wrong.

Still another example of this kind of study is the work of Gelman (1969). Gelman taught her subjects a large number of oddity problems (which require determining which one of three elements is different from the other two); the relevant dimension was size or number, but irrelevant dimensions such as color were also present. For example, in one problem there were three sticks, two of the same length and one shorter, but all the same color. Color was thus irrelevant to the problem, and the children had to focus upon size to attain the solution. Gelman found that a large proportion of her non-conserving children became conservers after the oddity problem training. She did not, however, diagnose how close these children were to attaining conservation prior to the training. Nevertheless, this study provides the most powerful evidence yet obtained for a perceptual as opposed to an operational interpretation of conservation.

Language Interpretations. The role of language in the solution of Piaget-type tasks has been explored from a number of different points of view, including direct tutelage on the correct verbal responses to the Piaget items (Kohnstamm, 1967; Sinclair-DeZwart, 1967). In general, the role of language seems to vary with the nature of the particular task used. Deaf children, without language competence, attain conservation at about the same age as hearing subjects (Furth, 1966). [Use of nonverbal procedures with normal children does not appear to make conservation easier (Wohlwill and Lowe, 1962).] Sinclair-DeZwart (1967) found that children who spontaneously described objects as tall *and* narrow or short *and* fat were conservers, and children who simply described objects as "big" or "little" did not conserve. However, training children to use the operational verbal formulas ("longer and narrower") did not affect their success on the conservation task. In contrast, Almy et al. (1966) reported that conservation was attained a year later in lower class children than in middle class children; this might be attributable to language deficit.

In classification problems, however, the situation is more dramatic. With such problems, which often include pictorial materials, children from culturally deprived or disadvantaged homes usually do much more poorly than middle class children. Sigel, Anderson, and Shapiro (1966a) and Sigel and McBane (1967) found that lower class Negro children were inferior to middle class Negro children in the ability to label pictorial materials. When content is important on a Piaget-type task, socioeconomic and cultural differences will probably be greater than when content is not important. This effect will be attributable at least in part to the great variations in linguistic training between, say, lower class Negro children and middle class white children (Bernstein, 1961).

Learning Interpretations. Piaget (1967) holds that the attainment of concrete operations and the attendant conservation, classification, and seriation concepts have an "optimal" time of development. Furthermore, although he believes that acceleration is possible, he also feels that the price paid for such acceleration may be too high. Acceleration is one goal of trying to train children to succeed on Piaget-type tasks, but it is not the only one nor the most important one. Many investigators who have carried out training studies have been concerned about whether or not such concepts as conservation can be taught in the traditional manner. If they can, then there would be no need to appeal to logical operations or "optimal periods of development."

In considering this kind of training or teaching study, however, the difference between what Flavell and Wohlwill (1969) called "performance" and "competence" must be made clear. Performance is the child's behavior in particular situations, and can be affected by a host of different factors. For example, a child who is unsure of his response on the conservation problem may look to the examiner for clues. If he finds such clues his performance may be successful, but it would not be a true index of his competence in conservation (it would be more an index of his competence in reading the examiner's clues). Obviously, it is easier to change a child's performance than his competence, and controls such as delayed posttests and tests for the generalizability and transfer of the training effects are required to determine whether training has genuinely altered the child's competence.

Unfortunately, not many of the training studies have taken this distinction seriously into account. Even so, many of the early attempts to train children on Piaget-type tasks were largely unsuccessful. In a study by Wohlwill and Lowe (1962) on number conservation, four groups of children were trained. One group was given trials in which they counted equal sets of elements in different spatial arrays. Another group had additional practice that illustrated that adding or taking away elements did indeed change the numerical quantity. A third group was trained to see that a set of elements spaced farther apart or closer together did not change in number. The fourth group was a nontraining control. Results showed that although all children made progress on a nonverbal measure of conservation of number, there was virtually no improvement on a verbal test of number conservation.

Perhaps the most extensive series of early training studies was carried out by Smedslund (1961a, 1961b, 1961c) on weight conservation. One of these experiments is of particular interest because it clearly exemplifies the competence-performance distinction mentioned above. Smedslund tested a group of children who demonstrated weight conservation on a pretest, and a group of children who did not manifest weight conservation on the pretest but who did do so after two training sessions. After this initial training and testing phase, the two groups participated in a modification of the training procedure, with two clay balls one of which was made into a sausage. In this procedure, children were allowed to verify the equal weights on a scale. Smedslund, however, surreptitiously removed a piece of the clay as he rolled it into a sausage. The children who had demonstrated conservation on the pretest tended to continue to maintain that the weights were equal, even when the scales did not confirm this, but most of the children who had acquired conservation in the training sessions reverted to perceptual explanations of the nonequivalence of the ball and sausage.

Although the results of these early studies were largely negative, more recent investigators have reported more positive results (Brison, 1965; Gelman, 1969; Kingsley and Hall, 1967; Sigel, Roeper, and Hooper, 1966b; I. D. Smith, 1968; Zimiles, 1966). However, not all of these investigators controlled for how advanced the children were before training. The work of Brison and Zimiles is of particular interest because motivation was manipulated. In the Brison study, the child's task was to get the most juice for

himself after the juice was poured into containers of different sizes. This experience seemed to facilitate conservation. Motivation or *need* to conserve may turn out to be one of the most important variables in conservation performance.

In classification problems, which have been the concern of recent investigations, the effects of training are much more clear-cut. In a carefully controlled study of children's ability to deal with class inclusions ($A + A' = BB - A' = A$, where A might be boys, A' girls, and B children), Kohnstamm concluded:

> *Briefly, the subjects to whom the standard inclusion problem had to be taught were as a group inferior in three ways to the groups who either discovered the solution immediately or after a series of related problems in durability, resistance to counter suggestion and composition of a good inclusion item. However, there were many taught subjects who performed as well as the non-taught subjects in the first two of these criteria and some who did as well in all three. (Kohnstamm, 1967, p. 144.)*

Recently, Inhelder (1968) has reported that she and other co-workers of Piaget have also been concerned with instruction and have carried out extended training experiments. They have tried to devise procedures that would engage the child's interest and that would bring about spontaneous discrimination and coordination of relations. Although they have had some success, the amount of improvement is always relative to the child's level of development at the time training was undertaken. Older children move more quickly and with less training than do younger children.

In general, the training studies emphasize that success on Piagetian tasks is a complex matter and that the success of training will vary with at least (a) the child's level of development at the start of training, (b) the training method employed, (c) the particular tasks used, (d) the amount of training, and (e) the criteria used to evaluate success (e.g., delayed posttests and tests of generalization, transfer, and resistance to extinction). It is therefore not yet possible to make any general statements about the teachability of the concepts assessed by the Piagetian tests.

Relation of Performance on Piagetian Tasks to Other Variables

Intelligence. Piaget's tests are avowedly concerned with intelligence, but with a kind of intelligence different from that assessed with standard intelligence tests (IQ tests). Many IQ tests, such as the Stanford-Binet and the Wechsler scales, contain tests of many different abilities, including perception, language skills, and sensorimotor coordination. For Piaget, however, intelligence refers exclusively to rational processes such as reasoning, problem solving, and concept formation. Not surprisingly, therefore, the correlations between performance on Piaget-type tests and performance on IQ tests are not exceptionally high.

Several investigators have reported correlations between Piaget-type tasks and IQ measures. Using a concept test, based in part upon Piaget-type tests, Beard (1960) obtained a correlation of .38 between performance and Stanford-Binet MA (mental age). Elkind (1961d) quantified several of Piaget's conservation tests (number, continuous and discontinuous quantity) and obtained a correlation of .43 with full-scale IQ on the Wechsler Intelligence Scale for Children. Correlations with various subtest IQs seemed to vary with the cognitive content of the subtest. Similarly, Dodwell (1961) used a Piagetian test of logical classification, and obtained a correlation of .34 with IQ. With a somewhat different approach, Hood (1962) observed that children with MA of less than five years almost never showed conservation, but children with MA of eight or nine years were almost always conservers. Goldschmid (1967) reported similar results.

In short, the Piagetian tests and IQ tests overlap to a certain extent but do not tap the same range of mental abilities. By and large, the Piagetian tests are more narrow and are limited to the assessment of cognitive processes, and IQ tests measure much else besides. In practical terms, what this probably means is that the Piagetian tests would predict general IQ well at the extremes—the very bright or very dull—but would be much less diagnostic of general intelligence in the middle range of mental ability.

Personality. The relation between performance on Piagetian tests and personality variables has only recently begun to attract the attention of researchers. For example, Inhelder (1968) reported results on Piagetian tests with psychotic children, and American work of this kind was recently reported by Goldschmid (1967, 1968). In one investigation (Goldschmid, 1967), a battery of Piagetian tests was given to normal children and to emotionally disturbed children; the emotionally disturbed children, who were on the average two years older than the normal children, were at about the same level of conservation behavior. This result was not clear-cut, however, because the emotionally disturbed children also had lower IQs, which could have been the critical variable.

In another study, Goldschmid (1968) gave a large battery of Piagetian tests and personality measures to children of middle class background. Goldschmid reported: "children with a high level of conservation tend to be (1) more objective in their self-evaluation, (2) described more favorably by their teachers, (3) preferred by their peers, (4) less dominated by their mothers, and (5) seen as more attractive and passive, than children with a low level of conservation" (Goldschmid, 1968, p. 579). In interpreting these results, the problem of IQ is again a factor because the same kinds of differences are found between high IQ and low IQ children. The results are suggestive, however, and much more work of this kind is to be expected in the future.

References

Almy, M., Chittenden, E., and Miller, P. *Young children's thinking.* New York: Teachers College, Columbia University, Bureau of Publications, 1966.

Bernstein, B. Social structure, language and learning. *Educational Research,* 1961, 3, 163-176.

Brison, D. W. Acquisition of conservation of substance in a group situation. Unpublished doctoral dissertation, University of Illinois, 1965.

Bruner, J. S. On the conservation of liquids. In J. S. Bruner, R. R. Olver, P. M. Greenfield *et al., Studies in cognitive growth.* New York: Wiley, 1966. Pp. 183-207.

Charlesworth, W. R. The development of the object concept: A methodological concept. Paper presented at the meeting of the American Psychological Association, New York, September 1966.

Dodwell, P. C. Children's understanding of number and related concepts. *Canadian Journal of Psychology,* 1960, 14, 191-205.

Dodwell, P. C. Children's understanding of number and related concepts: Characteristics of an individual and of a group test. *Canadian Journal of Psychology,* 1961, 15, 29-36.

Elkind, D. The additive composition of classes in the child. *Journal of Genetic Psychology.* 1961a, 99, 51-57.

Elkind, D. The development of quantitative thinking. *Journal of Genetic Psychology,* 1961b, 98, 37-46.

Elkind, D., Barocas, R., and Rosenthal, R. Concept production in adolescents from graded and ungraded classrooms. *Perceptual and Motor Skills* 1968, **27**, 1015-1018.

Flavell, J.H., and Wohlwill, J. F. Formal and functional aspects of cognitive development. In D. Elkind and J. H. Flavell (Eds.), *Studies in cognitive development: Essays in honor of Jean Piaget.* New York: Oxford University Press, 1969, Pp. 67-120.

Furth, H. G. *Thinking without language: Psychological implications of deafness.* New York: Free Press, 1966.

Gelman, R. Conservation acquisition: A problem of learning to attend to relevant attributes. *Journal of Experimental Child Psychology*, 1969, **7**, 167-187.

Glick, J., and Wapner, S. Development of transitivity: Some findings and problems of analysis. *Child Development*, 1968, **39**, 621-638.

Goldschmid, M. L. Different types of conservation and nonconservation and their relation to age, sex, IQ, MA and vocabulary. *Child Development*, 1967, **38**, 1229-1246.

Goldschmid, M. L. The relation of conservation to emotional and environmental aspects of development. *Child Development*, 1968, **39**, 579-589.

Goodnow, J. Problems in research on culture and thought. In D. Elkind and J. H. Flavell (Eds.), *Studies in cognitive development: Essays in honor of Jean Piaget.* New York: Oxford University Press, 1969. Pp. 440-462.

Goodnow, J., and Bethon, G. Piaget's tasks: The effects of schooling and intelligence. *Child Development*, 1966, **37**, 573-582.

Greenfield, P. M., Reich, L. C., and Olver, R. R. On culture and equivalence: II. In J. S. Bruner, R. R. Olver, P. M. Greenfield *et al.*, *Studies in cognitive growth.* New York: Wiley, 1966. Pp. 270-318.

Hood, B. H. An experimental study of Piaget's theory of the development of number in children. *British Journal of Psychology*, 1962, **53**, 273-286.

Inhelder B. Recent trends in Genevan research. Paper presented at Temple University, Fall 1968.

Inhelder, B., and Piaget, J. *The growth of logical thinking from childhood to adolescence.* New York: Basic Books, 1958.

Kingsley, R. C., and Hall, V. C. Training conservation through the use of learning sets. *Child Development*, 1967, **38**, 1111-1126.

Kohnstamm, G. A. *Teaching children to solve a Piagetian problem of class inclusion.* The Hague: Mouton, 1967.

Laurendeau, M., and Pinard, A. *La pensée causale.* Paris: Presses Universitaires de France, 1962.

Lovell, K. *The growth of basic mathematical and scientific concepts in children.* London: University of London Press, 1961.

Mehler, J., and Bever, T. J. Cognitive capacity of very young children. *Science*, 1967, **158**, 141-142.

Mermelstein, E., and Shulman, L. S. Lack of formal schooling and the acquisition of conservation. *Child Development*, 1967, **38**, 39-52.

Peluffo, N. Les notions de conservation et de causalité chez les infants prevenant de differents milieux physiques et socio-culturels. *Archives de Psychologie*, 1962, **38**, 75-90.

Piaget, J. *The psychology of intelligence.* London: Routledge & Kegan Paul, 1950.

Piaget, J. *The construction of reality in the child.* New York: Basic Books, 1964.

Piaget, J. Notes on learning. Lecture delivered at New York University, Winter 1967.

Schaffer, H. R. Objective observations of personality development in early infancy. *British Journal of Medical Psychology*, 1958, **31**, 174-183.

Sigel, I. E., Anderson, L. M., and Shapiro, H. Categorization behavior in lower and middle class Negro preschool children: Differences in dealing with representation of common objects. *Journal of Negro Education.* 1966a, Summer, 218-229.

Sigel, I.E., and McBane, B. Cognitive competence and level of symbolization among five year old children. In J. Hellmuth (Ed.), *The disadvantaged child.* Seattle Special Child Publications, 1967, Pp. 433-453.

Sigel, I.E., Roeper, A., and Hooper, F. H. A training procedure for acquisition of Piaget's conservation of quantity: A pilot study and its replication. *British Journal of Educational Psychology*, 1966b, **36**(3), 301-311.

Sinclair-DeZwart, H. *Acquisition du language et developpement de la pensée.* Paris: Dunod, 1967.

Smedslund, J. The acquisition of conservation of substance and weight in children. II. External reinforcement of conservation of weight and of the operations of addition and subtraction. *Scandinavian Journal of Psychology*, 1961a, **2**, 71-84.

Smedslund, J. The acquisition of conservation of substance and weight in children. III. Extinction of conservation of weight acquired "normally" and by means of empirical controls on a balance scale. *Scandinavian Journal of Psychology*, 1961b, **2**, 85-87.

Smedslund, J. The acquisition of the conservation of substance and weight in children. IV. An attempt at extinction of the visual components of the weight concept. *Scandinavian Journal of Psychology*, 1961c, **2**, 153-155.

Smith, I. D. The effects of training procedures upon the acquisition of conservation of weight. *Child Development*, 1968, **39**, 515-526.

Vernon, P. E. Environmental handicaps and intellectual development. Part I and Part II. *British Journal of Educational Psychology*, 1965, **35**, 9-20, 117-126.

Wallach, L., Wall, J., and Anderson, L. Number conservation: The roles of reversibility, addition, subtraction, and misleading perceptual clues. *Child Development*, 1967, **38**, 425-442.

White, B.L. The initial coordination of sensorimotor schemas in human infants: Piaget's ideas and the role of experience. In D. Elkind and J. H. Flavell (Eds.), *Studies in cognitive development: Essays in honor of Jean Piaget.* London and New York: Oxford University Press, 1969. Pp. 237-256.

Wohlwill, J. F. Responses to class inclusion questions for verbally and pictorially presented items. *Child Development*, 1968, **39**, 449-466.

Wohlwill, J. F., and Lowe, R. C. Experimental analysis of the conservation of number. *Child Development*, 1962, **33**, 153-167.

Zimiles, H. The development of conservation and differentiation of number. *Monographs of the Society for Research in Child Development*, 1966, **31**, No. 6.

11
MIDDLE CHILDHOOD:
PERSONALITY AND SOCIAL DEVELOPMENT

The developmental pace during middle childhood is relatively slow and steady, but the elementary school years are far from insignificant for personality and social development. As a youngster graduates from the dependency of his early childhood and enters school, his world expands in many directions. Perhaps most importantly, his peers and adults other than his parents now begin to play an increasingly important part in his interpersonal relationships.

In the first article selected for his chapter, Long, Henderson, and Ziller discuss the developmental changes of middle childhood in the context of changes in a child's conception of himself. They define five aspects of how people perceive themselves in relation to others—individuation, esteem, power, identification, and social dependency—and they report the results of a study in which they compared children in Grades 1 to 6 on each of these personality characteristics.

Campbell in the second selection reviews research concerned with the peer culture of middle childhood. The material abstracted from his article proves a good picture of the ways in which a child's activities in the company of other children contribute to his personality and social development. Also included is a summary of those variations in the peer-group situation that often lead to individual differences in how children are influenced by it.

BARBARA H. LONG, EDMUND H. HENDERSON, and ROBERT C. ZILLER

Developmental Changes in the Self-Concept During Middle Childhood*

The years of middle childhood are some-times considered a relatively dormant period during which the structures of personality established in early childhood remain more or less stable. Such a view-point tends to overlook important changes which normally occur between the ages of 6 and 12. Intellectually, the child becomes literate, and according to Piaget's formulations, acquires the opera-tional systems of a mature intelligence on a concrete level (Piaget, 1950; Flavell, 1963). Physical and motor development are also occurring. As the child increases in size and motor coordination, he nor-mally acquires athletic and manipulative skills. Socially, the child's world is ex-panding. His increased intellectual abili-ties permit a greater independence and mobility, and a reciprocal relationship with peers, in which the child is able to share goals, accept complementary re-sponsibilies, and appreciate the view-points of others (Piaget, 1926; Hunt, 1961). Relationships with peers become salient (Ojemann, 1953), and interests in peer organizations high (Jersild and Tauch, 1949).

The acquisition of these new intellect-ual, physical and social skills suggest that there will be a corresponding change in the personality of the child during this period of development. Specifically, it is proposed that developmental changes in the child's conception of himself occur during these years. Since the self-concept is assumed to be an important agent for the organization of perceptions, the as-similation of experiences, and the deter-mination of behavior (Jersild, 1960), such developmental changes in the self-concept are of both theoretical and practical concern.

Previous Research

Developmental studies of the self-concept have been extremely limited. A search of the literature failed to reveal such a study focused upon the years from 6 to 12. Although numerous studies related to the self-concept have been carried out with subjects at various points, within this age range (e.g., Davids and Lawton, 1961; Kagan, Hasken, and Watson, 1961; Horo-witz, 1962), Wylie's (1961) observation that variations in instruments, conditions, and subjects among these studies prevent the construction of even a tentative de-velopmental scheme appears true today.

Many investigations of the self-concept of children have employed verbal tech-niques. When verbal responses are stud-ied, the limited vocabularies of children restrict the range of responses, and thus

*From the *Merrill-Palmer Quarterly*, 1967, 13, 201-215. Reprinted by permission of the authors and the Merrill-Palmer Institute.

the extent of assessment. In addition, verbal ability as such, since it varies widely among individuals and increases with age, may interfere with valid measurement. Verbal instruments, such as rating scales and Q-sorts, are also highly visible to the child. Socially desirable, rather than objectively valid, responses may thus be elicitied. (Schaie, 1963; Jersild, 1960). For example, Perkins' findings (1958) (derived from Q-sorts for self and ideal-self) of greater self-ideal congruency both over a two-month period of time and between the fourth and sixth grades, may perhaps be attributable to a greater ability of the older subjects and the second-trial subjects to remember the initial Q-sort. Finally, as Kelly (1955) has suggested, a person (and we may add, especially a child) "is not necessarily articulate about the constructions he places upon his world." Self and social constructs may not be symbolized by words.

Self-Social Schemata

A self-social theory of personality assumes that a self-identity is derived from interpersonal orientations and experiences (Adler, 1927; Mead, 1934; Sullivan, 1953; Kelly, 1955). Similarities and contrasts with other people in the immediate social environment are considered necessary for a clear conception of the self. The self is assumed, as Piaget suggests (see Flavell, 1963), to be an "object among objects" and to be defined chiefly in relation to others.

Since the individual's orientations to the environment are largely social, self-other conceptions may be important mediating agents for perceptions and cogni-

tions. It is suggested that social stimuli are interpreted and given personal meaning on the basis of a set of topological schemata, possibly sub-verbal, consisting of self-other configurations. The self-concept is thus seen as a multidimensional set or constellation of constructs involving other persons.

Five such self-social constructs are considered in this paper: individuation, esteem, power, identification, and social dependency. These components of the self-social system do not constitute an exhaustive list, but rather exemplify various aspects of the self-social schemata which seem of particular interest in relation to development during middle childhood. Theoretical and operational definitions of these components are presented below.

METHOD

The present study applied a nonverbal method to the study of the self-concept in middle childhood. In this method, the subject selected and arranged symbols to represent himself in relation to salient other people. It was assumed that individuals can communicate various aspects of their self-social schemata symbolically, and that certain symbolic patterns have common meanings. The assumption was made, for example, that physical distance in the test represented psychological distance within the child's life space. Hierarchies of power or dimensions of importance or value were also assumed to be reflected in specific symbolic patterns, as were degree of self-differentiation and social dependency. The arrangement of concrete stimuli by the subject were thus thought to mirror his cognitive schemata. The validity of these assumptions was supported by a variety of findings (summarized below) related to the construct validity of various tasks employed.

The Children's Self-Social Constructs Test (CSSCT) was developed for this study from nonverbal tasks used in two earlier studies (Ziller, Megas, and De-Cencio, 1963; Henderson, Long and Ziller, 1965) and from the self-Social Symbols Tasks (Ziller, Alexander, and Long, 1964), a minimally verbal test of self and social constructs. In adapting these tasks for elementary school children, the following criteria were met: (1) all instructions were oral; (2) all responses were nonverbal. The test was administered to the subjects in groups and took approximately one-half hour to complete.

Test-retest (over one week) reliability coefficients from 61 fourth-, fifth-, and sixth-graders (not the present sample)[1] ranged from +.26 to +.87, with a median of +.49. A brief description of each item, evidence related to validity, and hypotheses relating each to development in middle childhood, follow.

Individuation

Individuation was defined as the degree to which a person differentiates himself from his peers. The extremes of this dimension were considered to be "like"

and "different from" others. Our measure of individuation included a large circular area containing a randomly placed array of small circles, representing "other children." The subject was asked to select one of two circles at the bottom of the page to represent himself. The choice of a circle "different" from those representing peers (i.e., shaded) was interpreted as a higher degree of individuation.

Evidence supportive of validity was found in an unpublished study in which 27 pairs of twins chose significantly fewer (p <.05) of the "different" circles to represent the self than did a control group of non-twins matched for sex, age, and class in school. Children who had moved frequently were also found to represent the self significantly (p < .05) more often as "different" than those who had lived in a single community all their lives (Ziller and Long, 1964).

Hypothesis 1. Although the individuation of the self is considered to be a subjective perception, social experiences, such as those in which the person is clearly "different" from others in a group (as a boy among girls), are thought to influence it. Such self-differentiating experiences would presumably increase with age, as the self is confronted with a succession of groups of others. A positive relationship between age and individuation is thus hypothesized for the years of middle childhood.

Self-Esteem

Self-esteem was defined as the value or importance attributed to the self in comparison with others. This dimension was conceived of as a rank-ordering of persons, in which the self may assume a posi-

[1] The authors are indebted to Dr. Howard E. Lamb, University of Delaware, for these data. Later work with an expanded version of the test, in which items are repeated from two to ten times, revealed split-half reliability coefficients ranging from .65 to .94 with a median of .85 for a group of 81 fifth graders.

tion ranging from first to last. Our measure of self-esteem consisted of a row of eight circles representing children. The subject was asked to select one of the circles to represent himself. Positions to the left were assumed to represent a higher degree of self-esteem. This assumption was supported by a finding of Morgan (1944) that the stimulus to the left in a row of stimuli was ranked as more important that those appearing further to the right.

Evidence supporting the validity of this task was found in an earlier study of ours (Henderson, Long, and Ziller, 1965) in which children arranged various arrays of people into rows. To a significant degree ($p < .001$) the "smartest" child was placed to the left, and the "dumbest" and "bad" child to the right. In a second array, mother and father were placed to the left and teacher and neighbor to the right ($p < .001$). In a third group "home" and "school" were placed to the left, "pencil" and "game" to the right ($p < .001$). Further evidence of validity was provided by a sample of 48 children who placed the self significantly ($p < .02$) further left among a group of children than they did among a group of adults. The findings that neuropsychiatric patients placed the self significantly further to the right than did normals ($p < .001$) (Ziller, et al., 1964b), and that sociometric isolates placed the self significantly ($p < .005$) further to the right than did sociometric stars (Ziller, et. al., 1964a) also supported the validity of this task.

Hypothesis 2. Because physical size and intellectual, motor and social skills increase with age in middle childhood, it is proposed that the child's conception of his own importance will increase as he grows older. A positive relationship between self-esteem and age is thus hypothesized.

Power

Power of the self in relation to certain authority figures was assumed to be a perception of the self as superior, equal, or inferior to the other person. In the measures of power, a higher position on the vertical plane was assumed to represent greater power. This assumption was supported by the findings of Osgood, et. al. (1957) that ratings on a "high-low" dimension had a high loading on a "power" factor. It was also consistent with a cultural metaphor associating power with a "high" position. In this task, the subjects were given a circle representing the self, which was surrounded by a semicircle of other circles. The subjects were asked to select a circle to represent another person (father or teacher, in the present study), (1) directly above, (2) diagonally above, (3) even with, (4) diagonally below, or (5) directly below the circle representing the self. The responses were scored from one to five, with a higher score indicating a lower position for the other person. Evidence supporting the validity of this task was found in an earlier study in which three samples of eighth-graders (N's = 83, 60, 76, respectively) placed teacher in a significantly higher position ($p < .01$ in all cases) than friend (Ziller and Long, 1964).

Hypothesis 3. In general, a child can be expected to perceive himself as less powerful than his parents or teachers. As he grows older, however, the perceived power of the self should tend to increase. In middle childhood, then, a progressive egalitarianism in relation to father and teacher is hypothesized. It is proposed that, relative to teacher and father, the self increases in power with time.

Identification

Identification of the self with particular other persons was defined as the placement of the self in a "we" category with the other person (cf. Parsons, 1955). Heider (1958) has suggested that when a person indicates that two objects "belong together," it may be assumed that a concept relates them. Thus, placing the self in close proximity to the other person was assumed to indicate a high degree of identification with him.

Two kinds of tasks measuring identification were included in this study. In the first, the subject was presented with two gummed circles (a red one for the self, and a green one for a friend). He was asked to paste them on a blank sheet of paper in any way he likes. The distance between the circles was measured in centimeters, with less distance assumed to represent more identification.

In a second task, the subject was presented with a row of circles with another person (mother, father, teacher) located on the circle to the extreme left. He was then asked to select one of the remaining circles to represent the self. In this task, distance was measured by counting the number of circles intervening between the self and other, with less distance again assumed to indicate more identification.

Evidence supporting the validity of this latter task has been found in a recently completed study (Long and Henderson, in press). Children living in fatherless homes were found to be signifi-cantly less identified with father ($p <$ .02) than children of the same age and socio-economic class whose fathers were present in the home. A second finding was that children rated by their teachers as being "shy with teacher" were significantly less identified with teacher ($p <$ .05) than those rated as "friendly with teacher."

Hypotheses 4, 5, 6, 7. As the child proceeds through elementary school, and an increasing proportion of his time is spent in peer activities, one can assume that he will come to identify more with his friends and less with his parents and teachers. Greater identification with friends, and less with mother, father and teacher, is thus hypothesized as a correlate of increased age in middle childhood.

Social Dependency

Social dependency was assumed to be the degree to which the person perceives himself as a part of a group of others, as opposed to a perception of the self as a separate entity. It was thought that tendencies toward the group may reflect either succorant or affiliative motives. In the measure of social dependency, the subject was presented with a paper containing three circles (representing parents, teachers, and friends) arranged as the apexes of an equilateral triangle. He was then given a gummed circle representing self and asked to paste it anywhere on the paper — only not on top of any of the other circles. Location of the self within, rather than outside of the triangular area was assumed to reflect a perception of the self as dependent upon, or as part of, the group of others.

Hypothesis 8. It is believed that experiences of independent activity will lead to a perception of the self as independent of others. It is expected that such experiences will increase with age, as will the child's ability to satisfy his own needs. A negative relationship between social dependency and age is thus hypothesized.

Sex-Difference Items

No hypotheses regarding sex differences in individuation, self-esteem, and power were made in the present study. However, provision was made for measures on items of identification and social dependency where sex differences logically could be assumed to have a bearing. Three sex-difference hypotheses, briefly stated here, were thus proposed and tested.

Hypotheses 9, 10, 11. It is expected that girls will identify more with mother and less with father, and more with a female teacher, than boys. It is further hypothesized that boys will perceive the self as more independent than will girls.

Subjects and Design

The Children's Self-Social Constructs Test was administered to all students (373) in an elementary school in a semi-rural community in Maryland. The subjects were white; chiefly from middle-class homes; and slightly above average in I.Q. (mean Otis I.Q. for grades 1-6 = 112) and achievement (mean percentile for composite score from the Iowa Tests of Basic Skills for grades 3-6 = 68). They ranged in age from 6 to 13 years.

In order to reduce the sample to 26 boys and 26 girls (the maximum number possible) in each of the six grades,

random procedures were used to eliminate subjects.[2] A 2 x 6 (sex-by-grade) analysis of variance was performed upon the measures of power, esteem, and identification. Since the individuation and dependency measures consisted of dichotomous scores, chi squares were used to test for the effects of grade and sex on these variables. Intercorrelations between all measures were also obtained using a random sample of seven boys and seven girls from each grade.

RESULTS

Results in relation to sex and grade are summarized below. Means (for individuation and dependency, per cents) are shown in Table 1; analyses of variance in Table 2.

Individuation

As hypothesized, the representation of the self as "different" increased with grade in school (X^2 = 31.85; df = 5; $p <$ .001). In addition, a higher proportion of boys represented the self as "different" (X^2 = 15.45; df = 1; $p <$ .001).

Self-Esteem

A significant effect for grade was found in relation to self-esteem. The highest score was found in the first grade. There was a sharp drop in the second grade,

[2] For identification with friend, subjects' errors reduced the sample to 25 boys and 25 girls in each grade.

Table 1 Self-Concept Scores for Grades 1-6

Measure	Mean (or Per Cent) Score for Each Grade						
	1	2	3	4	5	6	Total
Individuation (per cent)							
Boys	21	32	47	36	65	82	47
Girls	24	19	30	37	18	45	28
Self-esteem							
Boys	4.7	2.9	3.0	4.3	3.6	3.8	3.7
Girls	4.6	3.4	4.3	4.2	3.5	4.2	4.0
Power—Father							
Boys	2.9	2.4	2.8	2.3	2.8	2.4	2.6
Girls	2.7	2.8	2.6	2.1	2.6	2.5	2.5
Power—Teacher							
Boys	2.2	2.3	2.5	3.4	2.2	2.4	2.5
Girls	2.4	2.5	2.4	3.1	2.8	3.0	2.7
Identification—Mother[a]							
Boys	8.3	7.3	7.5	9.2	7.9	9.2	8.4
Girls	9.1	8.1	9.0	9.5	9.7	9.6	9.2
Identification—Father[a]							
Boys	8.2	8.2	9.0	8.9	8.2	9.2	8.6
Girls	9.4	7.7	8.3	8.9	9.5	9.1	8.8
Identification—Teacher[a]							
Boys	6.8	6.5	5.9	5.6	4.0	4.4	5.5
Girls	7.3	8.3	7.5	8.1	7.1	6.6	7.5
Identification—Friend[a]							
Boys	4.3	1.9	2.4	6.4	5.0	7.0	4.5
Girls	2.1	.3	3.6	4.2	8.5	9.4	4.7
Dependency (per cent)							
Boys	36	59	47	55	45	71	51
Girls	47	53	53	67	64	72	59

[a]In the measures of identification, distance (in circles or centimeters) scores were subtracted from 10, in order that higher scores should represent greater identification.

which displayed the lowest score. Scores rose in the third and fourth grades, and declined somewhat in the fifth and sixth.

Power

No significant effects were found for

Table 2 Self-Concept in Relation to Grade and Sex: Analysis of Variance

Measure	SS	df	MS	F	p<
Self-esteem					
Grade	70	5	14.0	3.16	.01
Sex	6	1	6.0		
Interaction	18	5	3.6		
Error	1330	300	4.4		
Power–Teacher					
Grade	29	5	5.8	2.52	.05
Sex	4	1	4.0		
Interaction	9	5	1.8		
Error	699	300	2.3		
Identification–Mother					
Grade	98	5	19.6	5.24	.001
Sex	47	1	47.0	12.60	.001
Interaction	19	5	3.8		
Error	1123	300	3.8		
Identification–Father					
Grade	46	5	9.2	2.14	.06
Sex	3	1	3.0		
Interaction	46	5	9.2	2.14	.06
Error	1304	300	4.3		
Identification–Teacher					
Grade	124.6	5	24.9	4.64	.005
Sex	31.3	1	31.3	5.83	.05
Interaction	310.8	5	62.2	11.58	.001
Error	1609.4	300	5.4		
Identification–Friend					
Grade	1769.4	5	353.9	9.18	.001
Sex	2.9	1	2.9		
Interaction	393.5	5	78.7		
Error	11,099.3	288	38.5		

power in relation to father. Power of self in relation to teacher was found to relate to grade. The scores were relatively low in the first three grades, rose sharply in the fourth, and declined in the fifth and sixth to a level slightly above that found in the first three grades.

Identification

Significant effects for identification with mother were found for both sex and grade. Girls identified more with mother than boys. The changes over the grades were as follows: first-graders showed high identification; there was a sharp decrease in the second grade, which displayed least identification; after that, the general trend was for identification to increase and reach its peak after the third grade. The one exception was obtained with boys, who showed a second low point in identification with mother in the fifth grade.

For identification with father, an effect for grade and a sex-by-grade interaction, both of which approached significance, were obtained. First-graders were most closely identified with father, second-graders the least (although this difference is attributable to differences between the first- and second-grade girls). Scores increased after the second grade, with the highest mean scores found for the boys in the sixth grade and for the girls in the fifth.

In relation to identification with teacher, significant effects were found for grade, for sex, and for a sex-by-grade interaction. Girls were more closely identified with teacher than boys. (It should be noted that all teachers but one in this school were women). In the first three grades, a relatively high degree of identification with teacher was found. Thereafter, scores decreased gradually, with the lowest mean scores found in the sixth grade for the girls, the fifth grade for the boys.

There was little difference between the sexes on this measure in the first grade. Henceforth, the difference between the sexes increased until the sixth grade, where it declined again, possibly because the only male teacher in the sample taught a sixth-grade class.

A significant effect for grade was found in relation to identification with friend. Identification decreased between first and second grades, but increased thereafter. The greatest identification with friend was found in the sixth grade.

Social Dependency

A significant effect for grade ($X^2 = 13.50$; $df = 5$; $p < .02$) was found for social dependency. Contrary to the hypothesis, the trend from the first to sixth grade was for greater dependency the higher the grade in school.

Interrelationships

The various components of the self-concept measured by the Children's Self-Social Construct's Test, as in previous studies using this method, proved to be relatively independent of one another. Self-esteem was found to be positively associated with identification with mother ($r = +.22$, $p < .05$) and with teacher ($r = +.23$, $p < .05$). Social dependency was positively associated with power for the self in relation to teacher ($r = +.27, p < .05$) and negatively with esteem ($r = -.37$, $p < .01$). These last two relationships may have been influenced by grade effects, however, since the lowest grades had lower scores in both social dependency and power relative to teacher, and higher scores for esteem.

As in the previous studies, several significant relationships were found between the measures of identification. These were father vs. friend: $r = +.28, p < .01$; father vs. teacher: $r = +.24, p < .05$; father vs. mother: $r = +.61, p < .01$; and mother vs. teacher: $r = +.43, p < .01$. The response of placing the self close to others thus appears to have some generality. A significant positive relationship was also found between power of self in relation to father and in relation to teacher ($r = +.23, p < .05$).

DISCUSSION

Of the eight hypotheses related to developmental changes, four were confirmed. Greater individuation, power in relation to teacher,[3] and identification with friend, and less identification with teacher, were associated with advancing grade level. Also confirmed were the hypotheses related to sex differences in identification with mother and teacher. On both of these measures girls attained higher scores. All of these findings seem in harmony with the present interpretation of development in middle childhood.

Certain findings, which were not predicted, however, seem to require further interpretation. The significant effect of grade on self-esteem, for example, was largely due to the difference between the first and second grade. The first grade received the highest mean score and the second grade the lowest. These findings are in harmony with Gesell and Ilg's (1946) description of the brashness of the six-year-old, and the self-criticism of the seven-year-old, and seem relevant to Piaget's observations about the decline of egocentricity at about this time (see Hunt, 1961).

Among the girls, the second graders

[3] This effect, however, is largely attributable to differences among the girls, perhaps a further indicant of sex differences in relationships with teacher.

were also distinguished by the lowest mean scores for identification with parents and friend, and the highest mean scores for identification with teacher. Second-grade boys replicated this pattern for identification with mother and friend. This apparent movement away from parents and, in the case of the girls, toward teacher may represent a significant step toward social maturity. It is possible that the low esteem of the second-graders is related to this withdrawal from parents, since a certain amount of derived status (see Ausubel, 1958) and emotional support may be lost at this time.

After the second grade, contrary to the hypothesis, identification with parents increased. It is possible that this trend was due to a feeling among older children that they "should" put themselves closer to parents (the identification items are perhaps the most visible of the tasks). Another possible explanation is that with increasing maturity the category "family" is more clearly differentiated from that of "non-family."

Contrary to the original hypothesis, social dependency increased over grade level. Because this finding appeared so contradictory to prevalent ideas about social development in these years, it was decided to retest the sample with a second measure of social orientation. This measure, which was administered to all members of the original sample, consisted of a choice between an "alone" and a "group" participation in a number of activities. It was reasoned that social dependency would be shown by a preference for the group condition.

The questions were posed orally, and a box with a single X in it checked if the child liked to pursue the activity alone; a box with a number of X's designated a liking for the group experience. The activities included (1) a space trip, (2) a hike in the woods, (3) fishing, (4) a history project (for the upper three grades) or an Easter painting (the lower three grades). Test-retest reliability (over one week) was .67 for this measure.

An analysis of these data revealed significant effects for both sex ($p < .001$) and grade ($p < .001$). Girls chose to pursue more group activities than boys (thus confirming the original hypothesis related to greater independence for boys). Changes over the grades were as follows: Number of group activities was relatively high in first grade but declined in the second, where the lowest mean scores were found. Thereafter scores increased, with most group activities found in the fifth and sixth grades. Subjects who had placed the self outside the group in the original non-verbal measure were found to choose significantly fewer group activities than did those placing the self within the group ($p < .01$). The second measure of social dependency thus confirmed the original finding of a greater social orientation in the upper grades and provided evidence supporting the validity of the original task.

One explanation for these findings is that the measures reflect affiliative tendencies, so that the increase over the years represents an increased degree of socialization in the older child. This is consistent with Kuhn's findings (1960) of greater identification with social groups with increased age, between 7 and 24 years. A second explanation may relate increasing social orientation to the increasing number of group activities provided for upper elementary school chil-

dren in present-day culture. School, which is largely a group experience, occupies most of the day; and after-school life is also frequently organized into group activities, leaving little time for independent or solitary pursuits.

Certain unexpected differences between the sexes also appeared. The greater individuation of the boys was not found in an earlier study among eighth-graders (Ziller and Long, 1964), but seems provocative. It is possible that the greater freedom and mobility of boys in our culture provide a varied social experience which promotes individuation.

Another possible explanation of this effect is related to early identifications. According to Parsons' scheme (1955), infants of both sexes initially identify with the mother. A boy, however, must differentiate himself from his mother when he makes his initial identification with other males. The boys' greater degree of individuation may thus derive from the early necessity of separating himself conceptually from his mother. This explanation is in harmony with the present theoretical position relating individualism to experiences of differentiation (see Long, Ziller, and Henderson, 1966).

A second set of boy-girl differences, partially unpredicted, was those related to the measures of identification. As hypothesized, girls were significantly more identified with mother and teacher. Girls also identified more with mothers than with fathers ($p < .05$). These findings support the theoretical position which ascribes sex-role learning to identification with same-sex adults.

In this study, however, the boys did not identify significantly more closely with father than with mother, and were less closely identified with father than girls were with mother ($p < .05$). In comparison with girls, then, boys show a less close relationship with a same-sex parent. This relative alienation from father may stem from the usual greater absence of the father from the home, or from the ubiquitous female authority figure experienced by boys in this culture.

The boys in this study, about equidistant from father and further from mother and teacher than the girls, appear to be less identified with adults than girls. This finding is consistent with Mowrer's suggestion (1950) that socialization in this culture may be more difficult for boys than girls.

In attempting to integrate these varied findings into meaningful patterns of self-other orientations, one notes first differences between the sexes. The boys' greater individuation, independence, and alienation from adults seem to reflect norms in the present culture for the male to be self-reliant and less person-oriented than the female. For both sexes, the changes from the first grade to the second seem to represent a significant discontinuity requiring further investigation. After the second grade, the child appears to be growing closer to others (with the exception of teacher), higher in self-esteem,[4] and more individuated. Taken together, these findings support the premise that the self-concept is changing during middle childhood, and also demonstrate the usefulness of the present method. Further research is indicated to study these phenomena longitudinally and in relation to specific background factors and behavioral events.

SUMMARY

A self-social theory of personality was the basis for hypothesizing changes in the self-concept during middle childhood. Nonverbal measures of individuation, esteem, power, identification, and social dependency were administered to all pupils (373) in an elementary school. Grade in school was significantly related to individuation, esteem, social dependency, power relative to teacher, and identification with friend, father, mother, and teacher. Boys and girls differed significantly in individuation and identification with mother and teacher.

[4] A subsquent study (Long, Ziller, and Henderson, in press) investigating developmental changes of the self-concept in adolescence with the present method found this trend to continue until the twelfth grade ($p = .05$).

References

Adler, A. *The practice and theory of individual psychology.* New York: Harcourt, 1927.

Ausubel, D.P. *Theory and problems of child development.* New York: Grune & Stratton, 1958.

Davids, A., & Lawton, Marcia J. Self-concept, mother concept, and food aversions in emotionally disturbed and normal children. *J. abnorm.*

soc. Psychol., 1961, **62**, 309-314.

Flavell, J.II. *The developmental psychology of Jean Piaget.* Princeton, N.J.: Van Nostrand, 1963.

Gessell, A., & Ilg, Frances L. *The child from five to ten.* New York: Harper, 1946.

Heider, F. *The psychology of interpersonal relations.* New York: Wiley, 1958.

Henderson, E.H., Long, Barbara H., & Ziller, R.C. Self-social constructs of achieving and nonachieving   readers. *Reading Teacher,* 1965, **19**, 114-117.

Horowitz, Frances D. The relationship of anxiety, self-concept, and sociometric status among 4th, 5th and 6th grade children. *J. abnorm. soc. Psychol.,* 1962, **65**, 212-214.

Hunt, J. McV. *Intelligence and experience.* New York: Ronald Press, 1961.

Jersild, A.T. *Child psychology.* (5th ed.) Englewood Cliffs, N.J.: Prentice-Hall, 1960.

Jersild, A.T., & Tasch, R. J. *Children 's Interests.* New York: Bur. Publ., Teacher's Coll., Columbia Univ., 1949.

Kagan, J., Hasken, Barbara, & Watson, Sara. Child's symbolic conceptualization of parents. *Child Develpm.,* 1962, **32**, 625-636.

Kelly, G.A. *The psychology of personal constructs.* New York: Norton, 1955.

Kuhn, M.H. Self Attitudes by age, sex, and professional training. *Sociol.Quart.,* 1960, **1**, 39-55.

Long, Barbara H., Ziller, R.C., & Henderson, E.H. A study of individualism: some demographic and psychological correlates. *Social Forces,* 1966, **45**, 96-106.

Long, Barbara H., Ziller, R.C., & Henderson, E.H. Developmental changes in the self-concept during adolescence. *School Review,* in press.

Long, Barbara H., & Henderson, E. H. Self-social concepts of disadvantaged school beginners. *J. genet. Psychol.,* in press.

Mead, G.H. *Mind, self, and society.* Chicago: University of Chicago Press, 1934.

Morgan, J.J.B. Effect of non-rational factors on inductive reasoning. *J. exp. Psychol.,* 1944, **34**, 159-168.

Mowrer, O.H. *Identification: a link between learning theory and psychotherapy.* New York: Ronald Press, 1950.

Ojemann, R.H. *The child's society: clubs, gangs, cliques.* Chicago: Sci. Res. Assoc., 1953.

Osgood, C.E. Suci, G.J., & Tannenbaum, P.H. *The measurement of meaning.* Urbana, Ill.: Univer. Illinois Press, 1957.

Parsons, T. Family, structure and the socialization of the child. In T.

Parsons & R.H. Bales (Eds.), *Family, socialization and interaction processes.* Glencoe, III.: Free Press, 1955.

Perkins, H.V. Factors influencing change in children's self-concepts. *Child Developm.,* 1958, **29,** 211-230.

Piaget, J. *The language and thought of the child.* New York: Harcourt Brace,1926.

Piaget, J. *The psychology of intelligence.* New York: Harcourt Brace, 1950.

Schaie, K.W. The color pyramid test: A nonverbal technique for personality assessment. *Psychol. Bull.,* 1963, **60,** 530-547.

Sullivan, H.S. *The interpersonal theory of psychology.* New York: Norton, 1953.

Wylie, Ruth C. *The self concept.* Lincoln, Nebr.: Univer. Nebraska Press, 1961.

Ziller, R.C., Allexander, Marea, & Long, Barbara H. Self-social constructs and social desirability. Unpublished MS., Univer. Delaware, 1964a.

Ziller, R.C., Megas, J., & DeCencio, D. Self-social constructs of normals and acute neuropsychiatric patients. *J. consul. Psychol.,* 1964b, **20,** 50-63.

Ziller, R.C., & Long, Barbara H. Self-social constructs and geographic mobility. Unpublished MS., Univer. Delaware, 1964.

JOHN D. CAMPBELL

Peer Relations in Childhood*

The child is a member of two worlds: the world of adults and that of his peers. His

*From M. L. Hoffman and L. W. Hoffman (Eds.), *Review of Child Development Research,* Vol. 1, 1964. Reprinted by permission of the author and the Russell Sage Foundation.

experiences in each of these worlds are crucial aspects of his daily living and are significant agents in molding his subsequent development. This chapter focuses on research primarily concerned with one of these worlds, that of the peer culture of childhood. Discussion will center to a considerable extent, but not exclusively, on the middle years of childhood, on the elementary school-age child's relations with other children of approximately the same age and general development. Of the complex of factors involved in the total picture of peer relations, three principal facets have been singled out for consideration: (a) the role of the broader environmental context in which peer processes occur, (b) the peer group as a socializing agent, and (c) aspects of interpersonal influence within the peer group situation.

Although the broad environmental context need not be viewed as an integral part of peer relations, it is an important determinant of the impact of children's groups and affects the nature of relationships within them. Thus general cultural and subcultural factors and family influences serve to establish the framework within which peer relations operate, to set the stage on which the drama of peer relations unfolds. While this drama may have several themes, that concerned with the peer group's role as a socializing agent has been chosen for primary consideration here, for the task of growing up in a social world is a central one for childhood's middle years. Hence we may view the peer group as a determinant of acceptance and stability in social relations, as a contributor to the child's developing self-concept, and as one of the factors operating to form the child's attitudes and values concerning the world about him. The processes at work determining the group's influence in shaping the child in such respects are several. Those highlighted in a later portion of this chapter include characteristics of the situation, variations in children's susceptibility to influence, other children as influence agents, and the impact of the adult on children's peer groups. . . .

THE PEER GROUP AS A SOCIALIZING AGENT

Although the family is rightfully viewed as a prime influence in the child's individuality, his activities in the company of other children contribute to his developing picture of the social world, help to establish his identity, and provide him an opportunity for group experience relevant not only to present functioning but to future social relationships as well. The peer group has generally been recognized as a socializing agent, but it has not yet been given the same sort of systematic research attention that has been focused on the family. Bronfenbrenner has suggested that limited consideration of the socialization function of group processes in collective settings outside the family is attributable to

. . . the traditional emphasis in Western culture, reflected in scientific work, on the centrality of the parent-child relationship in the process of upbringing. It is this circumscribed conception which probably accounts for the fact that Western personality theory and research, highly developed as they are in comparison with their Russian counterparts . . . offer little basis for ready-made hypotheses bearing on processes and effects of socialization in collective settings (1962, p. 556).

Although much still needs study, several aspects of this area yield promising research results.

The child in the group is part of a

complex network of relations with other children in the environment. Each child observes and evaluates the events around him, responds with feelings of liking or disliking, acts in the situation, and is the recipient of actions of others. Through such processes as these the role of the individual child becomes established and the particular nature of the peer group as a social product emerges. The Robbers Cave experiment, a stimulating and productive study directed by Sherif, illustrates some general aspects of this process (Sherif, Harvey, White, Hood, and Sherif, 1961). Twenty-two fifth-grade boys, homogeneous with respect to such criteria as age, family background, and intelligence, were brought together as members of two separately functioning camp groups, generally isolated from the outside world. At the end of one week, these boys, initially strangers to one another, had formed cohesive groups. Ratings by adult observers showed that a stable status structure had been established within the seven-day period; differentiation of function had taken place along hierarchical lines. Joint participation of group members in pursuit of the common goals of camp led to the formation of stable attitudes about one another and about places and objects in the camp environment. Since such attitudes were shared by members of the group, norms governing behavior in various aspects of the situation were established concomitantly with the formation of the group structure itself. When the boys discovered the presence of another group of campers, this added a heightened awareness of group membership and an emphasis on group solidarity. The "natural history" of Sherif's experimental

groups reasonably closely approximates the pattern followed in many children's group situations. Such experiences contribute to the crystallization of the child's role and status among his peers, aid in establishing his own self-concept, and serve as an important resource for the formation of the child's attitudes and values concerning his social world.

Peer Acceptance and Stability of Peer Relations

As the description of Sherif's experiment suggests, early in a child's group experience his peers form an impression of him. On the basis of such impressions, the child is assigned status and is accepted or rejected accordingly.

What are the criteria for acceptance or rejection? These can conveniently be classed broadly as pertaining either to personality and social characteristics or to skills and abilities. Ample research information exists to indicate some of these factors that enter into children's assessments of one another. Among the personality and social characteristics contributing to differential status, friendliness and sociability are, as one would certainly expect, associated with acceptance (Feinberg, Smith, and Schmidt, 1958; Tuddenham, 1951), and social indifference, withdrawal, rebelliousness, and hostility are attributes of low-status or rejected children (Northway, 1944; G. H. Smith, 1950). In the area of skills and abilities, the picture continues to build up that the more intelligent and creative are generally more accepted by their age mates; the slow learners and the retarded, less well accepted (Baldwin, 1958; Barbe, 1954; Gallagher, 1958; Northway and Rooks,

1956; Peck and Galliani, 1962; Porter-field, and Schlicting, 1961). Body size, muscular strength, and athletic ability also appear as criteria for acceptance among boys (Clarke and Clarke, 1961; Tuddenham, 1951a). And developmental maturity is associated with prestige of adolescent girls (Faust, 1960). In general, the qualities evaluated positively by peers are similar at different ages, but some variation does occur during the course of development. For American children such changes are apparently more marked among girls. In comparing shifts in values placed on personality traits by twelve- and fifteen-year-old children, Tryon (1939) reported that values for girls underwent some revolutionary changes. For boys, the same three-year age difference revealed only minor shifts, slight changes in emphasis on particular values.

The evidence is clear that, once children have been constituted into a group, patterns of relationships are quickly established and remain stable over time. Young boys were asked to state friendship preferences on the first day of attendance in a summer camp and at weekly intervals thereafter. A week-to-week comparison of such choices showed considerable consistency of choice. Complete stability was not, of course, achieved at the very outset of group formation, but the progress was rapid; although patterns of personal preference altered frequently during the very earliest phases of camp, consistency of preference and stabilization of status of group members rapidly increased. (Hunt and Solomon, 1942). In groups that have been established for some time, stability in preferences is the rule. Singer (1951) reported that a high degree of constancy

in friendship choices among a group of seventh- and eighth-grade children throughout a year and a half of study. And among children in the second, third, and fourth grades, general acceptance was found to be about as constant over a three-year period as were measures of intelligence (Bonney, 1943).

As one might expect, stability of relationships is positively related to age (Horrocks and Thompson, 1946; Thompson and Horrocks, 1947). But even among preschool children, sociometric preferences remain reasonably consistent over ten- to twenty-day intervals (McCandless and Marshall, 1957). Emotional disturbance or its absence also enters as a factor. Hospitalized emotionally disturbed boys, ranging in age from seven to thirteen years, were significantly less stable in friendship patterns than were a group of campers and a group of schoolboys of approximately the same age (Davids and Parenti, 1958).

Relationships among children are, of course, also expressed along lines other than those of choice and rejection. Do children also show stability in the behavior they display in the group situation? The answer is yes, with reservations. Thus in an experimental study of sixteen pairs of preschool children, Gellert (1961) found that, despite a fair amount of intersession variability, children maintained reasonably consistent positions of dominance and submission, although such was not the case for the expression of resistance (that is, noncompliance, self-defense, and counterdomination). Somewhat different results were obtained with newly formed preadolescent groups (Campbell and M.R. Yarrow, 1961). In these groups there was stability over a two-week period in the extent to which children initiated friendly and aggressive behavior, but on two much less frequently occurring dimensions of interaction, assertive and submissive behavior, there was much less consistency. Other evidence in this study suggested that children's reputations were more stable than their behavior. Further, information on changes in reputation and behavior led to the inference that reputations, which were quickly established, shaped expectations and, in part, drew out behavior from the children that accorded with such expectations. Polansky, Lippitt, and Redl reached a similar conclusion in their "contagion" studies: "So far as we can tell . . .the relative 'prestige' assigned to an individual in his group will be a fairly powerful determinant of his own behavior" (1950, p. 347). Such interpretations as these point to the potentially powerful role that the group may play in shaping a child's social development.

Peer Acceptance and the Self-Concept

One of the most important and enduring functions of peer relationships is to help the growing child in his attempt to paint the picture of his own identity. Early in his group experiences, he becomes aware that his peers place him along particular lines, and, as he grows older, he develops proficiency in interpreting his own status in the eyes of other children (Ausubel, Schiff, and Gasser, 1952). That his assessment by others is related to his own self-picture is suggested by a number of studies. F.D. Horowitz (1962) found that, in the middle grades of elementary school, the less popular children tended to think less well of themselves. Rosen,

Levinger, and Lippitt (1960), studying boys in their early teens, obtained evidence supporting the view that a boy's desire for change in himself is partly contingent on the extent to which he is well liked and viewed by his peers as a desired role model. In his extensive study of high school students, Coleman (1961a) saw much the same phenomenon. Students having elite status in their schools (named as being in the leading crowd, as a desired friend, or as someone to be liked) were much less likely than others to want to "be someone different from myself." High status in the group may, then, be a source of a positive self-concept; lack of status and security, a source of dissatisfaction with one's self.

In which direction does the causal relation go? Does popularity lead to self-esteem, or does self-esteem lead to popularity? It is perfectly possible that both alternatives are true. That some of the freight of influence, however, *does* travel from the group's appraisal to the individual's self-assessment is suggested by a conclusion by Polansky and his colleagues that "by and large those children to whom prestige position is attributed are aware of the fact; their awareness is facilitated by the behavior of others toward them . . ." (1950, p. 334). Rosenberg's (1962) extensive questionnaire study of high school students lends further research support to this view. His data reveal that those students who were reared in a neighborhood in which the predominant religious affiliation was different from that of their own families were more likely to have low self-esteem, to report psychosomatic symptoms, and to have feelings of depression. Such children growing up in dissonant religious contexts more often reported having experienced discrimination, and such experiences of rejection presumably contributed to psychic disturbance.

It is clearly an oversimplification to suggest that acceptance by peers directly determines the extent of a child's self-esteem. More rigorous evidence on the nature of this relationship needs to be obtained. Further, it is probable that additional factors (including the extent to which adults reinforce the child's self-picture, and the importance of peer-group membership to the child) play an influential role. Yet the likelihood that a child's age mates may contribute to his developing identity is a possibility for the practitioner to consider in determining strategy for action with children's peer groups.

Attitudes, Values, and the Peer Group

Just as peer relations play a part in the formation of concepts of the self, so, too, do they influence the formation of attitudes and values. To some extent, of course, such influences cannot readily be separated from those of the broader social environment. Indeed, it is probable that such peer influences often do not counter, but rather tend to reinforce predominant values in the adult culture. Yet peer influences do indeed aid in forming and changing attitudes and values; this can be quite clearly inferred from a number of studies differing in general orientation and in methodological approach. In a charming description, supplemented by quotations from interviews with Swiss children, Piaget has described the way that the child, in simple social games such as marbles, learns the rules of the game. The peer group is the one social agency primarily responsible for this process; as Piaget states, ". . . we are in the presence of rules which have been elaborated by the children alone" (1948, p. 2). A.B. Wilson (1959) studied the influence of the predominant values in membership groups on the educational, occupational, and political values of high school students. He classified 13 schools into three categories in terms of the general socioeconomic level from which the student body came. He then examined the data obtained from the students to ascertain the extent to which their values reflected the socioeconomic level of their parents and the extent to which they reflected the predominant socioeconomic level of the student body of their high school. It was apparent that status characteristics of a student's parents did influence his values. Yet when such parental characteristics as occupation and education were controlled, the hypothesis was clearly sustained that the bulk of the students in a school affected the values of individual students whose parents came from social strata differing from that of a major portion of the students' families.

Coleman's (1960, 1961a,b) inquiries present a similar picture. He found that social climates influenced values concerning academic achievement. In schools where such achievement was valued by the peer group, academic excellence was more closely related to measures of intelligence than was the case in schools where academic performance was less valued. Moreover, the impact of the peer value system tends to show some increment with time. Thus freshman students in a private school in a seriously oriented university setting valued "good looks" as an attribute for membership in the leading crowd to about the same extent as did freshmen in other high schools. But, in this one school, the importance of this factor went down sharply over the course of the four years, whereas the pattern in the average of the other schools showed no such decline.

From "natural experiments" with children's groups comes further confirmation of the proposition that the group serves to shape attitudes and values. Two weeks of equalitarian contact in a racially integrated summer camp led to significant reduction in, but not elimination of, feelings of social distance (as expressed by friendship preferences) between negro and white preadolescents (Campbell and M. R. Yarrow, 1958). Among eleven-year-olds in international summer camps, a summer of such international living reduced ethnocentrism (Bjerstedt, 1961). Attitudes toward children differing in language and nationality were clearly more favorable. The work of Sherif and Sherif (1953) indicates the way in which group membership may influence interpersonal attitudes. After three days together in a summer camp, twelve-year-olds were separated into two experimental groups in which friendship preferences for members of the experimental in-group were substantially less than for those of the experimental out-group. When sociometric choices were again made after a five-day period in which the two groups lived in separate bunkhouses, the pattern of choice was reversed; preferences for the experimentally created in-group predominated. Such experiments as these show that favorable contact situations can modify interpersonal attitudes. How deeply seated or how permanent are

such changed orientations remains, of course, another question.

Such studies clearly support the proposition that the peer group is a potent factor in the child's coming to terms with his environment.[1] Some facets of the *process* by which aspects of the group experience operate to shape the child will be presented in the subsequent portion of this chapter.

INFLUENCE PROCESSES IN THE PEER GROUP

Patterns of peer relations show considerable variability. The individual child and the group as a whole are subject to a number of factors that tend to channel actions in particular directions. The forces at work are of various sorts. Some are inherent in the character of the situation; others derive from characteristics of children—as recipients of influence as well as influence agents; and when adults are participants, they too shape the course of children's functioning in groups. These various factors do not, of course, function in isolation from one another, but, for ease of dealing with available research information, each can reasonably be brought into central focus, while the others remain temporarily in the background.[2]

[1] For relevant consideration of the role of the peer group in shaping attitudes and values of delinquent youth, see Cloward and Ohlin (1960); Cohen (1955); and Sykes and Matza (1957).
[2] Influence processes at work in groups of children do not, of course, differ in kind from those operating among adults. Thus, while it is not included in the present discussion, much of the work on influence in adult groups would be of some relevance to the reader.

Situational Influences

At least five different types of situational factors exert some degree of control over individual and group functioning. First, the physical setting itself, the actual structure of the environment plays a meaningful part in determining the course of group relations. Among preadolescent campers who were initially strangers to one another, friendship preferences within the cabin were significantly influenced by the physical structure of the cabin (Campbell and M.R. Yarrow, 1958). Blood and Livant (1957) noted that not only was interaction concentrated heavily within cabin groups, but children actively used cabin space (by relocating bunks, and the like) to express relations, to implement friendships, and to secure protection.

One step removed from the physical characteristics of the situation is the process whereby different activity settings lead to differences in behavior. In studies of normal and disturbed children, Raush, Farbman, and Llewellyn (1960) found that specific settings tended to induce particular patterns of behavior. For both groups of subjects, food settings were associated with friendly actions and competitive games were associated with unfriendly behaviors. In a similar vein Gump, Schoggen, and Redl (1957) noted that milieu factors affected behavior and experience; the amount and quality of interaction of eleven-year-old campers were quite different in different activity settings. Consistent with this theme are Spiro's observations in an Israeli kibbutz. Noting that children's classroom behavior was highly informal, he attributed this in part to the fact that, for these children,

"the dormitory and the classroom building are one" (1958, p. 263). The situation became so defined that the lack of a physical transition from the setting for sleep and play to that for school was accompanied by a similar lack of psychological transition.

The clarity of definition of the task for the group member is a third factor affecting the nature of his response. Thus Berenda (1950), studying effects of group pressures on children's judgments of perceptual stimuli, and Patel and Gordon (1960), examining the extent to which children yielded to influence in a vocabulary test, found that the more ambiguous the stimulus, the greater the likelihood that children would accept the views of others. Further, Kitano (1962) reported that "problem children," as well as "normal children," showed a high degree of adjustment in situations where role expectations were clear and where prescriptions for performance were readily enforceable.

Still a fourth situational factor, the reward structure, has been shown to relate to group cohesiveness in experimental studies of children in the elementary grades (Lott and Lott, 1960). Three-member groups played a game in which some were rewarded, others were not. Those who were rewarded subsequently indicated more positive attitudes toward their fellow group members than did the unrewarded.

The fifth situational factor that plays a part in the influence process is the social structure. Group size was linked to consensus among Boy Scouts: smaller groups achieved more consensus after a discussion, and their members were more likely to change their views as a result of the discussion (Hare, 1952). Interpersonal communication is also affected by the social structure of the group. In a study of boys in a summer camp, Larsen and Hill (1958) concluded that the more stable the social structure, the greater was its influence on interpersonal communication.

Although no group leader could be reasonably expected to take into account all of the diverse elements that might influence the course of individual and group development, the continually mounting evidence for the role of situational factors suggests that this aspect of the interaction equation warrants much thoughtful consideration. An assessment of the setting, the activity, the clarity of the task, the rewards, and the social structure of the group may lead to specific program modifications that can be used to obtain desired consequences in individual and group performance.

Variations in Susceptibility to Influence

What children are most responsive to the various forces shaping behavior in the peer group? No blanket generalizations can be made, but research evidence throws light on the extent to which such characteristics as age and sex, status in the group, and personality factors are associated with susceptibility to influence.

Information on the role of age and sex presents a slightly inconsistent picture. But the one that does emerge suggests that, as one might expect, younger children are more susceptible to the views of others than are older children, and, in line with cultural stereotypes about differences between the sexes, girls are more

likely to yield to peer pressures than boys. Perceptual judgments of children under ten were more influenced by the reports of others than those of children over ten years old (Berenda, 1950). Patel and Gordon (1960) found girls more likely to accept suggestions than boys, and twelfth graders less likely to yield to influence than tenth or eleventh graders, but the trend was not strictly linear over the three grades. In a clinical evaluation of available data on the extent to which 48 adolescents conformed to the authority of their peers, Tuma and Livson (1960) concluded that, over the limited age range studied, girls apparently increased in conformity, while boys became slightly less conforming. Such a conclusion fits reasonably well with Coleman's (1961b) survey results, which showed, in general, that cliques and crowds had far greater importance for the high school girls studied than for the high school boys.

The extent to which the child is influenced by others appears to be linked with his status in the group. Among boys and girls in the third, sixth, ninth, and eleventh grades, those whom peers accorded low status in terms of leadership criteria were more likely to change their opinions when faced with a contrary judgment supposedly given by a peer (Harvey and Rutherford, 1960). When members of 27 cliques in a training school for delinquent boys judged perceptual stimuli, the group members ranking just below the leaders conformed more to views held by others than did either the leaders or the bottom ranking boys (Harvey and Consalvi, 1960). In yet another experimental situation, high school boys with indefinite status conformed more than did either popular or unpopular boys (R. S. Wilson, 1960). While one might like to see such experimental evidence supported with additional data coming from observations of more natural situations, the findings do suggest that status and status strivings help to account for conformity to the norms of the peer group.

The role of personality factors in children's susceptibility to influence when faced with an ambiruous judgmental situation has been indicated in two experiments using the autokinetic phenomenon as the judgmental stimulus. (This phenomenon, of course, effectively "socialized" by Sherif in 1935, is the illusory movement of an actual fixed pinpoint of light in an otherwise dark room.) In one of these experiments (Jakubczak and Walters, 1959), nine-year-old boys who were high on dependency (who were willing to accept help in tasks even when none was required) proved to be more susceptible to suggestions of others than boys who were low on dependency. In the second experiment (Walters, Marshall, and Shooter, 1960), adolescent boys who reported anxiety about being experimental subjects were more suggestible; that is, they conformed more in response to contrary judgments than nonanxious boys. We may contrast these findings with information from a comparison of hyperaggressive boys aged eight to ten and a matched group of normals studied in a residential therapeutic center (Raush, Farbman, and Llewellyn, 1960). Observation of behavior revealed that the normal children varied their behavior according to the social setting to a greater degree than did the hyperaggressive boys. Another way of

phrasing this finding is that normal boys often conformed more to situational demands than did the other group. The reasonable implication is that "conformity" is not solely the province of the anxious, the dependent, the maladjusted; unwilling conformity in the face of ambiguity may be so, but conformity to the socially accepted demands of clearly defined situations seems a perfectly healthy response for a child (or for an adult, for that matter).

Children as Influence Agents

Various personal characteristics have been singled out as associated with children's ability to affect the functioning of their peers. Intelligence relates significantly to children's social power, though the degree of the relationship is not nearly as profound as many an intellectual might wish (Zander and Van Egmond, 1958). Suggestions attributed to children in a higher age-grade status are more likely to be accepted than are those from children with lower age-grade status (Patel and Gordon, 1960). The child who is chosen with a high degree of frequency on sociometric measures is also the one who is observed to take definite stands on issues, insist on impersonal fairness, and enlist others to aid in controlling deviant group members (Jennings, 1947). Children who have power and influence are more likely than others to be perceived as possessing those characteristics valued by their peers (Gold, 1958). Summer campers who received high peer ratings on such qualities as athletic skill, independence of adults, and independence of social pressures were the more influential members of the camp group. They attempted to influence their peers more often than did low-power members, and they were also more successful in such influence attempts; other group members were more likely to imitate the behavior of these high-power members, were more likely to accept their direct attempts at influence, and were more likely to accept their direct attempts at influence, and were more likely to initiate deferential behavior toward them (Lippitt, Polansky, and Rosen, 1952; Polansky, Lippitt, and Redl, 1950).

While some of the information on characteristics of children who are able to influence others may at first glance seem obvious, careful scrutiny at times qualifies the obvious in an illuminating fashion. Lippitt and associates (1952) provide a case in point. Although perceived fighting ability was strongly associated with attributed power among boys in two different camps, neither height nor weight was significantly related to attributed power. In one of these camps, composed primarily of normal boys from middle-class homes, height and weight were significantly related to perceived fighting ability. But in the other, with more disturbed boys and boys coming from low-income families, no such relationship was found. In the former instance, actual fighting was a rarity, so that potential was assessed in terms of the most obvious cues. In the latter case, perception was based on actual performance, and this did not necessarily correlate very highly with physical size.

Interest understandably tends to focus primarily on the influence and power of the high status child; yet influence is not the exclusive property of the esteemed individual. For example, the single impul-

sive child, given the right circumstances, may be an important determiner of group action. Thus a "contagious" response in the group may result when the impulsive child triggers off an action the group is ready for but has not yet done (Polansky et al., 1950). Such children are peculiarly effective in stressful situations when their expressional freedom is in accord with the group needs of the moment. Furthermore the group itself has an impact. Berenda's (1950) experimental work indicated that children's judgments were subject to the pressure of the views of a majority of fellow group members.

Children's Peer Groups and the Adult

The impact of the adult may range from an effect on quite specific functioning of individual children to a broad, pervasive influence on the group as a whole. One of the landmark studies of the late 1930's clearly indicated that the adult leader's role was a strong determiner of social interaction and emotional development in several experimentally organized boys' clubs studies over an extended period of time (Lippitt and White, 1947). When adult experimenters adopted either "authoritarian" or "laissez-faire" leadership styles, boys expressed more irritability and aggression toward fellow group members than in groups with "democratic" leadership. There was greater group unity and less use of scapegoating as a channel of aggressive release in the democratic than in the authoritarian groups. Further, experimentally contrived absences of leaders revealed that work motivation was more leader-induced in authoritarian situations while the presence or absence of the leader in democratic groups had practically no effect on work motivation.

In a natural experiment examining racial desegregation among groups of pre-adolescent campers, adult leaders were viewed as pivotal figures in determining the success of this process (Yarrow and Yarrow, 1958). The adults influenced children's reactions to the initial ambiguity of the interracial setting by structuring activities, defining behavioral possibilities, and setting the tone of affective relations.

The extent to which an adult can influence sociometric status of specific children was experimentally verified by Flanders and Havumaki (1960). When 17 groups of tenth-grade students met for a single discussion session with a teacher-trainer not known to any of the students, the teacher gave praise for participation only to those seated in odd-numbered seats. Subsequently obtained sociometric information indicated that the praised students received more choices. The relevance of this finding becomes increased in the light of evidence that teachers' responses to high status children differ from their responses to those with low peer-ascribed status (Lippitt and Gold, 1959). This leads to the possiblity of a vicious circle, in which (a) the child may be negatively evaluated by teacher and peers alike; (b) such negative evaluations may mutually reinforce one another; (c) the child may become aware of his own rejected status in the eyes of others; and (d) he may respond in such a fashion that his behavior serves further to confirm his disvalued position in the group. While heightened awareness of group processes and personal evaluations would not alone be sufficient to permit the adult leader to circumvent the sort of situation just described, such an awareness might constitute a reasonable positive step toward the creation of an effective environment for the social and emotional development of the group members.

The Adult vs. the Peer Group?

Given evidence that adults and children alike are significant in plotting the course of peer relations, the query as to the relative impact of these two sources of influence readily arises. The issue is sometimes posed as a conflict between the world of the adult and that of the child, a conflict that presumably reaches its peak during adolescence. And many suggest that when the smoke has cleared from the battlefield, youth emerges victorious. Certainly support can be mustered for such a contention. Berenda's (1950) systematic experimentation has shown that children's judgments yield much more to the pressure of a majority of their classmates than to that of their teacher. At the broad descriptive level, Davis, Gardner, and Gardner (1941) have suggested that the clique has more influence over the behavior of its members than do parents. The cross-pressures and the way they are frequently resolved by the bright girl are described by Coleman (1961b) in his careful survey of school climates. Urged by parents and teachers to do well in school but faced with norms of the peer culture that dissuade them from a role of "brilliant student," many of the girls who could be top scholars are constrained not to work so hard. Rosen's (1955) research indicates that among a group of Jewish high school students, when attitudes of family and peer group conflicted concerning the use of kosher meat, the peer group tended to exert more influence.

Such evidence fits a picture suggesting that the child's peer group wields greater influence than do significant adults. But at the same time this should not be equated with a conclusion that a major intergenerational conflict, a conflict that is resolved by youth's compulsive conformity to the peer culture, is occurring. A number of studies clearly restrict such an interpretation. To a considerable extent children select friends on the basis of values acquired from their parents (Westley and Elkin, 1956). A convincing majority of the teenagers in Coleman's (1961b) extensive study reported that, despite a personal preference, they would not join a particular club in school if parents disapproved of the group. The adolescent's own values, in some respects, seem to be a compromise between the values of his parents and those of his peers as he sees them; further, his expectations about his subsequent adult values clearly approach those of his parents as perceived by him (Riley, Riley, and Moore, 1961). Thus whatever the gap between the generations, youth has every intention of bridging it. Such items as these are entirely consonant with Bandura and Walters' (1963) conclusion that there is no serious conflict of generations.

The seemingly contradictory bits of evidence cited in the two preceding paragraphs suggest that the query concerning the relative impact of the adult and the peer group and the amount of conflict between these influence agents has not yet been satisfactorily answered. However, at least a limited clarification is possible. To ask whether the adult or the peer group has more influence on the child may actually be an inappropriate way to frame the question. It is quite likely that the functioning of these two sources of influence is contingent on several factors, including the characteristics of the situation, those of the participants, and the particular attitudes, values, or behaviors that are the outcome issues in question. And while it would be inappropriate to ignore evidence of dissonance between the world of the adult and that of the child, it is probable that the differences between adult values and those of the peer group are ones of degree, rather than kind. A fuller recognition of *particular* differences may result when they are placed within a context indicative of *general* similarity of values.

References

Ausubel, D.P., Schiff, H.M., & Gasser, E.B. A preliminary study of developmental trends in socioempathy: accuracy of perception of own and others' status. *Child Developm.*, 1952, 23, 111-28.

Baldwin, W.K. The social position of the educable mentally retarded child in the regular grades in the public schools. *Except. Child.*, 1958, 25, 106-108.

Bandura, A. & Walters, R.H. *The social learning of deviant behavior.* New

York: Holt, Rinehart & Winston, 1963.

Barbe, W.B. Peer relationships of children of different intelligence levels. *Sch. & Soc.*, 1954, **80**, 60-62.

Berenda, R.W. *The influence of the group on the judgments of children.* New York: King's Crown Press, 1950.

Bjerstedt, A. Informational and non-informational determinants of nationality stereotypes. *Acta Psychol.*, 1961, **18**, 11-16.

Blood, R.O. & Livant, W.P. The use of space within the cabin group. *J. soc. Issues*, 1957, **13** (1), 47-53.

Bonney, M.E. The relative stability of social, intellectual, and academic status in grades II to IV and the inter-relationships between these various forms of growth. *J. educ. Psychol.*, 1943, **34**, 88-102.

Bronfenbrenner, U. Soviet methods of character education: Some implications for research. *Amer. Psychologist*, 1962, **17**, 550-564.

Campbell, J.D. & Yarrow, M.R. Personal and situational variables in adaptation to change, *J. soc. Issues*, 1958, **14** (1), 29-46.

Campbell, J.D. & Yarrow, M.R. Perceptual and behavioral correlates of social effectiveness, *Sociometry*, 1961, **24**, 1-20.

Clarke, H.H. & Clarke, D.H. Social status and mental health of boys as related to their maturity, structural, and strength characteristics. *Res. Quart. Amer. Assn. Hlth. Phys. Educ. & Recrn.*, 1961, **32**, 326-334.

Cloward, R.A. & Ohlin, L.E. *Delinquency and opportunity.* Glencoe, Ill.: Free Press, 1960.

Cohen, A.K. *Delinquent boys,* Glencoe, Ill.: Free Press, 1955.

Coleman, J.S. The adolescent subculture and academic achievement. *Amer. J. Sociol.*, 1960, **65**, 337-347.

Coleman, J.S. Social climates in high schools. *U.S. Office of Education Cooperative Res. Monogr. No. 4*, 1961a, OE-33016.

Coleman, J.S. *The adolescent society.* Glencoe, Ill.: Free Press, 1961b.

Davids, A. & Parenti, A.N. Time orientation and interpersonal relations of emotionally disturbed and normal children. *J. abnorm. soc. Psychol.*, 1958, **57**, 299-305.

Davis, A., Gardner, B.B., & Gardner, M.R. *Deep south.* Chicago: Univ. Chicago Press, 1941.

Faust, M.S. Developmental maturity as a determinant in prestige of adolescent girls. *Child Developm.*, 1960, **31**, 173-184.

Feinberg, M.R., Smith, M. & Schmidt, R. An analysis of expressions used by adolescents at varying economic levels to describe accepted and rejected peers. *J. genet. Psychol.*, 1958, **93**, 133-148.

Flanders, N.A. & Havumaki, S. The effect of teacher-pupil contacts involving praise on the sociometric choices of students. *J. educ. Psychol.*, 1960, **51**, 65-68.

Gallagher, J.J. Social status of children related to intelligence, propinquity, and social perception. *Element. Sch. J.*, 1958, **58**, 225-231.

Gellert, E. Stability and fluctuation in the power relationships of young children. *J. abnorm. soc. Psychol.*, 1961, **62**, 8-15.

Gold, M. Power in the classroom. *Sociometry*, 1958, **21**, 50-60.

Gump, P., Schoggen, P., & Redl, F. The camp milieu and its immediate effects. *J. soc. Issues*, 1957, **13** (1), 40-46.

Hare, A.P. A study of interaction and consensus in different sized groups. *Amer. Sociol. Rev.*, 1952, **17**, 261-267.

Harvey, O.J. & Consalvi, C. Status and conformity to pressures in informal groups. *J. abnorm. soc. Psychol.*, 1960, **60**, 182-187.

Harvey, O.J. & Rutherford, J. Status in the informal group: influence and influencibility at differing age levels. *Child Developm.*, 1960, **31**, 377-385.

Horowitz, F.D. The relationship of anxiety, self-concept, and sociometric status among fourth, fifth, and sixth grade children. *J. abnorm. soc. Psychol.*, 1962, **65**, 212-214.

Horrocks, J.E. & Thompson, G.G. A study of the friendship fluctuations of rural boys and girls. *J. genet. Psychol.*, 1946, **69**, 189-198.

Hunt, J. McV. & Solomon, R.L. The stability and some correlates of group-status in a summer-camp group of young boys. *Amer. J. Psychol.*, 1942, **55**, 33-45.

Jakubczak, L.F. & Walters, R.H. Suggestibility as dependency behavior. *J. abnorm. soc. Psychol.*, 1959, **59**, 102-107.

Jennings, H.H. Leadership and sociometric choice. *Sociometry*, 1947, **10**, 32-49.

Kitano, H.H.L. Adjustment of problem and nonproblem children to specific situations: a study in role theory. *Child Developm.*, 1962, **33**, 229-233.

Larsen, O.N. & Hill, R.J. Social structure and interpersonal communication. *Amer. J. Sociol.*, 1958, **63**, 497-505.

Lippitt, R. & Gold, M. Classroom social structure as a mental health problem. *J. soc. Issues*, 1959, **15**, (1), 40-49.

Lippitt, R., Polansky, N., & Rosen, S. The dynamics of power: a field study of social influence in groups of children. *Hum. Relat.*, 1952, **5**, 37-64.

Lippitt, R. & White, R.K. An experimental study of leadership and group life. In T.M. Newcomb & E. L. Hartley (Eds.), *Readings in social psychology.* New York: Holt, 1947, Pp. 315-330.

Lott, B.E. & Lott, A.J. The formation of positive attitudes toward group members. *J. abnorm. soc. Psychol.*, 1960, **61**, 297-300.

McCandless, B.R. & Marshall, H.R. A picture sociometric technique for preschool children and its relation to teacher judgments of friendship. *Child Developm.*, 1957, **28**, 139-148.

Northway, M.L. Outsiders: a study of the personality patterns of children least acceptable to their age mates. *Sociometry*, 1944, **7**, 10-25.

Northway, M.L. & Rooks, M. McC. Creativity and sociometric status in children. *Sociometry*, 1956, **18**, 450-457.

Patel, A.S. & Gordon, J.E. Some personal and situational determinants of yielding to influence, *J. abnorm. soc. Psychol.*, 1960, **61**, 411-418.

Peck, R.F. & Galliani, C. Intelligence, ethnicity and social roles in adolescent society. *Sociometry*, 1962, **25**, 64-72.

Piaget, J. *The moral judgment of the child.* Glencoe, Ill.: Free Press, 1948.

Polansky, N., Lippitt, R., & Redl, F. An investigation of behavioral contagion in groups. *Hum. Relat.*, 1950, **3**, 319-348.

Porterfield, O.V. & Schlichting, H.F. Peer status and reading achievement. *J. educ. Res.*, 1961, **54**, 291-297.

Raush, H.L., Farbman, I., & Llewellyn, L.G. Person, setting, and change in social interaction. II. *Hum. Relat.*, 1960, **13**, 305-322.

Riley, M.W., Riley, J.W., & Moore, M.E. Adolescent values and the Riesman typology: an empirical analysis. In S.M. Lipset & L. Lowenthal (Eds.), *Culture and social character, the work of David Riesman reviewed.* Glencoe, Ill.: Free Press, 1961. Pp. 370-385.

Rosen, B.C. Conflicting group membership: a study of parent-peer-group cross pressures. *Amer. Sociol. Rev.*, 1955, **20**, 155-161.

Rosen, S., Levinger, G., & Lippitt, R. Desired change in self and others as a function of resource ownership. *Hum. Relat.*, 1960, **13**, 187-193.

Rosenberg, M. The dissonant religious context and emotional disturbance. *Amer. J. Sociol.*, 1962, **68**, 1-10.

Sherif, M. A study of some social factors in perception. *Arch. Psychol., N.Y.*, 1935, No. 187.

Sherif, M., Harvey, O.J., White, B.J., Hood, W.R. & Sherif, C.W. *Intergroup conflict and cooperation: the robbers cave experiment.* Norman: ,Univ. Oklahoma Press, 1961.

Sherif, M. & Sherif, C.W. *Groups in harmony and tension.* New York: Harper, 1953.

Singer, A., Jr. Certain aspects of personality and their relation to certain group modes, and constancy of friendship choices. *J. educ. Res.*, 1951, **45**, 33-42.

Smith, G.H. Sociometric study of best-liked and least-liked children. *Element. Sch. J.*, 1950, **51**, 77-85.

Spiro, M.E. *Children of the Kibbutz.* Cambridge: Harvard Univ. Press, 1958.

Sykes, G.M. & Matza, D. Techniques of neutralization: a theory of delinquency. *Amer. Sociol. Rev.*, 1957, **22**, 664-670.

Thompson, G.G. & Horrocks, J.E. A study of the friendship fluctuations of urban boys and girls. *J. genet. Psychol.*, 1947, **70**, 53-63.

Tryon, C.M. Evaluation of adolescent personality by adolescents. *Monogr. Soc. Res. Child Developm.*, 1939, No. 23.

Tuddenham, R.D. Studies in reputation: III. Correlates of popularity among elementary school children. *J. educ. Psychol.*, 1951, **42**, 257-276.

Tuma, E. & Livson, N. Family socio-economic status and adolescent attitudes to authority. *Child Developm.*, 1960, **31**, 387-399.

Walters, R.H. Marshall, W.E., & Shooter, J.R. Anxiety, isolation, and susceptibility to social influence. *J. Pers.*, 1960, **28**, 518-529.

Westley, W.A. & Elkin, F. The protective environment and adolescent socialization. *Social Forces*, 1956, **35**, 243-249.

Wilson, A.B. Residential segregation of social classes and aspirations of high school boys. *Amer. Sociol. Rev.*, 1959, **24**, 836-845.

Wilson, R.S. Personality patterns, source attractiveness, and conformity. *J. Pers.*, 1960, **28**, 186-199.

Yarrow, L.J. & Yarrow, M.R. Leadership and interpersonal change. *J. soc. Issues*, 1958, **14**, (1), 47-50.

Zander, A. & Van Egmond, E. Relationship of intelligence and social power to the interpersonal behavior of children. *J. educ. Psychol.*, 1958, **49**, 257-268.

12
/\\IDDLE CHILDHOOD:
INDIVIDUAL AND GROUP DIFFERENCES

Of the many different factors that contribute to individual and group differences in children, one of the most significant is culture. The characteristics of a child's culture affect not only his language, outlook, and values, but also many aspects of his thinking and concept formation. In the first of the following two selections, Vernon describes and summarizes the extensive cross-cultural research that has been done on the development of intellectual abilities. Vernon provides a thoughtful and balanced presentation of what are some very difficult and complex issues. In particular, he points with considerable sensitivity to a major new advance in cross-cultural research, namely, concern for the context in which children are assessed and recognition of how this context can influence their performance.

Another important determinant of individual differences is birth order. Birth-order effects, like cultural influences, play a part in child development from infancy through adolescence; however, we have included this topic in our section on middle childhood because this is the age when many of these effects first become pronounced. In the second selection that follows, Havassy-DeAvila provides a critical review of research in this area, covering the relationship of birth order to child-rearing practices, affiliation, dependence, conformity, intelligence, achievement, and alcoholism. As she notes, research findings support some of the classical views while also suggesting that birth order is a very complex phenomenon, the effects of which are not always easy to predict.

PHILLIP E. VERNON

Intelligence and Cultural Environment*

... Much of the controversy regarding differences in abilities between ethnic groups and subgroups has arisen because the term 'intelligence' is ambiguous. It is used here to refer to the effective all-round cognitive abilities to comprehend, to grasp relations and reason (Intelligence B), which develops through the interaction between the genetic potential (Intelligence A) and stimulation provided by the environment. One must also distinguish constitutional equipment, that is the potential as affected by pre-natal or other physiological conditions; and Intelligence C—the results obtained on various intelligence tests, which provide merely a limited sample of the Intelligence B displayed in behaviour and thinking at home, at school, at work. There is strong evidence that differences in Intelligence B and C between individuals within one culture are largely—certainly not wholly—genetically determined. But when environmental differences are more extreme, as between ethnic groups, their effects predominate. This does not mean that there are no innate racial differences in abilities, but they are probably small

and we have no means of proving them. Differences between subgroups such as social classes are partly genetic, not wholly environmental.

Current conceptions of cognitive growth derive largely from the work of Piaget, Hebb and Bruner. From the initial sensory-motor reflexes of the newborn, a succession of more complex and adaptive schemata or skills are built up through the impact of environmental stimulation on the maturing nervous system and through the infant's active exploration and experiment. Thus a series of stages or successive reorganisations can be recognised in the child's perception, speech and thinking, through which different children progress at different rates. (Bruner's enactive, iconic and symbolic modes of coding differ in important respects from Piaget's sensory-motor, pre-operational, concrete and formal stages, but both are useful in describing intellectual development.) Moreover more backward groups typically fail to progress as far as others along this scale, and though they may develop lower-order skills which are highly effective for survival, their reasoning capacities remain similar in many ways to those of younger children, or even regress through lack of appropriate stimulation. That is they learn to be unintelligent, instead of acquiring the skills that constitute intelligence. An important implication is that man has by no

*From P. E. Vernon, *Intelligence and cultural environment*, Part VI, 1969. Reprinted by permission of the author and Methuen and Company.

means reached the limits of his mental powers; there is immense room for improvement at the lower end of the scale, and also the possibility of more effective "techniques" at the top end.

General intelligence is merely the common element in a whole host of distinguishable, but overlapping, cognitive abilities. When dealing with homogeneous or highly selected populations, it is profitable to study different mental faculties and abilities along special lines, adopting the factorial models of Thurstone and Guilford. But with more heterogeneous populations, and particularly when considering different ethnic groups or subgroups, the common element or g factor tends to dominate. And there are advantages in following the hierarchical or group-factor model, which successively subdivides more specialised types of ability. This implies that, while we should certainly try to study a wide variety of mental functions in contrasted ethnic groups or subgroups, we are most likely to discover conditions that affect general or all-round ability; then those that favour or inhibit verbal and educational as contrasted with perceptual, spatial and practical abilities, and later the smaller (but still quite broad) group factors such as number, memorising, fluency or creativity, etc. Intelligence B cannot be precisely defined since it refers to the totality of our schemata, but its essence lies in the more generalised thinking skills, which can be applied to a wide variety of problems. . .

What then do we mean by the potential ability of an underdeveloped group or individual? It is not Intelligence A or constitutional potential, since these cannot be assessed and are of use only in so far as previous environment has developed them. Equally the conventional expedient of contrasting achievement measures with intelligence test scores (verbal or non-verbal) is beset with fallacies. Abilities at different types of test often differ, and by surveying these patterns of abilities in the light of the individual's or group's physical and cultural background, education and motivation, the psychologist can often arrive at useful diagnoses and remedial proposals. If plausible reasons can be suggested either for general backwardness or for unevennesses in performance, and if the remedial measures at the disposal of the community can be shown to, or reasonably be expected to, work, then that person or group has potentiality.

We have also surveyed the major environmental factors which have been found to influence the development of intellectual abilities, concentrating on recently published investigations. Most studies consist of cross-sectional comparisons of groups or individuals who differ in respect of many interacting conditions, and these do not readily demonstrate the effects of any particular condition. The methologically superior experimental approach, where one condition is changed and other factors are kept constant, and the longitudinal follow-up of a sample who undergo various conditions, have their own difficulties. Thus even in the case of relatively clear-cut conditions such as malnutrition during pregnancy or later, and debilitating diseases, our knowledge is scrappy and often indirect. The incidence of dietary deficiencies is worldwide, especially in the low-income countries, and it is found that they can cause permanent impairment to the brain at the formative stage of pregnancy and early infancy, and seriously reduce later intellectual capacity. After this stage, poor health and nutrition or endemic diseases, though often associated with poor performance, do not seem to affect mental growth as such.

Particular stress is laid by most psychologists on the sensory stimulation, opportunities for activity, and the emotional relationships of the first year or two of life, as basic to later psychological development. But the evidence, apart from that of animal experiments, is unconvincing. While it is clear that extreme social deprivation has traumatic effects on human infants, probably the ordinary range of social and physical environments (even among relatively primitive groups) provides adequate stimulation. In other words, conceptual and linguistic deprivation during the period from about one-and-a-half years and throughout childhood, when children should be building up their concepts of objects and their relations, labels and thinking skills, may be more important than so-called sensory or perceptual deprivation. And while the preschool and early school periods are crucial, the modifiability of intellectual capacities by changed conditions even in adolescence has been underestimated.

Certain types of visual discrimination are strengthened in environments where they are important for survival. But the evidence for the effects of ecological environment (e.g. "carpenteredness" vs. rounded, and open-vista vs. closely filled) on susceptibility to illusions is conflicting. Perceptual development seems to depend to a greater extent on social norms, education and acculturation. Clearly however many African peoples have difficulties with analytic perception of figures and pictures, and with three-dimensional interpretation. This deficiency is not found among other quite backward groups such as Eskimos. Its origins are obscure, and it may be remediable by appropriate training, but the main explanation would seem to lie in lack of visual-kinaesthetic experience and of encouragement of play and exploration throughout childhood.

The interactions of language with thinking are highly complex and controversial. But a child's language, which is wholly shaped by his cultural group, must be intimately involved in his perceptions and conceptualisations of the world. Hence his intellectual development is highly vulnerable to poverty of linguistic stimulation, and to the inadequacies of the mother-tongue—in many societies—as a medium for education. Bernstein's analysis of "formal" and "public" language codes describes the extremes of a continuum which is typical not only of the British socioeconomic classes, but applies in many respects to technological as against more primitive cultures. Bernstein brings out also the close connection between linguistic training and cultural values: the formal code is associated with internalised controls (Superego formation), high educational aspirations and planning for the future; the public code with externally imposed discipline and with less purposeful attitudes to life.

Infant rearing practices and maternal deprivation may cause temporary emotional traumata, and seem to be associated with certain cultural traits. But their long-term effects on personality and particularly on the development of abilities, are more dubious. A number of investigations indicate that socialisation practices and the home "climate" during preschool and school years are more influential. The "democratic" but demanding home climate makes for better intellectual progress than the over-protective, the autocratic or the "unconcerned" homes. The work in this area of Witkin and his colleagues provides important evidence that the encouragement of resourcefulness and independence in growing children leads to greater clarity and differentiation of perceptions and concepts, while maternal over-protection tends rather to favour verbal abilities. It is not clear whether it is general intelligence or spatial abilities which are chiefly affected, nor what parts are played in causation by social-class differences, by sex or temperament, or by masculine identification, etc. However Witkin's generalisations have fruitful applications to differences between cultural groups, e.g. Eskimos and certain African groups.

Turning then to intellectual progress at school: the major researches in the UK of E. Fraser, Wiseman and Warburton, and J.W.B. Douglas, are outlined. These show that, although the handicaps of poverty are much less marked than 40 years ago, socioeconomic class and its associated conditions of child care, neighbourhood morale, and good or poor schooling, still make substantial differences to children's intelligence and achievement. Even between 8 and 11 years the differential between the middle-class and lower-working class child becomes progressively greater. But the most important factor of all appears to be the cultural level of the home and the parents' interest in and aspirations for their children's education. Hence the fur-

ther improvements that we would desire in material conditions, social welfare and schooling, will not of themselves eliminate the handicaps of the lower working and less educated classes.

Much the same factors are shown to be significant by research in the USA, though the major differences there are not so much between socioeconomic classes as between ethnic and linguistic groups, i.e. between whites and negroes or recent immigrants. American negroes tend to score in the low 80s on tests of intelligence and achievement, though there are considerable geographic variations, and differences on different types of test. Moreover younger children perform better and show a cumulative deficit at later ages. Negroes are at least as handicapped in non-verbal or spatial tests as in verbal abilities, though relatively better in simple number and rote learning tests; and this may be attributable to familial factors such as the frequent absence of masculine identification models for boys. The interpretation and implications of observed differences in abilities have given rise to even more heated controversy in the USA. At the same time there have been valuable positive efforts to reduce the handicaps of "disadvantaged" children by compensatory or introductory schooling, or by integrating schools of different ethnic composition. It is too early to say how successful these measures are in improving general intellectual growth and scholastic performance, or whether the effects of home upbringing and of intergroup suspicions are too strong.

There is rather little evidence of the effects of different kinds of schooling, or of studying different subjects in different ways, on general mental growth. But it is clear that sheer amount of schooling, even—in backward countries—of low quality education, helps to promote both school achievement and the kind of reasoning measured by non-verbal tests. Also if such schooling is unduly delayed, the possibilities of mental growth deteriorate. The acquisition of lower-order schemata opens up the way to higher-order thinking, but they can also become rigidified and block further progress. Likewise in western countries the level of adult intelligence depends on the kind and amount of intellectual stimulation provided by the adolescent's secondary schooling and occupation. The notion of optimal or critical periods for learning probably has less applicability to conceptual than to sensory-motor functions, and greater importance should be attached to motivational factors — to the maintenance or repression of curiosity, and to the child's or young adult's aspirations and prospects of advancement. In this sense growth depends on the future as well as on the past.

Cultural groups and subgroups are exceedingly varied, and so also must be their effects on the intellectual growth of their members. A number of attempted classifications or typologies are examined, and it seems reasonable to regard the Puritan ethic of the western middle class as producing the greatest development of intelligence, in contrast both to western lower class and to the "less civilised" cultures. The two latter differ in important respects, but the less civilised can be subdivided into hunting and agricultural types, which coincide rather closely with Witkin's field-independent and dependent; i.e. they are to some extent linked with the major group-factors of spatial and verbal abilities.

The evidence in the preceding Part that Intelligence B is built up in response to environmental stimulation and is therefore affected in many ways by cultural differences does not mean that tests constructed in western cultures are always worthless elsewhere. Despite the valuation of different skills in different ethnic groups, all groups have increasing need for complex, symbolic thinking. Researches in Africa and other countries in fact show that adaptations of western tests possess promising validity in assessing educational aptitudes and work effectiveness, though this may be partly because they are measuring language skills required for advanced schooling in the former situation, or acculturation and cooperativeness with white employers in the latter. Correlations with job efficiency assessments (which tend to be unreliable) are low, but this is true in western cultures also. However tests may often be inappropriate not so much because they do not measure useful abilities as because they are also greatly affected by unfamiliarity with the materials, or with the testing situation, or by other irrelevant "extrinsic" factors.

Cross-cultural comparisons are unavoidable when members of different cultural groups or subgroups, who have very likely been reared under different conditions and are differently handicapped, are in competition for the same schooling or same jobs. Different regression equations, or different norms or cut-offs for acceptance, may be needed for such groups. Another legitimate cross-cultural application is for studying the effects of different background conditions on abilities . . . .

Unsophisticated testees are handicapped in many ways by lack of relevant experience, failure to understand the instructions, and absence of the motivations and sets which sophisticated testees bring with them to the testing situation. However the distinction between these extrinsic factors, and intrinsic factors which affect the underlying ability, is only a relative one. Probably it is best defined in terms of how readily the handicap can be overcome, e.g. by better conditions of administration. A bimodal score distribution or the piling up of low scores among "non-starters" is another useful indication of extrinsic difficulties. Also differences in the order of item difficulty may show that a test is measuring different things in different groups. However a number of investigations of practice effects among Africans indicate that these are not so large as is sometimes supposed, particularly when the testees have received some schooling. The results are comparable to those obtained with unsophisticated testees in the UK, and the same kind of measures used to familiarise British children with tests can be applied or extended. The suggestion that abilities should be judged from scores on several successive administrations, i.e. from learning curves, is technically unsound.

It is obviously far more difficult to transfer western-type tests to relatively unacculturated groups, with little or no schooling, and the psychologist may have to confine himself to individual testing with specially constructed materials, under informal conditions. However Biesheuvel's work shows that it is possible to get across performance tests to groups of linguistically heterogenous and illiterate adults; and Schwarz has formulated a series of useful principles for giving group tests, e.g., to applicants for technical training, which amount to teaching the testees beforehand precisely what they have to do. For most purposes it would be better to construct new tests based on materials and conditions appropriate to the culture concerned, than to adapt western ones, though this is difficult in view of the shortage of trained personnel. It is essential to validate old or new tests locally and to devise an appropriate system of norming.

In attempting to assess the educational potential of immigrant children, verbal tests are preferable to non-verbal or performance — either standard tests in English if they can communicate in it, or if not then similar tests in their own tongues. Alternatively a varied battery should be given and the results interpreted in the light of their educational, linguistic and social history, i.e. clinically. Objective tests of achievement are being produced in many developing countries and used on a large scale for secondary school selection. Less progress has been made with aptitude tests, e.g., for technical training, largely because, in the absence of suitable background experience, the skills needed for technical work are too undeveloped to provide a basis for worthwhile tests.

Also described are the present writer's investigations in which a battery of varied group and individual tests was applied to small groups of 10-12-year boys in England, Scotland (the Hebrides), Jamaica, Uganda and Canada (Indians and Eskimos). All the boys were being educated in the English medium. The chief aim was —

not to show that some groups are more backward than others — but to link up patterns of scores on different types of tests with differences of background. No intelligence tests as such were used. The main categories were:

(a) Verbal and educational — arithmetic, silent reading and English, oral vocabulary, rote learning and learning of meaningful information.
(b) Induction — versions of the Shipley Abstraction and the Matrices test.
(c) Conceptual development — sorting and labelling, and a series of Piaget tasks dealing with conservation and other concepts.
(d) 'Creativity' tests of fluency and imagination.
(e) Perceptual and spatial tests, including Kohs Blocks, Embedded Figures, Bender-Gestalt, Porteus Mazes and Draw-a-Man.

In interpreting what the tests measure, reference is made to previous evidence of their validity, and to factorial analyses of the scores in several groups. The scores on each test were converted into Deviation Quotients or Standard Scores (similar to IQs), on the basis of the distributions in the English group, so that relative performance on different tests could be compared. Each boy was also interviewed, usually by a local teacher, to obtain information on his background, home, schooling, interests and vocational aspirations.

Within the English group, the g factor, or general ability in all the tests, correlated highly with an assessment of Cultural Stimulus in the home, and to a lesser extent with Socioeconomic level and with Planfulness or Purposiveness of

the home; but there was no correlation with Stable vs. Broken homes. The educational, verbal, perceptual and practical group factors, measured by particular groups of tests, also gave small correlations with several background conditions, though there was only limited support for the hypothesis that masculine dominance in the home and encouragement of initiative are associated with perceptual-spatial abilities.

Small groups of delinquent boys in an Approved School, and maladjusted children, gave unusual patterns of scores. The delinquents were very low in educational attainments, but also in the two Induction tests and certain perceptual tests. Their oral vocabulary, concept development and rote learning were rather better (quotients in the 80s); on some performance tests they scored in the 90s, and their performance on creativity tests was close to average. The maladjusted boys were specially backward in arithmetic, less so in verbal abilities; they were near average in concept development and in most spatial-perceptual tests and above average in creativity. The poor reasoning of the former, and the well-developed ability of the latter to deal with concrete notions of space, conservation, etc. — in contrast to their disturbed emotional and social relations — suggest that a wide-ranging battery of ability tests may be valuable diagnostically. In addition the Drawing and Creativity tests have projective possibilities. Socioeconomic level, Planfulness and Regular Schooling were found to correlate moderately with verbal and educational performance, but not Broken Home or Parental Tension. Patterns of family relationships, mother or father dominance and affection or rejection, together with neurotic, aggressive or other syndromes, seemed to be related to test scores, but in no clear-cut manner.

A group of Scottish Hebridean boys was tested in or near Stornoway, Isle of Lewis; half of them were from English-speaking, half from Gaelic-speaking, homes. Apart from the linguistic differences, both groups are of interest as growing up in a relatively isolated community, free from the rush of modern civilisation. There are strong traditions of responsible and provident living, of rather rigid upbringing, and respect for formal education. The Gaelic-background group was handicapped in oral vocabulary, the Sorting test and Piaget, but did not differ significantly from the English-background boys in other respects. Both were superior to English norms in scholastic achievement and learning tests, though there was some restriction in originality. The test correlations were unusual in showing no distinction between g and verbal abilities. This does not seem to be due so much to linguistic heterogeneity as to a strong contrast between the more culturally stimulating and sophisticated homes vs. the more traditional and restricted.

Turning now to our deprived groups — two of African and two of indigenous Canadian origin: we will first summarise the cultural and other characteristics most likely to affect their ability development, and then compare and discuss the test results. Jamaica is a country in transition from a primitive agricultural to a technological economy, and the population ranges from extremely poor, largely illiterate and superstitious rural communities — descendents of African slaves — to a well-educated middle class, often of mixed descent. The sample of boys for testing was drawn from schools representing all levels. The mother tongue of the majority is a kind of pidgin English which considerably impedes education, and primary schooling tends to be irregular, of poor quality, and far too formal and repressive of initiative. Family life is apt to be unstable, female-dominated and likewise conformist and authoritarian.

Uganda is basically a rural subsistence economy, with a low standard of living and much malnutrition, though the writer's sample was derived mainly from urbanised East Africans living in or near to Kampala, i.e. a relatively acculturated group. As in many African countries there is a diversity of tribes with different dialects. Education is mainly conducted in English, though the language is seldom used by the children outside the classroom. Schooling is available only for about one third of this age group, but it is greatly prized. Because of the language difficulties (among teachers as well as pupils) and the strong motivation, and for historical reasons, education tends to be highly mechanical. But the major differences between African and western intelligences probably arise more from the emphasis on conformity and social integration as against individual responsibility and internal controls; and from the acceptance of magical beliefs which inhibit analytic perception and rational thinking.

Canadian Indians and Eskimos are equally disadvantaged linguistically, though English has greater currency in transactions with the white culture, and is freely used by Eskimo boys in and outside school. The quality of schooling is good also, especially in our Eskimo sample, though attendance may be delayed or irregular. The majority of families live at a low economic and cultural level, and show the traditional improvidence, or generous sharing now, rather than planning for the future. Vocational prospects for the boys are poor, partly because of geographical difficulties and partly because of the reputation of the indigenes for shiftlessness; also because of the apathy and demoralisation consequent on the breakdown of the traditional hunting economies and, in the case of reservation Indians, their continued resentment and resistance to acculturation. At the same time, the traditional child-rearing practices and values mean that boys of 10-12 years are still trained for resourcefulness and show strong identification with hunting and other masculine pursuits. This was most marked among a sample of Eskimo boys boarding at a school hostel, whose families still tend to live on the land rather than in settlements.

Table 1 provides a crude summary of the main handicaps thought to operate in nine of the above groups or subgroups, together with the main features of their test score patterns. In the top half are listed assessments of environmental conditions, *relative to those of children in western cultures.* Inevitably these are somewhat subjective, though backed up by the descriptions of these groups in preceding chapters.[1] Below, the groups are first graded on all-round ability, and then for *relatively* better or poorer performance on particular sets of tests, i.e., they are *compared with their own means* rather than with English standards. All-round ability is roughly graded, a single minus indicating a mean quotient of about 87-93, a double minus about

80-85. It should be pointed out that most of these groups are *not* representative samples. They are drawn from school attenders only; some groups are a little older than others; and the Ugandans, in particular, come mainly from urbanised families of above average socio-economic level.

Nevertheless there is clearly a general correspondence between the numbers of adverse conditions and overall performance: the main exceptions, who score lower than might be expected from their backgrounds, are the three most socially maladjusted groups — Maladjusted, Delinquents and Indians. It may be seen that the assessment of Cultural Stimulus is most diagnostic of all-round ability; most other variables overlap but show greater discrepancies (for example, Ugandans are among the lowest scorers though relatively high socioeconomically). Had we had a considerably larger number of groups and more objective techniques of comparing their relative standing on these environmental conditions, it would have been interesting to correlate each condition with the group scores.

Several other fairly close correspondences are apparent. Thus the lan-

[1] Perceptual-kinaesthetic stimulation is, perhaps, the most dubious. It is meant to refer to availability of toys, manipulable objects, and rich and varied non-verbal experiences. Clearly this is something which is lacking in African upbringing; but are not Eskimos, living in the Arctic, also deprived in this respect? And it hardly seems fair to equate the tranquillity of life in the Hebrides, and its somewhat reduced contacts with modern civilization, with this type of deprivation.

Table 1 *Environmental Conditions and Test Score Patterns in Nine Groups*

Conditions	Maladj.	Delin.	Hebr. Engl.	Hebr. Gael.	Jamaica	Ugandan	Indian	Esk. Town	Esk. Host.
Socioeconomic level		−			−		−	−	−
Providence-planfulness		−	+	+			−	−	−
Cultural Stimulus		−	+		−	−	−	−	−
Language				−	−	−	−		
Adequacy of Schooling			+	+	−	−			
Progressive vs. formal	+		−	−	−	−			
Encouragement of initiative						−	−	+	+
Home security and stability	−	−				−			−
Perceptual-Kinaesthetic stimulation			?−	?−	−	−			
Health, Nutrition					−	−		−	−
Deficiencies in: All-round level	−	− −			− −	− −	− −	−	−
Induction		−			−		−		+
School attainments	−	−	+	+			−	−	−
Oral English and comprehension				−	−	−	−	−	−
Conservation	+			−	+	−	−	−	
Memorising	−		+	+	+	+	−		
Fluency and originality	+	+				+		+	+
Practical-spatial	+		−	−	−	−	+	+	+
Perceptual	−		−	−		+			
Drawing		+			+	+	+	+	+

guage rating, based on lack of English in the home, is naturally related to deficiency in Oral English and Comprehension, though not so closely to School Attainments or to Fluency. Formality of schooling always tends to produce superior performance in Memorising (i.e. the Word Learning test + Spelling), but good School Attainments in English and arithmetic seems to be more related to the Providence or Planfulness rating of the average home. On the non-verbal side, the connections are less clear-cut, and give only limited support to the hypothesis that spatial ability is favoured by a hunting economy, or by cultures which train for initiative. Performance on the perceptual tests (mainly Embedded Figures, Design Reproduction and Mazes) does not correspond with any of the environmental variables. However practical-spatial ability (Kohs, Formboard and Picture Recognition) does tend to go with Encouragement of Initiative, and to some extent with Perceptual-Kinaesthetic Stimulation. Inductive ability also seems to be related to Initiative. What we can say is that there is a closer resemblance in test score patterns between Jamaicans (descended from West Africans) and East Africans, also between Indians and Eskimos, than across these two groups. Although our tests fail to pin down very clearly the essential ability factors in which they differ, Kohs Blocks — which mainly measures inductive + spatial ability — comes nearest to doing so. Thus 66 per cent of all the Jamaicans and (highly selected) Ugandans as against 22 percent of Indians and Eskimos scored under 10 points on this test. In contrast the Jamaicans and Ugandans were much superior in Word Learning and Arithmetic despite roughly equivalent linguistic handicap.

The results of our enquiries show that we cannot afford to ignore the factor of general retardation. On the whole these groups and those inidividuals who are most backward in, say, linguistic tests also tend to be below average on all other types of tests. Nevertheless there are considerable irregularities in score patterns, and we have made a little, though not very much, progress in explaining why particular groups do some things much better than others.

Some of the main results in particular groups are as follows: the Jamaicans, in common with others, were noticeably more successful on standard classroom tests of English (including multiple-choice vocabulary) and arithmetic than on oral comprehension of language. Thus western tests of verbal intelligence and achievements are less unsuitable, e.g. for school selection purposes, than might be supposed, though naturally western norms are apt to be misleading. Much more striking is their deficiency on non-verbal materials such as Matrices, Kohs and Formboard (the latter test probably being additionally affected by conditions of health and nutrition), though relatively high on perceptual and drawing tests. They differ most markedly from Africans on the Piaget tasks, probably due to their greater sophistication, their many contacts with British and American cultures, the absence of tribalism and fewer magical beliefs. But there were big differences on most of the tests between the urban boys, who were within the normal English range (except in comprehension and induction) and the rural ones who are much less touched by modern civilisation. Somewhat as in the Hebridean groups, there was a closer correlation between verbal and other abilities than in English groups, suggesting that schooling and acculturation are necessary to development on the perceptual-spatial side. This may arise when many of the homes provide little stimulus to any kind of intellectual development, or even repress such development.

The Ugandan group was the most handicapped of any in oral vocabulary, although they were supposed to have been taught in English for five years. This seemed to be due, at least partly, to their unfamiliarity in analysing words out of context. But the effects of their very formal schooling were manifest in high spelling and rote memorising. A particular retardation was noted also in the conservation items of the Piaget tests, and in three-dimensional interpretation of pictures, both of which confirm previous observations of African abilities. On the other hand there was no general retardation on the spatial-perceptual side; Gottschaldt Figures, for example, Drawing and Mazes were within the normal range. The structuring of abilities differed markedly from that in other groups: instead of verbal abilities (in English) permeating intellectual development generally, they were relatively distinct from other types of ability — inductive, practical-perceptual and imaginative. There seems to be a clear need for greater integration of their learning of English with daily life, based on less mechanical, more active, methods; also for the introduction of greater opportunities for concrete, practical training to compensate for the inadequacies of psychomotor stimulation in the homes.

The interests of the majority of Eskimo and Indian boys still lie mainly in hunting, trapping, fishing or riding and ice-hockey. But those who were tested were attending good schools, on the Canadian pattern, and had made some progress in classroom English, less in oral comprehension, in Piaget-type concepts or in arithmetic (where they are handicapped by "the new" mathematics). In most other respects Eskimos who have had some exposure to schooling tend to score within the normal range, and are generally superior to the Indians, partly because of the greater apathy and uncooperativeness of most Indian families. Eskimo hostel boarders do better than those living in settlements on tests of induction and concept development, indicating that these abilities are promoted by the more resourceful and independent mode of existence. Indians are particularly restricted in imaginative ideas, i.e. they receive no encouragement to think "divergently." All groups are good at drawing, and their relatively high scores on spatial tests suggest mechanical potentialities. An unusual feature of the general factor in Eskimo test scores was that it does not correlate with cultural and economic characteristics of the homes, but does with amount of schooling. Probably therefore it is much less developed among the indigenous population who obtain less regular or no schooling. In the Indians, on the other hand, it correlated highly with an assessment of the initiative or morale vs. apathy of the boy and his family . . . .

References

Bernstein, B.B. Social class and linquistic development: A theory of social learning. In A.H. Halsey, *Education, Economy and Society.* Glencoe: The Free Press, 1961, 288-314.

Biesheuvel, S. The study of African ability. *African Stud.*, 1952, II, 45-58, 105-117.

Bruner, J.S. The course of cognitive growth. *Amer. Psychologist*, 1964, 19, 1-15.

Brunner, J.S. The growth of mind. *Amer. Psychologist*, 1965, 20, 1007-1017.

Douglas, J.W.B. *The Home and the School.* London: McGibbon and Kee, 1964.

Fraser, E. *Home Environment and the School.* London: University of London Press, 1959.

Piaget, J. *The Psychology of Intelligence.* London: Routledge, 1950.

Schwarz, P.A. *Aptitude Tests for Use in Developing Nations.* Pittsburgh: American Institute for Research, 1961.

Warburton, F.W. The ability of the Gurkha recruit. *Brit. J. Psychology,* 1951, **42**, 123-133.

Wiseman, S. *Education and Environment.* Manchester University Press, 1964.

Wiseman, S. Environmental and innate factors and educational attainment, in J.E. Meade and A.S. Parkes, *Genetic and Environmental Factors in Human Ability.* Edinburgh: Oliver and Boyd, 1966, 64-80.

Witkin, H.A. and Dyk, R.B. et al. *Psychological Differentiation: Studies of Development.* New York: John Wiley, 1962.

BARBARA E. HAVASSY—DEAVILA

A Critical Review of the Approach to Birth Order Research*

Interest in birth order, or ordinal position, has been concentrated primarily on finding birth order differences, i.e., characteristics which are thought to be differentially distributed among those of different birth ranks. This interest in differences can be seen in the earliest birth order studies (e.g., Mitchell, 1866) as well as in the more recent ones.

Though the spectrum of work on birth order differences is broad both in terms of the number of years during which they have been studied and the type of differences studied; just how birth order functions in relation to demonstrated differences between siblings is no better understood today than it was in the late 19th century. In fact, one characteristic which early and recent birth order studies have in common is their lack of attention to the processes which underlie birth order differences. That is, the research on birth order has been markedly atheoretical. Moreover, those theoretical formulations which do exist in birth order research are *ad hoc,* following from a specific study and based on a specific set of data. Such a

*From the *Canadian Psychologist,* 1971, **12**, 282-305. Reprinted by permission of the author and the Canadian Psychological Association.

situation would not be undersirable if one researcher's *ad hoc* theory served as a theoretical basis for another's study. But such a systematic methodical approach is rarely found in the ordinal position literature.

This emphasis on differences, combined with the general failure to ask the "why" questions about birth order, has led to widespread ambiguity and equivocality in the birth order literature.

This paper will argue that the appropriate target of psychological investigation with respect to birth order is not the gathering of differences, but the investigation of the psychological processes which result in birth order differences. To this end, we will critically review some of the literature and problem areas related to it. Then we will suggest a means of directing psychological inquiry to the question of the origin of birth order differences.

REVIEW OF THE LITERATURE

The characteristic which seems to best typify the literature is inconsistency. As space does not permit an exhaustive review, the following studies were included on the basis of two criteria: they illustrate the equivocality encountered in the literature and they are of psychological relevance. Many are considered "classic" birth order studies. The review covers the following research topics: child-rearing practices; affiliation, dependence and conformity; intelligence and achievement; and alcoholism.

Child-Rearing Practices

Researchers who attempt to explain birth order differences generally locate their source in varying child-rearing practices and parental attitudes toward children of different birth orders within the same family. It is not difficult to accept the idea that child-rearing practices and attitudes of parents can vary from early to later borns and given that they do, this would have great importance for birth order differences.

In perhaps the most widely known work on birth order, that by Schachter (1959), there are several *ad hoc* theoretical formulations with regard to varying child-rearing practices associated with ordinal position differences. Schachter believes that "the first birth is an event of profound psychological and philosophical importance for the parents and that later births are events of considerably less moment [1959, p. 79]." He suggests that the greater importance of the first birth in combination with the inexperience and insecurity of new parents will result in over-protection and inconsistent treatment of the first born child.

Warren (1966) also has theorized with respect to the relationship of child-rearing techniques to birth order differences. He has said:

Firstborns, for some period of their life, have only adult models in their immediate family and are free from competition from siblings for parental attention. Later-born children find more competition for parental attention and have older siblings as well as adults as models [Warren, 1966, p. 39].

Altus (1966) attributed part of the cause of birth order differences to varying child-rearing practices. He states that:

the most prominent of the presumed social 'causes' is likely to be the differential parental treatment accorded children of different ordinal positions, to greater 'conscience' development, greater dependence on adult norms, and higher expectations of achievement falling to the lot of the first born [Altus, 1966, p. 48].

The empirical studies on birth order and child-rearing practices are not numerous. One of the earlier studies was Lasko (1954), who compared ratings of mothers' behavior (Fels Parent Behavior Scales) towards first born and second born siblings when each of the sibs was of the same age. On only 2 of the 21 variables on which the mother-child relationship was rated did first and second borns differ significantly; no more than would be expected by chance alone. What is of interest is the pattern of significant correlations found between ratings of mothers' behavior toward the first and second born children. The correlations indicate a significant consistency in the mothers' policies and techniques of managing her children, but no consistency in the quality of her emotional relationship. This finding, combined with differences on "warmth" variables (e.g., "approval") which favor the second child (though they are not statistically significant), led Lasko to believe that parent behavior toward the first born child, on the average, is less warm and more restrictive and coercive than with the second child.

These correlational patterns between first and second borns hold up, though less distinctly, in a comparison of second and third born children (Lasko, 1954). Lasko (1954) suggests that the mother develops an attitude of warmth combined with strictness as she has more children. Furthermore, these and other data led Lasko to conclude that the mother's behavior toward the second child does not tend to change systematically as the child grows older, whereas such changes do occur in the treatment of the first child in the direction of reduced mother-child interaction.

Rosen's (1964) data indicate a relationship between ordinal position and age of training in independence mastery, which generally tends to support the notion of reduced mother-child interaction for first borns. Of the only children, 55% were trained "early"; of the oldest children, 54% were trained "early"; while 43% of the intermediate children, and 32% of the youngest were trained "early." The measure employed was 7 of the 20 items of the Winterbottom (1958) test. Rosen (1964) did not indicate why these particular 7 items were selected. Furthermore, these results should be accepted only conditionally as no tests of difference between the groups were reported.

Hilton (1967) had observers rate mother-child interaction during a task sequence for the child with the mother as an onlooker. Mothers of first born children were rated more involved in their child's performance than mothers of later borns ($p<.05$). In spite of instructions to remain unobtrusive, mothers of first and only children were more likely to signal their child to start working than were mothers of later borns (by X^2, $p<.005$). Mothers of first borns also gave more task-oriented suggestions throughout the task sequence than did mothers of later borns ($p<.001$). Furthermore, of 18 mothers who disregarded instructions to remain seated while their child performed the task, 15 were mothers of first born and only children (by X^2, $p<.08$). It appears then, that the mothers of first and only children were more interfering than mothers of later born children. Mothers of first born children were also more extreme in their affect towards the child (number of overt demonstrations of love, $p<.001$); as well as more inconsistent than later borns' mothers (degree of maintenance of demonstrations of love over two experimental sessions, $p<.001$). In addition, when mothers of first borns discovered that their child was doing poorly (an experimental manipulation), they exhibited a significant decrement in level of verbal support which was not the case for mothers of later borns ($p<.03$).

By showing the fluctuations of a mother's behavior towards the first child and how relatively more stable the behavior is towards the second child, Hilton provided some support for Lasko's (1954) conclusion that mothers' behavior toward the first child tends to change, while the treatment of the second child tends to be stable.

Another study concerned with the same general phenomena is by Sears, Maccoby & Levin (1957). In interviewing mothers of five year olds, they found many significant birth order differences in child-rearing practices. In obtaining these differences, however, there was no control for family size. When family size was controlled, significant results were inconsistent and sporadic. Nevertheless, there are some general patterns to be found in the data which should be noted. First, fewer youngest children tend to be breast-fed. The difference is probably not

reliable for two-child families ($p = .12$), but in three-child families more oldest children were breast-fed than middle or youngest children ($p<.05$). Second, in two-child families there is a tendency for mothers to begin the first child's bowel training earlier than the second child's ($p<.05$). This difference is not found in three-child families. Last, it appears that mothers are more generally pleased over the first pregnancy than later ones ($p = .02$ for two-child families and $p<.01$ for three-child families).

Henry (1957) studied the way children view these differences in parental treatment. His findings suggest that the disciplining of the older child is perceived by children as being transferred from mother to father as family size increases. Youngest males in the 9th and 10th grades and youngest females in the 11th and 12th grades were more likely to say their mother was the disciplinarian than oldest males and females in the same grades ($p<.01$ for each sex separately.)

Thus, it seems that first born children are somehow special with respect to parental treatment, although exactly how they are is not agreed upon. A closer examination of the data cited above reveals little consistency with respect to what is different about treatment of first borns. Three examples illustrate this point. First, is the question of whether parents overprotect first borns. Schacter (1959) says they do; Rosen (1964) found that first borns are generally trained to be independent at an earlier age than are later borns; Hilton's (1967) data show mothers of first borns to be interfering; while Lasko's (1954) data indicate mothers who are"babying" and "protective" tend to be so with both first and second born children. Second, is the question of whether first borns are preferred children. The Sears et al. (1957) data indicate that they are (that mothers are more pleased about the first pregnancy than about later ones); whereas Lasko's (1954) data indicate that the first born has a less warm relationship with his mother than does the later born. Third, is the alleged inconsistent treatment of first borns proposed by Schacter (1959). Just what is entailed by inconsistent treatment is unclear. Hilton (1967) found mothers to behave inconsistently towards their frist borns across two experimental situations; whereas Lasko (1954) found mothers to behave inconsistently across two children, i.e., the emotional relationship of mothers to their second borns could not be predicted from their relationship to first borns. Is the issue that parents' treatment of second borns cannot be predicted from their treatment of first borns, or is it that they are inconsistent in their treatment of first borns, or both? Although some of Lasko's (1954) data led her to conclude that parental treatment of the second child does not change systematically while that of the first does, this does not clear up the question.

Affiliation, Dependence, and Conformity

The researcher who first juxtaposed the concepts of affiliation, dependence, and conformity with birth order was Schacter (1959). He found that under stress only and first born females tended to withdraw ($p < .01$). Schachter's (1959) further experimentation indicated that the result persisted.

Affiliation. Although the birth order differences appeared to be stable for Schacter (1959), a replication of his experimental design conducted soon after Schachter's results were published (Weller, 1962) failed to obtain the results of the original study. The only difference between the two studies was that the subjects attended different universities.

Whatever the true relationship between birth order, stress, and affiliation, Schachter's (1959) research on ordinal position had great heuristic value deriving from the two explanations he proposed to account for his findings. The first is that affiliation in times of stress serves as a direct reduction of anxiety. The second attributes such affiliation to the desire to determine the "appropriate" reaction to the situation. Three studies, representative of the many stimulated by these explanations of affiliative behavior under stress are discussed below.

Wrightsman (1960) in examining these two explanations in an experimental situation similar to Schachter's (1959) found that the first explanation, direct reduction of anxiety, was observed only for first born subjects ($p < .05$). The second explanation held true for the entire sample ($p < .05$). Thus, it would appear that under stress, a fairly common reaction is to seek out others in order to find out what others are feeling. But, such seeking out of others appears to provide more actual reduction of anxiety for first borns than for others.

Gerard & Rabbie (1961) examined the explanation that the tendency to affiliate under stressful situations arises from the person's desire to compare his fear or anxiety with that of others. The results of this study partially support Schachter's (1959) findings: first born women, under stress, expressed stronger desires to be with others than did later born women ($p<.01$). Yet, the tendency for later born women to withdraw, as reported by Schachter was not found; almost all of the women in the study chose to be with others. Furthermore, for the males in this sample ($n = 29$), the tendency was reversed: of the 19 males who sought to be with others when under stress, later born males generally had a stronger desire to be with others than did only or first born males ($p<.07$), though the reliability of this difference is questionable.

Ring, Lipinski & Braginsky (1965) also conducted research concerning the direct anxiety reduction and emotional comparison explanations of affiliation put forth by Schachter (1959). They assumed that first borns have a greater need for both self-evaluation (emotional comparison) and anxiety reduction than do later borns. The experimentally manipulated variables were "opportunity for anxiety reduction" and "ease of self-evaluation." With respect to birth order, they found several interesting results. Close inspection of then, however, reveals they are not as unequivocal as they initially appear. For example, first borns became less calm (self-rated) while "waiting for an experiment" with others (confederates) as compared to later borns ($.02<p<.05$), and after the prearranged interaction with confederates in the waiting room, they were still less calm than later borns ($p<.0005$). If we can say "less calm" is equivalent to "more anxious," then it appears that first borns did not find reduced anxiety in affiliation as compared to later borns (in contrast to the Wrightsman (1960) finding). Although Ring et al. (1965) obtained the self-ratings on anxiety, they did not use these but employed the self-ratings on "calm" because they felt that "calm" is much less ambiguous a word than "anxious." They cite no data to support this contention.

Another aspect of the Ring et al. (1965) data would indicate that first borns converge toward the perceived emotional level of others more than do later borns. But this conclusion, based on two findings, is questioned for the following reasons. First, the conclusion is based on a three-way analysis of variance (ANO-VA) of "convergence" scores, with ordinal position effect significant at $p<.05$. However examination of cell means for the four experimental conditions indicates that in one condition there was no difference on convergence scores between first borns and later borns (means -5.00 vs. -5.90), and in another condition first borns actually tended to converge less than later borns (-11.43 vs. -1.67). It was only in the remaining two conditions where the differences indicating first borns tend to converge more than later borns (10.00 vs. -23.33 and 26.67 vs. -9.17) are found. Thus it can be seen that the main effect of ordinal position is actually due to the behavior of first borns in two experimental conditions. Ring et al. (1965) do not report performing any post-hoc comparisons of their cell data.

Second, the conclusion was based on a finding for all subjects who changed on the "calm" self-rating. All first borns in this group moved toward the confederates' perceived level of calm whereas only half of the later borns did ($p = .01$). However, these subjects comprise only part of the sample (45%), i.e., those who did change on the "calm dimension."

Therefore, results from this analysis cannot be generalized to all first and later borns.

A study directed at the relationship between birth order and affiliation but employing a different procedure from the studies mentioned above, was done by Sampson & Hancock, (1967). They administered a modified version of the Edwards Personal Preference Schedule (EPPS—Edwards, 1953) to high school students from one- and two-child families. An ANOVA was performed on the EPPS need affiliation (nAff) items using ordinal position, sex of subject, and sex of sibling as the independent variables. There were no significant differences found, i.e., only, first and second borns, males and females, and subjects with male and female siblings did not score differently on the EPPS nAff items. Neither did groups made up of the combination of these variables differ on their scores.

A similar study utilizing college students' responses on the EPPS nAff items was performed by Waters & Kirk (1967). Subjects were divided into six groups on the basis of sex and birth order. An ANOVA performed on the scores indicated a significant difference between sex means, but no significant variation according to birth order groups.

So far, in the studies reported here, there are three studies partially supporting Schachter's (1959) finding — Gerard & Rabbie (1961), Ring et al. (1965), and Wrightsman (1960), but two of these (Ring et al., 1965 and Wrightsman, 1960) are in disagreement with each other. A study similar to the previous three, Zimbardo & Formica (1963), failed to find any relevant birth order differences. Furthermore, one replication of the original Schachter (1959) experiment (Weller, 1965) completely failed to obtain similar results; and two studies found no birth order differences in nAff as measured by the EPPS (Sampson & Hancock, 1967; Waters & Kirk, 1967). Thus we find the affiliation birth order area a confusing mass of data entangled with methodological problems — sharp contrast to the apparent clarity of the Schachter (1959) data. Such clarity seems difficult to reconcile in light of the confusion which has followed Schachter's research.

Dependence and Conformity. It was Schachter's work (1959) which brought the possible relationship of ordinal position to dependence to light. Schachter's (1959) position with respect to birth order and dependence appears to be based on three studies: that of Dean (1947), Gewirtz (1948), and Haeberle (1958).

In Dean's (1947) study, first born children were judged by their mothers to be more dependent than second born children. However, this finding must be tempered by consideration of the fallibilities of retrospective data. In the Gewirtz (1948) study, teachers rated second and later born children as being less dependent than only and first born children. In the study conducted by Haeberle (1958) at a therapeutic nursery school, a sample of three to six year olds was rated on overt dependency behavior. Only and first born males (together) had significantly higher dependency ratings than later born males ($p<.05$). Females showed no significant difference. For both sexes combined first born and only children were significantly more dependent than later borns ($p<.01$).

Schachter's position then, with respect

to dependence and birth order is that greater dependence, as defined by the "extent to which the individual uses or relies on other persons as sources of approval, support, help, and reference (Schachter, 1959, p. 82)," is developed in first borns. Furthermore, it is this dependence which is believed to mediate the relationship between birth order and affiliation. Though Schachter takes this position, he does not indicate how dependence is different from affiliation, for the "extent to which an individual uses or relies on others . . ." is, or can be, the extent to which he affiliates. Schachter does not indicate how he would differentiate affiliative from dependent behavior in a given situation.

In some recent research, stimulated in part by Schachter, Hilton's (1967) observers rated first borns as significantly more dependent than other children ($p<.001$). First borns also were more likely to cling to their mothers when they were told to sit at a table while their mothers went into the next room (by X^2, $p<.05$). They were more likely to persist in this behavior when they had been told to return to the table than were later borns (by X^2, $p<.05$). Finally, they were more likely to ask for direct help and reassurance than were later borns (by X^2, $p<.05$). Are these behaviors affiliation or dependence?

The confusion between dependence and other constructs in birth order research has given rise to results which are equivocal. For example, in the previously cited study by Sampson & Hancock (1967), the scores of subjects (from one- and two-child families) on the EPPS need Autonomy (nAut) items were compared via a three-way ANOVA. A significant main effect of ordinal position was found ($p<.001$). Sampson & Hancock (1967) claim to have found first borns scoring higher than second borns with the "only-child groups . . . fall(ing) at the extremes of their own sex grouping (p. 404)," i.e., only child males being the lowest scoring (lowest nAut) of all males. All that may be safely concluded from the reported cell difference tests (Scheffé, 1959), however, is that only children scored significantly lower than other birth order groups. There are no cell differences reported which would indicate that first borns score significantly higher than second borns. In fact, examination of cell mean scores indicate that second born males with a female sib score higher than first born males with a female sib. Nevertheless, if first borns did score significantly higher than second borns on nAut, this result would be difficult to interpret in light of the frequent finding that first borns are more dependent than second borns.

The following study further demonstrates the entanglement of dependence with other constructs, in this case conformity. As will be seen, what is called conformity may just as easily be called dependence, especially if Schachter's definition is applied.

Becker, Lerner & Carroll (1964) introduced a large or small payoff for a correct judgment in the Asch (1956) situation. They hypothesized that first borns tend to be influenced by normative pressures to conform, while later borns, because of their experience with other siblings, tend to be influenced by informational pressures to conform. The small payoff, given only after the entire series of judgments were made, was thought to offer incentive to resist "normative" pressures to conform. The large payoff was thought to enhance the apparent credibility of other judges (confederates), thus influencing the later borns to conform and providing the early born with an incentive to resist normative influences. The introduction of these payoffs did consistently affect the amount of yielding. First, in the control (no reward) condition, only and first borns yielded more than later borns. A small payoff led to less yielding than in the control situation for both early and later borns ($p = .05$). However, only and first borns showed the greatest reduction in yielding ($p = .006$). In contrast to expectations based on the Schachter (1959) data, later borns yielded more than early borns ($p < .01$) in the large payoff condition and more than later borns in the small payoff condition ($p < .01$). First borns' yielding behavior differed little from the small payoff to the large payoff condition.

Taking a view of the entire section on affiliation, dependence, and conformity, it becomes apparent that in the search for birth order differences, conceptual definition and clarity have been overlooked. The definitions of these three personality constructs, affiliation, dependence, and conformity are similar enough that we must ask how these three are different. One approach to this problem of conceptual definition is the multi-trait-multi-method matrix for convergent and discriminant validation proposed by Campbell & Fiske (1959). They make the point that in measuring need to affiliate, conformity and dependence, for example, by the same method, it is important to show that the respective scores are not correlated. Furthermore, in accordance with

the concept of convergent validation (Campbell & Fiske, 1959), one needs to show that different measures of need to affiliate, for example, correlate higher with each other than with similar measures of different constructs such as dependence. Without statements about the constructs along these lines, little meaning can be attached to statements pertaining to these constructs and their relationship to birth order.

Intelligence and Achievement

These two topics have been of interest for a long time to researchers concerned with birth order, e.g., Galton (1874), Ellis (1904). Earlier studies are concerned with eminence and birth order and more recent studies have to do with test performance (intelligence or achievement) and birth order.

Intelligence. Studies examining the relationship of birth order to intelligence fall into one of three categories: those which find first born and only children to be more intelligent than later borns, those showing the opposite, and those which fail to find birth order differences. Material related to these three relationships is reviewed below.

A study showing birth order differences which is representative of many birth order-intelligence studies is that by Thurstone & Jenkins (1929). A total of 1000 Stanford-Binet tests were analyzed by birth order. Thurstone & Jenkins (1929) found that average IQ increases slightly with birth order as far as the eighth born child. They also found that the variability of intelligence increased with the order of birth.

In a more elaborate approach. Hsiao

(1931) ran a study comparing the IQ of first borns to that of second borns. Hsiao's (1931) sample was 2121 first and second borns, including some first and second borns of the same family (to control for possible differences in hereditary factors of different families). The sample received four different measures of intelligence: the Stanford-Binet, the Terman Group Test of Mental Ability, the National Intelligence Test, and the Abbreviated Stanford-Binet. The analysis revealed that once the greater chronological age of the older child was corrected for, no IQ differences existed between first and second borns. It should be noted here that Hsiao controlled for the following sources of bias: family size, sex ratio of different ordinal positions, and errors of classification of first borns.

More recently, Jones (1954) argued that the supposed disadvantages of first borns, i.e., less experienced nurture by parents, less social stimulation (no older siblings) and less economic security of parents, etc., actually have a negligible effect on the mental development of the first born. Jones claims that those who have found differences between ordinal positions have made an error in interpreting their data arising from the inverse relation of birth rate and social status. Families of higher social status have fewer but more intelligent children. So, in a sample where family size is not controlled for, first and second born children will appear to have higher IQ than later borns. When family size is controlled, Jones indicates that the first born's often found unfavorable showing is because many intelligence tests are so standardized that IQ tends to drop slightly with age (Jones, 1954). This produces a lower average IQ

among earlier born children since they tend to be older when they are tested. A final error in interpretation causes later borns to appear less bright than first borns. This error arises from the fact that older maternal age, which is associated with later birth order, is also associated with a slightly greater incidence of certain types of mental defect (Jones, 1954). This often causes unfavorable IQ showing for later borns. "When these and other methodological difficulties are controlled, no birth order differences in intelligence occur in normal samples (Jones, 1954, p. 668)."

In illustration of Jones' point concerning the controlling of these methodological difficulties, is a study by Maxwell and Pillner (1960). They tested the younger siblings of a random sample of Scottish eleven year olds as they reached eleven years of age. Initially, they found the average intelligence of the younger siblings to be lower than that of the original sample. Among the explanations given for this finding is that there were losses of siblings from the subjects of the original sample which were not randomly distributed for intelligence or family size. The sibling sample was biased towards the larger families. For example, in two-child families, 44.25% of the subjects had siblings tested while in the eight-child families 90% of the subjects had siblings tested. When this difference is eliminated by taking the "average" sibling IQ per subject (and not entering each individual sibling's IQ into the correlation) the IQ differences between the subject and their siblings drop out. The resulting mean difference between subjects and "average" siblings is only about 1.3 IQ points, which is not statistically significant.

An additional study showing no birth order differences is Burton (1968). Burton (1968) analyzed birth order-intelligence data on 43,352 high school seniors (part of the Project TALENT sample). In 32 comparisons of first versus last borns' intelligence scores, controlled for sex, family size and socioeconomic status (SES), there were 15 in which first borns scored higher and 10 in which last borns scored higher. Burton (1968) indicates that though all of these differences are statistically siginificant, the mean difference in standardized intelligence scores between first and last born is 1.64, comparable to 3.28 IQ points — not a difference leading one to claim first born superiority over last born.

Thus, which birth rank members tend to appear more intelligent depends on how the study is performed. The point made by Jones (1954) that when methodological difficulties are controlled, no birth order differences in intelligence appear in normal samples is well made.

Achievement. Galton (1874) and Ellis (1904) conducted studies involving birth order and eminence. Both of these early studies showed an over-representation of first borns in the eminent category. Chen and Cobb (1960), in a review of the literature, found several studies which also indicate that first borns (excluding only children) outnumber youngest children in samples of eminent people. In a study of 261 eminent American men (Bowerman, 1947), the ratio of oldest to youngest was 2.0 (expected ratio is 1.0). Examination of the birth order of the first 33 presidents of the United States yielded a ratio of 2.0 for oldest to youngest. In a sample of 99 English men of science, the ratio of oldest to youngest

was 1.7 (Galton, 1874). A study of (male and female) British genius (Ellis, 1926) yielded a ratio of 1.4. Finally, a survey of 506 contemporary scientists yielded a ratio of 1.3, oldest to youngest (Chen & Cobb, 1960).

The recent investigations into the issue of eminence have been conducted primarily by two men — the first is Schachter (1963). He argues that the relationship of eminence to birth order derives from the fact that first borns are overrepresented in the college population, a finding which is not as stable as Schachter's data would indicate. He examined birth order data of college and graduate school samples, of a Minnesota high school sample and of a West German sample. In samples of college students, there were overrepresentations of first borns, but this did not hold true for the German sample. The percent of first borns in the college and graduate school samples was greater than the percent of first borns born in the years in which these subjects were born. This overrepresentation is to some extent reliable, as Schachter found the percent of first born undergraduates for the past twenty years at Columbia University to exceed the percent of first born children born in the appropriate years in the general population. When he controlled for economic factors by use of family size, Schachter (1963) still found a preponderance of first borns. The "why" of this relationship of birth order to college attendance thus remains unclear.

Altus (1966) is the second contemporary researcher concerned with birth order and eminence (college attendance and achievement). He gathered data at the University of California, Santa

Barbara, for four years (1960-1963) on all entering freshman (Altus, 1965). Of the 1817 students of two-child families, 63% were first born. Of those from three-child families, 50% were first born. Of those from four-child families, 49.7% were first born. Altus (1966) further reports that at Yale University, 61% were first born; and at the University of Minnesota a little over 50% were first born.

However convincing these data may appear, it should be noted that there is little or no control for SES in these studies. Although both Altus and Schachter do control for family size, such a procedure is indirect, at best, in controlling SES.

In contrast to these two studies, Bayer (1966) carefully controlled for SES by means other than family size. This study may be the only study to do so. In controlling for SES, he found birth order differences other than those reported by Schachter (1963) and Altus (1965a, 1966) and was unable to replicate their results. Using a complex index of SES based on items having to do with family income, the number of specified family possessions, etc., Bayer divided his national sample of high school seniors (50,000) into four SES groups. These four were designated as low, low middle, high middle and high status. When the percent of students in college one year after high school was analyzed by ordinal position, family size, sex and SES, Bayer (1966) found only children to be the most likely to attend college, while children of intermediate ordinal positions were the least likely to attend college. First borns emerged as no more likely to attend college than last borns coming from the same size family and SES group. While those in the two upper SES groups did have a greater tendency to go to college, the birth order findings were stable across all SES groups.

A recent review of birth order and school-related behaviors (Bradley, 1968) makes the point that there is a "redoubtable link" between birth order and college attendance, e.g., first borns are over-represented in college populations, and presents studies to illustrate this "link". However, what Bradley (1968) fails to consider is SES: the studies he cites rarely control for socioeconomic class. When they do, it is only by controlling for family size.

Need Achievement (nAch) or the motivation to achieve has been of great interest with respect to its possible relation to birth order. Winterbottom (1958) found nAch to be related to mothers' child-rearing practices (independence training and rewards and punishments) or at least to the avowed child-rearing practices. If one agrees that stable birth order differences may be due to child-rearing practices which vary within a family according to ordinal position, then it becomes meaningful to hypothesize the existence of birth order differences in nAch.

Sampson (1962) found a tendency for first born males and females to have high nAch and for later born males and females to have low nAch (by $X^2, p<.05$) as measured by the French (1958) Test of Insight. However, when analyzing males and females separately, the differences between first and second borns were not significant. In a later review of the literature, Sampson (1965) cites several studies (Elder, 1962; Pierce, 1959; etc.,) indicating a tendency of first borns achieving more in school, and thus tentatively concludes that the first born has a greater need to achieve than the later born.

In a study conducted on a sample of high school students from two-child families, Sampson & Hancock (1967) claim they found a significant difference in nAch between first and later borns. They measured nAch by a slightly modified version of the EPPS and found a significant main effect for ordinal position ($p<.001$) and a significant interaction between subjects' sex and sibling sex ($p<.005$). However, as there were three ordinal position groups (only children, first borns, and second borns), one cannot tell from the significant main effect which of these three groups differs from the other. As Sampson & Hancock (1967) do not report any post hoc comparisons between cells, one cannot locate the actual source of variance or interpret the results. On the basis of the data presented, however, it appears unwarranted to say first borns have a higher nAch than second borns.

Alcoholism

The entry into psychological literature of alcoholism in connection with birth order appears to have resulted from Schachter's (1959) work. He hypothesized that because first born females under stress wanted to be with others and later born females withdrew, later borns would be overrepresented in the ranks of alcoholics. (Alcoholism is envisioned by Schachter as a non-social way of handling stressful problems.) He cites part of Bakan's (1949) data on male alcoholics as supporting his hypothesis.

Bakan (1949) presented birth rank analyses of two samples of male alcoholics with a record of alcoholic offences, primarily public intoxication. The first sample contained 1493 males. The obtained distribution of birth ranks (no only children) was compared with a theoretical distribution (based on the hypothesis that the probability of any individual being in any birth rank is the same). The null hypothesis was rejected ($p<.001$). Examination of the deviations from theoretical frequency indicates that the sample of male "alcoholics" contained more later borns than expected.

Bakan's (1949) second sample consisted of 100 males (no only children) with known family size. In this case, the null hypothesis was retained, i.e., there was no significant difference between theoretical and obtained distributions. It should be noted that Schachter (1959) does not cite these latter data. An additional Chi square test performed between theoretical and obtained distributions of birth ranks 7 to 12 was large enough to be significant at the .05 level. That is, the likelihood of alcoholics from the birth ranks of seven to twelve in the alcoholic population is greater than expected under the equal probability hypothesis.

Smart (1963) is critical of the birth order-alcoholism link as put forth by Schachter (1959). He is critical of Bakan (1949) because his sample was not a "known" alcoholic group and he did not correct for family size. The criticism leveled at Schachter (1959) is (1) that he relied solely on Bakan's data to substantiate the link between alcoholism and birth order; (2) that he failed to correct Bakan's data for family size (e.g., by the

Greenwood-Yule method, see MacMahon, Pugh & Ibsen, 1960); and (3) that he assumed birth orders one through three to be "early born" and four and later to be "later born."

Smart (1963) retested Schachter's (1959) hypothesis concerning alcoholism and birth order with corrected birth order and family size data from a well-defined group of alcoholics. One of Smart's hypotheses was supported: the sample contained a significantly larger number of persons from large families than expected ($p<.05$). Nevertheless, no birth order differences were exhibited by the sample.

Adding more confusion to the issue, Chen & Cobb (1960) computed the ratio of eldest to youngest in seven alcoholic samples. In three, the eldest outnumber the youngest by ratios of 1.7, 1.2, and 1.1. In another three, the oldest are underrepresented by ratios of 0.6, eldest to youngest. In only one sample, alcoholics in treatment in an outpatient clinic, was the ratio 1.0.

Some research which attempts to unravel the relationship between alcoholism and birth order is that of de Lint (1964). His study of 276 female alcoholics admitted to an alcoholism clinic during a ten-year period revealed that being last born was related significantly to parental absence (one or both) during the first five years of childhood. His data show that an overrepresentation of last borns in the alcoholic sample is due to an overrepresentation of persons raised by one or no natural parents ($p<.001$). When absence of parent(s) is controlled, birth order has no relation to incidence of alcoholism. Thus, it may be assumed that the variable operating in the relation of alcoholism to birth order is actually parent absence.

As can be seen, it is difficult to draw a conclusion with respect to alcoholism and birth order. This is perhaps because the issue is not nearly as simple as Schachter (1959) would make it seem. From all appearances, the Bakan (1949) finding on which Schachter (1959) bases his argument is confounded by family size and sample selection bias. Also, results from the seven samples of alcoholics analyzed by Chen & Cobb (1960) are, no doubt influenced by factors determining which alcoholics are found at the various institutions from which the samples were drawn. The de Lint (1964) finding will probably do much to uravel the relationship (or lack of it) between birth order and alcoholism. .

References

Altus, W. D. Birth order and academic primogeniture. *Journal of Personality and Social Psychology,* 1965, **2**, 872-876.

Altus, W. D. Birth order and its sequelae. *Science,* 1966, **151**, 44-49.

Asch, S. E. Studies of independence and conformity: A minority of one against a unanimous majority. *Psychological Monographs,* 1956, **70** (9, Whole No. 416).

Bakan, D. The relationship between alcoholism and birth rank. *Quarterly Journal of Studies in Alcoholism,* 1949, **10**, 434-440.

Bayer, A. E. Birth order and college attendance. *Journal of Marriage and the Family,* 1966, **28,** 480-484.

Becker, S. W., Lerner, M., & Carroll, Jean. Conformity as a function of birth order, payoff and type of group pressure. *Journal of Abnormal and Social Psychology,* 1964, **69,** 318-323.

Bowerman, W. G. *Studies in genius.* New York: Philosophical Library, Inc., 1947. Cited by Chen & Cobb, S., Family structure in relation to health and disease. *Journal of Chronic Diseases,* 1960, **12,** 544-567.

Bradley, R. W. Birth order and school-related behavior: A heuristic review. *Psychological Bulletin,* 1968, **70,** 45-51.

Burton, D. Birth order and intelligence. *Journal of Social Psychology,* 1968, **72** *(2nd* half), 199-206.

Campbell, D. T., & Fiske, D. W. Convergent and discriminant validation by multitrait-multimethod matrix. *Psychological Bulletin,* 1959, **56,** 81-105.

Chen, E., & Cobb, S. Family structure in relation to health and disease. *Journal of Chronic Diseases,* 1960, **12,** 544-567.

Dean, Daphne A. The relation of ordinal position to personality in young children. Unpublished master's thesis, State Univer. of Iowa, Iowa City, 1947. Cited by Schachter, S., *The psychology of affiliation.* California: Stanford University Press, 1959, 85.

de Lint, J. E. Alcoholism, birth order, and socializing agents. *Journal of Abnormal and Social Psychology,* 1964, **69,** 457-458.

Edwards, A. L. *Edwards Personal Preference Schedule.* New York: Psychological Corporation, 1953.

Elder, G. H., Jr. Family structure: The effects of size of family, sex composition and ordinal position on academic motivation and achievement. In *Adolescent achievement and mobility aspirations.* (mimeo) Chapel Hill, North Carolina: Institute for Research in Social Science, 1962, 59-72. Cited by Sampson, E. E. The study of ordinal position: Antecedents and outcomes. In B. Maher (Ed.), *Progress in experimental personality research.* Vol. 2 New York: Academic Press, 1965. Pp. 175-228.

Ellis, H. *A study of British genius.* London: Constable Press, 1904.

Festinger, L. A. A theory of social comparison processes. *Human Relations,* 1954, **7,** 117-140.

Galton, F. *English men of science.* London: MacMillan & Co., 1874.

Gerard, H. B. & Rabbie, J. M. Fear and social comparison. *Journal of Abnormal and Social Psychology,* 1961, **62,** 586-592.

Gewirtz, J. L. Dependent and aggressive interaction in young children. Unpublished doctoral dissertation, State Univ. of Iowa, Iowa City, 1948. Cited by Schachter, S., *The psychology of affiliation.*

California: Stanford University Press, 1959.

Haeberle, Ann. Interactions of sex, birth order, and dependency with behavior problems and symptoms in emotionally disturbed preschool children. Paper read at Eastern Psychological Assocation, Philadelphia, 1958. Cited by Schachter, S. *The psychology of affiliation.* California: Stanford University Press, 1959.

Henry, A. F. Sibling structure and perception of the disciplining role of the parents. *Sociometry,* 1957, **20,** 67-74.

Hilton, Irma. Differences in the behavior of mothers toward first- and later-born children. *Journal of Personality and Social Psychology,* 1967, **7**(3, part 1), 282-290.

Hsiao, H. H. The status of the first born with special reference to intelligence. *Genetic Psychology Monographs,* 1931, **9,** 1-118.

Jones, H. E. Environment and mental development. In L. Carmichael (Ed.), *Manual of child psychology.* New York: Wiley, 1954. Pp. 631-696.

Lasko, Joan K. Parental behavior towards first and second children. *Genetic Psychology Monographs,* 1954, **49,** 97-137.

MacMahon, B., Pugh, T. & Ibsen, J. *Epidemiologic methods.* Boston: Little, Brown and Company, 1960.

Maxwell, J. & Pillner, A. E. The intellectual resemblance between sibs. *Annals of Human Genetics,* 1960, **24,** 23-32.

Pierce, J. V. *The educational motivation of superior students who do and do not achieve in high school.* U.S. Office of Education, Department of Health, Education and Welfare, November, 1959. Cited by Sampson, E. E., The study of ordinal position: Antecedents and outcomes. In B. Maher (Ed.), *Progress in experimental personality research.* Vol. 2. New York: Academic Press, 1965. Pp. 175-228.

Ring, K., Lipinski, C. E. & Braginsky, D. The relationship of birth order to self-evaluation, anxiety reduction, and emotional contagion. *Psychological Monographs,* 1965, **79** (10, Whole No. 603).

Rosen, B. C. Family structure and value transmission. *Merrill Palmer Quarterly,* 1964, **10,** 59-76.

Sampson, E. E. Birth order, need achievement, and conformity. *Journal of Abnormal and Social Psychology,* 1962, **64,** 155-159.

Sampson, E. E. & Hancock, F. T. An examination of the relationship between ordinal position, personality, and conformity: An extension, replication, and partial verification. *Journal of Personality and Social Psychology,* 1967, **5,** 398-407.

Schachter, S. *The psychology of affiliation.* California: Stanford University Press, 1959.

Schachter, S. Birth order, eminence, and higher education. *American Sociological Review,* 1963, **28,** 757-768.

Scheffe, H. *The analysis of variance.* New York: Wiley, 1959.

Sears, R. R., Maccoby, E., & Levin, H. *Patterns of child rearing.* Evanston, Illinois: Row, Peterson, 1957.

Smart, R. G. Alcoholism, birth order, and family size. *Journal of Abnormal and Social Psychology,* 1963, **66,** 17-23.

Thurstone, L. L. & Jenkins, R. L. Birth order and intelligence. *Journal of Educational Psychology,* 1929, **20,** 641-651.

Warren, J. R. Birth order and social behavior. *Psychological Bulletin,* 1966, **65,** 38-49.

Waters, K. K. & Kirk, W. E. Birth order and EPPS affiliation. *Journal of Psychology,* 1967, **67,** 241-243.

Weller, L. The relationship of birth order to anxiety: A replication of the Schachter findings. *Sociometry,* 1962, **25,** 415-417.

Winterbottom, Marian R. The relation of need for achievement to learning experiences in independence and mastery. J. W. Atkinson (Ed.), *Motives in fantasy, action, and society.* Princeton, New Jersey: Van Nostrand, 1958. Pp. 453-478.

Wrightsman, L. S., Jr. Effects of waiting with others on changes in level of felt anxiety. *Journal of Abnormal and Social Psychology,* 1960, **61,** 216-222.

Zimbardo, P. & Formica, R. Emotional comparisons and self-esteem as determinants of affiliation. *Journal of Personality,* 1963, **31,** 141-162.

13
MIDDLE CHILDHOOD:
ABNORMAL DEVELOPMENT

During middle childhood, mental retardation (see Chapter 5) and childhood schizophrenia (see Chapter 9) continue to be the two most important patterns of serious psychological impairment, and each tends to become more apparent and incapacitating as the impaired child struggles with the mounting demands of school and peer relationships. Likewise, as noted in the Wender article in Chapter 9, minimally brain-damaged preschool children usually exhibit various kinds of learning disability, and these learning handicaps account for a significant proportion of school-age maladjustment.

The articles that follow are concerned with two patterns of abnormal development that are particularly likely to appear first during middle childhood. One is school phobia, which is uniquely related to the school-age years and which represents the most common childhood manifestation of phobic reactions. Frick reviews in his article the nature of this condition, its origin in various sources of anxiety, and aspects of its diagnosis, treatment, and prognosis. The second pattern of disturbance, discussed in the Toolan article, is depression. Toolan notes that depression in younger people is frequently overlooked, and he illustrates with case examples some of the many ways in which children and adolescents may evidence underlying depression, including boredom, fatigue, physical complaints, antisocial behavior, and suicide attempts.

WILLARD B. FRICK

School Phobia: A Critical Review of the Literature*

Broadwin (1932) conceived of the following behavior to be a form of truancy: "The child is absent from school for periods varying from several months to a year. The absence is consistent. At all times the parents know where the child is. It is with the mother or near the home. The reason for the truancy is incomprehensible to the parents and the school. The child may say that it is afraid to go to school, afraid of the teacher, or say that it does not know why it will not go to school." As a description of this phenomenon there has been little basic change or improvement. However, Johnson et al. (1941) initiated the term "school phobia" as a more descriptive one, and recognized that there were definite differences between a truant child and the truly phobic child. These differences have been supported and clarified in subsequent studies. In this introduction we distinguish between truancy and school phobia before proceeding to a review of the literature on the latter phenomenon.

In comparing a study of 32 phobic children by Thompson (1948) with a study of similar design carried out by

Mohr (1948) on 40 truant cases, we find in the latter study a syndrome based on severe deprivation where the aggression is "so primitive that the child feels driven not only to evade the school but to evade his parents as well." Out of these 40 truant cases 32 were from seriously disturbed or broken homes. In school phobias we find, generally, a less severely emotionally-crippled child but one who seeks escape from his own hostile impulses which he has projected onto the school situation. The studies cited and others indicate that phobic children rarely come, as do truants, from broken homes or severely deprived environments. In a comparative study done on the two groups Warren (1948) studied 8 phobic children along with 12 cases of truancy. For the truant group he found a great number of debilitating factors in the social environment, a lower level of intelligence, more difficulties in school, and a much lower level of anxiety. The truants not only ran away from home and school but frequently lied and stole. In a more recent investigation comparing 50 school phobics with 50 truant children and using a control group, Hersov (1960) found that the children in his truancy group more often experienced maternal absence during infancy and paternal absence in later childhood. From these studies and other observations it is clear that the two groups present marked differences in the

*From the *Merrill-Palmer Quarterly*, 1964, **10**, 361-373. Reprinted by permission of the author and the Merrill-Palmer Institute.

dynamics of their respective syndromes.

Following Broadwin's (1932) early recognition and description of school phobia 30 years ago, there have appeared over 40 articles covering virtually every aspect of the problem. Increasing interest in the phenomenon within the past few years is indicated by the fact that approximately 30 of the total number of articles have been written within the last ten years. Also, at least two writers, Thompson (1948) and Eisenberg (1958a), report rather decisive increases in the number of cases of school phobia seen in clinics in recent years. Eisenberg reports that the rate of clinic admissions of school phobia to the Johns Hopkins Children's Psychiatric Service rose from four cases per 1,000 admissions in 1948 to 17 per 1,000 in 1956. In another article Eisenberg (1958b) states that the current rate of admissions was 30 per 1,000. This does not necessarily mean that there has been an actual increase in the incidence of school phobia. Increased interest and understanding of the phenomenon must have a bearing on what has been observed. For example, Waldfogel et al. (1957) report an almost phenomenal increase in referrals of school phobic children from a Boston suburban area after a special clinic unit was established in cooperation with teachers and administrators of the school system.

In the following review the material will be divided into three sections: I. Developmental data on school phobic children; symptomatology, personality dynamics, and etiology; II. Diagnosis, treatment, and prognosis; III. Interpretations and theoretical considerations.

DEVELOPMENTAL DATA

Although there are basic theoretical issues and conflicts in interpretation, there is throughout the literature on school phobia a remarkable unanimity in the results and conclusions of a variety of exploratory and descriptive studies. The disturbance is rather dramatic with definite and classical features and the descriptions and etiological hypotheses advanced early by Broadwin (1932) and Johnson et al. (1941) have served as a paradigm for all later thinking and investigations. Throughout the literature there is consistent reference to the latter study and it is to be considered a classic.

Most investigators have found that the manifestations of school phobia appear early. Studies by Goldberg (1953) and Thompson (1948) place the great majority of these children between the ages of five and ten years of age. This is confirmed by a more recent investigation by Rodriguez, et al. (1959) where 27 of 41 cases were from five to ten years of age at the time of referral. Two British writers (Davidson, 1961; Hersov, 1960b), however, have reported that the most common time of onset in their studies was at the age of 11 or shortly thereafter. Both attribute this frequent age of onset to the fact that most 11-year-olds in England are transferring from the junior school to the senior school. This transfer seems to be accompanied by much anxiety and provides a common precipitating factor for the susceptible ones.

Consistently, in all studies these phobic children tend to be average or above in intelligence. Goldberg (1953) reports that 8 out of 12 children studied were bright. Twenty of the 41 cases were above average in the study by Rodriguez et al. (1959). Only three fell below average. Other studies vary slightly, but the generalization can be made that school phobic children possess adequate academic ability or general intelligence. There are, however, some conflicting reports concerning their achievement. Jacobsen (1948) reports that retardation was slight in her group. Van Houten (1948) confirms this by finding no previous difficulties in school for any of the 12 children studied. Ten were regarded as doing well in school and only one girl was an achievement problem. In the Thompson study (1948) of 32 cases referred from an area in Brooklyn during a ten-year period, however, all but two children were retarded in reading or arithmetic or both.

Earlier studies by Van Houten (1948), Thompson (1948), and Jacobsen (1948) reported consistently more cases of school phobia among girls than boys. An assumption grew that this was, for some reason, a characteristic distribution. Subsequent and more recent studies, however, indicate that incidence is evenly distributed among girls and boys. Waldfogel et al. (1957) concluded that their recent distribution of 28 boys and 25 girls is representative and contradicts the previous impression. This is more recently confirmed by the writer, who found that the number of boys exceeded girls by 22 in a tally of 452 cases reported in the literature.[1] Such shifts in sex distribution

[1] A few reports did not present the sex distribution.

could very well be due to the capricious variations in sampling, and a more detailed look at the populations being sampled would be warranted in the future.

All studies concerned with the symptomatology and syndrome of this illness are in agreement that it does not represent a clear-cut entity but reflects an overall neurotic pattern. There is, first of all, a pervasive anxiety in these children with all of the concomitant symptoms including a wide range of fears and psychosomatic complaints (one of the chief justifications presented for avoiding school). There are frequent tantrums, habit disorders, and pre-phobic unhappiness at school. Agras (1959) has observed a strong depressive trend in these children, and Davidson (1961) in her study of 30 cases reported depression to be a marked feature in 23 children. Twelve of the mothers also displayed this symptom. Infantile behaviors are frequent at home. In school, however, phobic children tend to be shy and self-conscious and "acting out" behavior is rare.

Coolidge et al. (1957) isolated two almost equally divided subgroups, the neurotic and characterological, in a study of 21 cases of school phobia. The neurotic group is characterized by a dramatic and acute onset but the ailment is not pervasive and the children are able to express affect and fantasy freely. The primary conflict in the neurotic group grows out of autonomy needs in relation to the mother. The authors found the characterological group more severely disturbed: "The school phobic symptom was instead the culmination of a relentless process rather than any marked change." The chief conflict within the latter group, so Coolidge and his associates feel, is a symbiotic tie to the mother. There is little support for such a dichotomy except that a similar difference is noted between school phobic children and phobic adolescents. Adolescents seem to fit more nearly the "characterological" description given above. Without more evidence it appears that the difference might be explained on the basis of degree of severity of the disturbance rather than any basic difference in symptoms or nature of the illness. In commenting on the paper by Coolidge, Johnson (1957) questions the need for such a division of cases, feeling that the latter group (characterological) is just more insidious. Waldfogel et al. (1957) also suggest that a continuum is more probable. In a very recent study of school phobia in adolescence, Coolidge et al. (1960) observed that in adolescent school phobia there has invariably been an early history of the school phobic symptom which usually subsided spontaneously. Though the disturbance in adolescence is usually severe, early family relationships parallel the pattern found in younger children with school phobia. This tends to lend support to the suggestion of Waldfogel and his colleagues.

Most investigators agree as to the dynamics that give rise to school phobia. The drama is played in the complex and neurotic interaction between mother and phobic child. There is revealed in the early life history of the mother an inaequately resolved dependency relationship with the maternal grandmother, with concomitant feelings of repressed resentment and inadequacy. Such mothers find a source of gratification in one or more of their children, playing out their many infantile needs and conflicts in this rela-

tionship. "Having suffered, we are unconsciously or consciously seeking revenge, often against one as helpless as we were when we initially suffered. This usually means that the adult revenge is directed toward a child, if there is a child" (Robinson et al., 1955).

In an effort to fulfill the partial deprivation within her own childhood, there is a distorted interpretation of her infant's needs, and the mother makes it difficult for the child to achieve a healthy resolution of his dependency. In many subtle ways strivings for independence are rejected until the child, in some measure, succumbs. Both become strongly ambivalent in their feelings toward the other. Vacillating, contradictory behavior is extreme on the part of the mother as she goes through the cycle of counteracting her guilt. The child inevitably becomes dependent on his mother but with little feeling of support from her inconsistent behavior. He, too, goes through his cycle of dependency, hostility, and severe guilt feelings which are reflected in many neurotic maneuvers. There is both guilt over hostile impulses and over strivings for independence. Each learns to exploit the other's guilt feelings. Coolidge et al. (1962) have recently emphasized the importance of hostility as a genetic agent in school phobia. They present, in detail, an excellent discussion of the origins and development of hostile impulses in these parents and children.

Thompson (1948), Suttenfield (1954), and others either explicitly state or imply that this mother-child conflict represents a basic rejection of the child by the mother. Waldfogel et al. (1957), however, believe that too much emphasis has been placed on explaining school phobia as a result of unconscious maternal rejection. In their experience there is an identification with the child that is rooted in a strong, affectionate attachment. They do not interpret this as an attempt to deny hostility as in reaction formation; rather, they emphasize the mother's basic feeling of incompetence in being a "good" mother and her difficulty in "feeling" the role spontaneously. Thus, the mothers seem to meet these intense feelings of incompetence with over-protective devices.

The fathers are seen by all observers to be passive and subjected to the dominance of their wives. Thompson (1948) describes them as ". . . gentle, kindly men who have accepted the domination of their wives." Talbot (1957) contends that along with his wife, the father has failed to emancipate from his own family. Waldfogel et al. (1957) stress the father's inability to define clearly his paternal position and believe that these mothers and fathers are also looking to each other for gratification of their own dependency needs. That there is sufficient complementarity of neurotic need satisfaction in these marriages is shown by the fact reported above, that parents of school phobic children rarely break up their homes through separation or divorce.

With minor variations most writers agree with the major points of the dynamics discussed above. Equally unanimous is the opinion that school phobia is symptomatic of an intense separation anxiety (Robinson et al. 1955; Estes and Haylett, 1956; Wallinga, 1959). This separation seems to be a mutual anxiety on the part of both mother and child, but Waldfogel et al. (1957) emphasize that "there can be little doubt that the mother's problem around separation antedates the problem in the child."

Basic to the development of school phobia, then, is a neurotic dependency struggle (both intrapsychic and in interaction) between mother and child. Eventually, the child must struggle with intense dependency needs, erratic and guilt-producing strivings for independence, and frightening feelings of hostility (partially denied and displaced) toward the mother. This emotion-laden atmosphere is sooner or later ignited by some apparently innocuous and transitory situation which arouses intense anxiety within the child. A brief illness, change of school, harsh word from the teacher, loss of friend, birth of sibling, etc., have all been reported as precipitating factors in the onset of school phobia. Most of these precipitating factors seem relatively minor (Goldberg, 1953) and do not appear to be essentially different in kind or intensity from incidents that most children experience at some time during the course of schooling (Eisenberg, 1958a). In the majority of cases, however, the fear is usually attached to the school situation in some way and not infrequently is directed toward the teacher. Anger associated with hostile wishes is thus displaced onto the school by these dependent children.

Davidson (1961) emphasizes the strongly ambivalent relationship between mother and child. Phobic reactions occur, she believes, when the balance (tolerance for hostility) of this ambivalence is disturbed, frequently by the reappearance of the Oedipal conflict in pre-puberty.

Paralleling the child's heightened anxiety, Johnson et al. (1941) reported a simultaneous increase of anxiety in the mother because of a threat to her security. More recently, Coolidge et al. (1962) have reported a similar observation. That there is this specific and simultaneous threat to the mother at the time of the child's heightened anxiety has not been confirmed or even considered by other writers. There might well be such cases, but they do not seem to be frequent or else have gone unrecognized. Of course, as Estes and Haylett (1956) point out, as soon as the child flees the school in favor of the mother, she immediately begins to exploit the situation by fostering the dependency of the child upon her.

DIAGNOSIS, TREATMENT, AND PROGNOSIS

Diagnostically, school phobia ranges from a relatively simple and "normal" situational reaction at one end of the spectrum to a severely neurotic or even psychotic pattern at the other (Rodriguez et al., 1959). Adequate differential diagnosis, therefore, is vital. The more severely disturbed school phobics in one study (Goldberg, 1953) have been diagnosed as psychoneurotics suffering from anxiety hysteria. Goldberg recognizes the great range of neurotic disorders associated with school phobia and suggests that they will usually give a mixed diagnosis including anxiety neurosis, the obsessive-compulsive patterns, and a small number of borderline schizophrenics.

In treatment and handling, the issue around which there seems to be the most controversy is the one of pressure versus non-pressure in getting the child to remain in, or return to, school. Hanvik (1961) believes that homebound instruc-

tion is very unwise for the school phobic child since it tends to solidify the symptoms of non-attendance. Klein (1945) favors pressure to a point but rejects harsh treatment. He regards failure to get the child back in school promptly as encouraging primitive regression and a generalization of the phobia. Klein suggests that just getting the child in the school building, even though he may not visit the classroom, is a great help. The child may at first stay in an office, help the staff, or read and draw in another room in his progress toward re-establishment in his own classroom. Thompson (1948) on the other hand feels that any semblance of pressure is dangerous when working with the child and his parents. Talbot (1957) agrees with this position and favors an established treatment relationship before the child is sent back to school.

Waldfogel et al. (1957) have observed that once the child has returned to school it becomes difficult to continue therapy since there will be no felt need for it and returning to school provides the parents with a rationalization for discontinuing treatment. Eisenberg (1958b), however, reports that he has not experienced this difficulty. In a more recent discussion of this issue Rodriguez et al. (1959) favor a very early return to school if at all possible. They feel that early return has definite therapeutic value because (1) it focuses on the primary issue of separation; (2) it emphasizes the core of health in the child and reassures the family while a de-emphasis on back to school suggests a "sickness" in the child; (3) getting the child in school sends him back to a growth-promoting environment.

There is a measure of plausibility in

each of these points of view. Until one has a firm basis for deciding among them, therefore, it seems wise to let factors such as degree of illness of both mother and child, nature of the mother-child relationship (is the mother capable of letting the child achieve an early return to school?), degree of resistance to therapy, and the total school situation decide the best course of action. The points by Rodriguez et al. seem pertinent and reasonable if other factors also favor an early return.

Johnson et al. (1941) were the first to emphasize treatment with both mother and child. All agree that is is not only desirable to see that the mother gets treatment but in many cases it is a necessity. According to Estes and Haylett (1956) thorough treatment of the mother is essential to prevent her from involving another of her children in the neurosis. Such a shifting of the problem seems to occur most frequently when a phobic child achieves a greater degree of health and the mother remains untreated. It is sometimes difficult to get the mother to undergo psychotherapy since she must first face the fact that she is personally involved in an emotional disturbance. In treating the mother, Waldfogel et al. (1957) emphasize the delicate task of satisfying the dependency needs of the mother, yet not to the point where she will become over-anxious and hostile and discontinue treatment.

In treating the school phobic child various approaches and emphases have been advised, ranging from brief, on-the-spot treatment in the school for mild situational difficulties (Waldfogel et al., 1959) to analytic first-aid (Sperling, 1961) or in-patient care for more serious cases (Warren, 1948). There has been one report of psychoanalytic treatment of a school phobic child (Bornstein, 1949). This report, however, focuses mainly on problems of theory and technique in child analysis. Therapeutic considerations in treating school phobias in the young adult are discussed by Levenson (1961).

Release of hostility, tension, and guilt; indulgence of dependency needs; and helping the children see the relationship between infantile attitudes and fixations and their own fantasies (thus relating the two in consciousness) have all been mentioned frequently as important goals in therapy with the phobic child. In recent therapeutic efforts with school phobic children Waldfogel et al. (1957) stress early focus on symptoms, with a gradual translation of the fear of going to school to fear of separation from mother. Symptom focus, fantasy focus, and integration of symptom and fantasy with interpretation constitute their three-phase treatment of school phobic children. These writers also emphasize the importance of termination as a therapeutic experience for the child. At this time support and strong encouragement of independence are recommended.

Generally speaking, the prognosis for school phobic children is very good. The favorable outlook seems related, however, to severity of the disorder, age of the child, and length of time between onset of the phobic reaction and beginning of treatment. Using the criteria of "back in school" and general syndrome improvement, Jacobsen (1948) judged 30 cases as follows: 9 with satisfactory improvement, 13 with partial improvement (back in school), and 8 cases of unsatisfactory adjustment. Children in kindergarten and first grade with above average intelligence and children who were willful, demanding, and aggressive were more responsive to treatment and tended to make a better adjustment than others. In a follow-up study of 41 cases Rodriguez et al. (1959) report that prognosis is much graver for older children with school phobia. With 27 children younger than 11 there was 89 per cent success, as judged by a return to regular school attendance. Of those 11 and older only 37 per cent returned to school successfully. This led Rodriguez and his associates to conclude: "Separation problems in a child of 6 or 7 do not portend the same degree of illness as they do in a child of 11 or 12." This supports the previously cited observation of school phobia in adolescents.

In an effort to determine the effectiveness of early identification and therapeutic intervention in school phobia (Walfogel et al., 1959), it was found that there was a noticeable difference between the 16 children who were given brief therapy in school immediately following onset of symptoms and the 11 children who, for various reasons, received no therapy. In a follow-up study 14 of those who had had benefit of brief therapy were symptom-free and had been symptom-free since termination of contact. Only 3 children were symptom-free, however, in the 11 cases receiving no therapeutic intervention.

In spite of the fact that there appeared to be some bias in the selection of the groups — i.e., there was some suspicion that the 11 children who received no therapy were, on the whole, more disturbed — the results are impressive and warrant a carefully-controlled study.

INTERPRETATIONS AND THEORETICAL CONSIDERATIONS

The Problem of Labeling

Curiously, there appear several criticisms of attaching the term "school phobia" to the phenomenon under discussion. Wallinga (1959) calls the term a "misnomer" when applied to the disturbance. Robinson et al. (1955) find the term inappropriate, and Estes and Haylett (1956) prefer "separation anxiety" when referring to this common core of symptoms. Miller (1961) also objects to the term "phobia", believing that it focuses too strongly on the elements of anxiety and not enough on "the manipulative and controlling quality of the child's relatedness to his parents." Many who object to the term school phobia feel that it emphasizes the symptoms rather than conveying the underlying nature of the disorder.

These objections have been called curious since, by classical definition, a phobic reaction is a displacement of anxiety and frightening impulses onto a phobic object. This is exactly what we have in school phobia. The term phobia, whenever used, has never been a description of underlying dynamics but serves to highlight the intense anxiety and process of displacement involved. Waldfogel et al. (1957) consider this process of displacement of anxiety to be the main mechanism of symptom formation in school phobia: "The fear may be attached to the teacher, the other children, . . . or almost any detail of school life." Although Eisenberg (1958b) approves of Johnson's concern with dynamics underlying "school phobia," he feels that "the phenomenologic definition has the virtue, however, of stressing the symptomatic manifestations by which the syndrome may be identified. It involves no commitment to an exclusive theory of causation." This reviewer agrees and considers this type of separation anxiety to present a sufficient number of unique symptoms in reacting to the school environment to justify the label "school phobia." It would only serve to confuse the issue to discontinue its use.

General Separation Anxiety Versus Intrinsic School Factors

A related issue is whether school phobia is merely a general separation anxiety, or whether there are important intrinsic school factors involved in the process of displacement. From the very beginning of the literature, Broadwin (1932) recognized the importance of the teacher in the process: "Perhaps because the teacher is a substitute mother, she is able to direct towards herself the love and hate instincts of the child and thus cause the child to be overwhelmed by anxiety and guilt." Broadwin goes on to stress that the teacher is not actively at fault in bringing about these conflicts. Klein (1945) also emphasizes school factors when he says that "all of the child's worries, fears, anxieties, self-consciousness, feelings of inadequacy, his relations to his parents, to his siblings, and to himself, tend to gain reflection in the school situation." Suttenfield (1954) believed that avoiding school and its anxieties, plus getting to stay at home with mother and siblings, were the major forces in the five school phobic children she studied. She saw a repetition of maternal rejection in the school situation.

In discussing the teacher's role in the neurotic conflict of children, Dombrose (1955) stresses that the teacher becomes a parent substitute for children and that "the neurotic child acts as if they were identical." He adds that the neurotic child may try to resolve conflicts with real parents by making use of the teacher and that the teacher may be the center of much unwarranted love and hate.

In a recent study of 50 cases of school phobia, Hersov (1960b) found that an expressed fear of the teacher was elicited in only 11 children and fear of schoolmates in 14 cases. Some of the children he studied felt quite safe once they were actually inside their class rooms. He noted, "The fear was more often at its height prior to leaving home for school or during the journey to school; it was more of a fear of leaving home and going to school than of being at school." Hersov seems to feel that his study favors the hypothesis of a general separation anxiety. His observations are interesting and provide avenues worthy of further investigation. As his report stands, however, it seems to this reviewer that he is merely showing that, besides a phobic reaction toward school, there is also a large element of fear and anxiety in leaving the mother. A crucial question, here, might be: Would these children have reacted with the same fear response if they were going away to a place other than schools and classrooms?

Although Estes and Haylett (1956) remarked that "children with separation anxiety or so-called school phobia do not go to the park or the movies or the ball game or any other place when they are absent from school," there appears to be no empirical verification of this.

This reviewer hypothesizes that in school phobia we are not dealing just with a general separation anxiety, as indicated above — in which the park, the movies, and the ball game can be equated with the school environment — but rather with a unique and dynamic relationship between intrinsic school factors, intrapsychic conflict, and debilitating influences at home. We seriously question Robinson et al. (1955) who say that "in actuality, the problem is not fear of school or anything pertaining to school, but is the child's separation anxiety activated by leaving the mother on going to school." One thing is certain. We do need more research in this area.

School Phobia and Chronic School Failure

Those of us who have worked directly with children in the schools have deplored the number of "normal" children in school who do little more than just exist. They are unable to concentrate and direct their energies to the stimulation and demands of the classroom and usually remain chronically retarded in achievement throughout their school careers. It is possible that many of these children actually represent another less dramatic form of school phobia that we might call "emotional absenteeism"? This possibility has been implied in a small number of articles. Talbot and Henson (1954) in a study of five cases representing emotional conflict interfering with the continuous learning process say: "The social findings revealed that each boy was protecting himself against an anticipated impending disaster by the defense

mechanism of ceasing to learn. The particular disaster feared on the conscious level was characterized by illness, death, divorce, and the passivity of femininity."

In a survey of cases of school failure Aguilera and Keneally (1954) found tense parent-child relationships where teachers are blamed by parents, and where the children frequently see their teachers as mother-like figures with concomitant transference of negative feelings and emotional blocking.

In one of the most recent commentaries on the relationship between school phobia and other less dramatic forms of school difficulty, Waldfogel et al. (1957) recognize, "The chronic insidious school phobia where the child's overall adjustment is far less sound, but the absences have been neither frequent nor dramatic enough for the school or the parent to consider treatment."

Why do some children literally run away from school in the case of school phobia, while others are able to tolerate school but must escape in psychological ways? Hitchcock (1956) in a study comparing 13 boys with chronic inability to learn with a like number of boys with school phobia found use of denial much more frequent in the former group, with a need to maintain positive feelings for the teacher. The phobics, on the other hand, were more conscious of their fears and could more readily displace their hostility onto the teacher. Could this be one significant factor in determining which children overtly escape school by literally running home (those who are able to undergo the strongest displacement and utilization of teacher as parent substitute) and which are able to tolerate, by use of denial, the school and the teacher? In both types of cases, it seems, we may be dealing with over-dependency and failure to develop an autonomous functioning within the family. Certainly these studies do seem to indicate that we are dealing with more than mere separation anxiety unrelated to the school situation. As Hitchcock says, "It is easier and less painful to renounce the right to succeed than to deal with the hostility, anxiety, and guilt associated with self-assertion." It appears that it is this characteristic need to avoid success that the phobic child and the learning-inhibited child are both expressing.

A final hypothesis this reviewer would like to pose is that the teacher's personality is an important variable in determining which children are able to physically tolerate the school. Certainly teachers will react differently to the personalities of potential school phobics. One teacher is fearful of their exaggerated love and hate, another is able to accept these children and their needs for such expression. Perhaps, too, some teachers are capable of satisfying the dependency needs of a potentially phobic child in an appropriate manner, while in interaction with another teacher the child is frightened away. Admittedly, we are raising questions more than providing answers. It is important that well-designed studies start providing some tentative answers to these issues.

References

Agras, Stewart. The relationship of school phobia to childhood depression. *Amer. J. Psychiat.*, 1959, **116**, 533-536.

Aguilera, Augusto, & Keneally, Katherine G. School failure — psychiatric implications. *J. Child Psychiat.*, 1954, 3 88-92.

Bornstein, Berta. The analysis of a phobic child. *Psychoanal. Stud. Child,* 1949, **3 & 4** 181-226.

Broadwin, Irsa T. A contribution to the study of truancy. *Amer. J. Orthopsychiat.*, 1932, **2**, 253-259.

Coolidge, J.C., Hahn, Pauline B., & Peck, Alice. School phobia: neurotic crisis or way of life. *Amer. J. Orthopsychiat.*, 1957, **27**, 296-306.

Coolidge, J.C., Willer, Mary Lou, & Tessman, Ellen. School phobia in adolescence: a manifestation of severe character disturbance. *Amer. J. Orthopsychiat.*, 1960, **30**, 599-607.

Collidge, J.C., Tessman, Ellen, Waldfogel, S., & Willer, Mary Lou. Patterns of aggression in school phobia. *Psychoanal. Stud. Child,* 1962, **17**, 319-333.

Davidson, Susannah. School phobia as a manifestation of family disturbance: its structure and treatment. *J. Child Psychol. Psychiat.*, 1961, 1(4), 270-287.

Dombrose, L.A. Do teachers cause neurotic conflict in children? *Ment.*

Hyg., N. Y., 1955, **39**, 99-110.

Eisenberg, Leon. School phobia: A study of the communication of anxiety. *Amer. J. Psychiat.,* 1958a, **114**, 712-718.

Eisenberg, Leon. School phobia: diagnosis, genesis, and clinical management. *Pediat. Clinics of N. Amer.,* 1958d, **5**, 645-666.

Estes, H.R., & Haylett, Clarice H. Separation anxiety. *Amer J. Psychother.,* 1956, **10**, 682-695.

Goldberg, Thelma. Factors in the development of school phobia. *Smith Coll. Stud. soc. Work,* 1953, **23**, 227-248.

Hanvik, L.J. The child who is afraid of school. *Element. Sch. J.,* 1961, **62**, 27-33.

Hersov, L.A. Persistent non-attendance at school. *J. Child Psychol. Psychiat.,* 1960a, 1 (2), 130-136.

Hersov, L.A. Refusal to go to school. *J. Child Psychol. Psychiat.,* 1960b, 1 (2), 137-145.

Hitchcock, Alice B. Symbolic and actual flight from school. *Smith Coll. Stud. soc. Work,* 1956, **27**, 1-33.

Jacobsen, Virginia. Influential factors in the outcome of treatment of school phobia. *Smith Coll. Stud. soc. Work,* 1948, **18**, 181-202.

Johnson, Adelaide M., Falstein, E.I., Szurek, S.A., & Svendsen, Margaret. School phobia. *Amer. J. Orthopsychiat.,* 1941, **11**, 702-711.

Johnson, Adelaide M. Discussion of paper by Coolidge et al. *Amer. J. Orthopsychiat.,* 1957, **27**, 307.

Klien, Emanuel. The reluctance to go to school. *Psychoanal. Stud. Child,* 1945, **1**, 263-279.

Levenson, E. A. The treatment of school phobias in the young adult. *Amer. J. Psychother.,* 1961, **15**, 539-552.

Leyton, Donald A. Assessment of school phobia. *Ment. Hyg., N. Y.,* 1962, **46**, 256-264.

Miller, J. P. The child who refuses to attend school. *Amer. J. Psychiat.,* 1961, **118**, 398-404.

Mohr, Irma. Fears in relation to school attendance, a study of truancy. *Bull. nat. Assn. Sch. soc. Workers,* 1948, **24**, No. 1.

Robinson, D. B., Duncan, Glen, & Johnson, Adelaide M. Psychotherapy of a mother and daughter with a problem of separation anxiety. *Proc. Staff Mtngs, Mayo Clin.,* 1955, **30**, 141-148.

Rodriguez, A., Rodriguez, M., & Eisenberg, Leon. The outcome of school phobia: follow-up study based on 41 cases. *Amer. J. Psychiat.,* 1959, **116**, 540-544.

Sperling, Melitta. Analytic first-aid in school phobias. *Psychoanal. Quart.,* 1961, **30**, 504-518.

Suttenfield, Virginia. School phobia: A study of five cases. *Amer. J. Orthopsychiat.,* 1954, **24**, 368-380.

Talbot, Mira, & Henson, Isabelle. Pupils psychologically absent from school. *Amer. J. Orthopsychiat.*, 1954, **24**, 381-390.

Talbot, Mira. Panic in school phobia. *Amer. J. Orthopsychiat.*, 1957, **27**, 286-295.

Thompson, Jean. Children's fears in relation to school attendance. *Bull. nat. Assn. Sch. soc. Workers*, 1948, **24**, No. 1.

Van Houten, Janny. Mother-child relationships in 12 cases of school phobia. *Smith Coll. Stud. soc. Work*, 1948, **18**, 161-180.

Waldfogel, S., Coolidge, J. C., & Hahn, Pauline B. The development, meaning, and management of school phobia. *Amer. J. Orthopsychiat.*, 1957, **27**, 574-580.

Waldfogel, S., Tessman, Ellen, & Hahn, Pauline B. A program for early intervention in school phobia. *Amer. J. Orthopsychiat.*, 1959, **29**, 324-332.

Wallinga, J. V. Separation anxiety. *Lancet*, 1959, **79**, 258-260.

Warren, W. Acute neurotic breakdown in children with refusal to go to school. *Arch. Dis. Childh.*, 1948, **23**, 266-272.

JAMES M. TOOLAN

Depression in Children and Adolescents*

Depression is a common problem in adult psychiatry. Every worker is familiar with the classical signs of depression: retardation in mental and physical activity; insomnia; feelings of depression, apathy, worthlessness, and nihilism as well as

*From the *American Journal of Orthopsychiatry*, 1962, 32, 404-415. Reprinted by permission of the author and the American Orthopsychiatric Association.

suicidal preoccupation. In addition we are accustomed to encounter physiological symptoms such as anorexia and constipation. Similar clinical pictures are rarely encountered in children and adolescents— at least until 16 or 17 years of age. In fact, the absence of the usual clinical picture has led most psychiatrists to the erroneous conclusion that depression does not occur in younger people (1). It is true that children and adolescents may appear to be depressed for short periods of time, but rarely for more than a few hours at a time. As a matter of fact it is amazing to adults how very quickly most teen-agers recover from their transitory periods of unhappiness. One minute life has no meaning and the next, the youngster is on top of the world. Chronic depressive reactions occur very rarely.

This does not mean to imply that children and adolescents do not experience depressions or that depressions do not constitute a significant aspect of the child's life. On the contrary, I shall attempt to show in this paper that depression is a most important problem in childhood and in adolescence, and one which is unfortunately often overlooked. We have to cease thinking in terms of adult psychiatry and instead become accustomed to recognizing the various manifestations by which depression may be represented in younger people.

In infants depression is often evidenced by eating and sleeping disturbances, colic, crying and head-banging. It is of interest that the mothers of such infants are frequently depressed and/or anxious. These complaints come usually to the attention of the pediatrician, seldom to the psychiatrist. At a somewhat later age, withdrawal, apathy and regression may be evidence of the same difficulty. These symptoms may often be encountered in emotionally deprived infants (2). In severe cases emotional deprivation may lead to permanent emotional and intellectual impairment and even to death. As the child grows somewhat older, behavioral problems begin to displace depressive feelings: temper tantrums, disobedience, truancy, running away from home, accident proneness; masochism, as indicated by the child who

manages to get beaten up by the other children; self-destructive behavior. The youngster is convinced that he is bad, evil, unacceptable. Such feelings lead him into antisocial behavior, which in turn only further reinforces his belief that he is no good. The youngster will often feel inferior to other children; that he is ugly and stupid. All of the above-described symptoms should be considered as evidence of depression.

The following histories will illustrate typical cases:

Case 1.

A 28-year-old woman entered therapy for severe headaches and recurrent severe depressive reactions. She had been aware of the latter since she was graduated from college at 20 years of age. She could give no reason why she should have become depressed at that time, adding that she had many more reasons to be depressed when she had been living at home. In reviewing her early history she recalled having been a serious behavior problem from an early age. Her parents often had to tie her with a rope to control her, at 2-3 years of age. She would have severe temper tantrums, attack her brother with any object at hand, pull her own hair, and run out into the street without her clothes on. She was such a problem child that most of the other children were forbidden by their parents to play with her. By the time she entered grammar school the patient had become much more docile; in fact she was one of the best-behaved children in the school. Accompanying this change was a gradual withdrawal from other youngsters which reached a climax at the beginning of adolescence. During this time she indulged in a great deal of fantasy — to the exclusion of everything except schoolwork, at which she excelled. She would picture herself as a very attractive, popular girl, whereas in reality she was a shy, frightened, obese youngster with no friends. When she entered college she decided upon a career in the theater and enrolled in the school of dramatics, where much to her surprise she met with encouragement on the part of the faculty. She managed to lose about 30 pounds, to dress more fashionably, and for the first time in her life to attract the attention of young men. Just at that time she developed migraine headaches and shortly thereafter severe recurrent depressions.

Case 2.

A 12-year-old boy was seen at the request of his mother. She complained that he was obese, a compulsive eater, enuretic, fecally incontinent, and troublesome at home, as he constantly picked on his two younger sisters. She added that he was very disturbed in his relationships with other children. He refused to participate in their activities and, a student of superior talents, he would always point out their inadequacies in the scholastic area. When seen, Michael was a sullen, negativistic fat boy who stoically maintained he had no problems and didn't wish to see me. At the mother's insistence, however, he continued in therapy. For weeks the sessions consisted of brief recitals of the superficial events of the week, always phrased in the most optimistic terms: "Everything was fine." Chess was our only avenue of contact. Very gradually he began to reveal himself. He really didn't

have any friends, he would like to compete in sports but he wasn't good enough. Each forward step would be followed by two steps backward in his usual fashion of denying all difficulties. He realized he was overweight but couldn't control his appetite. Maybe he wet his bed and soiled his pants but not often and less than before (a bare-faced fabrication). Eventually he could discuss his great shame over such infantile behavior, how horrible he felt when everyone called him "Stinky." As time passed he began to mention that he had never been like the other fellows; he never remembered being happy. He often fantasied being dead and everyone being sorry for their behavior toward him.

Then, for the first time, he began to talk of his parents; how close he was to his mother, how he could get anything he desired from her. Slowly his attitudes to his father emerged. The latter, a successful dentist, was a cold, aloof, distant, hostile person who seldom was at home and on these occasions constantly berated his wife and son. He called the latter lazy, fat, incompetent, a baby. He would beat him, bribe him — all to no avail. Eventually the boy's hostile, angry feelings, which had been so long repressed, emerged. He would like to kill the father but was terrified of him. Why couldn't he and mother live by themselves? As these feelings were explored the youngster changed dramatically. He lost 25 pounds, ceased wetting and soiling, began to relate to his peers and for the first time tried out for a team, which he made, much to his amazement. That summer at camp (which incidentally accepted him back only at the urgent request of the therapist) he surprised everyone by his friendly, outgoing behavior and received a citation as the most improved camper.

Case 3.

A 13-year-old boy came to the attention of the Children's Court because of repeated truancy, fighting with other children, and running away from home. When interviewed he appeared to be a tough, calloused, belligerent youngster, indifferent to the feelings of others. He was the youngest child of a large family whose father was a chronic alcoholic, the mother a prematurely tired, discouraged woman overwhelmed by her problems. Initial attempts to involve the boy in a therapeutic relationship seemed futile, but it was noticed that despite his apparent negativistic attitude he continued to attend his sessions faithfully. He constantly tested the therapist by belligerent, provocative statements, as though desiring to be rejected. One of the aides on the ward noticed that he was a capable athlete, especially proficient at boxing. When this was mentioned to him his eyes lit up, and for the first time he appeared alert and interested. Then he shrugged it off with, "What's the use? I'd never get anywhere." It soon became evident that he felt doomed to be a failure like his father, that he regarded himself as no good. Once he expressed this as follows:

"I'm just a bastard. I have no feelings for anyone. Sometimes when I've been in a gang fight I wish I could get shot or stabbed to death — get it over quickly. It would serve me right."

He spoke initially with affection of his mother, how hard-working and noble she was. Gradually, however, other feelings emerged. "She should have left my father. She said she stayed for us kids. Some joke. How did his drinking and beatings help us?" It then became clear that his running away from home was an attempt to let his mother know how unhappy he was and also to punish her. "That was the only time she showed any interest. But in a few days she forgot about it and then everything was the same as before." Therapy revealed that his intensely angry feelings against his parents led him to regard himself as bad and evil. Such an attitude would propel him into aggressive, antisocial behavior, which in turn made him feel more evil and guilty. Assisted by therapy, Joe was able to return home and to school, where for the first time he ceased being troublesome and turned his interests to sports — joining the school basketball team.

In the latency child and especially in the adolescent we seldom see a clear picture of depression. Boys especially have a need to hide their true feelings, particularly any soft, tender, weak sentiments. Denial is one of the most characteristic mechanisms used by the adolescent, and this mechanism both on a conscious and an unconscious level is of great assistance in the avoidance of depressive feelings. At times the teen-ager may deliberately mask his true feelings by a pretense of happiness and exhibit the picture of a smiling depression. Such youngsters believe in the old adage, "Laugh and the world laughs with you, cry and you cry alone." Others utilize a reversal of affect and develop a manic-like facade. It is of interest that many comedians, both amateur and professional, are usually depressed individuals.

Rather than the usual clinical picture of depression in the adolescent, we encounter a set of symptoms which I prefer to call "depressive equivalents." Boredom and restlessness are exhibited by the adolescent to a remarkable degree. He appears uninterested in anything one moment, then is preoccupied with trivia the next. He loses interest quickly even in his most prized activities and then frenetically seeks something new to entertain him. He must be constantly busy, otherwise he is bored to distraction. He cannot stand to be alone, ever for a short period of time. He seeks constant stimulation. The phonograph, television, radio, telephone, friends, parties, all provide an opportunity to escape from the dreadful boredom that threatens to engulf him.

Persistent boredom is never a normal reaction and almost always is evidence of anxiety and/or depression. Adults, of course, often exhibit similar symptoms. An adult patient who worked in show business was accustomed to get to bed at about three or four o'clock in the morning. If by any chance he was alone before that time he would frantically seek companionship, calling up his friends or going to a bar or restaurant where he was certain to meet someone he knew. Being alone was unbearable.

The current interest of adolescents and young adults in the Beatnik way of life reflects their feelings of emptiness, isolation and depression. Believing themselves alienated from others, they band together, hoping to gain some support and relief from their distressing symptoms. Poetry sessions, mood sessions, walking sessions, alcohol, marijuana, mescaline, sexual promiscuity and perversions are all resorted to in the vain attempt to relieve their symptoms. These efforts may give transitory solace but eventually they are doomed to failure and then suicide may loom as the only solution. The following case is typical of such individuals:

Case 4.

A 15-year-old female was admitted to the hospital on her own request because of suicidal fears. An attractive youngster, she appeared several years older than her age. History revealed that she had been a behavior problem since age 7. She had had frequent fights with other children, was truant from school and disobedient at home. A bright child, her academic record was very erratic. At 14 she ran away from home to live in Greenwich Village. There she enjoyed a Beatnik existence for a short period of time; indulged in long talking sessions, mood sessions, and poetry readings. Constantly dissatisfied, she attempted also to find satisfaction by promiscuous sexual activity. As time passed she became increasingly depressed. Marijuana was attempted but provided only temporary relief. Suicide appeared the only solution but she decided, upon the advice of friends, to give psychotherapy a trial before making a final decision. In interviews with her therapist she became aware of a deep sense of loneliness, depression and despair. She realized that she had had occasional awareness of these feelings before but had, until recently, been able to ward them off by her frenetic behavior. As therapy progressed she was able to give up her pseudosophisticated facade and behave more as a normal 15-year-old.

Hand in hand with boredom, the teenager frequently complains of fatigue.

He alternates between overwhelming fatigue and inexhaustible energy. Undoubtedly some of this fatigue is physiological, being the result of the very rapid growth processes taking place at this time. We should always be suspicious, however, when the fatigue in a physically healthy youngster appears out of proportion to his activity and when it interferes with his normal activity. It is also noteworthy when the adolescent complains of being excessively tired upon awakening in the morning after an adequate amount of sleep. We are all accustomed to observing this symptom in adult patients suffering from depression. Hypochondriasis and bodily preoccupation have also frequently to be considered as evidence of depression, as is also the case in many involutional depressions.

Case 5.

Simon, age 12, was seen in consultation at the suggestion of his pediatrician. The latter was concerned because the youngster was constantly complaining of various physical ailments, which after examination proved to be either grossly exaggerated or totally imaginary. A slender, frail child, he came eagerly to the interview, desirous of discussing his problems. He stated that he had been worried about his health for the past two or three years. Initially he would become frightened whenever he had a minor physical illness, such as an upper respiratory infection. He felt that he would become seriously ill and die. As time passed he began to worry over trivial matters such as a muscle cramp or slight feelings of fatigue. During the past month he had been very alarmed, believing that he had leukemia.

This fear had begun after a class in biology at school in which the teacher described the symptoms of leukemia. He related that since that time he had had trouble falling asleep and felt anxious most of the day.

History revealed that he was an only child whose father had been killed in an airplane accident shortly after his birth. He had lived with his mother, who had never rewed and remained constantly attached to the image of her dead husband. The youngster grew up closely attached to the mother and also preoccupied with the image of the dead father. He had no close friends, although he maintained a superficial acquaintance with one or two boys younger than himself. As therapy progressed it became evident that this youngster had introjected the image of a dead father whom he both idolized and hated for deserting him. Strong incestuous ties to the mother gave rise to guilt feelings. He realized during therapy that he had seldom been happy, that he had always expected to die young (obvious identification with the dead father). As treatment progressed the somatic preoccupation was displaced by a frank depressive reaction which could then be handled directly.

Many depressed youngsters complain of difficulty in concentration. In fact, this is one of the chief presenting complaints to the school physician and should always be taken seriously, else within a very short time an otherwise capable student may fail out of school, to the amazement of parents and faculty alike. Confronted with such a problem the conscientious student will often spend long hours on his studies with little benefit. He will see others achieving better grades with much less effort and will soon become convinced that he isn't capable enough to master his work. Discouraged, he will then cease working, go frequently to the movies, spend hours watching television, and often end up by being accused of failing because he was a playboy.

Anyone who has worked with adolescents is well aware of their propensity for acting out. This, plus denial, is their main method of handling problems. Rather than face a problem, they will run away from it. This can be a most distressing obstacle to therapy but is met even more frequently in the daily activity of adolescents. The average teen-ager may appear to be frightfully concerned with his feelings and some appear to discuss them with their friends, but most of the time these discussions are on very superficial topics. It is a rare occasion for a teen-ager to discuss significant problems with anyone, himself included. In fact, these insignificant matters enable him to avoid facing really important problems. The adolescent talks constantly but, again, only about the most mundane matters. He may at times appear interested in "deep" problems such as philosophy, poetry, and the like, but this is usually only a cover for the things that really concern him. One has only to listen to some of these "world shaking" conversations for a few minutes to verify this statement.

The acting out of some adolescents may lead to serious delinquent behavior. The work of Kaufman (3) has shown that many a delinquent youngster is literally running away from himself. Anyone who has successfully treated delinquents has been struck by the very severe underlying depression which often frightens the patient away from therapy. The same situation is seen also in the character disorders of adults, who in many ways resemble adolescents in their behavior, in their defensive mechanisms, and in their response to therapy. These delinquents suffer from a severely impoverished self image and a profound emptiness of ego comparable to the emptiness of the schizophrenic ego. Any activity, no matter how dangerous or destructive, is better than facing this horrible image of oneself. It is still a mystery why one person succumbs to a psychosis and another is able to maintain his psychic equilibrium by means of psychopathic behavior. On a less serious level we may see many a youngster who, frightened of his image of himself as inadequate and as a weakling, attempts to prove that he is a tough guy by being the most aggressive one in the gang and by engaging in dangerous activity to prove that he is not afraid. Many a young man has joined the Marines, Paratroops or other dangerous outfits to prove his worth to himself.

Case 6.

Richard, a 16-year-old boy, was seen at the urgent request of his parents, who had become alarmed at evidence of increasingly delinquent behavior on his part. This had recently culminated in his suspension from school following an incident during which he struck a teacher. The boy, the elder of two children, came from a comfortable middle-class family in a suburb of New York City. He had always been somewhat small for his age — a matter of deep concern to him. A poor athlete, he tended to shun all competitive sports. He was extremely shy and frightened in the presence of girls, whom he avoided despite obvious interest. The parents noted that about six months previously he had lost all interest in his schoolwork and in his usual friends, and had begun to associate with a delinquent street gang from a distant neighborhood. At this time he evidenced a distinct personality change. He appeared cocky and self-assured, while all previous signs of anxiety disappeared. His parents had recently become aware that he had engaged in several gang fights during one of which he had been stabbed with a knife.

When first seen, Richard looked like a typical hoodlum, cigarette hanging out of the corner of his mouth, black leather jacket, tight-fitting black dungarees. He was glib and expressed his disinterest in the whole procedure. He had no problems, except his parents, who were prejudiced against his new friends. The only help he needed was to get them to leave him alone. He hated school and was happy that he had been suspended. He was pleased to converse about his gang, bragging about their delinquent activities and his own prowess in fighting. I asked him if he ever became frightened during such fights and was surprised when after much hesitation he replied, "Yes, I'm afraid I will lose control and kill someone." He went on to explain that he was losing his temper with increasing frequency and that he had not intended to strike the teacher but the latter had pushed him and then he lost his head. I remarked that perhaps this was important and also that it would obviously interfere with his plans to pursue a career in the Navy as he had intended for several years.

As therapy progressed, it was readily apparent that this patient was a frightened, anxious, chronically depressed youngster. He recalled how unhappy he had been prior to joining his gang, how inferior he had felt compared to other fellows, how scared he had been in the presence of girls, how stupid he had appeared at school, how worried that he would never amount to anything. Following his entry into the gang and by means of a vicarious identification with their supposed strength, he had felt different. "For the first time in my life I felt alive. I was a different person. I no longer worried, wasn't afraid of anyone." He began to go out with girls and felt equal to the challenge in that area. As therapy continued, a crucial period occurred when he became aware of the significance of the gang in relieving his previous depressions. He wanted to give them up but was afraid of the consequences, namely, that he would again become depressed. He finally was able to do so but only at the expense of a return of his previous feelings until these could be properly handled.

In many adolescents and adults we encounter sexual acting out as a method of relieving their depressive feelings. Such a person frenetically seeks contact with another human being by means of sexual intercourse, the only method of relating that he knows. Quite often, as in the case of the alcoholic, this activity produces only further depression and guilt, which once again he attempts to relieve by further sexual acting out.

Some children and adolescents who feel neglected and unloved by their parents may turn to animals as love objects. These youngsters are able to love and care for animals and in turn feel needed by the animal. They do not fear rejection by the animal as they do by human beings. As an example I might cite the case of a 17-year-old girl who was referred to the clinic because of scholastic difficulties. In the course of the psychiatric interview she began to speak of her interest in animals, especially horses. She spent most of her free time at a nearby stable caring for and riding horses. They and her dog were her only close relationships. Disappointed in her parents, she turned to animals, who, she felt, needed her and loved her. Her aspirations for the future consisted of becoming a veterinarian.

In many youngsters it is important to differentiate between a depressive and schizoid withdrawal. Such a differentiation is important for both therapy and prognosis. The depressive withdrawal does not ordinarily consist of as complete a rejection of reality with autistic fantasy as does the schizoid withdrawal.

One can gain much valuable assistance in the recognition of depressive reactions in both children and adolescents by means of dreams and fantasy material. Fantasies of being unloved and unwanted are frequently encountered. They may be tied in with the family romance, as such youngsters find it difficult to identify with any members of their family. Ask them whom they resemble either physically or psychologically and they will often say, "No one." When asked who loves them best in the world they will often answer, "God" — not a human being. They will fantasy their death, with their parents and other significant persons being very sorry for having mistreated them. Dreams will often reveal a preoccupation with dead persons or of being attacked and injured. It is especially significant when the youngster dreams of a dead person beckoning him to join the dead person in the other world. Dreams and fantasies often relate to body emptiness or dissolution and loss of either inner or outer parts of the body. This is not castration anxiety but refers to loss of a significant relationship. These fantasies and dreams are often expressed in sado-masochistic terms. . . .

It should be mentioned at this point that manic-depressive reactions are seldom if ever seen in children. Kanner (4) states that they are exceedingly rare before 15 or 16 years of age. Kasanin and Kaufman (5), in a series of 6,000 admissions, described only four affective psychoses before 16 years of age. All four had their initial onset after 14 years of age. The youngest child in whom we have been able to make such a diagnosis was 16 years of age. In the cases we have personally observed the initial clinical picture is usually that of a manic rather than a depressive one. Manic-like reactions are often described in children and adolescents, but closer observation usually shows that we are dealing either with a hyperactive, organic brain-damaged youngster or with an excited schizophrenic child. An interesting theoretical point is raised by the absence of manic episodes in adolescence. It is a common observation that denial is frequently used by adolescents as a means of handling their problems. Why, then, might we ask, does it not lead to a manic picture, as commonly occurs in adults? . . .

SUICIDE

It might not be amiss to make some mention of suicide at this point. Although suicide is rare in children under 10 years of age, it is far from uncommon in the adolescent age group. In fact, suicide is the fifth cause of death in the 15 to 19 age group in this country (6). When we come to examine suicidal attempts, we find even more dramatic evidence of its frequency in adolescence. According to Landrum (7) adolescents make 12 percent of all suicidal attempts. He gives a ratio of 10 females to 1 male. Our studies at Bellevue confirm these data. Suicidal attempts represent one of the most frequent reasons for admission to the psychiatric service for adolescent girls but is rather infrequently encountered on the boys' service.

There have been very few clinical studies of attempted suicide in adolescents. The most extensive, by Balser and Masterson (8), indicated that 23 of 37 suicidal patients were diagnosed as having schizophrenia. This has not been our experience at Bellevue. The majority of our patients fall into the character and behavior group. These represent immature, impulsive youngsters who react excessively to stresses often of a minor nature. When these patients are studied in more detail, however, they show many of the previously described symptoms of depression: restlessness, boredom, compulsive hyperactivity, sexual promiscuity, truancy, behavioral difficulties at home, running away from home. Quite often these suicidal attempts are manipulative in nature, directed against the parents and expressing the fantasy, "You will be sorry when I am dead. You will see how badly you treated me." Many of these youngsters had the same fantasy when they ran away from home. At times the suicidal attempt is a dramatic and last-ditch attempt to call attention to the child's problems in the hope that effective help will then be forthcoming. We have also encountered suicidal attempts as expressing: 1) a desire for peace and a nirvana-like existence, 2) a desire to join a dead parent, 3) a reaction to a hallucinatory command. These last three are usually responsible for the more serious attempts and are seen in the more disturbed youngsters. It is our belief that suicidal thoughts and attempts are either ignored or undervalued in adolescents because of the erroneously accepted tenet that adolescents do not become depressed — *ergo*, suicide is unlikely. If we can successfully recognize the signs by which depression is manifested in younger persons, we will then be in a position to prevent many serious suicidal attempts.

DISCUSSION

We must now pose the question why the clinical picture of depression should differ so markedly at different age levels. We are not in a position at this time to give a complete answer but we can offer some speculative thoughts on the problem. It would appear that the common denominator in all depressive reactions is loss of the desired love object, whether this be in fact or in fantasy. Such object loss will produce serious reactions at any age but the end result will depend upon the developmental level at which it first makes its effect felt. We agree with Rochlin (1) that in general the more serious consequences will occur in younger individuals. This, of course, is in conformity with the genetic principles of personality development. In the younger child the disturbances will primarily affect the development of the ego in all its various functions. The child will find it difficult or impossible to form the object relationships which are such a necessary part of his future psychic development. Such a deficit may lead to a lack of further development or even to severe regression. This lack of ego development will seriously impair the emotional and intellectual potential of the growing organism. It will, in addition, cause serious disturbances in the child's ability to identify with meaningful figures in his environment.

Such a disturbance in the process of identification will of necessity produce profound disorders in the development of the superego and the future personality structure. Where the disturbance arises during the latency and adolescent periods, it will lead the child to hate the lost object, who, he feels, has betrayed and deserted him. These hostile feelings can only lead to further serious conflict. The child still needs his parents, as he is still realistically dependent upon them for love and support. In fact the more he is neglected by the parents, the greater is his need for them. The child will desperately cling to the forlorn hope that they will change and give him the love he so desperately needs. Consequently repression and denial are utilized in the hope of warding off the devastating knowledge of his parents' role in his difficulty. The child would prefer to consider himself bad than to acknowledge the badness of his parents and the resultant impossibility of their changing. In assuming the burden of evil, he attempts to absolve the parents. Such an evil self-image can only, as described previously, lead the child to evil acts, which in turn reinforce his image of himself as an evil, horrible person.

As the child's reality testing improves with his advancing age, he finds it increasingly difficult to maintain his belief in the innocence of his parents. As a result, his hostility toward them increases, as do his guilt feelings. Simultaneously, the processes of identification and introjection have been progressing in the formation of the superego. Thus as these processes reach their maximum development (which does not occur until late adolescence [9]), much of the hostility previously directed toward the parents is directed toward their introjects within the child — leading to the clinical picture of depression seen in older adolescents and adults. In brief, we can state that the depressive person is constantly struggling with the opposing forces of love and hate (10).

SUMMARY

In this paper I have attempted to show that although depression, as measured by the usual clinical standards of adult psychiatry, is rarely seen in children and adolescents, depressive feelings are by no means uncommon. It must be recognized, however, that the clinical picture will vary with the age and developmental level of the child. A description is offered of the most common manifestations of depression in each age group. There is a discussion of the therapeutic problems such patients present and a theoretical explanation of the reason the clinical picture differs from that seen in adults. Recognition of such problems in children and adolescents can advance our theoretical knowledge and can enable us to prevent many suicidal attempts as well as to be more effective in our therapeutic efforts.

References

1. Rochlin, Gregory. *The Loss Complex.* J. Am. Psychoanal. Ass., 7: 299-316, 1959.
2. Spitz, Rene. "An Inquiry into the Genesis of Psychiatric Conditions in Early Childhood," in *The Psychoanalytic Study of the Child,* Vol. I, pp. 53-74. New York: Internat. Univ. Press, 1945.
3. Kaufman, Irving, and Lora Heims. *The Body Image of the Juvenile Delinquent.* Am. J. Orthopsychiatry, 28: 146-159, 1958.
4. Kanner, Leo. *Child Psychiatry.* Springfield, Ill.: Thomas, 1946.
5. Kasanin, Jacob, and M. R. Kaufman. *A Study of the Functional Psychoses in Childhood.* Am. J. Psychiatry, 9: 307-384, 1929.
6. Bakwin, H. *Suicide in Children and Adolescents.* J. Pediat., 50: 749, 1957.
7. Landrum, F.C. *A Thousand Cases of Attempted Suicide.* Am. J. Psychiatry, 13: 479, 1938.
8. Balser, B., and J.F. Masterson. *Suicide in Adolescents.* Am. J. Psychiatry, 116: 400-405, 1959.
9. Toolan, James M. "Changes in Personality Structure During Adolescence," in *Science and Psychoanalysis* (Jules H. Masserman, Ed.), Vol. III. New York: Grune & Stratton, 1960.
10. Fairbairn, William R.D. *An Object-Relations Theory of the Personality.* New York: Basic Books, 1954.

14
ADOLESCENCE:
PHYSICAL AND MENTAL GROWTH

In our society adolescence is roughly the age period from 12 to 18. In functional terms adolescence is usually considered to begin with the physical changes that usher in puberty and to end when a young person enters the work force, marries, or in some other way establishes his independence as an adult. The adolescent period is marked by extremely rapid growth in height and weight — the adolescent "growth spurt" — and by many other significant bodily changes, especially those that constitute physical sexual maturation. All of these changes require a young person to make new accommodations that affect both his orientation toward the world and his conception of himself.

In the first article that follows Tanner discusses some of the hereditary and environmental factors that influence physical growth and reviews what is known of the relative importance of these factors. Although many of the points Tanner makes pertain to individual and group differences among adolescents, which is the subject of Chapter 16, his article includes considerable normative data about the timing and rate of adolescent growth changes. It should also be noted in connection with Tanner's article that the bulk of current research suggests that a lower limit has been reached with regard to age of puberty. Over most of the last century the beginning of puberty became a progressively earlier event from one decade to the next, but this trend now appears to be at an end. Thus young women today reach puberty at about the same age as their mothers did.

The second selection by Elkind is concerned with some of the quantitative and qualitative aspects of intellectual growth in adolescence. Because of the dramatic physical changes that take place during the adolescent years, the equally dramatic but less visible intellectual changes in teenagers are often overlooked or minimized. Yet the intellectual changes that occur in adolescence are every bit as important for understanding adolescent development as the physical transformations. Elkind identifies in his article some of the major ways in which adolescent behavior is influenced by the new forms of thinking that emerge in the teenage years.

Interaction of Hereditary and Environmental Factors in Controlling Growth*

Many factors are known which affect the rate of development. Some, like the body build of the children, are chiefly hereditary in origin and act by hastening or retarding physiological maturation from an early age. Others, such as season of the year, psychological stress, or dietary restriction, originate in the environment and simply affect the rate of growth at the time they are acting. Others again, such as socio-economic class, reflect a complicated mixture of hereditary and environmental influences.

The height or weight or body build of a child or of an adult represents always the resultant of both the genetical and environmental forces, together with their interaction. It is a long way from the possession of certain genes to the acquisition of a height of 6 feet. In modern genetics it is a truism that any particular gene depends for its expression firstly on the internal environment as created by all the other genes, and secondly on the external environment. Furthermore, the interaction of genes and environment may not be additive; that is to say, bettering the nutrition by a fixed amount may not produce a 10 per cent. increase in height in all persons irrespective of their genetical constitution, but instead a 12 per cent. rise in the genetically tall and an 8 per cent. rise in the genetically short. This type of interaction, wherein a particular environment proves highly suitable for a child with certain genes, and highly unsuitable for a child with others, is called multiplicative. . . . It is exceedingly difficult to specify quantitatively the relative importance, therefore, of heredity and environment. In general the

*From Chapter 6 of J. M. Tanner, *Education and physical growth*, 1961. Reprinted by permission of the author, the University of London Press, and International Universities Press.

nearer optimal the environment the more the genes have a chance to show their potential actions, but this is a general statement only and undoubtedly many more subtle and specific interactions occur, especially in growth and differentiation.

Hereditary factors, however, are clearly of immense importance in the control of growth and they will be discussed first. . . . The effects of race and climate and season of the year will then be given, and lastly the effects of nutrition, illness, exercise, psychological disturbance, socio-economic class and family size.

GENETICS OF GROWTH

The genetical control of rate of growth is manifested most simply in the inheritance of age at menarche.[1] Identical twin sisters, with the same genes, reach menarche an average of 2 months apart. Non-identical twin sisters, with the same proportion of different genes as ordinary sisters,

---

[1] For many studies on growth rate age at menarche is used. This is partly because it is a definite landmark in the great majority of girls and partly because valid means and standard deviations can be obtained for different groups by the cross-sectional method of simply asking all the girls between the ages of 9 and 17, say, whether or not they have yet menstruated. This avoids the difficulty of depending on memory. Because age at menarche is distributed in a population in a Gaussian or near-Gaussian curve (except for a very few excessively retarded individuals, probably pathological) a probit or logit transformation can be made on data of the have/have-not menstruated variety and the means and standard deviations thus estimated.

reach menarche an average of about 10 months apart. The sister-sister and mother-daughter correlation coefficients are both about 0.4, which is only slightly below the same correlations for height. These are indications that a high proportion of the variability of age at menarche in populations living under West European conditions is due to genetical causes. Further, the inheritance of age at menarche is probably transmitted as much by the father as the mother, and is due not to a single gene but to many genes each of small effect. This is the same pattern of inheritance as that shown by height and other body measurements.

This genetical control evidently operates throughout the whole process of growth and the conclusions regarding age at menarche apply equally to rate of development in general. Skeletal age, for example, shows a very close resemblance in identical twins at all ages. In fact, under reasonable environmental circumstances, the genetical control extends down to many of the details of the velocity and acceleration curves. This is demonstrated by the records of three sisters given in Figure 1. The heights are plotted on the left against chronological age and on the right against developmental age as represented by years before and after maximum velocity of adolescent growth. Two of the sisters have curves which are almost perfectly superimposable one on the other except that they are on a different time base, one being almost a year in advance. These two sisters differ radically therefore in one parameter of their growth curve, but little in the other parameters. There is additional evidence also that genes controlling *rate* of growth are wholly or partly

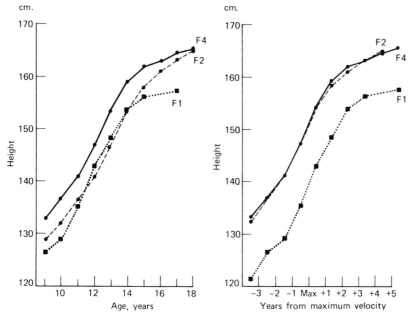

Figure 1. *Growth in height of 3 sisters. Left, height plotted against chronological age; right, against years before or years after maximum velocity. Note the coincidence of curves of F2 and F4 when equated for developmental age, right. [Data from Ford (1958). From Tanner, Human Growth, Pergamon Press.]*

independent of those controlling *final size* achieved.

The time of eruption of the teeth, both deciduous and permanent, is genetically controlled, and there is some evidence that the order in which teeth calcify and erupt is hereditarily determined also. This is important, as it implies the existence of hereditary factors acting locally on one or a few teeth only, an example of local growth gradients discussed above, which in the majority of cases are evidently genetically determined.

We have already seen ... that not all genes are active at birth. Some express themselves only in the physiological surroundings provided in the later years of growth. It is very probable, for example that the magnitude as well as the time of the adolescent spurt is genetically controlled, perhaps by genes causing secretion of large or small amounts of androgenic hormones. Such genes may have excited no effect before the moment when the pituitary gland signals the beginning of androgen secretion.

Genes whose expression is age-limited in this way may well be responsible for the fact ... that children grow to resemble their parents more as they grow older, relatively as well as absolutely. In fact, the curve for the correlation of parents' height with the height of their children at increasing ages is very similar to that of a child's height with his own height when adult. . . . The correlation is very low at birth and rises sharply to about 3 years, by which time evidently much of the genes' contributions to the child's growth is manifest. This is chiefly mentioned here, however, because a similar parent-child curve has been reported for the correlations of I.Q. measurements (Bayley, 1954; Honzik, 1957; though see Kagan and Moss, 1959). It may well have the same explanation. That the increasing resemblance of parents' and children's I.Q.s is due primarily to genetical factors is shown by the fact that foster-children increase their correlations with the I.Q. of their real mother, even though separated from her, while their correlations with the foster-mother's I.Q. remain unchanged throughout growth (Skodak and Skeels, 1949).

RACE AND CLIMATE

There are racial differences in rate and pattern of growth leading to the differences seen in adult build. Some of these are clearly genetically determined, while others depend perhaps on climatic differences and certainly on nutritional ones.

Contrary to popular belief climate seems to have little direct effect on rate of growth. The average at menarche of upper socio-economic class Nigerian schoolgirls has been recently reported as 14.3 years and that of Eskimo girls as 14.4 years. There is no difference in menarcheal age between girls in the hot humid areas of Central India and those in the hot but dry area of Northern Nigeria. Burmese girls living under good nutritional and medical circumstances in a relatively wealthy town with a hot weath-er temperature of 112°F., had an average menarcheal age of 13.2 years (for refs. see Tanner, 1961), which is very similar to figures reported for girls in Western Europe.

Kraus (1954) has compared the heights and weights of children aged 6 to 11 in three American Indian tribes living in Arizona with those of the local American whites. Despite being in worse economic and probably nutritional circumstances the American Indian children were at all ages heavier for their height than the whites. Similarly, the Maori are shorter and stockier than New Zealand whites at all ages from 5 onwards. By contrast, African negroes, and particularly the Nilotics, are lighter at all ages for their height than whites, and in many of the series studied this could hardly be due to nutritional deprivation (Roberts, 1960).

Negroes, in West Africa, East Africa and the United States, are ahead of whites in skeletal ossification at birth. This can scarcely be due to better economic or nutritional circumstances or to better prenatal care: it is almost certainly genetic. It is associated with advancement of motor behaviour, so that negro children in America are ahead of the white norms in passing milestones such as sitting up, crawling and vocalizing, and in Uganda are ahead on the Gesell baby tests. The advancement, both of skeletal and motor development, disappears by about the third year, at least in Africa. This is partially and perhaps wholly due to the effect of inadequate nutrition.

The permanent teeth also erupt an average of a year earlier in negroes than in whites, and this despite the fact that by the time these teeth erupt the skeletal maturity has fallen behind that of the whites by a similar or greater amount. Presumably the economic privation has less effect on the teeth, whose buds have been laid down earlier and whose growth is in most circumstances more resistant to malnutrition and disease, probably because it is less affected by hormonal alterations in the blood. At all events, this is an added example of the distinction between tooth maturity and general skeletal maturity.

SEASON

In most human growth data a well-marked seasonal effect on velocity can be seen. Growth in height is on average fastest in spring and growth in weight fastest in autumn. This applies at all ages after the first year. According to the majority of the data the average velocity of height from March to May is about twice that from September to October.

The months of greatest increase in weight in the Northern Hemisphere are usually September to October and in these months the weight increment may be four or five times the weight increment in March to May. A small percentage of children actually lose weight in the spring months. There is, however, some rather inconclusive evidence that well-nourished children show a smaller seasonal difference in weight gain than the less well-nourished.

The trends described are the average curves obtained from many children followed longitudinally. Relatively few individual children have curves which coincide with these; the time of year at which different individuals have their seasonal

peak varies considerably and so also does the degree to which seasonal peaking occurs at all. In some individuals' records regular seasonal fluctuations occur, as illustrated in Figure 2 for a pair of identical twins whose height velocity was consistently greater in the February-August periods than in the August-February ones. But in other children little sign of any seasonal effect is seen. Probably the effect is chiefly due to variations in hormone secretion, with individual differences caused by differences in endocrine reactivity.

NUTRITION

Malnutrition during childhood delays growth, as is shown from the effects of famine associated with war. In Figure 3 the heights and weights of school children in Stuttgart, Germany, are plotted at each year of age, for the years 1911 to 1953. There is a uniform increase at all ages in both measurements from 1920 to 1940 (see the next chaper on this), but in the later years of the Second World War this trend is sharply reversed as the food intake of the children became restricted. After 1947 conditions greatly improved and this is reflected in the increased size of the children who by 1953 had at most ages reached or exceeded the 1939 level.

Children have great recuperative powers, provided the adverse conditions are not carried too far or continued too long. During a short period of malnutrition the organism slows up its growth and waits for better times; when they arrive growth takes place unusually fast until the genetically determined growth curve is reached or approached again, and then

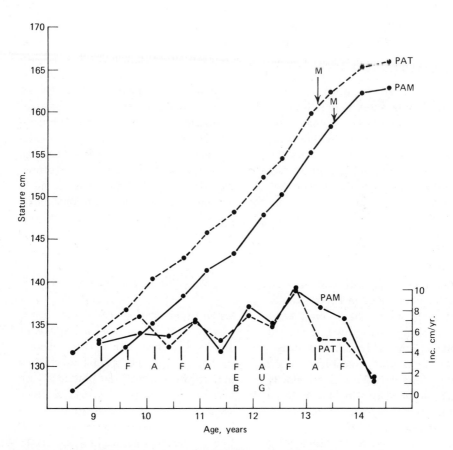

Figure 2. *Growth in height of identical twin girls, showing seasonal effect on rate of growth. (From Tanner, Growth at Adolescence, Blackwell Science Publications: Oxford.)*

it is subsequently followed. During this "catch-up" phase, following supplementation of the diet of children previously malnourished, height, weight and skeletal maturity are caught up at the same or nearly the same rate, so that the final state is probably little, if at all, distinguishable from what it would have been had no short period of malnutrition occurred (Widdowson and McCance, 1954). Chronic malnutrition can certainly retard and diminish growth and result in a small-sized adult. In cattle alternation of periods of good feeding and periods of underfeeding may alter the final shape and tissue composition as well as the overall size, according to the timing of the periods, the fastest-growing tissues suffering most. There is little evidence that this occurs in either acute or chronic malnutrition in man however. Japanese children brought up in California, for example, and better fed there than in Japan grow faster, and become larger

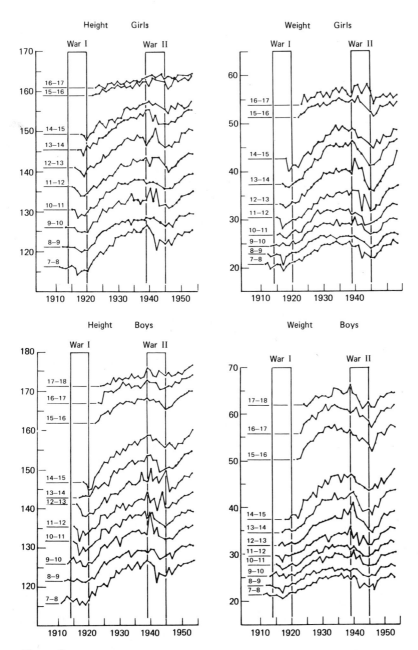

Figure 3.

than Japanese in Japan; but their proportions of leg and trunk remain the same (Greullch, 1957).

One of the most arresting findings in this field in recent years has been the discovery that boys and girls differ in their ability to withstand malnutrition or illness. Girls are less easily thrown off their growth curves by adverse circumstances than boys. The control of their growth is better stabilized. This is believed to be due to their possession of two X chromosomes rather than one, since it is known in animals (which also show this sex difference) that genetic factors are responsible for this regulation of growth in the face of adversity.

It is perhaps due to this, as well as to their more retarded development, that more boys than girls are seen in most remedial clinics, and that more boys than girls are persistent bed-wetters (Blomfield and Douglas, 1956). It is not known to what extent this increased vulnerability applies to behavioural matters, or to the neurological basis underlying them.

ILLNESS

Minor and relatively short illnesses such as measles, influenza and even antibiotic-treated middle ear infection or pneumonia cause no discernible retardation of growth rate in the great majority of well-nourished children. In children with a less adequate diet they may cause some disturbance, though this has not been securely established. Often the children with continuous colds, ear disease, sore throats and skin infections are on average smaller than the others, but inquiry reveals that they come from economically depressed and socially disorganized homes where proper meals are unknown and cleanliness too much trouble. The small size is more likely to be due to malnutrition than to the effects of the continued minor diseases (Miller, Court, Walton and Knox, 1960).

Major illnesses which take the child to hospital for a month or more or keep him in bed at home for several months may cause a considerable slowing down of growth. The mechanism by which they do so varies from one disorder to another; in a number changes in endocrine balance are probably involved and in particular an increase in hydrocortisone secretion from the adrenal glands which if sufficient is known to slow down growth. When recovery takes place a "catch-up" period may occur, during which growth rates may reach twice the normal rate for the child's age. A chronic disease may result in a considerable reduction in body size, just as does chronic malnutrition; but body proportions seem to be largely unaffected, as shown by comparison of identical twins one with and the other without the chronic disease in question.

EXERCISE

Though some writers have claimed that exercise increases the rate of growth or enlarges permanently the muscles, the published evidence is not sufficiently critical to allow of any firm conclusion. In adults muscles enlarged by heavy weight-lifting exercise soon regress to the pre-existing level when the exercise is stopped (Tanner, 1952) and there is little to suggest that muscular exercise in children would cause a lasting muscular enlargement. Much more research, and in particular more critical and adequately designed research, is needed in this field before any conclusions can really be drawn.

PSYCHOLOGICAL DISTURBANCE AND GROWTH RATE

That adverse psychological conditions may cause a degree of retardation in growth is a thought that readily comes to mind. Clear-cut experiments on this are very hard to find, however, and opinions in this field tend to be based more on the wish than the experimental fact. The clearly controlled study made by Widdowson (1951) is therefore all the more valuable.

In studying the effect of increased rations on orphanage children living on the poor diet available in Germany in 1948 she had the rare opportunity of observing the change brought about by replacement of one sister-in-charge by another. The design of the experiment was to give orphanage B a food supplement after a six months' control period and to compare the growth of the children there with those in orphanage A, which was not to be supplemented. As shown in Figure 4, however, the result was just the reverse of what was expected; though the B children actually gained more weight than the A children during the first, unsupplemented, six months, they gained less during the second six months despite actually taking in a measured 20 per cent. more calories. The reason appeared to be that at precisely the six-month mark a certain sister had been transferred from A to become

head of B. She ruled the children of B with a rod of iron and frequently chose mealtimes to administer to individual children public and often unjustified rebukes, which upset all present. An exception was the group of eight favourites (squares in the figure) whom she brought with her from orphanage A. These eight always gained more weight than the others, and on being supplemented in B gained still faster. The effect on height was less than that on weight, but of the same nature. "Better," quotes Widdowson, "a dinner of herbs where love is than a stalled ox and hatred therewith."

Possibly similar factors may explain in part some of the observations made on gains in height and weight in school children during term-time as opposed to holidays (though it must be emphasized that the sister's treatment of the children was really shocking and constituted a severe emotional stress not to be compared with the occasional reprimand; the occasional reprimand to one child may be a severe pressure to another, however). In certain day and boarding schools the rate of growth in height and weight has been shown to be less during term, and particularly during the second half of term, than in the holidays (Friend, 1935; Allan, 1937, 1939; Friend and Bransby, 1947). Schools differ in this respect. In two out of three private boarding schools investigated boys aged 13 to 16 had term-time gains in height and weight which were only half as much as the holiday gains; but in the third school term and holiday gains were equal (Widdowson and McCance, 1944).

These comparisons seem to be independent of seasonal effects. Many criticisms could be levelled at the techniques,

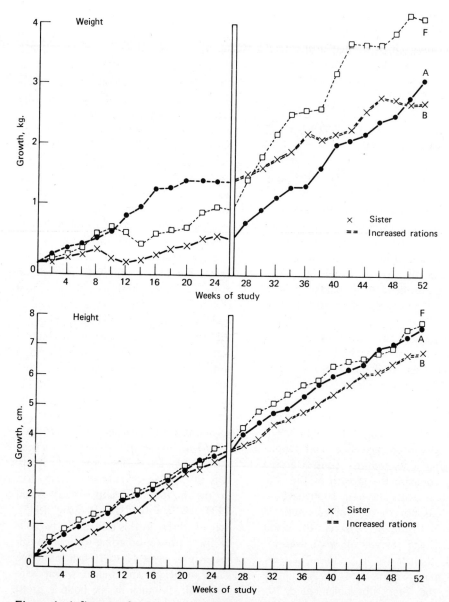

Figure 4. *Influence of sister-in-charge S on growth in weight and height of orphanage children. Presence of S marked by X plots, increased rations by ==. Orphanage B diet supplemented at time indicated by vertical bar, but sister simultaneously transferred to B(- - -) from A(—). Note magnitude of growth follows presence or absence of sister, not amount of rations. Top curves (□...□) are for 8 favourites of sister, transferred with her to B from A. [Redrawn from Widdowson (1951). (From Tanner, Growth at Adolescence, Blackwell Sci. Publ.: Oxford.]*

expecially for measuring height, used in the older investigations where very small increments are being studied. Many alternative explanations, nutritional and other, could be found for the results. Nevertheless, the subject is of potential importance and some further careful and more detailed studies—distinguishing bone, muscle and fat growth, for example, instead of lumping them all together as body weight—would provide educational authorities with valuable data on various aspects of the schools concerned.

SOCIO-ECONOMIC CLASS: SIZE OF FAMILY

Children from different socio-economic levels differ in average body size at all ages, the upper groups being always larger. In most studies socio-economic status has been defined according to the father's occupation, though in recent years in Great Britain it is becoming clear that this does not distinguish people's living standards as well as it used to; an index reflecting housing conditions is becoming a necessary adjunct, since these vary widely within occupational classes.

The difference in height between children of the professional and managerial classes and those of unskilled labourers is currently about an inch at 3 years, rising to 1½ or even 2 inches at adolescence. In weight the difference is relatively less (from 1 to 8 lb. in most data), since the lower socio-economic class children have a greater weight for height, due to greater relative breadth of skeleton and probably also of muscles. In Figure 5 the heights and weights of a random sample of all

11-year-old Scottish children are plotted in relation to socio-economic class and family size (see below). Classes I-III here represent professional persons, employers and salaried staff, Class IV non-manual wage earners, and so on down to Class VII, unskilled manual workers. The tendency for the better-off children to be larger is visible for all family sizes.

The greater part of the height difference is due to earlier maturation of the well-off classes, though some is due to their being larger as adults. Menarche occurs three months earlier in grammar school girls in Bristol than in girls in secondary modern schools there (Wofinden and Smallwood, 1958). In Copenhagen there is a difference of two months in menarcheal age between the daughters of professional and managerial classes and those of unskilled workmen. Permanent tooth eruption also occurs earlier in the more favoured groups. The difference between children in well-off and average families amounts to some three months in date of eruption, averaged over all the teeth.

The causes of this socio-economic differential are probably multiple. Nutrition is almost certainly one, and with it all the habits of regular meals, sleep, exercise and general organization that distinguish, from this point of view, a good home from a bad one. The growth differences are more related to home conditions than to the economic conditions of the families, and home conditions reflect to a considerable degree the intelligence and personality of the parents.

Berry and Cowin (1954) have found that although there were consistent weight differences, associated with parents' social class, in 14-year-old boys in

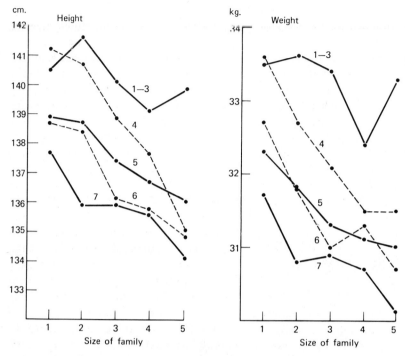

Figure 5. *Relation between height and weight of 11-year-old children and size of family, in different socio-economic classes in Scotland in 1947. Classes marked 1-3, 4, 5, 6, and 7. [Data from Scottish Council for Research in Education, 1953. (From Tanner, Growth at Adolescence, Blackwell Sci. Publ.: Oxford.)]*

grammar and in secondary modern schools, still larger differences existed between grammar and secondary modern 14-year-olds whose fathers had the *same* occupation. The weights of boys whose parents were in the Registrar-General's occupational classes I and II, III, IV, and V, were in grammar school 116, 110, 108 and 104 lb., and in secondary modern school 105, 103, 103 and 102 lb. respectively. Thus it seems that a high weight is more associated with a boy's ability to get into grammar school (usually by examination at age 11) than with the occupational class of his parents. We do

not know whether this relation between intelligence and size reflects a genetical effect on both, or whether both superior weight and intelligence come from excellence of early child care.

There is little published data on heights and weights of pupils of different educational streams in comprehensive and other schools, though a great deal must certainly exist in school records. Analysis of such data would be useful, especially if the I.Q. of the child, the father's occupation and housing conditions and some measure of the child's developmental age were also recorded. Some teachers tend to believe that the earliest maturers are not the grammar school boys but the lower stream ones. This may be a 'clinical' impression derived from a few short, muscular, early-maturing, highly noticeable and not too bright lads. It may be misleading in terms of averages. But perhaps not; the situation may well be more complex than outlined here.

The size of the family exerts an effect on the size of the children, at least in worse-off groups of the population (see Figure 5). The more mouths to feed and children to bother about, the less well the feeding, and perhaps the general care, is carried out.

References

Allan, J. Influence of school routine on the growth and health of children. *Lancet*, 1937, 1, 674–675.

Allan, J. Growth of children in day schools. *Lancet*, 1939, 1, 1300–1301.

Bayley, N. Some increasing parent-child similarities during the growth of children. *Journal of Educational Psychology*, 1954, 45, 1-21.

Berry, W. T. C., and Cowin, P. J. Conditions associated with the growth of boys, 1950-51. *British Medical Journal*, 1954, 1, 847-851.

Blomfield, J. M., and Douglas, J. W. B. Bedwetting: Prevalence among children aged 4-7 years. *Lancet*, 1956, 1, 850-852.

Friend, G. E. *The schoolboy: A study of his nutrition, physical development and health*. Cambridge: Heffer, 1935.

Friend, G. E., and Bransby, E. R. Physique and growth of schoolboys. *Lancet*, 1947, 2, 677-681.

Greulich, W. W. A comparison of the physical growth and development of American-born and native Japanese children. *American Journal of Physical Anthropology*, 1957, 15, 489-515.

Honzik, M. P. Developmental studies of parent-child resemblance in intelligence. *Child Development*, 1957, 28, 215-228.

Kagan, J., and Moss, H. A. Parental correlates of child's I. Q. and height: A cross-validation of the Berkeley Growth Study results. *Child Development*, 1959, 30, 325-332.

Kraus, B. S. *Indian Health in Arizona*. Tucson, Arizona: University of Arizona Press, 1954.

Miller, F. J. W., Court, S. D. M., Walton, W. S., and Knox, E. G. *Growing up in Newcastle-upon-Tyne: A continuing study of health and illness in young children within their families*. London: Oxford University Press, 1960.

Roberts, D. F. Effects of race and climate on human growth as exemplified by studies on African children. In J. M. Tanner (Ed.), *Human growth*. Vol. 3. London: Pergamon, 1960.

Skodak, M., and Skeels, H. M. A final follow-up study of one hundred adopted children. *Journal of Genetic Psychology*, 1949, 75, 85-125.

Tanner, J. M. The effect of weight-training on physique. *American Journal of Physical Anthropology*, 1952, **10**, 427-462.

Tanner, J. M. *Growth at adolescence.* (2nd ed.) Oxford: Blackwell Science Publications, 1961.

Widdowson, E. M. Mental contentment and physical growth. *Lancet*, 1951, **1**, 1316-1318.

Widdowson, E. M., and McCance, R. A. Growth at home and at school. *Lancet*, 1944, **2**, 152-153.

Widdowson, E. M., and McCance, R. A. Studies on the nutritive value of bread and on the effect of variations in the extraction rate of flour on the growth of undernourished children. *Medical Research Council Special Report*, No. 287, 1954.

Wofinden, R. C., and Smallwood, A. L. *Annual Report Principal School Medical Officer to City and County of Bristol Education Committee*, 1958.

DAVID ELKIND

Quantitative and Qualitative Aspects of Cognitive Growth in Adolescence*

THE COURSE OF MENTAL GROWTH

Perhaps the most famous study dealing with the course of mental growth across a long age span was an investigation published three decades ago by Jones and Conrad (1933). The study was instigated in part by the statement, made shortly

*From Chapter 6 of J. F. Adams (Ed.), *Understanding adolescence*, 1968. Reprinted by permission of the author and Allyn and Bacon, Inc.

after the First World War, to the effect that the mental ability of the average white draftee was equal to that of a thirteen-year-old child. This statement contradicted the notion that the mental ability of the average adult was comparable to that of a sixteen-year-old as indicated by the Terman (1916) revision of the Binet Scale. The aim of the Jones and Conrad study was to answer the question as to the peak of mental growth in a more systematic way than had hitherto been attempted.

In this carefully controlled and executed investigation, the Army Alpha Intelligence Test was administered to 1191 subjects who ranged in age from 10 to 59. For our purposes the most important finding was that mental growth increased rapidly until about the age of sixteen, after which the rate of growth became much slower. After the age of 21 the curve for mental ability began to move downward. In interpreting their results, Jones and Conrad took into account many non-intellectual factors that might possibly have affected their findings. They considered, for example, the fact that older persons might be handicapped with respect to younger ones because the Alpha is primarily a speed test and because older people tend to work more slowly than do younger people. Jones and Conrad were able to show, however, that the results held even for tests where no time pressure was involved. In summary, for the abilities tapped by the Army Alpha and for the populations studied (mostly persons from rural towns in New England), these findings with respect to the curve of mental growth would seem to have a certain measure of validity, and they have been supported in a general way by Shock (1951).

More recent work has, however, suggested that these initial findings have to be qualified in several ways. As Jones (1955) himself is quite willing to concede, the decline of intellectual functions will vary with the educational level of the subjects and with the nature of the mental abilities in question.

In a study of Thorndike (1948) it was found that mental test scores for individuals who are attending school continue to increase at least until the age of 20. Similar findings have been reported by Burns (1966), who retested 80 university graduates who had been tested on two previous occasions—during teacher training in 1930-33 when their age was 22½, and again in 1955 when their age was 47. The mean age at the third testing was 56. In general, Burns found that verbal skills such as vocabulary showed very little deterioration with age while number skills did show deterioration. Burns comments on the fact that the verbal skills may have been maintained because at least 60% of the subjects were engaged in teaching—which supposedly would serve to provide exercise for verbal skills.

These findings suggest that those persons who continue in intellectual pursuits during their adult lives may show less deterioration in some mental abilities than those adults who are not so engaged. This finding is probably complicated by the fact that the pursuit of an academic career is usually associated with higher intelligence and that persons of better than average ability may show less deterioration with age than persons of average ability. In this regard the findings of Owens (1953) with college graduates and of Bayley and Oden (1955) with gifted adults suggest that high intelligence as well as an academic profession is a hedge against the deterioration of some mental abilities.

All these studies are consistent in showing that verbal skills tend to deteriorate less rapidly than mathematical skills. An interesting hypothesis to account for the different developmental and decline patterns of varied mental abilities has been offered by Trembly (1964). He argues that each mental ability shows a period of rapid early growth after which it reaches a plateau and then proceeds to decline. In addition, each mental ability shows a distinct rate of growth, age of maturity, age of decline and rate of decline. Trembly argues further that those mental abilities which appear earliest in individual development show longer plateaus and less rapid decline at older age levels than do later appearing mental abilities. In support of this position, he cites tonal memory, which has a plateau of 30 years, and contrasts it with inductive reasoning, which appears much later in development and manifests a plateau of only three years.

This hypothesis is in keeping with the position of Jones (1955), who argues that those abilities that are maintained with little deterioration tend to reflect "the mere accumulation of verbal or factual inventories" while the abilities which show decline with age, such as mathematical reasoning and analogies, have more to do with high level mental processes. In this connection Jones (1955) cites Whitehead, "The imagination is most active between the ages of 19 and 35 and we mostly keep going thereafter, on whatever fizz we have experienced then." Such a view is supported by the fact that in science and in the arts the really great discoveries and creations are most often the work of young men.

THE DIFFERENTIATION OF ABILITIES

One of the debates that seems to be perennial within developmental psychology is whether growth proceeds by differentiation or by integration. This debate has been carried on at the biological, physiological, and psychological levels without ever having been completely resolved at any level. In some cases the debate revolves more around a definition of terms that upon different interpretations of the data. Differentiation, for example, can mean either specialization of function or increased complexity of functioning or both! Likewise, integration can refer either to the unity of an organization or to its simplicity or to both at the same time. With respect to the issue of differentiation vs. integration of intelligence with age, the debate would appear to be factual as well as verbal.

In order to make clear the issue of differentiation with respect to intellectual functioning, it is necessary first to recall Spearman's (1923) theory of intelligence. According to Spearman, performance on any mental task involves a general or g factor present in all mental operations plus specific s factors unique to the mental operations called forth by different types of tasks. The issue with respect to the differentiation of abilities in adolescence concerns the relative amounts of g and s factors involved in specific mental tests at different age levels. Although these factors are extracted by the rather complex mathematical procedures of factor analysis, we need not understand those procedures to grasp the issues involved.

One of the first investigators to advocate the differentiation hypothesis with respect to adolescent intelligence was Burt who wrote:

With younger children, and particularly, it would appear, with younger girls, one can demonstrate little but the existence of the general factor (i.e., g); with

*older school children and particularly
with college students, little but specific
talents or specialized interests (Burt,
1962/1921, p. 359).*

J.M. TANNER

This statement was based on factor analytic data which showed that the amount of the general factor in tests of verbal, arithmetical and manual ability decreased markedly with age while the reverse held true for the specific factors.

Support for this differentiation point of view came from Garrett (1946), who was primarily concerned with the nature of mental organization. In one study reported by Garrett (1946) 9, 12 and 15-year-old children were tested for memory, verbal, and number abilities. The degree to which the general or g factor was involved in these tests dropped from .31 among the youngest boys to .12 among the oldest boys, and for the girls the amount of g dropped from .31 among the youngest to .19 among the oldest. Garrett also reports other studies (which suggested comparable results) and postulated the following hypothesis: "Abstract or symbol intelligence changes in organization as age increases from a fairly unified and general ability to a loosely organized group of abilities or factors" (Garrett, 1946, p. 373).

Other investigators have found similar trends. Balinsky (1941) tested subjects ranging in age from 9 to 59 and found that the number of factors increased between the ages of 9 and 29 but declined thereafter. Thurstone and Thurstone (1941) also obtained evidence for differentiation with age. These investigators found six primary mental abilities among kindergarten children, seven among seventh grade children, and nine among

such factors among college students. Although arrived at by somewhat different methods and tests, these results are in general agreement with those of Burt (1962/1921) and Garrett (1946) with respect to the differentiation of mental abilities during adolescence.

Unfortunately, at least for those who like their science neat, other investigators have obtained evidence which contradicts the differentiation hypothesis in the sense that it points toward the notion that intelligence becomes more integrated with age. Cohen (1959), for example, tested children aged 7-6, 10-6, and 13-6 with the Wechsler Intelligence Test for Children (WISC) and found no evidence for the differentiation hypothesis. He argues that the same factors appear in the intellectual functioning of children and adults, and that adults show more of the general factor than do children. Likewise, Cropley (1964) tested 10 and 12-year-old children on the WISC and found comparable factor structures and a tendency for increasing integration with age. While these results might be questioned (on the basis of the methods used to extract the factors), as they stand they raise difficulties for the differentiation hypothesis. Perhaps a theory which postulates a general to specific to general development across the whole life span (Green and Berkowitz, 1964) may help resolve the problem. In addition, the utilization of uniform methods for extracting factors and uniform criteria for interpreting them would be helpful.

It is not possible at the present time to come to any clear-cut conclusion about the differentiation of abilities in adolescence although the bulk of the evidence seems to favor differentiation over integration at least during the adolescent period. All that we can do, as a parting shot at the problem, is to present a statement by Burt which helps to clarify the issues involved and provides a cautionary note as well:

Judging from my own data, I should readily agree that, after the age of puberty, it is not easy to find evidence for further differentiation of abilities, *though a differentiation of* interests *is often discernible. That, however, cannot affect the hypothesis with which we are here concerned—namely, that between late infancy and early adolescence, there is a definite increase in specialization in ability due, not to education, but to maturation. At the same time,* it would be a gross oversimplification to describe mental development in terms of a single sweeping principle—whether of increasing differentiation or increasing integration—or to assume that any such principle must hold good of all mental processes and of every individual. *(our italics) (Burt, 1954, p. 85)*

THE CONSTANCY OF THE IQ FROM CHILDHOOD TO ADOLESCENCE

On the surface, it might seem that an answer to the problem of whether or not the IQ remains constant over long time periods would be relatively easy to answer. All one needs to do is test the same subject as a child and again as an adolescent and then compare the results of the two examinations. In fact, however, the problem is complicated by many different factors, some of which come from the nature of the tests and some

from the nature of the subject. Let us first consider the difficulties which are inherent in the tests.

The kinds of defects inherent in mental tests which make difficult the comparison of the performances of the same individual are illustrated by the 1937 revision of Stanford Binet (Terman and Merrill, 1937). Pinneau (1961), for example, has shown that by virtue of the way in which the test was constructed, a person who maintained the same relative standing with respect to his age group from childhood to adolescence would nonetheless have attained a different IQ score in adolescence than he did in childhood. The reason is statistical and has to do with the fact that the amount of variability at the two developmental periods differs. In addition, the correlation between the scores obtained by the same person on a particular intelligence test will vary as a function of the ages at which the examinations were given and as a function of the time interval between the examinations. Scores attained during the pre-school period, for example, tend to correlate less highly with scores attained during adolescence than do scores attained during the elementary period (Honzik, MacFarland and Allen, 1948).

Another major consideration in attempting to evaluate the constancy of the IQ is the kinds of experiences the individual has undergone. Since the IQ measures achievement as well as underlying capacity, any factors which affect achievement will also affect the IQ. Environmental experiences which make for self-confidence, which provide or deprive the individual of ample and effective stimulation for learning, may markedly affect the extent of the young person's intellectual achievements. Environmental circumstances, moreover, do not remain constant throughout childhood and adolescence. The family may move, the young person may become a member of a group which is for or against school, or he may encounter a teacher who sets a spark to his intellect or who, contrariwise, kills his interest in learning. All of these factors and more can and do affect performance on intelligence tests and make it difficult to say how stable the IQ will remain from childhood to adolescence.

For all these reasons, changes in IQ with age are probably the rule rather than the exception. It is also true, however, that a certain amount of constancy does occur. Correlations between IQ's attained in childhood and those attained in adolescence are on the order of .60, and the correlations between IQ's attained in adolescence and adulthood on the order of .80 (Bradway and Thompson, 1962). While the knowledge of the IQ of a child may not be sufficient to predict exactly what his IQ will be as an adolescent, it does enable us to make a better than chance guess as to what his relative standing in adolescence will be. And, in general, the more extreme the IQ at childhood, whether in a low or high direction, the more accurate will be the prediction. The greatest changes in IQ occur among those who score in the average range between 90 and 110, but even though there is an absolute change in score, the chances are that the person will remain in the average category. Put differently, if we think of IQ standing in terms of gross categories such as above average, average and below average, rather than in terms of absolute scores, then the

IQ does remain relatively stable from childhood through adolescence. It is only when we think of the IQ in terms of absolute numerical scores that we must reject the notion of IQ constancy. The reader will also find Nichol's chapter, on the issue of the contributions of heredity and environment, a valuable supplement to his thinking in this area.

SEX DIFFERENCE IN INTELLIGENCE AND MENTAL ABILITY

The literature on differences between boys and girls in intelligence in general and in cognitive abilities and interests in particular is enormous, and no attempt will be made to survey that material here. In a comprehensive summary of the findings up to 1954, Terman and Tyler made the following points which appear equally valid today:

1. If there are differences in general intelligence between the sexes, they cannot be identified by means of our present tests.

2. Girls tend to excel on verbal types of problems, boys on quantitative or spatial problems.

3. School marks almost universally indicate superior achievement for girls. Achievement tests, however, while they show girls to be superior in all kinds of language material, show boys to be superior in science and mathematics.

4. Vocational aptitude tests show boys as higher in mechanical, girls in clerical, aptitudes.

5. Ability differences are most apparent at the older age levels in children. Most of these differences do not show up

in the pre-school period. (Terman and Tyler, 1954, p. 1068 Slightly modified version of original wording)

From the point of view of our particular focus, cognitive development in adolescence, Terman and Tyler's last point is of particular interest. Although sex differences in achievement appear prior to adolescence, they become particularly prominent during this age period. This is especially true in the areas of scientific knowledge and achievement. The performance of high school students on science tests has repeatedly shown that boys perform at a much higher level on these tests than do girls (Jordan, 1937; Edgerton and Britt, 1944, 1947). These differences are much less marked at the elementary school level. The writer, for example, found no sex differences between elementary school boys and girls with respect to certain quantity concepts (Elkind, 1961a) but significant differences between the sexes on quantity concepts among high school and college students (Elkind, 1961b, 1962). The differences among the older groups were consistently in favor of the boys. In the same vein, King (1963) examined the responses of 5-17 year old children to twenty science questions and found no sex differences for elementary school children but significant sex differences for secondary school children.

In all likelihood, these sex differences in scientific achievement which appear in adolescence reflect differences in interest rather than differences in mental ability. In one of the aforementioned studies of the writer (Elkind, 1962) it was found that the girls had higher mean IQ's than the boys even though they had more

primitive quantity concepts. The results of Project Talent point in the same direction. Flanagan found, for example, that high school "boys did better than girls in physical science information, but their superiority was not nearly so great as in related nonacademic areas such as electricity and electronics" (Flanagan, 1964, p. 3-116). Flanagan argues that, "Boys did better than girls on the mechanical reasoning test (an aptitude measure) but not as much better as would have been commensurate with their superiority in mechanical information if the latter superiority had been wholly attributable to differences in aptitude" (Flanagan, 1964, p. 3-116). The adoption of adult sex roles in adolescence could thus serve to channel interests and activities and could help account for the divergence of the sexes with respect to scientific achievement. In summary we can conclude with some assurance that adolescence is a period during which differences in certain areas of academic achievement become the most marked. . . .

COGNITIVE MANIFESTATIONS OF FORMAL OPERATIONAL THOUGHT

Let us now consider some of the cognitive manifestations of formal operational thinking and some of its affective consequences.

Differentiation of Thought and External World

The growth of thought from infancy through adolescence is marked by a progressive differentiation of thought and reality. At each level of development this differentiation poses a unique problem and a unique solution. The infant begins, for example, by treating objects as if they no longer existed when they were out of sight. By the end of infancy, on the other hand, he shows, by his active search for hidden objects, that for him objects now have a permanence which is independent of their immediate sensory presence or absence (Piaget, 1954). From about the age of 2 to 6, the child begins to deal with subject-object differentiation at a new level. This period begins with the use of symbols and signs but without a clear understanding of the relation between signifier and what is signified. The pre-school child thinks that the name of the object resides in the object and has always been the name of the object.[1] He also believes that an object can have only one name and has difficulty understanding how people can call his baby brother "Robert" when in fact his name is "Bobby." Towards the end of this period the child discovers that names are arbitrary designations, as shown by the advent of *name calling* during the elementary school period. Thus a new level of subject-object differentiation has been reached, this time on the plane of the symbol and its referent.

During the period of concrete operational thinking (ages 6-7 to 11-12) the child encounters the problem of subject-object differentiation on still another

plane. The advent of concrete operations makes possible elementary deductive thinking and hence the construction of concrete hypotheses about reality. At this stage the child does not recognize the hypothetical character of his conclusions and assumes that they have a measure of physical fixedness while reality has a degree of hypothetical arbitrariness. At this stage the child does not recognize that his notions have to be tested against the evidence and instead behaves as if the facts must be made to fit the hypotheses. Towards the end of childhood and the beginnings of adolescence, however, one sees a new subject-object differentiation. The adolescent recognizes the arbitrariness of his hypotheses and the necessity of testing them against the evidence.

Some concrete experimental data may help to illustrate the differences between the thought of children and adolescents in this regard. In an experiment by the writer (Elkind, 1966), children (8-9 years of age) and adolescents (13-14 years of age) were presented with a concept attainment task. The materials were pictures of wheeled and non-wheeled tools and wheeled and non-wheeled vehicles. The pictures were presented in pairs such that a wheeled tool or vehicle was always coupled with a non-wheeled tool or vehicle. Choice of a wheeled tool or vehicle always made a light go on, whereas the choice of a non-wheeled tool or vehicle never resulted in the light going on. The task for the subject was to find the kind of card which would make the signal light go on every time.

The results clearly illustrate the difference between adolescent and child thought. Only half of the children were able to arrive at the notion that it was the

[1] The child at this stage behaves in the manner of the scholar who when asked why noodles are called noodles replied, "Well, they are white like noodles, soft like noodles and they taste like noodles."

choice of wheeled objects which made the light go on. Furthermore, it took those children who did succeed almost all of the allotted 72 trials to arrive at the correct solution. On the other hand, *all* of the adolescents solved the problem and many did so in as few as 10 trials. The reason for this difference was quite clear from the spontaneous verbalizations made during the course of the trials. Adolescents raised hypotheses such as "maybe it's transportation" and then "no it must be something else, I'll try . . ." By constantly raising hypotheses and checking them against whether or not the light went on they quickly solved the problem. The children, however, seemed to get fixated on either the tool or vehicle hypothesis which was so strongly suggested by the pictures. These subjects kept trying to find ways they could reconcile this hypothesis with the cards that made the light go on. Moreover, when asked what the rule was that made the light go on, even those children who failed on the majority of trials still gave a rule as if it were a correct one. To test the strength of this hypothesis some children were shown a negative instance, for example if they said "things that move" they were shown a horse and a wheelbarrow where the choice of horse did not make the light of on and the choice of wheelbarrow did. Under this circumstance a common reply was, "Well, the horse moves in a different way."

It was clear, then, that the child stuck with his hypothesis and would not give it up in the face of the evidence. Indeed, the evidence was reinterpreted to fit the hypotheses! These findings support the view that the child, as compared to the adolescent, does not clearly differentiate his hypotheses from reality. Other data which support this conclusion have been provided by Weir (1964). In Weir's investigation, subjects from nursery school through high school were confronted with an apparatus on which there were three knobs. They were instructed that when the correct knob was pressed, a reward would drop into a small chute beneath the knobs. The machine was so adjusted that only one of the knobs "paid off" and this only 66% of the time. The *best* or maximizing solution was thus the simplest, "keep pushing the knob which paid off before."

The results differed from what is usually found in developmental investigations in the sense that there was not a regular improvement with age. In fact, the nursery school children were the most successful of all, although the adolescents ran them a close second. The elementary school children, however, had the most difficulty with the problem. Weir's examination of the qualitative aspects of the situation made clear what was going on. The young children simply persevered on the knob which paid off regardless of whether or not it paid off on a particular trial. The adolescents, on the other hand, initially adopted complex strategies in the sense that they assumed there were elaborate patterns of knob pressing to be discovered. They soon gave these strategies up, however, and began pressing only the pay-off knob. The difficulty encountered by the elementary school children resulted from the fact that they adopted a strategy—"if you win you shift and if you lose you shift"—from which they did not deviate despite the fact that this strategy did not succeed!

As in the previous study, the results of

Weir's investigation strongly suggest that while the elementary school child raises hypotheses about physical events, he does not test these against the facts. Indeed, he seems unaware of the hypothetical quality of his strategy and seems to feel that it is imposed from without rather than constructed from within. It is for this reason that the child appears to be more rigid than the adolescent in certain problem-solving tasks. The adolescent, with his awareness of the arbitrariness of his hypotheses and of their mental quality, is ready to give them up to produce others. This ability to discriminate between thought and reality is derived from the capacity to take all of the possibilities in the situation into account, and it is the awareness of *possibility* that marks the true differentiation between thought and reality.

Utilization of Abstract Concepts

One of the most regular observations with respect to adolescent thought is that it is more abstract than that of the child. In this context, *abstract* usually means thinking which is more general and more divorced from immediate experience than is the thought of the child. This difference is most clearly illustrated in the kinds of definitions children and adolescents give for the same terms. With respect to a concept like *time*, for example, a ten year old youngster is likely to define it in a static, specific sense, as "it is something that the watch tells," or as "time means the clock" or as "a clock tells time." By the age of 15, however, time is defined as, "time is stable, it is what we don't have too much of," or "time is sort of like an interval of space"

(Gesell, Ilg, and Ames, 1956). Comparable differences in definition have been observed with respect to a wide variety of vocabulary items (Feifel and Lorge, 1950).

Differences in level of abstraction between adolescents and children can also be observed when they are asked to deal with complex class concepts such as the concept of religious denomination. In one study (Elkind, 1963) elementary school and junior high school children were asked a variety of questions about their religious denomination which in this case was Protestant. One of the questions asked was, "Are all boys and girls in the world Protestant?" The routine answer of the children was "no" and this was usually explained by a statement such as, "Well, some of my friends are not Protestant," or "I know a boy who is not Protestant." By the age of twelve and thirteen, however, the typical response was usually, "No, because there are different religions in the world."

Although the differences between the replies of children and of adolescents to such questions are intuitively clear, it might be well to spend a few words on making these differences more explicit. If one looks at the child's explanations closely, it becomes immediately obvious that while they are correct as far as they go, they are incomplete. It is true enough that not all boys and girls in the world are Protestant and that acquaintance with non-Protestants is evidence for this conclusion. This explanation, nonetheless, does not take into account all of the *possible* non-Protestant children. To say, on the other hand, that there are "other religions" does take care of all the other children in the world. The same incompleteness can be seen in children's definitions of most concepts as in their definitions of the concept of time, mentioned earlier. While it is true "that a clock tells time," it is also true that a calendar tells time. The definitions of the older children with respect to time attempt to provide notions which will take into account all the different kinds of time measures.

The major difference, then, between the definitions given by children and those given by adolescents is that the definitions of the adolescents take into account all of the instances and non-instances of the concept whereas the definitions of children take account of only some of the positive and negative instances. The completeness of definitions given by adolescents would seem to derive from their capacity for formal operational thinking. It is combinatorial logic which enables the adolescent to deal systematically with all of the possible positive and negative instances of a concept and thus to arrive at a definition which is both complete and precise.

Interpretation of Literary and Graphic Materials

Still another way in which formal operational thought is manifested is in the interpretation of literary and graphic materials. The usual procedure in investigations of this kind is to present subjects of different ages with literary passages or graphic materials and then to question the subjects about them.

In a study by Peel[2] the following

[2] Peel, E. A. *The Pupil's Thinking.* London: Oldbourne Press, 1960, pp. 117-120. Used by permission.

passage was read by children from 8 to 15 years of age who were also shown a picture of the Stonehenge site.

Stonehenge. Stonehenge is in the south of England, on the flat plain of Salisbury. There is a ring of very big stones which the picture shows. Some of the stones have fallen down and some have disappeared from the place. The people who lived in England in those days we call Bronze Age Men. Long before there were any towns, Stonehenge was a temple for worship and sacrifice. Some of the stones were brought from the nearby hills, but others which we call Blue Stones, we think came from the mountains of Wales.

The questions asked of the children were as follows:

Question 1: Do you think Stonehenge might have been a fort and not a temple? Why do you think that?

Question 2: If the stones were rolled into position, what do you think has become of the rollers?

Question 3: What do you think has happened to the missing stones?

Here are some of the replies from children at different age levels:

A: aged 7:7

1. A temple (Why?) Because people live in it.

2. They've fallen down. People might have knocked them down. (Explanation of rollers) They'd broken.

3. They've fallen down. People have rolled them somewhere. (Why?) So they could live in them.

B: aged 9:1

1. I think it might have been to stop the enemy charging through. (Why do you think that?) It looks like it. The bricks would stand up. The enemy could

not force through quick enough and they'd be killed.

2. They've thrown them away in a little river to the big sea. (There isn't a river there.) They carried them to the river and got sunk.

3. They must have sunk in the ground. (They dug around there and they couldn't find any.) They must have been used by the people that came after.

D: aged 14:0

1. I think it would be a temple because it was a round formation with an altar at the top end, and at a certain time of the year, the sun shines straight up a path towards the altar, and I think that it was used for the worship of the sun god. There was no roof on it so that the sun shines right into the temple. There is a lot of hard work and labour in it for a god and the fact that they brought the blue stones from Wales.

2. The rollers would be wooden and they probably rotted away by now.

3. The wear of the weather, the wind and sun have crumbled them to dust in the ages. (Do you think anything else might have happened?) A warring tribe might have come and knocked some down and took some away. (What for?) Just to get revenge on the tribe.

E: aged 14:11

1. I doubt it. I shouldn't think so. It seems rather open for a fort. It doesn't seem large enough either. It does seem rather small. You wouldn't need a fort in the middle of Salisbury Plain. It's deserted. There's not many people about. There's not likely to be any trouble around there.

2. It depends if they were made of wood they might have rotted and maybe if they were circular stones they may

have been buried. I doubt if they would have been taken away. They would have had to shape stones. I think they would have used wood.

3. They may possibly have worn away through weather. I don't mean completely worn away but worn down like the small ones in the picture. There are a lot of stones lying down. There might have been enough to make up the circle. (Some have disappeared.) Maybe some have been taken away to be examined to see how long its been standing. Is it proved that it was completed? (People think it was completed.)

If one compares the responses of the children with those of the adolescents several differences can immediately be seen. First of all, the child does not deal with the situation as a whole, but rather focuses upon one dominant feature of the situation. To illustrate, the child (B) who said that Stonehenge was a fort explained this solely on the basis of the fact that the "stones would stand up." The adolescent, on the other hand, considers the situation from many different points of view simultaneously, as (E) said, "it seems rather open for a fort. It doesn't seem large enough either... You wouldn't need a fort on Salisbury Plain ..." Thus, while the child bases his interpretation on one or at most a few concrete aspects of the situation, the adolescent bases his judgment on many different considerations, some of which are far removed from the actual data presented.

Another difference between the responses of the children and the adolescents is reflected in the language with which they express their answers. The child expresses himself as if he were stating a fact. One child (B) said of the rollers, "They've thrown them away in a little river to the big sea. . . .They carried them to the river and they went to the sea and they got wet and sunk." Although this is just an hypothesis, the child states it as if it were a fact. The adolescent, on the other hand, states his conclusions in much more tentative language. D says "the rollers would be wooden and they probably rotted away by now." These differences in the responses made to literary material by children and adolescents show in still a different way the effects of formal operational thought in enabling the adolescent to deal with all the possibilities in the situation and to differentiate between thought and reality. Similar results have been found with materials and questions dealing with the social sciences (Case and Collinson, 1962) and with religion (Goldman, 1965).

One observes comparable differences between adolescent and child thought in the interpretation and production of graphic materials. In an early study, Shaffer (1930) presented children and adolescents with political cartoons and asked them to write about what the cartoons meant. Shaffer found that it was not until the age of 12-14 that children got beyond the literal meaning of the cartoon to its metaphorical meaning. The inability of young children to deal with metaphoric expression has also been demonstrated in their reactions to poetry (Pyle, 1935).

Why should children have difficulty in dealing with metaphor when adolescents can take it in their stride? In metaphor, one and the same word or figure takes on a double meaning. In political cartoons,

for example, the donkey and elephant symbolize much more than animals, and the same holds true for the "bears" and "bulls" in stock market cartoons. The grasp of metaphor presupposes the ability to recognize parallels between quite disparate things such as political parties and donkeys and elephants. It also presupposes that the figure can be separated from its literal representation. This ability, to see the many possible meanings of a concrete figure, no matter how removed these meanings may be from its literal interpretation, is once again a product of the combinatorial potential of formal operational thought.

The findings with respect to the interpretation of realistic pictures and the drawings of young people parallel the results obtained with cartoons and other metaphoric materials. Vernon (1948) has shown that the reactions to realistic pictures can be grouped according to three age related stages. Young children (4-6 years) merely *enumerate* the elements of the picture; somewhat older children (7-10) *describe* the picture in the sense of attempting to relate the elements of the picture to another in an objective way. It is only towards adolescence, however (11-12), that children begin to truly *interpret* the pictures in the sense of attributing motives and feelings to the depicted characters. With respect to graphic productions, Harris (1964) among others has shown that as children get older, their drawings become more differentiated in the sense that more and more details are taken into account. Here again, both with respect to the interpretation and production of realistic pictures, we see that the adolescent tends to take account of all, or at least most, of the possibilities present in graphic materials while the child focuses primarily on one or several salient aspects of the configuration.

The effects of formal operational thought, the ability to deal with all the possibilities in the situation, can thus be seen in the differential between thought and reality and in the definitions given to concepts and in the interpretations of literary and graphic materials.

References

Balinsky, B. an analysis of the mental factors of various age groups from 9 to 60. *Genetic Psychology Monographs,* 1941, **23,** 191-234.

Bayley, N., and Oden, M. H. The maintenance of intellectual ability in gifted adults. *Journal of Gerontology,* 1955, **10,** 91-107.

Bradway, Katherine P., and Thompson, Clare W. Intelligence at adulthood: A twenty-five year follow-up. *Journal of Educational Psychology,* 1962, **53,** 1-14.

Burns, R. B. Age and mental ability: re-testing with thirty-three years' interval. *British Journal of Educational Psychology,* 1966, **36,** 116.

Burt, C. The differentiation of intellectual ability. *British Journal of Educational Psychology,* 1954, **24,** 76-90.

Burt, C. *Mental and scholastic tests.* London: Staples Press, 1962/1921.

Case, D., and Collinson, J.M. The development of formal thinking in verbal comprehension. *British Journal of Educational Psychology,* 1962, **32,** 103-111.

Cohen, J. The factorial structure of the WISC at ages 7-6; 10-6; and 13-6. *Journal of Consulting Psychology,* 1959, **23,** 285-299.

Cropley, A. J. Differentiation of abilities, socio-economic status, and the WISC. *Journal of Consulting Psychology,* 1964, **28,** 512-517.

Edgerton, H. A., and Britt, S.H. Technical aspects of the Fourth Annual Science Talent Search. *Educational and Psychological Measurement,* 1947, **7,** 3-21.

Elkind, D. Children's discovery of the conservation of mass, weight and volume. *Journal of Genetic Psychology,* 1961a, **98,** 219-277.

Elkind, D. Quantity conceptions in junior and senior high school students. *Child Development,* 1961b, **32,** 551-560.

Elkind, D. Quantity conceptions in college students. *Journal of Social Psychology,* 1962, **57,** 459-465.

Elkind, D. The child's conception of his religious denomination III: The Protestant child. *Journal of Genetic Psychology,* 1963, **103,** 291-304.

Elkind, D. Conceptual orientation shifts in children and adolescents.

Child Development, 1966, **37**, 493-498.

Feifel, H., and Lorge, L. Qualitative differences in the vocabulary responses of children. *Journal of Educational Psychology,* 1950, **41**, 1-18.

Flanagan, J.C. , *Project talent: The American high school student.* Pittsburgh: University of Pittsburgh, 1964.

Garrett, H. E. A developmental theory of intelligence. *American Psychologist,* 1946, **1**, 372-378.

Gesell, A., Ilg, F. L., and Ames, L. B. *Youth: the years from ten to sixteen.* New York: Harper & Row, 1956.

Goldman, R. J. The application of Piaget's schema of operational thinking to religious story data by means of the Guttman scalogram. *British Journal of Educational Psychology,* 1965, **25**, 158-170.

Green, R. F., and Berkowitz, B. Changes in intellect with age: II. Factorial analysis of Wechsler-Bellevue scores. *Journal of Genetic Psychology,* 1964, **104**, 3-18.

Honzik, M. P., MacFarlane, J. W., and Allen, L. The stability of mental test performance between two and eighteen years. *Journal of Experimental Education,* 1948, **17**, 309-324.

Jones, H. E., and Conrad, H. S. The growth and decline of intelligence. *Genetic Psychology Monographs,* 1933, **13**, 223-298.

Jones, H. E. Age changes in adult mental abilities. In: Conrad, H. S. (Ed.) *Studies in human development.* New York: Appleton-Century-Crofts, 1966.

Jordan, A.M. Sex differences in mental traits. *High School Journal,* 1937, **20**, 254-261.

King, W.H. The development of scientific concepts in children. *British Journal of Educational Psychology,* 1963, **23**, 240-252.

Owens, W.A., Jr. Age and mental abilities: A longitudinal study. *Genetic Psychology Monographs,* 1953, **48**, 3-54.

Peel, E.A. *The pupil's thinking.* London: Oldbourne Press, 1960.

Piaget, J. *The construction of reality in the child.* New York: Basic Books, 1954.

Pinneau, S.R. *Changes in intelligence quotient: Infancy to maturity.* Boston, Mass.: Houghton Mifflin, 1961.

Shaffer, L.F. *Children's interpretations of cartoons.* Contributions to Education, No. 429. New York: Teacher's College, Columbia University, 1930.

Shock, N.W. Gerontology (later maturity). *Annual Review of Psychology,* 1951, **2**, 353-370.

Spearman, C. *The nature of "intelligence" and the principles of cognition,* London: Macmillan, 1923.

Terman L.M. *The measurement of intelligence.* Boston: Houghton Mifflin, 1916.

Terman, L.M., and Merrill, Maud A. *Stanford-Binet Intelligence Scale.* Boston: Houghton, Mifflin, 1937.

Terman, L.M., and Tyler, Leona E. Psychological sex differences. In: Carmichael, L. (Ed.) *Manual of child psychology.* New York: Wiley, 1954.

Thorndike, R.L. Growth of intelligence during adolescence. *Journal of Genetic Psychology,* 1948, **72**, 11-15.

Thurstone, L.L., and Thurstone, Thelma G. Factorial studies of intelligence. *Psychometric Monographs,* 1941, No. 2.

Trembly, D. Age-curve differences between natural and acquired intellectual characteristics. *American Psychologist,* Abstract,1964, **19**, 546. Paper delivered to the APA's 72nd Annual Convention, Sept. 4-9, 1964, Los Angeles.

Weir, M.W. Developmental changes in problem solving strategies. *Psychological Review,* 1964, **71**, 473-490.

15
ADOLESCENCE:
PERSONALITY AND SOCIAL DEVELOPMENT

Personality and social development during the adolescent years revolves around three kinds of events. First, a teenager's earlier progress in attaining mastery and self-reliance now culminates in a striving for psychological independence from his parents. Many aspects of adolescent behavior reflect the needs of teenagers to be their own person, to determine their own values and plan their own destiny, and many individual differences among young people are a function of the extent to which they have become capable of exercising such independence.

Second, the importance attached to peer relationships in middle childhood now becomes increasingly attached to dating and heterosexual relationships, and the ways in which adolescents learn to handle relationships has considerable bearing on their eventual level of social maturation. Third, the adolescent years are the time when young people begin to consolidate a sense of their personal identity, that is, a reasonably clear, consistent sense of who they are and where they are going. The process of identity formation involves adolescents in numerous kinds of decisions concerning the particular social roles, value systems, and life goals to which they want to commit themselves.

No brief selection of articles can discuss all of these aspects of adolescent personality development. The two selections we have chosen for this chapter are instead concerned with a broad look at the nature of adolescence. The material by Douvan and Adelson is taken from the last chapter of their book, *The Adolescent Experience*, in which they report data obtained from interviews with approximately 3500 teenage boys and girls in various parts of the United States. This selection summarizes their major conclusions and findings with respect to the future life orientation of these adolescents, their independence strivings, their peer-group and heterosexual ties, and their patterns of family interaction. Douvan and

Adelson stress some clear sex differences they observed in these areas, and they make a case for what they call the "homogenization" of American adolescents.

In the second selection Weiner elaborates on one of Douvan and Adelson's themes, namely, that a psychology of adolescence should be attuned to normative adolescent development and not be distorted by generalizations based on the characteristics of certain special groups of young people. Weiner describes a number of popular but erroneous conclusions about what teenagers are like, including the Douvan and Adelson view that they are homogenized. He also reviews available data concerning teenage sexual behavior and drug use to illustrate the kinds of discrepancy between fact and impression that have arisen in recent years.

ELIZABETH DOUVAN AND JOSEPH ADELSON

Integrating Themes*

There remain only the tasks of summarizing major conclusions and findings and of tying together the main threads that run through our observations of American adolescents. Most of what we have to say in this final chapter has been stated somewhere earlier in the book, or is at least implicit in the book's structure and organization. At this point we hope to draw the various themes together, to clarify and interpret some of the major

*From Chapter 10 of E. Douvan and J. Adelson, *The Adolescent Experience*, 1966. Reprinted by permission of the authors and John Wiley and Sons.

findings.

The adolescent in our view is both pushed and pulled toward the future. The psychic conflicts of the period, with their regressive dangers, assemble the power of the past to urge the child to leave family and childhood. The prospect of independence and adulthood urges him to become his own man. He will move on the strength of this attraction, but if it should fail, he still has behind him the tail wind of all the childhood dangers to be escaped. We suggested at the beginning of our studies that this thrust to the future is crucial to the adolescent experience, that without some such tie to adulthood, the adolescent experience has no substance, and that the child's ability to integrate a concept of his adult future would be a key solution on which a great part of his adolescent adaptation would depend.

Our studies have confirmed and strengthened this general conception. The future is by no means a remote or irrelevant prospect to American adolescents. It is crucial as it is absorbed, integrated, and expressed in current activities and attitudes. In one form or another, the future orientation appears again and again as a distinguishing feature of youngsters who are making adequate adolescent adaptations. A faulty time perspective consistently marks the groups in our studies who were isolated analytically by other measures of ego weakness or lack of personal integration.

The style and focus of future orientation differs sharply for boys and girls. The two groups focus their interest on different aspects of future identity, and they differ also in the style of expression. Boys tend to concentrate on the vocational future and their style is all business—concrete, crystallized, tied to reality, if not always realistic. They think of job preparation and channels, and of their own capabilities and tastes for particular work roles. They think of the future in an instrumental way—"This is what I think my future will be because this is what I think I am and what the job world looks like to me." It is not surprising to find that boys' vocational goals are not much colored by dreams of glory. For the most part the jobs boys choose represent modest advances over their fathers' positions, and they are jobs with which the boys have had some personal contact. Boys who have no clear vocational plans or

whose job goals are deviant in some way (for example, downward-mobile or glamour based) have less instrumental and realistic notions of steps toward their goals, and are likely to show a pattern of personal maladjustment in their current lives.

Girls focus on the interpersonal aspects of future life—on marriage and the roles of wife and mother. They are not without notions about channels and instrumental acts appropriate to their goals, but the ideas they have are less concrete than boys'. They are less concerned with real skills than boys are, and more concerned with social and interpersonal reality, as we would expect from the nature of their goals. Their reasons for choosing particular jobs reveal that girls want jobs that express feminine interests and provide a social setting for meeting prospective husbands.

Beyond this interpersonal emphasis, girls seem to bridge the present and future much more with fantasy than with reality-tied or concrete plans. The girl is less likely to say of the future, "This is what I think I will be," than she is to say, "I hope my life will be like this." The boy checks and conditions his goals by the step-by-step instrumental procedures they imply; the girl leaps more directly in fantasy to the goal. And this makes good sense—for her the procedures are equally ambiguous, whether the goal is simple or grand. What she will become does not depend in any direct or simple way on her own instrumental acts, it depends rather on the man she marries.

A clear concept of her adult femininity, of feminine goals and interpersonal skills, functions for the girl like the vocational concept for the boy. It bridges the worlds of adolescence and adulthood, brings the future concretely into current life, and allows the future to contribute meaning and organization to adolescent activities and interests. Girls who have relatively clear notions about and goals in adult femininity show a high degree of personal integration. Those girls who specifically reject a feminine future are troubled adolescents.

The different stances boys and girls assume toward the future is expressed most simply and directly in our analysis of mobility aspirations. Mobility aspiration for the boy is no idle dream, it is rather the concrete expression of a boy's faith in himself. The goal he chooses is realistic in light of his talent and opportunities, but is not overblown. And it is cast in the phrasing of reality—What is the job like? What activities and demands does it encompass, what training does it require? What are my abilities and opportunities, do they provide me access to the field?

The girl's mobility aspirations are less formed and less fettered by reality. She need not test her desire against her own talent and skill, since these will not be crucial determinants of her future status. Her access to higher status will come through marriage. For most of these girls (except those few older girls who have already experienced a lasting, meaningful relationship with a boy) marriage itself has so little reality that the difference between a "good" or socially advancing marriage and any marriage at all is not significant. Since it is all a dream, in any case, one may as well dream big. Girls' mobility plans are less careful than boys', less cautioned by an assessment of opportunity. They are more simply dreams.

The imminence of adulthood, the im-posing need to master and incorporate some elements of adult identity into current life (at least in fantasy), means that the child must alter his relationship to his family in some important ways. He must begin to detach himself from the family and develop some measure of independence in behavior, emotions, values, and beliefs. The process of detachment has traditionally been described as high drama—the rebellious adolescent pressing for enlarged independence and continually confronting conservative, dynastic parental control. We shall have more to say later about the detachment as it seems to develop in American adolescents, and about the appropriateness of this traditional model to the reality of American family life. At this point it is enough to say that the process as we observe it seems less dramatic and full of conflict than tradition and theory hold, and to point out again a significant difference between boys and girls.

Our findings regarding the issue of independence indicate that the urge to be free, to be one's own master, is almost exclusively a masculine stirring. Up to the age of eighteen girls show no great press for independence, certainly no need to confront authority or insist on the right to develop and distinguish independent beliefs or controls. The difference appears in our descriptive findings about adolescents' attitudes toward themselves and their family relationships. It also emerges analytically when we look at the relationship of developing independence to other areas of personal growth. In boys, the measure of independent functioning achieved relates clearly to other areas of development—to the integration of a future concept, to upward-mobility aspirations and general achievement strivings, to current adolescent adjustment. These relationships do not hold for the girls. Feminine integration does not demand a strong bid for independence during the adolescent period. Indeed we find that girls' attitudes toward parental control do not even relate very strongly to the nature or style of that control.

Close to the issue of detachment, and theoretically the central mechanism for realizing separation, is the issue of adolescent peer group ties. Here again we have the impression that the importance of the peer group has been exaggerated in theory and in much of popular complaint about adolescents. Our data again indicate that boys and girls differ both in the extent of their allegiance to the peer group and in the particular uses they make or peer ties. Boys more often hold allegiance to the group as such, conceive the group as a coherent and loyal band offering support to members and having an authority of its own. Boys recognize "the gang" as a force that could lead a boy to break rules; they think of getting into a "bad gang" as a danger to be avoided.

Girls use peer relationships differently. They are not as tied to a group as such, nor are they as sensitized to the pressure of "the gang" (except possibly in issues of taste). In general girls are more attracted to close two-person friendships. The loyalty of the best friend is the loyalty the girl depends on, needs, and seeks. In belonging to groups, the girl does not seek a band to support her as she makes a play for freedom—rather, she uses the group as a resource for finding close individual friendships. She is always on the lookout for prospective best friends. The individual friendship transcends the group (although it may exist in a group setting), and becomes the center of mutual self-exploration through shared intimacy. In their concepts about friendship and in the intimacy of their friendships, girls are more higly developed than boys. In fact, the interpersonal seems to be the central area of growth for girls during adolescence. Our evidence indicates that the girl's development in the interpersonal sphere is the pivotal feature around which her adolescent adjustment focuses. A measure of interpersonal development was our best predictor of ego integration in girls.

We have stressed the importance of the future in adolescent adjustment, but we do not mean to underestimate the impact of the child's past on his resolution of adolescent tasks. His particular past in a particular family with its own style of interaction enters and critically affects the youngster's encounter with all of the adolescent problems. Two clear family patterns appear in our studies—the democratic family style and an autocratic or authoritarian style. In the democratic family, parents allow the adolescent a fair degree of autonomy, include the child in important decisions affecting his own behavior, and tend to use psychological and verbal discipline. Authoritarian parents set rules without consulting the children, allow little autonomy, and tend to use physical techniques for enforcing discipline. The effects of the family pattern on the adolescents are apparent, strong, and consistent. The democratic families produce adolescents who are unusually self-reliant, poised, and effective. They are free to criticize and disagree with parents, but have generally warm companionship with them. In the authoritarian families the adolescents are on the surface compliant; beneath the surface (in responses to projective measures) they are rebellious and impulsive. They tend to have an externalized morality, to define morals as what one can get away with. They are less effective and less poised in their general bearing.

The findings from our studies point to the homogenization of American adolescence across regional boundaries and, by and large, across social class lines as well. We were struck by the lack of impressive differences among these population groups. It seems that the peculiar conflicts of the age itself and the force of modern mass communications have combined to cast a universal form for the adolescent experience—a form heavily invested with middle-class values. Adolescent interests and activities, family patterns and moves toward independence, are much the same in all regions, in all social classes. Among standard background variables, only religion yielded differences that are large, consistent, and consistently interesting.

These, briefly, are the substantive findings from our studies. Beyond these conclusions supported directly by data, what can we say we have learned from the studies? We like to think that years invested bear a yield in wisdom and insight that extend beyond the relatively narrow range of empirical findings. Some broader conclusion and speculation should be part of the reward for so much demanding attention to detail.

We have two such broad comments to make, both representing insights we gained from the research, both having to do with the aptness of standard theoretical formulations of the adolescent experience. The two areas that focus these comments are first, the importance of sex differences in adolescence; and, second, the nature of the adolescent experience as it occurs in the middle range of American children.

Our initial approach to the study of adolescence, while tied theoretically to psychoanalysis, rested also on developmental descriptive notions that have dominated child psychology and particularly the study of adolescence. We hoped to go beyond the mere description of change, and to use theory to clarify sources of variation in the form and pace of adolescent change. Nonetheless, we conceived these changes, however they might vary, as organized around certain developmental tasks posed for all children in our culture somewhere near the close of childhood. The tasks we noted were the ones we have described in earlier chapters—regulating instincts; dissolving infantile dependencies and integrating new areas of autonomy; developing stable object ties, particularly heterosexual ties; coming to terms with the superego; and exploring identity possibilities.

This conception of adolescent challenges established the outlines of our investigation, and we had at the outset some notions about the factors, including sex, that would determine different forms of the developmental crisis and its outcome. We were quite sure that achievement and occupational choice would be more crucial to the boy, that social and interpersonal issues would play a larger role in girls' preoccupations and would more surely gauge the girl's personal integration at adolescence.

What we did not anticipate was the

force of the sex variable, the extent to which it defines and shades all aspects of the developmental crisis. Since all children undergo radical biological changes at puberty, and presumably also derivative instinctual changes, we assumed that the new task of regulating these instincts would also be met by all children. This would require some reworking of internal controls, some changes in self-regulation. The nature of the solutions might vary, but they would all be responses to a unifying problem and would share at least the rough outline and structure that this problem establishes.

In fact we find that the adolescent crisis for boys and girls differs in almost every regard—in the statement of developmental tasks, not just how they are phrased, but whether they arise during the era at all; in the general direction of solution alternatives available to the child, and in the individual solution expressions achieved by youngsters in our society.

One may see commonalities, of course. But our studies suggest that the observation of similarity in this case requires such a high level of abstraction, and such a cost to the richness of one's description and understanding of adolescent reality, that the transaction loses its relevance and value. So, for example, we know that puberty brings basic biological changes to girls as well as boys. Mead (1955) has even pointed to the more decisive nature of feminine puberty changes. Yet to conclude from this that boys and girls face similar problems psychologically in the regulation of instinctual energy seems to strain too much reality from the situation. At some level the drives increase and must be managed in both sexes, but our findings point to the conclusion that the drive is so successfully excluded from consciousness by the large majority of girls that they do not in any relevant psychological sense confront an impulse problem comparable to boys' during the adolescent years. This difference, in turn, influences the reworking of controls, the development of autonomy, and the resolution of dependencies—producing sex-determined differences in both pace and process.

The key terms in adolescent development for the boy in our culture are the erotic, autonomy (assertiveness, independence, achievement), and identity. For the girl the comparable terms are the erotic, the interpersonal, and identity. Differences between the two sets of problems are larger and more complex than a single discrepancy implies; for this discrepancy is so central that it reverberates through the entire complex. For the girl the development of interpersonal ties—the sensitivities, skills, ethics, and values of object ties—forms the core of identity, and it gives expression to much of developing feminine eroticism. Feminine sexuality, consciously inhibited from active and direct expression, seeks more subtle, limited, and covert expression. The search for popularity, the effort to charm, all of the many and varied interpersonal ties which serve as setting for the girl's practice in winning and maintaining love—these engagements filter and express a good deal of the girl's erotic need. We have noted that greater intensity and importance of girls' like-sexed friendships when compared to their friendships with boys or to boys' like-sexed friendships. And we have held that the intimate friendship between girls serves a number of functions, all tied to the girl's need to explore and understand her sexual nature as well as her individuality. It is primarily through these serial, episodic, intimate two-somes that the girl comes to terms with her sexual nature and gradually sorts elements of identification from aspects of individuality to form an identity. The tie to objects is both the key to her erotic realization and also the mechanism through which she arrives at an individuated personal identity.

For the boy, on the other hand, the integrated capacity for erotic ties and the solution of the identity challenge demand separation and autonomy. What the girl achieves through intimate connection with others, the boy must manage by disconnecting, by separating himself and asserting his right to be distinct. His biological sexual nature is more explicitly and individually stated than the girl's. It has less compelling interpersonal features, depends less on the existence of a fully developed object relation and it insists on the resolution of certain authority problems in order to gain expression. The boy can know sexual gratification outside a full or fully developed love relationship, but his sexual realization depends on severing infantile ties and asserting his independence of them. Without autonomy, the boy's sexual realization suffers the constant hazard of crippling castration fears. To achieve full status as a sexual adult, the boy must clarify the difference between himself and his father and assume the status of the father's independent peer. The girl's adult sexuality, on the other hand, depends on an intricate and little understood process of consolidating a satisfactory identification with her own mother.

The identity problem is also phrased differently for boys and girls in our culture, and the distinction again revolves around their different requirements for object love and for autonomy. We have noted that feminine identity forms more closely about capacity and practice in the personal arts, and we have seen in our findings evidence that the girl's ego integration co-varies with her interpersonal development. Masculine identity, in contrast, focuses about the capacity to handle and master nonsocial reality, to design and win for oneself an independent area of work which fits one's individual talents and taste and permits achievement of at least some central personal goals. The boy's ego development at adolescence already bears the mark of this formulation and reflects his progress in mastering it. Identity is for the boy a matter of individuating internal bases for action and defending these against domination by others. For the girl it is a process of finding and defining the internal and individual through attachments to others.

The normative descriptive approach to adolescent psychology is not the only one in which sex variation has been overlooked. When we look at the developing literature on identity and the self-concept, we note again the predominance of a masculine formulation. The most advanced psychoanalytic theorists often fail to note what seems to be an imposing distinction, at least to judge from the results of our studies and other recent research.

In Erikson's statement of the developmental tasks of adolescence and early adulthood, the problem of individual identity is put before that of intimacy—and there is a compelling logic to this order. For how, one asks, can the individual form a genuine tie to another, a contact of depth and intimacy, unless the outlines of his individual being have been established and fortified; how can we speak of two individuals merging in intimacy unless we start with two individuals?

Yet psychic phenomena do not always follow logic in so orderly a manner. We know that in many people, the working through of identity issues continues well beyond the early adult years and that in some cases, at least, intimacy has been achieved in some degree before the individual has developed the kind of continuity and integrity of self which an identity resolution implies.

This, we would argue, is much more commonly the tone of feminine identity formation. The girl is more likely to gain a developed identity in consequence of intimacy rather than as a precursor of it. Out of her intimate connections to others, through processes of identification and projection, the woman comes to know her own individuality and to solve the question of who she is. The reasons for this arrangement lie both in the nature of feminine psychic development and in the much simpler and more obvious realm of social reality. For the fact is that in our culture at least the need to marry and find acceptance and love exert such pressure on the young girl that we can hardly imagine her having the time and energy to invest in identity-resolution until she has gained some measure of security in a stable love relationship. To do so may even involve hazards to her marriage eligibility. Too sharp a self-definition and too full an investment in a unique personal integration are not con-sidered highly feminine; they are often thought to be unattractive in a young woman.[1]

The girl, then, is likely to arrive at an identity resolution through the interpersonal, and, then, only after she has reached some relatively satisfactory integration of intimacy and the erotic. The boy's tasks are ordered differently—his identity depends on his achieving autonomy—an acceptable integration of assertiveness and self-direction. His identity demands and forms around these qualities; beyond this, no erotic resolution except denial is available to him until he has established a degree of freedom from external control.

We have perhaps overstated the difference between boys and girls. The girl has experienced some degree of separation before she enters the intimate friendships of adolescence—after all, all social development consist of rhythmic and complementary processes of differentiation and integration, of separating from and connecting with objects. The boy, on the other hand, has been tied in more or less intimate (although immature) relationships with others up to the adolescent strike for autonomy. But the tone and order of development that begins in adolescence and concludes in maturity—these, we contend, differ sharply for the two sexes. We have seen the derivative effects of the difference in our studies—the areas of achievement, autonomy,

---

[1] Mirra Komarovsky (1946) has reported interviews with college women in which the girls themselves reveal that they are consciously avoiding too clear and invested self-definitions because of the fear of becoming ineligible for marriage.

authority and control focus and express boys' major concerns and psychological growth; the object relations—friendship, dating, popularity and the understanding and management of interpersonal crisis—hold the key to adolescent growth and integration for the girl. The internalization of feminine goals also has important implications for the girl's development. Here too the goal is to form a lasting tie to another, and is not an individual achievement in the sense that the boy's vocational goal is.

We conclude, then, that there is not one adolescent crisis, but two major and clearly distinctive ones—the masculine and the feminine. If we are to think of adolescence as a relatively delimited period, we must conclude that some of the traditionally conceived problems of the period (for example, detachment from external authority, the resolution of primitive object ties) are not a part of the feminine phrasing of adolescence. If we conceive impulses to be drives that have some reasonably direct impact on conscious thought and behavior, we may even question the traditional concept of adolescence as a time of turbulent instinctual struggle as far as the girl is concerned. While we cling to the notion that somewhere beneath compliance and repression there lies a heart of fire, our impression from the study of girls is that for them adolescence is less infused with impulse and more focused on form than any traditional conception of the era could have led us to expect.

If sex differences led us to reconsider traditional conceptions of adolescence, the normative findings from our studies also made us think twice about the received version of the period. Most contemporary comment on adolescence focuses on two conspicuous but atypical enclaves of adolescents, drawn from extreme and opposing ends of the social class continuum, and representing exceptional solutions to the adolescent crisis. These are, on the one hand, the delinquent, and on the other, the sensitive, articulate, middle-class adolescent on whom the psychoanalytic view is almost exclusively based.

Now in most ways these types could not be more dissimilar. The estranged lower-class youngster relies largely on alloplastic solutions to the adolescent crisis, living out mutely, in urgent yet aimless acts of violence or bravado, a sullen resentment against the middle-class world and its values. The estranged upper-middle-class youngster is largely autoplastic in response; subject to acute intrapsychic upheavals which are expressed in neurotic symptoms, affect storms, character eccentricities, and a general value ferment. Paradoxically, these two extremes are alike, and their likeness is in being different from the normative adolescent—the adolescent of the core culture. The extremes are alike in showing an unusual degree of independence from the family; they are alike in disaffection, in acting out or thinking out a discontent with the social order; they are alike, above all, in that they adopt radical solutions to the adolescent task of ego-synthesis.

We want to suggest that one cannot generalize these processes to the adolescent population at large. The adolescent at the extremes responds to the instinctual and psychosocial upheaval of puberty by disorder, by failures of ego-synthesis, and by a tendency to abandon earlier values and object attachments. In the normative response to adolescence however, we more commonly find an avoidance of inner and outer conflict, premature identity consolidation, ego and ideological constriction, and a general unwillingness to take psychic risks. The great advantage of the survey technique is that it allows us to study these adolescents who make up the middle majority, who evoke neither grief nor wonder, and who all too often escape our notice.

Let us begin with the question of autonomy and conflict. In the traditional view, the child at puberty is under great pressure to detach himself from the family emotionally, to find a pattern of disengagement. The instinctual revival brings with it a return of Oedipal dangers and temptations. The home is a "hothouse" and the boy at least must discover a way out, a means of escaping his dependent status in the family, and even more urgently, the dimly recognized drives and feelings toward his parents. This is the psychosexual irritation which pushes the child from home, leading him to negotiate or battle with the parent for greater freedom. The confict of generations is joined. We add to this a psychosocial pull—the child's need to forge an individual identity—those needs which draw the child toward the future. These forces give the peer group at adolescence its critical importance. Peer group and culture supplant the family as the locus of authority and the giver of norms. Through his immersion in the peer group, through the incorporation of peer ideals and values, the youngster gains the support he needs to win autonomy from the family. And the peer group provides a haven in which the delicate task of

self-exploration and self-definition can be accomplished.

This view of adolescence has a good deal to recommend it, but our reading of the interviews suggests that it needs revision in some important particulars if we are to apply it to the middle majority. This view exaggerates the degree of conflict between parent and child; it wrongly estimates the autonomy issue; and it misinterprets the role of the peer group. The normative adolescent tends to avoid overt conflict with his family. Now this is not to say that conflict is not present; but it is largely unconscious conflict, those under-surface resentments which do not necessarily liberate or enlarge the personality, but which, paradoxically, increase the child's docility toward his parents. Even when we do find overt conflict one senses that it has an "as if" quality to it, that it is a kind of war game, with all the sights and sounds of battle but without any blood being shed. More often than not the conflicts will center on trivia, on issues of taste—clothing, grooming, and the like. One can argue that these issues are trivial only to the adult, that they are, however, of great symbolic importance in the adolescent's quest for autonomy. True; but one can reply that parent and child play out an empty ritual of disaffection, that they agree to disagree only on token issues, on teen issues, and in doing so are able to sidestep any genuine encounter of differences.

Much the same is true of autonomy. There are autonomies and autonomies. The American adolescent asks for and is freely given an unsual degree of behavioral freedom—the right to come and go, to share in setting rules, and so on. But it is far more problematic whether he asks for or achieves a high degree of emotional autonomy, and it is even more doubtful that he manages much in the way of value autonomy. Indeed, the ease with which the adolescent acquires behavioral freedom may tend to interfere with the achievement of emotional and ideological freedom, for reasons we shall turn to in a moment. As to the peer group, its supposed functions—as an arena for the confrontation of the self, for the testing and trying out of identities—are present for many adolescents, but for many more the peer group is used for the learning and display of sociability and social skills. The peer culture is all too often a kind of playpen, designed to keep the children out of harm's way and out of the parents' hair. It may not work out this way; the children may begin throwing toys at each other, or, what is worse, may begin throwing them at the grownups in the living room. But generally it does work out just this way. The peer group, with its artificial amusements and excitements, more often acts to hinder differentiation and growth.

This is especially evident in the area of values and ideology. The traditional idea of the adolescent experience has it that the youngster becomes involved in an intense concern with ethics, political ideology, religious belief, and so on. The moral parochialism of early childhood was thought to be smashed by the moral fervor and incipient cosmopolitanism of adolescence. The youngster's need to detach himself from the family and its view of the moral and social order, his need to redo the ego-superego constellation, his need to find new and more appropriate ego ideals, his need to use ideology as a solution for instinctual problems—all these needs came together, so it was thought, to produce a value crisis somewhere in the course of the adolescent career. This pattern can be found in adolescence, but it is found in a bold, sometimes stubborn, often unhappy minority. Our interviews confirm a mounting impression from other studies, that American adolescents are on the whole not deeply involved in ideology, nor are they prepared to do much individual thinking on value issues of any generality. Why is this so? We would guess this is true because to think anew and differently endangers the adolescent's connection to the community, his object attachments, and complicates the task of ego synthesis.

We can sum up in the language of personality theory. The inherent tensions of adolescence are displaced to and discharged within the matrix of peer group sociability. Intrapsychically the defenses and character positions adopted are those which curtail experience and limit the growth and differentiation of the self—repression, reaction-formation, and certain forms of ego restriction. These two modes of dealing with inner and outer experience join to produce a pseudoadaptive solution of the adolescent crisis, marked by cognitive stereotypy, value stasis, and interpersonal conformity. It is a solution which is accomplished by resisting conflict, resisting change, resisting the transformation of the self. It settles for a modest resynthesis of the ego—closely along the lines of the older organization of drives, defenses, values, and object attachments. It is characterized by an avoidance of identity-diffusion through identity-coarctation.

These rather dismal conclusions on the

contemporary adolescent character are akin to those stated by Edgar Friedenberg in his brilliant book, *The Vanishing Adolescent.* Adolescence, he says, is disappearing as the period in which the individual can achieve a decisive articulation of the self. Nowadays the youngster, in his words, "merely undergoes puberty and simulates maturity." If this amiable but colorless form of adolescence is indeed a new thing in our country, then we would have to single out as one important reason the extraordinary attenuation of today's adolescence. Given the long preparation required for advanced technical training, given the uselessness of the adolescent in the labor market—parent and child settle down for a long, long period of time during which the child will, in one way or another, remain a dependent being.

Traditionally, adolescence has been the age in which the child readied himself to leave home; and when we read accounts of adolescence in the earlier part of this century we very often note between father and son a decisive encounter, a decisive testing of wills, in which the son makes a determined bid for autonomy, either by leaving home, or threatening to do so, and meaning it. The adolescent then had little of the freedom he has today; he was kept under the parental thumb, but he used his captivity well, to strengthen himself for a real departure and a real autonomy. Nowadays the adolescent and his parents are both made captive by their mutual knowledge of the adolescent's dependency. They are locked in a room with no exit, and they make the best of it by an unconscious *quid pro quo*, in which the adolescent forfeits his adolescence, and instead becomes a teenager. He keeps the peace by muting his natural rebelliousness through transforming it into structured and defined techniques for getting on people's nerves. The passions, the restlessness, the vivacity of adolescence are partly strangled, and partly drained off in the mixed childishness and false adulthood of the adolescent teen culture.

References

Komarovsky, M. Cultural contradictions and sex roles. *American Journal of Sociology,* 1946, **52,** 184-189.
Mead, M. *Male and female.* New York: Mentor, 1955.

IRVING B. WEINER

Perspectives on the Modern Adolescent*

According to some authorities, today's teenagers constitute a youth culture that is cut off from and at odds with the adult world. Among the imputed hallmarks of this youth culture are sloth, sloppiness, sexual promiscuity, drug abuse, and insistence on immediate gratification, mixed with a liberal dose of bad manners, disrespect for authority, and renunciation of traditional values. Whereas some writers view these aspects of youthful alienation with alarm, proponents of the "counter culture" and "Consciousness III" regard them as signs of social progress. A third group of writers disagrees entirely with the notion of a youth culture, asserting instead that adolescents as an essentially unique age group are a vanishing species. From this point of view the adolescent generation, beneath its superficial trappings, is a dull, stereotyped, unimaginative segment of our population that shrinks from individuality and prematurely adopts identities prescribed or modeled for them by their parent. Each of these positions has led to overdrawn conclusions about the nature of the modern adolescent, particularly with respect to his sex behavior and drug use, and a more balanced perspective is necessary to separate myth from reality.

*From *Psychiatry*, 1972, 35, 00-00. Reprinted by permission of the author and the William Alanson White Psychiatric Foundation.

THE YOUTH CULTURE

The notion of the youth culture in modern American emerged from the studies of Coleman (*The Adolescent Society*), Keniston (*The Uncommitted: Alienated Youth in American Society*) and Pearson (*Adolescence and the Conflict of Generations*) and had led to a recent spate of books decrying its existence, of which Feuer's *The Conflict of Generations* and Mead's *Culture and Commitment: A Study of the Generation Gap* are two of the more prominent. These writers attribute teenage alienation to such influences as a breakdown of family organization and parental authority, a rapidly changing world that exposes teenagers to experiences their parents cannot understand, the long apprenticeship between childhood and adulthood in a complex technological society, and teenage disaffection for a hypocritical, materialistic adult generation that has failed to eliminate war, injustice, and human misery.

The youth culture is generally seen as arising because teenagers have nowhere to turn except to themselves to find a sense of group belongingness and a set of values with which they can feel comfortable. Unappreciated by their elders and denied adult prerogatives, they look to each other for status and support and pointedly refuse to think, act, talk, dress, and comport themselves as the adult generation would like them to. "Don't trust anyone over 30" and "Screw the establishment" have become mottoes of the youth culture, and many observers feel that it is urgent that adults find some way to communicate across the generation gap before young people take over and tear down the institutions on which our society is founded. As contemporary as such concerns are, it is interesting to note how closely they were shared by Shakespeare's old shepherd in *The Winter's Tale*, who had this to say about adolescents:

"I would there were no age between ten and three-and-twenty, or that youth would sleep out the rest; for there is nothing in the between but getting wenches with child, wronging the ancientry, stealing, fighting" (Act III, Scene iii).

In assessing the accuracy of this perspective on youth, it is first necessary to emphasize the oversimplification inherent in any reference to "the youth culture." To the extent that adolescents differ from adults in any uniform fashion, the teenage population comprises not one but multiple cultures. There is a world of difference between the values and behavior of a group of 17-year-old black boys in New York's Harlem, a group of 13-year-old white girls in suburban Detroit's Grosse Point Shores, a group of teenage 4H Clubbers in rural Kansas, and a group of adolesent Chicanos in southern California. The fact is that youngsters of different age and sex, representing different ethnic and social class backgrounds, and coming from different sections of the country are likely to think and act as differently from each other as they do from adults.

Lipset and Raab (1970) have recently pointed out in this regard that no more than 10 percent of youth are really bent on renouncing or revamping the structure of our society, and that these youngsters are primarily college or college-bound students whose parents also hold liberal political attitudes. Thus revisionary youth protesting against the establishment comprise only a small segment of our adolescent population and are more likely to share political activism with their parents than to be rebelling against their parents' values (see also Block, Haan and Smith, 1968).

A less visible but equally large group of dissident youth come from conservative working-class and lower-middle-class families whose major concern is preventing any erosion of their hard-won security and prerogatives. These young people, far from deploring traditional society, are as intent as their parents on preserving and intensifying societal norms and resisting any concession to liberal activists.

Still a third segment of dissatisfied youth consists mainly of black and other culturally disadvantaged youngsters who want to preserve the system essentially as it is but improve their chances of getting into it and enjoying a piece of the action. Thus most militant black leaders and their youthful followers are pressing not for doing away with the American System, but for more black power in it—blacks in government, blacks in the upper echelons of business and finance, black control of programs for black people, and equal educational and occupational opportunities for blacks. The political gaps among these three elements in the youthful generation are considerably bigger than any gap between them and their parents: "Politically . . . the basic direction of the younger generation is in most cases the same as that of their parents; they go with the parental grain rather than against it" (Lipset and Raab, 1970, p. 38).

There is little evidence to support the widespread impression that most teenagers are in revolt against the values of their family and society. The notion of a normative "identity crisis" that causes teenagers to behave in a confused, unpredictable, and undisciplined manner bordering on psychopathology has been laid to rest by a mass of empirical data, even though it persists in the thinking of many clinicians. These data, as reviewed by Offer (1969, Chaps. 11-13) and Weiner (1970, Chap. 2), indicate (1) that adolescent turmoil is an infrequent phenomenon and reflects psychopathology rather than normal development when it occurs, (2) that most adolescents consolidate their personal identity gradually and without any major disruptions in the continuity of their self-concept or behavioral style, (3) that most adolescents respect their parents, want to be like them, and maintain relatively harmonious relations with them and other adults, and (4) that the majority of high school boys and girls feel that they are an integral part of the community in which they live and report that their main sources of concern are achievement and study habits, not sports or recreation or popularity or instant gratification.

THE COUNTER CULTURE AND CONSCIOUSNESS III

Two currently influential writers, Roszak and Reich, have taken positions that place the "youth culture" in numerical perspective, but at the same time extol and glorify those very aspects of youthful alienation that Feurer, Mead, and many other adults are concerned about. Roszak, a historian (The Making of a Counter Culture), and Reich, a law professor (The Greening of America), concur that revisionist or revolutionary youth comprise only a small minority of young people at present. However, both authors argue at length that radical youth capture what is best in the human spirit, that they are the wave of the future, and that they represent our only hope for survival.

According to Roszak (1969), the counter culture is a revolt against the totalitarian, dehumanizing atmosphere of our contemporary technocracy, a society in which bigness and complexity compel its citizens to defer on all matters to those who know better. The counter culture calls into question the validity of the conventional scientific world view, it denies the existence of an objective consciousness, and it seeks to replace technical and industrial values with a "profoundly personalist sense of community." Roszak's views of the importance of the counter culture and of youth's role in it are unequivocal:

"... most of what is presently happening that is new, provocative, and engaging in politics, education, the arts, social relations (love, courtship, family, community), is the creation either of youth who are profoundly, even fanatically, alienated from the parental generation, or of those who address themselves primarily to the young, (p. 1) . . . I am at a loss to know where, besides among *these dissenting young people and their heirs of the next few generations, the radical discontent and innovation can be found that might transform this disoriented civilization of ours into something a human being can identify as home. . .If the resistance of the counter culture fails, I think there will be nothing in store for us but what anti-utopians like Huxley and Orwell have forecast (pp. xii-xiii)."*

Reich (1970) similarly sees the younger generation as the vanguard of revolt against a "Corporate State" that "dominates, exploits, and ultimately destroys both nature and man." The Corporate State is the heir of Consciousness I, which Reich defines as the every-man-for-himself, survival-of-the-fittest mentality, and is rooted in Consciousness II, which surrenders individuality to a dehumanized corporate heriarchy and responsibility to a bureaucracy that is accountable to no one. Consciousness III, which is the key to refurbishing or "greening" America so as to bring back our freedom, vigor, humanity, and sense of community, is difficult to define succinctly; Reich says that to describe it systematically and analytically would be to engage in an intellectual process that Consciousness III rejects. Essentially, Consciousness III liberates the person from automatically accepting the imperatives of society and frees him to build his own philosophy and values; it declares that the individual self is the only true reality; it postulates the absolute worth of every human being; and it rejects the concept of excellence and comparative merit by refusing to classify people or evaluate them by general standards (pp.

225-227).

Reich argues vigorously for the transcendental importance of Consciousness III: "And only Consciousness III can make possible the continued survival of man as a species in this age of technology" (p. 353). As for the role of youth in this revolution, and the gloriousness of "youth culture," Reich is equally explicit:

"This is the revolution of the new generation. Their protest and rebellion, their culture, clothes, music, drugs, ways of thought, and liberated life-style are not a passing fad or a form of dissent and refusal, nor are they in any sense irrational. The whole emerging pattern, from ideals to campus demonstrations to beads and bell bottoms to the Woodstock Festival, makes sense and is part of a consistent philosophy. It is both necessary and inevitable, and in time it will include not only youth, but all people in American (p. 4)."

It is beyond the scope of this paper to debate the social philosophy advocated by Roszak and Reich. However, both authors extol a certain type of youthful behavior and exhort all young people, and indeed all America, to behave similarly, and in this regard they demonstrate a psychological naiveté that is quite germane to the topic of accurate perspectives on adolescence.

First, Roszak and Reich have an exaggerated impression of the innovativeness and depth of commitment reflected in many aspects of youthful behavior. In the quotation above, Reich includes tastes in clothes and music among adolescent behaviors that express a consistent philosophy and are not a passing fad. Later in his book he elaborates the selection of clothes by young people to express their freedom, affinity with nature, and rejection of affluence, and he pays particular attention to bell-bottom trousers as a means of expressing feelings through the body and giving the ankles freedom "as if to invite dancing right on the street" (pp. 234-237).

What is missing here is the recognition that most teenage tastes in clothes, music, and the like are not created de novo out of adolescent ingenuity and expressiveness. Rather, they are more often the product of adult inventiveness and opportunism, mainly in the form of entertainers, manufacturers, and promoters who are successful in convincing young people that what the merchandisers have to offer is "now" and "with it." That the young decide what kinds of clothes and music they enjoy is neither here nor there. The point is that they are the *consumers* and not the *creators* of taste, and what they choose to consume is likely to change often enough to keep a step ahead of their boredom and satiation and the promoter's slacking profits—just as the bell-bottoms with which Reich is enthralled were the pipe-stem jeans of a few years ago, and short skirts were long skirts and were short skirts before that, and the jerk was once the jitterbug, and so forth. Reich appears to feel that current tastes, because they are wedded to a whole new consciousness, are going to be permanent. History and our knowledge of adolescent psychology suggest that he is mistaken.

Second, both Roszak and Reich include among the youthful behaviors they glorify some that clinicians recognize as

reflecting psychopathology—psychopathology not merely in the sense of being deviant, but also in the sense of previous interpersonal difficulty and underachievement and a current history of anxiety and depression, identity diffusion, inability to experience intimacy, failure of self-realization, and pervasive unhappiness. Thus Roszak pays tribute to youth "who are profoundly, even fanatically, alienated," and Reich credits psychedelic drugs as being "One of the most important means for restoring dulled consciousness" (p. 258) and lists them as among the necessary and rational elements of the revolution that is to green America. Yet clinicians have identified profound alienation as a symptom of psychological disturbance that may presage personality breakdown (Halleck, 1967; Weiner, 1970, Chap. 2; Wise, 1970), and there is mounting evidence, to be presented shortly, that drug use, aside from its possible harmful effects, is the pastime of the teenage fringe and not of the masses or the likely leaders of the new generation.

THE VANISHING SPECIES

In striking contrast to writers who deplore the youth culture and all it is presumed to stand for or glorify it as our hope for salvation, other observers define the probems of today's youth as their lack of verve and cultural individuality. This view of contemporary youth was introduced by Friedenberg (*The Vanishing Adolescent*), whose thesis is that adolescent identity formation proceeds mainly through conflict with society, whereas modern technological society idealizes the organization man (Reich's Consciousness II) and has little tolerance for boat-rockers. Thus our society no longer fosters "real" adolescents struggling to define themselves, but rather is turning out conformist youngsters homogeneously identified with school and other institutional values, and adolescence as a unique developmental period is becoming obsolete.

The main support for this view of adolescence is provided by Douvan and Adelson (1966), whose research team interviewed a broadly representative sample of over 3000 teenagers. Douvan and Adelson concluded from their data that contemporary youth are indeed tending toward homogeneity, with a preference for conformity over conflict, for playing it safe and resisting change rather than experimenting or taking chances, and for premature identity consolidation. They also reported that apparent adolescent rebellion in their subjects consisted primarily of superficial disagreements with their parents about relatively trivial matters—hair length, style of dress, curfews, choice of friends, use of the family car—and did not involve major confrontations, disaffection, or controversy about fundamental standards of conduct and decency.

These data have served as an important corrective to the notion of a normatively alienated youth culture: "What generation gap?" asks Adelson (1970); "an overwhelming majority of the young—as many as 80%—tend to be traditionalist in values." However, the implication that adolescents routinely turn out to be stodgy, stilted, overconforming carbon copies of their parents also needs some correction. First, premature identity con-

solidation does not appear to be any more universal than an identity crisis. Follow-up studies of the teenagers interviewed by Offer and his colleagues suggest that relatively few adolescents opt for identity foreclosure. Even as 19- and 20-year olds, the majority of these youngsters still had only a moderate sense of their personal identity and were constructively engaged in role experimentation and self-assessment (Offer, Marcus, and Offer, 1970).

Second, identity foreclosure, like identity diffusion, appears to reflect maladjustment rather than normal development when it occurs. In studies of college students, Marcia (1966, 1967) and Marcia and Friedman (1970) found significant differences between those who exemplified early identity foreclosure and those who had achieved identity gradually following an extended period of uncertainty about future commitments. Compared to identity achievement youngsters, identity foreclosure subjects were more authoritarian, more likely to set unrealistically high goals for themselves and maintain these goals even in the face of failure, and more vulnerable to experimental manipulations of their self-esteem. Other work suggests that college students with identity foreclosure tend to be less task-oriented and to receive lower grades than students of similar ability who have achieved identity gradually (Cross and Allen, 1970).

Third, the incompatibility that Friedenberg postulates between modern society and adolescence as a unique developmental period, whatever its sociological ramifications, makes little psychological sense. No degree of adolescent conformity or homogeneity alters the fact that teenagers face certain developmental tasks peculiar to their age and that their lives are consequently oriented around different needs, different priorities, and different types of activities than the lives of children and adults. Adjusting to physical sexual maturation, learning to handle dating and heterosexual relationships, gaining psychological independence from parents, and planning one's educational and vocational future are tasks of adolescence that define it as a unique developmental period, regardless of how many youngsters prematurely foreclose their identity.

The uniqueness of adolescence brings us back to the question of the youth culture, and here there are some additional things to be said. Despite empirical evidence to the contrary, the notions of "adolescent rebellion" and the "generation gap" not only persist in clinical parlance, but also captivate the news media and become fixed in the public mind. The delinquent, the runaway, the addict, the Yippie, the flower person, the unwed mother, the malcontent, and the lost soul make better copy than the youngster who is unobtrusively going about the business of growing up. Likewise, the downtown shopper who sees dozens of scraggly, unwashed, and boorish youngsters loitering on the street corners easily loses sight of the thousands who are at that moment sitting in a classroom, practicing with the football team, working at a part-time job, taking a music lesson, or helping around the house.

It is the focus of newspapers, magazines, television, and the movies on what is most spectacular and sensational rather than on what is most typical about adolescent behavior, together with the individual memory for what is most shocking and repugnant rather than what is most common and ordinary, that nourish overgeneralized conceptions of adolescent rebellion and the generation gap. Two areas of teenage behavior that have come in for a lion's share of journalistic overemphasis and adult preoccupation are sex and drug use. A look at recent data in these two areas will further illustrate the need to balance current perspectives on adolescence against the weight of fact.

SEX BEHAVIOR

In this day of increasingly liberal attitudes toward nudity, pornography, and extramarital sexuality, it has become commonplace to accuse our youth in particular of moral decadence. The press dramatizes sexual swingers as if they were representative of all young people, and professional journals compound this fiction by carrying assertions that teenagers no longer have any regard for virginity (Hurlock, 1966), and that premarital intercourse has become a perfunctory aspect of the adolescent dating system (Glassberg, 1965).

Such imprecations have little relation to reality. The most thorough assessment of premarital sexual behavior in the United States is provided by Reiss (1967, 1969), who reports that, contrary to widespread belief, there has been no appreciable increase in the proportion of nonvirginity among unmarried young people since the 1920s. Furthermore, the changes toward permissiveness that have taken place in recent years have been closely tied to affection and have neither fostered nor sanctioned promiscuity. Reiss emphasizes that permissiveness without affection has very few followers; unfortunately, however, it makes attractive grist for the popular media mill, and hence the public gets misled as to the number of people who endorse it.

Although Reiss' data and observations pertain to middle-class youngsters, lower-class youngsters hold similar attitudes. Rainwater (1966, 1969) reviews evidence that both lower-class boys and lower-class girls are more likely to have premarital sexual relations than middle-class boys and girls, but that a double standard is the rule among lower-class as well as middle-class youth. Fewer lower-class girls than middle-class boys have had premarital intercourse, and the virginity of lower-class girls is highly valued and protected within their family and peer group.

More recent data from selected samples suggest that the incidence of premarital intercourse among college girls may have risen in the past decade, somewhat more than Reiss' earlier impressions. Studies by Kaats and Davis (1970) and by Luckey and Nass (1969) report a 60% frequency of intercourse among unmarried male college students, which is essentially the same figure that has existed since World War I, but an incidence approaching 40% for a sample consisting primarily of junior and senior co-eds, which represents an increase from the 20-30% figure observed in most studies of college girls during the 1950s and early 1960s. Yet these studies lend no support to the notion that adolescents have rejected virginity and accepted intercourse as perfunctory aspect of dating.

In the Luckey and Nass study, which

involved 1398 students drawn from a representative sample of 21 colleges and universities, 70% of the boys and 40% of the girls said it would "trouble" them to marry a person who had previously had intercourse with someone else. In the Kaats and Davis survey, only 28% of the coeds felt that their having intercourse, even with someone they loved, would be approved by their friends. And Bell and Chaskes (1970), studying co-eds in a large urban university, found a 39% incidence of premarital intercourse among girls who were engaged, 28% for those who were going steady, and 23% for those who had a dating relationship with their sexual partner.

In general, then, the evidence demonstrates that notions of rampant free love among teenagers simply do not hold water. Young people have more permissive attitudes toward sex than in the past, but they link this new permissiveness to love and affection. Thus today's youth are more likely than previously to consider sexual intercourse within the context of a close, trusting, exclusive, and relatively enduring relationship, but they continue firm in their rejection of casual, indiscriminate, or promiscuous sexuality.

Two other recent sources of information help to distinguish normative patterns of teenage sexuality from myths about youthful licentiousness. In a national survey by the Merit Publishing Company (1970) of 22,000 high-achieving high school juniors and seniors, 42% indicated their approval of premarital sexual intercourse but only 18% of the boys and 15% of the girls reported having participated in it. Although this sample of able students cannot be taken as representative of all adolescents, it does confirm how far nonvirginity is from being the norm among academically successful teenagers.

Second, the problem of the unwed teenage mother has not increased nearly as disproportionately as is commonly supposed. National statistics (U. S. Department of HEW, 1967) reveal that the rate of illegitimate births in the United States between 1940 and 1967 increased *less* among 15- to 19-year-old girls than for any other age range between 20 and 39. Over this period the illegitimacy rate per 1000 unmarried women rose from 7.1 to 18.7 among 15- to 19-year-olds, but from 9.5 to 38.6 for 20- to 24-year-olds, from 7.2 to 41.4 for those 25-29, from 5.1 to 29.8 for age 30-34, and from 3.4 to 15.3 for age 35-39.

DRUG USE

There is little question that an increasing number of young people have been attracted to marijuana, amphetamines, LSD, and related drugs in recent years. This upsurge in drug use has led to enormous public concern and widespread belief that taking some sort of drug is fast becoming a universal teenage fashion. We read in *The New York Times* that on the college campus "Marijuana is the common denominator among all groups" (Darnton, 1971), and the Movement to Restore Decency Committee tells us that 25% of young Americans are on drugs and that their numbers are increasing by 7% per month (Hober, 1971)—which would mean 84%, or almost double, each year.

Teenage drug addiction, when it occurs, is a grave clinical and public concern. However, reliance on less than adequate sampling has inflated the results of many incidence surveys of teenage drug use, and highly publicized adolescent deaths due to drug overdose have led to exaggerated conclusions about the prevalence of youthful drug abuse. Imperi, Kleber, and Davie (1968) demonstrated this kind of discrepancy between fact and impression by comparing the actual incidence of drug use among Yale and Wesleyan students they surveyed with estimates of incidence given by students. The observed incidence was considerably lower than student estimates, and Imperi and her co-author suggest that students who are involved with drugs overestimate campus use to justify their own behavior—that is, "everybody else is doing it." To the extent that this is the case, journalists who investigate campus drug use by interviewing student drug users will get responses that appear to justify captions like "Smoking Pot a Student Way of Life."

A somewhat different picture of teenage drug use emerges if one excludes studies with restricted samples and polls reported in newspapers and magazines and looks just at recent large-scale studies done by reliable social scientists. Surveys of 10,364 students attending Sacramento State College (Morrison, 1969), 3010 at Carnegie-Mellon University in Pittsburgh (Goldstein, 1970), 2145 at Ithaca College, New York (Rand, 1968), and 26,111 at nine schools in the Denver area (Mizner, Barter, and Werme, 1970) indicate that approximately 25% of college students have used marijuana at some time, 12% have used amphetamines, and 5% have tried LSD. Furthermore, of students who report ever having used marijuana, amphetamines, or LSD, 40-50% state that they have stopped using them. In other words, it appears that three-fourths of college students have never tried drugs at all and that only half of those who have tried them have become repetitive users.

At the high school level, observed teenage drug use has varied with the locale being studied (see Table 1). Among 47,000 high school students in Utah, the reported incidence of any marijuana use was 12.2%, for amphetamine use 10%, and for LSD use 4.9% (Governor's Citizen Advisory Committee on Drugs, 1969). For 1300 high school youngsters in Montgomery County, Maryland (Joint Committee on Drug Abuse, 1970) and 800 in Madison, Wisconsin (Udell and Smith, 1969), about one fifth had tried marijuana; less than 8%, amphetamines; and

Table 1 Percentage of High School Students Reporting Any Previous Use of Marijuana, Amphetamines, or LSD

Locale and Year	N	Marijuana	Amphetamines	LSD
Utah, 1969	47,182	12.2	10.0	4.9
Montgomery County, Md., 1970	1,348	18.7	7.8	5.9
Madison, Wisconsin, 1969	781	22.6	5.4	5.8
Suburban NYC, 1971	1,704	24.0	12.0	10.0
San Mateo County, Cal., 1970	25,756	42.9	20.0	14.4

less than 6%, LSD. For 1704 respondents in a suburban New York City community, representing over 90% of that community's 15- to 18-year-old population, the rates of previous use were 24% for marijuana, 12% for amphetamines, and 10% for LSD (Tec, 1971). And in San Mateo County, California, 25,756 high school students reported previous use rates of 42.9% for marijuana, 20% for amphetamines, and 14.4% for LSD (San Mateo County Department of Public Health and Welfare, 1970). For high school as well as for college students, however, these reports of ever having used a drug do not necessarily indicate current use. In the Montgomery County study, for example, almost 40% of the youngsters who had used marijuana or LSD had quit after trying them, and two thirds of those who had experimented with amphetamines had never used them again.

The San Mateo County study merits further comment in two respects: (1) it is the only large-scale study that has surveyed youthful drug use in the same population in three successive years—1968, 1969, and 1970—and provided comparisons over these years; and (2) the three-year data from the study indicate a leveling-off or decline in drug use rates. From 1968-1969 the San Mateo youngsters' reported incidence of any drug use during the previous year increased by 7.6% for marijuana, 4.3% for amphetamines, and 4.2% for LSD. For 1969-1970, however, the percent of reported use increased only 2.5% for marijuana and *decreased* for both amphetamines (by 0.9%) and LSD (by 1.5%). These changes may not be reliable enough to indicate a permanent downward trend in drug use. However, as Richards and Carroll (1970) point out in discussing these San Mateo data, west coast schools were the first to experience the onslaught of drug use, and the 1970 findings may well presage a general stabilization or rates of declining student interest in drugs.

Finally, in addition to demonstrating a lower rate of teenage drug use than is commonly supposed, available data also indicate that drugs have relatively little appeal for well-adjusted youngsters. In a study of almost 9000 junior and senior high school students drawn from throughout metropolitan Toronto, Smart, Fejer, and White (1970) consistently found that the youngsters who were most likely to be using drugs were those who were doing least well academically, were least involved in school activities, and were most inclined to spend their evenings and weekends hanging around with friends rather than in organized activities.

This indication that the small minority of teenagers who use drugs consists primarily of fringe youngsters who are not doing well in the classroom or in extracurricular activities is supported by the rates of marijuana use among the 22,000 able high school juniors and seniors in the Merit survey. These academically successful youngsters showed regional differences similar to those reflected in the Utah, Maryland, New York, and California studies, but in each case their incidence figures were lower than those for the general high school population. They reported higher rates of marijuana use in northeastern (15%) and western (13%) states than in the midwest (8%), south (5%), and southwest (5%), and their marijuana use was more common in suburban (13%) and urban (10%) communities than in rural and small-town America (5%).

In concluding this brief overview of teenage drug use, I must report on the usual reaction when I present these kinds of data to professional colleagues: "Very interesting; but of course we know that drug use is a pervasive and spreading phenomenon, and there are probably other studies that show this more fully." But there is no such cache of "other studies" that I have steadfastly chosen to ignore or carelessly managed to overlook. I have kept reasonably abreast of the literature and have made use of current compilations of studies graciously supplied by the Drug Abuse Center of the National Institute of Mental Health (Berg, 1970). It seems to me that behavioral scientists may share with the general public some difficulty in hearing facts about teenagers that conflict with impressions they have formed on some other basis.

I do not wish to minimize the presence and potential seriousness of drug abuse problems in substantial numbers of young people. However, I do wish to make the point that a proper perspective on drug use must be maintained, so that (1) the use of drugs is not considered a normative feature of growing up in modern times and (2) the drug-abusing adolescent is regarded as a confused, disturbed, and probably alienated young person in need of professional help.

For a generally balanced perspective on the modern adolescent, then, it is necessary to recognize that he belongs neither to a rebellious youth culture nor to an overconforming vanishing species; that the manner in which groups of young people approach the developmental tasks of adolescence often makes them as different from each other as they are from adults; and that alienation, protest, sexual promiscuity, and drug abuse are neither normal nor normative patterns of adolescent behavior and assertions to the contrary suffuse reality with myth.

References

Adelson, J. *Time*, August 17, 1970. P. 35.

Bell, R. R., and Chaskes, J. B. "Premarital Sexual Experience Among Coeds, 1958 and 1968," *Journal of Marriage and the Family* (1970) 32:81-84.

Berg, D. F. "Illicit Use of Dangerous Drugs in the United States: A Compilation of Studies, Surveys, and Polls," Bureau of Narcotics and Dangerous Drugs, U. S. Department of Justice, September, 1970.

Block, J. H., Haan, N., and Smith, M. B. "Activism and Apathy in Contemporary Adolescents," in J. F. Adams (Ed.), *Understanding Adolescence: Current Developments in Adolescent Psychology.* Boston: Allyn and Bacon, 1968. Pp. 198-231.

Coleman, J. S. *The Adolescent Society.* New York: Free Press of Glencoe, 1961.

Cross, H. H., and Allen, J. G. "Ego Identity Status, Adjustment, and Academic Achievement," *Journal of Consulting and Clinical Psychology* (1970) 34:288.

Darnton, J. "Many on Campus Shifting to Softer Drugs and Alcohol," *The New York Times,* Jan. 17, 1971.

Douvan, E., and Adelson, J. *The Adolescent Experience.* New York: Wiley, 1966.

Feuer, L. S. *The Conflict of Generations.* New York: Basic Books, 1969.

Friedenberg, E. Z. *The Vanishing Adolescent.* Boston: Beacon, 1959.

Glassberg, B. Y. "Sexual Behavior Patterns in Contemporary Youth Culture: Implications for Later Marriage," *Journal of Marriage and the Family* (1965) 27:190-192.

Goldstein, J. "The Social Psychology of Student Drug Use: Report on Phase One," A Report on the Carnegie-Mellon University Drug Research Project, June, 1970.

Governor's Citizen Advisory Committee on Drugs, State of Utah. "Drug Use Among High School Students in the State of Utah," Sept. 1969.

Halleck, S. L. "Psychiatric Treatment of Alienated College Students," *American Journal of Psychiatry* (1967) 124:642-650.

Hober, N. Letter to the Editor, *Rochester Democrat and Chronicle,* Jan. 9, 1971.

Hurlock, E. B. "American Adolescents Today—A New Species," *Adolescence,* (1966) 1:7-21.

Imperi, L. L., Kleber, H. D., and Davie, J. S. "Use of Hallucinogenic Drugs on Campus," *Journal of the American Medical Association* (1968) 204:1021-1024.

Joint Committee on Drug Abuse, Montgomery County, Md. "A Survey of Secondary School Students' Perceptions of and Attitudes Toward Use of Drugs by Teenagers," Final Report, March 10, 1970.

Kaats, G. R., and Davis, K. E. "The Dynamics of Sexual Behavior of College Students," *Journal of Marriage and the Family* (1970) 32:390-399.

Keniston, K. *The Uncommitted: Alienated Youth in American Society.* New York: Harcourt, Brace, and World, 1965.

Lipset, M. L., and Raab, E. "The Non-Generation Gap," *Commentary* (1970) 50:35-39.

Luckey, E. B., and Nass, G. D. "A Comparison of Sexual Attitudes and Behavior in an International Sample," *Journal of Marriage and the Family* (1969) 31:364-379.

Marcia, J. E. "Development and Validation of Ego-Identity Status, " Journal of Personality and Social Psychology (1966) 3:551-558.

Marcia, J. E. "Ego Identity Status: Relationship to Change in Self-Esteem, 'General Adjustment,' and Authoritarianism," *Journal of Personality* (1967) 35:119-133.

Marcia, J. E., and Friedman, M. L. "Ego Identity Status in College Women," *Journal of Personality* (1970) 38:249-263.

Mead, M. *Culture and Commitment: A Study of the Generation Gap.* New York: Doubleday, 1970.

Merit Publishing Company. *National Survey of High School High Achievers,* 1970.

Mizner, G. L., Barter, J. T., and Werme, P. H. "Patterns of Drug Use Among College Students," *American Journal of Psychiatry* (1970) 127:15-24.

Morrison, R. L. "Preliminary Report on the Incidence of the Use of Drugs at Sacramento State College," May 15, 1969.

Offer, D. *The Psychological World of the Teenager.* New York: Basic Books, 1969.

Offer, D., Marcus, D., and Offer, J. L. "A Longitudinal Study of Normal

Adolescent Boys," *American Journal of Psychiatry* (1970) 126:41-48.

Pearson, G. H. J. *Adolesence and the Conflict of Generations.* New York: Norton, 1958.

Rainwater, L. "Some Aspects of Lower Class Sexual Behavior," *Journal of Social Issues* (1966) 22:96-108.

Rainwater, L. "Sex in the Culture of Poverty," in C. B. Broderick and J. Bernard (Eds.), *The Individual, Sex, and Society.* Baltimore, Md.: Johns Hopkins Press, 1969. Pp. 129-140.

Rand, M. E. "A Survey of Drug Use at Ithaca College," presented at the American College Health Association Annual Convention, May, 1968.

Reich, C. A. *The Greening of America.* New York: Random House, 1970.

Reiss, I. L. *The Social Context of Premarital Sexual Permissiveness.* New York: Holt, Rinehart and Winston, 1967.

Reiss, I. L. "Premarital Sexual Standards," in C. B. Broderick and J. Bernard (Eds.), *The Individual, Sex, and Society.* Baltimore, Md.: Johns Hopkins Press, 1969. Pp. 109-128.

Richards, L. G., and Carroll, E. E. "Illicit Drug Use and Addiction in the United States," *Public Health Reports,* (1970) 85:1035-1041.

Roszak, T. *The Making of a Counter Culture.* New York: Doubleday, 1969.

San Mateo County Department of Public Health and Welfare. "Five Mind-Altering Drugs," Research and Statistics Section, 1969.

San Mateo County Department of Public Health and Welfare. "Five Mind-Altering Drugs (Plus One)," Research and Statistics Section, 1970.

Smart, R. G., Fejer, D., and White, J. "The Extent of Drug Use in Metropolitan Toronto Schools: A Study of Changes from 1968 to 1970," Addiction Research Foundation, Toronto, October, 1970.

Tec, N. "Drugs Among Suburban Teenagers: Basic Findings," *Social Science and Medicine* (1970) 5:77-84.

Udell, J. G., and Smith, R. E. "Attitudes, Usage and Availability of Drugs among Madison High School Students," University of Wisconsin Bureau of Business Research and Service, Madison, Wisconsin, July 1969.

U.S. Department of Health, Education and Welfare. *Vital Statistics of the United States, 1967.* Vol. I. *Natality.*

Weiner, I. B. *Psychological Disturbance in Adolescence.* New York: Wiley, 1970.

Wise, L. J. "Alienation of Present-Day Adolescents," *Journal of the American Academy of Child Psychiatry* (1970) 9:264-277.

16
ADOLESCENCE:
INDIVIDUAL AND GROUP DIFFERENCES

Whereas many intellectual and personality differences among children emerge clearly before they reach adolescence, it is during the adolescent years that individual differences in the physical domain become most pronounced. At no other time in life are individuals of the same chronological age so varied in physical size, appearance, and degree of maturation. These individual differences in growth rate and degree of physical maturity can have important and lasting psychological consequences, primarily because adolescents tend to be very self-conscious and highly sensitive to the attitudes and reactions of other people to their physical appearance. This same adolescent self-consciousness about appearance is involved in one of the most significant group differences among young people, which is the problem in identity formation experienced by adolescents who are black or belong to some other minority group.

The first paper that follows, based on a follow-up study of the adult status of subjects previously examined as adolescents, deals with the psychological effects of early and late maturation in adolescent boys. This study illustrates the fruitfulness of longitudinal research and documents the immense debt owed to researchers like Mary Cover Jones who have had the foresight and persistence to conduct such investigations. Her study also bears the mark of the careful investigator who does not prematurely opt for compelling hypotheses but instead reports all the facts as they are, even at the expense of being unable to draw simple conclusions.

In the second paper Proshansky and Newton thoughtfully review some of the literature concerning the complex question of how black young people arrive at a sense of identity in an essentially white society. The paper highlights the many difficulties, ambiguities, and contradictions that face Negro children and adolescents who are striving to attain a sense of self-worth and self-esteem in a society that often says their skin color does not warrant such attitudes. Among the important points Proshansky and Newton make is the fact that social scientists have vastly overgeneralized the problems of blacks in America, especially in terms of not sufficiently appreciating the wide class and cultural differences that exist within the black community itself.

MARY COVER JONES

The Later Careers of Boys Who Were Early- or Late-Maturing*

A previous study (7) compared two groups of boys who had been classified as physically accelerated or retarded, in terms of skeletal age. These groups represented approximately the 20 per cent at each extreme of a normal public school sample. The comparison showed differences in physical growth, sexual maturing, and in a number of psychological measures, and led to the conclusion that ". . . those who are physically accelerated are usually accepted and treated by adults and other children as more mature. They appear to have relatively little need to strive for status. From their ranks come the outstanding student body leaders in senior high school. In contrast, the physically retarded boys exhibit many forms of relatively immature behavior: this

*From *Child Development*, 1957, 28, 113-128. Reprinted by permission of the author and the Society for Research in Child Development.

may be in part because others tend to treat them as the little boys they appear to be. Furthermore, a fair proportion of these give evidence of needing to counteract their physical disadvantages in some way—usually by greater activity and striving for attention, although in some cases by withdrawal" (p. 146.).

It is clear that early- or late-maturing may have a considerable bearing upon the social life and personal adjustment of some individuals during the middle years of their adolescence. Perhaps of greater importance, however, is the inquiry as to longer-term effects or relationships in adult life, and on this point no evidence has previously been offered.

The subjects who participated in the original study are now in their early thirties. Contacts have been maintained with many of the group during the intervening years; in a systematic follow-up study beginning in 1954 current data have been obtained for 20 of the early-

and late-maturing boys, out of an original sample of 32.

ADOLESCENT DIFFERENCES

Figures 1 to 7 present data from the adolescent period for the original groups, and for the subsamples available in the present study. Figure 1 shows the distri-bution of skeletal ages (at around chrono-logical age 17) for the early- and late-maturing. Each circle represents an individual case: the black circles those included in the follow-up and the open circles those who have dropped out.[1] It can be seen that the new selection has not substantially altered the maturity differ-ential of the two groups.

Figures 2 and 3 present cumulative

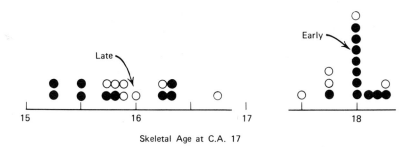

Figure 1. *Skeletal ages at 17 years, of the late-and early-maturing.*

records for height and weight in terms of standard scores at ages 12 to 17. Standard scores (in which 50 is taken as the mean and 10 as the SD) are indicated on the left vertical axis, and percentiles on the right. In these and the following figures, the points on connecting lines represent averages for the follow-up group, consist-ing of 11 early- and 9 late-maturing individuals. The adjacent points denote averages for the original 16 early- and 16 late-maturing.

The early-maturing tend to fall at the 75 percentile or above, and the late-maturing at the 25 percentile or below, with differences which are at a maximum at around 14 years, when the early-maturing are on the average approxi-mately 8 inches taller and 34 pounds heavier.

In these physical measures the adoles-cent data for the follow-up sample are similar to those of the original sample, and this is also shown in Figure 4, based on a measure of static dynamometer strength (right grip).

---

[1] Skeletal age was assessed from X-rays of the hand and knee, using Todd standards. Of the 12 cases lost from the original sample, three have died, one has not been located, one is non-cooperative, three have been scheduled but not yet seen in the follow-up and the remaining four have moved away and are for the time being unavailable because of resi-dence abroad, or in other states.

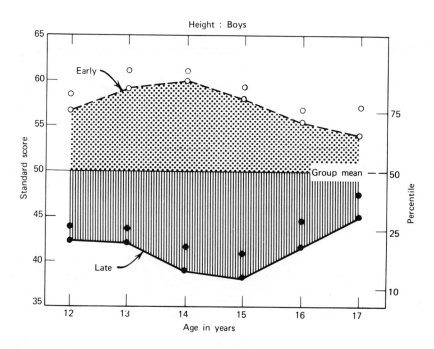

Figure 2. *Height comparisons for two contrasting groups.*

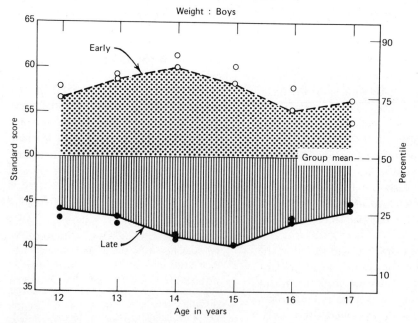

Figure 3. *Weight comparisons.*

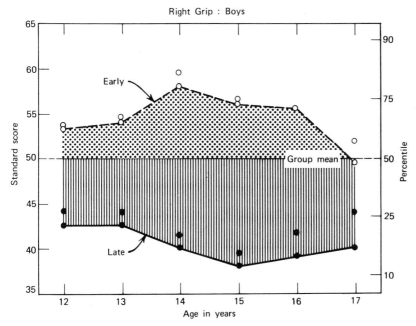

Figure 4. *Strength comparisons.*

Other physical comparisons included Greulich's (6) 5-point standards of maturity (rated by physicians from pubic hair and external genitalia) and Bayley's ratings of androgeny (1). On the Greulich scale the late-maturing boys at age 14 averaged only 2.0, well below the norm; while the early-maturing averaged 4.5, or close to the scale maximum. In the androgeny assessments, the early-maturing were nearly all in the "masculine" or "hyper-masculine" zone, while approximately half of the late-maturing were classified as "asexual," "bisexual," "hypo-bisexual," or physically "disharmonious." In these as in other respects the follow-up samples yielded distributions similar to those of the original study.

With such marked adolescent differences in size, strength, masculine conformation, and associated athletic abilities, we might also predict, in our culture, average differences in reputational status and in some aspects of self-acceptance. In the original study comparisons were presented, at an average age of 16, for a series of ratings made in "free play" situations. The early-maturing were judged to be more attractive in physique and as showing more attention to grooming. They tended to be more relaxed, more matter-of-fact and less affected in their behavior. Differences were significant at the .05 level for each of these traits; for a number of other characteristics, such as interest in the opposite sex, and "good naturedness," quite consistent differences were obtained over nine semesters of observation. The late-maturing were significantly more expressive, but their small-boy eagerness was also

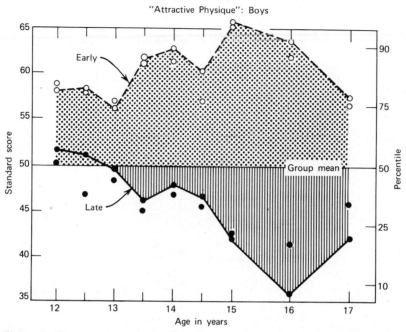

Figure 5. *Comparative ratings of "attractive physique."*

associated with greater tenseness and more affected attention-seeking mannerisms.

Figure 5 represents average measures for attractiveness of physique, based on independent ratings by three staff members. Figure 6 gives similar cumulative records for an illustrative aspect of expressive behavior (eagerness). The early-maturing are centered close to the average in this characteristic while the late-maturing are judged to be more juvenile and less poised in their expressiveness, especially in the middle years of adolescence. Similar results were found for such characteristics as "animated," "talkative," and "uninhibited."

On behavior items suggesting a large component of self-acceptance (being relaxed, unaffected and matter-of-fact) the early-maturing were rated higher at the end of the study, with the late-maturing becoming increasingly "tense" and "affected" in the high school years.[2] Figure 7 illustrates this for the characteristic which we have called "matter-of-fact." Both groups fluctuate around the average in this trait until age 16 when they separate noticeably, the early-maturing falling on the favorable or well-adjusted side, and the late-maturing on the attention-seeking or show-off side of the scale. Similar wide separation at ages

[2] A study of the Thematic Apperception Test responses at age 17 suggests that early-maturing boys tend to be more self-accepting and to feel less threatened than late-maturing. These data will be presented in a forthcoming article by Paul H. Mussen and Mary Cover Jones.

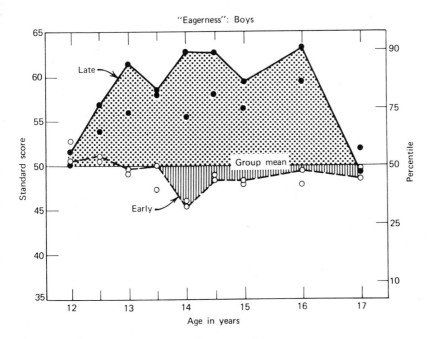

Figure 6. *Comparative ratings of "eagerness."*

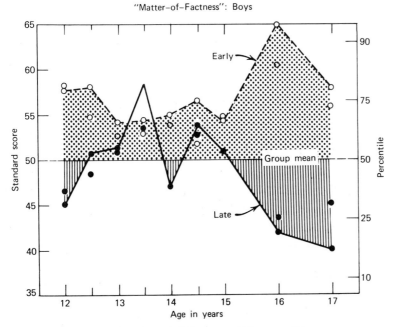

Figure 7. *Comparative ratings of "matter-of-factness."*

16 and 17 has been found for the trait "unaffected-affected" and for "relaxed-tense." In these, as in other relevant psychological measures, the follow-up groups had adolescent records similar to those of the original study; the loss of cases has not substantially changed the selection.

ADULT DIFFERENCES

We may now consider the adult characteristics of the early- and late-maturing, as observed at an average age of 33 years. As was predicted at age 17, the differences in gross size tend to disappear. The early-maturing average only half an inch taller, at 5 feet 10 inches; and 7 pounds heavier, at 172 pounds. These differences are not significant. In body build, the prediction is that the early-maturing would be more mesomorphic. The tendency is in this direction, but the differences are not significant. The chief thing to note is the wide range of physiques within each group (both in adolescence and in adulthood) and the marked consistency over the years. A slight change is apparent in the direction of greater mesomorphy in eight of the nine late-maturing and they now present a somewhat more developed and sturdy appearance.

Some differences would be expected in constitutional indices of masculinity. Among the late-maturing, the majority of the original study and of those included in the follow-up were rated as having a deficiency in masculine development, at age 17. At age 33, however, Sheldon ratings of gynandromorphy (8) in the two groups showed considerable overlap and only a small and nonsignificant difference in favor of the early-maturing.

Personality differences in adult life have been examined with reference to a number of criteria. Two sources of data to be considered here are Gough's California Psychological Inventory and the Edwards Personal Preference Schedule. The first of these, the C.P.I., attempts to appraise aspects of character and temperament which are significant for social living and interpersonal behavior and which are related to personal maturity and creative achievement. Eighteen scales are available which describe individuals in terms of social responsibility, tolerance, flexibility, academic motivation, self-control[3] and the like (3).

Most of the above scales did not show significant differences between the groups. One outstanding exception is the scale entitled "good impression," (interest in, and capacity for, creating a "good impression" on others) (4). Differences here favored the early-maturing with a significance at the .006 level.

Some of the interpretative phrases associated with high scores on this scale include: "is turned to for advice and reassurance; fatherly; is concerned with making a good impression; is persistent in working toward his goal." High scorers on this "Gi" scale are also designated as responsible, cooperative, enterprising, sociable and warm.

In our groups the early-maturing tend in addition to obtain higher scores on the C. P. I. scales for socialization, dominance, self-control and responsibility. Although none of these shows differences

---

[3] "Self-control" is indicated by a low score on the impulsivity scale.

at a significance level better than .07, it is true that the early-maturing have high average scores and present a consistently favorable personality picture with regard to these important social variables.

The phrases and adjectives associated with high scores on these five scales (good impression, socialization, dominance, self-control, and responsibility) remind us strikingly of the social behavior and personal traits attributed, by their peers and by adults, to the early-maturing boys in adolescence. For the total group of 43 boys thus far included in the follow-up, a correlation of .50 (significant at the .01 level) was found between the "good impression" score on the C.P.I., and their level of skeletal maturity 18 years earlier. The corresponding Pearson r for the socialization[4] score at age 33, and skeletal maturity at age 15, was .40, significant at the .01 level. For these correlations skeletal quotients were computed (skeletal age over chronological age),to make allowance for slight differences in the age at which the skeletal X-rays were obtained.

One other scale yields an interesting difference, significant at the .05 level. This is the scale for what has been termed "flexibility." Those who score high on this scale are described by Gough as tending to be rebellious, touchy, im-

<hr/>

[4]This "socialization" scale was first presented by Gough (5) and described as a scale for "delinquency." It is now scored in the opposite direction so as to emphasize the "socialization" side of a socialization-asocialization continuum. In a validation study lowest scores were obtained by those nominated as high school "best citizens"; highest scores by delinquents.

pulsive, self-indulgent, assertive, and also insightful. Low scorers are described as deliberate, methodical, industrious, rigid, mannerly, overly-controlling of impulses, compliant. In these terms, the late-maturers tend to be more "flexible" than the early-maturers.

We might hazard the guess that some of the little boy behavior—the impulsiveness, playfulness and also the "touchiness" repeatedly noted in late-maturing adolescents is mirrored in the description of high scorers on this scale. We might speculate further that in the course of having to adapt to difficult status problems, the late-maturers have gained some insights and are indeed more flexible, while the early-maturing, capitalizing on their ability to make a good impression, may have clung to their earlier success pattern to the extent of becoming somewhat rigid or over-controlled.

The Edwards Personal Preference test shows relatively few significant differences between the two groups. This is a self-report device which measures 15 variables named from Murray's list of needs (2).

On the Edwards test, two of the scales are discriminating for our groups at the 4 and 5 per cent levels respectively. The early-maturing group scores high on the *dominance* scale: "to be a leader, persuade, argue for a point of view," while the late-maturing score high in *succorance*: "to seek encouragement, to be helped by others, to have a fuss made over one when hurt." For the total group of 40 who took the Edwards test at around age 33, skeletal maturing at age 17 correlated .40 with dominance, and −.48 with succorance (both significant at the .01 level). Table 1 summarizes the

Table 1 Summary of Statistical Findings for the Follow-up Comparisons

	Physical Measures: Means			
	Late		Late	
	Age 14	Age 33	Age 14	Age 33
Height..................	5 ft. 8 in.	5 ft. 10 in.	5 ft.	5 ft. 9½in.
Weight	126.9 lb	172 lb.	93.2 lb	155 lb.
Endomorphy*.....	2.6	3.1	3.1	3.3
Mesomorphy*.....	4.5	4.6	3.9	4.3
Ectomorphy*	3.4	3.4	3.7	3.7

	Psychological Scales				
	Means		Signif. of		Signif.
	Early	Late	Difference†	r‡	Level
California Psychological Inventory					
Good Impression.........	25.6	15.7	.006	.50	<.01
Flexibility....................	9.7	13.8	.05	−.23	<.01
Deliquency§	13.9	20.3	.07	−.40	<.01
Impulsivity.................	17.1	23.4	.13	−.31	<.05
Dominance................	31.7	27.4	.17	.26	
Responsibility	32.9	30.0	.19	.35	<.05
Edwards Personal Preference Schedule					
Dominance.................	19.4	12.6	.04	.40	<.01
Succorance.................	7.1	12.4	.05	−.48	<.01

*Rating on 7-point scale; 7 is high.
†Significance level, Wilcoxon Rank Test.
‡Pearson product-moment correlation with skeletal age / chronological age, at 15 years.
§A low score indicates "socialization."

statistical findings for the follow-up comparisons.[5]

To those of us who have known these young men for over 20 years, some of the most interesting questions remain to be answered. What have been their successes and failures in achieving occupational and personal goals? All are married, and in each group the present number of children averages 2.3. Socio-economic ratings, based on homes and neighborhoods, show no differences for the two groups. There are no significant differences in average educational level, although a slightly higher proportion of

[5] Statistical analysis of the data was completed under a research grant from the Department of Education, University of California.

the later-maturing have college degrees and the only college teacher is in this group.[6]

There is some indication that more of the early-maturing have attained vocational goals which are satisfying and status-conferring. Among this group five are in professional careers; four are executives; one is a skilled mechanic and one in a clerical position. Of the executives, three are in positions of somewhat impressive status.

Among the late-maturing, four are in professions, two are still university students, two are salesmen, and one is a carpenter. None has attained an important managerial position and several, by their own account and the nature of their work, seem somewhat precariously unsettled.

In the former study descriptive pictures were given of late-maturing boys who illustrated contrasting behavior patterns of attention-seeking activity and of withdrawal. It may be appropriate here to summarize individual records for several of those at the early- and late-maturing extremes.

Tom, a late-maturing boy as described in a previous article (7), was at the age of 13 a chubby small boy, very rosy of cheek, sparkling eyed, laughing and dimpled. He was gay, active, good-humored, emotionally volatile. Even as a senior in high school he was still a "little boy." His voice had not changed. At a time when most of his classmates were paying care-

ful attention to cleanliness and grooming he often came to school with dirty hands and in misfit clothes. He was likely to get into childish scuffles; physically, however, he was not able to cope with his classmates, and would sometimes break down and cry when things went badly.

Unlike most of the physiologically retarded group, he seemed not to be anxious about his immaturity. Growth continued during his college years, when he added four inches to his height, and 20 pounds to his weight. As a graduate student Tom began to play baseball on an intramural team and for the first time, according to his own report, was able to hold up his end of the game. So impressed was he with his own physical gains (there had never been any doubt about his mental abilities) that he raised his sights in regard to vocational goals, achieved a graduate degree and joined the academic ranks as a college teacher.

The interviewer who saw him most recently at the age of 33 described him as: "A genial smiling young man, well integrated, mature, observant, well satisfied with his life situation." He is making excellent progress professionally, and achieving recognition among his colleagues. We now feel that we were justified in the impression gained during his high school years, that Tom was able to cope with the problems of late-maturing without permitting these to create a basic feeling of handicap.

Lonnie, on the other hand, was a late-maturing boy whose physical deficiencies in size and athletic prowess were a persistent source of tension and anxiety. His activity pattern was expressed in excessive verbalizations, which became more aggressive and compulsive as he

[6] The writer is indebted to Mr. Read Tuddenham who secured much of the interview material through a grant from the Office of Naval Research.

progressed through adolescence.

Excerpts from a staff group confer-ence after a camping trip illustrate this point:

(W.J.C.) Lonnie was by far the most talkative in this very talkative crowd. . . . Saturday night after most of the boys had gone to sleep Lonnie turned to a question which had to do with the history of religion. He pursued the sub-ject with vehemence.

(M.C.J.) On Sunday morning when we were just finishing breakfast, Mr. G. mentioned a friend who had been work-ing with a growth-promoting hormone. He had hardly uttered a sentence when Lonnie, who had been at the next table, suddenly appeared by his side.

(J.C.) This led to further discussion throughout the day and on Monday, at school. . . . He was again on the subject of the hormone. He wanted to offer himself as a subject because he had always been small and underweight, "skinny." . . .

(T.C.) Lonnie talks with ceaseless energy, with a good deal of ego at stake . . . "I know a fellow who is a grandson of a Senator. But when we argue I can beat him every time with cold facts—statis-tics."

In a current interview many of the same characteristics of restless energy emerged. The interviewer commented that he was hard to rate because of tendencies which were superficially in contradiction to each other. He seemed self-centered, self-sufficient, and with a strong drive for autonomy, but was also dependent on his wife and "socially-minded" in the sense of having abstract interests in groups, social issues, etc. "He seems to have achieved a fairly stabilized adjustment—if not a conventional one.

Seems able to work toward long term goals because he has considerable per-sonal freedom. He is tense, rebellious, intellectual, too bent on satisfying his own needs in relationships to relate well to groups either as a member or a leader."

When asked what he would do differ-ently if he had the last 15 years to live over again, Lonnie replied that he would have gone ahead as fast as possible with academic work. "As it was I was out for Adventure with a capital A and Experi-ence with a capital E—a hollow sort of goal which doesn't satisfy. I travelled a lot but could have done as much living just around the corner."

Late-maturing was merely one of Lonnie's problems, but it led to an impaired status which was an immediate source of frustration, and of rebellious compensatory strivings. These patterns are still apparent in his adult life, although he now seems to take a more realistic view of the roles which are possible for him.

A third late-maturing boy, with a very different set of behavior patterns, was Charles—one of the two brothers de-scribed in the earlier publication as social-ly inconspicuous, extremely quiet and self-contained. Although not especially noticed or approved by his peer group, he had a variety of substantial individual interests, and congenial family ties.

Charles is described as "Frank and open in expression, individualistic, and outspoken, primarily an introvert. Though somewhat odd, he is probably fairly well liked by his associates. He seems relatively insecure, requiring sup-port and reassurance. He expresses both hostility and dependence in relation to authority figures. . . . He is mildly self-centered, somewhat imperceptive of others' feelings."

In his own description of current activities, he observed, "My job requires relatively little contact with people. I like it this way. . . . My wife is not overly fond of people. . . . My wife and I are very congenial, we talk over everything together."

Charles, who used to be so shy about girls, so retiring and quietly accepting of his own physical deficiencies, now seems to have established a way of life similar to that of his parents, and one which meets his needs with reasonable adequacy.

Howard was early-maturing. In the eyes of adult observers and classmates, he was advantaged in this respect as well as in family background and personal endowment. He was the younger of two boys from a home well above average in financial security, community status, and interpersonal compatibility.

He was well-liked by both boys and girls but although Howard had the same best friend for many years he seemed less dependent upon social ties than was the case with most youngsters of his age. "The girls would like him to take more interest in them," wrote one observer in the ninth grade. He learned to dance in the eighth grade but was a little shy at first with girls.

By the ninth grade he had lost his shyness, but led too busy a life with his own individual projects and his family's activities to be more than casually interested in girls or to accept more than a few of the many party invitations which he received. "He is a grand-looking boy and the girls feel it a great loss that he is not more interested in them."

Even in his senior year at high school when one girl seemed to be steadfastly claiming his attention, he was described as follows at a staff conference after a party which involved both swimming and dancing: "In his customary manner, Howard left Clare to her own devices and went to join the boys in the pool. He enjoys athletic activities even more than devotion to his lady love. . . . I have a feeling that any girl who goes with Howard will have to stand for that arrangement . . ."

Referring to his social development 15 years later he said, "My interest in girls was not any problem in high school."

Throughout the years of the study, descriptions of Howard stressed his maturity in relation to the group: "Has always been one of the largest and best looking. . . . His prestige among boys is quite marked, with no striving on his part (age 14.4). . . . Howard, like several of his friends this semester, seemed to have reached the stage of 'putting away the childish.' They sat and talked after lunch while the other boys played ball. He has unquestioned prestige, though he seems unaware of it . . ." (14.9).

"Howard is large, seems much more mature than almost any of our group (15.9). . . . Considerable maturity of manner, talked at length to H. E. J., and as an equal, about cameras and photographic equipment" (16.0). A student assistant in the physiology laboratory, impressed with Howard as a 16-year-old said: "He doesn't attempt to make a show of himself or his accomplishments although he now holds the record for vital capacity of 6.40 liters and of 3 minutes 37 seconds for holding his breath."

In spite of the fact that others recognized his accelerated maturity from the time he was in elementary school, Howard, in retrospect, described his own development as physically retarded.

A possible clue to this erroneous belief comes from his position in the family, as the younger boy. His father was past middle age when Howard was born and according to his own analysis of the situation, it was the older brother who had received the understanding and attention of a young, vigorous, active father. Howard missed this when he was growing up. It was his older brother who, in turn, furnished the active, interested companionship in which Howard may have felt a fatherly, as well as a brotherly quality. He certainly compared himself to this older brother and may have, growing up in the shadow of this comparison, thought of himself as inadequate in many ways, including rate of maturing. An interpretation of his response to the Murray pictures suggests that this is so:

Age 17: Howard's conflict seems to lie in his inability to reconcile his position as an individual with his position as a member of his family. . . . He tells of his fear that he is inadequate as a family member. His relationship to his older brother is basic to his difficulty. He is impressed with his older brother's superiority. Howard is far from the inadequate person he imagines himself to be in comparison with his brother. It seems likely that he does not feel inadequate except when measuring himself against his exaggerated notion of his brother's accomplishment.

In other circumstances, while his demands on himself are high, he appears to be able to meet them. In his struggle to emulate his brother he has developed qualities basic to superior performance.

He shows determination and persistence, a high level of energy, and the capacity to direct and maintain effort toward the goal he sets for himself. In the stories, he exaggerates his weakness but he indicates, as well, his strength.

As an adult in his early thirties, Howard seems to have come to realize his potentialities. "I've developed a good deal more self-confidence. . . . I feel I have had enough education and experience to tackle a job that I have some feel for, so I'm optimistic. In my work, I'm in a dominant position and you build up self-confidence. In college, fraternity life and athletics helped, too."

The interviewer summarizes: "Mr. F. has strong needs for acquisition and mastery. He is dominant, active, a leader and autonomous. It would be hard to keep him down."

Bob provides another example of the socially advantaged early-maturing boy. An only son in a prosperous upper-middle-class family, Bob had a pattern cut out for him to follow. He was expected to enter his father's business. His mother knew exactly how she wanted him to grow toward manhood and what course to pursue in fulfilling this goal. "I will not have a dirty boy," she said on one occasion. But this meant that he had to wash up after strenuous play, not that activity was prohibited. She understood that boys like to ride bicycles, build boats, and later, drive cars; that they are happy when playing with neighborhood boys in the backyard as preadolescents, and that as adolescents their social interests include girls, dancing, parties. Creditable scholarship and practice in leadership were encouraged in school.

All of these goals were easily attained.

Bob was slightly above the average of our group in intelligence and achievement tests. He was rated consistently on the favorable side, in a wide range of social and personal characteristics. Classmates placed him very high in leadership and popularity. In self-report, he was consistently on the well adjusted side—above the eightieth percentile for the group in all categories, which implied family, social, school and personal satisfactions.

After 15 years, Bob has achieved the realization of his own and his family's goals: "I enjoy my work very much . . . it's a business of my father's that I've always been interested in going into." To the question about how he might live his last 15 years over again he responded: "I'd do them about the same."

Two interviewers, a man and a woman, reveal their own somewhat different biases when summing up their impressions of Bob: The male psychologist wrote: "Mr. A is a tanned, dark-haired, immaculately dressed business man, self-assertive, confident in general bearing but not quite at ease during the interview. He is satisfied with himself and the mores of his business milieu . . . a rigid personality with little insight, little ability to relax and enjoy himself. He puts business first. He has no conflict since he faces no difficult external problems."

The woman who interviewed Bob reacted as follows: "Mr. A fits happily into the 'ideal' stereotype of a successful upper-middle-class business man with no strain and with none of the unfavorable connotations. Although he has social ambitions not yet attained and lets work invade leisure time to a minor extent, he does not seem under pressure about his work. His range of interests are not wide

or differentiated. . . he accepts the stereo type of upper-middle-class without much thought. . . his interests are social (in the sense of personal enjoyment) rather than directed along power lines . . . he exhibits more freedom from anxiety than any subject I have seen so far."

Unlike the two preceding cases, Rod was an early-maturing boy with persistent difficulties in social adjustment. These stemmed in part from a family background which was a handicap in a school where acceptable behavior followed upper-middle-class standards.

In our first records (at 10.5 years) he was described as tall and thin, talkative and outgoing with adults, friendly with strange boys whom he was meeting for the first time. These characteristics were continued during the period of the study.

But from the classroom and the playground came reports of difficulties. While some of the attributes ascribed to him by classmates were socially desirable—"a leader, daring, active in games, happy and enthusiastic," he was also said to be a fighter, lacking in a sense of humor about himself, inclined to be extremely bossy, and attention-seeking. His friendship relations must have been unsatisfactory also, in the early adolescent years, since he mentioned five boys as best friends but was mentioned by none of them in return. He was quarrelsome in games.

During a period of exceptionally rapid growth, in the seventh and eighth grades, this rough and quarrelsome behavior seemed to increase. Rod's superior size and strength provided an easy means of dominating others. "Rod seems driven by an urge to tease; the other boys do not like him very well but cannot dispute his attacks since none of the group approaches his size." Although recognized as a stormy adolescent, often using physical aggression as a defense against his feelings of social inadequacy, he gradually learned to channel his energies in more acceptable directions. He was active in games, and gained some prestige as an athlete. As the other boys caught up with him in size and strength, he was less tempted to draw them into situations involving bullying or fighting. He became more popular, and although still considered "bossy," he was less of a show-off and more considerate of others.

Usually the physical build and stature of early-maturing boys is attractive. During the middle years of adolescence this was not the case with Rod, whose growth in weight did not keep up with his growth in height. He was embarrassed rather than pleased by his height; he worried about it, and seemed to slump as he sat and to stoop as he walked.

In the later years of high school he gained better proportions and began to be rated as "good-looking." He became an expert dancer, and although still preferring athletics he was now frequently included in mixed parties. His classmates rated him as a leader, and as having a good sense of humor.

Thus we see that a boy from "across the tracks" at first used the physical competence accompanying early-maturing as a means of asserting himself in an environment in which he felt ill at ease. He was disliked for his undisciplined behavior, and his physical power was a liability rather than an asset.

By the end of adolescence, however, he had learned more effective social techniques. His size and strength were not to be disregarded, and his classmates began to perceive him in a more favorable light.

After high school Rod saw service in the Pacific—a handsome, swashbuckling soldier who wrote of his adventures to various members of the study staff. He is now settled down as a business man. Interviewers describe him as devoted to his wife and three children, hard-working, ambitious. He impressed an interviewer as not being very perceptive about or concerned with other people's opinions, except as having a general wish to make a good impression. "Interests in others' motivations and his own are relatively superficial. He expresses his feelings impulsively without much anxiety; seems to be able to disregard the needs of others but is probably warm to those close to him. Perhaps he is too self-centered to care much about group activity and does not seem to care for the kind of prestige which he would get from exploiting a group."

Though friendly he was thought to be a little defensive about having no recreational or cultural interests to report. He said, "I have three main interests: the family, the business, and sports." But an account of his daily living revealed that the business got most of his attention. He was able to report fair financial success as the result of his devotion to work. He described with some pride the house which he owns: "It is supposed to be elite. I lived on the wrong side of the tracks too long. But now where I live each house has its own patio and there are lots of swimming pools in the subdivision."

SUMMARY AND CONCLUSION

Boys who had been classified as physically accelerated or retarded in terms of skeletal age during adolescence were compared as young adults at age 33, to determine the long-term effects of rate of maturing upon personality.

Although some cases were lost from the original sample, the data for the follow-up group as reconstituted showed no substantial alteration in the adolescent differentials of the early- and late-maturing.

For the original sample and for the subsample available in the present study, analysis of ratings by adults and classmates indicated that the early-maturing boys were significantly more attractive in physique, more relaxed, poised and matter-of-fact. Consistent differences in other characteristics, such as interest in the opposite sex and "good-naturedness," were obtained over nine semesters of observation. Late-maturing boys were described as more expressive, active, talkative, eager, attention-getting.

The physical differences noted for these boys at adolescence have tended to disappear in adulthood. Personality characteristics as appraised by the California Psychological Inventory and the Edwards Personal Preference Schedule have shown a number of significant differences on the various scales for which the tests are scored (e.g., higher scores for the early-maturing on measures of "good impression" and "socialization"). Where such differences were found, they tended to describe the young adults much as they had been described in adolescence.

No differences were found between the early- and late-maturing in present marital status, family size or educational level. A few of the early-maturing have made exceptionally rapid progress as junior executives and a few of the late-maturing are still somewhat unsettled, vocationally.

The foregoing presentation of data and the case summaries remind us again of the conclusions to the original study which stressed individual differences within each group, resulting from the complex interplay of factors. During the adolescent period late-maturing is a handicap for many boys and can rarely be found to offer special advantages. Early-maturing carries both advantages and disadvantages. In our culture it frequently gives competitive status, but sometimes also involves handicaps in the necessity for rapid readjustments and in requiring the adolescent to meet adult expectations which are more appropriate to size and appearance than to other aspects of maturing. The adolescent handicaps and advantages associated with late- or early-maturing appear to carry over into adulthood to some extent, and perhaps to a greater extent in psychological than in physical characteristics.

References

1. Bayley, Nancy, & Bayer, Leona M. The assessment of somatic androgyny. *Amer. J. phys. Anthrop.*, 1946, **4**, 433-462.

2. Edwards, A.L. *Edwards Personal Preference Schedule.* New York: Psychological Corporation, 1954.
3. Gough, H.G. *The California Psychological Inventory.* Stanford: Consulting Psychologists' Press, Copyright 1951.
4. Gough, H.G. On making a good impression. *J. educ. Res.,* 1952, **46**, 33-42.
5. Gough, H.G. Systematic validation of a test for delinquency. *Amer. Psychol.,* 1954, **9**, 380. (Abstract)
6. Greulich, W.W., *et al.* Somatic and endocrine studies of puberal and adolescent boys. *Monogr. Soc. Res. Child Develpm.,* 1942, 7, No. 3.
7. Jones, Mary C., & Bayley, Nancy. Physical maturing among boys as related to behavior. *J. educ. Psychol.,* 1950, **41**, 129-148.
8. Sheldon, W.H., Stevens, S.S., & Tucker, W.B. *The varieties of human physique.* New York: Harper, 1940.

HAROLD PROSHANSKY AND PEGGY NEWTON

The Nature and Meaning of Negro Self-Identity*

SOURCES AND CONSEQUENCES OF CONFLICT IN NEGRO SELF-IDENTITY

... In the previous section we had begun to consider the substantive nature of the Negro's self-identity, that is, what he thinks and feels about himself as a person. To expand and elaborate on this topic in this section, we shall consider both the conditions that foster a Negro self-identity and the consequences of this identity for the behavior and experience of the individual. In undertaking such a discussion, it is necessary to specify its limitations, which are imposed by the type of available research on Negro self-identity.

The research on Negro self-identity has tended to be sporadic rather than systematic. Much has been written about the self-image of the Negro. Those writing in the field have generally agreed on the

*From Chapter 5 of M. Deutsch, I. Katz, and A. R. Jensen (Eds.), *Social class, race, and psychological development,* 1968. Reprinted by permission of the authors and Holt, Rinehart and Winston, Inc.

nature of the Negro's identity conflicts, however, the basis of their statements has usually been anecdotal evidence and general descriptions of the "plight of the Negro" instead of carefully collected empirical data. To complicate the picture further, we find that most of the existing data focuses on the lower-class Negro; therefore, these findings cannot be generalized to apply to Negroes in other social class categories. In addition, most studies of the self-identity characteristics of lower-class Negroes have made comparisons with middle-class whites, thus making it virtually impossible to separate the race and social class factors.

The urban slum dweller, whether white or Negro, faces problems with self-image in a society which values individual initiative, success, and status. However, some properties of the self-identity of the lower-class Negro reflect his unique place in the social hierarchy.

We may ask about the self-image of Negroes who have achieved middle-class and upper-class status. There are undoubtedly significant class-associated differences in family structure and in attitudes toward the dominant white society, which influence the child's self-image and identification, his school achievement, and his eventual occupational status. Unfortunately the empirical research on these social class differences is extremely limited. On the basis of a comparison of intelligence test scores of Negro and white subjects from three social class levels, Deutsch and Brown (1964) suggest, " . . . the influence of racial membership tends to become increasingly manifest and crucial as the social class level increases" (p. 27). They propose that lower-class status has a similar effect

on Negroes and whites, but while higher status tends to bring the white increased "participation in the cultural mainstream," the Negro of similar status is often denied such participation because of his race.

The concentration of research and theory on the lower-class urban Negro has perpetuated a narrow and limited view of Negro identity. Although research has usually been confined to the urban slum dweller, there has been a tendency to generalize these findings, applying them to all Negroes, regardless of social class or geographical location. We would expect that Negroes who had achieved occupational and economic success would be confronted by a different order of identity conflicts than the lower-class Negro. It would seem likely that the accomplishments and status of middle-class Negroes would merely redefine rather than eradicate the stigma of their racial group membership. Research on middle-class and upper-class Negroes is needed both to clarify these questions and to suggest the scope and complexity of the issue of Negro identity.

A further shortcoming of the existing research has been in its problem-centered approach. In dealing with a lower-class urban population, researchers have tended to look for "problems," emphasizing negative elements of identity and seeing differences from white middle-class norms as "problems." As we shall point out in the final section of this chapter, there *are* positive and compensatory aspects of Negro identity. These positive elements of identity need to be given a larger place in research and theoretical formulations. In our concluding section, we shall consider those aspects and conditions of the Negro dilemma that strengthen rather than weaken his tie with his own racial group; we shall look at the potentially integrative rather than divisive forces in the development of Negro self-identity.

THE NEGRO SELF-IMAGE: ITS EFFECTS ON BEHAVIOR AND EXPERIENCE

The Negro who feels disdain or hatred for his own racial group is expressing at some level of awareness disdain or hatred for himself. Where the self-image is rooted in and structured by this kind of self-rejection, we can expect negative effects on the behavior and experience of the individual. In the discussion that follows, we shall look at some of the research which deals with the consequences of self-hatred and rejection. For the purpose of convenience, we shall consider the studies under two categories: "personality adjustment" and "achievement orientation." By the term, "personality adjustment," we mean how the Negro reacts to and copes with his underlying sense of inferiority or lack of self-esteem. Although the Negro's achievement orientation may also be seen as a mode of adjustment in response to a negative identity, we shall consider these topics separately.

Personality Adjustment

Perhaps the "real tragedy" for the American Negro lies less in the inferior, passive, and servile role he is forced to play, and more in the fact that he comes to believe in this role. His self-image not only reflects this role structure but also confirms and supports it. As Pettigrew (1964b) points out, by judging himself the way others do, " . . . the Negro may grow into the servile role; in time the person and the role bacome indistinguishable" (p. 25).

Many theorists have noted that the Negro does not find satisfaction in passive compliance with the demands of a white society. The Negro who conforms to these demands and consequently rejects himself pays a high price. A report by the "Group for the Advancement of Psychiatry" suggests that beneath the Negro's mask of compliance lie anger, resentment, and fear (1957). In hiding his feelings, the Negro may suffer serious psychological consequences, such as distorting his capacity for expressing his feelings or actually lowering his "potential for affectivity" (Kardiner and Ovesey, 1962).

Kardiner and Ovesey (1962) hypothesize that the Negro bears an inescapable "mark of oppression," which reflects his strong identification with whites, who are simultaneously hated. This conflict leads to aggression which is channeled into compensatory defensive maneuvers. In a study of the responses of 100 nine- to fourteen-year-old Negro and white boys on the Thematic Apperception Test (TAT), Mussen (1953) found that the Negro boys tended to perceive the world as hostile and threatening, while the white boys were more likely to view the world as a friendly place. Palermo (1959) found greater anxiety among Negro children in the fourth to sixth garde than he did among a corresponding group of white children. In their study of the Rorshach and TAT protocols of 25 adult Negroes, Kardiner and Ovesey (1962) reported that their respondents showed a strong need to aviod "meeting reality head on" by denying, distorting, or simplifying provocative tension-producing situations.

The thread of consistency running through the studies cited above is sustained by Deutsch's extensive study of Negro and white lower-class children in grades four through six (1960). Deutsch found that the Negro children generally had more negative self-concepts, and were more passive, more morose, and more fearful than their white schoolmates. When the Negro child was aggressive, it was usually in some covert manner.

In the face of adversity, the Negro feels more than the frustration engendered by the caste system. His anger is intensified — particularly in the Negro male — by his sense of powerlessness (Drake, 1965). When hostility is expressed, it is often through indirect means. Among lower-class Negroes aggression is frequent, the chain of victimization is perpetuated, and the lower-class Negro is exploited by both whites and fellow Negroes. Other outlets for aggression are juvenile delinquency and crime, both of which provide means of "striking back" at the white society.

Covert or indirect expressions of hostility are only one form of response to the frustration and sense of powerlessness experienced by the Negro. The need to escape is frequently manifested in the form of excessive use of alcohol, drugs, and gambling (Drake, 1965). A far more subtle form of escape embodies the old adage, "If you can't beat them, join them." Some Negroes, in effect, escape by "turning white."

In the case of the very light-skinned Negro, this desire may actually be accomplished by "passing." Other Negroes may attempt to "look white" by using hair straighteners and skin bleaches. Drake (1965) suggests that this rejection of Negroid features reflects a reaction to the stereotype of the primitive and savage African. The preference for light skin also has traditional foundations in this country. Since plantation days the light-skinned Negro has been favored and granted special privileges, particularly in middle-class and upper-class society. We also find that parents tend to favor a light-skinned child (Coles, 1967; Grambs, 1964), and that dark-skinned men often try to marry wives of a lighter skin color (Kardiner and Ovesey, 1962).

Psychologists have shown great interest in the defensive strategy of "turning white" and in its implications for mental health and personality adjustment. Perhaps this interest stems in part from the fact that "passing" represents a blatant expression of self-rejection and a denial of reality. Parker and Kleiner (1965) note a large body of research documenting the unhealthiness in aspiring to be white: "Almost every clinical study of psychopathology among Negroes indicates that the Negro who is not identified with other members of his group, or who aspires to 'be white,' is relatively more prone to manifest various forms of mental ill health" (p. 157).

In spite of some serious methodological problems, Parker and Kleiner's own research raises some important speculative questions about the dynamics of racial identification. As a measure of racial identification, Parker and Kleiner asked their Negro subjects how they would feel about a friend who tried to "pass." They found that Negroes in psychiatric hospitals tended to be strongly identified with Negroes or not identified with Negroes, while Negroes in the community tended to be ambivalent about their racial identification. On the basis of this finding, Parker and Kleiner suggest that ambivalence may be "realistic and adaptive" for the Negro, but that extreme reactions or "polarization of racial identification" are likely to be psychopathogenic. In their opinion " . . . the psychiatrically healthy Negro is an individual with conflicts about his racial identification. It is the mentally ill person who tends to remove this constant conflict from conscious awareness" (p. 160). The logic implicit in this statement is that if the conflict about his racial identification becomes unbearable, the individual may deny the conflict entirely (either strongly identifying with or rejecting his racial group) and become mentally ill.

While it seems apparent that a denial of the conflict over identification is unhealthy, it cannot be assumed that conflict and ambivalence are healthy. Certainly, in light of the conditions that the Negro faces in America, such ambivalence is understandable. The crucial questions become: "How severe is the conflict?" and "How does the individual deal with this conflict?"

It seems obvious that individual Negroes will find various means of dealing with this conflict. When faced with a severe form of this conflict, not all individuals will become psychotic; some will resort to drugs, alcohol, violence, or other forms of escape. Many of these individuals, who certainly cannot be considered psychiatrically healthy, will remain in the community. Therefore, a

judgment of mental health, based solely on whether or not an individual is in a psychiatric hospital, is open to serious question. We may also predict that some of the individuals in the community who are ambivalent about their racial identification may not be able to continue to function with this conflict and may later become psychotic or adopt another "unhealthy" way of dealing with the conflict.

After examining the evidence available on the Negro and his conflicts over identification and also on the possibilities for positive identification, we would hypothesize that the psychiatrically healthy Negro is one who basically identifies with Negroes, but who is aware of and realistic about the problems facing him in a "white man's" society. This form of identification with Negroes is to be distinguished from the extreme "defensive" or reactive form of identification in which the individual denies that there are problems in being Negro. Unfortunately the Parker and Kleiner study does not distinguish between these two forms of identification with the Negro group and does not describe individuals in the community sample who have "identified" with Negroes. It would be interesting to know if some of these individuals fit our description of a Negro who is positively identified with his race and yet realistic about his opportunities, as a Negro.

Achievement Orientations.

Human motivation involves a complex set of processes. Conceptually, an analysis of motivation includes analyses of the individual's end or goal, the strength of his desire, the value placed on the end, and his expectancy of achieving the end. In his consideration of achievement motivation in a modern industrial society, Rosen (1959) has suggested that achievement is dependent on three factors, which he labels collectively, the "achievement syndrome." The first factor is McClelland's "achievement motive," which Rosen (1956) has defined as involving "a personality characteristic . . . which provides an internal impetus to excel" (p. 204). The second dimension, "achievement-value orientations" involves a concern with social mobility and a development of patterns of behavior, such as "deferred gratification," which aid in the pursuit of long-term goals. The third dimension, "educational and vocational aspirations" are the levels of academic and occupational achievements *desired* by parents for their children and desired by the children themselves. According to Rosen, high achievement depends on appropriate levels on all three of these dimensions.

Employing variations of Murray's TAT measure of *n* Achievement, investigators have found that Negro children are lower in achievement motivation than white children. Mussen (1953) found that Negro boys, aged nine to fourteen, scored significantly below their white counterparts on *n* Achievement and also on *n* Understanding, a category which is intended to tap activities such as thinking, reflecting, and speculating. In measuring the achievement motivation of boys from six ethnic groups, Rosen (1959) reported that Negro boys were significantly lower in *n* Achievement than boys from four other ethnic groups: Jewish, white Protestant, Greek, and Italian.

Evidence suggests that *n* Achievement is related to social class as well as to ethnicity. In his study Rosen (1959) found that there were significant social-class differences among his subjects; he also discovered that social class was more strongly related to achievement motivation than was ethnicity. In addition, he found that Negro subjects in the top two social classes (I-II, according to a modified version of Hollingshead's Index of Social Position) were significantly higher in *n* Achievement than Class IV-V white Protestants. Rosen suggests that this relatively high Negro score may be indicative of the "strong motivation necessary for a Negro to achieve middle class status in a hostile environment" (1959, p. 53).

Rosen (1959) has explored "achievement-value orientations" through the use of personal interviews with mothers who were asked to agree or disagree with items which reflected various orientations in child rearing: active versus passive, individual versus collective, and present versus future. It seems that the active, individual, and future orientations in child rearing are most conducive to the achievement of long-term goals. Rosen found that among the six ethnic groups that he studied, Negro mothers ranked fourth in "achievement-value orientations." This score was significantly lower than that of the Jewish mothers, who ranked highest in achievement values; however, the score of Jews was not significantly higher than the scores of Greeks and of Protestants, who were in the next two ranks.

Social class is also significantly related to achievement-value orientations. As might be expected, members of higher social classes tend to have high achievement-value orientations, and conversely, those in lower-class levels have relatively low scores on achievement-value orientation (Rosen, 1959).

Many investigators have explored the third dimension of Rosen's "achievement syndrome": occupational and educational levels of aspiration. However, studies of the aspiration levels in Negro and white children and their parents have been inconsistent in their findings. In comparison with whites, Negroes have been shown to have high or low, and realistic or unrealistic, levels of aspiration.

For example, in a study of junior high school students in a small industrial town in Pennsylvania, Wylie (1963) found that Negro children generally had lower self-estimates or levels of aspiration for their schoolwork ability than did white children. However, when Negro and white subjects from lower socioeconomic levels were compared, there were no race differences. In contrast, in a somewhat similar study, Boyd (1952) reported very different results when he compared the aspiration levels of Negro and white students, matched for age, IQ, and socioeconomic status. He discovered that Negro children predicted relatively higher performances on arithmetic and target tests than did white children. Furthermore, in comparison with the white children, the Negro children had higher occupational ambitions, desired more foreign trips, and more frequently stated that they expected to be "above average" students in high school. In discussing his results, Boyd suggests that Negro children may have higher aspiration levels because of insecure feelings or because they have developed better defense mechanisms than white children and are, therefore, able to tolerate a greater discrepancy between predicted and actual performance.

To confuse the literature further, Rosen found that Negro mothers had low occupational, but high educational, aspirations for their sons. When Rosen asked the mothers, "How far do you *intend* your son to go in school?" 83 percent of these mothers mentioned college. This percentage was not significantly different from those of the Jews, Greeks, or white Protestants, but it was significantly higher than those of the Italians and French Canadians. However, when Negro mothers were given a list of occupations and were asked if they would "be satisfied" if their sons were in these occupations, they expressed satisfaction with more low-status occupations than did any other group of mothers.

In some ways Rosen's measure of vocational aspiration is a negative one, since it seems to elicit the lower limit rather than the upper limit of aspiration. Because of the Negro's traditional lack of vocational opportunity, Negro mothers may be more accepting of low-status occupations than mothers from other ethnic groups. There may be a wide *range* between the vocation a Negro mother would most like her son to follow and a vocation with which she would be satisfied if her son actually did follow it. This possibility has been suggested by other studies, showing that Negro mothers and their sons have high vocational aspirations, although many researchers have labeled such aspirations as "unrealistically high."

In part, the contradictions in findings on the Negro's level of aspiration can be explained by differences in such factors as the samples studied, the indices used for measuring the level of aspiration, and the geographical setting. However, the studies are somewhat clarified, if we consider, whenever possible, the distinction between *desired* and *expected* occupational or educational attainment. The importance of these distinctions is illustrated in a study by Weiner and Murray (1963), who compared the educational aspiration levels of middle- and lower-class parents. Weiner and Murray point out that both middle-class and lower-class parents have high levels of aspiration for their children's education. However, the concept of education has a different meaning for each social class. The key difference in meaning lies in the realistic expectations of achieving the goal. Weiner and Murray note that if middle-class and lower-class parents are asked if they want their child to attend college, both groups of parents will answer "yes." However, the middle-class parent will answer "yes" with the full expectation that his child will attend college, while the lower-class parent may hope that his child will go to college, but he will not actually expect it.

It is possible that in studies which have reported a high aspiration level for Negroes, researchers have been measuring what their subjects desire rather than what they expect. Perhaps measures of aspiration level which reflect what the subjects expect may yield lower levels of aspiration and may be more realistic. However, it is important to stress that even when a Negro's aspirations are based on his expectations, they may be distorted in light of his actual abilities and, more importantly, the opportunities available to him.

This situation is seen clearly in C.S. Johnson's (1941) study of rural Negro youth in the South. Johnson found that 58.8 percent of the boys and 65.3 percent of the girls preferred professional occupations. Of these youth, 26.4 percent of the boys and 48.8 percent of the girls actually *expected* to follow such occupations. In this case the subjects' expectations were not much more realistic than their desires. Johnson concluded: "The gap between occupational expectation and reality is at present so great as to suggest that the expectation itself borders on fantasy" (p. 223). Johnson also suggested that the desires and expectations for these occupations represented an attempt at escaping an unpleasant environment.

Ausubel and Ausubel (1958) have drawn similar conclusions about the aspiration levels of Negro children, basing their ideas on implications drawn from studies comparing lower- and middle-class children. They suggest that the lower-class child's expressed levels of vocational and academic aspiration do not necessarily reflect his "real or functional levels of striving." His aspirations seem to show a lack of realistic judgment because of continued failure and low social status; therefore, a high level of aspiration is likely to represent an attempt to bolster self-esteem by presenting an image of "aiming high" rather than actually striving for high educational or occupational goals. In the Ausubels' view, the conditions experienced by the lower-class child are intensified for the segregated Negro child. These interpretations are generally supported by Deutsch's (1960) study of the occupational aspirations of lower-class Negro and white fourth-, fifth-, and sixth-graders.

Deutsch (1960) found that *both* Negro

and white boys tended to have unrealistic aspirations for high prestige occupations. Although it might be expected that Negro boys would be less realistic than white boys in these choices, only 26 percent of the Negro boys in contrast with 38 percent of the white boys, expressed interest in high prestige professions. In comparison with the boys, the aspirations of the girls were much more realistic and the occupational desires of the Negro girls were significantly higher than those of the white girls. While 25 percent of the Negro girls indicated a preference for white-collar jobs, such as secretary or bookkeeper, only 4 percent of the white girls showed an interest in this type of job. However, the Negro girls were less interested than the white girls in the housewife-mother role and in the movie star-actress category.

In a study whose findings stand somewhat apart from those previously cited, Lott and Lott (1963) reported that Negro students had high but realistic levels of occupational aspiration. A comparison of Negro and white high school seniors in Kentucky showed significant differences in both occupational desires and expectations. The major differences between the occupational desires of the Negro and white boys were in "glamour" jobs, such as pilot or politician, and in the clerical-sales-skilled-trade field of jobs. While 27 percent of the white boys expressed interest in a "glamour" job, only 12 percent of the Negro boys did. While 18 percent of the white students desired work in the clerical-sales-skilled-trade area, 39 percent of the Negro students wanted a position in this field. An even sharper contrast was seen in the fact that 15 percent of the whites versus 40 per-

cent of the Negroes expected to be in the clerical-sales-skilled-trade field ten years later.

The Negro boys showed somewhat exaggerated or unrealistic aspirations in their desires to enter professional or business fields; 41 percent of the Negro boys and 46 percent of the white boys wanted a professional or business career. However, only 30 percent of the Negroes, in contrast with 41 percent of the whites, actually expected to attain this type of job.

The occupational aspirations of the Negro girls described by Lott and Lott (1963) were consistent with those reported by Deutsch (1960) despite the age differences in the two samples. These findings suggest that the aspirations of these girls reflect their perceptions of their role as women—a role which places economic independence above the role of housewife and mother. In the Lott and Lott study (1963), 17 percent of the white girls and none of the Negro girls wanted to assume the roles of wife and mother. Furthermore, 54 percent of the Negro girls, but only 31 percent of the white girls, wanted a professional job, such as teaching or social work.

Although Deutsch (1960) and Lott and Lott (1963) have reported similar findings about the aspirations of Negro girls, their results differ sharply from most of the other research in this field. Lott and Lott conclude that their Negro subjects' plans for the future were realistic in terms of available opportunities. They suggest that the difference in their findings may lie either in changing social conditions or in particular factors operating in the environment of a border community.

Another relevant factor in explaining differences in the "realism" of the Negro's aspirations may be a "knowledge of the means of achievement." To understand how this factor might operate, we need to distinguish between dreams or desires and expectations. Dreams or desires, by definition, function to transcend reality; they are a source of hope and a salve against pain. In contrast, expectations are grounded in reality; they reflect the world "as it is," not the world "as it might be." A problem arises when expectations become identified with dreams and a person expects what he has little or no possibility of achieving. We would hypothesize that this situation is likely to occur when a person has little "knowledge of the means of achievement," that is, when he does not know how to achieve his goal, or when he does not recognize that his dream is unattainable. When the dream and expectation are not separated, the aspiration level is likely to be unrealistically high. The orientation toward the future would seem to reflect an emphasis on the goal, rather than on the "means of achieving the goal." Following this line of reasoning, we could infer that the Negro youth studied by Lott and Lott (1963) had a "knowledge of means," which enabled them to have realistic expectations about their occupational futures.

The significance of a "knowledge of means" is illustrated in a study of parents and their children in a suburb of New York City. The researchers Weiner and Graves (1960) found that parents and children from the lower socioeconomic status (SES) had occupational aspirations similar to those of parents and children from a middle socioeconomic level. In both SES groups most parents and children were interested in one of the professions. However, when the children from the lower SES group were asked how far they expected to go in school, 52 percent expected to go through college and 33 percent expected to finish only high school. Even more revealing was the fact that only 37 percent of the lower SES subjects were enrolled in college preparatory courses. In contrast, 95 percent of the middle SES students intended to go through college and 100 percent of these students were taking the college preparatory curriculum.

In line with Weiner and Murray, Drake (1965) cites evidence suggesting that lower-class and lower-middle-class Negro parents often have high aspirations for their children but no clear idea of how to implement these plans. He proposes that Negro students in segregated high schools and colleges are often unaware of the opportunities and techniques for advancement.

Preliminary evidence indicates that many of these "techniques for advancement" can be taught effectively in short periods of time. "Cram" courses in how to pass qualifying exams and how to meet job requirements—for example, filling out applications, being interviewed, and so on—have succeeded in increasing the numbers of Negroes in several fields (National Urban League, 1966; Davis, 1967). The often dramatic success of short-term educational programs supports the contention that many Negroes have high motivation for achievement but lack the more pragmatic, but also necessary, "knowledge of the means of achievement."

References

Ausubel, D.P., and P. Ausubel. Ego development among segregated Negro children. *Mental Hygiene*, 1958, **42**, 362-369. (Republished in A.H. Passow (ed.), *Education in depressed areas*. New York Teachers College, Columbia University, Bureau of Publications, 1963, pp. 109-131.)

Boyd, G.F. The levels of aspiration of white and Negro children in a non-segregated elementary school. *Journal of Social Psychology*, 1952, **36**, 191-196.

Coles, R. It's the same, but it's different. *Daedalus*, 1965, **94**, 1107-1132. (Republished in T. Parsons and K. B. Clark (eds.), *The Negro American*. Boston: Beacon Press, 1967, 254-279.)

Coles, R. *Children of crisis: A study of courage and fear*. Boston: Atlantic-Little, Brown, 1967.

Davis, C.H. Personal communication. November 1967.

Deutsch, M. Minority group and class status as related to social and personality factors in scholastic achievement. Monograph No. 2. Society of Applied Anthropology, 1960.

Deutsch, M., and B. Brown. Social influences in Negro-white intelligence differences. *Journal of Social Issues*, 1964, **20**, 24-35.

Drake, St. C. The social and economic status of the Negro in the United States. *Daedalus*, 1965, **94**, 771-814. (Republished in T. Parsons and K.B. Clark (eds.), *The Negro American*. Boston: Beacon Press, 1967, 771-814.)

Grambs, J.D. "The self-concept: Basis for reeducation of Negro youth." In W.C. Kvaraceus, J.S. Gibson, F. Patterson, B. Seasholes, and J.D. Grambs, *Negro self-concept: Implications for school and citizenship*. New York: McGraw-Hill, 1964, 11-34.

Group for the Advancement of Psychiatry. Psychiatric aspects of school desegregation. New York: Group for Advancement of Psychiatry, 1957.

Johnson, C.S. *Growing up in the black belt*. Washington, D.C.: American Council on Education, 1941. (Republished: New York: Shocken, 1967.)

Kardiner, A., and L. Ovesey. *The mark of oppression*. Cleveland, Ohio: World, 1962.

Lott, A.J., and B.E. Lott. *Negro and white youth*. New York: Holt, Rinehart and Winston, 1963. (Republished as "Negro and white children's plans for their futures" in J.I. Roberts (ed.), *School children in the urban slum*. New York: Free Press, 1967, 347-361.)

Mussen, P.H. Differences between the TAT responses of Negro and white boys. *Journal of Consulting Psychology*, 1953, **17**, 373-376.

National Urban League. *Education and race*. New York. National Urban League, 1966.

Palermo, D.S. Racial comparisons and additional normative data on the Children's Manifest Anxiety Scale. *Child Development*, 1959, **30**, 53-57.

Parker, S., and R.J. Kleiner. *Mental illness in the urban Negro community*. New York: Free Press, 1965.

Pettigrew, T.F. Father-absence and Negro adult personality: A research note. Unpublished paper. Cited by T.F. Pettigrew in *A profile of the Negro American*. Princeton, N.J.: D. Van Nostrand, 1964*a*, **20**.

Pettigrew, T. F. *A profile of the Negro American*. Princeton, N.J.: D. Van Nostrand, 1964*b*.

Rosen, B.C. The achievement syndrome: A psychocultural dimension of social stratification. *American Sociological Review*, 1956, **21**, 203-211. (Republished in J.W. Atkinson (ed.), *Motives in fantasy, action, and society*. Princeton, N.J.: D. Van Nostrand, 1958, 495-508.)

Rosen, B. C. Race, ethnicity, and the achievement syndrome. *American Sociological Review*, 1959, **24**, 47-60. (Republished in J.I. Roberts (ed.), *School children in the urban slum*. New York: Free Press, 1966, 327-346.)

Weiner, M., and M. Graves. A study of educational and vocational aspirations of junior high school pupils from two socioeconomic levels (Dittoed paper). White Plains, N.Y., Board of Education, 1960. (As cited by M. Weiner and W. Murray, "Another look at the culturally deprived and their levels of aspiration," in J.I. Roberts (ed.), *School children in the urban slum*. New York: Free Press, 1967, 296.)

Weiner, M., and W. Murray. Another look at the culturally deprived and their levels of apiration. *Journal of Educational Sociology*, 1963, **36**, 319-321. (Republished in J.I. Roberts (ed.), *School children in the urban slum*. New York: Free Press, 1967, 295-310.)

Wylie, R.S. Children's estimates of their schoolwork ability as a function of sex, race, and socioeconomic level. *Journal of Personality*, 1963, **31**, 204-224.

17
ADOLESCENCE:
ABNORMAL DEVELOPMENT

Because adolescents confront a number of challenging developmental tasks—adjusting to physical maturation, achieving independence from parents, establishing rewarding heterosexual relationships, and consolidating personal identity—adolescence inevitably brings with it moments of anxiety, turmoil, and uncertainty. These moments are not tantamount to psychopathology, however, nor is adolescence a time of heightened susceptibility to psychological disturbance. Available data indicate that adolescents are just about as likely as adults to suffer moderate or severe impairments of their school, work, and/or social functioning due to psychological disturbance, at the rate of about 20 percent of the population.

The vast majority of this significant psychological disturbance beginning in adolescence is accounted for by five conditions, three of which have been discussed in earlier chapters. The most serious of these conditions is schizophrenia, the subject of the Goldfarb paper in Chapter 9. Although schizophrenia beginning in adolescence has more in common with adult schizophrenia than with the childhood form of the disorder discussed by Goldfarb, the basic personality impairments and contributing factors he outlines pertains to schizophrenia at all ages. Hence we elected not to devote further space to schizophrenia in this chapter, even though it is generally regarded as the number one mental health problem in the world today. The other two adolescent conditions discussed earlier are depression, particularly as reflected in suicidal behavior, and school phobia. The Frick and Toolan articles on these subjects in Chapter 13 cover both the middle childhood and adolescent years.

The two remaining and most frequent patterns of abnormal development in adolescence are academic underachievement and delinquent behavior. To review these topics we have abstracted two chapters from

Weiner's *Psychological Disturbance in Adolescence.* Included in these selections are detailed descriptions of what these developmental problems consist of and what factors appear to cause them.

IRVING B. WEINER

Academic Underachievement*

According to Lichter et al. (1962, p. 2) 40% of all children in the United States fail to complete high school, and of these school drop-outs more than half possess at least average intellectual ability. This tragic waste of youthful potential highlights the social importance of academic underachievement, and learning difficulties have been observed to participate prominently in the psychological disturbances of the young.

The able youngster who cannot or will not utilize his intellectual potential may irretrievably surrender educational and occupational attainments that would otherwise be within his grasp. Data from the Fels Research Institute confirm a high positive correlation between involvement in intellectual activities at age 10 to 14 and achievement behavior in the adult

*From Chapter 7 of I. B. Weiner, *Psychological Disturbance in Adolescence,* 1970. Reprinted by permission of the author and John Wiley and Sons.

years 20 to 29 (Moss and Kagan, 1961). Hess (1963), who assessed boys and girls as high school seniors and again eight years later, similarly found a significant positive association between academic achievement in high school and subsequent occupational level and upward mobility.

In addition to considering such long-range implications of academic underachievement it is important to recognize that underachieving patterns may emerge early in a youngster's school career and be firmly entrenched by the time he reaches adolescence. In a study of equally bright achieving and underachieving high school students who had been classmates from the first grade on Shaw and McCuen (1960) found that the underachieving boys had tended to receive lower grades than the achieving boys beginning in the very first grade. The underachieving boys had dropped to a significantly lower performance level by grade 3 and had demonstrated increasingly poorer achievement in each consecutive year up to grade

10. A similar but later developing pattern was found for the underachieving girls, who began to receive lower grades than those of the achieving girls in grade 6 and declined to a significantly lower performance by grade 9.

The apparently progressive nature of underachievement has also been noted by Marcus (1966), who observed numerous cumulative effects of learning difficulty in bright 12- to 14-year-old youngsters he studied. The poor background of these students in subject matter they had previously failed, their depreciated image of themselves as students, and their loss of motivation and pleasure in learning had contributed to progressively larger gaps between capacity and performance as their underachievement persisted from one year to the next. . . .

SOCIOCULTURAL DETERMINANTS

For many underachieving adolescents the discrepancy between their academic performance and their intellectual capacity reflects social and cultural influences that have little to do with individual organic or psychological disturbances. Following Rabinovitch (1959) the sociocultural determinants of academic underachievement can be roughly classified under the headings of *motivation* and *opportunity*.

Motivation

Sociocultural motives influence academic performance primarily through the attitudes and orientations the young person brings to his academic pursuits. The youngster whose behavior is guided primarily by nonintellectual values and non-academic goals is minimally motivated to exercise his scholastic talents. The association of such motivational variables with underachievement has been demonstrated in a number of empirical studies; for example, Pierce and Bowman (1960), in comparing equally bright high-achieving and low-achieving 10th and 12th grade boys and girls, found that (a) on an interview measure the achievers were rated significantly higher on strength of educational motivation than the underachievers, and (b) on a semantic differential the concepts *school, work,* and *imagination* were valued significantly more highly by the achievers than by the underachievers.

Hathaway and Monachesi (1963, p. 115) similarly report that, of 824 male and 671 female high school drop-outs they studied, 33% of the boys and 21% of the girls gave "lack of interest" as their main reason for quitting school. The only reason given more frequently by either sex was marriage or illegitimate pregnancy, which was given by 53% of the girls. In contrast, failing grades were mentioned as the main reason for dropping out by only 12% of the boys and 5% of the girls.

Noneducational values and goals typically originate in certain demonstrable patterns of parental and peer-group influence. The youngster whose parents depreciate the relevance of education to occupational attainment or success in life, view the school as an essentially foreign or hostile institution, and neither praise his scholastic successes nor deplore his failures is unlikely to develop much intrinsic achievement motivation relative to school. Such parental influences have been confirmed in studies (Morrow and

Wilson, 1961; Wilson and Morrow, 1962) of achieving and underachieving high school boys of equal intelligence and socioeconomic status, which demonstrated (a) that the parents of the achievers were generally more encouraging with respect to achievement, (b) that the families of the achievers more actively fostered intellectual interests in their sons and positive attitude toward teachers and toward the school, and (c) that the achievers were less inclined than the underachievers to express negative attitudes about school or to view their teachers as unreasonable or unsupportive.

Whereas lower class and certain minority group families may explicitly depreciate education and distrust the school as a middle class institution (see Katz, 1967), it is not unusual for lower class and especially middle class parents of underachieving adolescents overtly to espouse educational values while covertly communicating to their youngster that his underachievement makes little difference. Typical in this regard is the self-made man who, having succeeded in the business world despite minimal schooling or a poor academic record, berates his son for his low grades and distaste for school but nevertheless considers him a "chip off the old block." Such tacit approval of academic underachievement by a youngster's parents seldom fails to find expression in subtle but clear messages that reinforce the adolescent's disdain for the benefits of scholastic diligence. . . .

Although academically unmotivated youngsters may take pains to avoid the inconvenience and embarrassment of frank failure, they see little reason to exert themselves beyond what is necessary just to get by. Their life experience has yielded no associative links between academic achievement and inner satisfaction, expectation of reward, or a feeling of progressing toward meaningful long-term goals. Indeed Hummel and Sprinthall (1965) have observed that bright underachieving high school students are relatively unlikely to perceive their school work in terms of future consequences, whereas good achievers tend to regard academic tasks as a necessary route to their life goals and to approach them purposefully. Studies with college students by Todd, Terrell, and Frank (1962) have similarly confirmed that, particularly among male students, significantly fewer underachievers than normal achievers regard doing well in coursework as important to the attainment of their long-range objective.

Participation in a peer group that endorses nonintellectual values further reinforces the effects of family attitudes that ignore or depreciate the importance of academic achievement. In a survey of several high schools Coleman (1960) found a clear relationship between the extent to which scholastic success was valued by the student body and the number of bright students among the top achievers; for example, in schools where athletic excellence was especially valued many good students appeared to avoid high achievement for fear that it might detract from their popularity.

Negative peer-group influence associated with lower class anti-intellectual values has been graphically depicted by Evan Hunter in *The Blackboard Jungle*. The youngsters in the school he describes utterly disdain discipline and learning in the classroom both because they cannot see education as benefiting them in any way and because they take shared pleasure in frustrating the efforts of their middle-class teachers to instruct them. The teacher hero of Hunter's novel is dumbfounded when he learns that some of his most apparently dull and exasperatingly inattentive students have demonstrated superior intelligence on aptitude measures. . . .

Another important sociocultural determinant of academic motivation is the prevailing definition of sex roles in the youngster's subculture. In some groups academic effort and attainment are viewed as essentially feminine, and the high school boy who is conscientious and successful in his studies risks being labeled not only as "brain" or "grind" but also as "sissy," "fairy," "teacher's pet," or some other pejorative that implies he is less than all boy. In this vein Wilson and Morrow (1962) found that underachieving boys explicitly regarded academic achievement as incompatible with being a "regular guy" or a "good Joe," and Hathaway and Monachesi (1963, p. 102) have demonstrated in fact that high school boys who do well in their studies are more feminine in their interests, as measured by the MMPI (Minnesota Multiphasic Personality Inventory), than their less academically successful peers.

In other groups, particularly during the late high school and college years, scholastic excellence and career-mindedness are considered masculine characteristics, and the girl who values her studies above her social life — especially if she is preparing to enter such predominantly masculine fields as engineering, law, and medicine — may find her femininity called in question by her family and friends. Parents who doubt the compati-

bility of femininity and academic striving often reserve their special pride for the intellectual achievements of their sons and take little interest or pleasure in their daughters' educational plans and accomplishments. The considerable negative reinforcement that is experienced by able girls in such circumstances frequently dulls their academic enthusiasm and results in underachievement.

Modern movements away from these traditional sex-role definitions appear to be abrogating their influences, however. The premium that is placed in contemporary society on maximum educational advancement for all talented people has done much to eliminate such earlier concepts as the "gentleman's C" and the essential restriction of career-minded girls to teaching, nursing, and social work. Nevertheless in the individual instance it is clinically relevant to explore the extent to which a youngster's reluctance to employ his or her full intellectual potential derives from some feeling that by so doing he will compromise his sexual identity. . . .

Opportunity

Able youngsters who are otherwise motivated to achieve in school may be prevented from realizing their goals by sociocultural factors that impede their learning or hinder their studying. Among the most widely publicized of these factors is the failure of elementary education to prepare youngsters adequately for high school and college work. In an underequipped, understaffed school with crowded classrooms, taught by poorly trained, disinterested, or otherwise inadequate teachers, the child may lose irretrievable ground in developing the basic academic skills and study habits he needs to realize his academic potential. The youngster who gets to high school without having learned, for example, to multiply, read fluently, or take examinations and the late adolescent who enters college without ever having had to write a composition or conduct a laboratory experiment are ill-prepared to meet the educational demands that await them.

Even the youngster who has had the benefit of attending good schools may become inadequately prepared for educational advancement if illness or changes of school disrupt the continuity of his learning; for example, changing in midyear from one school where his class is about to embark on an intensive study of fractions to another school where the class has just finished fractions and is starting on decimals can leave a youngster chronically deficient in his understanding of fractions. In the bright youngster such a deficiency might well pass unnoticed until he suddenly fails algebra some years later.

Academic underachievement can also result from extracurricular circumstances that detract from a youngster's attention to his school work. The student who must work long hours at a job or assume burdensome responsibilities in the home may simply lack the requisite time and energy to do justice to his studies, even though he has the ability and the will to do well. Even the lack of a private or reasonably quiet place to study may determine a youngster's failure to maintain the grades of which he appears capable. Mundane as such matters seem, their potentially significant contribution to underachievement obligates the clini-

cian to consider their possible role in academic underachievement before he presumes organic or psychological determinants.

PSYCHOLOGICAL DETERMINANTS

The major psychological determinants of academic underachievement, as elaborated below, comprise two somewhat different patterns of disturbance: (a) developmental and psychopathological states that have no specific relationship to learning but handicap a youngster's educational efforts by generally restricting his personality functioning and (b) specific learning aversions and psychological syndromes defined primarily by a reluctance or refusal to achieve.

Developmental and Psychopathological States

The developmental states that impair scholastic performance include several aspects of cognitive, physical, and emotional immaturity. An adolescent youngster's level of cognitive maturity influences his academic progress primarily in relation to his capacity for abstract thinking. This educationally significant aspect of cognitive maturation in adolescence was first elucidated by Piaget (Inhelder and Piaget, 1958, Chapter 18; see also Muuss, 1967), whose work demonstrated that important developments in cognitive functioning normally occur during adolescence.

Specifically, Piaget observed that not until the early teen years do most youngsters begin to advance from the primarily concrete operations that characterize the thinking of children to the formal operational thinking that typifies mature cognition. These cognitive developments greatly expand the youngster's capacity for abstract thinking: now he becomes able to manipulate relationships between ideas verbally, in the absence of concrete props; to deal with possibilities, hypotheses, and even contrary-to-fact ideas as well as with facts; to take his own thought as an object and reason about it; and to formulate and grasp notions of how things might be as well as how they are (see Ausubel and Ausubel, 1966; Elkind, 1967, 1968).

In concert with these developmental changes the academic demands that are placed on adolescents increasingly require them to assume such abstract attitudes. High school teachers generally formulate their methods of instruction, examination, and grading with the exceptation that their students will possess such cognitive capacities. Consequently an otherwise normal adolescent whose cognitive maturation is lagging behind that of his peers may be handicapped in his studies by a temporary inability to abstract at grade-level.

The classroom problems of cognitively immature youngsters can be readily illustrated. The eighth-grader whose science teacher begins by saying, "Imagine that the earth is flat," cannot appreciate what follows if he is unable to progress beyond perplexedly recalling that in the sixth grade he was taught the earth is unquestionably round. Similarly, whereas a 10-year-old may define "time" specifically in terms of the clock — that is, in hours, minutes, and seconds — for the 15-year-old "time" becomes an abstract interval defined as "a measurement of space" (Gesell, Ilg, and Ames, 1956, pp. 63 and 247). Thus the 15-year-old whose recitation responses and examination answers reflect such relatively concrete orientations as "time is what the clock tells" is almost certain to receive lower grades than his equally intelligent peers whose normal rate of cognitive development allows them to think abstractly of time as "an interval of space."

The association of delayed physical maturation with learning difficulty has been noted among others by deHirsch (1963), who reports that a significant proportion of the underachieving adolescents seen at the Pediatric Language Disorder Clinic of Columbia-Presbyterian Medical Center are passive and infantile youngsters who are physiologically immature and often appear young and small for their age. The negative impact of physical immaturity on academic performance is typically mediated through the anxiety that attends delayed or arrested growth. Delayed development of puberty usually generates sufficient dismay to disrupt a broad range of a youngster's personality functions, including his capacity to concentrate on his school work.

Considerable empirical data have confirmed the generally adverse personality effects of delayed puberty. Studies of several hundred adolescent boys by Schonfeld (1950), Mussen and Jones (1957, 1958) and Weatherly (1964) have demonstrated that late-maturing boys are more likely than their normally developing peers to suffer serious doubts as to their adequacy, to be personally and socially maladjusted during adolescence, and to have more difficulty in achieving the transition from childhood to adulthood. Jones and Mussen (1958) report that late-maturing girls similarly have a depreciated view of themselves. For girls, however, they also found considerable evidence that early as well as late maturation may be anxiety provoking. Particularly in early adolescence the rapidly developing girl may so outstrip her peers in height and secondary sexual characteristics that for a time she experiences a distressing sense of selfconsciousness and isolation.

The role of emotional immaturity in poor school performance has been demonstrated primarily in relation to vocational attitudes, which constitute a meaningful index of maturity level (Crites, 1965). Available evidence suggests that an adolescent's failure to formulate appropriate long-range occupational goals, as a reflection of emotional immaturity, depletes his intrinsic motivation to achieve at capacity; for example, in the already mentioned Todd, Terrell, and Frank (1962) study of college students significantly more normal achievers of both sexes had decided on a specific vocational goal than had students whose grades were well below their placement on aptitude-test scores.

In related work with a large random sample of high school boys Douvan and Adelson (1958) found that psychological immaturity — as defined by infantile, dependent ties to parents, vulnerability to conflict, and underdeveloped capacities for judgment, impulse control, and delay of gratification — was associated with a likelihood of downward mobility. Specifically, immature boys more often than their peers aspired to levels of adult work ranking lower in the hierarchy of skills

and status than their fathers' vocations. . . .

With regard to psychopathological states, finally, it is important to recognize that any form of anxiety state, by disorganizing, distracting, and preoccupying a youngster, may vitiate his academic efforts:

"The natural learning impetus, of which curiosity and attention are a part, is frustrated by tensions in thinking and doing. It is a herculean task to direct one's energies in two directions. When one is self-absorbed and deeply concerned with internal anxiety which calls for constant vigilance, how can the natural impetus to learn be as free and resilient as it should be, and as it is in the secure individual?" (Liss, 1949, pp. 503-504). . . .

Specific Aversions and Syndromes

Specific aversions to the learning process typically reflect certain negative implications that are unconsciously associated by the individual with learning. The origin of academic underachievement in unconscious implications of the learning process has been elaborated mainly by psychoanalytic writers; for example, Fenichel (1945, p. 181) suggests that there are two major reasons "why an ego may be induced to keep its intellect permanently in abeyance": (a) a repression of sexual curiosity that blocks normal interests in thinking and knowing, and (b) the equation of thinking with sexual functions so that the inhibition of thinking has the meaning of castration or its avoidance.

Lorand (1961) has more recently explicated the role of mishandled childhood curiosity and sexual preoccupation in learning problems that arise after puberty. She notes that adolescents who are struggling with repressed or unsatisfied childhood curiosity about bodily and sexual functions may have particular difficulty in concentrating on such subjects as biology, even though their learning in other courses proceeds apace. As for adolescents who tend to become preoccupied with sexual fantasies or masturbatory impulses during solitary intellectual activity, she continues, the very process of studying, whatever the subject matter, may become so anxiety laden and inefficient as to bring their academic progress to a standstill.

Aggressive fantasies can also inhibit a youngster's application to his studies; for example, Sperry, Staver, and Mann (1952) note that a student with pressing concerns about aggression may have difficulty in understanding *Treasure Island* because its violence frightens him. Similarly a youngster who is uncomfortable with his aggressive impulses may panic at the dissection of animals and thus do poorly in biology, or be so appalled by warfare that he cannot concentrate on his history assignments or on Caesar's *Gallic Wars* in Latin class.

Other dimensions of specific unconscious handicaps to learning are discussed by Blanchard (1946) and Liss (1941a). In reviewing various psychoanalytic conceptions of academic underachievement Blanchard suggests that errors in school work, especially in reading, may serve as disguised ways of gratifying repressed impulses; that is, some aspects of inaccurate school work may derive from the same kinds of unconscious influence to which Freud (1901) attributed certain types of forgetting, mistakes in speech,

reading, and writing, and erroneously carried out actions. Liss stresses that the learning process may take on sexual connotations that suffuse it with taboo implications, and he also points out that learning may carry with it unconscious implications for the responsibility of utilizing it that discourage academic attainment.

Although the inhibiting effects of such specific unconscious implications of learning are generally quite plausible to the dynamically oriented clinician and personality theorist, there are unfortunately no adequate data concerning how frequently they contribute to adolescent underachievement. The author's experience would suggest that even within the group of underachieving youngsters whose difficulties are primarily psychological rather than organically or socioculturally determined the vast majority of achievement problems can be adequately understood in terms of the maladaptive patterns of family interaction discussed in the next section, without hypothesizing specific unconscious implications of the learning process itself. . . .

Psychological syndromes consisting primarily of a reluctance of refusal to achieve commonly reflect maladaptive patterns of family interaction involving hostility, rivalry, and passive-aggressive behavioral styles. Each of these elements has been identified in clinical work with underachieving adolescents. Dudek and Lester (1968) and Parens and Weech (1966) present evidence that the focal conflict among underachieving young people usually involves anxiety engendered by aggressive wishes; Liss (1941b) elaborates the academically inhibiting effect of concerns about competing with parents or siblings; and Kotkov (1965) and Rubinstein, Falick, Levitt, and Ekstein (1959) describe their observations of specific learning-failure syndromes characterized by a youngster's utilization of passive-aggressive maneuvers to resolve his conflicts with his parents and to maintain control of aggressive desires he fears to express.

Considerable additional clinical and research data tend to confirm the roles of hostility, rivalry, and passive-aggressive behavior in psychologically determined underachievement. Although none of these elements is specific for learning problems, their combined impact is so frequently conducive to academic underachievement, especially in families that value education, that underachievement can often be predicted for youngsters in whom such problems coexist. Learning difficulties that are determined by unresolved hostile impulses toward family members, fears of competing with parents and siblings, and passive-aggressive proclivities thus constitute a fairly specific pattern of psychological disturbance, which for purposes of discussion can be labeled *passive-aggressive underachievement.*

PASSIVE-AGGRESSIVE UNDERACHIEVEMENT

This section draws on clinical and research literature to review more fully the manner in which hostility, rivalry, and passive-aggressive behavior operate to prevent young people from realizing their academic potential.

Hostility

Kirk (1952) has inferred from her counseling experience with underachieving college students that the passive-aggressive underachiever tends to be (a) expending considerable energy to avert any awareness or explicit expression of angry feelings, (b) struggling in particular with pronounced anger at family members who are demanding or expecting his success, and (c) utilizing academic failure as a means of indirectly aggressing against his parents. This association between restrained hostility and academic underachievement has been confirmed in studies by Sutherland (1952, 1953), Shaw and Brown (1957), and Shaw and Grubb (1958). In studies of bright underachieving high school boys with a variety of projective test, interview, teacher rating, and parental report measures Sutherland found that aggressive feelings were more frequently a source of guilt and anxiety for them than for a control sample and that they were significantly less able to give direct, effective expression to their negative feelings than the control youngsters. In the Shaw studies personality measures administered to high- and low-achieving college freshmen and high school sophomores, all of whom were at the 75th percentile or above on aptitude tests, demonstrated (a) more pronounced hostility among the underachievers and (b) the underachievers' preference to express their hostility in hypercritical attitudes toward others rather than in overt behavior.

Other studies of underachieving youngsters have located the particular origin of their anger in the resentment of parental authority they perceive as restrictive and unjust. Morrow and Wilson (1961) and Davids and Hainsworth (1967) report that low-achieving high school boys, more so than their equally intelligent but academically successful peers, describe their parents as restrictive, severe, and controlling:

"From our clinical experience working with these teenagers, we know that issues concerning control and discipline are of vital importance to them. Not only in casual conversations, but also in discussions recorded in group psychotherapy sessions, we have heard many of these boys describe their unresolved conflicts over yielding to adult authority or rebelling against it" (Davids and Hainsworth, 1967, p. 36).

Interestingly, however, questionnaire data provided by the mothers of Davids and Hainsworth's subjects revealed a fuller endorsement of controlling attitudes among the achievers' mothers than among the mothers of the underachievers. Drews and Teahan (1957) similarly found that the mothers of high-achieving junior high school boys and girls were more authoritarian and restrictive toward their children than the mothers of low achievers. These findings suggest that the passive-aggressive underachiever's resentment of parental control represents not so much a high level of parental authoritarianism as a disparity between the youngster's perception of what his parents' attitudes are and what he would like them to be.

Teahan (1963) has in fact demonstrated (a) that the mothers of underachieving college freshman girls are more strongly committed to domination and the use of discipline than are their daughters, (b) that the fathers of underachiev-

ing college freshman boys have more possessive and domineering attitudes than do their sons, and (c) that neither of these disparities characterizes the attitudes of normally achieving students and their parents. Comparable data are reported by Mutimer, Loughlin, and Powell (1966), who provide evidence that achieving girls identify more closely with their mothers than underachieving girls and that achieving boys are more completely identified with their fathers than underachieving boys.

Although incomplete parental identification is by no means specific to underachievement, its frequency among underachievers is consistent with one of the common precipitants of resentment and subsequent retaliatory underachievement: the parental imposition on a youngster of academic goals that he does not share. For example, the son of a lawyer or physician may be encouraged and expected to follow in his father's footsteps, despite his being uncertain of what he would like to do or perhaps preferring to become a history teacher or an architect. Even if he has no problem in identifying with the same-sex parent, a youngster may find himself unwilling or unable to accept his family's standards of behavior and success. A girl who is the only, the oldest, or the brightest child in her family may be selected to become their standard-bearer as a successful professional person, even though she would rather pursue a nonprofessional career or perhaps not even attend college. When such youngsters are unable to challenge or contravene their parents' demands openly, they frequently utilize underachievement to frustrate the parents' aspirations. . . .

The passive-aggressive underachiever's discomfort with direct expression of hostility and resentment typically originates in three kinds of developmental experience that foster strong aversion to assertive or angry behavior. First, children who have been consistently punished for angry outbursts tend to become relatively passive youngsters who refrain from overtly assertive behavior. Having learned to fear the consequences of expressing anger directly, such youngsters frequently adopt a pervasive passive-aggressive stance in which inactivity is the hallmark of underlying anger. . . .

Rivalry

Problems with rivalry frequently contribute to inaction in achievement settings and avoidance of the competitive pursuit of excellence. Specifically, passive-aggressive underachievers typically suffer from fears of failing or fears of succeeding that generate a number of academically inhibiting defensive maneuvers. These characteristic defensive efforts can best be elaborated in relation to the fears of failure and success that prompt them.

Fear of Failure. Many passive-aggressive underachievers so doubt their own abilities that they erect elaborate defenses to buffer any possible confrontation with the experience of having failed. Most notably the youngster with a prominent fear of failure sets unrealistically high goals for himself and then works only half-heartedly to achieve them. In this way he provides himself two sets of rationalizations by which he can deny his limitations and dismiss any suggestion that he has actually been a failure. First, although his unrealistically high goals

virtually guarantee his failure to reach them, to himself and others he can assert, "Of course I didn't do as well as I had hoped, but look at what I was aiming for — I can really be proud of myself for aspiring to such high goals, and I have no reason to feel embarrassed at not achieving them." Second, his abridged effort allows him to claim, "I didn't really put much time in on my studies, you know, and if I had really cared or worked hard, I could have done a lot better." Were such a youngster to set goals realistically within his grasp and work diligently toward them, he would then risk failure without having such excuses available to cushion the anxiety that would ensue.

The student who fears failure generally takes few such risks. He seldom risks being wrong, he seldom admits having worked hard even if he has, and he utilizes his purportedly limited effort to pride himself on what he has been able to accomplish without truly extending himself. As the insightful father of one underachieving boy put it, "I think he's afraid to work hard, because if he tried hard and still wasn't doing well, he would really have to feel terrible."

Berger (1961) has documented the association of such reaction patterns with underachievement among superior high school students who began to underachieve when they reached college, apparently in response to anticipating that they might no longer be able to maintain superior grades. Berger also selected a comparison group of college freshmen with similarly good high school records who, in contrast to the underachievers, seemed relatively able to accept their limitations: they denied extremely high standards, were willing to exert and acknowledge maximum effort even in the face of possible failure, and took pleasure in hard work. These latter students were found to earn significantly higher college grades than the comparably bright youngsters whose inability to accept their limitations indicated fear of failure.

Academically crippling concerns about competition frequently arise at transition points that confront a student with more difficult subject matter or more demanding academic standards than he has previously experienced. Thus for the able youngster who doubts his scholastic talents the transitions from grammer school to junior high school to senior high school to college may so enhance his fear of failure as to precipitate retreat from competitive effort and consequent underachievement. Similarly the youngster who transfers from one school to another and perceives his new classmates as brighter, more industrious, or better prepared than his former peers may be precipitated into underachievement at this point in his schooling.

The discouraging impact of the transition from high school to college has been elaborated by McArthur (1961), who describes the dilemma of the college student whose family and friends expect him to maintain the same relative excellence he displayed in high school, despite the fact that he is now competing only with students who had equally good high school records. Such youngsters often suffer what McArthur calls "big league shock" when they realize the nature of their competition, and their despair of ever being able to compete successfully in the college environment leads many of them to retreat from the competitive effort. In contrast the group of "compe-

tent" adolescents studied by Silber et al. (1961) generally acknowledged and were prepared for the fact that they probably could not expect to maintain the same grade-point average in college that they had earned in high school.

Intrafamilial concerns about competition are also characteristic in underachieving youngsters whose self-defeating approach to their studies reflects fear of failure. Whatever his potential, the youngster who fears failure has usually suffered from unfavorable comparisons with a successful parent or sibling whose abilities he cannot match. Directly stated or implied disappointment that a youngster does not live up to family standards often is involved in his eschewing the endeavor that would earn him grades commensurate with his ability ("What's the use of trying? I could never do as well as my brother did anyway"). In this context Coleman and Hewett (1962) found eight of their underachieving adolescent patients to have strong feelings of failure and inadequacy, and to have a problematic relationship with their father, who in each case was a highly successful man disappointed by his son's lackluster performance in school. . . .

Fear of Success. Fear of success consists of the expectation that achievement will bring with it negative consequences far more distressing than the failure to achieve. Such paradoxical effects of success were first elaborated clinically by Freud (1916, pp. 311-331), who described patients apparently "wrecked by success." These people had become psychologically disturbed precisely upon the attainment of successes for which they had long and arduously labored. As more recently elaborated by Schuster

(1955), the mental association of success with punishment and retaliation may not only prevent a person from enjoying what he has achieved but also induce him to abandon his aspirations or undo his successes.

It is through the abandonment of otherwise appropriate aspirations and the recourse to self-defeating maneuvers that the individual who fears success is likely to become an underachiever and never realize his innate potential. Although such aversion to success may develop in the setting of a family atmosphere that discourages aggressive striving, fears of success that are powerful enough to result in academic underachievement derive primarily from problems of intrafamilial rivalry. Specifically, a youngster who perceives his parents as dreading his competition and envying his attainments tends to expect disapproval, rejection, and retaliation in the wake of success. The degree of his distress and aversion to achievement depends on the degree to which he regards his parents as relatively unsuccessful or less able than himself. In this respect the underachiever who fears success differs markedly from the fear-of-failure youngster, whose difficulties have usually been intensified by unfavorable comparisons between himself and more successful members of his family.

Such fear-of-success patterns of family interaction have been frequently noted in clinical studies of academic underachievers. Sperry et al. (1958) observed both prominent guilt and anxiety about competitive and acquisitive impulses in the boys they studied and a general family feeling that the father was something less than an unqualified success. Many of these fathers presented a superficial picture of having been successful in life but nevertheless considered themselves failures, primarily in relation to goals they had not realized, to the more significant accomplishments of their friends, and to circumstances that threatened their self-image as breadwinners, such as their wives' working. Grunebaum et al. (1962) further note that the fathers of underachieving boys, in addition to depreciating themselves despite objective indications to their having been successful, tend (a) to view their sons as competitors, particularly for their wives' support and admiration and (b) unconsciously and covertly to subvert their son's achievement strivings in an apparent effort to protect themselves from even greater feelings of having failed.

The characteristic approaches to achievement-related situations of youngsters who fear success contrast interestingly with the coping maneuvers employed by the student who is more prominently concerned with failure. The youngster who fears failure is likely to set very high goals and then, by exerting little effort to reach them, escape the anxiety of a near-miss, and he takes pains to impress on others that his ability is in reality much greater than his attainments would suggest. The underachiever who fears success, on the other hand, publicly disparages his own abilities, even when they are considerable ("There's no sense in my trying to get into the advanced science section, I could never make it"); he sets very limited, unrealistically low goals for himself ("I'll be very happy to get a C average, and that's all I'm working for"); and he curtails his efforts as soon as he reached his minimal goals ("I was lucky to get through high school; why should I try college and just flunk out?"). By such attitudes toward his work the youngster who fears success avoids the accomplishments that he feels might threaten his parents or endanger his own security and sources of affection.

The onset of fear-of-success underachievement in the late high school or early college years very commonly relates to mixed feelings about going to college and thereby surpassing high-school-educated parents. A boy whose father was prevented from reaching college by intellectual, financial, or other limitations, for example, may regard attending college as an aggressive triumph over his father that could undermine the father-son relationship. Familial preoccupation with what the father might have attained if he had had the chance for college exacerbates such anxieties, and a youngster may become particularly prone to disruptive fears of academic success if he regularly receives the paternal message, "Now you'll be able to do all the things I never could." Although such messages manifestly imply pride and encouragement, they can latently convey feelings of disappointment, envy, rejection, and even anger: "My way of life isn't good enough for you, so now you'll become a highbrow intellectual, and it will never be the same between us again."

Commonly in such situations a capable youngster, by sudden neglect of his studies, will either do poorly in college after a strong high school performance or tail off in his high school work sufficiently to compromise his chances of getting into college. On occasion the fear-of-success aversion to attending college involves nonacademic as well as academic areas in which a youngster is reluctant to surpass his parents. Thus for an athletic boy, college may mean opportunities for achievement in sports that his father never had, and for an attractive girl the campus life may represent social outlets never available to her mother. Youngsters with concerns in these areas may simply sabotage their chances for athletic or social success when they reach college, thus becoming athletic or social underachievers; or they may unconsciously utilize academic underachievement to keep themselves out of college, thereby resolving the conflict by leaving the field.

Passive-Aggressive Behavior

Passive-aggressive behavior consists of purposeful inactivity intended to vent underlying feelings of anger and resentment that cannot be expressed directly, save at the price of considerable anxiety. Most underachieving youngsters whose school problems are primarily psychological in origin demonstrate such behavior patterns, and, perhaps consistently with the notable incidence of academic underachievement passive-aggressive personality is by far the most commonly diagnosed personality disorder among adolescents seen in outpatient clinics. . . .

The passive-aggressive youngster, then, is one who is angry but fights back by inaction, rather than outwardly. He exerts control not by commission of disobedient acts, but by failure to do what is expected of him or what might please others. He frustrates and provokes the important people in his world by just sitting there. To his teachers and parents he seems lazy, disinterested, and unmotivated — a stubborn lump they would like to build a fire under.

This behavioral style determines the typical academic pattern of the passive-aggressive underachiever. Studies by Frankel (1960) and Wilson and Morrow (1962) substantiate that underachievers study less than their equally intelligent peers, delay completing their assignments, and reserve their enthusiasm for hobbies and activities that are unrelated to school. Underachievers "forget" to write down assignments, study the wrong material in preparation for examinations, turn in test papers in which they have "overlooked" a section or an entire page, sit silently through class discussions, and in dozens of similar ways compromise their chances of achieving commensurately with their abilities.

Such academic attitudes are typically reflected in the passive-aggressive underachiever's profile of intellectual functioning as measured by psychological tests. Specifically, the passive-aggressive underachiever characteristically performs less well on intellectual tasks that require previous school learning and concentrated effort than on tasks that can be handled with a relatively effortless application of general social knowledge or specific abilities unrelated to school learning. . . .

References

Ausubel, D. P., and Ausubel, P. Cognitive development in adolescence. *Review of Educational Research,* **36**: 403-413, 1966.

Berger, E. M. Willingness to accept limitations and college achievement. *Journal of Counseling Psychology,* **8**: 140-144, 1961.

Blanchard, P. Psychoanalytic contributions to the problems of reading disabilities. *Psychoanalytic Study of the Child,* **2**: 163-187, 1946.

Coleman, J. C., and Hewett, F. M. Open-door therapy: A new approach to the treatment of underachieving adolescent boys who resist needed psychotherapy. *Journal of Clinical Psychology,* **18**: 28-33, 1962.

Coleman, J. S. The adolescent subculture and academic achievement. *American Journal of Sociology,* **65**: 337-347, 1960.

Crites, J. O. Measurement of vocational maturity in adolescence: I. Attitude Test of the Vocational Development Inventory. *Psychological Monographs,* **79**: (whole No. 595), 1965.

Davids, A., and Hainsworth, P. K. Maternal attitudes about family life and child rearing as avowed by mothers and perceived by their underachieving and high-achieving sons. *Journal of Consulting Psychology,* **31**: 29-37, 1967.

deHirsch, K. Two categories of learning difficulties in adolescents. *American Journal of Orthopsychiatry,* **33**: 87-91, 1963.

Douvan, E., and Adelson, J. The psychodynamics of social mobility in adolescent boys. *Journal of Abnormal and Social Psychology,* **56**: 31-44, 1958.

Drews, E. M., and Teahan, J. E. Parental attitudes and academic achievement. *Journal of Clinical Psychology,* **13**: 328-332, 1957.

Dudck, S. Z., and Lester, E. P. The good child facade in chronic underachievers. *American Journal of Orthopsychiatry,* **38**: 153-160, 1968.

Elkind, D. Egocentrism in adolescence. *Child Development,* **38**: 1025-1034, 1967.

Elkind, D. Cognitive development in adolescence. In J. F. Adams, ed., *Understanding Adolescence: Current Developments in Adolescent Psychology.* Boston: Allyn and Bacon, 1968, pp. 128-158.

Fenichel, O. *The Psychoanalytic Theory of Neurosis.* New York: Norton, 1945.

Frankel, E. A comparative study of achieving and underachieving high school boys of high intellectual ability. *Journal of Educational Research,* **53**: 172-180, 1960.

Freud, S. (1901). The psychopathology of everyday life. *Standard Edition,* Vol. VI. London: Hogarth, 1960.

Freud, S. (1916). Some character-types met with in psychoanalytic work. *Standard Edition,* Vol. XIV. London: Hogarth, 1957, pp. 311-333.

Gesell, A. L., Ilg, F. L., and Ames, L. B. *Youth: The Years from Ten to Sixteen.* New York: Harper, 1956.

Grunebaum, M. G., Hurwitz, I., Prentice, N. M., and Sperry, B. M. Fathers of sons with primary neurotic learning inhibitions. *American Journal of Orthopsychiatry,* **32**: 462-472, 1962.

Hathaway, S. R., and Monachesi, E. D. *Adolescent Personality and Behavior.* Minneapolis, Minn: University of Minnesota Press, 1963.

Hess, R. D. High school antecedents of young adult achievement. In R. E. Grinder, ed., *Studies in Adolescence.* New York: Macmillan, 1963, pp. 401-414.

Hummel, R., and Sprinthall, N. Underachievement related to interests, attitudes, and values. *Personnel and Guidance Journal,* **44**: 388-395, 1965.

Hunter, E. *The Blackboard Jungle.* New York: Simon and Schuster, 1954.

Inhelder, B., and Piaget, J. *The Growth of Logical Thinking from Childhood to Adolescence.* New York: Basic Books, 1958.

Jones M. C., and Mussen, P. H. Self-conceptions, motivations, and interpersonal attitudes of early- and late-maturing girls. *Child Development,* **29**: 491-501, 1958.

Katz, I. The socialization of academic motivation in minority group children. *Nebraska Symposium on Motivation,* **15**: 133-191, 1967.

Kirk, B. A. Test versus academic performance in malfunctioning students. *Journal of Consulting Psychology,* **16**: 213-216, 1952.

Kotkov, B. Emotional syndromes associated with learning failure. *Diseases of the Nervous System,* **26**: 48-55, 1965.

Lichter, S. O., Rapien, E. B., Siebert, F. M., and Sklansky, M. *The Drop-outs: A Treatment Study of Intellectually Capable Students Who Drop out of High School.* New York: Free Press of Glencoe, 1962.

Liss, E. Learning difficulties: Unresolved anxiety and resultant learning patterns. *American Journal of Orthopsychiatry,* **11**: 520-524, 1941a.

Liss, E. The failing student. *American Journal of Orthopsychiatry.* **11**: 712-717, 194lb.

Liss, E. The psychiatric implications of the failing student. *American Journal of Orthopsychiatry,* **19**: 501-505, 1949.

Lorand, R. L. Therapy of learning problems. In S. Lorand and H. I. Schneer, eds., *Adolescents: Psychoanalytic Approach to Problems and Therapy.* New York: Hoeber, 1961, pp. 251-272.

McArthur, C. C. Distinguishing patterns of student neuroses. In G. R. Blaine and C. C. McArthur, eds., *Emotional Problems of the Student.* New York: Appleton-Century-Crofs, 1961, pp. 54-75.

Marcus, I. M. Family interaction in adolescents with learning difficulties. *Adolescence,* **1**: 261-271, 1966.

Morrow, W. R., and Wilson, R. C. Family relations of bright high-achieving and under-achieving high school boys. *Child Development,* **32**: 501-510, 1961.

Moss, H. A., and Kagan, J. Stability of achievement and recognition seeking behaviors from early childhood through adulthood. *Journal of Abnormal and Social Psychology,* **62**: 504-513, 1961.

Mussen, P. H., and Jones, M. C. Self-conceptions, motivations, and interpersonal attitudes of late- and early-maturing boys. *Child Development,* **20**:243-256, 1957.

Mussen, P. H., and Jones, M. C. The behavior-inferred motivations of late- and early-maturing boys. *Child Development,* **29**:61-67, 1958.

Mutimer, D., Loughlin, L., and Powell, M. Some differences in the family relationships of achieving and underachieving readers. *Journal of Genetic Psychology,* **109**: 67-74, 1966.

Muuss, R. E. Jean Piaget's cognitive theory of adolescent development. *Adolescence,* **2**: 285-310, 1967.

Parens, H., and Weech, A. A. Accelerated learning responses in young patients with school problems. *Journal of the American Academy of Child Psychiatry,* **5**: 75-92, 1966.

Pierce, J. V., and Bowman, P. H. Motivation patterns of superior high school students. *The Gifted Student.* Washington, D.C.: Cooperative Research Monograph No 2, U.S. Department of Health, Education, and Welfare, 1960.

Rabinovitch, R. D. Reading and learning disabilities. In S. Arieti, ed.,

American Handbook of Psychiatry, Vol. I. New York: Basic Books, 1959, pp. 857-869.

Rubinstein, B. O., Falick, M. L., Levitt, M., and Ekstein, R. Learning impotence: A suggested diagnostic category. *American Journal of Orthopsychiatry*, **29**: 315-323, 1959.

Schonfeld, W. A. Inadequate masculine physique as a factor in personality development of adolescent boys. *Psychosomatic Medicine*, **12**: 49-54, 1950.

Schuster, D. B. On the fear of success. *Psychiatric Quarterly*, **29**: 412-420, 1955.

Shaw, M. C., and Brown, D. J. Scholastic underachievement of bright college students. *Personnel and Guidance Journal*, **36**: 195-199, 1957.

Shaw, M. C., and Grubb, J. Hostility and able high school under-achievers. *Journal of Counseling Psychology*, **5**: 263-266, 1958.

Shaw, M. C. and McCuen, J. T. The onset of academic underachievement in bright children. *Journal of Educational Psychology*, **51**: 103-108, 1960.

Silber, E., Hamburg, D. A., Coelho, G. V., Murphey, E. B., Rosenberg, M., and Pearlin, L. I. Adaptive behavior in competent adolescents: Coping with the anticipation of college. *Archives of General Psychiatry*, **5**: 354-365, 1961.

Sperry, B. M., Staver, N., and Mann, H. E. Destructive fantasies in certain learning difficulties. *American Journal of Orthopsychiatry*, **22**: 356-365, 1952.

Sperry, B. M., Staver, N., Reiner, B. S., and Ulrich, D. Renunciation and denial in learning difficulties. *American Journal of Orthopsychiatry*, **28**: 98-111, 1958.

Sutherland, B. K. The sentence-completion technique in a study of scholastic underachievement. *Journal of Consulting Psychology*, **16**: 353-358, 1952.

Sutherland, B. K. Case studies in education failure during adolescence. *American Journal of Orthopsychiatry*, **23**: 406-415, 1953.

Teahan, J. E. Parental attitudes and college success. *Journal of Educational Psychology*, **54**: 104-109, 1963.

Todd, F. J., Terrell, G., and Frank, C. E. Differences between normal and underachievers of superior ability. *Journal of Applied Psychology*, **46**: 183-190, 1962.

Weatherly, D. Self-perceived rate of physical maturation and personality in late adolescence. *Child Development*, **35**: 1197-1210, 1964.

Wilson, R. C., and Morrow, W. R. School and career adjustment of bright high-achieving and under-achieving high school boys. *Journal of Genetic Psychology*, **101**: 91-103, 1962.

IRVING B. WEINER

Delinquent Behavior*

... This chapter first reviews distinctions between sociological and psychological patterns of delinquency in relation to studies of adaptive and maladaptive delinquency, social and solitary delinquency, and lower and middle class delinquency. Later sections then discuss and illustrate the patterns of neurotic, characterological, and psychotic and organic disturbance that are found in primarily psychological delinquency. The final portion of the chapter is devoted to the treatment of these various types of delinquent behavior.

SOCIOLOGICAL AND PSYCHOLOGICAL DETERMINANTS

Variations in the nature and essential motives of delinquent acts have stimulated numerous efforts to categorize delinquent behavior along social-psychological lines.[1] Three important dichotomies of delinquent behavior emerging from this work contrast adaptive with maladaptive delinquency, social with solitary delinquency, and lower class with middle

class delinquency. Although these dichotomies do not represent truly discrete behavior patterns, the data concerning them clarify the major distinctions between sociological and psychological determinants of delinquency.

Adaptive and Maladaptive Delinquency

Jenkins (1955, 1957) has defined adaptive delinquency as motivated, goal-oriented behavior involving learning from experience; and maladaptive delinquency as frustration-induced behavior that is rigid, stereotyped, and refractory to punishment. Using the terms "socialized delinquent behavior" and "unsocialized aggressive behavior" to denote the adaptive and maladaptive patterns, respectively, Jenkins (1957, pp. 534-535) summarizes their essential differences as follows:

"With socialized delinquency, we have a predatory minority subculture in which acquisitive desires for what is most easily achieved by theft may be reinforced by the prestige which attaches to successful delinquency—or the contempt, loss of status and social rejection which may attend a refusal to participate. We are dealing with planful, normally motivated, easily understandable behavior. With the unsocialized aggressive, on the other hand, we have gross failure of conscience or inhibitions of any sort in a highly

*From Chapter 8 of I. B. Weiner, *Psychological Disturbance in Adolescence*, 1970. Reprinted by permission of the author and John Wiley and Sons.
[1] Ferdinand (1966) reviews in detail most of the published typologies of delinquency.

frustrated individual with a low frustration tolerance, unrestrained impulsiveness and bitter resentments and hostilities. "

Jenkins derived this distinction from data collected on 500 youngsters seen at the Michigan Child Guidance Institute, 300 delinquent boys committed to the Warwick, New York, training school, and 300 youngsters admitted to the Child Psychiatry Service at the University of Iowa. In the original Michigan study, done in 1941, three clinically meaningful clusters of youngsters were identified: 70 who manifested such characteristics as bad companions, gang activities, cooperative stealing, furtive stealing, habitual school truancy, running away, and staying out late at night and were called *socialized delinquents;* 52 who displayed such behavior as assaultive tendencies, starting fights, cruelty, defiance of authority, malicious mischief, and inadequate guilt feelings and were labeled *unsocialized agressive* children; and 73 marked by seclusiveness, shyness, apathy, worrying, sensitiveness, and submissiveness who were classified as *overinhibited* (Jenkins, 1964). Jenkins found relatively little overlap among the behaviors associated with these three categories, and most of the 300 delinquent boys in the initial Warwick study also proved readily classifiable as socialized delinquent, unsocialized agressive, or emotionally disturbed (Jenkins and Glickman, 1947).

Jenkins' distinction between the socialized delinquent and unsocialized agressive patterns, which has been incorporated into the recently revised psychiatric nomenclature *(Diagnostic and Statistical Manual of Mental Disorders, 1968),* also extends to background factors that ap-

pear to differentiate the two groups. Both the Michigan data (Jenkins, 1957, 1966) and observations in the Iowa sample (Jenkins, NurEddin, and Shapiro, 1966) suggested a relationship between unsocialized aggressive behavior and developmental problems related to maternal rejection from infancy or early childhood on. The unsocialized aggressive youngsters seemed never to have experienced a sense of being loved or wanted by their mothers. The socialized delinquent boys and girls, on the other hand, were not as likely to have experienced deficient mothering during their early years as inadequate parental care in their later childhood. Socialized delinquency was generally associated with unsupervised development in a disorganized home located in a deteriorated, high-delinquency neighborhood, with neither parent providing much in the way of direction or guidance during the preadolescent and adolescent years.

Social and Solitary Delinquency

The distinction between social and solitary delinquency was suggested by Lindesmith and Dunham's (1941) differentiation between *socialized* and *individualized* criminality: the socialized delinquent collaborates with others to commit criminal acts that are endorsed by his subculture and earn him status and recognition within it, whereas the individualized delinquent acts alone for personal and private reasons to perpetrate crimes that violate codes of acceptable behavior within his social milieu. According to Lindesmith and Dunham, the social delinquent is usually a psychologically normal person who shares antisocial values with his subcultural group, whereas the individual criminal is most often psychologically disturbed.

Subsequent work has tended to confirm such differences between social and solitary delinquent youngsters; for example, Randolph, Richardson, and Johnson (1961) found significantly higher scores on eight of the nine clinical scales of the MMPI among individually delinquent than among socially delinquent boys. Cowden (1965) reports that individual delinquent girls experience significantly higher levels of guilt and anxiety than girls whose delinquency has involved participation in delinquent peer-group activities. And Brigham, Ricketts, and Johnson (1967) obtained more deviant descriptions of maternal behavior, indicating disturbed relations with female authority figures, from solitary than from social delinquents.

These data indicate a close parallel between the social-solitary dimension of delinquency and Jenkin's adaptive-maladaptive continuum. Social and adaptive delinquency both constitute primarily sociological problems in which the antisocial norms of a deviant subculture generate delinquent behavior in its loyal, well-integrated, relatively stable members. Solitary and maladaptive delinquency, in contrast, emerge as essentially psychological problems in which delinquent behavior derives from individual disturbances in the absence of ostensible subcultural support.

Although most writers subscribe to such a distinction between primarily sociological and primarily psychological patterns of delinquency, this dichotomy has typically been couched in imprecise terms. From a broad sociological perspec-

tive most cooperative delinquency is neither adaptive nor independent of frustration. Concerning adaptations, some behavioral scientists do regard group delinquency largely as normative lower class behavior that represents a consistent, adaptive adherence to norms and values at variance with middle class standards and is thus coincidentally, rather than intentionally, antisocial (Kvaraceus and Miller, 1959; Miller 1958). Yet most emphasize that delinquent subcultures are deviant within any social class and serve no adaptive function beyond the immediate confines of the gang:

"Many of the delinquent behaviors of adolescents seem totally devoid of a social purpose which could be understood or accepted by adults. . . . The behavior of the delinquent is incongruent with the goals of the middle classes and can be considered a mockery or perversion of such goals. It is also at times alien to the goals of the lower class adult population, who are sometimes as disturbed as middle class adults by the unreasonable nature of juvenile crime" (Halleck, 1967, p. 116).

. . .As for frustration, the major sociological analyses of gang and subcultural delinquency stress the role of common frustrations in the genesis of social delinquent acts. This emphasis is particularly clear in the "reaction formation" theories of subcultural delinquency advanced by Cohen (1955) and by Cloward and Ohlin (1960). Cohen interprets subcultural delinquency as the eventuation of frustrated efforts to attain middle class status and prerogatives in a reactive endorsement of antisocial values. Through this reaction pattern, Cohen continues, a youngster can "retaliate against the norms at whose impact his ego has suffered, by defining merit in terms of the opposite of those norms and by sanctioning aggression against them and those who exemplify and apply them" (p. 168). Cloward and Ohlin similarly argue that "pressures toward the formation of delinquent subcultures originate in marked discrepancies between culturally induced aspirations among lower class youth and the possibilities of achieving them by legitimate means" (p. 78).

The "cultural transmission" theories of subcultural delinquency also invoke a prominent element of frustration. Shaw and McKay (1942), for example, who describe delinquency as a group tradition transmitted from older youngsters to younger ones in neighborhoods where parental authority is ineffective, traced the lack of constructive parental influence in the Chicago neighborhoods they studied in part to the frustrated efforts of native-born youngsters to identify comfortably with the standards of their immigrant parents.

These and other major contributions to the sociology of subcultural delinquency have recently been reviewed by Glaser (1965) and Short (1965) and are not elaborated here. It should be noted, however, that social-disability interpretations of delinquent behavior pertain primarily to the disadvantaged youngster and cannot account for the delinquent acts of youngsters with broad social, cultural, and economic horizons. Social-disability theories of delinquency are further compromised by clear evidence (a) that most lower class youths do not become chronically delinquent and (b) that patterns of relationship within their

individual families significantly influence the likelihood of antisocial behavior in young people (see Glueck and Glueck, 1962, pp. 97-136; Nye, 1958; Peterson and Becker, 1965; Wirt and Briggs, 1959).

Yet it is just as simplistic to overlook sociological determinants of delinquency in favor of exclusively psychological hypotheses. To the extent that shared frustrations of lower social class membership can generate cooperative delinquency, psychological approaches are no more adequate than sociological formulations to explain all delinquent behavior. It has been suggested, for example, that a delinquent is a youngster "who never was properly or healthfully related to his family" (Church, 1944, p. 144) or whose "ego has failed in its fundamental role of synthesizing agent and mediator" (Bernabeu, 1958, p. 386), and that "if one is even to begin treating delinquents, it is absolutely necessary to recognize the pervasiveness of his personality distortions" (Schulman, 1955, p. 35). Such views fail to embrace the adaptive-social type of delinquency that develops primarily in deteriorated neighborhoods and is relatively independent of significant psychological disturbance or problems of early socialization. . .

Lower Class and Middle Class Delinquency

Delinquent behavior has been studied and interpreted primarily as a lower class phenomenon; for example, the extensive contributions of Glueck and Glueck (1950, 1956, 1960, 1962) are based largely on comparisons between 500 reform school boys, almost all of whom were drawn from underprivileged neighborhoods, and a control sample of nondelinquent boys from comparable neighborhoods. Glueck and Glueck attribute their selection of such a disadvantaged population to their particular interest in determining what factors would predict nondelinquency even in the face of adverse social conditions that are often presumed to augur against it (1950, pp. 14-15).[2]

Research with such restricted samples overlooks delinquent behavior among middle class youth and tends to yield results that say more about lower class life than about the origins of delinquency. Thus Glueck and Glueck (1950, pp. 109-110) report that delinquency is significantly associated with lack of cultural refinement in the home and lack of family ambition, yet "cultural refinement" was absent in 82% of their nondelinquents' homes (as against 92% for delinquents) and "family ambition" was negligible for 70% of the nondelinquents (90% for delinquents).

When differences between lower class and middle class delinquency have been considered, the usual tendency has been to regard adaptive-social delinquency largely as a lower class phenomenon and maladaptive-individual delinquent behavior as the characteristic form of delinquency among middle class, socially advantaged youngsters. For example, Cohen (1955, p. 73) and Cloward and Ohlin (1960, p. 28) concur that delinquent subcultures arise primarily within the working class, and Randolph et al. (1961) present some evidence that solitary delinquents are more likely to come from the upper socioeconomic levels. As these writers acknowledge, however, such a class distinction is far from exclusive.

In the first place it is obviously as possible for a lower class as a middle class youngster to engage in individual delinquent acts motivated by underlying psychological disturbances. Second, middle class youngsters are no strangers to delinquent gangs, even though the primary locus of delinquent subcultures is in working-class neighborhoods; for example, Robins (1966, p. 189) reports that in her large clinic sample 26% of the boys from better neighborhoods had participated in "trouble-making" gangs, as compared with 53% of the boys from slum areas. According to Wattenberg and Balistrieri (1952), furthermore, at least one form of group delinquency, auto theft, occurs more commonly among advantaged than lower class youngsters.

The task remains, then, to account for delinquency in the absence of the social and economic disadvantages to which delinquent behavior, especially when cooperative, has so frequently been attributed. Elkind (1967) suggests that middle class delinquency is essentially antifamilial rather than antisocial and represents retaliation against parents whom the youngster feels to be subverting his needs to their own. Cohen (1955) interprets male delinquency in middle class families as efforts to cope with basic sex-role anxieties by exhibiting masculine assertiveness. Other hypothesized sources of delinquent behavior in the middle class adolescent, as reviewed by Shanley (1967), include resentment of maternal dominance in the home, impatience with the protracted dependency of middle

[2] For a critical review of the Gluecks' work and other prediction studies of delinquency the reader is referred to Briggs and Wirt (1965).

class adolescents on their parents, the upward diffusion of lower class values antithetical to achievement through deferred gratification, and ineffective early childhood training combined with inadequate parent-child relationships during adolescence.

However relevant such variables might be to delinquency, none is specific for delinquency or even unique to the middle class social context. In fact, the more closely the distinction between middle class and lower class delinquency is examined, the more such a distinction appears to consist of little more than the difference in socioeconomic status of the delinquent. Bohlke (1961) has challenged even this distinction by suggesting that many apparently "middle class" delinquents come from families that have lower class backgrounds and values or are downwardly mobile. . . .

It is furthermore apparent that lower class and middle class youths commit essentially the same kinds of delinquent acts. Nye, Short, and Olson (1958, p. 27) report no generally significant social class difference in the delinquent behavior admitted by several hundred high school boys and girls representing a broad socioeconomic range. Herskovitz, Levine, and Spivack (1959) reviewed the offenses of middle class delinquent adolescents at the Devereux Foundation and found the nature of the delinquent acts to be almost entirely consistent with the offenses typically observed among lower class delinquents, with the exception of auto theft (slightly more common among middle class delinquents) and burglary (committed more often by lower class offenders). Herskovitz et al. conclude that, with these two exceptions, "delinquency seems to be delinquency, irrespective of slums or suburbs, material advantages or underprivilege, gangs or no" (p. 473).

DELINQUENCY AS A NEUROTIC SYMPTOM

The symptomatic expression of psychological conflict through delinquent behavior usually represents (a) communication of needs that the youngster cannot otherwise impress on his environment, (b) the effects of inadvertent parental fostering of antisocial behavior, and (c) "scapegoating," the unconscious selection of a particular youngster to receive the family's implicit encouragement to delinquency. As illustrated below, these three influences often interact in motivating an individual adolescent to antisocial behavior.

Communication of Needs

A youngster who commits delinquent acts is often attempting to elicit environmental response to pressing needs that are being overlooked or ignored. The specific needs most commonly underlying such neurotic communicative efforts are needs to be punished, needs to be recognized, admired, and accorded status, and needs to receive help.

Need for Punishment. The utilization of delinquent behavior to communicate needs for punishment was first explicated in psychoanalytic studies of individuals whose motivation to illegal acts seemed rooted in guilt feelings. As suggested by Freud (1916, pp. 332-333) and later elaborated by Alexander (1930) and

Friedlander (1947, pp. 149-150), the "criminal from a sense of guilt" violates the law specifically in order to be caught and punished. Such offenders usually harbor guilt over previous transgressions, real or fantasied, for which their punishment provides the needed expiation that has not previously been exacted by their environment.

Other psychoanalytic writers (e.g., Johnson and Szurek, 1952) contend that the criminal who desires to be caught is much less likely to be reacting to a sense of guilt than he is to be groping for protection against committing more or even worse crimes. William Heirens, the infamous teenage murderer of two women and a six-year-old girl whose body he dismembered, vividly demonstrated this phenomenon when he scrawled in one of his victim's apartments, "For heaven's sake catch me before I kill more; I cannot control myself" (see Kennedy, Hoffman, and Haines, 1947). Nevertheless, the demonstrable implications of masochistic needs for a variety of maladaptive behaviors (see Bergler, 1959; Reik, 1941) justify attention in the individual case to the possibility that a youngster's antisocial behavior is motivated by unfulfilled needs to be punished.

Needs for Recognition, Admiration, and Status. The needs to be recognized, admired, and accorded status are frequently communicated through delinquent acts by youngsters who feel isolated or ignored in their family and peer groups. Misbehavior generally draws attention to its perpetrator, and a youngster dismayed at the limited impact he is making on his environment may correctly anticipate that a detected delinquent act will command the attention of teachers, police, and other important adults; will forcibly engage his parents in court, school, or clinical deliberations concerning him; and will enhance his notoriety among his peers.

In this last regard Erikson (1956, p. 88) has noted in his concept of the "negative identity" that many adolescents would prefer to be "somebody bad" than "not-quite-somebody." The "masculine proving" ascribed to some male delinquency by Cohen, by Bloch and Niederhoffer, and by others illustrates such a quest for identity through deviant behavior, and Blaine and McArthur (1961) have similarly interpreted the colorful anti-establishment behavior of some college students as attempts to establish a definite public identity. Certainly the very small minority of college students who have battled police and vandalized property during the campus demonstrations of the late 1960s, whatever their professed motivations, have earned themselves a degree of public attention they would otherwise have been unlikely to command.

Among girls, needs for identity and recognition frequently contribute to sexual delinquency. "Feminine proving" girls sometimes seek through intercourse and pregnancy to bolster their sense of femininity and publicly proclaim their womanhood. For many unwed pregnant adolescents studied, for example, by Visotsky (1966) and Gottschalk et al. (1964), engaging in intercourse represented being attractive and feminine, and pregnancy was associated with peer-group respect for girls who have a lover and become pregnant by him. Conversely, Vincent (1961, pp. 253-254) concludes from an extensive research project that the development of a positive self-identity from infancy through adolescence effectively deters illegitimate pregnancy. . . .

Need for Help. A youngster who recognizes in himself psychological disturbances that are not sufficiently appreciated by others may utilize delinquent behavior to communicate his need for help. Such a youngster may have directly petitioned his parents for professional help with the matters troubling him. Yet some parents are unable to accept the possibility of psychological disturbance in their family and respond to such requests by depreciating the severity of the problem; others are embarrassed that their child might need psychotherapy and encourage him to work things out by himself with "common sense"; and still others resent the implication that their ministrations are inadequate and insist that, if he needs to talk to someone, "that's what parents are for." A youngster thus rebuffed often resorts to public antisocial acts to convince his parents of his needs and to elicit the insistence of teachers, police, or judges that he receive professional counsel.

In many other instances a troubled youngster feels too embarrassed or estranged from his parents to confess concern about his psychological state, even when he could anticipate a positive response to his request for professional guidance. Especially if the overt manifestations of his disturbance are subtle and fleeting or his parents are generally oblivious to matters he does not directly bring to their attention, a dramatic or illegal act may be his only way to communicate his need and receive the desired help. . . .

Parental Fostering of Antisocial Behavior

Although an adolescent's conscience may at times motivate him to delinquent behavior through which he seeks punishment to assuage burdensome guilt feelings, such "punitive superego" factors play a much smaller role in generating antisocial acts than the relative lack of superego strictures and controls. In the symptomatically delinquent youngster such defects in conscience tend to be highly selective rather than pervasive, a phenomenon that was formalized by Adelaide Johnson (1949) in her concept of "superego lacunae."

The lacunar superego is neither absent nor generally weak, but rather, together with some normal and perhaps even some punitive aspects, it contains circumscribed gaps, or "lacunae." It is these gaps that allow an otherwise conforming youngster to engage in certain specific kinds of delinquent act without hesitation, guilt, or remorse (Giffin, Johnson, and Litin, 1954). Beginning with the work of Szurek (1942), clinical investigation has traced such selective superego defects to the implicit fostering of parents who covertly stimulate and inadvertently reinforce antisocial behavior in their youngsters.

Covert Stimulation. Covert stimulation to delinquent behavior commonly proceeds through two somewhat different patterns of family interaction. In one pattern the parents display superego defects in their own behavior and thereby present a lacunar model with which their child comes to identify. Generally law-abiding parents who, for example, regularly take unjustified deductions on their income tax returns or drive over the speed limit communicate to their youngster the acceptability of such illegal acts. When the parent additionally takes obvious pleasure in his law breaking ("I've figured out a nifty way to charge off our vacation as a business expense"), blandly dissembles when apprehended ("Honest, officer, I had no idea I was going over 35"), and remains unabashed if proved guilty ("It was worth a try; I'll be more careful next time"), he teaches his youngster that flaunting the law may be desirable as well as acceptable. Similarly, when a youngster has regularly been made partner to various deceptions ("Scrunch down so you won't look so tall, and maybe we can get you in at half-fare"), he is likely to conclude that lying and cheating are appropriate and expected modes of behavior. . . .

In the other pattern of covert stimulation parents whose overt behavior is above reproach but who harbor latent antisocial impulses implicitly encourage their children to act out their impulses for them. Such parents typically incite delinquent behavior by unnecessary prohibitions that (a) identify the specific transgressions that will provide them vicarious gratification and (b) communicate an anticipation that their youngster will commit them. Parents who vigorously and repetitively caution their youngster against driving recklessly, drinking, fighting, stealing, misbehaving sexually, or hanging around with unsavory companions convey their expectation that he will do one or another of these things. Especially when he has previously given them no cause for such concern, the youngster is likely to interpret this expectation as the parents' wish that he misbehave, which it usually is. He

may then decide to please them by fulfilling their expectations, and their subsequent protests or overt dismay will seldom alter his perception of their secret pleasure in his escapades. . . .

Inadvertent Reinforcement. Once a delinquent act has been committed, whether parentally abetted or otherwise stimulated, parental sanctions figure prominently in reinforcing the antisocial behavior and implicitly encouraging its repetition. The parent who sanctions superego lacunae lacks basic conviction that particular delinquent behaviors are wrong, and he accordingly disciplines his misbehaving youngster in an ambivalent, inconsistent manner that tacitly communicates approval. He varies protracted periods of permissiveness with sudden angry outbursts and punishments that are disproportionate to the offense. He deplores the delinquent behavior but collaborates to prevent its being detected; should the youngster be caught, he minimizes the significance of the offense to the authorities. He accepts flimsy excuses for misdeeds and describes them to others in a tone of bemused tolerance. He criticizes the outcome of the offense but pays scant attention to the offense itself: "If you had to speed, why did you have to do it right in the center of town where you were sure to be caught," or "Next time you want to get sloppy drunk, do it at home and don't make a public spectacle of yourself," or "If you want to fight, you could at least tangle with a kid you can handle."

These and similarly ambivalent parental responses have been consistently observed by Johnson and Szurek (1954), Johnson and Burke (1955), and Carek, Hendrickson, and Holmes (1961) in their work with adolescents manifesting parentally sanctioned delinquency. Johnson (1959, p. 846) comments specifically on the demeanor of the sanctioning parent as he learns of his youngster's antisocial tendencies:

"The entranced parental facial expression apparent to the child describing a stealing episode, a sexual misdemeanor, or a hostile attitude toward a teacher conveys to the child that the parent is achieving some pleasurable gratification. No amount of subsequent punishment will act as a deterrent against the recurrences of the acting out. A child wishes to do the thing which he senses gives the parent pleasure, even though he may be punished."

Although the evidence for parental sanctioning of delinquent behavior is largely clinical, it is of interest to note some supportive empirical data reported by Gallenkamp and Rychlak (1968). These investigators administered to the parents of delinquent boys and nondelinquent controls a "sanctioning of delinquent behavior" scale comprising items on parental expectations, parental discipline, and parental modeling of antisocial behavior. The parents of the delinquent boys demonstrated noticeably more sanctioning of delinquent behavior than the parents of the controls, and comparisons between just the fathers of the two groups yielded a highly significant difference in the expected direction. . . .

Selecting a Scapegoat

Parental fostering of delinquent behavior is usually concentrated on one or more children in the family who are selected as scapegoats. It is this youngster in particular to whom illegal acts are confided with pride, whose aid is enlisted in perpetrating various deceptions, and who bears the brunt of his parents' unnecessary prohibitions and ambivalent responses to misdeeds. As within other social or political units, the scapegoat thus selected and victimized soon becomes essential to the group's equilibrium. In emerging as the family "black sheep" and the bane of his parents' existence the youngster who is encouraged to delinquent behavior serves his family's needs in several ways: he discharges antisocial impulses that might otherwise be disconcerting to his parents; he allows his parents and siblings to enhance their self-image by contrasting their "record" with his; and through his penchant for getting into trouble he provides a ready cause to which any family difficulties or dissension can be attributed. He unites his family in common concern about his misbehavior, and they are spared from having to squabble with each other by being able to direct all squabbling at him. These dynamics of the scapegoating phenomenon have been related by Counts (1967, p. 67) to the resolution of some family crisis:

"Scapegoating an adolescent is selected as the means of solving the crisis. Pressure is brought to bear by the parents, and the youngster acts in some impulsive and self-defeating manner. The family equilibrium may or may not be reestablished by this action; but if it is restored, the new equilibrium will generally be predicated on the fiction that the family is in difficulty because of the

disruptive behavior of the adolescent member, and not because of some underlying problem related to one or both parents."

The scapegoating phenomenon helps to explain the fact that often only one of the children of delinquency-fostering parents displays antisocial tendencies. Just as interfamily differences can explain why some but not all youngsters growing up in a deteriorated, high-delinquency neighborhood become delinquent, intrafamily differences account for one child of fostering parents but not his siblings becoming delinquent. The special parent-child relationship that encourages antisocial behavior is reserved for the youngster selected as scapegoat, and his siblings are spared significant exposure to the parents' superego-lacunae sanctioning attitudes.

Several considerations influence which youngster is selected by his parents for the parental fostering that renders him delinquency prone. Above all, the scapegoated youngster typically stands out from his siblings in some way that is important to the parents. He may have provoked their anger by being an unplanned or unwanted child; by being a boy when they wanted a girl, or vice versa; or by being sickly or for some other reason making unusual demands on their time, energy, and resources. As noted by Johnson (1949), the child who becomes scapegoated for having angered his parents gratifies them not only by acting out their forbidden impulses but also by being caught and punished, which satisfies their hostile, destructive feelings toward him.

In other instances the scapegoat is chosen and victimized on the basis of positive traits that distinguish him from his siblings; for example, parents with unresolved conflicts about being surpassed by their children may select the brightest, ablest, or most talented of their youngsters as the object of their covert encouragement to self-defeating antisocial behavior. Still other delinquency-fostering parents appear to be threatened by the youngster who most resembles them. Whether because he challenges their own identity more than their other children or because he demonstrates more clearly their undesirable traits, the youngster most resembling his parents has been found in clinical investigations of families with scapegoated children to be the one who is frequently selected for this role (Vogel and Bell, 1960). . . .

DELINQUENCY AS A CHARACTERO-LOGICAL ORIENTATION

Psychologically determined delinquent behavior occurs in some youngsters not as a neurotic symptom but as the reflection of an asocial characterological orientation. This characterological pattern—in which acquisitive, aggressive, and pleasure-seeking impulses are translated into immediate action—is variously labeled *psychopathic personality, sociopathic personality, impulse-ridden personality,* and, in the most recent psychiatric nomenclature, *antisocial personality (Diagnostic and Statistical Manual, 1968).*

Psychopathic personality was first distinguished from neurosis and psychosis and elaborated clinically by Hervey Cleckley (1959, 1964), whose *The Mask of Sanity* appeared in 1941. Cleckley identified psychopathy as a condition that is marked by persistent and inadequately motivated antisocial behavior, irresponsibility, pathological lying, inability to accept blame, failure to learn by experience, incapacity for love, inappropriate or "fantastic" reactions to alcohol, lack of insight, shallow and impersonal responses to sexual life, self-defeating behavior, and unexplained life failures, all in the absence of neurotic anxiety or impaired cognitive capacities. The work of Cleckley and other early contributors is reviewed by McCord and McCord (1964, Chapter 2), who summarize the defining characteristics of psychopathy as follows:

"The psychopath is asocial. His conduct often brings him into conflict with society. The psychopath is driven by primitive desires and an exaggerated craving for excitement. In his self-centered search for pleasure, he ignores restrictions of his culture. The psychopath is highly impulsive. He is a man for whom the moment is a segment of time detached from all others. His actions are unplanned and guided by his whims. The psychopath is aggressive. He has learned few socialized ways of coping with frustrations. The psychopath feels little, if any, guilt. He can commit the most appalling acts, yet view them without remorse. The psychopath has a warped capacity for love. His emotional relationships, when they exist, are meager, fleeting, and designed to satisfy his own desires. These last two traits, guiltlessness and lovelessness, conspicuously mark the psychopath as different from other men" (pp. 16-17).

The last part of this description is particularly important, because it is above all the psychopath's underdeveloped conscience and inability to identify with other people that distinguish him from other disturbed persons. Jenkins (1960, p. 323) likewise concludes from his studies of delinquent behavior that guiltlessness and lovelessness are the essential defining characteristics of psychopathy: "The psychopath lacks the capacity for loyalty and is distinguished from others by this lack."

These two central characteristics of psychopathic personality disorder distinguish psychopathy from antisocial behavior in general and from professional criminality. Because of his generally asocial, aggressive attitudes, limited frustration tolerance, and lack of concern for the welfare of others, the psychopathic individual is highly prone to commit antisocial acts. As the above definition indicates, however, it is his defective conscience and incapacity for loyalty that mark his personality disturbance, rather than any particular frequency of antisocial acts. Neurotically and psychotically disturbed people may be as repetitively and seriously antisocial as the psychopath, and Robins (1966, p. 159) reports that even in the most antisocial group of youngsters in her large sample a diagnosis of sociopathy was made in only about half the cases.

As for criminality, most workers in the field concur that there is little necessary relationship between the professional criminal and the psychopath. Whereas psychopaths may become inveterate criminals, most professional criminals demonstrate capacities for planning, exerting self-control, and learning from experience that are not shared by psychopaths, and many are free from the intense aggression, impulsivity, guiltlessness, and shallow emotional relationships that mark psychopathy:

"The contrast between the psychopath and the professional criminal is far greater than the contrast between the professional criminal and the law-abiding citizen. Both of the latter normally pursue occupational goals, one legal, the other illegal. Both are in part motivated by the desire for financial gain, either as a means or as an end in itself. Both learn by experience. Both plan their behavior and modify and adapt it according to the circumstances which they meet. Both understand each other far better than either can understand the psychopath" (Jenkins, 1960, p. 321). . . .

Origins of Psychopathic Personality Disturbance

There is considerable evidence that psychopathic personality disturbance most commonly arises in the setting of early and severe parental rejection that generates deep reservoirs of anger, resentment, suspicicion, and distrust. The youngster who is deprived from an early age of his parents' affection and interest develops little capacity for interpersonal warmth and compassion, seldom expects consideration or nurturance from others, and feels little restraint in unleashing his bitterness and hostility against a world he experiences as hostile and uncaring. . . .

Such early disturbed parent-child relationships, especially maternal failure to gratify an infant youngster's emotional needs, have also been observed in clinical studies of characterologically antisocial

youngsters by Bender (1961), Berman (1959), Bowlby (1944), and Friedlander (1949, pp. 89-90). These and other studies indicate the following:

1. That the vast majority of psychopaths have been rejected in childhood.

2. That aggression is the dominant reaction to such rejection.

3. That rejected or institutionalized children often, though not invariably, exhibit psychopathic personality disturbance (see McCord and McCord, 1964, pp. 70-83).

Discipline. Parental rejection in the case of the budding psychopath typically involves not only maternal deprivation in early childhood but also the parents' subsequent failure to provide adequate discipline and supervision. Robins (1966, pp. 167-168) reports that only 9% of the youngsters in her sample who were disciplined adequately or strictly by both parents were diagnosed as sociopathic as adults. In contrast, where one or both parents were described as too lenient 29% of the youngsters were diagnosed as sociopathic as adults, and where one or both exerted no discipline at all 32% became sociopathic. McCord and McCord (1959, p. 77) similarly report a positive relationship between parental disinterest, leniency, and inconsistent discipline and subsequent convictions for illegal acts, and the aggressive boys in the Bandura and Walters (1959) study were found to have been subjected to many fewer restrictions, demands, and controls than the control youngsters.

Other work has demonstrated the particular importance of the father's failure to discipline in the genesis of characterological delinquency. Becker et al. (1959) observed more arbitrary discipline in the families of uncontrollably aggressive youngsters they studied than in the parents of a control sample of normal youngsters, with the fathers much more often failing to enforce regulations. Anderson (1968) reports considerably more paternal deprivation in the histories of 15- to 18-year-old delinquent boys than in those of nondelinquent controls. The difference between Anderson's groups both in the actual absence of the father and "under the roof alienation" from the father had begun to appear as the boys passed age 4 and had become highly significant by age 12.

In assessing parental strictness, however, it is important to distinguish between physical abuse and harsh discipline. Random parental cruelty and physical abuse serve no disciplinary purpose and communicate to a youngster his parents' essential disinterest in him, whereas severe punishment addressed to a specific misbehavior, however much resented at the time, demonstrates parental concern and capacity to exert authority. It is similarly erroneous to mistake the cold, stern parent for a rejecting parent. The cold, stern parent, despite his undemonstrativeness, often conveys through his painstaking surveillance and legislative rulings an abiding interest in his youngsters' welfare. Thus in addition to noting an inverse relationship between adequate or strict discipline and subsequent sociopathy, Robins (1966, p. 161) found that physical abuse yielded a slightly elevated rate of sociopathy, but that the children of cold, stern parents who were not physically abusive demonstrated a particularly low incidence of subsequent sociopathy.

Parental Fostering. Beyond failing to gratify their youngster's emotional needs early in life and neglecting to discipline and supervise him adequately in childhood and adolescence, the parents of the psychopathic youngster have usually encouraged him to aggressive, delinquent, and irresponsible behavior through the same patterns of parental fostering observed in symptomatic delinquency: by setting antisocial models, by anticipating delinquent behavior before it has occurred, and by responding ambivalently to such behavior once it has begun (see pp. 494-496). The role of parental fostering in psychopathy has been documented in the clinical experience of Kaufman et al. (1963) with over 800 antisocial youngsters seen in various court and child guidance clinics. Concerning the impulse-ridden, character-disordered delinquent youngsters in their sample Kaufman et al. conclude, "The parents of this group largely tend to be impulse-ridden, character-disordered personalities themselves, and either directly by their actions or covertly condone and stimulate the delinquency in their child" (p. 316).

Robins (1966, pp. 160-161) presents corroborating evidence that perhaps the most reliable predictor of sociopathy is growing up in a home in which the parents, particularly the father, are prominently antisocial. In families where the parents had no known psychological disturbances or had demonstrated non-antisocial behavior disorders, one of every seven youngsters in her child patient sample developed subsequent psychopathy. However, when the father or mother had a history of arrest or desertion, or when the father was chronically unemployed, about one-third of these disturbed youngsters were later diagnosed as sociopathic personality, and a significantly increased risk of sociopathy also occurred when the father drank excessively or had failed to support his family. For both boys and girls, interestingly, paternal antisocial behavior was the more significant predictor of subsequent sociopathy; although having a behaviorally disturbed mother in addition to an antisocial father slightly increased the likelihood of sociopathy in the child, the risk of sociopathy when only the mother displayed behavior problems was no greater than when she did not.

Despite superficial appearances to the contrary, identification seldom plays a significant role in such familial incidence of psychopathy. Not only does the developing psychopath by definition lack capacity to identify with others, but the dominant importance of the father's pathology for nascent psychopathy in girls as well as boys transcends the sex-role influences usually associated with identification. Rather, the striking relationship between paternal psychopathy and antisocial personality formation appears to derive primarily from the pathogenic child-rearing practices of the anti-social father: the psychopathic father is a particularly likely candidate to ignore his children and to abdicate his disciplinary responsibilities for them.

The major role of pathogenic child-rearing rather than identification in producing psychopathy is also reflected in the Robins data. She reports that the relationship between paternal and child sociopathy is markedly diminished when discipline and supervision have nevertheless been adequate, whereas about as many children without antisocial fathers as with them become sociopathic in the absence of adequate discipline and supervision (p. 170). Robins furthermore suggests that the frequently reported relationship of broken and discordant homes to delinquency (see Glueck and Glueck, 1950, pp. 115 and 261; Monahan, 1957; Nye, 1958, pp. 41-52) may also constitute a derivative effect of the antisocial father's impact on his family. Specifically, the characterological aberrations of the antisocial father may simultaneously generate both antisocial behavior in his children and marital disharmony eventuating in a broken or discordant home (Robins, 1966, p. 179). . . .

References

Alexander, F. The neurotic character. *International Journal of Psycho-analysis*, 11: 292-311, 1930.

Anderson, R. E. Where's Dad? Parental deprivation and delinquency. *Archives of General Psychiatry*, 18: 641-649, 1968.

Bandura, A., and Walters, R. H. *Adolescent Aggression: A Study of the Influence of Child-Training Practices and Family Interrelationships.* New York: Ronald, 1959.

Becker, W. C., Peterson, D. R., Hellner, L. A., Shoemaker, D. J., and Quay, H. C. Factors in parental behavior and personality as related to problem behavior in children. *Journal of Consulting Psychology,* **23**: 107-118, 1959.

Bender, L. Psychopathic personality disorders in childhood and adolescence. *Archives of Criminal Psychodynamics,* **4**: 412-415, 1961.

Bergler, E. *Principles of Self-Damage,* New York: Philosophical Library, 1959.

Berman, S. Antisocial character disorder: Its etiology and relationship to delinquency. *American Journal of Orthopsychiatry,* **29**: 612-621, 1959.

Bernabeu, E. P. Underlying ego mechanisms in delinquency. *Psychoanalytic Quarterly,* **27**: 383-396, 1958.

Blaine, G. R., and McArthur, C. C. Basic character disorders and homosexuality. In G. R. Blaine and C. C. McArthur, eds., *Emotional Problems of the Student.* New York: Appleton-Century-Crofts, 1961, pp. 100-115.

Bloch, H. A., and Niederhoffer, A. *The Gang: A Study in Adolescent Behavior.* New York: Philosophical Library, 1958.

Bohlke, R. H. Social mobility, stratification inconsistency, and middle-class delinquency. *Social Problems,* **8**: 351-363, 1961.

Bowlby, J. Forty-four juvenile thieves: Their characters and homelife. *International Journal of Psychoanalysis,* **25**: 19-53, 107-128, 1944.

Briggs, P. F., and Wirt, R. D. Prediction. In H. C. Quay, ed., *Juvenile Delinquency: Research and Theory.* Princeton, N. J.: Van Nostrand, 1965, pp. 170-208.

Brigham, J. C., Ricketts, J. L., and Johnson, R. C. Reported maternal and paternal behaviors of solitary and social delinquents. *Journal of Consulting Psychology,* **31**: 420-422, 1967.

Carek, D. J., Hendrickson, W., and Holmes, D. J. Delinquency addiction in parents. *Archives of General Psychiatry,* **4**: 357-362, 1961.

Church, A. S. Adolescence and juvenile delinquency. *Nervous Child,* **4**: 142-146, 1944.

Cleckley, H. M. Psychopathic states. In S. Arieti, ed., *American Handbook of Psychiatry,* Vol. I. New York: Basic Books, 1959, pp. 567-588.

Cleckley, H. *The Mask of Sanity,* 4th edition. St. Louis: Mosby, 1964.

Cloward, R., and Ohlin, L. E. *Delinquency and Opportunity: A Theory of Delinquent Gangs.* New York: Free Press of Glencoe, 1960.

Cohen, A. K. *Delinquent Boys: The Culture of the Gang.* Glencoe, Ill.: The Free Press, 1955.

Counts, R. M. Family crises and the impulsive adolescent. *Archives of General Psychiatry,* **17**: 64-71, 1967.

Cowden, J. E. Differential test responses of two types of delinquent girls under authoritarian and permissive conditions. *Journal of Clinical Psychology,* **21**: 397-399, 1965.

Diagnostic and Statistical Manual of Mental Disorders, 2nd edition. Washington, D.C.: American Psychiatric Association, 1968.

Elkind, D. Middle-class delinquency. *Mental Hygiene*, 51: 80-84, 1967.

Erikson, E. H. The problem of ego identity. *Journal of the American Psychoanalytic Association*, 4: 56-121, 1956.

Ferdinand, T. N. *Typologies of Delinquency: A Critical Analysis*. New York: Random House, 1966.

Freud, S. (1916). Some character-types met with in psychoanalytic work. *Standard Edition*, Vol. XIV. London: Hogarth, 1957, pp. 311-333.

Friedlander, K. *The Psycho-Analytic Approach to Juvenile Delinquency*. New York: International Universities Press, 1947.

Friedlander, K. Latent delinquency and ego development. In K. R. Eissler, ed., *Searchlights on Delinquency*. New York: International Universities Press, 1949.

Gallenkamp, C. R., and Rychlak, J. F. Parental attitudes of sanction in middle-class adolescent male delinquents. *Journal of Social Psychology*, 75: 255-260, 1968.

Giffin, M. E., Johnson, A. M., and Litin, E. M. Specific factors determining anti-social acting out. *American Journal of Orthopsychiatry*, 24: 668-684, 1954.

Glaser, D. Social disorganization and delinquent subcultures. In H. C. Quay, ed., *Juvenile Delinquency: Research and Theory*. Princeton, N.J.: Van Nostrand, 1965, pp. 27-62.

Glueck, S., and Glueck, E. T. *Unraveling Juvenile Delinquency*. New York: Commonwealth Fund, 1950.

Glueck, S., and Glueck, E. *Physique and Delinquency*. New York: Harper and Bros., 1956.

Glueck, S., and Glueck, E. *Predicting Delinquency and Crime*. Cambridge, Mass.: Harvard University Press, 1960.

Glueck, S., and Glueck, E. *Family Environment and Delinquency*. Boston: Houghton-Mifflin, 1962.

Gottschalk, L. A., Titchener, J. L., Piker, H. N., and Stewart, S. S. Psychosocial factors associated with pregnancy in adolescent girls: A preliminary report. *Journal of Nervous and Mental Disease*, 138: 524-534, 1964.

Halleck, S. L. *Psychiatry and the Dilemmas of Crime*. New York: Harper and Row, 1967.

Herskovitz, H. H., Levine, M., and Spivack, G. Anti-social behavior of adolescents from higher socio-economic groups. *Journal of Nervous and Mental Disease*, 125: 1-9, 1959.

Jenkins, R. L. Adaptive and maladaptive delinquency. *Nervous Child*, 11: 9-11, 1955.

Jenkins, R. L. Motivation and frustration in delinquency. *American*

Journal of Orthopsychiatry, **27**: 528-537, 1957.

Jenkins, R. L. The psychopathic or antisocial personality. *Journal of Nervous and Mental Disease,* **131**: 318-334, 1960.

Jenkins, R. L. Diagnoses, dynamics, and treatment in child psychiatry. *Psychiatric Research Report, American Psychiatric Association,* **18**: 91-120, 1964.

Jenkins, R. L. Psychiatric syndromes in children and their relation to family background. *American Journal of Orthopsychiatry,* **36**: 450-457, 1966.

Jenkins, R. L., and Glickman, S. Patterns of personality organization among delinquents. *Nervous Child,* **6**: 329-339, 1947.

Jenkins, R. L., NurEddin, E., and Shapiro, I. Children's behavior syndromes and parental responses. *Genetic Psychology Monographs,* **74**: 261-329, 1966.

Johnson, A. M. Sanctions for superego lacunae of adolescents. In K. R. Eissler, ed., *Searchlights on Delinquency.* New York: International Universities Press, 1949, pp. 225-245.

Johnson, A. M. Juvenile delinquency. In S. Arieti, ed., *American Handbook of Psychiatry,* Vol. I. New York: Basic Books, 1959, pp. 840-856.

Johnson, A. M., and Burke, E. C. Parental permissiveness and fostering in child rearing and their relationship to juvenile delinquency. *Proceedings of Staff Meetings, Mayo Clinic,* **30**: 557-565, 1955.

Johnson, A. M., and Szurek, S. A. The genesis of antisocial acting out in children and adults. *Psychoanalytic Quarterly,* **21**: 323-343, 1952.

Johnson, A. M., and Szurek, S. A. Etiology of antisocial behavior in delinquents and psychopaths. *Journal of the American Medical Association,* **154**: 814-817, 1954.

Kaufman, I., Durkin, H., Frank, T., Heims, L. W., Jones, D. B., Ryter, Z., Stone, E., and Zilbach, J. Delineation of two diagnostic groups among juvenile delinquents: The schizophrenic and the impulse-ridden character disorder. *Journal of the American Academy of Child Psychiatry,* **2**: 292-318, 1963.

Kennedy, F., Hoffman, H. R., and Haines, W. H. A study of William Heirens. *American Journal of Psychiatry,* **104**: 113-121, 1947.

Kvaraceus, W. C., and Miller, W. B. *Delinquent Behavior, Culture, and the Individual.* Washington, D.C.: National Educational Association, 1959.

Lindesmith, A. R., and Dunham, H. W. Some principles of criminal typology. *Social Forces,* **19**: 307-314, 1941.

McCord, W., and McCord, J. *The Psychopath: An Essay on the Criminal Mind.* Princeton, N.J.: Van Nostrand, 1964.

Miller, W. B. Lower-class culture as a generating milieu of gang delinquency. *Journal of Social Issues,* **14**: 5-19, 1958.

Monahan, T. P. Family status and the delinquent child: A reappraisal and some new findings. *Social Forces,* **35**: 250-258, 1957.

Nye, F. I. *Family Relationships and Delinquent Behavior.* New York: Wiley, 1958.

Nye, F. I., Short, J. F., and Olson, V. J. Socio-economic status and delinquent behavior. In F. I. Nye, ed., *Family Relationships and Delinquent Behavior.* New York: Wiley, 1958, pp. 23-33.

Peterson, D. R., and Becker, W. C. Family interaction and delinquency. In H. C. Quay, ed., *Juvenile Delinquency: Research and Theory.* Princeton, N.J.: Van Nostrand, 1965, pp. 63-99.

Randolph, M. H., Richardson, H., and Johnson, R. C. A comparison of social and solitary delinquents. *Journal of Consulting Psychology,* **25**: 293-295, 1961.

Reik, T. *Masochism in Modern Man.* New York: Farrar Strauss, 1941.

Robins, L. N. *Deviant Children Grown Up: A Sociological and Psychiatric Study of Sociopathic Personality.* Baltimore: Williams and Wilkins, 1966.

Schulman, I. Dynamics and treatment of antisocial psychopathology in adolescents. *Nervous Child,* **11**: 35-41, 1955.

Shanley, F. J. Middle-class delinquency as a social problem. *Sociology and Social Research,* **51**: 185-198, 1967.

Shaw, C. R., and McKay, H. D. *Juvenile Delinquency and Urban Areas.* Chicago: University of Chicago Press, 1942.

Short, J. F. Social structure and group processes in explorations of gang delinquency. In M. Sherif and C. W. Sherif, eds., *Problems of Youth: Transition to Adulthood in a Changing World.* Chicago: Aldine, 1965, pp. 155-188.

Szurek, S. Notes on the genesis of psychopathic personality trends. *Psychiatry,* **5**: 1-6, 1942.

Vincent, C. E. *Unmarried Mothers.* New York: Free Press of Glencoe, 1961.

Visotsky, H. M. A project for unwed pregnant adolescents in Chicago. *Clinical Pediatrics,* **5**: 322-324, 1966.

Vogel, E. F., and Bell, N. F. The emotionally disturbed child as a family scapegoat. *Psychoanalysis and the Psychoanalytic Review,* **47**: 21-42, 1960.

Wattenberg, W., and Balistrieri, J. Automobile theft: A favored group delinquency. *American Journal of Sociology,* **57**: 575-579, 1952.

Wirt, R. D., and Briggs, P. F. Personality and environmental factors in the development of delinquency. *Psychological Monographs,* No. 73 (Whole No. 485), 1959.